QUICK REFERENCE GUIDE

THE LAW OF
ENTERTAINMENT
AND
BROADCASTING

AUSTRALIA
The Law Book Company
Brisbane * Sydney * Melbourne * Perth

CANADA
Carswell
Ottawa * Toronto * Calgary * Montreal * Vancouver

AGENTS:
Steimatzky's Agency Ltd., Tel Aviv;
N.M. Tripathi (Private) Ltd., Bombay;
Eastern Law House (Private) Ltd., Calcutta;
M.P.P. House, Bangalore;
Universal Book Traders, Delhi;
Aditya Books, Delhi;
MacMillan Shuppan KK, Tokyo;
Pakistan Law House, Karachi, Lahore.

THE LAW OF

ENTERTAINMENT

AND

BROADCASTING

By

VINCENT NELSON LL.B

of the Inner Temple, Barrister
Ashworth Scholar in the Inner Temple

LONDON
SWEET & MAXWELL
1995

Published in 1995 by
Sweet and Maxwell Limited of
South Quay Plaza, 183 Marsh Wall,
London E14 9FT
Computerset by Interactive Sciences, Gloucester
Printed and bound in Great Britain by
Hartnolls Ltd., Bodmin

No natural forests were destroyed to make this product:
only farmed timber was used and re-planted

A CIP catalogue record for this book is
available from the British Library

ISBN 0 421 50150 2

©
VINCENT NELSON
1995

FOREWORD

To the general public, and even perhaps to some legal practitioners, entertainment law conjures up visions of film stars or television personalities suing journalists and newspapers to recover astronomical damages for libel. This valuable book should quickly cure any such misconception.

In part the book shows, by reference to decided cases, how general principles of law have been applied in the entertainment field. In part, and perhaps even more valuably, it gathers together a mass of material, not readily available to most practitioners, specifically governing this important area of economic life. To those called upon to consider the difficult and often novel problems which arise in this field the book will be a boon.

Vincent Nelson is superbly qualified for his task. He has behind him years of full-time practical experience in television and broadcasting. And he has current practical experience of legal practice. He brings to his legal analysis a deep insight into the practical realities of the entertainment world.

The book deserves the warmest welcome. The show can go on – with the benefit of sound legal advice.

The Rt. Hon. Sir Thomas Bingham
Master of the Rolls.

PREFACE

The last decade has seen a rapid growth in the means of delivering entertainment to the consumer. Examples are satellite television, cable television, music on demand via cable and the imminent commencement of video on demand. This has had two results. First, there has been a marked increase in the demand for programming and music for such media and secondly, the legal problems facing managers of such businesses and their legal advisers have become increasingly complex. This work is intended to assist in the resolution of such legal problems in so far as they relate to entertainment and broadcasting.

The law relating to the subject-matter of this work can be found, *inter alia*, in the areas of the law of contract, the law of tort, intellectual property law, the Broadcasting Act 1990, and other statutes, and increasingly the laws of the European Union. Thus, in producing a work relating to entertainment law there is a danger that one may produce a book which is over-weighted in respect of one particular area of law or which is excessively long. I have sought to avoid this mischief by selecting those areas of the law which experience has shown to be of most practical importance to practitioners in entertainment law and managers of entertainment businesses. In adopting this approach I am mindful of the fact that there may often be a fine dividing line between what is included and what is omitted. However, it is hoped that the omissions will not detract from the usefulness of this work to the user.

Although this work is primarily intended for practitioners and lawyers working within the entertainment industry, it is hoped that it will be useful to students who are increasingly choosing to study entertainment and media law as a degree option.

Finally, a work of this nature would not be complete without acknowledgements, or credits as they are referred to in the entertainment industry. I would like to thank my colleague in chambers, Sean Wilken, for his scholarly contribution to the preparation of the section of this work relating to the regulation of broadcasting; Craig Barlow and Alan Maclean for their assistance in respect of the preparation of Restraint of Trade; and Theresa Villiers for her assistance in respect of Assignment and Licences. I would also like to thank my publishers for their co-operation and expert guidance throughout the preparation of this work.

Most importantly, I would like to thank my wife, Ina, and my children, Oliver, Saffron and Edward, for their support, patience and understanding without which this work would not have been possible.

Preface

The law as stated is as at October 1994. As usual, any mistakes are, of course, entirely mine.

Vincent Nelson
39 Essex Street
Outer Temple
London WC2R 3AT.

CONTENTS

PART I—ENTERTAINMENT CONTRACTS

Contents

PART II—COPYRIGHT AND RELATED RIGHTS

Contents

Contents

Contents

Contents

Contents

Contents

Contents

TABLE OF CASES

(References are to paragraph number)

xix

Table of Cases

Table of Cases

Table of Cases

Table of Cases

Table of Cases

Table of Cases

Table of Cases

Table of Cases

Table of Cases

Table of Cases

Table of Cases

Table of Cases

TABLE OF STATUTES

(References are to paragraph number)

li

Table of Statutes

TABLE OF STATUTORY INSTRUMENTS

(References are to paragraph number)

RULES OF THE SUPREME COURT

TABLE OF EUROPEAN MATERIALS

EEC Treaty

E.C. Directives

TABLE OF EUROPEAN CASES

PART I

ENTERTAINMENT CONTRACTS

FORMATION OF CONTRACTS

Note. For a detailed treatment of other areas relating to the formation of contracts which are not dealt with in this work reference should be made to one of the standard works on the law of contract.[1]

1. Elements of Contract

General. An entertainment contract, like any other contract, will be **1.01** valid and enforceable where there are "(1) two or more separate and definite parties to the contract; (2) those parties [are] . . . in agreement, that is there must be a consensus ad idem; (3) there must be an intention to create legal relations . . . [and] (4) the promises of each party [is] . . . supported by consideration, or by some other factor the law considers sufficient".[2]

2. Offer and Acceptance

(a) *Options*

General. Contracts of options are a common feature of the entertain- **1.02** ment industry. For example, in the film and television sectors of the industry a producer may seek to acquire and develop simultaneously

---

[1] See, *e.g. Chitty on Contracts* (Sweet & Maxwell, 26th ed., 1989) Vol. 1.
[2] *Halsbury's Laws of England* (Butterworth, 4th ed.) Vol. 9, para. 203. See generally *Chitty on Contracts* (26th ed.) Vol. 1, chap. 2 for a detailed examination of these elements.

for production a number of literary or dramatic works. It would not be cost effective to pay the full purchase price for such works due to the fact that only a very few of the works developed with a view to production are actually so produced. Thus, for example, the option price for the film rights to a best selling novel may be acquired by a producer for 10 per cent. of the purchase price. The purchase of such an option will often give a producer the opportunity to adapt the novel into a screenplay and to raise the necessary finance to produce the anticipated film and thus to pay the option price payable upon the exercise of the option.[3]

1.03   **Nature of an option.** An option is an offer by the grantor to enter into a contract with the grantee, which, if given for consideration or contained in a deed, may be irrevocable but in any case remains open for acceptance until it is revoked.[4] A contract of option must therefore conform to all the requirements of a binding contract in that there must be an agreement between the parties as to the terms of the contract of option and there must be consideration which is recognised by the law. However,

> " . . . once consideration has been given or the option granted by deed, there comes into existence a unilateral obligation on the part of the grantor . . . The obligation so created is conditional (1) upon the grantee's demand for its performance and (2) upon tender by the grantee of the agreed price, but of itself it creates no rights on the part of the grantor. The grant of the option creates no obligation on the part of the grantee-only a right to demand performance of his obligation by the grantor. In the absence of such demand he assumes no obligation, conditional or otherwise."[5]

1.04   **Consideration.** Where the contract of option specifies the consideration payable upon the exercise of the option little difficulty arises. Where however the contract of option provides no fixed consideration payable on the exercise, nor a clear basis for determining the consideration payable on exercise, nor any means of quantifying that basis, the contract of option may be void for uncertainty. At least three types of option may

---

[3] See also *post.*, Chap. 8, "Films", para. 8.13, "Acquisition of underlying rights".
[4] *Stromdale & Ball Ltd v. Burden* [1952] 1 Ch. 223, 235; *Mountford v. Scott* [1973] 3 W.L.R. 884. See also *Varty v. British South Africa Co.* [1965] 1 Ch. 508 at 523, where it was said that to speak "of an enforceable option as an 'irrevocable offer' is juristically a contradiction in terms, for the adjective 'irrevocable' connotes the existence of an obligation on the part of the offeror, while the noun 'offer' connotes the absence of any obligation until the offer has been accepted"; revsd. on other grounds [1966] A.C. 381, H.L.; *cf. Helby v. Matthews* [1895] A.C. 471, H.L.
[5] *Varty v. British South Africa Co.* [1965] 1 Ch. 508 at 522, C.A., *per* Diplock L.J. revsd. on other grounds [1966] A.C. 381, H.L.

be distinguished where such uncertainty may arise. First, the option may be exercised simply at "a price to be agreed". In that case, no formula for quantifying the consideration being laid down by the contract of option, prima facie the contract of option will be void as being a mere contract to make a contract, or a contract dependent upon the making of an agreement.[6] The second type of option is one expressed to be exercisable at a price to be determined according to a stated formula without any effective machinery being provided for working out that formula. In such a case, where the parties disagree as to the application of the formula, the court has jurisdiction to determine the manner in which the formula is to be applied.[7] Thirdly, the option may be one which provides both a formula and the machinery, as for example arbitration. In such a case it may be permissible for the machinery to cure a defect in the formula. However, it may not be permissible for the machinery to provide such a cure where the defect is of a fundamental character or would be such as would result in the machinery executing an agreement which is not what the parties intended.

Exercise of option. The terms on which the option is granted are treated by the courts as strict conditions, failure to comply with which render the option, and the rights conveyed by it, ineffectual.[8] However, the parties may elect, either expressly or by implication, to waive such a defect in performance. **1.05**

(b) *Contracts of first refusal or pre-emption*

Distinction between contracts of first refusal and pre-emption. A contract of "first refusal" is one whereby the grantee has the right to be offered, by the grantor, prior to the same being offered to any other party, the opportunity of refusing or accepting a "fair and reasonable offer" by the grantor to sell to the grantee the subject-matter of the contract of first refusal.[9] Whereas a contract of "pre-emption" is a contract whereby the grantee is given a right to enter into a contract at a price and on terms acceptable to the grantor offered to the grantor by some person other than the grantee in respect of the subject-matter of the right of pre-emption.[10] An illustration of the latter type of contract **1.06**

---

[6] *King's Motors (Oxford) Ltd. v. Lax* [1970] 1 W.L.R. 426.
[7] *Brown v. Gould* [1972] Ch. 53.
[8] *Helby v. Matthews* [1895] A.C. 471, H.L.; *Hare v. Nicholl* [1966] 2 Q.B. 130, 141, 148, C.A.; *Holwell Securities Ltd. v. Hughes* [1984] 1 W.L.R. 155, 159, C.A. See also Mowbray, "Who can exercise an option" (1958) 74 L.Q.R. 237.
[9] *Manchester Ship Canal Co. v. Manchester Racecourse Co.* [1901] 2 Ch. 37, C.A.; *Gardner v. Coutts & Co.* [1968] 1 W.L.R. 173; *Smith v. Morgan* [1971] 1 W.L.R. 903.
[10] *Manchester Ship Canal Co. v. Manchester Racecourse Co.* [1901] 2 Ch. 37, C.A.; *Gardner v. Coutts & Co.* [1968] 1 W.L.R. 173; *Smith v. Morgan* [1971] 1 W.L.R. 803; *Fraser v. Thames Television Ltd.* [1984] Q.B. 44.

would be the case where a film company is granted the right to acquire the film rights in a novel by "matching" any offer acceptable to the author made by any other producer wishing to acquire such novel.

1.07 **Distinction between contracts of "first refusal" "pre-emption" and "option".** Under an option, only one step is normally needed to constitute a contract, namely, the exercise of the option. Under a right of first refusal or pre-emption, two steps will usually be necessary, the making of the offer in accordance with the right of first refusal or pre-emption, and the acceptance of that offer. The failure to provide either a price or a formula for ascertaining the price is accordingly far more serious in the case of an option than under a pre-emption.

1.08 **Price payable by grantee where contract of first refusal.** Where the grantee of the right of first refusal wishes to give the grantee the option of exercising his right of first refusal the obligation on the grantor is no more than to make an offer to the grantee to enter into an agreement at a price and terms at which the grantor is willing to enter into a contract: if that offer is accepted by the grantee there will be a contract at a price and upon terms which have been agreed.[11] The grantor must, however, act bona fide in defining the price to be included in the offer[12] but there is no obligation to offer the property at market value or at such value as the court may determine.[13]

(c) *Contracts to negotiate*

1.09 **General.** It is a common practice in the entertainment industry that parties enter into agreements containing clauses requiring them to enter into good faith negotiations for the conclusion of a new agreement or a collateral agreement affecting a subject matter of the agreement. In the light of the decision in *Walford v. Miles*[14] it is clear that such an agreement is unenforceable because it lacks the necessary certainty. Furthermore, a "duty to negotiate in good faith is as unworkable in practice as it is inherently inconsistent with the position of a negotiating party . . . while negotiations are in existence either party is entitled to withdraw from those negotiations, at any time for any reason. There can thus be no obligation to continue to negotiate until there is a 'proper reason' to withdraw."[15]

---

[11] *Manchester Ship Canal Co. v. Manchester Racecourse Co.* [1901] 2 Ch. 37, C.A.; *Smith v. Morgan* [1971] 1 W.L.R. 803.
[12] *Manchester Ship Canal Co. v. Manchester Racecourse Co.* [1901] 2 Ch. 37, C.A.; *Smith v. Morgan* [1971] 1 W.L.R. 803.
[13] *Smith v. Morgan* [1971] 1 W.L.R. 803.
[14] [1992] 2 A.C. 128, H.L.
[15] *Ibid.* at 138.

Duty to negotiate – when enforceable. The decision in *Walford v.* **1.10**
Miles[16] would indicate that where A, for good consideration, undertakes to use *best endeavours* to negotiate an agreement with B such an
undertaking is enforceable.[17] Similarly, where the parties seek a so-
called "lock-out" agreement and A, for good consideration, undertakes,
for a specified period, not to negotiate with anyone except B with regard
to the subject-matter of the proposed contract, such an undertaking will
be enforceable.[18] However, an undertaking by A, for good consideration, that for *such time as is reasonable* he will not negotiate with any
other person than B with regard to the subject-matter of the proposed
contract will be unenforceable.[19] Similarly, where A, for good consideration, undertakes to *negotiate in good faith* to reach an agreement with B
such undertaking is unenforceable.[20]

(d) *Letters of intent*

General. It is a common practice within the film and television industry **1.11**
for development and contracting of personnel to commence prior to the
conclusion of a production agreement in order to enable the preliminary stages of production to start so as to meet proposed exhibition
dates. Often the preparatory work for such a film production will commence upon the receipt by the producer of a letter of intent from the
exhibitor or television company indicating its intention to enter into a
contract to finance the film. Experience shows that, notwithstanding the
good intentions of the parties, substantial difficulties may arise as to
conclusion of the intended contract and in such circumstances the
question may arise as to the contractual effect, if any, of the letter of
intent.

Quantum meruit **or damages – significance of concluded contract.** **1.12**
Where work is done as a result of a request contained in the letter of
intent, it will not matter whether a contract did or did not come into
existence, because, if the party claiming, who has acted on the request,
is simply claiming payment his claim will usually be based on a
quantum meruit, and it will make no difference whether that claim is
contractual or quasi-contractual. Where, however, one party is claiming
damages for breach of contract, the success of such a claim will depend
on the question whether any contract was concluded. In *British Steel*

---

[16] [1992] 2 A.C. 128, H.L.
[17] *Ibid.* at 139.
[18] *Ibid.* at 139.
[19] *Ibid.* at 140.
[20] *Ibid.* at 138. *cf. Channel Home Centers, Division of Grace Retail Corporation v. Grossman*
(1986) 795 F. 2d 291 where it was held that an obligation to negotiate in good faith could
be enforceable. It is to be noted, however, that the U.S. authorities are not in agreement
as to whether such undertakings are enforceable.

Corp. v. Cleveland Bridge and Engineering Co. Ltd.,[21] Goff J. analyzed the nature and effect of such letters and observed that

> "[t]here can be no hard and fast answer to the question whether a letter of intent will give rise to a binding agreement: everything must depend on the circumstances of the particular case . . . As a matter of analysis the contract (if any) which may come into existence following a letter of intent may take one of two forms: either there may be an ordinary executory contract, under which each party assumes reciprocal obligations to the other; or there may be what sometimes is called an 'if' contract, *i.e.* a contract under which A requests B to carry out a certain performance and promises B that, if he does so, he will receive a certain performance in return, usually remuneration for his performance."[22]

If a contract is entered into by the parties subsequent to the letter of intent, the work done will be treated as having been performed under that contract; if no contract is entered into which can be ascertained by the court, "the law . . . imposes an obligation on the party making the request to pay a reasonable sum for such work as has been done pursuant to the request . . . ".[23] Where, however, it is clear from the letter of intent or the circumstances of the case that the letter of intent is not a request to do work and there is no intention to induce the carrying out of work by the sending of the letter and work is nevertheless carried out but no contract is concluded as anticipated, then, it is submitted, no claim in *quantum meruit* will lie against the party issuing the letter of intent.

(e) *Output agreements*

1.13　There may be a standing offer on the part of, for example, a television company or film studio to accept such programmes as may be produced by a production company or producer up to a certain number of hours in a particular year within a particular category of programme or film. Such offers are generally known in the film and television industries as "output agreements". The offeror may revoke this offer unless there is consideration for the offer or where it is made under seal[24] but if before revocation a film in the terms of the agreement is produced, a contract comes into existence for that film and the television company must accept it.[25]

---

[21] [1984] 1 All E.R. 504.
[22] *Ibid.* at 504, 509.
[23] *Ibid.* at 504.
[24] *Offord v. Davies* (1862) 12 C.B., N.S., 748; *G.N. Railway v. Witham* (1873) L.R. 9 C.P. 16, 19; *Dickinson v. Dodds* (1876) Ch.D. 463. See also *infra*, para. 1.16 *et seq.*, "Formalities of Contract".
[25] *G.N. Railway v. Witham* (1873) L.R. 9 C.P. 16.

If no film is produced during the period[26] or if fewer films are delivered than the probable amount indicated in the preliminary discussions leading up to the agreement, whether because the films are licensed to another contractor or otherwise,[27] the television company has no action for breach of contract.

Such contracts of indefinite or very long duration may be construed as determinable upon reasonable notice, particularly if they are affected by inflation.[28]

(f) *Agreement subject to execution of formal contract – when binding*

The practice has arisen in some sectors of the entertainment industry **1.14** whereby the parties having reached agreement as to the terms of the proposed transaction, whether by documents or letters or otherwise, stipulate that such agreement is subject to the execution of a formal agreement. In such circumstances it is a question of construction whether the execution of the formal contract is a "condition or term of the bargain or whether it is a mere expression of the desire of the parties as to the manner in which the transaction already agreed to will in fact go through. In the former case there is no enforceable contract either because the condition is unfulfilled or because the law does not recognise a contract to enter into a contract. In the latter case there is a binding contract; the reference to the more formal document may be ignored" and the agreement will be immediately binding.[29]

3. Consideration

In the ordinary entertainment contract the general rules of the law of **1.15** contract apply as to the requirement and definition of consideration. However, where an impresario or producer engages an "artiste"[30] to perform, " he is promising two things: he is giving consideration which consists of two different elements; firstly, a salary which he promises

---

[26] See *R. v. Demers* [1900] A.C. 103, P.C.

[27] See *Att.-Gen. v. Stewards & Co. Ltd.* (1901) 18 T.L.R. 131, H.L.

[28] *Re Spenborough Urban District Council's Agreement; Spenborough Corporation v. Cooke, Sons & Co. Ltd.* [1968] Ch. 139; *Staffordshire Health Authority v. South Staffordshire Waterworks* [1978] 1 W.L.R. 1387; *cf. Kirklees M.B.C. v. Yorshire Woollen* (1978) L.G.R. 448.

[29] *Von Hatzfeldt-Wildenburg v. Alexander* [1912] 1 Ch. 284; see also *Oxford v. Provand* (1868) L.R. 2 P.C.; 16 E.R. 472, P.C.; *Rossiter v. Miller* (1878) 3 App. Cas. 1124 H.L.; *Coope v. Ridout* [1921] 1 Ch. 291; *Rossdale v. Denny* [1921] 1 Ch. 57; *Chilingworth v. Esche* [1924] 1 Ch. 97; *Bunker-Smith v. Freeza Meats Ltd.* [1987] BTLC 20; *Branca v. Cobarro* [1947] K.B. 854, C.A.; *cf.* "subject to contract" as used in relation to the sale and purchase of land where the term is strictly applied notwithstanding the fact that the parties have agreed the terms of the purchase and/or sale.

[30] An "artiste" is to be taken to mean all creative persons who earn their living by attracting the public to their work: *Tolnay v. Criterion Film Productions* [1936] 2 All E.R. 1625.

the artiste for his services, and secondly, the opportunity to play in public some part which will attract attention."[31] The implied contractual consideration for the artiste's work to be seen in public has been generally characterised as the "right to publicity".[32] For these purposes an "artiste" is any person who makes a living by attracting the public to their works and would include authors, actors, directors, composers and musicians.[33]

However, the authorities show that consideration does not move from the artiste to the impresario or producer in the form of publicity.[34] This is justified upon the premise that an impresario is a business man rather than an artiste and consequently the enhancement of his reputation does not depend upon being seen by the public.[35] However, it can be argued that an impresario, as much as an artiste, depends upon being perceived by the public as someone who is able to deliver public entertainment at the time and by the artistes advertised.

4. Formalities of Contract

(a) *Contracts requiring writing*

1.16 An entertainment contract may, like any other contract, be written, oral or partly oral and partly in writing. However, there are three exceptions to this general principle which are worthy of mention in the context of the entertainment industry. These are first, contracts for the assignment of copyright, secondly, exclusive licences and thirdly, contracts for the provision of independent television and radio services.

1.17 **Contracts for the assignment of copyright.** An assignment of the legal or equitable interest in copyright is not effective unless it is in writing signed by or on behalf of the assignor.[36]

1.18 **Exclusive licences.** An exclusive licence whereby the copyright owner authorises the licensee to the exclusion of all other persons, including the person granting the licensee, to exercise a right which would

---

[31] *Withers v. General Theatre Corporation* [1933] 2 K.B. 537, *per* Greer L.J. at 554; *Re Gollomb* (1931) 144 L.T. 301; see also *Ackland v. World Screenplays, The Times,* February 23, 1950, where the same principles were applied in respect of a screenplay writer. Publicity may be the entire consideration: *Fechter v. Montgomery* (1863) 33 Beav. 22; *Bunning v. Lyric Theatre Ltd.* (1894) 71 L.T. 396.

[32] *Marbe v. George Edwardes* [1928] 1 K.B. 269, C.A.; *Clayton v. Oliver* [1930] A.C. 209; *Withers v. General Theatre Corporation* [1933] 2 K.B. 536, C.A.; *Fielding v. Moiseiwitsch* (1946) 175 L. 265.

[33] *Tolnay v. Criterion Film Productions, Ltd.* [1933] 2 All E.R. 1625.

[34] *Fielding v. Moiseiwitsch* (1946) 175 L.T. 265.

[35] *Ibid.*

[36] Copyright, Designs and Patents Act 1988, s.90(3); *Roban Jig & Tool Co. Ltd. v. Taylor* [1979] F.S.R. 130, 143. See "Assignments and Licences", *post,* para. 7.01 *et seq.*

wise be exclusively exercisable by the copyright owner must be in writing signed by or on behalf of the copyright owner.[37]

Contracts for the provision of independent television services. A **1.19** licence granted for the provision of independent television services or independent radio services must be in writing.[38]

(b) *Deeds*

The assignment of the copyright in a work is often by deed. Such a **1.20** document has the advantage that it has a 12-year limitation period[39] and does not require consideration to render it enforceable. An instrument is not a deed unless it makes it clear on its face that it is intended to be a deed by the person making it or, by the parties to it, whether by describing itself as a deed or expressing itself to be executed or signed as a deed or otherwise,[40] and it is validly executed as a deed by that person, or where more than one, one or more of the parties.[41] Where the deed is executed by an individual there is no longer any necessity for the deed to be sealed.[42] Where the deed is executed by a company, sealing will, however, continue to be necessary.[43] An instrument is validly executed as a deed by an individual "if, and only if"[44]:

(a) it is signed:

  (i) by him in the presence of a witness who attests the signature; or

  (ii) at his direction and in his presence and the presence of two witnesses who attest the signature; and

(b) it is delivered as a deed[45] by him or a person authorised to do so on his behalf.

---

[37] Copyright, Designs and Patents Act 1988, s.92(1). "Rights in Performances". See *post*, para. 14.01 *et seq.*
[38] Broadcasting Act 1990, s.3(1), s.86(1).
[39] Limitations Act 1980, s.8(1).
[40] Law of Property (Miscellaneous Provisions) Act 1989, s.1(2)(a).
[41] *Ibid.*, s.1(2)(b).
[42] *Ibid.*, s.1(1)(b).
[43] But see Law of Property (Miscellaneous Provisions) Act 1989, s.1, and Companies Act 1985, s.36A(4) (inserted by Companies Act 1989, s.130) which provides that the signing of a document by both the director and secretary of the company or by two directors, has the same effect as attaching the seal.
[44] *Ibid.*, s.1(3).
[45] "Delivery" in this connection does not mean "handed over" to the other side. It means delivered in the old legal sense, namely, an act done as to evince an intention to be bound. Even though the deed remains in the possession of the maker, or of his solicitor, he is bound by it if he has done some act evincing an intention to be bound. He may, however, make "delivery" conditional: in which case the deed is called an "escrow" which becomes binding when the condition is fulfilled.

5. Capacity of Parties

1.21 **Minors.** A person who has not attained the age of 18 years is for the purposes of the law a minor.[46] As a general rule contracts entered into by a minor are voidable at the instance of the minor. Exceptions to this rule are contracts for necessaries and other contracts such as contracts for services if they are on the whole for the minor's benefit.[47] This is particularly important in relation to young entertainers who enter into agreements with managers, recording companies and music publishers.

A young musician, for example, can become a world figure whilst still a minor, but may remain in obscurity unless he obtains the services of managers and agents to look after his business affairs. If he contracts to receive such services he is doing no more than is necessary to enable him to use his talents and earn his living, and such contracts are in that respect analogous to a contract of service, and binding upon him, if on the whole for his benefit.[48] In deciding whether the contract is for the minor's benefit the court will look at the surrounding circumstances. Important considerations will be whether the agreement enables the minor to make a start as an entertainer[49] or is in restraint of trade[50] or harsh and oppressive.[51]

1.22 **Companies.** Where a person deals with directors of a company the Companies Act 1985 provides that "[i]n favour of a person dealing with the company in good faith,[52] any transaction decided on by the directors is deemed to be one which it is in the capacity of the company to enter into, and the power of the directors to bind the company is deemed to be free of any limitation under the memorandum and articles of association".[53] Furthermore, "[a] party to a transaction so decided on is not bound to inquire as to the capacity of the company to enter into the transaction or as to any such limitation on the powers of the directors, and is presumed to have acted in good faith unless the contrary is proved".[54] The secretary of a company has ostensible authority to enter

---

[46] Family Law Reform Act 1969, s.12.

[47] *Slade v. Metrodent* [1953] 2 Q.B. 112; *Mills v. I.R.C.* [1975] A.C. 38, H.L.

[48] *Denmark Productions Ltd. v. Boscobel Productions Ltd.* (1967) 111 S.J. 715, revsd. on other grounds [1969] 1 Q.B. 699; *Chaplin v. Leslie Frewin (Publishers), Ltd.* [1966] Ch. 71.

[49] *Chaplin v. Leslie Frewin (Publishers) Ltd.* [1966] Ch. 71, C.A.

[50] See "Restraint of trade", para. 5.01 *et seq.*

[51] *De Francesco v. Barnum* (1889) 43 Ch.D. 165.

[52] Lack of good faith in somebody entering into transactions with a company will be found either in proof of actual knowledge that the transaction was *ultra vires* the company or where it can be shown that such person could not in view of all the circumstances, have been unaware that he was party to a transaction *ultra vires*: *International Sales and Agencies Ltd. v. Marcus* [1982] 3 All E.R. 551 at 559.

[53] Companies Act 1985, s.35(1).

[54] Companies Act 1985 s.35(2). See also *TCB Ltd. v. Gray* [1986] Ch. 621.

into contracts connected with the administrative side of his company's affairs.[55] He will therefore have no authority to enter into entertainment contracts unless such authority is expressly given by the directors of the company.

Partnerships. Every partner is an agent of the partnership and his **1.23** partners for the purposes of the business of the partnership and has ostensible authority to enter into contracts for carrying out in the usual way business of the kind carried on by the partnership.[56] For example, if the relationship between members of a pop group is one of partnership,[57] a contract made by one member on behalf of all the other members will be binding on the group as a whole[58] if such contract is for the carrying on of the business of the group in the usual way (*e.g.* the booking of appearances and the entering into contracts with managers); but a contract made by one member as an individual is not binding upon the remainder of the group.

---

[55] *Panorama Development (Guildford) Ltd. v. Fidelis Furnishing Fabrics Ltd.* [1971] 2 Q.B. 711, C.A.
[56] Partnership Act 1890, s.5. See generally *Lindley on Partnership* (Sweet & Maxwell, 15th ed., 1984), chap. 12.
[57] See *Page One Records Ltd. v. Britton* [1968] 1 W.L.R. 157 and *Peterson v. Gibb* (1969) 113 Sol. Jo. 894 where it was held that the relationship between members of a pop group resembled a partnership but was anomalous in that it was not actually a partnership. Whether a pop group is a partnership will depend upon the facts of the case. See also *Stuart v. Barrett* [1994] E.M.L.R. 448.
[58] Partnership Act 1890, s.9.

EXCUSES FOR NON-PERFORMANCE

Note. In this chapter it is proposed to deal briefly with (a) frustration of contract and (b) economic duress with particular reference to entertainment agreements. Where a particular subject is not dealt with or given detailed treatment it is recommended that reference is made to one of the standard works on contracts.[1]

1. Frustration

2.01 **The doctrine.** The relevant legal principles of frustration have been clearly and authoritatively set out in the "classic statement of the doctrine"[2] to be found in the speech of Lord Radcliffe in *Davis Contractors Ltd. v. Fareham U.D.C.*[3]:

> " . . . frustration occurs whenever the law recognises that without default of either party a contractual obligation has become incapable of being performed because the circumstances in which performance is called for would render it a thing radically different from that which was undertaken by the contract. *Non haec in foedera veni*. It was not this that I promised to do."

In determining whether frustration has occurred the "question . . . is not whether one case resembles another but whether applying Lord Radcliffe's enunciation of the doctrine, the facts of the particular case . . . do or do not justify the invocation of the doctrine".[4]

---

[1] *Chitty on Contracts* (Sweet & Maxwell, 26th ed., 1989), Vol. 1.
[2] *Pioneer Shipping Ltd. v. B.T.P. Tioxide Ltd. (The Nema)* [1982] A.C. 724 at 744, H.L.; see also *National Carriers Ltd. v. Panalpina (Northern) Ltd.* [1981] A.C. 675, H.L.
[3] [1956] A.C. 696; see also *Pioneer Shipping Ltd. v. B.T.P. Tioxide Ltd. (The Nema)* [1982] A.C. 724 at 744, 751, H.L.
[4] *Ibid.* at 752.

Express terms. "[T]here can be no discharge by supervening impossi- **2.02**
bility if the express terms of the contract bind the parties to
performance, notwithstanding that the supervening event may occur".[5]
This principle is, however, subject to the qualification that it is a question of construction whether the parties intended the express term to
apply to the supervening event which has occurred.[6] The principle was
illustrated thus by Asquith L.J. in *Parkinson & Co. Ltd. v. Commissioners
of Works and Buildings*[7]:

> "A contract often provides that in the event of "delay" through
> specified causes, the contract is not to be dissolved, but merely sus-
> pended yet such provision has been held not to apply where the
> delay was so abnormal, so pre-emptive as to fall outside what the
> parties could possibly have contemplated in the suspension
> clause."

Thus, unless the words are clearly expressed to apply to the event in
issue they will be construed as limited to the normal moderate occurrence of the event contemplated by the express term.

Self-induced frustration. Reliance cannot be placed on a self-induced **2.03**
frustration.[8] This principle does not, however, require the party claiming to be discharged to prove that the frustrating event was not due to
his neglect or default.[9]

Effect of frustration. Where frustration occurs the contract is automati- **2.04**
cally terminated "because at that date its further performance becomes
impossible in fact in circumstances which involve no liability for
damages for the failure on either party".[10]

Operation of the doctrine

(i) *Illness or death: Contracts for personal services*

Entertainers. Where the contract is for personal services, both parties **2.05**
are taken to have known and contemplated at the time of entering into
the contract that the performance of the services is dependent upon the

---

[5] *Joseph Constantine SS. Line Ltd. v. Imperial Smelting Corp.* [1942] A.C. 154 at 163, H.L.
[6] *Jackson v. Union Marine Insurance Co. Ltd.* (1874), L.R. 10 C.P. 125; *Metropolitan Water
Board v. Dick, Kerr & Co.* [1918] A.C. 119, H.L.; *Bank Line Ltd. v. A. Capel & Co.* [1919]
A.C. 435, H.L.; *Sir Lindsay Parkinson Ltd. v. Commissioners of Works* [1949] 2 K.B. 632 at
665; *Kodros Shipping v. Empresa Cubana (The Evia) (No. 2)* [1983] 1 A.C. 736, H.L.
[7] [1949] 2 K.B. 632, C.A.
[8] *Bank Line, Ltd. v. A. Capel & Co.* [1919] A.C. 435 at 452, H.L.
[9] *Joseph Constantine Steamship Line, Ltd. v. Imperial Smelting Corporation, Ltd.* [1942] A.C.
154 at 179, H.L.
[10] *Fibrosa Spolka Akcyjna v. Fairbairn Lawson Combe Barbour Ltd.* [1943] A.C. 32 at 70, H.L.;
Hirji Mulju v. Cheong Yue Steamship Co. [1926] A.C. 497 at 505, H.L.; *National Carriers Ltd.
v. Panalpina (Northern) Ltd.* [1981] 1 A.C. 675 at 712, H.L.

performer continuing in a condition of health to make it possible for him to render the services. If, through death or illness, the performer is unable to perform such services the contract is discharged unless there are express terms to the contrary.[11] This is illustrated by *Robinson v. Davison*[12] where the plaintiff entered into an agreement with the defendant whereby he undertook that his wife would play at a concert to be given by the plaintiff on a specified date. On the day in question she was unable to perform through illness. The contract contained no express term as to what was to be done in case of her being too ill to perform. The plaintiff sued the defendant for breach of contract and it was held that the illness frustrated performance of the contract. Kelly C.B. observed that:

> "The law is . . . well stated in *Taylor v. Caldwell* . . . by Blackburn J. The learned Judge says . . . : 'There are authorities which we think establish the principle that where, from the nature of the contract, it appears that the parties must from the beginning have known that it could not be fulfilled, unless when the time for the fulfillment of the contract arrived some particular specified thing continued to exist, so that, when entering into the contract, they must have contemplated such continuing existence as the foundation of what was to be done; there, in the absence of any express or implied warranty that the thing shall exist, the contract is not to be construed as a positive contract, but as subject to an implied condition that the parties shall be excused, in case before breach performance becomes impossible from the perishing of the thing without default of the contractor.' I think this principle is directly applicable here; the parties must have known their contract could not be fulfilled unless the defendant's wife was in a state of health to attend and play at the concert on the day named."

2.06   Where the contract consists of an obligation to perform personal services over an extended period, performance of the contract will be frustrated where the performer cannot perform his obligations with the continuity contemplated by the contract. In *Condor v. The Barron Knights, Ltd.*[13] the plaintiff was engaged in December 1962 for a period of five years as a drummer by the Barron Knights. By the terms of the contract he was required to be available to perform on seven nights a week. In January 1963, the plaintiff became ill. The doctor treating the plaintiff informed the defendants that the plaintiff would suffer a

---

[11] *Boast v. Firth* (1868) L.R. 4 C.P. 1; *Farrow v. Wilson* (1869) L.R. 4 C.P. 744; *Robinson v. Davison* (1871) L.R. 6 Exch. 269; *Poussard v. Spiers & Pond* (1876) 1 Q.B.D. 410; *Condor v. The Barron Knights, Ltd.* [1966] 1 W.L.R. 87.
[12] (1871) L.R. 6 Exch. 269.
[13] [1966] 1 W.L.R. 87.

serious mental breakdown if he worked more than four nights a week. The defendants formed the view that it would not be possible to employ the plaintiff for four nights a week only and dismissed him. The plaintiff, who considered he was fit to work seven nights a week, brought an action for damages for wrongful dismissal. It was held that "fitness involves not merely being able to do all the work . . . it involve[s] the ability to do it without the likelihood of such damage to health and so as, within the contract, to continue with the continuity which the contract contemplated."

The court found that there was a "virtual certainty that at the end of a week or a very short period" of working seven nights a week there would be another breakdown. Consequently, it was in a business sense impossible for him to continue to perform or for the defendants to have him perform the terms of the contract as a member of the group.

However, a performer's contract will not necessarily be frustrated in the event of temporary illness. Frustration will only occur where the fulfillment of the performers obligations in the future would be either impossible or if rendered a thing radically different from that undertaken by him and accepted by the producer, record company or impresario.[14] The question whether it is so frustrated is a question of mixed fact and law to be determined by an analysis "on the one hand, [of] the terms of and construction of the contract read in the light of the existing circumstances, and on the other hand [of] the events which have occurred".[15]

If an actor is unable to attend rehearsals due to illness so that it is reasonably doubtful whether he is able to appear in the part on the first night, the agreement might be thereby frustrated.[16] This principle would appear to be equally applicable to the production of a film. If it is reasonably clear that an entertainer will be unable, due to illness, to comply with the production schedule for the film the contract may in such circumstances be frustrated.

A difficult question arises as to whether the death or illness of one member of a group will frustrate an agreement by the group to perform on a specified date or over a specified period. If all the members are significant members in their own right it may be that the agreement to perform is determined by the death or illness of one member. It is a question of degree. However, it is submitted that unless the illness or death is that of the lead performer, or a significant member of the group

---

[14] *Marshall v. Harland and Wolff Ltd.* [1972] 1 W.L.R. 899.
[15] *Denny, Mott and Dickson Ltd. v. James Fraser & Co. Ltd.* [1944] A.C. 265 at 274–275, H.L.
[16] *Poussard v. Spiers and Pond* (1876) 1 Q.B.D. 410. See *Said v. Butt* [1920] 3 K.B. 497 at 501: "A first night is . . . an event of great importance. The result of a first night may make or mar a play . . . A first night, therefore, is a special event with special characteristics."

the agreement will not be rendered radically different from that contracted for.[17]

2.07 Management. The death or illness of the manager or member of the management employing the artiste does not necessarily put an end to the contract, unless the contract is for the performance of personal services by such person. Thus where an impresario contracts a performer to perform at a concert or theatre and dies before the performance, absent contractual terms to the contrary, the death will not put an end to the contract because it is immaterial who pays the performer provided he is paid.[18]

Where the personal manager of an artiste is unable through illness or other reasons beyond his control to render his contractual services to an artiste for such period as to render impossible the operation object and purpose of the contract, the personal relationship will be destroyed and both parties will be discharged from their obligations under it.[19]

Further, where an artiste enters into a contract with a partnership or company in which personal services (for example, personal management) are to be rendered to the artiste by the partnership, company or a specified individual in such entities, the dissolution of partnership, winding up of the company or the termination of the employment of the individual will, in the absence of contractual provision to the contrary, operate to terminate the contract.[20]

(ii) *Extra expense*

2.08 Substantial increases in costs either by reason of failure to adhere to a production schedule or in some cases currency movements often occurs in some sectors of the entertainment industry: in particular the film and television industry. However, the fact that there has been an unforeseen increase in the cost does not of itself frustrate the venture.[21] So, for example, the fact that the cost of a film may escalate due to factors beyond the control of a producer is not of itself a factor frustrating performance of the production agreement.

Further, performance of a contract is not frustrated by currency movements:

"The parties to an executory contract are often faced, in the course of carrying it out, with a turn of events which they did not at all

---

[17] *Glinseretti v. Richards, The Times,* January 26, 1907, C.A.; *Harvey v. Tivoli, Manchester, Ltd.* (1907) T.L.R. 592, C.A.

[18] *Phillips v. Alhambra Palace Co.* [1901] 1 K.B. 59.

[19] *Morgan v. Manser* [1948] 1 K.B. 184. See also *post*, Chap. 4, "Music Agreements".

[20] *Sales v. Crispi* (1913) 29 T.L.R. 491.

[21] *Larrinaga & Co. Ltd. v. Societe Franco-Americaine des Phosphates de Medulla, Paris* (1922) 38 T.L.R. 739; *Tsakiroglou & Co. Ltd. v. Noblee Thorl G.m.b.H* [1962] A.C. 93 at 115.

anticipate – a wholly abnormal rise or fall in prices, a sudden depreciation of a currency . . . Yet this does not in itself affect the bargain they have made."[22]

Such price rise or fall or depreciation in currency will only frustrate performance of the contract if a consideration of the terms of the contract, in the light of the circumstances existing when it was made, shows that the parties never agreed to be bound in a fundamentally different situation which has unexpectedly emerged.[23]

(iii) *Delay*

"Whether or not delay is such to bring about frustration must be a **2.09** question to be determined by an informed judgment based upon all the evidence of what has occurred and what is likely thereafter to occur. Often it will be a question of degree whether the effect of delay suffered, will be such as to bring about frustration of the particular adventure in question."[24] It is therefore possible that unforeseen delay caused, for example, by strike or illness may frustrate performance of an agreement. In the case of an agreement to produce a film, delays are of common occurrence due to, *inter alia*, failure to adhere to shooting schedule and illness. Whether or not such causes are sufficient to frustrate performance of the agreement must be subject to the test laid down by Lord Roskill in *Pioneer Shipping Ltd v. BTP Tioxide Ltd (The Nema)*. Delay is a common occurrence in the entertainment industry. The parties can and often do make contingency plans for such occurrences. It is therefore submitted that delay will frustrate a contract only where the cause of the delay is so abnormal or pre-emptive that the parties could not have made provision for such an event in the preparation of the production schedule.

2. Economic Duress

Economic duress is an evolving principle whose boundaries have not **2.10** yet been fully determined. Such duress can occur where a party to a contract is forced by the other party to renegotiate the terms of the contract to his disadvantage and has no alternative but to accept the new terms.[25] Practical experience shows that there is a tendency in the entertainment industry towards the variation of pre-existing contractual

---

[22] *British Movietonews Ltd. v. London and District Cinemas Ltd.* [1952] A.C. 166 at 185, H.L.
[23] *Ibid.* at 185.
[24] *Pioneer Shipping Ltd. v. B.T.P. Tioxide Ltd. (The Nema)* [1982] A.C. 724 at 752, H.L.; see also *Chitty on Contracts* (26th ed.) Vol. 1, para. 1657.
[25] See, *e.g. B & S Contracts and Designs Ltd. v. Victor Green Publications Ltd.* [1984] I.C.R. 419; *Atlas Express Ltd. v. Kafco (Importers & Distributors) Ltd.* [1989] 1 All E.R. 641.

obligations by means of commercial pressure. However, in a contractual situation commercial pressure is not enough. There must be some factor which could in law be regarded as a coercion of will so as to vitiate consent[26]:

> "In determining whether there was a coercion of will such that there was no true consent, it is material to inquire whether the person alleged to have been coerced did or did not protest; whether, at the time he was allegedly coerced into making the contract, he did or did not have an alternative course open to him such as an adequate legal remedy; whether he was independently advised; and whether after entering the contract he took steps to avoid it. All these matters are . . . relevant in determining whether he acted voluntarily or not."[27]

Thus, where a plaintiff seeks to set aside a transaction he must establish that he entered into the agreement unwillingly but not necessarily under protest, though the absence of protest will be highly relevant; that he had no realistic alternative but to submit to the defendant's demands; that his apparent consent was exacted from him by improper pressure exerted by or on behalf of the defendant; and that he repudiated the transaction as soon as the pressure was relaxed.[28]

3. Discharge by breach

2.11 A breach of a primary obligation[29] will, in the absence of contractual terms to the contrary, give rise to the right to put an end to the remaining primary obligations agreement in two circumstances. These circumstances are

> " . . . (1) [w]here the event resulting from the failure by one party to perform a primary obligation has the effect of depriving the other party of substantially the whole benefit which it was the intention of the parties that he should obtain from the contract, the party not in default may elect to put an end to all primary obligations of both

---

[26] *Pao On v. Lau Yiu Long* [1980] A.C. 614 at 635, P.C.; *Universe Tankships Inc. of Monrovia v. International Transport Workers Federation* [1982] I.C.R. 262, H.L.; *Alex Lobb Ltd. v. Total Oil* [1983] 1 W.L.R. 87 at 93, on appeal [1985] 1 W.L.R. 173 unaffected on this point; *B & S Contracts and Design Ltd. v. Victor Publications Ltd.* [1984] I.C.R. 419, C.A.

[27] *Pao On v. Lau Yiu Long* [1980] A.C. 614 at 635, P.C.

[28] *Ibid.* at 635; *Universe Tankships Inc. of Monrovia v. International Transport Workers Federation* [1982] I.C.R. 262, H.L.; *Alec Lobb Ltd. v. Total Oil* [1983] 1 W.L.R. 87 at 93, on appeal [1985] 1 W.L.R. 173 unaffected on this point; *B. & S. Contracts and Design Ltd. v. Victor Green Publications Ltd.* [1984] I.C.R. 419, C.A.

[29] Primary obligations are the legal obligations arising out of the contract between the parties "to procure that whatever he has promised will be done is done", *per* Lord Diplock *Photo Productions Ltd. v. Securicor Ltd.* [1980] A.C. 827 at 849, H.L.

parties remaining unperformed. (If the expression "fundamental breach" is to be retained, it should in the interests of clarity, be confined to this exception.) (2) Where the contracting parties have agreed, whether by express words or by implication of law, that *any* failure by one party to perform a particular primary obligation ('condition' in the nomenclature of the Sale of Goods Act 1893), irrespective of the gravity of the event that has in fact resulted from the breach, shall entitle the other party to elect to put an end to all primary obligations of both parties remaining unperformed. (In the interests of clarity . . . 'breach of condition' should be reserved for this exception.)"[30]

The circumstances giving rise to the right to repudiate an agreement and whether a term is a condition, warranty or innominate term will depend upon the construction of the contract and the facts of each case. It is not proposed to undertake in this work a detailed treatment of the law relating to discharge of contracts. It is therefore recommended that reference be made to one of the standard works on the subject.[31]

---

[30] *Photo Productions Ltd. v. Securicor Ltd.* [1980] A.C. 827 at 849, H.L.
[31] See *Chitty on Contracts* (26th ed.) Vol. 1, para. 1701.

DAMAGES

1. Introduction

3.01 **Distinction between remoteness of damage and measure of damage.** A claim for damages raises two questions. First, what kind of damage entitles the plaintiff to recover compensation. This question concerns the remoteness of damage. Secondly, is the damage sufficiently proximate. This second question concerns the measure of damages and does not arise for consideration until it has been determined by the rule of remoteness whether that head of damage can be brought into consideration at all.

2. Remoteness of Damage: The Rule in *Hadley v. Baxendale*

3.02 **The rule.** The rule that governs remoteness of damage was stated as follows by Alderson, B., in delivering the judgment of the Court of Exchequer in *Hadley v. Baxendale*:

> "Where two parties have made a contract which one of them has broken, the damages which the other party ought to receive in respect of such breach of contract should be such as may fairly and reasonably be considered either arising naturally, *i.e.* according to the usual course of things, from such breach of contract itself, or such as may reasonably be supposed to have been in the contemplation of both parties, at the time they made the contract, as the probable result of the breach of it."[1]

This formulation contains two limbs. The first limb of the rule deals with normal damage that occurs in the usual course of things; the second with damage which arises because of special circumstances.

---

[1] (1854) 9 Exch. 341 at 354.

Under the first limb the aggrieved party is only entitled to recover such part of the loss actually resulting as was at the time of the contract in the reasonable contemplation[2] of the defaulting party as liable to result from the breach in the ordinary course of things: "The first part of the rule contains the necessity for the knowledge of certain basic facts . . . On this limited basis of knowledge the horizon of contemplation is confined to things "arising naturally", *i.e.* according to the usual course of things."[3] What arises in the usual course of things is "what reasonable business men must be taken to have contemplated as the natural and probable result if the contract was broken. As reasonable business men, each must be taken to understand the ordinary practices and exigencies of the other's trade or business."[4]

The second limb applies where "special circumstances were communicated by the Plaintiffs to the Defendants, and thus known to both parties, the damages resulting from the breach of such a contract, which they would reasonably contemplate, would be the amount of injury which would ordinarily follow from a breach of contract under these special circumstances so known and communicated".[5]

It has been said that the mere fact of knowledge cannot increase liability and is only important if it forms part of the contract.[6] However, it would appear to be "sufficient if, on the basis of the knowledge of the special circumstances communicated to the defendant, the reasonable man in the defendant's position at the time of the contract would have understood that by making the promise in those circumstances he was assuming responsibility for the risk of the type of loss in question".[7]

The following principles are applicable in respect of both limbs of the test laid down in *Hadley v. Baxendale*. First, the question of what was in the reasonable contemplation of the parties is to be judged at the time of the contract. Thus, damages will not be awarded under the second limb unless the plaintiff has particular evidence to show that at the time of entering into the contract the defendant knew the special circumstances relied upon. Secondly, in order to make the contract breaker liable it is

---

[2] *per* Lord Reid *Koufos v. Czarnikow* [1969] 1 A.C. 351 at 388, H.L.; see also *Victoria Laundry v. Newman Industries* [1949] 2 K.B. 528, C.A.; but see *Parsons Ltd. v. Uttley Ingham & Co.* [1978] 1 Q.B. 791 at 807 where Scarman L.J. said that the difference between "reasonably foreseeable" and "reasonably contemplated" "is semantic not substantial".

[3] *Koufos v. Czarnikow* [1969] 1 A.C. 350 at 416, H.L.

[4] *Monarch Steamship Co. Ltd. v. Karlshamns Oljiefabriker (A/B)* [1949] A.C. 196 at 224.

[5] *Hadley v. Baxendale* (1854) 9 Ex. 341 at 354; *Victoria Laundry v. Newman Industries Ltd.* (1949) 2 K.B. 528, C.A.; *Koufos v. Czarnikow* [1969] 1 A.C. 351.

[6] *British Columbia Saw-Mill Co. Ltd. v. Nettleship* (1868) L.R. 3 C.P. 499 at 509, *per* Willes J.

[7] *Chitty on Contracts* (26th ed.) Vol. 1, para., 1798.This test is supported by dicta of Bridge L.J. in *G.K.N. Centrax Gears Ltd. v. Matbro Ltd.* [1976] 2 Lloyd's Rep. 555 at 580 and Goff J. in *Satef-Huttenes Albertus S.p.A. v. Paloma Tercera Shipping Co. S.A.* [1981] 1 Lloyd's Rep. 175 at 183–184.

not necessary that he should actually have asked himself what loss was liable to result from a breach of the kind which subsequently occurred. It suffices that, if he had considered the question, he would as a reasonable man have concluded that the loss of the type[8] in question was liable to result.

3. Measure of damages

3.03 **Principles upon which damages are awarded.** "The underlying rule of the common law" is that "where a party sustains a loss by reason of a breach of contract, he is, so far as money can do it, to be placed in the same situation, with respect to damages, as if the contract had been performed."[9] Generally, therefore, the plaintiff is entitled to be put into the position he would have been in if the contract was performed. However, the injured party is under no obligation to make a claim for damages; he may elect to claim for wasted expenditure rather than loss of profits.[10]

3.04 **Wasted expenditure.** A plaintiff has an unfettered right to elect to claim loss of profit or the expenditure thrown away or wasted by reason of the defendant's breach of contract.[11] The plaintiff cannot, however, claim both: he must elect between them.[12] If the plaintiff claims wasted expenditure he is not limited to expenditure incurred after the contract was concluded he may also claim pre-contractual expenditure provided that such expenditure was in the reasonable contemplation of the parties as likely to be wasted if the contract was broken.[13]

However, the plaintiff is not entitled to succeed in respect of a claim for wasted expenditure where, even had the contract not been broken by the defendant, the returns earned by the plaintiff's exploitation of the subject of the contract (*e.g.* a film or record) would not have been sufficient to recoup that expenditure.[14] The burden of proof on this

---

[8] The "party who has suffered damage does not have to show that the contract-breaker ought to have contemplated, as being not unlikely, the precise detail of the damage or the precise manner of its happening. It is enough if he should have contemplated that damage of damage *of that kind* is not unlikely": *Christopher Hill Ltd. v. Ashington Piggeries Ltd.* [1969] 3 All E.R. 1496 at 1524, C.A., reversed [1972] A.C. 441 without affecting this point.

[9] *Koufos v. Czarnikow Ltd.* [1969] 1 A.C. 350 at 414, H.L., citing Parke B. in *Robinson v. Harman* (1848), 1 Exch. 850.

[10] *Anglia Television Ltd. v. Reed* [1972] 1 Q.B. 60, C.A.; *C.C.C. Films (London) Ltd. v. Impact Qudarant Films Ltd.* [1985] 1 Q.B. 16.

[11] *Ibid.*

[12] *Ibid.*

[13] *Anglia Television Ltd. v. Reed* [1972] 1 Q.B. 60, C.A.; *Lloyd v. Stanbury* [1971] 1 W.L.R. 535.

[14] *C. & P. Haulage v. Middleton* [1983] 1 W.L.R. 1461, C.A.; *C.C.C. Films (London) Ltd. v. Impact Quadrant Films Ltd.* [1985] 1 Q.B. 16.

issue is on the defendant: in other words it is not up to the plaintiff to show that the venture would have been profitable but up to the defendant to show, on a balance of probabilities, that the plaintiff would not have recouped his expenditure even if the contract had been fully performed.[15]

It is perhaps no coincidence that the most significant cases on wasted expenditure have occurred in respect of entertainment contracts. In the case of the performing arts considerable expenses may be incurred in, for example, developing[16] a film, contracting directors, film crew and artistes, and hiring locations before principal photography has begun. Even where a prominent performer plays the lead part it is often difficult to say at what stage, if at all, a film will break even or make a profit.

In such circumstances an action based on the principles laid down in *Anglia Television Ltd. v. Reed* and *C.C.C. Films (London) Ltd. v. Impact Quadrant Films Ltd.* has a number of advantages. First, where the producer is able to provide evidence of his expenditure he will prima facie be entitled to this sum whereas a claim for loss of profits may be difficult to substantiate and subject to reduction to take account of the speculative nature of the expected returns from, for example, a film or record album. Secondly, it will be difficult for the defendant, who bears the burden of proof, to show that the film or record would not have recouped its expenditure, in any event, so as to deprive the plaintiff of his right to recover his wasted expenditure.

4. Mitigation of Loss

The general principle is that, so far as possible, a party who has proved   **3.05**
a breach of a bargain to supply what he contracted to get is to be placed, as far as money can do it, in as good a situation as if the contract had been performed. However, "this first principle is qualified by a second, which imposes on a plaintiff the duty of taking all reasonable steps to mitigate the loss consequent on the breach, and debars him from claiming any part of the damage which is due to his neglect to take such steps".[17] But, "this second principle does not impose on the plaintiff an obligation to take any step which a reasonable and prudent man would not ordinarily take in the course of his business. But when in the course of his business he has taken action arising out of the transaction, which action has diminished his loss, the effect in actual diminution of the

---

[15] *C.C.C. Films (London) Ltd. v. Impact Quadrant Films Ltd.* [1985] Q.B. 16.

[16] See *post*, Chap. 8, "Films" for a description of this process.

[17] *British Westinghouse Electric and Manufacturing Co. Ltd. v. Underground Electric Railways Co. of London Ltd.* [1912] A.C. 673 at 689, H.L.

loss he has suffered may be taken into account even though there was no duty on him to act."[18]

Any loss resulting from such reasonable steps is recoverable.[19] The onus of proof is on the defendant to prove any failure to mitigate.[20]

These principles are generally applicable to entertainment contracts. However, the position of an artiste calls for particular consideration. In *Clayton-Green v. De Corville*[21] the plaintiff had been engaged by the defendant to play a leading part in a new play and he attended some rehearsals. Later, the defendant himself formed the view that the plaintiff was not suitable for the particular part, but offered him another part in the same play at the same fee, which the plaintiff declined to take. McCardie J, in holding that the plaintiff's refusal was not unreasonable said:

> "An actor's life differed much from the life of a business man. If the latter bought well and sold at a profit he might be indifferent to the approval of the public and might smile at the asperity of critics. But an actor lived on the whisper of public approbation. He might use the language of Pope and say, 'A breath revives him or a breath o'erthrows.' He must therefore choose his parts. He must consult the tastes and whims of the public. It was well and cogently observed by Dr. Johnson that: 'Those who live to please must please to live.' Versatility was lightly spoken of by laymen. That quality was not only permissible but often requested in the days of stock companies . . . But the case was now quite different under modern theatrical methods, as with striking development of specialised reputations in the West End theatres. It was now only an actor of dominant position who could safely embark upon the perilous seas of unchecked versatility. But an actor in the position of the plaintiff must choose characters. He could not be an histrionic Autolycus, a mere snapper-up of parts."

With the advent of television and the cinema, versatility is not now as perilous as in the 1920s and is often considered to be the mark of an actor of note. However, due to the fact that an actor lives by his reputation with the public it is submitted that the dicta of McCardie J. is still of general application. However, the question whether a part is suitable

---

[18] *British Westinghouse v. Underground Railways Co.* [1972] A.C. 673 at 689, H.L., referring to James L.J. in *Dunkirk Colliery Co. v. Lever* (1878) 9 Ch.D. 20 at 25, C.A.; *London and South of England Building Society v. Stone* [1983] 1 W.L.R. 1242.

[19] *British Westinghouse v. Underground Railways Co.* [1912] A.C. 673 at 691, H.L.; *The World Beauty* [1970] P. 144, C.A.; *Pagnan (R.) Fratelli v. Corbisa Industrial* [1970] 1 W.L.R. 306, C.A.; *Koch Marine v. D'Amica Societa Di Navigazione* [1980] Lloyd's Rep. 75 at 88.

[20] *British Westinghouse v. Underground Railways Co.* [1912] A.C. 673, H.L.; *Garnac Grain Co. Inc. v. Faure & Fairclough Ltd.* [1968] A.C. 130 at 1140, H.L.

[21] (1920) 36 T.L.R. 790.

is a question of fact for the court to decide in the light of the reputation of the actor, the type of character he ordinarily plays and his audience.

5. Loss of Publicity

General principle. An artiste will be entitled to damages for loss of   **3.06**
publicity where a breach of contract deprives him of the opportunity of appearing in public if that appearance would have enhanced his reputation. However, damages will not be recoverable for damage to a reputation already existing by not allowing an artiste to obtain publicity in accordance with his contract.[22] The principle was stated thus by Greer L.J. in *Withers v. General Theatre Corporation Ltd.*[23]:

> "I take it to be common ground that for a breach of contract . . . the damages are limited to the pecuniary loss arising from the breach of contract; and however clear it may be that the person whose contract has been broken suffers general damages for loss of reputation he cannot get anything in respect of that loss . . .
>
> There is an exception to this rule, and that is with regard to an agreement by an artiste who engages to perform at a theatre or music-hall, and I understand the exception has this effect: When a proprietor of a music hall or theatre engages an artiste to perform, he is promising two things: he is giving a consideration which consists of two different elements; first, a salary which he promises the artiste for his services, and secondly, the opportunity to play in public some part which will attract attention . . . For the loss of opportunity of impressing the public . . . and so enhancing or maintaining his reputation, he is also entitled to recover damages . . ."

The approach of the Court of Appeal would suggest that damages for the loss of the opportunity of enhancing or maintaining a reputation is limited to actors and actresses. However, in *Tolnay v. Criterion Film Productions Ltd.*[24] where the plaintiff, who was a scriptwriter, was deprived of a screen credit by a reason of the defendant's repudiation of a screenwriting agreement it was held that the principle applied to all creative artistes who earned their living by attracting the public to their

---

[22] *Marbe v. George Edwardes* [1928] 1 K.B. 269, C.A.; *Herbert Clayton and Jack Waller Ltd. v. Oliver* [1930] A.C. 209, H.L.; *Withers v. General Theatre Corporation* [1933] 2 K.B. 536, C.A.; *Tolnay v. Criterion Films* [1936 2 All E.R. 1625; *Ackland v. World Screenplays, The Times,* February 23, 1950.

[23] *Withers v. General Theatre Corporation* [1933] 2 K.B. 536 at 554, C.A.; approved *Herbert Clayton and Jack Waller Ltd. v. Oliver* [1930] A.C. 209, H.L.

[24] [1936] 2 All E.R. 1625. See also *Ackland v. World Screenplays, The Times,* February 23, 1950.

3.06 *Damages*

work. Therefore, the principle will apply, *inter alia*, to actors, composers, musicians, writers and directors.

3.07 Remoteness and measure of damages. In *Herbert Clayton and Jack Waller Ltd. v. Oliver*[25] the House of Lords laid down the test in respect of the remoteness for loss of publicity as follows:

> " . . . the old and well established rule applies . . . damages are those that may reasonably be supposed to have been in the contemplation of the parties at the time when the contract was made, as the probable result of its breach, and if any special circumstances were unknown to one parties, the damages associated with and flowing from such breach cannot be included. Here both parties knew that as flowing from the contract the plaintiff would be billed and advertised as appearing at the Hippodrome, and in the theatrical profession that is a valuable right."

In assessing the quantum of damages it is competent for the court to consider the success of the production or the popularity of the venue of the place of public entertainment and the fact that in the ordinary course the plaintiff would be credited and advertised as appearing.[26] The stage which the artiste has reached in his career at the time of breach is a relevant consideration when assessing damages. The fact that he is at an early stage and may have become established as a result of the publicity may be a factor increasing the quantum of damages.[27]

In *Tolnay v. Criterion Film Productions*[28] Goddard J. was of the view that the loss of publicity to an actor is more serious than in the case of a playwright or screenwriter. It would appear that the inference to be drawn from this conclusion is that, subject to the matters to be taken into consideration in assessing damages, the quantum of damages to be awarded to an actor would be greater if the same film were cancelled resulting in a breach of the author's and actor's contract. It is submitted that this conclusion is correct. The enhancement of an actor's career, and thus his living, is dependent upon appearing before the public whether on the stage or on film. A playwright or screenwriter's success does not depend entirely upon the perception of his work by the public. It is often the case that an author will be contracted to write several scripts during the course of the year of which only one may be reproduced in the form of a film or theatrical production. The unused scripts are considered on their merits and may nevertheless enhance the reputation of the author amongst the commissioners of such scripts. If they

---

[25] [1930] A.C. 209 at 220, H.L.
[26] *Ibid.*
[27] *Ackland v. World Screenplays, The Times,* February 23, 1950.
[28] [1936] 2 All E.R. 1625.

28

are of high quality the commissioners will consider him as a candidate for further scripts which they may require. The fact they have not been produced as a film or theatre production may be as a result of a number of reasons principal amongst which is the inability to obtain sufficient money to fund the production.

Producer and impresario. An impresario or producer is not entitled to **3.08** damages for loss of publicity caused by the contractual failure of an artiste to appear. A producer or impresario is a businessman and not a creative artiste.[29]

6. Screen Credit

This is merely the carrying into operation of the contractual duty to give **3.09** publicity to the artiste. Where the producer in breach of contract fails to provide the contracted credits he is liable in damages for the loss of publicity by the artiste.[30] It is submitted that it is an implied term of an artiste's agreement with a producer or impresario that he will receive a credit. The right to publicity can only be given real meaning if the name of the artiste as well as his appearance is put before the public. If his performance is anonymous there can be no enhancement of reputation. This is particularly the case where the artiste is relatively unknown or is a scriptwriter.

---

[29] *Fielding v. Moiseiwitsch* (1946) 175 L.T. 265.
[30] *Ackland v. World Screenplays, The Times,* February 23, 1950.

MUSIC AGREEMENTS

1. Personal Management Agreements

4.01 General. A performer employs a personal manager to advance his professional career and administer his business affairs. With few exceptions, especially in the pop industry, performers have neither the time nor the inclination to undertake these activities and in general, if they are to have any great success, must have experienced managers. The specific terms and conditions to be included in such agreements are outside the scope of this work. Reference should therefore be made to a standard work dealing with the terms and conditions to be inserted in such agreements.[1] The areas to which the manager and performer should, however, pay particular regard prior to entering into such an agreement, are:

(a) the provision of independent and experienced legal advice to the performer prior to him entering into such an agreement,[2] and

(b) ensuring that the agreement is fair so as not to be in restraint of trade.[3]

4.02 Nature of management agreement. Where a manager provides his expertise in developing the career of the performer and receives a share of the income of the performer on a commission basis the relationship between the parties is "more a joint venture, almost approaching the relationship of partners than anything else."[4] The relationship is not, however, a partnership nor, clearly, apart from express contractual provision, is it one of employer and employee. Each party is in essence

---

[1] See Bagehot, R., *Music Business Agreements* (Sweet & Maxwell, 1989).

[2] As to which see generally "Undue Influence", *post*, Chap. 5.

[3] See generally "Restraint of Trade", *post*, Chap. 5.

[4] *Page One Records Ltd. v. Britton* [1968] 1 W.L.R. 157 where counsel for the group submitted that the manager was an employee but this was rejected by Stamp J.; *Petersen v. Gibb* (1969) 113 Sol. Jo. 894; *O'Sullivan v. Management Agency Ltd.* [1985] 1 Q.B. 428, *per* Waller L.J. at 472.

contributing their respective skills to a joint venture which, depending on the terms of the agreement, is under the control of the manager.[5]

Duty of parties. The relationships between a performer and his per-   **4.03**
sonal manager requires a high degree of mutual confidence between them. Consequently, there is an implied term in all such agreements that neither party will do anything which he could reasonably foresee would destroy that confidence.[6] The duty of confidence places the manager in a fiduciary position.[7] Thus, he may not put himself in a position where his personal interests conflict with his duty to promote the career of, and provide independent guidance and advice, to the performer.[8] The breach of such a term amounts to a repudiation of the management agreement.[9]

2. Music Publishing Agreements

General. The general law of contract applies to music publishing   **4.04**
agreements. The terms which are generally incorporated into such agreements will vary according to the performer and the music publisher. A consideration of such terms is outside the scope of this work and reference should be made to one of the standard works dealing with the drafting of such agreements.[10] There are, however, a number of specific aspects of music publishing agreements which should be considered.[11]

Form of publishing agreement. Where the agreement consists of an   **4.05**
assignment of copyright or an exclusive licence writing is required.[12] No particular form for such writing is required.

---

[5] *Page One Records Ltd. v. Britton* [1968] 1 W.L.R. 157; *Peterson v. Gibbs* (1969) 113 Sol. Jo. 894. *Cheese v. Thomas* [1994] 1 W.L.R. 129, 137, C.A.
[6] *Denmark Productions Ltd. v. Boscobel Productions Ltd.* [1969] 1 Q.B. 699; *Page One Records Ltd. v. Britton* [1968] 1 W.L.R. 167; *O'Sullivan v. Management Agency Music Ltd.* [1984] 1 Q.B. 428, C.A.
[7] See *post*, para. 6.04.
[8] *O'Sullivan v. Management Agency and Music Ltd.* [1985] Q.B. 428; *Elton John v. Richard Leon James* [1991] F.S.R. 397
[9] *Denmark Productions Ltd. v. Boscobel Productions Ltd.* [1969] 1 Q.B. 699, C.A.; see also *Page One Records Ltd. v. Britton* [1968] 1 W.L.R. 167; *Elton John v. Richard Leon James* [1991] F.S.R. 397; *O'Sullivan v. Management Agency and Music Ltd.* [1984] 1 Q.B. 428, C.A.
[10] See, *e.g.* Bagehot, R., *op. cit., ante,* para. 4.01, n.1.
[11] Reference should also be made to the sections in this work relating to "Undue Influence" and "Restraint of Trade" and "Agreements between Copyright Owners and Licensees" which are of importance in relation to the effective formation of such agreements.
[12] Copyright, Designs and Patents Act 1988, ss.90(3), 92(1). For the distinction between an assignment and a licence, see also, *post*, Chap. 7.

4.06 Nature of music publishing agreement. A conflict arises in a music publishing agreement between the interests of the music publisher and the composer. The music publisher on the one hand, when making decisions on whether, when and how to exploit the compositions, wishes to be at liberty to take the view that publication is not justified immediately, or at all, or that there should be publication but accompanied only by a low level of promotional effort and expense. The composer on the other hand usually wishes his compositions to be published immediately with maximum publicity and promotional effort. This freedom of the publisher to consult its own interests, which might be in conflict with those of the composers, was recognised by Lord Reid in *A. Schroeder Music Publishing Co. Ltd. v. Macaulay*[13] when he observed:

> "It was argued that there must be read into this agreement an obligation on the publisher to act in good faith. I take that to mean he would be in breach of contract if by reason of some oblique or malicious motive he refrained from publishing work he would otherwise have published . . .
> I do not think that a publisher could reasonably be expected to enter into any positive commitment to publish future work by an unknown composer. Possibly there might be some general undertaking to use his best endeavours to promote the composer's work. But that would probably have to be in such general terms as to be of little use to the composer."

Thus it would appear that where there is no absolute obligation imposed on the publisher to exploit a work, a court will be slow to impose an obligation which would stultify the exercise by the publisher of his commercial judgment.

In *Elton John v. Richard Leon James*[14] Nicholls J. in considering such a possible conflict said:

> "I do not think that the publisher's freedom to consult its own commercial interest in balancing expense and risk against prospects of success is inconsistent with the existence of fiduciary duties . . . The object sought to be achieved by exploitation is maximising the pool of royalties received by the publisher and in which the composer would share. In seeking to attain that object, in which the parties have a joint interest, the publisher is entitled to exercise its own commercial skill and judgment; but in so doing the publisher

---

[13] [1974] 1 W.L.R. 1308.
[14] *Elton John v. Richard Leon James* [1991] F.S.R. 397.

is not free to pursue its own commercial interests (as distinct from the joint interest)."[15]

The fiduciary duties envisaged by Nicholls J. arise where "copyrights **4.07** are assigned to a publisher, and to become its property, but with the intention that the would be exploited by the publisher, which would have complete control over the method of exploitation not for its benefits alone but for the joint benefit."[16] In such circumstances the relationship gives rise to "an arrangement in the nature of a joint venture, and the writers would need to place trust and confidence in the publisher in the manner in which it discharged its exploitation function".[17] This fiduciary duty does not, however, oblige the publisher to exploit compositions which, having regard to its assessment of the prospects of success and the expenses of promotion, it considers not commercially justified. If, however, exploitation is carried out it must be in a manner which the publisher honestly considers to be for the joint benefit of the parties.[18]

Thus, it is submitted, a publisher is entitled to exercise its commercial skill and judgment in good faith in deciding whether, and the manner in which, a composition should be published. It is submitted that the test of whether there has been a good faith exercise of commercial skill and judgment is that of a reasonable and prudent board of directors acting properly in the interests of the company and applying their minds to their contractual obligations to the artiste. However, in respect of any composition which the publisher, in exercising its commercial skill and judgment in good faith, decides actually to exploit that exploitation must be carried out in a manner which will result in the maximum return to the pool of royalties from which the writer and the publisher will share. The publisher may not pursue its own commercial interest by exploiting the composition through, for example, its own subpublisher if in so doing that sub-publisher receives remuneration in excess of that which can be obtained in an arm's length transaction with an independent sub-publisher. This fiduciary duty also places the publisher under a duty not to make for itself any profit not brought into account in computing the writer's royalties unless this is clear to the composer prior to the signing of the agreement and on which he has obtained independent advice.

Restraint of trade. Reference should be made to Chapter 5, "Restraint of **4.08** Trade".

---

[15] *Ibid.* at 433–434.
[16] *Ibid.* at 433.
[17] *Ibid.* at 433.
[18] *Ibid.* at 433.

3. Recording Agreements

4.09 General. The general law of contract applies to the formation and termination of recording agreements. The terms and conditions of such contracts will vary depending upon the performer and the record company. In general, such contracts will be exclusive recording contracts between the performer and the person with whom he enters into the contract. Persons having the benefit of such exclusive recording contracts are now accorded specific protection under the Copyright, Designs and Patents Act 1988.[19]

A detailed examination of the terms and conditions generally incorporated into such agreements is outside the scope of this work. Reference should, therefore, be made to one of the specialist works on the drafting of such agreements.[20] However, the following aspects of such agreements merit some comment.

4.10 Restraint of trade and undue influence. These subjects are dealt with at Chapters 5 and 6 respectively.

4.11 Duty of record company with regard to exploitation of recording of performances. It is submitted that an exclusive recording agreement is, like a music publishing agreement, in the nature of a joint venture giving rise to a duty of confidence with regard to the exploitation of the sound recordings of the performers' performance. Consequently, the duty of the record company with regard to the exploitation of the sound recording will be the same duty as that imposed on the music publisher in the exploitation of a composition.

4.12 Recording costs. Generally, a recording contract will require the recording company to pay the costs of recording and producing the sound recording. Such costs will, however, be recoupable as a first charge on the gross receipts payable to the performer from the sale of the sound recordings. Where the record company has sole discretion as to the expenditure to be incurred in the recording and production of the recording, the recoupment provisions have the potential of working to the considerable detriment of the performer. Therefore, where the record company is endowed with such sole discretion, it is an implied term of the recording contract that the recording and production costs will be reasonable.[21]

---

[19] Reference should be made to "Rights in Performances", *post*, Chap. 14, for a detailed survey of the definition of and the law relating to "exclusive recording contracts".
[20] See Bagehot, R., *op. cit.*, *ante*, para. 4.01, n.1.
[21] *Zang Tumb Tuum Records Ltd. v. Johnson* [1993] E.M.L.R. 61.

CHAPTER 5

RESTRAINT OF TRADE

Note. In this chapter the general principles applicable to restraint of trade will be considered with particular reference to composers and performers' contracts. For ease of reference the word performer will be used to describe both.

General Principles

The legal principle may be stated thus: All interference with the indi- **5.01** vidual's liberty of action in trading, and all restraints of trade themselves, if there is nothing more, are contrary to public policy and therefore prima facie void.[1] The restraint will only become enforceable if the restriction is reasonable as between the parties and does not offend against public policy.[2] Thus, in every case which attracts the operation of the doctrine it is necessary to consider first whether the restraint went farther than to afford adequate protection to the party in whose favour it was granted; secondly, whether it can be justified as being in the interest of the party restrained; and, thirdly, whether it must be held contrary to public policy. The onus of establishing that the contract is reasonable as between the parties is on the proponent of the contract, while the onus of establishing that, although reasonable as between the parties, it is nevertheless contrary to public policy, lies on the party challenging the contract.[3]

---

[1] *Nordenfelt v. Maxim Nordenfelt Guns & Ammunition Co. Ltd.* [1894] A.C. 535, H.L. This is a basic proposition and must be approached with some caution in the light of the doubt about whether the restraint is void, voidable or unenforceable. See under "Void Voidable or Unenforceable" *ante*, para. 5.20.

[2] *Nordenfelt v. Maxim Nordenfelt Guns and Ammunition Co.* [1984] A.C. 535, H.L.

[3] *Herbert Morris Ltd v. Saxelby* [1916] 1 A.C. 688 at 700, 707–708, H.L.; *Esso Petroleum Co. Ltd. v. Harper's Garage (Stourport) Ltd.* [1968] A.C. 269, H.L.

5.02 **The Restraint.** Precisely what constitutes a "restraint requiring justification" is difficult to state.

In *Petrofina (Great Britain) Ltd. v. Martin*[4] the Court of Appeal attempted to describe the essential characteristics of such a restraint of trade. Lord Denning M.R. defined it as:

> " . . . any contract which interferes with the free exercise of his trade or business, by restricting . . . the work he may do for others".[5]

Diplock L.J., as he then was, described it in the following terms:

> "A contract in restraint of trade is one in which a party (the covenantor) agrees with the other party (the covenantee) to restrict his liberty in the future to carry on trade with other persons not parties to the contract in such manner as he chooses."[6]

However, neither of these definitions are exhaustive and they are liable to mislead. Diplock L.J.'s exposition, taken literally, is far too wide. It has been pointed out[7] that "any exercise of contractual freedom is likely to impose some limitation on future contractual capacity – if I agree to sell my only car to X, I am no longer free to agree to sell it to Y", and that although the words used by Diplock L.J. are wide, "only the egregious cases" are intended to be caught by the restraint of trade provisions.

In *Esso Petroleum Co. v. Harper's Garage (Stourport) Ltd.*,[8] the House of Lords encountered similar difficulties in attempting to formulate a precise definition and ultimately refrained from doing so, favouring a more pragmatic approach.[9] Lord Morris found the *Petrofina* formulations "helpful" but stressed that they were not an acid test of the ambit of the restraint of trade doctrine. Lord Reid, with whom Lord Morris of Borthy-Gest and Lord Hodsen agreed, was of the opinion that the doctrine of restraint of trade should be limited. He stated the principle thus:

> "Restraint of trade appears to me to imply that a man contracts to give up some freedom which otherwise he would have had."

The application of this definition would have the effect that if the contract does not have the effect of restricting a pre-existing freedom there is no restraint of trade which requires justification. Lord Wilberforce was content to declare that "[t]he common law has often (if

---

[4] [1966] Ch. 146.
[5] *Ibid.* at 169.
[6] *Ibid.* at 180.
[7] Davies P.L., "Post Employment Restraints: Some Recent Developments" (1992) J.B.L. 490.
[8] [1968] A.C. 269, H.L.
[9] For a convenient summary of the speeches see *Chitty on Contracts* (26th ed.) at paras. 1191.

sometimes unconsciously) thrived on ambiguity and it would be mistaken, even if it were possible, to try to crystallise the rules of this, or any, aspect of public policy into neat propositions. The doctrine of restraint of trade is one to be applied to factual situations with a broad and flexible rule of reason."[10]

This broad and flexible approach was adopted in *Stenhouse Ltd. v. Philips*,[11] where Lord Wilberforce defined a restraint of trade in very broad terms. He observed that:

> "Whether a particular provision operates in restraint of trade is to be determined not by the form the stipulation bears, but, as the statement of the question itself shows, by its effect in practice."[12]

The application of the doctrine is particularly difficult in cases where **5.03** the restraint endures during the period of engagement. Lord Reid took the view that:

> "Whenever a man agrees to do something over a period he thereby puts it wholly out of his power to exercise any trade he pleases during that period. He may enter into a contract of service or may agree to give his exclusive services to another: then during the period of the contract he is not entitled to engage in other business activities. But no one has ever suggested that such contracts are in restraint of trade except . . . where the servant had agreed not to work for anyone else but might have been given no work and received no remuneration for considerable periods and thus have been deprived of a livelihood."[13]

This distinction was reiterated by Lord Reid in *A. Schroeder Music Publishing Co. Ltd. v. Macaulay*[14]:

> "Any contract by which a person engages to give his exclusive services to another for a period, necessarily involves extensive restrictions during that period of the common law right to exercise any lawful activity he chooses in such a manner as he thinks best. Normally, the doctrine of restraint of trade has no application to such restrictions: they require no justification. But if contractual restrictions appear unnecessary or to be unreasonably capable of enforcement in an oppressive manner, then they must be justified before they can be enforced."

Thus, it would appear that restrictions on trade during the currency

---

[10] [1968] A.C. 269 at 331.
[11] [1974] A.C. 391.
[12] *Ibid.* at 402G.
[13] *Esso Petroleum Co. Ltd. v. Harper's Garage (Stourport) Ltd.* [1968] A.C. 269 at 294, 298, 306, 307, 324, 327, H.L.
[14] [1974] W.L.R. 1309 at 1314, H.L.

of the contract do not have the quality of restraints of trade unless there is discovered something too unilateral or exorbitant. Lord Pearce[15] stated the distinction thus:

> "The doctrine does not apply to ordinary commercial contracts for the regulation and promotion of trade during the existence of the contract, provided that any prevention of work outside the contract, viewed as a whole, is directed towards the absorption of the parties services and not their sterilisation . . .
>
> When a contract only ties the parties during the continuance of the contract, and the negative ties are only those which are incidental and normal to the positive commercial arrangements at which the contract aims, even though those ties exclude all dealings with others, there is no restraint of trade within the meaning of the doctrine and no question of reasonableness arises. If, however, the contract ties the trading activities of either party after its determination, it is a restraint of trade, and the question of reasonableness arises. So, too, if during the contract one of the parties is too unilaterally fettered so that the contract loses its character of a contract for the regulation and promotion of trade and acquires the predominant character of a contract in restraint of trade. In that case . . . the question whether it is reasonable arises."[16]

Lord Pearce's distinction between absorption and sterilisation is open to criticism in that it confuses the definition of what is a restraint with what is reasonable. Whether the restraint amounts to absorption or sterilisation is an important consideration in respect of reasonables and was an important factor in this respect in *A. Schroeder Music Publishing Co. Ltd. v. Macaulay.*

5.04   These definitional difficulties crystallised in *Silvertone Records Ltd. v. Mountfield.*[17] It was argued that a recording contract for the provision of exclusive services was not a restraint of trade but merely the absorption of the defendants' output and as such not in itself a restraint. This argument echoed Lord Pearce's distinction in *Esso Petroleum Co. Ltd. v. Harper's Garage* between sterilisation and absorption. In *Silvertone Records v. Mountfield* the defendants were expressly prohibited from

---

[15] *Ibid.* at 328.
[16] In *Instone v. A. Schroeder Music Publishing Co. Ltd.* [1974] 1 All E.R. 171 at 177, the Court of Appeal criticised this approach as "puzzling . . . for the very discovery [of terms oppressive, too unilateral or exorbitant] would appear to pre-empt the decision on reasonableness" and refused to apply it. However, the distinction was affirmed by the House of Lords in *A. Schroeder Music Publishing v. Macaulay* [1974] 1 W.L.R. 1308 at 1314, H.L. *per* Reid L.J. with whose speech Viscount Dilhorne, Lord Simon and Lord Kilbrandon concurred (H.L.). See also *Watson v. Praeger* [1993] E.M.L.R. 275 where Scott J. accepted this analysis as representing the law.
[17] [1993] E.M.L.R. 152.

undertaking musical recordings for anybody other than the plaintiffs: on any view this is restriction not absorption and the argument was, it is submitted, rightly rejected.

Nevertheless, it remains to be seen whether a contract which imposes a timetable of obligations, but without a separate restriction forbidding the performer contracting with others, would be held to be a restraint of trade. *Silvertone* suggests that the courts will not be blinded by the form of an agreement, but will instead enquire into the practical consequences of the agreement. Thus:

> "If an artist is effectively able to be prevented from reaching the public over a prolonged period I find it unrealistic to say that this is not a contract in restraint."[18]

However, this view may go too far. In principle there is a difference between a promise not to do any work for anyone other than the other party and a promise to do a certain amount of work for him with a freedom to work for anyone else at the same time. In the former there is an exclusive prohibition. Whereas in the latter there is no prohibition at all other than a practical one. If the performer fails to perform his obligations he will be liable for damages. However, where the obligation to record is such that it would be physically unrealistic to expect the performer to record elsewhere, there is prima facie a restraint of trade.

The Interest. In determining the reasonableness of a restraint between **5.05** the parties it is essential first to identify the "interest" the party imposing the restraint wishes to protect. The interest assumes this importance because unless it is a legitimate interest, the courts will strike down the restraint. It is well established that the court will not enforce a restraint which goes further than affording adequate protection to the legitimate interests of the party in whose favour it is granted. A common approach is that a restraint which seeks solely to prevent competition will never be regarded as reasonable and is thus void[19] but this is not a reliable test because of its subjective nature. The correct and more reliable approach is first to ascertain what were the legitimate interests of the plaintiff which they were entitled to protect and then to see whether the restraints were more than adequate for that purpose.[20] What were the legitimate interests and whether the restraint is more than adequate for the protection of those interests are both questions of fact depending largely on the nature of the business and/or industry under consideration.[21] Further, the interest which it is sought to protect must subsist at

---

[18] *Ibid.* 160.
[19] *Morris (Herbert) Ltd. v. Saxelby* [1916] 1 A.C. 688, *per* Lord Atkinson: "no person has an abstract right to be protected against competition per se in his trade or business."
[20] *Esso Petroleum Co. Ltd. v. Harper's Garage (Stourport) Ltd.* [1968] A.C. 269 at 301, 319, H.L.
[21] *Ibid.* at 301.

the time the contract is made. In *Gledhow Autoparts Ltd. v. Delaney*,[22] Diplock L.J. said:

> "It is natural . . . to tend to look at what in fact happened under the agreement; but the question of the validity of a covenant in restraint of trade has to be determined at the date at which the agreement was entered into and has to be determined in the light of what may happen under the agreement, although what may happen may cover many possibilities which in the result did not happen. A covenant of this kind is invalid *ab initio* or valid *ab initio*. There cannot come a moment at which it passes from the class of invalid into that of valid covenants."[23]

5.06   For example, a worldwide record restraint imposed in 1985 may not be enforceable if, in 1985, there was no worldwide interest to protect.[24] It would be irrelevant that a worldwide interest was subsequently acquired.[25] Where the business comprises a record company, the legitimate interest may be found in[26]:

(1) the desire to sell as many records as possible[27];

(2) the desire to ensure that there is an even and adequate flow of product;

(3) the desire to plan ahead;

(4) the desire to have available a proven successful product for as long as possible;

(5) where the company operates on an international basis, the desire and need to be able to compete on equal terms in an international environment against other record companies;

(6) the desire to be known for continued high calibre releases by long term successful artistes in order to maintain a reputation with consumers, dealers and unsigned artistes;

(7) the desire and need to recover the investment made in a particular artist;

(8) the desire to make a profit on investment;

---

[22] [1965] 1 W.L.R. 1366.
[23] *Ibid.* at 1377; *cf. Shell U.K. v. Lostock Garage Ltd.* [1976] 1 W.L.R. 1187, *per* Lord Denning M.R., to the effect that if a clause is subsequently found to operate unreasonably or unfairly, the court may nevertheless hold it to be invalid.
[24] *cf. Strange (S.W.) Ltd. v. Mann* [1965] 1 W.L.R. 629.
[25] *cf. Lyne-Pirkis v. Jones* [1969] 1 W.L.R. 1293, where it was suggested that if, at the time the agreement is made, business expansion is within the contemplation of the parties, then the court may take into account the parties expectation in determining the reasonableness of the restraint.
[26] *Panayiotou v. Sony Music Entertainment (U.K.) Ltd.* (the *George Michael* case) [1994] E.M.L.R. 229. See *post*, para. 5.27 *et seq.*
[27] See also *Petrofina (Great Britain) Ltd. v. Martin* [1966] Ch. 146 at 188E.

(9) the need to have available sufficient product to finance (a) losses on unsuccessful product,[28] and (b) the fixed costs of the infrastructure;

(10) the desire to accumulate property rights as an asset;

(11) the desire to have a supply of successful product in the future at reasonable and predictable prices.

A music publishing company would also, it is submitted, *mutatis mutandis*, have the same legitimate interests. In regard to managers, it is submitted that (3), (6), (7) and (8) would amount to legitimate interests.

(a) *Reasonableness of the restraint: the test*

In *Esso Petroleum Co. Ltd. v. Harper's Garage (Stourport) Ltd.* Lord Reid stated the approach as follows: **5.07**

> "So in every case it is necessary to consider first whether the restraint went farther than to afford adequate protection to the party in whose favour it was granted, secondly whether it can be justified as being in the interests of the party restrained, and, thirdly, whether it must be held contrary to the public interest."[29]

For the purpose of this test all the provisions of the contract must be taken into consideration.[30]

Reasonableness: Between the Parties. The restraint is only legitimate, and thus justifiable, in so far as it is reasonably necessary to protect some commercial or proprietary interest and is reasonable as between the parties. This requires a balancing exercise between the competing interests of the covenantor to trade freely and the covenantee to receive the full benefit of his bargain. The test has been formulated in the following terms.[31] **5.08**

> "As long as the restraint to which he subjects himself is no wider than is required for the adequate protection of the person in whose favour it is created, it is in his interest to be able to bind himself for the sake of the indirect advantages he may obtain by so doing."

Thus, the court adopts a broad approach and recognises that the benefits of the transaction must be viewed as a whole. If the covenantee would not have entered into the contract but for the covenant, it may well have been in the covenantor's interests to give the covenant in order to induce the covenantee to enter into the agreement.

---

[28] *cf. Zang Tumb Tuum Records Ltd. v. Johnson* [1993] E.M.L.R. 61 at 74, C.A.
[29] [1968] A.C. 269 at 300, H.L., adopting the test laid down in *Nordenfelt v. Maxim Nordenfelt and Ammunitions Co.* [1894] A.C. 535, H.L.
[30] *A. Schroeder Music Publishing Co Ltd. v. Macaulay* [1974] 1 W.L.R. 1308 at 1316, H.L.
[31] *Herbert Morris Ltd. v. Saxelby* [1916] 1 A.C. 688, *per* Lord Parker at 707.

Whether any given restraint is wider than necessary will depend on the facts of each case but, in general the nature of the interest will set the parameter of the reasonableness of the restraint as between the parties. Thus, for example, the reasonableness of the restraint in regard to the area of the restraint will depend on the nature of the business and the fashion in which it is carried on. In general, a restraint which prevents a party from conducting "any other business" whatsoever, even within a limited locality, will be void because it is wider than necessary.[32] Conversely, where there are world wide interests, a world wide restraint will be upheld.[33]

5.09   The reasonableness of a restraint in regard to duration will, similarly, be tested against the nature of the protection required. In *A. Schroeder Publishing v. Macaulay*,[34] Lord Reid observed that:

> "The duration of an agreement in restraint of trade is a factor of great importance in determining whether the restrictions in the agreement can be justified."[35]

However, it is only a factor and should not be considered in isolation. In each case the court must examine the particular facts to determine whether, in the circumstances of the business when the agreement was made, the stipulated duration was more than adequate protection to the legitimate interests contended for.[36] If therefore, for example, a record company or a music publisher has a series of options which would extend an artiste's contract for successive periods, the court should look to, *inter alia*, the legitimate interest of the company in maintaining a stable and adequate flow of successful product so as to enable its business to run efficiently and economically. If the totality of such successive periods is no more than is adequate to protect the legitimate interests of the company then it should not matter to the court that the option provisions could be operated in a manner which is commercially unreasonable. The court should have regard to the fact that the company will have many artistes under contract with similar options and cannot afford to act oppressively without damaging the goodwill of the business.[37] If, in such circumstances, an artiste should choose to rely on the commercial probity and good sense of the record company or music publisher when entering into the agreement, a court should not, it is submitted, hold the agreement unreasonable because it is legally capable of some misuse. In such circumstances the court must, in order

---

[32] *Woods v. Thorburn* (1897) 41 Sol. Jo. 756.
[33] *Vancouver Malt & Sake Brewing Co. Ltd. v. Vancouver Breweries Ltd.* [1934] A.C. 181.
[34] [1974] 1 W.L.R. 1308.
[35] *Ibid.* at 1312G.
[36] *Esso Petroleum Co. Ltd. v. Harper's Garage (Stourport) Ltd.* [1968] A.C. 269 at 303, H.L.
[37] *Ibid.*; *A. Schroeder Music Publising Co. Ltd. v. Macaulay* [1974] 1 W.L.R. 1308 at 1313, H.L.

to reach a decision as to the fairness of the options and the potential duration, go on to consider whether the consideration is commensurate with the benefit secured to the artiste for such potential restraint.

Reasonableness between the parties also admits consideration of the equality of bargaining power between the parties.[38] Where one party exerts its commercial strength over another so as to take unconscionable advantage of the other's weakness, the agreement thereby produced will neither be reasonable nor in the interests of the weaker party and will not be enforced.[39]

The quantum of the consideration is relevant in determining the reasonableness of the restraint. In *Nordenfelt v. Nordenfelt*, Lord MacNaghton said:

> "It was laid down in *Mitchel v. Reynolds* [1 P.Wms. 181] that the court was to see that the restriction was made upon a good and adequate consideration, so as to be a proper and useful contract. But in time it was found that the parties themselves were better judges of that matter than the court, and it was held to be sufficient if there was legal consideration of value; though of course the quantum of consideration may enter into the question of the reasonableness of the contract."[40]

In *A. Schroeder Music Publishing Co. v. Macaulay*, Lord Diplock's test of fairness would, it appears, also require consideration to be taken into account in that the restrictions must both be reasonably necessary for the protection of the legitimate interests of the promisee and "commensurate with the benefits secured to the promisor under the contract".[41]

Consideration is particularly relevant when considering the length of the restraint. As a rule, and subject to a public policy long stop,[42] the

---

[38] *cf.* the statement in *N.W. Slat Co. v. Electrolytic Alkali Ltd.* [1914] A.C. 461 at 471, to the effect that a restraint cannot be unreasonable as between the parties if each has freely agreed to it. It is submitted that equality is merely one factor.

[39] *Esso Petroleum Co. Ltd. v. Harper's Garage (Stourport) Ltd.* [1968] A.C. 269 at 300, 305, 323–324, H.L. *A. Schroeder Music Publishing Co. v. Macaulay* [1974] 1 W.L.R. 1308 at 1316, H.L. "Unconscionable" in this context is to be taken to mean objectively unreasonable within the meaning of the text set out *ante*, para. 5.07.

[40] [1894] A.C. 535 at 565. Accordingly, it is respectfully submitted that *Chitty on Contracts* (26th ed.) at para. 1195, is potentially misleading because it fails to make clear that the adequacy of consideration is a factor relevant to the test of reasonableness. See also *Nordenfelt v. Maxim Nordenfelt Guns & Ammunition Co. Ltd.* [1894] A.C. 535 at 565 where Lord MacNaghten observed, "of course the quantum of consideration may enter into the question of the reasonableness of the contract".

[41] *A. Schroeder Music Publishing Co. v. Macaulay* [1974] 1 W.L.R. 1308 at 1315, H.L. See also *Amoco Australia Pty. Ltd. v. Rocca Bros. Engineering Pty. Ltd.* [1975] A.C. 561, P.C.

[42] See *Provident Financial Group Plc v. Hayward* [1989] I.C.R. 160. A substantial consideration may be contrary to the wider public interest and thus unenforceable in a case, *e.g.* where the restraint is against competition *per se*.

greater the consideration, the greater the justification for the duration of the restraint.[43]

5.10   Thus, the broad approach is one of fairness.[44] This permits, *inter alia*, consideration of the length of time it takes to bring a performer to the public and the investment his backers will have made in promoting his career. The paternal approach of the court to contracts entered into by young performers creates a conflict between the court's wish to uphold the freedom of contract and the desire to protect the weak and naive from powerful managers, publishers and recording companies. The difficulty has been articulated as follows:

> "On the one hand the law must protect the naive or weak minded from being exploited by those in a stronger position; on the other hand, the record industry is a particularly high risk business: the majority of the artists signed up by the companies will prove to be unsuccessful."[45]

5.11   Such an argument was considered by the Court of Appeal in *Zang Tumb Tuum Records Ltd. v. Johnson*.[46] Dillon L.J., considering the considerable investments made in promoting a performer's career, commented:

> "Pop musicians are promoted by the sales of their records, and obviously a recording company has difficulty in promoting a little known group when there are so many others seeking fame and fortune. Stringent provisions such as many of those in the recording agreement may be justifiable in an agreement of short duration. But the onus must, in my judgment, be on the recording company to justify the length of the term and the one sidedess of the provisions as to its duration."[47]

It was argued that because many new performers fail, and the fruits of a successful performer only come with time after the first successful record, the company was entitled to have a contract of long duration so as to gain the rewards of its considerable risks.

---

[43] *Esso Petroleum Co. Ltd. v. Harper's Garage (Stourport) Ltd.* [1968] A.C. 269 at 318, *per* Hodson, H.L.

[44] This is not altogether a satisfactory approach because as Wollcombe observes: "It does seem that in many of the cases the courts are looking at the fairness of the contract with hindsight of the success that the artist in question has achieved." *Op. cit., infra* at 189.

[45] Wollcombe, J.H., "Fairness versus certainty – pop goes the music contract" in [1987] 7 EIPRA 187.

[46] [1993] E.M.L.R. 61.

[47] *Ibid.* at 73.

However, Dillon L.J. dismissed this argument and pointed out that:

> "These arguments can feed on themselves, and lead logically to a submission that every recording agreement should last, at the company's option, for the whole lifetime of the Artist."[48]

Reasonableness: Public Policy. The majority of modern entertainment **5.12** cases which go before the court as allegedly being in restraint of trade are fought almost exclusively on the basis of whether they are reasonable as between the parties. However, it would appear that there is no clear distinction between what is reasonable on grounds of public policy and what is reasonable between the parties. Both limbs rest upon considerations of public policy. "There is one broad question: is it in the interests of the community that this restraint should, as between the parties be held to be reasonable and enforceable?"[49] It would appear, however, that public policy is partially shaped by commercial realities. Therefore, once it has been established that the restraint is reasonable as between the parties, it will be difficult to demonstrate that it offends public policy. Indeed, it has been said by the Privy Council that "once the Court is satisfied that the restraint is reasonable as between the parties [the] onus will be no light one".[50]

There may, however, in relation to agreements containing restraints, be wider issues affecting the interests of the public than those which relate merely to the interests of the parties.[51] In such circumstances the court must examine such wider considerations to see to what extent, if at all, it conflicts with the interest of the parties.

Conflict with public policy will depend on the prevailing policy and **5.13** extent of the clause itself. The position has been summarised by Lord Reid in *A. Schroeder Publishing v. Macaulay*[52] as follows:

> "The public interest requires in the interests both of the public and of the individual that everyone should be free so far as practicable to earn a livelihood and to give to the public the fruits of his particular abilities. The main question to be considered is whether and how far the operation of the terms of this agreement is likely to conflict with this objective."[53]

---

[48] *Ibid.* at 74.
[49] *Esso Petroleum Co. Ltd. v. Harper's Garage (Stourport) Ltd.* [1968] A.C. 269 at 324, *per* Lord Pearce (H.L.).
[50] *A-G of Commonwealth of Australia v. Adelaide Steamship Co.* [1913] A.C. 781 at 795.
[51] *Esso Petroleum Co. Ltd. v. Harper's Garage (Stourport) Ltd.* [1968] A.C. 269 at 340.
[52] [1974] 1 W.L.R. 1308, H.L.
[53] *Ibid.* at 1313.

(b) *Construction of restraint clauses*

5.14   The general principle can be stated thus:

> "Agreements in restraint of trade . . . must be construed with reference to the object to be attained by them . . . The court ought not to hold a just and honest agreement void, even when to enforce it would be just, simply because the agreement is unskillfully worded as apparently, or even really, to cover some conceivable case not within a mischief sought to be guarded against. Public policy does not require so serious a consequence to be attached to a mere want of accuracy of expression. To hold such an agreement wholly illegal and void is to lose all sense of proportion, and is not necessary for the protection either of the defendant or of the public."[54]

Nevertheless, the covenant[s] must not be uncertain in its terms.[55] The favoured approach is to construe contracts purposively so as to give effect to their object and intent. In the context of restraint of trade clauses this means that the courts are slow to create improbable and extravagant contingencies to render clauses unreasonable and void.[56]

5.15   In *Plowman (G.W.) & Son Ltd. v. Ash*,[57] a restraint was expressed in very wide terms. The former employee was restrained from canvassing "articles". The Court of Appeal held that notwithstanding the apparent wideness of the word "articles" it took on a meaning relative to the employer's business. Harman L.J. said:

> "True it is that in the covenant not to canvass there is no mention of the kind of goods in which the employer is dealing. But, in my judgment, you must regard the contract (as you always must) as a whole, and this is a contract for a sales representative in South Lincolnshire serving a firm which . . . is a corn and agricultural merchant and animal feeding stuffs manufacturer. In my opinion, it is no wider than that: the articles in which he may not canvass are the very articles in respect of which his employer employed him."[58]

However, in *Commercial Plastics Ltd. v. Vincent*,[59] the Court of Appeal struck down a restraint clause which had no words of limitation attached to it and presumably operated on a worldwide basis, whereas the employers business was exclusively within the United Kingdom. Pearson L.J. observed:

---

[54] *Haynes v. Doman* [1899] 2 Ch. 13 applied *J.A. Mont (U.K.) Ltd. v. Mills* [1993] F.S.R. 577.
[55] *Davies v. Davies* (1887) 36 Ch. D. 359.
[56] See *Rannie v. Irvine* (1844) 7 Man & G 969; *Nevanas (S.V.) & Co. Ltd. v. Walker and Foreman* [1914] 1 Ch. 413.
[57] [1964] 1 W.L.R. 568.
[58] *Ibid.* at 572.
[59] [1965] 1 Q.B. 623.

"It is unfortunate that a home-made provision, offered and accepted in good faith between commercial men and not in the least intended to be oppressive, has to be ruled out and declared void in a court of law for lack of the necessary limiting words."[60]

In *Littlewoods Organisation v. Harris*,[61] Lord Denning[62] suggested that   **5.16**
this view was *per incuriam*:

"It is important to observe that the court was not referred to the many cases where the courts have construed these clauses with regard to their object and intent. They have often inserted words of implied limitation so that they should not be held invalid as being too wide . . . [T]hat is one way of upholding a covenant which is intrinsically just and reasonable. It is a process of interpretation so as to cut down wide words to words of more limited scope. But there is another way. This is where the words are so wide that on a strict construction they cover improbable and unlikely events. All that should be done is that, if that improbable and unlikely event takes place the court should decline to enforce it."[63]

This view must now be regarded as the orthodox approach. It has recently been applied by the Court of Appeal in *Clarke v. Newland*[64] to read an implied limitation into the phrase "not to practice" so as to convert the promise into a promise not to practice as a general medical practitioner.

(c) *Severance*

The doctrine of severance applies in so far as the covenant is not really a   **5.17**
single covenant but is in effect a combination of several distinct covenants. In that case and where severance can be carried out without the addition or alteration of a word, it is permissible.[65] In *Mason v. Provident Clothing & Supply Co.* Lord Moulton stated the principle thus:

"It was suggested . . . that even if the covenant was, as a whole, too wide, the court might enforce restrictions which it might consider

---

[60] *Ibid.* at 647.
[61] [1977] 1 W.L.R. 1472.
[62] Megaw L.J. appears to agree at 1489C. See, however, the dissent of Browne L.J. at 1493B where he states: "Megaw L.J. takes the view that one can construe the agreement as containing the very much more elaborate limitations to which he has referred . . . I think this is re-writing the clause, and re-writing it so as to make enforceable that which would otherwise be unenforceable . . . I think this is something which this court can not do."
[63] *Ibid.* at 1481C, 1481H.
[64] [1991] 1 All E.R. 397. See also *J.A. Mont (U.K.) Ltd. v. Mills* [1993] F.S.R. 577 where *Clarke v. Newland* was not considered, but which implicitly adopted a similar approach.
[65] *Attwood v. Lamont* [1920] 3 K.B. 571, C.A.

reasonable (even though they were not expressed in the covenant), provided they were within its ambit . . . the court may, and in some cases will enforce a part of a covenant in restraint of trade, even though the covenant taken as a whole exceeds what is reasonable. But . . . that ought only to be done in cases where the part so enforceable is clearly severable".[66]

The clause will only be "clearly severable" where it is possible to delete words without affecting the meaning of the clause or as Millet J. has stated:

> "[A] contract can be severed if the severed parts are independent of one another and can be severed without the severance affecting the meaning of the part remaining."[67]

This is an application of the so called "blue pencil test".[68] The court is not prepared to re-write the contract, but where there are divisible obligations the court will be prepared to delete those which offend provided the others remain sensibly intact.[69]

5.18   The importance of this latter qualification has been emphasised by the Court of Appeal. In *Chemidus Wavin Ltd. v. Societe pour la Transformation et L' Exploitation des Resines Industrielles SA,*[70] Buckley L.J. said:

> "It seems to me that . . . one may well have to consider whether, after the excisions . . . have been made from the contract, the contract could be said to fail for lack of consideration or on any other ground, or whether the contract would be so changed in its character as not to be the sort of contract that the parties intended to enter into at all."[71]

Thus, the general rule is that the restraint clause can only be severed where (1) the unenforceable provision is capable of being removed without the necessity of adding to or modifying the wording of what remains; and (2) the remaining terms continue to be supported by adequate consideration; and (3) the removal of the unenforceable pro-

---

[66] [1913] A.C. 724 at 745, *per* Lord Moulton.
[67] *Business Seating Ltd. v. Broad* [1989] I.C.R. 729 at 734.
[68] *Goldsoll v. Goldman* [1915] 1 Ch. 292 is another illustration. There, the court deleted the words "real or" from a restraint which applied to "real or imitation jewellery".
[69] The importance of leaving the remainder intact was stressed by Lord Reid at 295D of *Esso Petroleum Co. Ltd. v. Harpers Garage (Stourport) Ltd.* where he said: "[I]n the ordinary case the courts will not remake a contract: unless in the special case where the contract is severable, it will not strike out one provision as unenforceable and enforce the rest".
[70] [1978] 3 C.M.L.R. 514.
[71] *Ibid.* at 520.

vision does not so change the character of the contract that it becomes wholly different to the contract the parties originally entered into.[72]

A recent innovation to avoid the difficulties associated with severance has been the inclusion of a clause, in contracts in restraint of trade, in the following terms:

> "The restrictions . . . are considered reasonable by the parties, but in the event that any such restriction found to be void would be valid if some part thereof were deleted or the period of application reduced such restriction shall apply with such modifications as may be necessary to make them valid or effective."

Such a clause appeared in the contract the subject of a dispute in *Hinton & Higgs (U.K.) Ltd. v. Murphy*.[73] The Outer House of the Court of Session held that this clause permitted the court of modify the agreement. Lord Dervaird said:

> "It has often been said that the courts will not make contracts for the parties. Here, however, as it seems to me the parties have agreed in advance they will accept as continuing to bind them such part of the arrangements which they have made as the court finds by deletion only to be alterations which permit the restriction to be regarded as reasonable. On my part I do not see why the court would refuse to perform that role, not being one of rewriting the contract but of selecting which version of it which the parties have, *inter alia*, made with each other and enabling the bargain as so modified to stand."

This view is open to criticism. First, the clause is an invitation to the court to re-write the agreement. This is contrary to public policy. As Moulton L.J. explained in *Mason v. Provident Clothing & Supply Co.*,[74] the courts are reluctant to come to the assistance of the party who has inserted the clause so as to discourage other persons from inserting such clauses. Otherwise, the party imposing the restraint has nothing to lose by litigating. He can rely on the court to make the agreement and enforce it against the weaker party:

> " . . . the Court would in the end enable them to obtain everything which they could have obtained by acting reasonably . . . [T]hey

---

[72] *Sadler v. Imperial Life Assurance Co. of Canada Ltd.* [1988] I.R.L.R. 388 at 392.
[73] [1989] I.R.L.R. 519.
[74] [1913] A.C. 724 at 746; see also *Silvertone Records Ltd. v. Mountfield* [1993] E.M.L.R. 152 at 168, where severance was specifically mentioned in clause 21.6 of the first agreement but the court refused, on the grounds of public policy, to allow the clause to operate.

hoped to paralyse the earning capabilities of the man if and when
he left their service, and were not thinking of what would be a
reasonable protection to their business, and having so acted they
must take the consequences."[75]

Secondly, such a clause offends against the principle of certainty. At
the time the contract is entered into it is uncertain which of the spectrum of restraints is binding and which is not. For example, if the
restraint was stated to operate for twenty years and the court held that
only 10 years was reasonable, could the court substitute 10 years? The
parties are being asked to contract today on the basis that tomorrow the
court will determine the duration of the contract. It is submitted that
such an arrangement is void for uncertainty.[76]

(d) *Void, voidable or unenforceable*

5.20 In describing the effect of a contract found to be in restraint of trade different judges have used different expressions at different times. In *Nordenfelt v. Maxim Nordenfelt Guns & Ammunition*[77] Lord MacNaghten laid
down the rule that since agreements in restraint of trade offend against
public policy, they are void. This has been interpreted to mean that a
contract in restraint of trade is void *ab initio*. Indeed it has been suggested that the authorities establish that it is now beyond challenge that
a contract in restraint of trade is void *ab initio*.[78]

However, modern authorities have avoided the use of the word
"void" and have instead preferred to refer to the effect of a contract in
restraint of trade as a "voidable" or "unenforceable". In *Esso Petroleum
v. Harper's Garage* Lord Reid observed that: "One must always bear in
mind that an agreement in restraint of trade is not generally unlawful if
the parties choose to abide by it: it is only unenforceable if a party

---

[75] Indeed, this approach has found modern favour. In *Sunshine Records (Pty) Ltd. v.
Frohling* (1990) 4 S.A. 782, Grosskopf J.A. refused to severe parts of the contract on the
basis given at 797A-B that: "[The record company] wanted a complete monopoly of the
respondents' professional activities without offering them anything substantial in
return, the recording contract, which is the contract whereby [they] obtained the most
important part of this monopoly, is unenforceable precisely because he was too
grasping. The Court should therefore not, I consider, be astute to assist . . . by holding
that the contract could validly have been enforced in part only."

[76] *Quaere* whether such a term is in essence a stipulation that the agreement should be
enforced so far as the law allows and therefore void for uncertainty; *cf. Davies v. Davies*
(1887) 36 Ch.D. 359, where the phrase "so far as the law allows" was held to render the
restraint void for uncertainty.

[77] [1894] A.C. 535 at 565, H.L. See also *Haynes v. Doman* [1899] 2 Ch. 13; *Greig v. Insole*
[1978] 1 W.L.R. 302.

[78] Guest, *Anson's Law of Contract* (O.U.P. 26th ed. 1984) p. 321, n.76. See also *Gledhow
Autoparts Ltd. v. Delaney* [1965] 1 W.L.R. 1366, C.A.

chooses not to abide by it".[79] The distinction between void voidable and unenforceable was considered in *O'Sullivan v. Management Agency and Music Ltd.*[80] Waller L.J. said:

> "The judge found that the publishing agreement and the Ebostrail agreement were both in unreasonable restraint of trade. The effect of such an agreement was considered in *Instone v. Schroeder Music Publishing Co. Ltd.* [1974] 1 All E.R. 171, affirmed in the House of Lords under the name. *A. Schroeder Music Publishing Co. v. Macaulay* [1974] 1 W.L.R. 1308. The Court of Appeal held that because the agreement was in unreasonable restraint of trade it was unenforceable in so far as it had not been carried. And Lord Reid, dismissing the appeal against that decision, concluded his speech with these words: '*It must therefore follow that the agreement so far as unperformed is unenforceable.*' the effect of this finding taken by itself is that the two agreements to which I have referred were unenforceable so far as they have not been performed and not void."

Thus it would appear that modern authorities would hold that agreements in restraint of trade are void only in the sense that, in so far as unperformed, they do not give rise to legally-enforceable obligations. They are not void in the sense that for all purposes they are treated as non-existent. This position is unsatisfactory. First, it conflicts with the principal that the time for determining whether the covenant is in restraint of trade is at the time the agreement is entered into. If at that time the agreement is entered into it is in restraint of trade it is invalid at the outset and of no legal effect.   **5.21**

Secondly, its effect is that a party may impose oppressive and unconscionable restrictions on a performer knowing, in the majority of cases, that the performer will not challenge those restrictions as being in restraint of trade until he has achieved some semblance of success. If the performer is successful in that challenge the party extracting the covenants will, nevertheless, obtain the benefits of the performer's success up to the time of judgment. In such circumstances it is submitted that the

---

[79] [1968] A.C. 269 at 297, H.L. It is noticeable that none of their Lordships used the expression "void" when referring to the effect of a contract in restraint of trade. See also *Attorney-General of the Commonwealth of Australia v. Adelaide Steamship Co. Ltd.* [1913] A.C. 781 at 797, P.C. where Lord Parker of Waddington stated: "It is only necessary to add that no contract was ever an offence at common law merely because it was in restraint of trade. The parties to such a contract, even if unenforceable, were always at liberty to act on it in the manner agreed." See also *A. Schroeder Music Publishing Co. v. Macaulay* [1974] 1 W.L.R. 1308 where Lord Reid described a contract in restraint of trade as unenforceable.

[80] [1985] Q.B. 428 at 469, C.A. See also Fox L.J. at 469 where he observed: "The fact that the agreements were in restraint of trade does not, in my view, render them void. They are unenforceable . . .". See also *Boddington v. Lawton, The Times,* February 19, 1994.

correct approach is that adopted by Diplock L.J.'s in *Gledhow Autoparts Ltd. v. Delaney*[81] where he observed that a " . . . covenant in restraint of trade has to be determined at the date the agreement was entered into and has to be determined in the light of what may happen under the agreement, although what may happen may cover many possibilities which in the result did not happen. A covenant of this kind is invalid *ab initio* or valid *ab initio*. There cannot come a moment at which it passes from the class of invalid into that of valid covenants".

(e) *Illustrations of the application of restraint of trade principles*

5.22 *Zang Tumb Tuum Records v. Johnson.*[82] An interesting illustration of the application of the principles laid down in *A. Schroeder Music Publishing Co. Ltd. v. Macaulay* is the case of *Zang Tumb Tuum Records Ltd. v. Johnson*.

The facts of the case were found to be as follows. Young members of a group were approached by the principals of group of companies comprising recording and publishing companies. In marked contrast to the members of the Group, the court found that the people in day to day control of both companies were experienced business people.[83] They were offered two separate, though related contracts: a publishing agreement[84] and a recording agreement. The recording company would not enter into either agreement unless, contemporaneously, there was a publishing agreement with the company's sister publishing company. It was a take it or leave it arrangement.

The Recording Agreement

5.23 The members of the Group were bound both jointly and severally. By clause 1 of the agreement they undertook to perform, record and deliver up fully edited and mixed masters to the company. The Group were essentially bound to record what, when and where the Company chose.[85]

By Clause 2 copyright in the Group's performances and other world rights in respect of manufacture, sale and marketing of records were assigned to the Company which had an absolute discretion to manufacture sell or market the records as they saw fit. There were, however, pro-

---

[81] [1965] 1 W.L.R. 1366 at 1377, C.A.
[82] [1993] E.M.L.R. 61.
[83] Though there was no suggestion of undue influence. The Group had a manager and a solicitor.
[84] In fact there were two publishing agreements, the first dated September 1, 1983, and the second dated May 11, 1984. The court held that since the second replaced the first in identical terms it was immaterial that there were two contracts because if the first were void for being in restraint of trade, so too the second.
[85] There was a provision which required the Company to consult with the Group. But in cases of conflict, the Company's Choices prevailed.

visions for the re-assignment of copyright in works which were not exploited.

By Clause 3 the agreement was expressed to last an initial term of May to November 1983. However, the agreement gave the Company irrevocable options to extend the contract period and the exercise of one option triggered a new option.

Each "contract period" was defined as the longer of one year or 120 days from the date on which the minimum recording commitment was satisfied. In total, if all the options were exercised, there were eight contract periods. The "minimum recording commitment" required the Group to deliver a single in each of the first three periods and an album in each of the next five periods.

By Clause 5 the Group nor any member thereof was to render any service to anyone which might be recorded or lead to a recording being made or released anywhere in the World. This restriction was to apply for five years after termination of the agreement.

Clause 6 provided that no one other than the Company was to manufacture or sell any recording embodying a performance of the Group or member thereof.

Clauses 8, 9 and 10 contained provisions with respect to the royalties and advances. Royalties were to be accounted for half-yearly, advances to the Group were triggered by certain events. Signing the recording agreement or delivering the master for the first single brought £250. Delivery of masters in respect of successive albums brought between £5,000 and £30,000. The Company could however, deduct from any royalties due to the Group unrecouped advances and recording costs.[86]

Clause 14(1)(b) provided that if a member left the Group, the Company could terminate the agreement with that member or the whole Group at its option.

By Clause 14(2), if the Group had any new members they were to sign a recording agreement in identical terms. If a member left the Group, the Company had the option, *inter alia*, of requiring the departing member to execute a new agreement with the Company.

By July 1985 a dispute was underway. Holly Johnson was concerned with regard to the spiralling cost of recording and the deduction of these costs from the royalties payable to the members of the Group. The first single cost £26,000, the first album £394,000 and the second album £760,000. In fact the Group had made no more recordings since April 1986 and by March 1987 the Defendant had ceased to be a member of

---

[86] Referring to the preceding clauses, Dillon L.J. commented: "Against that very stringent background, the crucial provisions of the recording agreement are, in my judgment, Clause 3 which . . . provides for the Minimum Recording Commitment and the provisions of Clause 14 which attempted to deal with the situation where, as happened, a member of the Group left the Group."

the Group. The music companies brought an action against the artist for a declaration that he was bound to the agreements.

The Court's Approach

5.24 The Court of Appeal adopted the test formulated by Lords Reid[87] and Diplock[88] in *A. Schroeder Music Publishing Co. v. Macaulay* and asked whether the contracts viewed as a whole were fair. The Court concluded that the terms were both unfair and one sided. Dillon L.J. said:

> "[I]t is pertinent to the oppressiveness of the recording agreement that if Clause 14.2 bears the construction . . . [counsel for the Plaintiff] puts forward, it would have the consequences (1) that if the Defendant, having left the Group, wants during the Term to form a new group with new partners he can only do so if his new partners are acceptable to the recording company and are prepared to agree with the recording company to be bound by all the outstanding terms of the recording agreement and conversely, (2) if the other members of the Group, want another singer, they can have one only if they find one who is acceptable to the recording company and is prepared likewise . . . to be bound by all the outstanding terms of the recording agreement."[89]

Further, the Court held that the potential duration of the agreement was such that it could not be upheld.

> "It is an agreement which could well last eight or nine years and during all that time, when their earnings potential would be likely to be at its highest, the members of the Group would be bound to record only for the recording company. But the recording company itself is free to terminate its obligations at any time by not exercising the next option."[90]

In the light of these criticisms the Court held that the recording and publishing agreements fell to be condemned together.

> '[T]he effect of the publishing agreement is that the defendant cannot perform any of his own compositions . . . without the consent of the publishing company as the owner of the copyright worldwide in such works. I can see no reasonable justification for such an additional restriction on the Defendant being required."

---

[87] *A. Schroeder Music Publishing Co. v. Macaulay* [1974] 1 W.L.R. 1308 at 1310A-B and 1313C–1314B.
[88] *Ibid.* at 1315H.
[89] *Zang Tumb Tuum Records v. Johnson* [1993] E.M.L.R. 61 at 72.
[90] *Ibid.* at 73.

The Competence of the Advisers

Counsel for the record company identified two matters which it was   **5.25**
contended amounted to legitimate interests. First, that it was reasonable and in the interests of the music industry and of all engaged in that
industry, that the artists whose records are successful should be tied to
the recording company so that the recording company's share of the
profits of their artists' successful records should compensate the recording company for the costs of other artists' unsuccessful records.

Secondly, that a second record of an artist's music will have better
chances of success if a first record of another composition of that artist
was successful. It would appear, however, that even if both factors
could be classified as legitimate interests, the benefits secured to the
artist under the contract were not commensurate with the restraint as to
duration and, also, the terms of the contract when considered as a whole
were more than adequate for the protection of such interests. The
cumulative effect of the contract was such that the artist had no control
over his music, the potential members of the group, and the cost of production with no obligation on the record company/publisher to exploit
the artist's work. Effectively, therefore, the future success or failure of
the artist was completely within the hands of the record company/pub-
lisher.

Silvertone Records v. Mountfield. A useful illustration of the effect of   **5.26**
competent legal advice is *Silvertone Records Ltd. v. Mountfield.* [91] The
facts were similar to *Zang Tumb*. The plaintiffs were part of the same
group of companies and had control of both recording and publishing
rights in the defendants' music. The defendants, at the time of entering
into recording and publishing agreements with the plaintiffs were
unknown. At the negotiation of the agreement the defendants were
represented by an inexperienced manager and lawyer with little or no
experience in the music industry. The plaintiffs were experienced in the
negotiation of music agreements. The Court was of the view that:

> " . . . as between the parties negotiating and entering the agree-
> ment there was immense inequality in bargaining power, negoti-
> ation ability, understanding and representation. It is, however,
> possible even if one person has superior knowledge and bargain-
> ing power for a fair agreement to be reached." [92]

It would appear therefore that although an experienced or inexperienced legal adviser is present throughout the negotiations, the question the court must nevertheless ask itself is whether at the time of the

---

[91] [1993] E.M.L.R. 152.
[92] *Ibid.* at 163.

conclusion of the contract it was fair. The lack of an experienced legal adviser may be evidence of inequality of bargaining power but it is not determinative of whether the agreement is unfair: the court must examine the substance of the agreement to determine whether it is in fact fair.

5.27 *Panayiotou v. Sony Music Entertainment (U.K.) Limited* **(the** *George Michael* **case).**[93] The most recent illustration of the operation of the doctrine of restraint of trade in relation to entertainers' contracts is the *George Michael* case which is discussed in this section (paras. 5.27–5.44) and reported in [1994] E.M.L.R. 229. This case is important in three respects. First, the performers' cases prior to the *George Michael* case have the common factor that the performers were young and relatively "unknown". The case is therefore an important illustration of the court's approach when the contract in issue is not the first contract (in the *George Michael* case, "the 1984 Agreement") when he was relatively unknown but a renegotiation of that agreement and its replacement by a second agreement ("the 1988 Agreement") which took into account the success of the performer since the conclusion of the first agreement.

In the *George Michael* case the court was faced with a performer who was a "star" who received a substantial fee in respect of an exclusive recording contract. Secondly, the court sought to give some consideration as to what amounts to the "legitimate interest"[94] of a recording company and thirdly, the definition provided by the court of the market for the services of a performer in the context of Article 85 of the Treaty of Rome.[95]

The Recording Agreements

5.28 The contract which was the subject of the dispute in *George Michael* was a recording contract entered into by Mr Michael and Sony Music and known as "the 1988 Agreement". This Agreement was in fact the result of the renegotiation of an earlier contract, known as the "1984 Agreement". This "renegotiation" factor was to prove crucial to the Court's findings both in relation to restraint of trade and Treaty of Rome Article 85 arguments raised by George Michael.

5.29 The 1988 Agreement included the following terms:

(1) Clause 2.01 provided for the sale, transfer and assignment to Sony Music of all Master Recordings made by Mr Michael during the currency of the Agreement.

---

[93] *Panayiotou v. Sony Music Entertainment (U.K.) Ltd.* [1994] E.M.L.R. 229.
[94] See *ante*, para. 5.06.
[95] See *post*, para. 5.46 *et seq.*

(2) Clause 2.02(a) provided for Sony Music to have exclusive copyright in the Master Recordings.

(3) Clause 2.02(b) provided for Sony Music to have unlimited rights to manufacture, sell and deal in records, cassette tapes and compact discs derived from the Master Recordings,

 " . . . or to refrain from any such manufacture sale or dealing . . .".

(4) Clause 3 provided for the agreement to continue for an "Initial Contract Period", with Sony Music having five consecutive options to extend the term of the agreement by a further contract period.

(5) Clause 15.14 provided, *inter alia*, that;

 " . . . in no event shall the Term hereof last from inception for longer than fifteen years by virtue of the provisions of this paragraph".

(6) Clause 4.01 provided that George Michael's "Minimum Delivery Commitment" was three albums during the Initial Contract Period and one album in each subsequent Contract Period.

(7) Clause 6 provided for, *inter alia*, a payment to Mr Michael of U$1 million on signing the agreement, a total of U$5 million in respect of the album *Faith* (the first of the possible eight albums under the Agreement), a U$3 million advance in respect of the second album, and further payments of not less than U$2 million in respect of each of the second to fourth albums.

(8) Clause 7 provided for royalty rates to Mr Michael which, importantly, were an improvement over those he was already receiving pursuant to the 1984 Agreement.

(9) Clause 11.01 provided that if in any Contract Period Sony Music failed to release an album within 180 days of the delivery of the Master Recordings, Mr Michael could by notice require such release, and, in default of subsequent release, the Agreement was to terminate automatically.

The alleged effect of the contract being in restraint of trade

George Michael, for the purposes of the High Court hearing, argued   **5.30** that if his restraint of trade arguments succeeded, the recording agreement would be rendered unenforceable insofar as it remained unperformed, rather than void *ab initio*. However, he reserved the right to argue in a higher court[96] that the true effect of the restraint being

---

[96] At the time of writing George Michael has indicated his intention of appealing the judgment of Mr. Justice Jonathan Parker.

found to be unreasonable would be to render the agreement void *ab initio*. In effect, therefore, George Michael was reserving the right to argue that the decision in, or at least the interpretation of, *Instone v. A. Schroeder Music Publishing Co. Ltd* was wrong.[97]

The Court's Approach

5.31 The Judge was bound by and adopted the test set out in *Nordenfelt v. Maxim Nordenfelt Guns and Ammunition*.[98] The Judge stated the approach as follows:

> " . . . the right approach for the court, once it is satisfied that the contract before it is a contract which is (in ordinary parlance) in restraint of trade, is to consider whether in all the circumstances sufficient grounds exist for *excluding* that contract from the application of the doctrine . . . If no sufficient grounds exist, the contract attracts the doctrine."

In other words, there is a presumption in favour of applying the reasonableness test once a restraint of trade (using the term colloquially) has been found.

5.32 In applying this test to the 1988 Agreement the Judge's initial conclusions were favourable to George Michael. He observed that:

> "As to the terms of the respective agreements [the 1984 and 1988 Agreements], it is beyond doubt that they contain restraints of trade, using that expression in the broad popular sense. As to whether they are also "restraint of trade" using that expression this time as a term of art to mean contracts which attract the doctrine of restraint of trade, on the authority of *Esso* I find myself unable to say that an agreement of the general type with which I am concerned . . . is dispensed from the necessity of justification under the doctrine of restraint of trade. In particular it does not seem to me that, as of today, it can be said that recording agreements of this type have 'passed into the accepted and normal currency of commercial or contractual . . . relations'."

5.33 However, fatally for Mr Michael's case on restraint of trade, Sony Music succeeded in excluding the 1988 Agreement from the rigours of the "reasonableness" test on public policy grounds.

Sony Music's argument was that since the 1988 Agreement was the result of a renegotiation of the 1984 Agreement, and since the 1984 Agreement was itself in the nature of a compromise in order to settle an

---

[97] See *ante*, paras. 5.20–5.21.
[98] See *ante*, para. 5.01.

earlier dispute in which Mr Michael was alleging a restraint of trade, and since there is a public policy interest in the upholding of bona fide compromises of disputes between parties, it would be contrary to public policy now to allow Mr Michael to resurrect issues identical to or similar in effect to those which the renegotiation and compromise had been intended to lay to rest.

Thus the role of public policy in the *George Michael* case was not to   **5.34** provide a secondary test of reasonableness once the restraint of trade had been found to be reasonable *as between the parties*.[99] Rather, the effect of public policy was to prevent the 1988 Agreement from ever becoming subjected to the reasonableness calculus in the first place.

Having so concluded, it was strictly unnecessary for the court to go on   **5.35** to consider whether the 1988 agreement passed the *Nordenfelt* test. However, the Judge went on to consider this question, in case his conclusion on the public policy argument regarding compromises was inapplicable to the case, and/or wrong.

Was there inequality of bargaining power?

George Michael alleged, as part of his case on the unreasonableness of   **5.36** the restraints, that there was an inequality of bargaining power as between himself and Sony Music in the negotiation of the 1988 Agreement. The alleged inequality took two forms:

(1) at all material times in the negotiations leading up to the 1988 Agreement Mr Michael assumed he was bound by the earlier agreement;

(2) the major record companies do not seriously compete in the deals they offer artists, in terms of royalty rates, or the minimum number of albums required.

The Judge accepted that in a renegotiation there is bound to be some   **5.37** inequality of bargaining power, since the performer is already bound contractually to the other party:

"In a renegotiation an artist cannot expect to be treated in exactly the same way as he would be if he were negotiating on the open market free from any contractual ties. There is bound to be a degree

---

[99] *cf. ante*, para. 5.12.

of discount to reflect the fact that the artist is already bound by an existing recording agreement."

5.38 As to the second basis of the alleged inequality of bargaining power, the Judge rejected George Michael's submission on the basis that similarities between contracts or clauses offered by different "majors" (*i.e.* major record companies) is not the result of any lack of competition between them but is the direct consequence of the fact

" . . . that the negotiation of recording agreements tends to be concentrated in the hands of a relatively small band of experienced professionals".

Did the 1988 Agreement go any further than was necessary for the adequate protection of Sony Music's interests? Was George Michael compensated for the restraints by the benefits accruing to him under the Agreement?

5.39 The 1988 Agreement was similar to an exclusive supply agreement, in that Sony Music had contracted to buy Mr Michael's entire output of Master Recordings during the currency of the 1988 Agreement. In addition, Sony Music also had what the Judge called "exclusivity of exploitation" in that Sony Music acquired all copyright in the Master Recordings.

5.40 As to the first exclusivity, that of supply, the Judge emphasised that a factor to be taken into account is the consideration which the covenantor receives for making the "restraining" covenant in the contract.

"It will be recalled that one element of the 'test of fairness' formulated by Lord Diplock in *Schroeder* is that the restrictions should be 'commensurate with the benefits secured to the promisor under the contract'. In the instant case, Mr Michael's financial terms under the 1988 Agreement reflected, among other things, Sony Music's entitlement to exclusivity of output of Master Recordings during the continuance of the agreement."

5.41 As to exclusivity of exploitation, the Judge rejected as a real possibility the prospect of Sony Music's simply taking merely formal steps of releasing an album without properly promoting it. As the learned Judge put it:

"Sony Music's commercial interests lay in exploiting Mr Michael's recordings to the full . . . the notion that as matters stood on 4 January 1988, there was a real risk that Sony Music might in effect 'put [Mr Michael's recordings] in a drawer and leave them there' (see Lord Reid in *Schroeder* at p. 1313D) is in my judgment far-fetched."

Moreover, the Judge went further, stating:

"I find difficulty in seeing how exclusivity of exploitation arising by reason of the outright sale and transfer of copyright can be classified as a restraint of trade at all . . . the sale and transfer of property rights is pre-eminently a matter of bargain. The proposition that there is some public policy interest in preventing an outright sale of a property right seems to me to be self-evidently unsustainable."

George Michael further complained that while Sony could terminate **5.42** the contract by declining to exercise an option, he had no such power. The learned Judge answered that complaint shortly:

"It is only if the artist is actually successful that the contract will continue for its full length. Thus if an artist does remain bound for the length of his contract, it will be virtually inevitable that the relationship will have been a commercially successful one for both sides. Thus, it cannot sensibly be suggested that if the 1988 Agreement runs its full course Mr Michael will thereby suffer financial or commercial hardship of any kind: indeed, the opposite is likely to be the case."

The Judge's conclusion on reasonableness

The Judge concluded that, if, contrary to his primary finding, the **5.43** restraint of trade doctrine did apply to the 1988 Agreement, the restraints imposed by the Agreement were reasonable, even without taking into account the fact that the 1988 agreement built on pre-existing restraints (which both parties believed to be enforceable when negotiating the 1988 Agreement) from the 1984 agreement. When the 1984 Agreement was taken into account, as the Judge concluded it must, the restraints in the 1988 Agreement were even further removed from the standard of unreasonableness required by the *Nordenfelt* test, since they built on pre-existing restraints contained in the 1984 Agreement, which both sides had assumed to be valid and enforceable. The learned Judge concluded:

"Taking all the above factors into account, reading the 1988 Agreement as a whole, and considering the cumulative effect of the restrictions which it contains – and doing so in the context of the surrounding circumstances as they where when it was signed – I conclude that its terms are justified. To put it another way . . . taking all the provisions of the 1988 Agreement into consideration I find that the restrictions contained in it are both reasonably necessary for the protection of the legitimate interests of Sony Music and commensurate with the benefits secured to Mr Michael under it."

5.44   As with all restraint of trade cases, the *George Michael* case turned to a significant degree on its facts. In particular, the fact that the agreement sued on was a renegotiation of an existing agreement proved crucial. In addressing some of the factors which had proved to be of particular importance in the case, the Judge concluded:

> " . . . it should be borne in mind in particular that the 1988 Agreement was a renegotiation of an earlier agreement; that by January 1988 Mr Michael was already an established artist who had just achieved enormous commercial success as a solo artist with his album "Faith"; that Mr Michael's aim in the renegotiation was to achieve parity 'with other superstars'; and that the essence of the renegotiation, as embodied in the 1988 Agreement, was a substantial improvement in Mr Michael's financial terms in exchange for additional product [*i.e.* more albums]."

5.45   **Conclusion.** The music cases which follow on from *A. Schroeder Publishing v. Macaulay*[1] establish no new principles of law. They are, however, illustrations of the factors the court will take into account when deciding whether the contract is fair. No definitive list can be compiled because the terms of each contract must be considered in the context of the duration of the contract, the consideration, the experience of the performer, the bargaining power at the time the contract was concluded and the extent of the duration. The cases do, however, have the common factor that the contracts were entered into at the time that the performers were young and "unknown". It remains to be seen what the position would be where the performer is a "star" who is able to choose among a number of competing companies and receives a substantial fee in respect of exclusive period contracts for recording and or publishing. In such circumstances it is submitted that the test of what is fair might not be as rigorous as in the case of an "unknown" performer.

(f) *European Community law and performers' contracts*

5.46   Article 85(1) of the Treaty of Rome is of relevance to performers agreements where the principle of restraint of trade is under consideration.[2] Article 85(1) provides as follows:

> "The following shall be prohibited as incompatible with the common market: all agreements between undertakings, decisions by association of undertakings and concerted practices which may affect trade between Member States and which have as their object

---

[1] [1974] 1 W.L.R. 1308, H.L.
[2] This Article is directly applicable in Member States and is incorporated into national domestic law by ss.2(1), 3(1) of the European Communities Act 1972.

or effect the prevention, restriction or distortion of competition within the common market, and in particular those which:

(a) directly or indirectly fix purchase or selling prices or any other trading conditions;

(b) limit or control production, markets, technical development or investment;

(c) share markets or sources or supply;

(d) apply dissimilar conditions to equivalent transactions with other trading parties, thereby placing them at a competitive disadvantage;

(e) make the conclusion of contracts subject to acceptance by the other parties of supplementary obligations which, by their nature or according to commercial usage, have no connection with the subject of such contracts."

Article 85(1) is the subject of a considerable number of decisions of **5.47** the European Commission and the European Court of Justice, the analysis of which is beyond the scope of this work.[3] However, following the decision of *Re: Unitel Film-Und Fernseh Produktionsgesellschaft mbH Co ("Rai/Unitel")*[4] a number of general principles emerge in relation to the application of Article 85 to performers' agreements.

First, a performer is capable of being an undertaking within the meaning of Article 85(1) when they exploit commercially their artistic performances: the fact that the performer may not render his services through a corporation or a partnership does not preclude his being an undertaking.[5] However, the question whether a particular performer constitutes an undertaking depends upon the economic implications of the agreement concerning the commercial exploitation of his artistic services.

Secondly, Article 85 is not applicable to a performers agreement which does not have an "appreciable effect" on trade between Member States. In many cases, particularly where little known performers are involved there is unlikely to be an "appreciable effect" but where the restraint is in respect of a highly successful performer there is a greater likelihood that such restraint may have an appreciable effect on trade between Member States. A successful performer's exclusive contract may therefore be rendered void[6] where there are economic or legal circumstances the effect of which is to restrict competition to an appreci-

---

[3] For such an analysis see, Bellamy and Child, *Common Market Law of Competition* (Sweet & Maxwell, 3rd ed., 1987) Chap. 2.
[4] [1978] O.J. L157; [1978] 3 C.M.L.R. 306.
[5] *Ibid.*
[6] Art. 85(2).

able degree or distort competition between Member States, regard being had to the characteristics of the market.[7] It is, however, important to be clear as to the market in which it is alleged competition has been or is intended to be prevented, restricted or distorted.

In the *George Michael* case, the relevant market for the purposes of considering whether his 1988 recording agreement was anti-competitive in its object or effect was not the record/CD market but the "raw material industry" (records being the end product obtained from, *inter alia*, the "raw material" of the artist's services), defined as the market for the services of recording artistes in the field of popular music." Once the market has been identified the next stage in the analysis is to identify whether there is a Community-wide market for such services. Only if there is such a market will Article 85 be engaged. If only a national or domestic market, it will not be so engaged.[8] This analysis of the relevant market and its terrestrial extent was of crucial importance in the *George Michael* case. The Judge found that on

> "the evidence before me . . . I can only conclude that there is no Community-wide market for the services of UK recording artists in the field of popular music, since . . . only in exceptional cases will UK recording artists sign to a non-UK record company."

In the present state of the market for the services of recording artists in the field of popular music, it may be difficult for an artist to successfully avail himself of Article 85. The position may not, however, be the same in respect of music publishing and the services of artists in the field of classical music. However, if the circumstances are such as to show that such exclusive licensing arrangements are necessary to ensure some degree of security against risks both for the performer and the music publisher or record company and are necessary, *inter alia*, because many such performers would not obtain record or publishing deals without such exclusive agreements and the market would thereby be impoverished and competition depressed the terms of the agreement may not, in itself, be such as to prevent, restrict or distort competition.[9]

Breach of Article 85 not only renders the agreement void, but also subjects the parties to the risk of substantial fines by the Commission. Those advising parties to an entertainment contract should not overlook the possibility of applying to the Commission for "negative clearance" (that is a declaration that Article 85 does not apply to the agreement), or of applying to the Commission for the purposes of obtaining exemption under Article 85(3).

---

[7] Case 262/81, *S.A. Compagnie Generale pour la Diffusion de la Television Coditel v. S.A. Cine Fog Films*: [1982] E.C.R. 3381.
[8] Case 22/78, *Hugin v. Commission*: [1979] E.C.R. 1869.
[9] *Ibid.*

CHAPTER 6

UNDUE INFLUENCE

1. Introduction

Distinction between restraint of trade and undue influence. In this 6.01
chapter the general principles applicable to undue influence will be considered with particular reference to entertainers' contracts. Questions of undue influence and restraint of trade often arise for consideration together in cases involving entertainers. The two principles are, however, distinct in that "in cases of undue influence, the Court intervenes, not because a party has sought to restrain trade of another beyond the limits of reasonableness, but because a party should not be held to an unfair bargain about which he has not been fully informed".[1]

2. The Doctrine

The Principle. The classic exposition of the doctrine is to be found in 6.02
Allcard v Skinner[2]:

"The question is . . . Does the case fall within the principles laid down by the decisions of the Court of Chancery in setting aside voluntary gifts executed by the parties who at the time were under such influence as, in the opinion of the court, enabled the donor afterwards to set the gift aside? These decisions may be divided into two classes . . . First, where the Court has been satisfied that the gift was the result of influence expressly used by the donee for the purpose; second, where the relations between the donor and

---

[1] *Armatrading v. Stone*, per Legatt J. (1984; unreported).
[2] (1887) 36 Ch.D. 145, C.A.; the case concerned a gift, which in the present connection "equally applicable *mutatis mutandis* to commercial transactions": *Elton John v. Richard Leon James* [1991] F.S.R. 397.

the donee have at or shortly before the execution of the gifts been such to raise the presumption that the donee had influence over the donor. In such a case the Court sets aside the voluntary gifts, unless it is proved that in fact the gift was a spontaneous act of the donor acting under circumstances which enabled him to exercise an independent will and which justifies the Court in holding that the gift is as a result of the free exercise of the donor's will. The first class of cases may be considered as depending on the principle that no one shall be allowed to retain any benefit arising from his own fraud or wrongful act. In the second class of cases the Court interferes, not on the ground that any wrongful act has been committed by the donee, but on the ground that of public policy, and to prevent the relations which existed between the parties and the influence arising therefrom being abused."[3]

Thus, undue influence is of two kinds: first, express, or as it is more usually known, actual, undue influence, and secondly, that which in certain circumstances is presumed from a confidential relationship; by which in this context is meant a relationship wherein one party has ceded such a degree of trust and confidence as to require the other, on grounds of public policy, to show that it has not been betrayed or abused.[4] It is the second class of case with which we are here concerned in this work.

6.03   **Nature and effect of presumption of undue influence.** Where the presumption arises it is not necessary to show that the relationship was one of domination of one party by the other: it is enough to show that the party in which the trust and confidence is reposed is in a position to exert influence over him who reposes it.[5] However, the presumption of influence is not perfected and remains inoperative until the party who has ceded the trust and confidence makes a gift so large, or enters into a transaction so large which is manifestly or unfairly disadvantageous[6] to the plaintiff and so improvident as not to be reasonably accounted for by the ordinary motives on which ordinary men act.[7] Although the *influence* might have been presumed beforehand, it is only at that point that it is presumed to have been *undue*. Where the presumption of undue influence has come into operation, the transaction will be set aside, unless it is proved, by those asserting the validity of the gift or transaction, to have been the spontaneous act of the grantor acting in

---

[3] *Ibid., per* Cotton L.J. at 171, approved *Inche Noriah v. Omar* [1929] A.C. 127, P.C.
[4] *Goldsworthy v. Brickell* [1987] 1 Ch. 378, C.A.
[5] *Ibid.,* explaining *National Westminster Bank plc. v. Morgan* [1985] A.C. 686.
[6] *National Westminster Bank plc. v. Morgan* [1985] A.C. 686, H.L.; *C.I.B.C. Mortgages Plc v. Pitt* [1993] 3 W.L.R. 802, H.L.
[7] *Goldsworthy v. Brickell* [1987] 1 Ch. 378, C.A.

circumstances which would enable him to exercise an independent will free of the influence of the grantor.[8]

Relationship giving rise to presumption of influence. The courts have **6.04** steadfastly refused to circumscribe by reference to defined limits the relationships which give rise to a presumption of influence.[9] The existence of a fiduciary relationship or special relationship must depend on the particular facts of each case.[10] Some guidance as to the essential characteristics of a special relationship giving rise to the presumption of influence can be obtained, however, from *Goldsworthy v. Brickell*[11] where Nourse L.J. observed that:

> " . . . there are many and various . . . relationships lacking a recognisable status to which the presumption has been held to apply. In all these relationships, whether of the first kind or the second, the principle is the same. It is that the degree of trust and confidence is such that the party in whom it is reposed, either because he is or has become an adviser of the other or because he has become entrusted with the management of his affairs or everyday needs or for some other reason is in a position to influence him into effecting the transaction of which complaint is later made".

The court has been ready to find that such fiduciary or special relationships exist in circumstances where a performer or composer relies on the guidance and advice of his manager, or contracts with a music publisher for the exploitation of his compositions.[12] In such circumstances it is assumed that the advice given by, for example, a manager or musical publisher, would by reason of the special relationship with a performer, carry more weight with, and be more likely of acceptance by the performer than the advice of a stranger, and consequently provides a sufficient degree of potential influence.

Burden of proof. The party seeking to have the transaction set aside by **6.05** reason of undue influence bears the onus of proving the existence of the special relationship giving rise to the presumption of influence.[13]

---

[8] *Allcard v. Skinner* 36 Ch.D. 145 at 171, C.A.; *Zamet v. Hyman* [1961] 1 W.L.R. 1442 at 1446, C.A.; *O'Sullivan v. Management Agency and Music Ltd.* [1985] 1 Q.B. 428, C.A.; *Goldsworthy v. Brickell* [1987] 1 Ch. 378 at 401, C.A.

[9] See, *e.g. Tufton v. Sperni* [1952] 2 T.L.R. 516; *National Westminster Bank plc. v. Morgan* [1985] 1 A.C. 686, H.L.; *Goldsworthy v. Brickell* [1987] 1 Ch. 378, (C.A.).

[10] *Lloyds Bank v. Bundy* [1975] Q.B. 326 at 341, C.A.; *Armatrading v. Stone* (1984) unreported) Legatt J.; *Goldsworthy v. Brickell* [1987] 1 Ch. 378, C.A.

[11] *Goldsworthy v. Brickell* [1987] 1 Ch. 378.

[12] *O'Sullivan v. Management and Agency Music Ltd.* [1984] 3 W.L.R. 448, C.A.; *Armatrading v. Stone* (1984; unreported); *Elton John v. Richard Leon James* [1991] F.S.R. 397.

[13] *Barclays Bank plc v. O'Brien* [1993] 3 W.L.R. 786.

6.06 **Rebuttal of presumption.** Where a special relationship is found to exist the "onus is . . . upon the party asserting the validity of the gift or transaction to show that they were in consequence of the free . . . exercise of will in the light of full information regarding the transaction.[14] Thus, the party asserting the validity of the transaction must show that it was entered into as a result of the donor "acting independently of any influence from the donee *and* with the full appreciation of what he was doing"[15] in the light of full information regarding the transaction.[16] There is no rule of law that where such a special relationship exists the influenced party should have independent advice at the time of entering into the impugned transaction in order to rebut the presumption.[17] Nevertheless, independent advice is an important factor in determining whether the transaction was as a result of the free exercise of will in the light of full information.

The absence or presence of independent advice although an important factor, is not, however a determinative factor. The Privy Council in *Inche Noriah v. Shaik Allie bin Omar*[18] pointed out that the grantor may rebut the presumption in any manner open to him on the facts and which enables him to persuade the court that the transaction was really the spontaneous act of a party, comprehending what he did and as a result of his own free will. If, however, the grantor should receive independent advice and either misunderstands the advice or is given possibly erroneous advice whereby he fails to appreciate or realize the financial implications and the detriment to himself involved in the transaction, a court will not set aside the transaction if the grantor otherwise understood the nature of the transaction and acted in the full exercise of his will.

6.07 Where independent advice is relied upon as the evidence in rebuttal of the presumption of undue influence the following principles can be discerned from the authorities. First, the adviser must be truly independent. This independence will not exist if the adviser acts for both par-

---

[14] *Allcard v. Skinner* (1887) 36 Ch.D 145, per Lindley L.J.; *Inche Noriah v. Shaik Allie Bin Omar* [1929] A.C. 127, P.C.; approved *Lancashire Loans Ltd. v. Black* [1934] 1 K.B. 380 at 413, C.A. per Lawrence L.J. See also *O'Sullivan v. Management Agency and Music Ltd.* [1985] 1 Q.B. 428 at 463, C.A.; *Armatrading v. Stone*; (1984; unreported); *Elton John v. Richard Leon James* [1991] F.S.R. 397; *Goldsworthy v. Brickell* [1987] Ch. 378, C.A.
[15] *Allcard v. Skinner* 36 Ch.D. 145 at 171, C.A.; *Inche Noriah v. Shaik Allie Bin Omar* [1929] A.C. 127 at 135, P.C.; *Lancashire Loans Ltd. v. Black* [1934] 1 K.B. 380, C.A.; *Zamet v. Hyman* [1961] 1 W.L.R. 1442, C.A.; *Goldsworthy v. Brickell* [1987] 1 Ch. 378, C.A.
[16] *O'Sullivan v. Management and Music Agency Ltd.* [1985] Q.B. 428, C.A.
[17] *Allcard v. Skinner* (1887) 36 Ch.D. 145; *National Westminster Bank plc. v. Morgan* [1985] A.C. 686, H.L.
[18] [1929] A.C. 127; *Lancashire Loans Ltd. v. Black* [1934] 1 K.B. 380 at 413, C.A., per Lawrence L.J. See also *Allcard v. Skinner* (1887) 36 Ch.D. 145 at 171; *Kali Bakhsh Singh v. Ram Gopal Singh* (1913) 30 T.L.R. 138 at 139.

ties to the transaction.[19] Secondly, the person seeking to rebut the presumption must show that the adviser satisfied himself that the transaction was one that was right and proper for the grantor to enter into and if he was not so satisfied that he advised the grantor not to go on with the transaction.[20] It is therefore insufficient for the adviser merely to endorse the views of the grantee as to the transaction without consideration of its terms. Thirdly, it is submitted that such independent advice must be rendered by an adviser who has experience and qualification in the area of activity contemplated by the transaction. Ultimately, the circumstances of the case must be examined to determine not only whether the person was truly independent but also whether the grantor received advice from a person qualified to give the particular advice in relation to the particular transaction.

Third party rights. The doctrine of undue influence is not limited to   **6.08**
cases where the influence is exerted to obtain a benefit for the person exerting the influence.[21] Thus, for example, where a person in a fiduciary position procures, by undue influence, contracts to be entered into with companies under his control and direction the companies will be affected by the doctrine of undue influence even though they themselves were not in a fiduciary relationship.[22] However, the right of a third party bona fide purchaser for value without notice would not in any event be affected.[23]

Effect of finding of undue influence. As a general proposition, if the   **6.09**
party who is presumed to exercise an influence obtains a benefit from his fiduciary position which is to the manifest disadvantage of the party influenced he must account to him for the benefit so obtained.[24] Where a contract is procured by undue influence it is prima facie void and the person influenced is entitled to have the contract set aside.[25] In such circumstances, "the court will do what is practically just [as between the parties] in the individual case even though *restitutio in integrum* is

---

[19] *Powell v. Powell* [1900] 1 Ch. 243; *Bank of Montreal v. Stuart* [1911] A.C. 120, P.C.; *Bullock v. Lloyds Bank Ltd.* [1955] 1 Ch. 317.
[20] *Powell v. Powell* [1900] 1 Ch. 243 at 247; *Permanent Trustee Co. of New South Wales Ltd. v. Bridgewater* [1936] 3 All E.R. 501 at 507, P.C.; *Bullock v. Lloyds Bank* [1955] 1 Ch. 317.
[21] *Bridgeman v. Green* (1757) Wilm. 58; *Bullock v. Lloyds Bank Ltd.* [1955] Ch. 317; *Bainbrigge v. Browne* (1881) 18 Ch.D. 188; *Lancashire Loans Ltd. v. Black* [1934] 1 K.B. 380, C.A.; *O'Sullivan v. Management Agency & Music Ltd.* [1985] Q.B. 428 at 464, C.A.
[22] *O'Sullivan v. Management Agency and Music Ltd.* [1985] 1 Q.B. 428 at 464, C.A.
[23] *O'Sullivan v. Mangement Agency & Music Ltd.* [1985] 1 Q.B. 428, C.A.; *Goldunell Ltd. v. Gallon* [1986] Q.B. 1184; see also *Chitty on Contracts* (Sweet & Maxwell, 26th ed., 1989), Vol. I, paras. 535 and 536.
[24] *Regal (Hastings) Ltd. v. Gulliver (Note)* [1967] 2 A.C. 134, H.L.
[25] *Erlanger v. New Sombrero Phosphate Co.* (1878) 3 App.Cas. 1218 H.L.; *Lloyds Bank v. Bundy* [1975] Q.B. 326, C.A.; *O'Sullivan v. Management Agency and Music Ltd.* [1985] 1 Q.B. 428, C.A.

impossible.''[26] Thus, in setting aside the agreements the question is not whether the parties can be restored to their original position; it is, what does the justice of the case require?

   This approach is wide enough, if it be necessary in the individual case, to accommodate the protection of third parties although the rights of bona fide purchasers for value would not in any event be affected.[27] Further, it does not apply the strict rule that the fiduciary must disgorge the whole profit without any allowance for the work without which the profit could not have been created. Once again the "justice of the individual case must be considered on the facts of that case. Accordingly, where there has been dishonesty or surreptitious dealing or other improper conduct . . . it might be appropriate to refuse relief; but that will depend upon the circumstances.[28] Thus, where the circumstances of the case permit, and justice as between the parties demand it, the court may grant the fiduciary a reasonable remuneration which may include some part of the profit of the venture, even though there may have been improper conduct on his part.[29]

6.10   In *O'Sullivan v. Management and Music Agency Ltd.*, the Court came to the conclusion that it would not be proper to exclude the defendants from receiving a share of the profits notwithstanding the fact that they had abused their fiduciary position. "[S]ubstantial justice between the parties"[30] required that such an award be made to the defendants to take account of the contribution to the plaintiff's success. However, the award did not take full account of the plaintiff's success because of the failure of the defendant to ensure that the contracts had between properly negotiated between fully advised parties. Thus, although the defendants had abused their positions this did not deprive them of a share of the profit. The circumstances of the case merely required that such abuse be reflected in the award to the defendant for their contribution to the plaintiff's success.

3. Laches and Acquiescence

6.11   **General**. Laches and acquiescence are common defences raised in undue influence actions involving entertainers.[31]

---

[26] *O'Sullivan v Management Agency Ltd.* [1985] 1 Q.B. 428 at 466, C.A.
[27] *Ibid.* at 467
[28] *Ibid.* at 468.
[29] *O'Sullivan v. Management Agency and Music Ltd.* [1985] 1 Q.B. 428, C.A.
[30] [1985] 1 Q.B. 428 at 469, C.A.
[31] See *e.g. Elton John v. Richard Leon James* [1991] F.S.R. 397; *Zang Tumb Tuum Records Ltd. v. Johnson* [1993] E.M.L.R. 61; *Armatrading v. Stone* (1984; unreported)

Relationship between laches and acquiescence and affirmation. Undue   **6.12**
influence is an equitable right and as such liable to be defeated by
equitable defences. The equitable defences which would usually be
regarded as being available to defeat such rights are laches and
acquiescence. By any of these two means the transaction could be
impliedly affirmed. The expressions are not uniformly used. The choice
of which term is used often depends on which more appropriately des-
cribes the attitude or conduct of a person after learning of the infringement of his rights. Doing nothing in that context may be said to be
acquiescence. Sometimes laches is taken to mean undue delay on the
part of the plaintiff in prosecuting his claim and no more. Sometimes
acquiescence is used to mean laches in that sense and sometime laches
is used to mean acquiescence in its proper sense, which involves a
standing by so as to induce the other party to believe that the wrong is
assented to.[32]

Laches. The classic formulation of the principle is to be found in *Lindsay*   **6.13**
Petroleum Company v. Hurd.[33] where Lord Selborne stated:

> "Now the doctrine of laches in Courts of Equity is not an arbitrary
> or a technical doctrine. Where it would be practically unjust to give
> a remedy either because the party has, by his conduct, done that
> which might fairly be regarded as equivalent to waiver of it, or
> where by his conduct and neglect he has, though perhaps not waiv-
> ing that remedy, yet put the other party in a situation in which it
> would not be reasonable to place him if the remedy were after-
> wards to be asserted, in either of these cases, lapse of time and
> delay are most material. But in every case, if an argument against
> relief, which would otherwise be just, is founded upon mere delay,
> that delay of course not amounting to a bar by any statute of limi-
> tations, the validity of that defence must be tried upon principles
> substantially equitable. Two circumstances, always important in
> such cases, are the length of the delay and the nature of the acts
> done during the interval, which might affect either party and cause
> a balance of injustice in taking the one course or the other, so far as
> related to the remedy."

To this formulation Lord Blackburn added this comment:

> "I have looked in vain for any authority which gives a more distinct
> and definite rule than this; and I think, from the nature of the
> inquiry, it must always be a question of more or less, depending on
> the degree of diligence which might reasonably be required, and

---

[32] *Goldsworthy v. Brickell* [1987] 1 Ch. 378, C.A.; *Armatrading v. Stone* (1984; unreported).
[33] (1873) 5 App.Cas. 221 at 239.

the degree of change which has occurred, whether the balance of justice or injustice is in favour of granting the remedy or withholding it."[34]

6.14   Thus, where a party becomes dissatisfied with the terms on which he entered into an agreement in which influence is presumed it behoves him to act promptly in seeking to have it set aside. However, so long as the special relationship lasts "so long is it necessary to hold that lapse of time affords no sufficient ground for refusing relief to the donor. But this necessity ceases when the relationship itself comes to an end."[35] If the performer desires to have the transaction declared invalid and set aside he ought to seek relief within a reasonable time after removal of the influence under which the transaction was made. If he does not, the inference is strong, and if the lapse of time is long the inference becomes inevitable and conclusive, that the performer is content not to impugn the contract and elects not to avoid it.[36]

This, is illustrated by *Elton John v. Richard Leon James*[37] where Elton John entered into publishing and recording agreements in 1967 which expired in 1972 and 1975 respectively. No intimation of a claim was made to, or a claim brought against, the defendant until 1982. It was held that there had been a lapse of time amounting to acquiescence which made it practically unjust to set aside the agreements in the light of the benefits which had been obtained by John under the agreements and the amount of work done under them by the defendant.

6.15   Acquiescence. Acquiescence differs according to whether the act acquiesced in is in progress or has been completed.

"If a person having a right, and seeing another person about to commit, or in the course of committing the act, and who might otherwise have abstained from it, to believe that he assents to its being committed he cannot afterwards be heard to complain of the act. This . . . is the proper sense of the term 'acquiescence', and in that sense may be defined as quiescence under such circumstances as that assent may be reasonably be inferred from it, and is no more than an instance of the law of estoppel by words or conduct. But when once the act is completed without any knowledge or assent upon the part of the person whose right is infringed, the matter is to be determined on very different legal considerations. A right of action has then vested in him which, at all events as a general rule, cannot be divested without accord and satisfaction, or release

---

[34] *Erlanger v. New Sombrero Phosphate Co.* (1878) 3 App.Cas. 1218 at 1279.
[35] *Allcard v. Skinner* (1887) 36 Ch.D. 145, at 187.
[36] *Ibid.* at 187.
[37] [1991] F.S.R. 397.

under seal. Mere submission to the injury for any time short of the period limited by statute for the enforcement of the right of action cannot take away such right, although under the name of laches it may afford a ground for refusing relief under some particular circumstances."[38]

Thus, in the case of a completed transaction the hallmark of acquiescence is a fixed, deliberate and unbiased determination that the transaction should not be impeached. This may be proved either by the lapse of time during which the transaction has been allowed to stand, or by other circumstances[39] but a positive act is not necessary to render the transaction unimpeachable.[40]

In *Willmott v. Barber*[41] Fry J. set out five criteria for establishing the **6.16** defence of acquiescence:

"A man is not to be deprived of his legal rights unless he has acted in such a way as would make it fraudulent for him to set up those rights. What, then, are the elements or requisites necessary to constitute fraud of that description? In the first place the plaintiff must have made a mistake as to his legal rights. Secondly, the plaintiff must have expended some money or must have done some act . . . on the faith of his mistaken belief. Thirdly, the defendant, the possessor of the legal right must know of the existence of his own right which is inconsistent with the right claimed by the plaintiff. If he does not know of it he is in the same position as the plaintiff, and the doctrine of acquiescence is founded upon conduct with knowledge of your legal rights. Fourthly, the defendant, the possessor of the legal right, must know of the plaintiff's mistaken belief of his rights. If he does not, there is nothing which calls upon him to assert his own rights. Lastly, the defendant, the possessor of the legal right, must have encouraged the plaintiff in his expenditure of money or in the other acts which he has done, either directly or by abstaining from asserting his legal right. Where all these elements exist, there is fraud of such nature as will entitle the court to restrain the possessor of the legal right from exercising it, but, in my judgment nothing short of this will do."

However, as laches and acquiescence are equitable principles, the governing consideration is whether in the circumstances it would be

---

[38] *De Bussche v. Alt* (1878) 8 Ch.D. 286 at 314.
[39] *Wright v. Vanderplank* (1856) 8 D.M. & G. 133 at 146, approved *Mitchell v. Homfray* (1881) 8 Q.B.D. 587, C.A.; *Allcard v. Skinner* [1887] 36 Ch.D 145 at 187, C.A.
[40] *Ibid.*
[41] (1880) 15 Ch. D. 96 at 105.

unfair to allow the plaintiff to assert or resurrect his legal rights.[42] This is the corollary of the approach adopted by Lindley J. in *Allcard v. Skinner*[43] which involved asking whether it would be fair and right to the defendant to grant the relief sought against him.

4. Undue Influence and the Music Cases

6.17 In *O'Sullivan v. Management and Music Agency Ltd.*,[44] a young and unknown composer entered into an exclusive management agreement with his manager. The manager also controlled a music agency and a publishing and recording company. A complex series of agreements was entered into between the performer and the recording and publishing companies. The performer applied for a declaration that the agreements were void and unenforceable.

The Court of Appeal held that the agreements were presumed to be the result of undue influence and were voidable. Dunn L.J. observed that "it was conceded that as the contracts were presumed to have been obtained by the undue influence of [the manager] and as the companies knew of [the manager's] confidential relationship with [the artiste], it would be inequitable for the companies to take any benefit from the contracts other than that which they would have obtained from a reasonably negotiated agreement."[45]

In the light of that concession, the factual matrix permitted the Court to go on to hold that:

> "[a]lthough the companies were not formally appointed managers by [the performer's manager], in fact they carried out most of the management functions and this was the intention from the outset. From the moment [the performer] joined [his manager] the affairs of [the performer] were run by the companies. They took it upon themselves to look after him . . . They knew they were dealing with a young and inexperienced man who was content to put himself entirely in their hands and relied entirely on them to give him a fair deal. They were responsible for the contractual arrangements and they were just as much in a confidential relationship to [the performer] as was [his manager] . . . ".[46]

This passage makes it clear that the fiduciary relationship between the

---

[42] *Taylor Fashions v. Liverpool Victoria Trustees Co. Ltd* [1982] Q.B. 133; *Amalgamated Investment and Property Co. Ltd. v. Texas Commerce International Bank* [1982] Q.B. 84, C.A.
[43] (1887) 36 Ch.D. 145, C.A.
[44] [1985] 1 Q.B. 428.
[45] *Ibid.* at 448A–B.
[46] *Ibid.* at 448G–H.

performer and the companies arose because the companies were little more than the alter ego of the manager.[47] On signing with his manager, the performer had from the beginning effectively been under the control of the companies. They had stepped into the manager's shoes. The companies performed the manager's duties towards the performer.

A variation of the facts in *O'Sullivan* occurred in the case of *Elton John* **6.18** *v. Richard Leon James*.[48] There, the artiste had entered into a publishing agreement four months before signing the management agreement with the same company. The publishing and recording companies were not therefore at the outset managing the artiste. Nevertheless, Nicholls J, held that a fiduciary duty arose for two reasons. First, because the arrangement can be viewed as a joint venture:

> "Thus, commercially, the arrangement was in the nature of a joint venture, and the writers would need to place trust and confidence in the publisher over the manner in which it discharged its exploitative function."

The second basis upon which a duty was imposed was upon the following factual basis:

> "When they first met Mr. James, Mr. John and Mr. Taupin were in awe of him . . . Being offered a contract by Mr. James was 'like a dream come true' to the two aspiring young men. They snapped at it, and had no hesitation in signing the contract (the 1967 publishing agreement) when it was in due course prepared and produced for signature by them and their respective parents."[49]

Having made this finding, Nicholls, J. concluded:

> "Did [Mr. James] assume a role of dominating influence? I consider that, brief though their acquaintance had been at this stage, he did. Once he had decided that the two young men, who like so many others were anxious to be signed by him, were worth pursuing and encouraging, he really took charge of the arrangements . . . what does emerge clearly is that Mr. James did not regard himself as obliged to give Mr. John or Mr. Taupin, nor did he give them, a thorough explanation of the terms of the proposed agreement."[50]

It is submitted that notwithstanding the reference by the learned

---

[47] As Wollcombe has acknowledged: "Where an artists' manager is in *de facto* control of the record company to whom the artist assigns the copyright in his sound recordings, as in the *O'Sullivan* case, then there is clearly an argument for extending the fiduciary duty to the record company."

[48] [1991] F.S.R. 397.

[49] *Ibid.* at 411.

[50] *Ibid.* at 451.

Judge to "dominating influence" the authorities do not indicate that the presumption of undue influence can only apply to a relationship in which one party assumes a role of dominating influence.[51] It is sufficient for a presumption of influence to arise to show that the party in whom the trust and confidence is reposed is in a position to exert influence over him who reposes it.[52]

6.19   *Elton John v. Richard Leon James* is not an extension of the principle applied in *O'Sullivan v. Management and Music Agency Ltd*. It is, however, a recognition of the fact that an established publishers and recording companies are capable of exercising undue influence on an artiste, especially an unknown and unestablished artiste, notwithstanding the fact that they are not in law the manager of the artiste, if they exercise all the practical functions of a manager, or through the fact that as record companies and music publishers they are in a position to influence the artiste to enter into the transaction. This is consistent with the fact that it is clear to an artiste that without a contract with a successful record or publishing company it would be difficult to succeed and that it is highly unlikely that an unestablished artiste offered such an opportunity by a record company or music publisher would not be influenced into entering such a transaction.

It is submitted therefore that a contract between an artiste and such entities will be presumed to be the product of undue influence and the burden of proof will be upon the record company or music publisher to prove that the contract was a result of the exercise of free will in the light of full information and advice regarding the transaction. The practical effect is that it is important to ensure not only that the artiste receives independent legal advice, but that the advice is competent and is reflected in the terms of the agreement.

---

[51] See *Goldsworthy v. Brickell* [1987] 1 Ch. 378 at 406 where Nourse L.J. in rejecting the requirement for such "dominating influence" said in relation to *National Westminster Bank plc. v. Morgan* [1985] A.C. 686, H.L.: "If, which I very much doubt, the House of Lords intended to hold the contrary, then I would respectfully disagree with them and point out that holding was not necessary to the decision of that case. I will add that it is to my mind inconceivable that their Lordships could have intended, *sub silentio*, to overrule not only *Tufton v. Sperni* [1952] 2 T.L.R. 516 but many other leading cases from *Huquenin v. Baseley*, 14 Ves. Jun. 273, onwards."

[52] *Goldsworthy v. Brickell* [1987] 1 Ch. 378, C.A.

CHAPTER 7

ASSIGNMENTS AND LICENCES

I. Introduction

(a) *Distinction between assignments and licences*

A producer, composer or record company seeking to secure or transfer **7.01** rights in a copyright work is faced with a choice between an assignment or a licence. Assignment involves a transfer of copyright or some relevant aspect of the copyright,[1] whereas a licence essentially involves a permission to do what would otherwise be an infringement.[2] The practical distinction between the two is, however, often blurred. This is especially so in the case of exclusive licences and assignments: section 101 of the Copyright, Designs and Patents Act 1988 provides that an exclusive licensee has, except against the copyright owner, the same rights and remedies in respect of matters occurring after the grant of the licence as if the licence had been an assignment. The distinction between a licence and an assignment, although "often slender"[3] is nevertheless real and has important consequences: for example, the assignment of the rights of copyright to a purchaser in good faith for value without notice of a prior assignment, whereas a licence is liable to be defeated by such a purchase.[4]

When the document is in plain terms an assignment or, as the case may be, a licence, no difficulty arises. However, where there is no such clarity the question into which of the categories of assignments and

---

[1] See *post*, para. 7.06, nn.24–29.
[2] *Frisby v. British Broadcasting Corporation* [1967] 1 Ch. 932 at 948; *Heap v. Hartley* (1889) 42 Ch.D. 461 at 470; see also *Musket v. Hill* (1840) Bing N.C. 694, *per* Tyndall C.J.: "a dispensation or licence properly passes no interest but only makes an action lawful which, without it, would have been unlawful".
[3] *Frisby v. British Broadcasting Corporation* [1967] 1 Ch. 933 at 947, *per* Goff J.
[4] See *post*, paras 7.08–7.09 and 7.18–7.19.

licences a particular agreement is to be placed falls to be determined upon the construction of that instrument.

7.02   The problem being to discover what the parties intended, the court is not bound by the construction put upon a particular phrase or phrases in another document.[5] Thus, no definitive guidance can be given, in the absence of express agreement as to the disposition of copyright, as to the ascertainment of whether the agreement is an assignment or licence. However, the following general principles appear from the authorities.

First, the court will generally construe the agreement as a licence where the consideration involves a continuing obligation on the part of the person to whom the right is granted to make payment to the grantor of royalties or a share of the profits from the exploitation of the grant of rights.[6] The corollary of this general principle is that where a single once and for all payment is made, an assignment will generally be inferred. Where, however, such a single payment is made, the terms of the agreement must nevertheless be closely examined to determine whether the agreement is designed to vest the copyright in the grantee or to grant a licence. Thus, for example, where in consideration of a single payment the owner of a copyright work grants the rights for one performance only together with an option to acquire wider rights this would indicate a licence notwithstanding the fact of the single payment.[7]

7.03   Secondly, the agreement will generally be construed as an assignment where it grants the rights to produce and perform a play, or exhibit a film, together with a stipulation that the right is to revert[8] to the grantor so as to become again his absolute property in the event of certain defined circumstances.[9] This is illustrated by *Messager v. British Broadcasting Company Limited*,[10] where the agreement between the parties stated that "[t]he licensor hereby grants to the licensee the sole and exclusive right of representing or performing the play in the United

---

[5] See, *e.g.* the comments of Scrutton and Bankes L.JJ. in *Barker v. Stokney* [1919] 1 K.B. 121 at 124, 133.

[6] *Stevens v. Benning* 1 K. & J. 168, Page Wood V.-C, affirmed 6 D.M. & G. 223; *Hole v. Bradbury* (1879) 12 Ch.D. 886; *Re St Jude's Musical Compositions* [1907] 1 Ch 651, C.A. But see text to *infra*, para. 7.03, n.8.

[7] *Frisby v. British Broadcasting Corporation* [1967] 1 Ch. 933 at 947.

[8] This is often referred to in the film and entertainment industry as a "recapture" provision and frequently provides for the reversion of the rights granted in the event that the producer should fail to commence principal photography of the works assigned with a specified period. A similar provision is "turnaround" clause which grants the grantor the right to call for the re-transfer of the rights to the grantor upon payment by him of an agreed sum.

[9] *Messager v. British Broadcasting Company Limited* [1929] A.C. 151, H.L.; *Loew's Incorporated v. Littler* [1958] 1 Ch. 650, C.A.

[10] [1929] A.C. 151, H.L.

Kingdom". There was also a clause which provided that "[i]f the play be not produced in London . . . within three months from this date all rights of representation . . . shall revert to and become again the absolute property of the licensor". The House of Lords held that in the circumstances there was an assignment of the right to perform the work and this was so notwithstanding the fact that there was a continuing obligation on the "licensee" to pay royalties and that the agreement referred to the grantor and grantee as "licensor/licensee" respectively.[11]

However, the absence of an express provision for reverter, or even the words "grant" or "assign" is of little consequence where the terms of the agreement are sufficient to constitute an assignment of copyright. Thus in *Chaplin v. Leslie Frewin*,[12] the Court of Appeal held that an agreement which granted "during the legal term of the copyright . . . the exclusive right of producing, publishing and selling the said work", which are the rights conferred on the owner of the copyright, was effective to constitute an assignment of copyright notwithstanding the absence of a reverter clause, or the use of the words "grant" or "assign" and the continuing obligation on the part of the grantee to pay royalties.[13]

2. Assignment

(a) *Formalities required for assignment*

Formalities necessary for legal assignment. Under English law, an   **7.04** assignment of any of the copyright in respect of any of the relevant acts, or different classes of acts,[14] is not effective to pass legal title to the right assigned unless it is in writing, signed by or on behalf of the assignor.[15] However, where the assignment is signed on behalf of the assignor, the person signing must have the authority of the assignor so to do.[16] Where the assignor is a company the requirement for a signature is satisfied by affixing its seal to the instrument effecting the assignment.[17]

---

[11] *Ibid.* at 157, see particularly, the brief judgment of Viscount Sumner.
[12] [1966] Ch. 71.
[13] *Ibid* at 94, *per* Danckwerts L.J.
[14] As to which see *post*, para. 7.06, n.24 and annotated text.
[15] Copyright, Designs and Patents Act 1988, s.90(3); agreements which do not comply with the statutory requirements may be effective to transfer an equitable interest: see post, para. 7.06, nn.19–23 and annotated text.
[16] *Beloff v. Pressdram* [1973] 1 All E.R. 241.
[17] Copyright, Designs and Patents Act 1988, s.176; see also Law of Property (Miscellaneous Provisions) Act 1989, s.1, and Companies Act 1985, s.36A(4) (inserted by Companies Act 1989, s.130) which provides that the signing of a document by both the director and secretary of a company or by two directors, has the same effect as attaching the seal.

Where these requirements are satisfied no particular form of words is prescribed by the Copyright, Designs and Patents Act 1988 to effect the assignment of copyright. However, where the document is not clearly an assignment, difficulties may arise as to whether, on a true construction of the instrument, the transaction amounts to an assignment or licence.[18]

7.05 Equitable assignment. Where the parties have orally agreed to assign copyright or the instrument of assignment is unexecuted this may give rise only to an equitable title to copyright, notwithstanding the fact that the consideration for the legal assignment has been paid.[19] Similarly, an agreement which provides for the execution of a formal assignment of copyright is likely to be effective as an agreement to transfer copyright and thus an equitable assignment.[20] A further assignment of the equitable interest so created will only be effective if in writing.[21]

An equitable assignee does not acquire the same rights as a legal assignee.[22] The right of an assignee in equity is liable to be defeated by a bona fide purchaser for value without notice of the equitable assignment.

Where the equitable assignee seeks to protect the rights acquired by him he may apply for interlocutory relief but the legal owner must be joined as a party to the proceedings before the action for infringement can proceed to trial.[23]

7.06 Partial assignments. The Copyright, Designs and Patents Act 1988 provides for the divisibility of the rights of copyright. Copyright is divisible and consequently assignable so as to apply to:

(a) one or more, but not all, of the classes of acts which, by virtue of the 1988 Act, the copyright owner has the exclusive right to do[24];

---

[18] See *ante,* paras. 7.01–7.03 for "Distinction between assignments and licences".
[19] *Wah Sang Industrial Co. v. Takmay Industrial Co. Ltd.* [1980] F.S.R. 303, C.A., Hong Kong.
[20] *Sims v. Marryat* (1851) 17 Q.B. 281.
[21] *Roban Jig & Tool Co. Ltd. v. Taylor* [1979] F.S.R. 130 at 143.
[22] See *post,* para. 7.09 and nn.43–53 for the "rights of legal assignee".
[23] *Performing Right Society v. London Theatre of Varieties Ltd.* [1924] A.C. 1, H.L.; *Merchant Adventures Ltd. v. M. Grew and Co. Ltd.* [1972] Ch. 242.
[24] Copyright, Designs and Patents Act 1988, s.90(2)(a). These acts are:
   (a) reproducing the work in any material form (s.17);
   (b) issuing copies of the work to the public (s.18);
   (c) performing, showing or playing the work to the public (s.19);
   (d) broadcasting the work or including it in a cable programme service (s.20);
   (e) making any adaptation of the work (s.21);
   (f) doing any of the above in relation to an adaptation (s.21(2)).

(b) part, but not the whole, of the period for which copyright is to subsist[25];

(c) one or more but not all of the territories to which the owner's copyright extends.[26] In respect of agreements entered into before August 1, 1989, there is specific statutory provision for the geographical division of copyright[27] the omission of the provision from the 1988 Act does not appear to affect the owner's power to grant rights in respect in respect of particular territories outside the United Kingdom.[28]

Thus, an author may assign to a producer the right to adapt his work into a dramatic work and reproduce it in the form of a film but nevertheless retain the right to, *inter alia* issue copies of his work to the public. Similarly, a composer may assign the right of reproduction to his publisher but retain the performing right which he will assign to the Performing Right Society if he is a member of that licensing body. This has the consequence that the term "the copyright owner" is context—driven in that the term is to be taken to mean the person who is entitled to the relevant aspect of copyright assigned to the assignee.[29]

Future copyright. Where a prospective owner[30] of future copyright,[31] by means of an agreement signed by him or on his behalf, purports to assign the future copyright (wholly or partially) to another person, then if, on the copyright coming into existence, the assignee or another person claiming under him would be entitled as against all other persons to have the copyright vested on him, the copyright vests in the assignee or his successor in title.[32] **7.07**

Thus, for example, where a composer enters into an agreement with publisher A for valuable consideration whereby he undertakes to assign the copyright in his works which may come into existence during the duration of the agreement, such compositions will automatically vest in A by reason of the agreement without further action on the part of the composer when he creates a work during the currency of the

[25] *Ibid.,* s.90(2)(b).
[26] *CBS United Kingdom Ltd. v. Charmdale Record Distributions Ltd.* [1980] F.S.R. 289 at 294.
[27] See Copyright Act 1956, s.36(2).
[28] If the agreement regulates the flow of copyright material between member states and grants the assignee any form of exclusivity, it may be void under the provisions of Article 85 of the Treaty of Rome: See *post*, Chap. 8, "Films".
[29] Copyright, Designs and Patents Act 1988, s.173(1).
[30] *Ibid.,* s.91(2): "prospective owner" is to be construed accordingly and includes a person who is prospectively entitled to copyright by virtue of an assignment of future copyright.
[31] *Ibid.,* s.91(2): "future copyright" means copyright which will or may come into existence in respect of a future work or class of works or on the occurrence if a future event.
[32] *Ibid.,* s.91(1).

agreement. Such an assignment also has the consequence that if the composer, subsequent to the agreement with A, agrees to assign copyright in his prospective composition to B, on coming into existence of the works they will vest in A regardless of whether B had notice of the prior assignment. Further, A may, subject to the terms of the agreement, assign his prospective rights under the agreement to X and on the coming into existence of the composition the copyright will vest in X or his successors.

An assignment of future copyright does not, however, apply to:

(1) an agreement made before June 1, 1957[33];

(2) an oral agreement[34];

(3) foreign copyrights.

Where an agreement for the disposition of future copyright was made before August 1, 1989, and where the person who would otherwise be entitled has died before copyright has come into existence, the right to it devolves as if it had subsisted immediately before death and he had then been the owner of the copyright.[35]

7.08 **Rights of Assignor.** Assignment, by its nature involves the transmission of ownership of the relevant aspect of copyright.[36] The assignor therefore relinquishes his right of copyright in the relevant aspect of copyright which has been assigned and, like anyone else, can be restrained by the assignee from infringing the aspect of the copyright which is the subject of the assignment.[37] Particular agreements may make provision for the return of ownership[38] in certain specified circumstances but even in the absence of such express or implied provisions, the assignor retains certain rights in respect of the work assigned. First, prima facie, an author retains the "moral rights" conferred by Chapter IV of the 1988 Act.[39] Secondly, an assignor retains certain common law rights. Thus, for example, he may sue for defamation,[40] malicious falsehood and passing off.[41] Thirdly, if part of the consideration for the assignment is the payment of royalties or a share in

---

[33] *Ibid.*, Sched. 1, para. 26(1).
[34] *Wah Sang Industrial Co. v. Takmay Industrial Co. Ltd* [1980] F.S.R. 303, C.A. Hong Kong).
[35] Copyright Act 1956, s.37(2) – repealed by Copyright, Designs and Patents Act 1988 but preserved in respect of agreements made prior to the commencement (August 1, 1988) of the 1988 Act: Copyright, Designs and Patents Act 1988 Sched. 1, para. 26(2).
[36] See *ante*, para. 7.06, n.24 and annotated text.
[37] Except to the limited extent to which the creator of an artistic work is allowed, by virtue of Copyright, Designs and Patents Act 1988, s.64, to copy aspects of his previous works.
[38] See, *e.g. ante*, para. 7.03, nn.8–10 and annotated text.
[39] See *post*, para. 15.01 *et seq.*
[40] See *post*, para. 21.01 *et seq.*
[41] For "passing off" see *ante*, para. 4.01 *et seq.*

profits, a fiduciary relationship is created between assignee and assignor, entitling the latter to an account.[42]

Rights of Assignee. If the copyright has been the subject of a valid legal   **7.09**
assignment,[43] the transferee obtains good title as against any
subsequent purported transferee regardless of whether the latter gave
value or had notice of the prior assignment.[44] Further, in the absence of
express provision to the contrary, it is in the sole discretion of the
assignee whether he proceeds to exploit the work.[45] Similarly, in the
absence of such contrary provision, the assignor may, in reproducing or
adapting the work, make additions, omissions or alterations,[46] and may
assign his interest at will.[47]

However, where the agreement is made "upon personal considerations",[48] and is thus a personal contract, it is not valid in the absence of
an express term to the contrary, for the assignee to assign to a third
party the rights acquired under the agreement.[49] For these purposes a
personal contract will exist where, for example, rights of copyright are
assigned to a music publisher by reason of its reputation, personal skill
and ability as a music publisher.[50] A personal contract will also be
inferred where the assignor is to have a share of the profits by way of
royalties in the work the subject of the assignment.[51] An individual
may have confidence in a limited company as well as an individual.
Thus, for these purposes, no distinction is to be drawn between an
agreement between, for example, an individual composer and an
individual assignee and assignor, and an individual assignor and a
limited company[52] or partnership.[53]

Reversionary rights. Where the author of a literary, dramatic, musical or   **7.10**
artistic work was the first owner of copyright in it, no assignment of the
copyright and no grant of any interest in it, made by him (otherwise

---

[42] *Elton John v. Richard Leon James* [1991] F.S.R. 397.
[43] *i.e.* complies with the formalities required by the Copyright, Designs and Patents Act
1988: see *ante*, para. 7.04 and nn.14–18.
[44] *cf.* the position where the assignment is an equitable one only; see *ante*, para. 7.05 and
nn.19–23.
[45] *Hole v. Bradbury* (1879) 12 Ch.D. 886; *A. Schroeder Music Publishing Co. Ltd. v. Macaulay*
[1974] 1 W.L.R. 1308, H.L. See *ante*, para. 4.06 *et seq.* for the duties of the assignee where
the assignor is entitled to receive a share of royalties.
[46] Subject to the residual rights of the assignor: see *ante*, para. 7.08 and nn.36–42.
[47] *Messager v. British Broadcasting Company Limited* [1929] A.C. 151, *per* Lord Hailsham
L.C. at 156.
[48] *Stevens v. Benning* (1855) 1 K. & J. 168 at 175; *Hole v. Bradbury* (1879) 12 Ch.D. 886 at 896.
[49] *Stevens v. Benning* (1855) 1 K. & J. 168; *Hole v. Bradbury* (1879) 12 Ch.D. 886 at 896;
Dorling v. Honnor Marine Ltd. [1964] 1 Ch. 560 at 568.
[50] *Stevens v. Benning* [1855] 1 K. & J. 168; *Hole v. Bradbury* (1879) 12 Ch.D. 886.
[51] *Stevens v. Benning* (1855) 1 K.B. 168; *Elton John v. Richard Leon James* [1991] F.S.R. 397.
[52] *Griffith v. Tower Publishing Co. Ltd.* [1897] 1 Ch. 21.
[53] *Hole v. Bradbury* (1879) 12 Ch.D. 886.

than by will) between July 1, 1912 and June 1, 1957,[54] is effective to vest in the assignee or grantee any rights with respect to the copyright in the work beyond the expiration of 25 years from the death of the author.[55] Any assignment made during this period, regardless of its terms, automatically comes to an end, in the absence of any assignment of the reversionary interest by the author after commencement after the expiration of the 25-year period; the copyright then reverts to the author's estate.[56]

The operation of this rule has the effect that the author's ability to assign in whole or in part and to grant interests by licence is restricted where he is the first owner of the copyright in a work. Any such assignment or grant cannot operate to vest in the assignee or grantee any right or interest in the copyright extending in time beyond the expiration of 25 years from the death of the author of the work; the reversionary interest for the remaining 25 years of the copyright term devolves, on the author's death, in his legal representative as part of his estate and, importantly, any agreement by the author as to the disposition of such reversionary interest is null and void.

The 25-year reversionary rights rule is, however, subject to a number of limiting statutory rules. First, it does not affect any of the following categories of dealings with the reversionary interests:

(a) an assignment of the reversionary interest by a person to whom it has been assigned[57];

(b) an assignment of the reversionary interest after the death of the author by his personal representatives or any person becoming entitled to it[58]; or

(c) any assignment of the copyright after the reversionary interest has fallen in.[59]

7.11   Secondly, it does not apply to the assignment of the copyright in a collective work or a licence to publish a work or part of a work as part of a collective work.[60] For these purposes, a "collective work" means a work in which copyright is capable of subsisting in the totality of the work in addition to and apart from any copyright which may exist in its constituent parts.[61] "The collective work is something which by original collocation or arrangement has a copyright of its own and it is the

---

[54] The commencements of the Copyright Acts 1911 and 1956 respectively.
[55] Copyright, Designs and Patents Act 1988, Sched. 1, para 27(1).
[56] *Ibid.*, Sched. 1, para. 27(2).
[57] *Ibid.*, Sched. 1, para. 27(3)(a).
[58] *Ibid.*, Sched. 1, para. 27(3)(b).
[59] *Ibid.*, Sched. 1, para. 27(3)(c).
[60] *Ibid.*, Sched. 1, para. 27(4).
[61] *Chappell & Co. v. Redwood Music Ltd.* [1981] R.P.C. 337, H.L.

assignment of *that* copyright that is excepted from the proviso".[62] An example of a collective work would be an anthology of short stories. Such a collection of copyright stories is capable of attracting a copyright separate from the individual stories. However, in the case of a song[63] where the lyrics are written by A and its music by B, the lyrics have a copyright, as does the music: the two copyrights are entirely separate from each other and cannot be merged. It follows that the song has no copyright and does not come within the meaning of a "collective work".

(b) *Assignment of agreements containing a right to royalties*

Assignment to a third party by the publisher. Where the owner of a **7.12** copyright work assigns his rights to, for example, a music publisher on terms which provide for the payment of a royalty and the music publisher in turn assigns the rights to a third party, the owner may, where the music publisher remains solvent, pursue him for damages if the third party fails to pay royalties and/or adequately to exploit the work.[64]

If, however, the music publisher becomes bankrupt or enters into insolvent liquidation, the assignor's rights against the third party is not without difficulty. The applicable principles were considered by the Court of Appeal in *Barker v. Stickney*[65] where Barker had assigned the copyright in his book to a publisher on terms which provided for a royalty and a lump sum payment and the publisher expressly covenanted not to assign the copyright except subject to the terms of the agreement. The publisher went into receivership and by its receiver assigned the copyright to Stickney without any stipulation as to payment of royalties. Three grounds were put forward by Barker in support of his claim against Stickney. First, an unpaid vendor's lien, secondly a charge on the copyright for the payment of the royalties and thirdly, a duty on the Stickney to perform the covenants in the agreement of which he had notice.

The court rejected Barker's claim based on a vendor's lien on the basis that a vendor's lien arises only where a person purports to convey property but the purchase money though due has not been paid. Although in law the conveyance is complete, it is not complete in equity but is subject to the right of the vendor to a lien upon the property for the amount of the unpaid purchase price. In the instant case, the consideration for the sale of the copyright was not the payment of royalties, which were not then due and might never become due. The consideration was the covenant of the purchasers to pay the royalties when they

---

[62] *Ibid.* at 348, *per* Lord Russell of Killowen.
[63] Meaning the musical work and the lyrics together.
[64] See *post*, paras. 7.20, 7.21, nn.94–97 for problems caused by its insolvent liquidation. See also *Elton John v. Richard Leon James* [1991] F.S.R. 397.
[65] [1919] 1 K.B. 121, C.A.

became due. The second ground was rejected on the basis that upon construction of the agreement it imposed no charge on the copyright and the third ground was rejected on the basis that a person acquiring a chose in action is not bound by mere notice of a personal covenant by his predecessor in title.

7.13   Thus it would appear that an original assignor may have a claim against a second assignee where on a construction of the agreement a charge is imposed on the copyright for the payment of the royalty, but has no right of action against a third party to whom the copyright has been assigned, notwithstanding the fact that the third party has notice of the obligation of the intervening assignor's obligation to pay royalties to the original first assignor.

However, there is a developing principle which holds that he who takes the benefit of a transaction must also take the burden. In *Tito v. Waddell (No. 2)*,[66] Sir Robert Megarry V.-C examined all the cases which could be said to exemplify the principle. Many were cases in which on the true construction of the instrument, enjoyment of the benefit was conditional on the assumption of the burden. However, he found some cases which he said[67] embodied the "pure principle" of benefit and burden. He stated the principle thus: "the right and the burden, although arising under the same instrument, are independent of each other: X grants a right to Y and by the same instrument Y independently covenants with X to do some act". This principle is, however, subject to limitations so as to prevent the subversion of the doctrine of privity of contract and the principle that an assignee of a contract or other chose in action is not bound to perform the obligations undertaken by the assignor. Thus, "[i]f the initial transaction has created benefits and burden which, on its true construction, are distinct, the question whether a person who is not an original party can take one without the other will prima facie depend upon the circumstances in which he comes into the transaction. If, for instance, all that is assigned to him is the benefit of the contract, and the assignor, who is a party to the contract undertakes to continue to discharge the burdens of it, it would be remarkable if it were to be held that the assignee could not take the benefit without assuming the burden. The circumstances show that the assignee was intended to take only the benefit, and that the burden was intended to be borne in the same way as it had been borne previously."[68]

Thus, the right of the covenantee to enforce his covenant against an assignee depends on the circumstances of a transaction to which he is

---

[66] [1977] Ch. 106 at 289, 299.
[67] *Ibid.* at 290.
[68] *Ibid.* at 302.

not a party. One must, however, be able to infer from that transaction that the assignee was intended to assume the burden.[69] If correct, this would explain *Barker v. Stickney*[70] where the assignment by the receiver contained no provision that the purchaser should pay royalties.

Thus, a copyright owner, such as, for example a composer, who wishes his work to be exploited by another in consideration of the payment of royalty, may seek to protect his interests by including express and clear words in the agreement, imposing a charge on the relevant copyright for payment of the royalties due to him under the terms of the assignment.[71] Alternatively, he might grant the relevant exploitation right conditional upon the payment of royalties, or a non-assignable licence conditional on payment of royalties.[72]   7.14

(c) *Insolvency of the publisher*

Where a copyright owner assigns the copyright in his work on terms that he is to be paid a royalty from the income received from its exploitation but the assignee subsequently becomes bankrupt he is entitled only to prove in the bankruptcy for damages for the royalty that was due to him under the terms of the contract.[73] The harshness of this rule was mitigated by section 60 of the Bankruptcy Act 1914 in respect of authors who assigned their copyright: the operation of the section prevented a trustee in bankruptcy from selling or authorising the sale of copies of the work, except where he ensured that the author received the same royalties as would have been payable by the bankrupt.[74] Although the provision has been repealed by the Insolvency Act 1985,[75] it continues in effect in relation to transactions entered into prior to December 29, 1986, by reason of the operation of paragraph 15 of Part II of Schedule 2 to the Insolvency Act 1986.   7.15

A copyright owner may seek to protect his right to royalties received

---

[69] *Law Debenture Corpn. v. Ural Caspian Ltd.* [1993] 1 W.L.R. 138.
[70] *Ibid.*, n.89. The "pure benefit and burden" principle was not argued in *Barker v. Stickney*. See *Tito v. Waddell (No. 2)* [1977] 1 Ch. 106 at 300.
[71] When dealing with companies, copyright owners should be aware of the registration requirements with respect to charges on copyright; see Companies Act 1985, s.396(1) (as amended by the Companies Act 1989); neither a liquidator, nor purchaser, for value, of an interest in the relevant asset, is bound by an unregistered charge falling within s.396 (*ibid.*, s.399).
[72] *Barker v. Stickney* [1919] 1 K.B. 121 at 133, *per* Scrutton L.J., C.A.
[73] *Re Richards* [1907] 2 K.B. 33; *cf. Lucas v. Moncrieff* (1905) 21 T.L.R. 683 where a licence granted in exchange for royalties was held to be terminated by the bankruptcy.
[74] This provision did not apply to publishers which were bodies corporate: *Re Health Promotion Ltd.* [1932] 1 Ch. 65.
[75] As consolidated in the Insolvency Act 1986.

by the assignee from the exploitation of the work prior to the bankruptcy or liquidation by requiring the same to be paid into a specially
designated "trust account" upon receipt by the assignee. In the event
that the assignee should become bankrupt or enter into liquidation
prior to the payment of the royalties to the copyright owner such "trust
funds" will not form part of the funds available for distribution to his
creditors.[76]

3. Licences[77]

7.16 **General.** A licence may fall into one of three classes. First, it may be a
purely gratuitous licence in return for which the grantor gets nothing
for the grant. Secondly, it may be a licence given for valuable consideration. This second category may itself be sub-divided into (a) cases
where the consideration is paid by a single lump sum on the grant of
the licence and (b) cases where the consideration is in the form of
periodic payments during the period of the licence. Thirdly, the licence
may take the form of an exclusive licence. A copyright owner may
licence others to do any or all of the acts which the 1988 Act gives him
the exclusive right to do.[78]

7.17 **Formalities required for the creation of licences.** For these purposes a
distinction should be drawn between exclusive licences and other
licences. An exclusive licence will only be created where it is:

(a) in writing; and

(b) signed by or on behalf of the copyright owner; and

(c) authorises the licensee to the exclusion of all other persons,
including the person granting the licence, to exercise a right
which would otherwise be exercisable exclusively by the copyright owner.[79]

No such formalities are required in respects of licences which are not
exclusive: such licences may therefore be oral or implied from the conduct of the copyright owner. In determining whether there is an
implied licence, the test to be applied is an objective one: namely

---

[76] *Carreras Rothman v. Freeman Mathews Treasure Ltd.* [1985] Ch. 207.
[77] See *ante*, para. 7.01 for the definition of a licence.
[78] As to which see *ante*, para. 7.06, n.24.
[79] Copyright, Designs and Patents Act, 1988 s.92(1).

whether, viewing the facts objectively, the words and conduct of the alleged licensor, as made known to the alleged licensee, in fact indicated that the licensor consented to what the licensee was doing.[80]

Rights of an exclusive licensee. An exclusive licensee under an agree- **7.18** ment made on or after August 1, 1989, has, except against the copyright owner, the same rights and remedies in respect of matters occurring after the grant as if the licence had been an assignment.[81] Such rights and remedies as the exclusive licensee is accorded as against infringers is concurrent with the rights of the copyright owner.[82] The exclusive licensee's rights are, however, liable to be defeated by a purchase of the relevant copyright by a purchaser in good faith for valuable consider- ation, without notice of the exclusive licence.[83] In such circumstances, as the exclusive licensee's rights against the owner are contractual only, the licensee's remedy would be an action against the copyright owner in contract for damages.

An exclusive licensee, under an agreement made between June 1, 1956 and August 1, 1989, may, in his own name, pursue infringers, apart from those deriving title from the copyright owner.[84]

Rights of other licensees. A licence granted by a copyright owner is **7.19** binding on every successor in title to his interest in the copyright, except a purchaser in good faith for valuable consideration and without notice (actual or constructive) of the licence or a person deriving title from such a purchaser.[85]

The licence passes no proprietorial interest in the work but only makes an action lawful which, without it would have been unlawful.[86] This has, as one of its consequences, the effect that a licensee may not sue for infringement of copyright without joining the copyright owner as co-plaintiff.[87]

A licensee has, unless the terms of the licence provides otherwise, the

---

[80] *Redwood Music Ltd. v. Chappell & Co. Ltd.* [1982] R.P.C. 109. See also *Mellor v. Australian Broadcasting Commission* [1940] A.C. 491; *cf. Performing Right Society v. Coates* (1924) Mac G.Cop.Cas (1923–28) 103.
[81] Copyright, Designs and Patents Act 1988, s.101(1).
[82] *Ibid.*, s.101(2). Section 102 makes a number of provisions for regulating procedure and apportioning damages between owner and exclusive licensee in respect of actions for infringement as to which see *post*, para. 13.21 *et seq.*
[83] *Ibid.*, s.90(4).
[84] Copyright Act 1956, s.19.
[85] Copyright Design and Patents Act 1988, s.90(4).
[86] See *ante*, para. 7.01, n.2 and annotated text for the nature and extent of the rights granted by a licence.
[87] *Neilson v. Horniman* (1909) 26 T.L.R. 188, C.A.

right to make alterations[88] this right is, however, subject to the author's power to object to derogatory treatment of his work.[89]

7.20 **Revocation of licences.** A gratuitous licence is revocable by reasonable notice given to the licensee,[90] notwithstanding the fact that the licensee has expended moneys in the belief that the licence will continue.[91] Where a licence is given for consideration, revocability depends on the construction of the contract in question including all the surrounding circumstances.

A licence coupled with an interest is, in general, irrevocable.[92] If the contract grants the licence for a specific period or for a specific purpose, it is generally irrevocable, for the duration of that period or purpose.[93] Where a contractual licence provides for periodic payments by way of royalties or profit sharing but contains no express provision for its termination it may be revoked on giving reasonable notice to the licensee.[94]

Where the licensor purports to revoke a revocable licence but gives insufficient notice of revocation, the licensee cannot ignore the revocation and treat the licence as still subsisting: he will not, however, be treated as a wrongdoer for continuing to do what the licence permitted him to do until the expiry of the period which constituted reasonable notice.[95]

7.21 **Construction of licences.** Where the instrument granting a licence is silent as to a matter in issue between the parties, or there is a contention as to the meaning of a provision or provisions in the licence, the task of construing the document falls to the court. The construction of each licence will depend upon its terms. However, one area which is of particular importance for the entertainment industry is the construction of licences in the light of technological developments. Many modern licence agreements sensibly make specific provision for media and methods of reproduction unknown at the time of contracting. In the absence of such provisions, the contract must be construed in order to

---

[88] *Frisby v. British Broadcasting Co. Ltd.* [1967] Ch. 932, where it was also stated that the courts would readily imply a term which limited this right to alter.
[89] Copyright, Designs and Patents Act 1988, s.80: see *ante*, para. 7.09, nn.45–46 and annotated text.
[90] *Winter Garden Theatre (London) Ltd. v. Millennium Productions Ltd.* [1948] A.C. 173 at 188, H.L.
[91] *Hart v. Hyam* (1916) MacG.Cop.Cas. (1911–16) 301.
[92] *Williams v. Feldman* (1913) MacG.Cop.Cas. (1911–1916) 98; *Hurst v. Picture Theatres Ltd.* [1915] 1, C.A.
[93] *Hurst v. Picture Theatres Ltd.* [1915] 1 K.B. 1 at 10, C.A., per Buckley L.J.; *Williams v. Feldman* (1913) MacG.Cop.Cas (1911–16) 98; *Winter Garden Theatre (London) Ltd. v. Millennium Productions Ltd.* [1948] A.C. 173.
[94] *Reade v. Bentley* (1858) 4 K. & J. 656.
[95] *Dorling v. Honnor Marine Ltd.* [1964] 1 Ch. 560 at 567.

ascertain whether the parties intended that the new development should be included in the rights licensed.

Thus, for example, in *Hospital for Sick Children v. Walt Disney Productions Inc.*,[96] the Court of Appeal observed that the right to reproduce a work in *"cinematography or moving picture films"* was capable of including the right to produce sound films. Sound films being but a genus of *"cinematography or moving pictures"* and an improvement upon the silent films which they have replaced, the expression would not normally exclude any improvements that might thereafter be invented in cinematographic technique and methods of production.[97] This case does not set down any rule of law in relation to the construction of licences but similar reasoning may well apply with respect to more modern developments such as video, satellite and cable and any future development of such technologies.

---

[96] [1968] Ch. 52, C.A.
[97] *Ibid.* at 78, *per* Salmon L.J.

PART II

COPYRIGHT AND RELATED RIGHTS

FILMS

1. Introduction

(a) *Definition of Film*

The Copyright Designs and Patents Act 1988 defines "film" as meaning **8.01**
a "recording on any medium from which a moving image may by any
means be produced".[1] This definition encompasses all known means of
recording visual images including film, videotape, disc. All recordings
involving a "moving image", including documentary, full length
feature films and television productions, will therefore be uses of
"film". Further, by defining a "film" by reference to a "moving image"
the definition is capable of covering any new development in technology.

(b) *Distinction between copyright in film and underlying rights*

In the creation of a film there is a separate copyright in the underlying **8.02**
literary (*e.g.* the novel) artistic and musical works on which the film is
based, or which form part of the film, and a separate copyright in the

---

[1] Copyright, Designs and Patents Act 1988, s.5(1).

"moving image" which is reproduced from the medium on which it has been recorded. Ownership of the physical material from which the "moving image" may be reproduced does not confer any ownership by way of copyright in the film unless an assignment of the copyright has also been made with the transfer of such physical ownership.

(c) *Owner of copyright in film*

8.03　**The 1988 Act.** The author of a film is the first owner of any copyright in it.[2] The Copyright, Designs and Patents Act 1988 Act provides that in the case of a film the "author" is the person "by whom the arrangements necessary for the making of the . . . film are undertaken".[3] Although the financial arrangements will be an important aspect,[4] it is submitted that "arrangements" in this context is to be taken to mean all the arrangements and not merely the financial arrangements necessary for the making of the film. It is to be noted that the definition of "author" makes no reference to the person who finances or commissions the film. Where the sole function performed by such persons consists of the commissioning or financing of the production of a film it is submitted that they do not make the arrangements necessary for making the film[5] in that the provision of finance cannot be said in the ordinary sense of the word to be the "arrangements" necessary for making the film. The obtaining of the finance or commission is itself a part of the arrangements necessary for making the film. Where the finance has been provided, or the film commissioned, the person who can be said to have made the arrangement in respect of such financing or commissioning is the person who procured the financing or commissioning. Article 2(1) of E.C. Directive 93/98[6] provides that on the coming into effect of the Directive the principal director of a film is to be considered as its author or one of its authors. Member States are obliged to pass legislation before July 1, 1995, giving effect to the Directive and may determine the date from which Article 2(1) is to apply provided that date is no later than July 1, 1997. However, a Member State need not apply Article 2(1) to films created before July 1, 1994 and retain a discretion as to the date (no later than July 1, 1997) from which Article 2(1) is to apply.

8.04　**Film industry practice.** Consideration of the practice of the film and television industries tends to indicate that, except in exceptional cases,

---

[2] *Ibid.*, s.11(1).
[3] *Ibid.*, s.9(2)(a).
[4] *Re F.G. (Films) Ltd.* [1953] 1 W.L.R. 483.
[5] *Beggars Banquet Records Ltd. v. Carlton Television Ltd.* [1993] E.M.L.R. 349.
[6] [1993] O.J. L209/9.

the production company ("the producer") will be the author. The producer will generally have as its business the production of films. This function will involve the creation of original ideas or the acquisition of copyright material or development of ideas in the public domain. The producer will prepare an outline or treatment based on such material and will, in general, use that material to obtain finance. Generally, a theatrical film distributor or television company will finance or commission the production of the film. Thereafter, the producer will commission a script, prepare a production schedule and budget. The producer will hire a director, individual producer[7] and the performers. The individual producer will generally carry out the task of booking locations, facilities, post-production facilities and crew. Where filming is to be on location overseas, a production company in the foreign country may be hired by the producer to organise the necessary facilities. The fact that a part of the arrangements is made by another production company at the request of the producers does not of itself deprive the producer of his designation as author.[8] It will therefore be seen that while the financing of the film production may be derived from the film distributor of the television company, the producer is the person who initiates the original concept, arranges the finance, the director, facilities and crew. In such circumstances it is clear that the producer is generally the person who undertakes the "arrangements necessary for the making of the . . . film".

A television company may on occasion appoint a production company to produce a film which has been brought to, or originated by the television company. In such circumstances, where the producer is required to select and arrange, for the appointment of the performers, crew, facilities and complete the post-production, the producer will be the author. However, each case must be examined on its own particular facts to determine who has undertaken the arrangements necessary for making the film.[9]

(d) *Duration of copyright in film*

Copyright in a film expires at the end of the period of 50 years from the end of the calendar year in which it is made, or if it is released[10] before the end of that period, 50 years from the calendar year in which it is
8.05

---

[7] "Individual producer" in this context means the person employed by the producer to manage the production on a day-to-day basis.
[8] *Beggars Banquet Records Ltd. v. Carlton Television Ltd.* [1993] E.M.L.R. 349; *Adventure Film Productions S.A. v. Tully* [1993] E.M.L.R. 376.
[9] *Beggars Banquet Records Ltd. v. Carlton Television Ltd.* [1993] E.M.L.R. 349.
[10] "Released" occurs in the case of a film or film sound-track, when the film is first shown in public: Copyright, Designs and Patents Act 1988, s.13(2)(b).

released.[11] Thus, where a film is made in 1990 but is not released, copyright expires at the end of 2040. If, however, it is released in 2030, although produced in 1990, copyright will expire at the end of 2080.

The term of copyright protection in respect of films published at commencement[12] of the 1988 Act, or films within section 13(3)(a) of the 1956 Act (*i.e.* films registered under former enactments[13] relating to registration films) is 50 years from the end of the calendar year in which it was published or registered.[14]

The term of copyright in films which were not published at the commencement of the Act, or not registrable under former enactments relating to registration, continues for a period of 50 years from the end of the calendar year in which the 1988 copyright provisions came into force.[15] If it is published during that period copyright in it continues until the end of 50 years from the end of the calendar year in which it is published.[16]

It is to be noted that the 1988 Act accords a separate copyright to the sound-track of a film.[17] A soundtrack of film which is protected as part of a film pursuant to section 13(a) of the Copyright Act 1959 at commencement[18] of the 1988 Act also acquires a separate copyright as a sound recording which subsists until the copyright in the film expires.[19]

(e) *Qualification for copyright protection*

8.06 **General.** It is a pre-condition of the subsistence of copyright in a film that:

---

[11] Copyright, Designs and Patents Act 1988, s.13(1). Art. 2(2) of E.C. Directive 93/98: [1993] O.J. L290/9, provides that from the coming into effect of the Directive (July 1, 1995) the terms of protection expires 70 years after the death of the last of the following persons to survive, whether or not these persons are designated as co-authors: the principal director, the author of the screenplay, the author of the dialogue and the composer of the music specifically created for use in the film. Where the country of origin of a work is a third country and the author is not a European Union national the term of protection granted by a Member State expires on the date of the protection granted in the country of origin of the work up to a maximum period of 70 years: Directive 93/98, Art. 7.

[12] August 1, 1989.

[13] *i.e.* Films Act 1960 and Films Act 1970 as amended by Films Act 1980.

[14] Copyright, Designs and Patents Act 1988, Sched. 1, para. 12(b); for the meaning of "published" see *infra*, para. 8.06.

[15] *Ibid.*, Sched. 1, para. 12(5).

[16] *Ibid.*

[17] *Ibid.*, Sched. 1, para. 8(1).

[18] August 1, 1989.

[19] *Ibid.*, Sched. 1, para. 8(1) and 8(2).

(a) the author was a "qualifying person"[20] when the film was "made"[21]; or

(b) it was first "published" in the United Kingdom, or a qualifying country.[22]

There is no definition in the 1988 Act of the word "made" in relation to films. However, it is submitted that where the author is not a "qualifying person" but becomes so prior to the final edited version of the film, copyright will subsist in the final version. If, however, a person is not so qualified, copyright protection may be acquired in the film by first publishing it in the United Kingdom or a Convention country.

"Publication" for these purposes means the issue of copies to the public[23] but does not include the film being shown in public or broadcast or included in a cable programme service.[24] Where the film is first published in a non-Convention country and is subsequently published within 30 days in a Convention country, it is regarded as published simultaneously in a qualifying country.[25] However, publication does not include "publication which is merely colourable and not intended to satisfy the reasonable requirements of the public." In *Frances, Day & Hunter v. Feldman & Co.*[26] Neville J. observed that publication will not be colourable if the person publishing the work is prepared to satisfy the demand of the public but "[y]ou need not advertise and you need not call the attention of the public to the fact that you have published".

Qualifying person. A "qualifying person means":   **8.07**

(a) a British citizen, a British Dependent Territories citizen, a British National (overseas), a British Overseas citizen, or a British protected person within the meaning of the British Nationality Act 1981[27]; or

(b) an individual domiciled or resident in, or a body incorporated under the laws of, the United Kingdom, Channel Islands, Isle of Man and Colonies[28];

---

[20] *Ibid.*, s.153(1).
[21] *Ibid.*, s.154(5)(a).
[22] *Ibid.*, s.155(1).
[23] *Ibid.*, s.175(1)(a).
[24] *Ibid.*, s.175(4)(c)(i).
[25] *Ibid.*, s.155(3).
[26] [1914] 2 Ch. 728.
[27] Copyright, Designs and Patents Act 1988, s.154(1).
[28] *Ibid.*, s.154(1)(b), s.154(1)(c).

    (c) an individual who is a citizen, or subject of domiciled or resident in a country specified in Schedule 1 of the Copyright (Application to other Countries) Order (S.I. 1994 No. 263)[29];

    (d) bodies incorporated under the laws of a country specified in Schedule 1 of the Copyright (Application to other Countries) Order.[30]

8.08   **Qualifying country.** A "qualifying country" for the purposes of publication is a country specified in Schedule 1 of the Copyright (Application to Other Countries) Order.[31–33]

2. Infringement

(a) *Primary infringement*

8.09   The owner of the copyright in a film has the exclusive right to do the following acts in the United Kingdom[34]:

    (a) to copy the work;

    (b) to issue copies of the work to the public;

    (c) to perform, show or play the work in public;

    (d) to broadcast the work, or include it in a cable programme service.

A person who carries out any of these activities, or authorises another so to do, without the authority of the copyright owner infringes the copyright in the work.[35]

(b) *Secondary infringement*

8.10   Secondary infringement of the rights in a film will take place by[36]:

    (a) importing an infringing copy;

    (b) possessing or dealing with an infringing copy;

    (c) providing means for making infringing copies;

---

[29] *Ibid.,* s.159; see Appendix A for the terms of the Order.
[30] *Ibid.,* s.159; see Appendix A for the terms of the Order.
[31–33] *Ibid.,* s.159; see Appendix A for the terms of the Order.
[34] See "Infringement of Copyright in Films and Music", *post*, Chap. 12.
[35] Copyright, Designs and Patents Act 1988, s.16(2).
[36] See *supra*, n.34.

(d) permitting use of premises for infringing performances;

(e) provision of apparatus for infringing performance, etc.

3. Film Production

Whatever, the intended place of first exhibition, the production of a   **8.11**
film[37] requires the maker to ensure that he has sufficient control over
the bundle of rights which comprise the constituent elements necessary
to produce and commercially exploit it. This section examines the constituent elements which make up a film.

(a) *A typical film production*

General. There are many complex permutations of the process of under-   **8.12**
taking "the arrangements necessary for the making of the . . . films".
The process for each project will depend on its own particular facts and
in particular the nature of the proposed film, the costs of production and
whether it is primarily intended for exhibition in the cinema or on
television. What follows is a simplified outline of the typical process
involved in the creation of a film.

Acquisition of underlying rights. In general, the first stage in the pro-   **8.13**
duction of a film is the acquisition[38] of the necessary legal rights in the
works on which the film is to be based. Such rights are usually referred
to in the entertainment industry as the "underlying rights" and generally consist of literary, dramatic, musical or artistic works.

Few ideas which are developed for the purposes of the creation of a
film reach the stage of actual production. However, where the film is to
be based on a copyright work the outright purchase of the necessary
rights to produce and exploit a film has disadvantages both to the producer and the copyright owner. For the producer the principal disadvantage lies in the fact that he has to maintain sufficient projects in
development to have a reasonable prospect of regularly producing
films. Consequently, a producer would find it extremely expensive to
pay the acquisition price for all the copyright works he has in his development portfolio, especially when the ratio of development to production is low. For the copyright owner, the principal disadvantage is that
he may find an outlet for his work sterilised where a producer fails to

---

[37] In this section the expression "film" or "film production" includes television
programmes and television programme production.

[38] Where the film is to be based on a work in the public domain it will be unnecessary to
acquire such rights. See under "Constituent elements in a film", *post*, para. 8.22 *et seq.*

find an exhibitor willing to fund its adaptation and transformation to the screen. For these reasons, the practice has developed in the film industry that, in general, a producer will at the outset only acquire a right to adapt the work into a dramatic work by way of screenplay together with an option to purchase the film rights during the agreed option period. The screenplay will then be available to the producer to enable him to solicit finance for the production of the film.

The option period will depend upon the nature of the work (for example, whether it is a successful novel), the reputation of the author and the reputation and track record of the producer. In general, the option period is 12 months and often extendable for further periods upon the payment of additional sums. The option price is normally 10 per cent. of the price payable upon exercise of the option for the films rights, and the option price is usually treated as on account of the price payable on the exercise of the option.

8.14 **Outline; treatment.** Having acquired the right of adaptation coupled with the option to make a film based on the work a producer will generally, either by himself or by commissioning a script writer, prepare an outline or treatment of the work on which it is proposed to base the film. An outline is, as its name implies, a short document giving a brief guide to the proposed film, whereas a treatment generally comprises a summary of the plot, sample dialogue and character analyses. Such documents are generally prepared for the purpose of raising finance for the next stage of the film production process or, where a theatrical film is concerned, to attract a star name who will make it easier to obtain financing for the film.

8.15 **Development.** Where the producer does not finance the screenplay himself he will generally approach an exhibitor, usually a television or feature film distribution company, for the initial finance to commission the screenplay and "develop" the acquired underlying rights. Where such funds are forthcoming, "development" will comprise the commissioning from a scriptwriter of a screenplay based upon the underlying idea or material, and the preparation of a production schedule and budget based upon the screenplay for the film. For the purposes of preparing the production schedule and budget the producer will appoint an individual producer or production manager who will be responsible for the supervision of the preparation of the production schedule and the budget based on the screenplay. In the process of the creation of a film the production schedule is an important stage in that it provides a clear indication of the requirements of the script and enables the financial costs of the production to be appraised.

The production schedule will comprise an analysis of the production requirements of the screenplay such as, for example, the cast, the number of days each cast member will be required during production of the film, the details of the types of locations that will be required, accommodation, storage facilities, crew costs and transport requirements. It is only when the full analysis of all the items required by the screenplay for the production of the film and the period of that requirement exists that a budget can be prepared showing how much will be required to produce and deliver the film.

Where the proposed film is for cinema distribution, it is common **8.16** practice for a producer to present the screenplay, production schedule and budget to a reputable completion guarantor company with a view to the completion guarantor providing a completion bond[39] for the film if it should be produced. Where a completion guarantor considers a project at this stage it will often provide a letter indicating that it has considered the screenplay, production schedule and budget and would be prepared to provide a completion bond for its production in accordance with the production schedule and budget. This letter can be of considerable assistance to a producer seeking finance in that it is an indication to a potential financier that the project is capable of being produced at the indicated price according to the production schedule. It is uncommon for this process to take place in the case of productions exclusively for television.

However, the advent of publisher-broadcasters is likely to cause completion guarantees to become of increasing importance as an assurance that the film will be produced and delivered without any call upon them to provide financing in excess of the agreed sum.

Finance. Only when the screenplay, production schedule and budget **8.17** have been prepared and considered by the exhibitor and found acceptable, will a binding commitment usually be given by an exhibitor or financier to provide finance for the actual production of the film. At this stage, where a film for the cinema is under consideration, a named star(s) and director will often have given letters of intent to participate if the film proceeds, and this will in many cases be an important condition of the financiers commitment to the film.

Exercise of option. Where the finance has been secured the producer **8.18** will normally exercise his option to acquire the right to make and exploit a film based upon the underlying rights.

---

[39] A completion guarantee is a contractual commitment from a completion guarantee company to a financier to procure that a film will be completed and delivered within budget, in accordance with the script and production schedule. For an interesting discussion of the nature of such a contract see Northrop in [1993] 5 Ent. L.R. 142.

8.19 Engagement of personnel. Where the production finance is secured the producer will formally engage the director and principal cast. The individual producer will be responsible for the hiring of the crew, the facilities and equipment necessary to shoot the film, and the securing of the filming locations required by the screenplay and production schedule.

8.20 Principal photography. Principal photography is the stage where filming of the production takes place based upon the production schedule or script.

8.21 Post production. Following principal photography, an important stage of production is the creation of the final edited version of the film synchronised with any library or commissioned music. The director and producer are generally responsible for supervising the editing of the film but ultimately the producer, in conjunction with the financing exhibitor or television company, will make the final decision as to the version to be exhibited, although his discretion may in some circumstances be subject to the intervention of the exhibitor, particularly where the subject of consumer protection is concerned. It is usually at this stage that any question of derogatory treatment of the director and screenplay writer's work might arise, assuming that no such infringement took place during shooting of the film.

(b) *Constituent elements of a film*

8.22 Having examined, in outline, the processes involved in the production of the film, consideration will now be given to the elements which comprise a film.

(i) *Underlying rights*

8.23 Categories of underlying rights. The underlying rights on which a producer may seek to base his film will generally fall into one of the following three categories:

(a) literary, dramatic or musical works which are in the public domain;

(b) original literary, dramatic or musical works which are protected by copyright;

(c) original literary, dramatic or musical works commissioned by the producer;

Where the work is protected by copyright the producer will need to ensure that he acquires the rights necessary to make and exploit the film. The right to issue copies of the work to the public, perform the work in public, broadcast or include it in a cable programme service are

104

all separate rights exclusive to the copyright owner. Thus, where the producer wishes to exploit the work by selling copies, exhibiting it in the cinema, broadcasting it or including it in a cable programme service, he will need expressly to acquire such rights in the work.

Works in the public domain

Works in the public domain. A literary, dramatic, musical or artistic **8.24** work which is not protected by copyright, or, where there is no copyright, protected as confidential information,[40] will, as a general rule, be in the public domain and can thus be used by a producer as the basis for a film. A work will not be protected by copyright unless is can be shown that it comes within one of the following categories of copyrightable works[41]:

(a) original literary, dramatic, musical or artistic works;

(b) sound recordings, films, broadcasts or cable programmes; and

(c) the typographical arrangement of published editions.

Facts in the public domain. Where a producer or writer bases a screen- **8.25** play or film on facts or incidents which are available from a non-copyright source but which are also incorporated in works protected by copyright he may use the copyright material so as to find the original source of the material contained in the copyright work, but in creating the script or film he must, if he has not acquired the right in the copyright work, compile his work from the original source material and not the copyright work.[42]

This principle is illustrated by *Harman Pictures N.V. v. Osborne*[43] where the plaintiffs who were film producers and distributors owned the film reproduction rights in a book entitled *The Reason Why* which deals with the Charge of the Light Brigade. The plaintiffs entered into discussions with the defendants who were also producers and distributors with a view to the defendants purchasing the plaintiffs rights in *The Reason Why*, or the plaintiffs undertaking a joint production based on it. The discussions came to nothing and the defendants proceeded to develop their own film based on the Charge of the Light Brigade and commissioned John Osborne who was a director of the defendant companies to write a screenplay. The screenplay contained marked

---

[40] See "Breach of Confidence" *post*, para. 17.20. Such works may also be protected under the law relating to passing off; see *post*, para. 18.31.
[41] Copyright, Designs and Patents Act 1988, s.1(1).
[42] *Pike v. Nicholas* (1869) 5 Ch.App. 251; *Moffat and Paige Ltd. v. Gill* 18 T.L.R. 547, C.A.; *MacMillan & Co. Ltd. v. Cooper* 40 T.L.R. 186 at 189, P.C.; *Poznanski v. London Film Productions Ltd.* [1937] MacG.Cop.Cas. 107.
[43] [1967] 1 W.L.R. 723.

similarities to *The Reason Why* in the choice of incidents. The defendants contended that the screenplay was based on original research from common sources without making any improper uses of the book. In the absence of an explanation from the screenplay writer of what sources he consulted and how he arrived at his selection, or by him taking one or two examples of common situations in the book and screenplay and giving an explanation of how the similarities occurred, an injunction was granted.

Thus, where a producer or screenplay writer proposes to use facts in the public domain which are also incorporated in a copyright work he should take care to ensure that he keeps a record of his sources in order that he is in a position to demonstrate that his work is based on a source other than the copyright work.

Original literary, or dramatic works protected by copyright

8.26 **Dramatisation of non-dramatic work.** Adaptation is an important part of the business of film production. Prior to the production of a film,[44] the producer will have to commission a screenplay. Where a producer proposes to use literary, dramatic or musical works which are protected by copyright as the basis for his film he will need to acquire the right of "adaptation" so as to enable him base his film on, or incorporate the material into, his film. As a general rule, it is an infringement of the copyright owner's rights if a producer makes a dramatic adaptation[45] (*e.g.* a screenplay) of a non-dramatic work[46] (*e.g.* a novel), or copies incidents which form a substantial part of such work, without the copyright owner's permission.[47] Such infringement will occur even if the purpose of the adaptation is to enable the producer privately to solicit financing from exhibitors or distributors for the production of a film based on the work following which an assignment of the film rights would be sought from the owner. What amount to a substantial part is a question of fact for the court.[48] In deciding whether the part is substantial the value as well as the quantity must be considered.[49]

---

[44] Particularly in the case where a feature film production is proposed where a leading performer will often wish to see the script or at least a treatment before agreeing to participate.

[45] See *post*, paras. 12.40–12.43 for "adaptation" generally.

[46] Copyright, Designs and Patents Act 1988, s.22(3).

[47] *Corelli v. Gray* (1913) 29 T.L.R. 570; *Kelly v. Cinema Houses Ltd.* [1928–35] MacG.Cop.Cas. 391; *Sutton Vane v. Famous Players Film Co. Ltd.* MacG.Cop.Cas. 6; *Glynn v. Weston Feature Film Co.* [1916] 1 Ch. 261; *Bolton v. British International Pictures Ltd.* [1936–45] MacG.Cop.Cas. 20; *Poznanski v. London Film Productions Ltd.* [1936–45] MacG.Cop.Cas. 233; *Harman Pictures N.V. v. Osborne* [1967] 1 W.L.R. 723; *Fernald v. Jay Lewis Productions* [1978] F.S.R. 499.

[48] *King Features Syndicate Inc. v. O. & M. Kleeman Ltd.* [1941] A.C. 417.

[49] *Hawkes & Son (London) Ltd. v. Paramount Film Service Ltd.* [1934] Ch. 593.

Thus, for example, in *Fernald v. Jay Lewis Productions Ltd.*[50] where the defendant reproduced four pages out of 126 of the plaintiff's novel *Destroyer from America* in his film *The Gift Horse*. Notwithstanding the fact the incident which the defendant was alleged to have reproduced covered only four pages out of 126 in the plaintiff's book, and only five to six minutes of the film, the court was of the view that the four pages amounted to a substantial part of the plaintiff's original work.

Protection of the idea or plot of a dramatic or non-dramatic work. No 8.27 copyright protection is accorded to the idea or motive of a novel or play. The copyright protected is in the combination of situations, scenes and incidents which constitute the particular expression or working out of the idea or theme.[51]

However, in order to amount to an infringement of the plaintiff's work, it is not necessary that the defendant should appropriate the dialogue of the plaintiff's work. It will be sufficient to amount to an infringement of copyright where a combination or series of dramatic events in a work have been taken from the like situation in the plaintiff's work, although no part of the dialogue of the defendant's work is similar to the plaintiff's work.[52] In considering the manner in which such an infringement might take place, Swinfen Eady L.J., in *Rees v. Melville*,[53] stated the guiding principle thus:

"In order to constitute an infringement it is not necessary that the words of the dialogue should be the same, the situations and incidents, the mode in which the ideas are worked out and presented may constitute a material portion of the whole play, and the court must have regard to the dramatic value and importance of what, if anything, is taken, even though the portion may in fact be small and the actual language not copied. On the other hand, the fundamental idea of two plays may be the same, but if worked out separately and on independent lines they may be so different as to bear no resemblance to one another."

Thus, a copyright infringement will occur where a film substantially

---

[50] [1975] F.S.R. 499; first reported *The Times*, February 6, 1953.
[51] *Sutton Vane v. Famous Players Film Co. Ltd.* [1928–35] MacG.Cop.Cas. 6 at 8, C.A.; see also *Rees v. Melville* [1911–16] MacG.Cop.Cas. 391, C.A.; *Dagnall v. British and Dominions Films Corp.* [1928–38] MacG.Cop.Cas. 391; *Wilmer v. Hutchinson & Co. (Publishers) Ltd.* (1936–45) MacG.Cop.Cas. 13; *Kelly v. Cinema Houses Ltd.* [1928–35] MacG.Cop.Cas. 362; *Holland v. Vivian Van Damm Productions Ltd.* [1936–45] MacG.Cop.Cas. 69.
[52] *Corelli v. Gray* (1913) 29 T.L.R. 570; on appeal 30 T.L.R. 116; *Kelly v. Cinema Houses Ltd.* [1928–35] MacG.Cop.Cas. 362; see also *Dagnall v. British and Dominions Film Corporation Ltd.* [1928–35] MacG.Cop.Cas. 391.
[53] [1911–16] MacG.Cop.Cas. 96 and 168, C.A.; *Bagge v. Miller* [1917–23] MacG.Cop.Cas. 179; *Bolton v. British International Pictures Ltd.* [1936–45] MacG.Cop.Cas. 20; *Poznanski v. London Film Productions Ltd.* [1936–45] MacG.Cop.Cas. 233.

reproduces one or more of the original situations, with or without the dialogue, of a prior work. There will, however, be no infringement if the works have been worked out independently of each other and the similarities are thus due to coincidences, common sources or common stock themes, incidents or characters.

Common stock themes, incidents and characters

8.28 **Protection granted.** Copyright protection may not be available when common stock themes, incident and characters are in evidence. In *Kelly v. Cinema House Ltd.*[54] Maugham J. stated the rational behind the denial of copyright protection to such subject matter:

> "The film writer who depicts upon the screen love-making in a car or a taxi-cab, or the chase of an evil doer in a phenomenally speedy vehicle, or the ways of the film counterpart of Delilah (the modern 'vamp') with a man, has no claim to such copyright in those scenes presented with different dialogue and a different setting. To hold the contrary, would be to give to a producer or a novelist not only a monopoly in an idea without merit of novelty. The Plaintiff in order to prove his right must at least establish that he is the **author** of the character or the idea in some possible sense of the word."

8.29 However, where common stock themes, incidents or characters have been combined so as to arrive at such a "degree of complexity" as to amount to an original work the work will be entitled to copyright protection.[55] In *Dagnall v. British and Dominion Film Corporation Ltd.*[56] the test of whether "common stock" themes, ideas or characters were entitled to copyright protection was stated to be whether they are so combined as to produce some original dramatic situation or situations of "a substantial character". There appears to be no real distinction between the tests "degree of complexity" and "substantial character". The essential question is whether the common stock themes, ideas or characters have been so combined to produce an original story or a novel new twist to the common theme or idea.

Whether or not the combination of the themes, ideas or character have reached the "degree of complexity" or is of "a substantial character" is one of fact and degree to be determined by the court. Where the work consists of a mixture of common stock ideas, themes and characters together with wholly new and original ideas and themes the task

---

[54] [1928–35] MacG.Cop.Cas. 391.
[55] *Corelli v. Gray* (1913) 29 T.L.R. 570 where it was held that the common stock ideas incorporated in the plaintiff's novel were of such complexity that it was practically impossible that it should have been arrived at independently by a second individual.
[56] [1928–35] MacG.Cop.Cas. 391.

may not be a difficult one, but where it consists solely in a series of common stock dramatic situations it is difficult to make from this such a novel selection and combination of situations as to be the subject of copyright, apart from the dialogue.[57]

Definition of common stock themes ideas and characters. It is a com- **8.30** mon characteristic of films that the subject matter tends to revolve around recurring situations, themes, and characters which have proved successful in the past. Such situations, ideas, themes, and characters have constituted the common stock from which producers have drawn their basic ideas for the creation of films. However, what constitutes a "common stock" situation, idea, theme or character cannot be defined with any precision and is better illustrated by examples.

In *Dagnall v. British and Dominions Film Corporation Ltd.*[58] where it was alleged that a film entitled *Almost Divorced* infringed two works respectively entitled *Divorced for a Year* and *Nearly Divorced* Clauson J. said:

> "It will have been guessed that the main subject-matter is divorce which involves the necessary ingredients of husband and wife. It almost of necessity involves a quarrel, if there is to be any romantic incident, or anything of humorous character, and it must end well and there must be reconcilement at the end, and it is equally necessary that there should be misunderstandings and the discovery of the one party by the other in situations which, to put it mildly, require explanation."

These matters remain common-stock ideas. To them must be added modern day common stock ideas such as are to be found in science fiction films such as *Star Trek* and *Star Wars*, namely inter-galactic travel and star wars.

Character from novel or screenplay. It is a common occurrence that **8.31** where a novel or film has proved successful, a sequel is produced in which the leading character in such novel or film plays a leading part in an otherwise completely different story. Examples of such sequels are Inspector Poirot from the Agatha Christie novels and Indiana Jones in the area of film productions. This gives rise to the important question whether such characters are entitled to copyright protection separately

---

[57] *Dagnall v. British and Dominions Film Corporation Ltd.* [1928–35] MacG.Cop.Cas. 391.
[58] (1928–35) MacG.Cop.Cas. 391; for further examples of cases instancing stock situations themes, ideas and characters, see *Sutton Vane v. Famous Players Film Co. Ltd.* [1928–35] MacG.Cop.Cas. 6; *Robl v. Palace Theatre* (1911) 28 T.L.R. 69; *Rees v. Melville* (1911–16) MacG.Cop.Cas. 168; *Manduit v. Gaumont British Picture Corporation Ltd.* [1936–45] MacG.Cop.Cas. 292; *Bagge v. Miller* [1917] MacG.Cop.Cas. 179; *Vining v. Evett* (1917–23) MacG.Cop.Cas. 189.

from the work in which they appear or whether protection, in so far as it is available, is only within the context of the story.

There is no settled view as to whether, and if so to what extent, copyright protection will be accorded to a fictional character taken out of the context of the plot in which it appears. It has been said that "there is no copyright in fictional characters in books, films or plays".[59] However, in *Kelly v. Cinema Houses Ltd.*,[60] in a judgment approved by the Court of Appeal, the question was expressly left open by Maugham J when he said:

> "If, for instance, we found a modern playwright creating a character as distinctive and remarkable as Falstaff, or as Tartuffe, or (to come to a recent classic) as Sherlock Holmes, would it be an infringement if another writer . . . were to borrow the idea and to make use of an obvious copy of the original? I should hesitate a long time before I came to such a conclusion . . . But whatever the answer may be . . . I am strongly of the opinion that there can be no infringement in such a case if the character . . . is devoid of novelty."

8.32   It is clear that Maugham J. had considerable doubts with regard to copyright protection being accorded, but it would appear that if copyright protection were to be accorded the starting point would be whether the character is "distinctive" or "novel". This would appear to accord with the approach of the leading United States case of *Nichols v. Universal Pictures Corp.*,[61] in which Judge Hand indicated that a fictional character is capable of copyright protection separate from the work in which it appears. He went on to observe:

> "If *Twelfth Night* were copyrighted, it is quite possible that a second comer might so closely imitate Sir Toby Belch or Malvolio as to infringe, but it would not be enough that for one of his characters he cast a riotous knight who kept wassail to the discomfort of the household, or a vain and foppish steward who became amorous of his mistress. These would be no more than Shakespeare's "ideas" in the play, as little capable of monopoly as Einstein's Doctrine of Relativity, or Darwin's Origin of Species. It follows that the less developed characters, the less they can be copyrighted; that is the penalty an author must bear from marking them too indistinctly."

---

[59] *O'Neill v. Paramount Pictures Corporation* [1983] C.A.T. 235; [1984] N.L.J. 338, C.A., *per* May L.J.

[60] [1928–35] MacG.Cop.Cas. 39.

[61] 45 F. 2d 119 (2nd Cir. 1930) approved *Columbia Broadcasting Sys., Inc. v. De Costa* 377 F. 2d 315 at 320 (1st cir. 1967); *cf Warner Bros. Pictures Inc. v. Columbia Broadcasting Sys., Inc.* 216 F. 2d 945 (9th Cir. 1954).

It has been suggested[62] that the American cases show that in deter- **8.33**
mining whether copyright protection should be accorded to a character
two questions must be answered: "First, was the character as originally
conceived and presented sufficiently developed to command copyright
protection, and if so, secondly, did the alleged infringer copy such
development and not merely a broader and more abstract outline."[63] It
is submitted that this approach is sound in principle and provides a
useful approach to resolving the protectability of characters. It enables
the court to look at the circumstances of the case and do justice where it
is clear that there is a marked similarity between the characters in two
works.

Where a fictional character is the subject of an animation ("cartoon")
the difficulties are not as pronounced. Such works may command protection as artistic works.[64]

Notwithstanding the doubt relating to the copyright protection
accorded to a fictional character protection may be available by an
action in passing off.[65]

Literary, dramatic works commissioned by the producer

Generally. Material commissioned by a producer will generally com- **8.34**
prise:

(a) original treatment or screenplay which is not based on any existing copyright material; or

(b) outline, treatment or screenplay based on copyright material.

Unless the writer is engaged by the producer under a contract of service as an employee[66] and writes the screenplay during the course of his
employment, the first owner of the copyright in the screenplay will be
the writer. Generally, where such material is commissioned from a
scriptwriter all rights of copyright are acquired by the producer by way

---

[62] See Nimmer: *Nimmer on Copyright*, section 2.12.
[63] *cf.* Kurtz in [1990] 2 Ent. L.R. 62 where it is argued that courts should "focus on
comparisons between characters, rather than on abstract consideration of the qualities
of the original character".
[64] *King Features Syndicate v. Kleeman Ltd.* [1941] A.C. 417.
[65] See "Passing Off", *post*, para. 18.31.
[66] There is no single satisfactory test governing the question whether a person is an
employee or is self employed but it would appear that the accepted test is whether the
person perform his services as a person in business on his own account. If he does, his
work as a scriptwriter for various film or television production companies must be
regarded as performed under a series of contracts for services, entered by him in the
course of carrying on his own business. If he does not, his work must be regarded as
performed under a series of contracts of employment with those companies: *Hall v.
Lorimer* [1992] 1 W.L.R. 959. See also *Ready Mixed Concrete (South East) Ltd. v. Minister of
Pensions and National Insurance* [1968] 2 Q.B. 497; *Market Investigations Ltd. v. Minister of
Social Security* [1969] 2 Q.B. 173; *Lee Ting Sang v. Chung Chi-Keung* [1990] 2 A.C. 374.

of future assignment. There are for these purposes, standard form industry agreements which may be utilised for the commissioning of the scriptwriter.[67]

8.35 Duties of the screenplay writer. Where a writer is commissioned to write a screenplay for a play or a film he is entitled to exercise his own taste and skill except in so far as some particular treatment has been defined by the terms of the contract under which he is engaged.[68] The script must not depart so far from the story on which the script is based as to result in it not being a script of the story, but it may be, and usually is, impossible for the writer to adhere rigidly to the underlying story and much is permissible in the way of alteration and addition for the purposes of adapting the story to the different medium in which it is to be produced.[69]

8.36 Secondary contributions. Where a producer commissions a screenwriter to write an original screenplay it is common practice in the television and film industry that the producer commissioning the scriptwriter provides the plot of the screenplay. Absent agreement as to the copyright ownership in the completed screenplay, the general rule is that one who employs another to write for him, and even suggests the subject and plot, does not become the proprietor of the copyright in the screenplay unless he contributes to the form in which the copyright exists[70]: in such cases the copyright will vest in the scriptwriter. In order to constitute the producer joint author of the screenplay there must be a pre-concerted joint design[71] in which the contribution of each author is not distinct from the other or authors.[72] The question whether a person is a joint author is one of fact to be determined by the court.[73]

A screenplay is often altered by the director and producer or script editor before or during the shooting of the film so as to enable the production to conform to the schedule or to meet the exigencies of production.[74] In such circumstances the question may arise, absent contractual

---

[67] For a detailed treatment of such standard form contracts, see Cotterell, L., *Performance: The Business and Law of Entertainment* (Sweet & Maxwell, 3rd ed., 1993) Part 7.

[68] *Ellis v. British Filmcraft Production Ltd.* [1928–35] MacG.Cop.Cas. 51.

[69] *Ibid.*

[70] *Levy v. Rutley* (1871) L.R. 6 C.P. 523; *Stannard v. Harrison* (1871) 24 L.T. 570; *Tate v. Thomas* [1921] 1 Ch. 503; *Shepherd v. Conquest* (1856) 17 C.B. 427; *Bagge v. Miller* [1917–23] MacG.Cop.Cas. 179; *Donoghue v. Allied Newspapers Ltd.* [1938] 1 Ch. 106.

[71] *Levy v. Rutley* (1871) L.R. 6 C.P. 523.

[72] Copyright, Designs and Patents Act 1988, s.10(1). See also *Copinger & Skone on Copyright* (Sweet & Maxwell, 13th ed., 1991) para. 7–1 *et seq.* as to "Works of Joint Authorship".

[73] *Tate v. Thomas* [1921] Ch. 503 at 511.

[74] In such a case the producer will need to bear in mind the scriptwriter's "moral rights". See "Moral Rights", *post*, Chap. 15.

agreement, as to the ownership of the altered script which forms the subject matter of the film. As a general rule, where scripts are produced by a scriptwriter and subsequently altered by corrections, additions or omissions made by another, it is a question of fact having regard to the character of the alterations and the circumstances in which they are made whether there is any independent work in respect of which the author of the altered version can claim to be the author or owner of the copyright, or whether the first author is, notwithstanding the alteration, the sole author and the owner of the copyright in the altered work as a whole.[75]

(ii) *Scenic effects*

Copyright does not exist in scenic arrangements as such, but only in so **8.37** far as those elements form part of a film or dramatic work which is itself capable of being the subject of copyright.[76] However, where the scenic arrangements are derived from prior drawings, copyright protection, as artistic works, may be available to such drawings. The ownership of the rights in the drawings will depend upon the contract between the producer and the set designer but absent such an agreement the rights in the drawings will belong to the set designer unless the set designer is employed by the producer under a contract of service and carries out the design in the course of his employment.

Where the film includes artistic works on public display,[77] the copyright in such works is not infringed by the making of a film,[78] or the issue to the public of copies of the film, or the broadcast or inclusion of such film in a cable programme service.[79]

(iii) *Title*

As a general rule a title is not an original literary work and is not suf- **8.38** ficiently substantial to justify a claim to protection, though in particular cases a title may be on so substantial a scale, and of so important a character, as to be a proper subject of protection.[80] In this context an "original literary work" is something that affords either information, instruction or pleasure in the form of literary enjoyment.[81]

---

[75] *Samuelson v. Producers' Distributing Co. Ltd.* [1932] 1 Ch. 201; see also *Levy v. Rutley* (1871) L.R. 6 C.P. 523.

[76] *Tate v. Fulbrook* [1908] 1 K.B. 821; *Tate v. Thomas* [1921] 1 Ch. 503.

[77] *e.g.* buildings, sculptures, paintings.

[78] Copyright, Designs and Patents Act 1988, s.62(2)(b).

[79] *Ibid.*, s.62(3).

[80] *Francis, Day & Hunter v. Twentieth Century Fox Corporation Ltd.* [1940] A.C. 112 at 123, P.C.; *Ladbroke (Football) Ltd. v. William Hill (Football) Ltd.* [1964] 1 W.L.R. 273; *Dicks v. Yates* (1881) 18 Ch.D. 76; *Lamb v. Evans* [1893] 1 Ch. 218; *Exxon Corpn. v. Exxon Insurance Consultants International Ltd.* [1982] 1 Ch. 119 at 138.

[81] *Exxon Corpn. v. Exxon Insurance Consultants International Ltd.* [1982] 1 Ch. 119 at 138.

It would appear that where a phrase forms part of a book or other copyright work protection will not be afforded to such work unless that word or phrase is a sufficiently substantial part of the copyright work.[82] So, for example, in *Francis, Day & Hunter v. Twentieth Century Fox Corporation Ltd.*,[83] where the defendant used the title of a song entitled "The Man Who Broke the Bank at Monte Carlo" as the title of their film without using any other words from the song, Lord Wright, delivering the advice of the Privy Council, in holding that a title was not infringed by its use as the title of a film which did not use any other part of the song, said:

"The theme of the film is different from that of the song, and their Lordships see no ground in copyright law to justify the appellants' claim to prevent the use by the respondents of these few words, which are too unsubstantial to constitute an infringement, especially when used in so different a connection."[84]

It should be noted, however, that although a phrase or word may not have the essential characteristics for protection as a subject of copyright, it may qualify for protection under the law relating to passing off.[85]

(iv) Performers[86]

Consent to recording and exploitation

8.39 For the purposes of film production, where a performer has not given his consent it is an infringement[87] of his rights:

(a) to make a recording of his qualifying performance[88];
(b) to exploit a recording by using it to show, or play in public, his qualifying performance, or to broadcast or include in a programme service such a performance.[89]

For infringement to occur the performer's consent must have been lacking on each of (a) and (b). There is no requirement that the necessary consent be in writing. Therefore, where a performer attends for the purpose of the recording of his performance he may be held to have

[82] *Ladbroke (Football) Ltd. v. William Hill (Football) Ltd.* [1964] 1 W.L.R. 273 at 286.
[83] [1940] A.C. 112.
[84] *Ibid.* at 123.
[85] See "Passing Off", *post*, para. 18.34
[86] Only those aspects of performers rights relevant to the production of films will be dealt with in this section. For a fuller survey of the law relating to performances see "Rights in Performances", *post*, Chap. 14.
[87] Copyright, Designs and Patents Act 1988, s.183.
[88] *Ibid.*, s.182. For meaning of "qualifying performance", see *post*, para. 14.08.
[89] *Ibid.*

given his consent to the recording.[90] It would, however, be prudent to obtain such consent in writing.

Where a performer has entered into an exclusive recording contract with a third party it will be necessary for the producer to obtain the consent of the party who has such exclusive recording rights together with an acknowledgement from such person that copyright in the performance for the film vests in the producer. This will be particularly important in respect of musical performers.

Engagement of performers and production personnel

General. General terms for the production of television and cinema films have been agreed between broadcasters, the organisations representing independent producers and directors and performers' trade associations, such as Equity. These agreements set out the minimum terms of payment and conditions for the employment of performers and the terms on which films may be transmitted and subsequently exploited. The scope and extent of these standard agreements are outside the scope of this work. For a discussion of such agreements reference should be made to a specialist work on the subject.[91] **8.40**

Children. Where a film is to include a person under 16 years old a licence will be required from the local authority in whose area the child resides.[92] Such a licence is not, however required where in the six months preceding the performance the child has not taken part in other performances in the theatre, on licensed premises, any broadcast performance, or a performance included in a programme service.[93] A local authority may not grant a licence in respect of a performance by a child under 13 years of age unless: **8.41**

(a) the licence is for acting and the part he is to act cannot be taken except by a child of "about his age"[94];

(b) the licence is for dancing in a ballet which does not form part of any other general entertainment and the part he is to dance cannot be taken except by a child "about his age"[95]; or

(c) his part in the performance is wholly or mainly musical and the

---

[90] *Mad Hat Music Ltd. v. Pulse 8 Records Ltd.* [1993] E.M.L.R. 172 at 179.
[91] For a detailed survey and commentary see Cotterell, L., *Performance: The Business and Law of Entertainment* (Sweet & Maxwell, 3rd ed., 1993) pp. 149–181 in respect of television productions and pp. 223–259 for theatrical films and videocassette.
[92] Children and Young Persons Act 1963, s.36 (as amended).
[93] *Ibid.*
[94] *Ibid.*, s.38(1)(a).
[95] *Ibid.*, s.38(1)(b).

nature of the performance is wholly or mainly musical, or the performance consists only of opera or ballet[96];

8.42   A child between the age of 14 and 18 may not perform abroad without the licence of a magistrate.[97] A licence in respect of a child under 14 may be granted provided his performance comes within (a) to (c) above. A licence may not, however, be granted by the magistrate unless he is satisfied:

  (a) that the application for the licence is made by or with the consent of his parent or guardian[98];

  (b) that he is going abroad to fulfil a particular engagement[99];

  (c) that he is fit for the purpose, and that proper provision has been made to secure his health, kind treatment, and adequate supervision while abroad, and his return from abroad at the expiration or revocation of the licence[1]

  (d) that the child has received a document, drawn up in language understood by him, setting out the terms and conditions of his employment.[2]

(v) *Music Synchronisation rights*

8.43 **Meaning of synchronisation rights.** There is no legal definition of "synchronisation rights". However, in the entertainment industry the expression is used to mean the right to record music as part of the soundtrack of a film.

8.44 **Commissioned music.** Where music is specially commissioned for a film a producer will need to acquire synchronisation rights in the music. The person from whom such rights are acquired will, in general, depend on whether the composer is subject to a music publishing agreement the terms of which provide for future assignment of copyright in his compositions. Where there is such agreement the producer will need to acquire the synchronisation rights directly from the music publisher. However, where the composer has no such agreement the producer will generally obtain an express assignment or licence of the synchronisation rights from the composer.

   Where the composer is a member of the Performing Right Society (PRS) the synchronisation right for feature films (as distinct from tele-

---

[96] *Ibid.*, s.38(1)(c).
[97] Children and Young Persons Act 1933, s.25 (as amended).
[98] *Ibid.*, s.25(2)(a).
[99] *Ibid.*, s.25(2)(b).
[1] *Ibid.*, s.25(2)(c).
[2] *Ibid.*, s.25(2)(d).

vision films) will be exercisable by the PRS. The producer will therefore have to obtain the necessary synchronisation licence for feature films from the PRS.

Performing rights in music. The PRS controls the performing rights, except grand rights,[3] in music. The performance of music to enable it to be recorded on the soundtrack of a film is not a public performance and therefore no licence is required. Where the public performance of a film is to take place in a cinema or other public place the producer is not required to obtain a licence from the PRS. In such circumstances the performance is made by the managers of the public place of performance and it is consequently their duty to obtain the necessary licences from the PRS. Where the film is broadcast in a programme service there are blanket licence agreements between the PRS and the BBC and the Independent Television Association covering performance in public. **8.45**

Non-commissioned music. Where a producer proposes to use an existing sound recording rather than specially composed music a synchronisation licence will be required from the owner of the sound recording, or the Mechanical Copyright Protection Society, which will often exercise such rights on his behalf. In addition, it will also be necessary to obtain a licence from the owner of the composition (or the PRS acting on his behalf). **8.46**

(vi) *Moral rights*

The factors to be taken into account by a film producer, authors and directors under this heading are dealt with under "Moral Rights" (see *post*, Chapter 15) to which reference should be made. It is worth noting, however, that the consideration of moral rights will require particular attention at the time that the script is altered, if at all, and at the time of the shooting of the film and post production of the film. **8.47**

(c) *Talent Shows, Game Shows and Soaps*

Distinction between "changed format rights" and "format rights". A distinction should be drawn between "changed format rights" and "format rights". The former generally comprises the sale (usually to a foreign producer) of scripts and recorded programmes of an already established programme or series of programmes, together with the right to adapt the scripts into the idiom and television style of the market-place at which it is aimed. In essence this is the grant and exercise of the right of adaptation. Where this takes place there is both copy- **8.48**

---

[3] For the meaning of "grand rights", see *post*, para. 9.19.

right in the original scripts and in the scripts which have been changed into a format suitable for the second country. An example of such a work is the creation of the successful United States version, *Three's Company*, of the British series *Robin's Nest* where a completely new series was produced using American actors but adopting the characters used in the British series.

The expression "format rights", as used in the entertainment industry, is a reference to the underlying idea or concept for a programme or series which forms a common element of a such programme or series of programmes. Such, idea or concept is usually in the form of rules for the presentation of a programme such as *Mastermind, Blind Date* or a game show. Such rules provide the programme with a structure for its presentation within which the participants compete.

8.49   **"Format rights" in game shows.** The extent to which a format for a talent show or quiz game show qualifies for copyright protection cannot be stated with any degree of clarity. It would appear, however, that a game show format is not entitled to protection as a dramatic work.[4] If, however, the format is reduced to writing or some other form susceptible of copyright protection and, in that form, expresses more than a general idea or concept it may qualify for copyright protection as a literary work.[5]

Where the format is so reduced into writing or other form it is submitted that it is that the "format rights" in talent shows and quiz games are susceptible of protection if two conditions are fulfilled. First, the detailed rules and structure of the programme from commencement of the programme to closing credits must be reduced to writing in the form of a script, or other written material, or be fixed in some other way. It has been suggested that in "the case of a game show the skeleton structure will comprise: (i) the name of the programme, (ii) the manner of the presentation, (iii) the sequence and type of incidents in the show, (iv) the repeated material (including catchphrases and distinctive movements) which links the incidents, (v) the distinctive props and set, (vi) the running order, and (vii) any material intended to manifest the connection between the individual programmes".[6] This represents a useful approach to recording and defining the nature of the content of the format rights. Secondly, the matters so delineated by the author

---

[4] Green v. Broadcasting Corporation of New Zealand [1989] 2 All E.R. 1056 at 1058, P.C.
[5] *Ibid.* at 1058.
[6] Lane and McD.Bridge, "The Protection of Formats under English Law" in [1990] 3 Ent. L.R. 96 and in [1990] 4 L.R. 131 which contains a useful and full analysis of the law relating to "formats". See also T. Martino and C. Miskin, "Format Rights: The Price is not Right" in [1991] 2 Ent. L.R. 31; P. Smith, "Format Rights: Opportunity Knocks" in [1991] 3 Ent. L.R. 63.

must be original in the sense that the ingredients which constitute the particular expression or working out of the idea or theme of the format should not consist merely of common-stock themes ideas or situations. If the ingredients consist of common stock ideas or themes the combination of those ideas must be such that it provides a novel or new twist in the old theme.

It is submitted that where the foregoing two conditions are satisfied the format will be entitled to copyright protection and an infringement will occur where a person copies the format as delineated and not merely a broader and more abstract outline.

"Format rights" in soaps". Where, however, the "format" is in respect **8.50** of "soaps", the considerations may be different. There are few detailed rules which can be reduced into a document or otherwise recorded for the conduct of each episode of the series and which can be said to be entitled to copyright protection. The common denominators in "soaps" will generally be the titles, the characters, and scenic effects. As a general rule the law does not afford copyright protection to titles,[7] scenic effects,[8] or characters.[9]

The central idea or theme of a soap generally revolves around the characters and their relationships with each other. However original such characters and their interrelations may be it is difficult to envisage a situation where copyright can exist in a format for the whole series. A format would, in such circumstances, only delineate the general nature of the characters. The situations in which they find themselves will, however, change from week to week. Thus, the combination of situations, scenes and incidents which constitute the particular expression or working out of the idea or theme will generally only be found in the script for each particular programme.

There is the added difficulty that, in general, soaps consist of common stock situations themes, ideas and characters which are not entitled to copyright protection unless they are so combined as to arrive at such a "degree of complexity,[10] or "substantial character,[11] as to amount to an original work and thus be entitled to copyright protection. Such combination is unlikely to be found in one document which defines the format for the series. In the light of these factors it is difficult to envisage circumstances in which the format for a "soap" will attract copyright protection.

---

[7] *Francis, Day & Hunter Ltd. v. Twentieth Century Fox Corporation Ltd.* [1940] A.C. 112.
[8] *Tate v. Fullbrook* [1908] 1 K.B. 821. See *ante*, para. 8.37 for "Scenic effects".
[9] But see *ante*, paras. 8.30–8.33 under "Character from novel or screenplay".
[10] *Correlli v. Gray* (1913) 29 T.L.R. 570. See also *ante*, paras. 8.28–8.29.
[11] *Dagnall v. British and Dominion Film Corporation Ltd.* [1928–35] MacG.Cop.Cas. 391. See also *ante*, paras. 8.28–8.29.

(d) *Production Agreements Practice*

The Production Agreement.[12]

8.51 **General.** Film production agreements are subject to the general law of contract. The parties to such agreements will vary according to the cost of production of the film, the sources of finance and whether the film is produced primarily for television or for the cinema. A description of the terms that may be found in such agreements is outside the scope of this work. However the following matters are often common and important features of production agreements.

8.52 **Budget.** The budget represents the basis on which financiers in the form of exhibitors and distributors have undertaken to provide finance. The Production Agreement will generally contain an undertaking by the producer to produce complete and deliver the film according to an agreed production schedule and budgeted cost of production. So as to ensure that this undertaking is complied with the agreement will invariably contain an undertaking by the producer to make, to the financier exhibitor or television company, daily reports with regard to the progress of the production (*i.e.* in terms of minutes of film produced each day) and weekly reports with regard to actual and estimated future expenditure to completion of the film. Completion in this context includes post-production and delivery.

8.53 **Banking.** The provision and expenditure of finance during the process of production is of especial concern to the financiers of the production. It is the general practice to include a clause in the production agreement requiring a producer to establish a production bank account, at an agreed bank, into which all funds relating to the production will be deposited and from which expenses relating to the film will be disbursed. The production and financing agreement should specifically provide that:

(a) the production bank account is to be designated a trust account in joint names of the producer and the financiers[13];

(b) the account as established requires the joint signature of a representative of the financier and the producer to effect a withdrawal from the account; and

(c) at the time of the establishment of the account the producer must obtain from the bank a written undertaking that any right of set-

---

[12] A detailed treatment of production agreements is outside the scope of this work. It is proposed to deal with only the more important aspects of such agreement in this work.
[13] See *ante*, para. 7.15 for the legal effect of such an account.

off it may have against the producer in respect of any debts not relating to the film will not be exercised against the production bank account.

Takeover, default and abandonment. The production agreement will generally include a clause entitling the financier to take-over or abandon a production in the event, *inter alia*, that the weekly reports indicate that the approved budget will be exceeded, or where there is an interruption or delay which cannot be remedied. Such a provision provides a useful protection to a financier from, *inter alia*, the requirement to continuing to finance a production where it is probable that it will not be completed without additional funds, exceeding those agreed, being provided by the financier or completion guarantor. **8.54**

4. Film exploitation

General. A description of the various forms and contents of distribution agreements is outside the scope of this work. What follows is a general description of the process of exploiting a completed film. The form of exploitation will vary according to whether the film is produced for television or cinema exhibition. In both cases distribution is, in general, characterised by the fact that distributors will seek to grant exclusive rights in respect of particular territories. This has the effect that where exclusive rights are granted to A in France, B, who has the rights in Germany, is not entitled to exploit the film in France without the permission of A.[14] **8.55**

Television. Where a film is produced for television the United Kingdom television company will in general act as the main distributor of the film throughout the world. It will generally appoint foreign agents or distributors in respect of territories outside the United Kingdom.[15] The agents or distributors will, in general, have the exclusive rights to license the broadcast of the particular film in the territory in which they are based and will receive a fee, calculated as a percentage of the licence fee received.

In territories such as, for example, the United States, the fee will vary according to whether the licence is with a television network, a cable channel or a regional broadcaster. In any event, the commission structure also has the effect that the United Kingdom distributor will also be entitled to deduct a commission for the sale. The remainder of the proceeds of the licence less costs of distribution such as prints, advertising

---

[14] See *post*, paras. 8.58–8.63, as to the effect of European Community competition law.
[15] Most United Kingdom television companies have long term agency or sub-distribution agreements with companies in the major television markets of the world.

and transport will comprise net profits. From this sum the financier, generally the television company, will be entitled to recoup the funds advanced for production together with interest. When such funds are recouped the producer will then be entitled to share in the net profits from distribution. In many cases, depending on the film, it will be many years before the producer receives any income from exploitation.

Cinema. Where a film is produced for initial exhibition in cinemas the distributor will take care to maximise the earnings of the film by ensuring that the film is first exclusively exhibited in cinemas. After cinema exhibition, it may then be released on video for an exclusive period and thereafter broadcast on television. However, the increasing success of satellite television in the United Kingdom means that it is increasingly becoming a major consideration for distributors when considering the order of exploitation.

The fee retained by the distributor will depend upon the arrangement reached with the producer and or financier, but by way of example, the following are two of the forms of remunerating a distributor.

First, the type of agreement may be in the form of an arrangement where the distributor is entitled to deduct and retain from the gross proceeds of distribution a distribution fee and distribution expenses in respect of certain agreed categories of expenses, the remainder of the distribution income being remitted to the producer or financier to be disbursed in the manner agreed between them.

Secondly, the arrangement may be in the form of an arrangement where the gross receipts from distribution are shared between the distributor and the financier/producer according to an agreed percentage, with the distributor bearing the costs of distribution out of his share.

(a) *Restraint of trade in film exhibitions in the cinema*

8.56   Prior to the passing of the Films (Exclusivity Agreements) Order 1989 it was common practice for distributors to undertake, when licensing a film for exhibition at a particular cinema, not to licence it for exhibition in certain other cinemas concurrently or prior to the exhibitor to which the undertaking was given; nor to allow certain forms of advertising by these cinemas before a date which is in effect agreed by the barring cinema. It was standard practice for licence agreements to mention the barred cinemas by name, or by specifying the area or distance within which all cinemas are thus barred, or by referring to the bars normally applied by the barring cinema.

8.57   **The Films (Exclusivity Agreements) Order 1989.** Article 4 of the Order provides:

"It shall be unlawful for an exhibitor to withhold or to threaten to withhold any order for exhibition of a film at a cinema on the ground that terms about exclusivity in respect of any other film have not been agreed or complied with."

"Terms about exclusivity" means terms restricting a distributor from authorising the exhibition of a film at a cinema.[16] By the terms of the Order, an exhibitor or distributor is prohibited from making or carrying out any agreement relating to the supply of any film for the exhibition at a cinema if the agreement contains or provides for terms about exclusivity applied or to be applied to more than one film.[17] These rules do not apply to an agreement if it relates to more than three films in respect of their exhibition at the cinema in question as a single programme[18] nor to an agreement to which the Restrictive Trade Practices Act 1976 applies or may apply.[19]

(b) *European Community law and film exploitation*

General. The assignment of exclusive licensing of the exclusive performance rights in a film or both for the cinema and television in respect of specific territories, is an important part of the commercial exploitation of the completed product. It is the ability to exercise these rights to the exclusion of other persons which lends a semblance of viability to the film industry, especially in the light of the soaring costs of the costs of producing films whether primarily intended for cinema or television. **8.58**

As was pointed out by Advocate General Reischl in *Compagnie Generale pour la Diffusion de la Television Coditel v. Cine-Vog Films*,[20] "films are often produced with the financial participation of the distributors . . . that does not happen unless there is a degree of security against risks: a distributor will be prepared to advance a lump sum for financing a film only if he is accorded an exclusive right of exhibition on one particular market". It is therefore of some importance to producers and financiers whether the exploitation and exclusive licensing of films on an exclusive territorial basis is capable of having the effect of restricting trade between Member States of the European Union and thus being in breach of the Treaty: principally Articles 30 to 34, 59 and 85 of the E.C. Treaty.

---

[16] The Films (Exclusivity Agreements) Order 1989.
[17] *Ibid.*, art. 3(1); the prohibition applied to the carrying out of an agreement in existence on April 4, 1989, including agreements in existence on February 28, 1989. Any distributor or exhibitor who was a party to such an agreement was required to terminate it before May 25, 1989: Art. 3(2).
[18] *Ibid.*, art. 3(4).
[19] *Ibid.*, art. 3(4). At the time of writing the Monopolies and Mergers Commission is undertaking further review of distribution of films to cinemas.
[20] Case 262/81: [1982] E.C.R. 3381 at 3412.

8.59 Distinction between existence and exercise of intellectual property rights. Article 36 of the Treaty permits exceptions to the principle of free movement of goods set out in Articles 30 to 34 for the purposes of, *inter alia*, the protection of industrial and commercial property, provided such restrictions do not constitute a means of arbitrary discrimination or disguised restriction of trade between Member States. The European Court of Justice has interpreted this as meaning that the E.C. Treaty does not affect the existence of property rights, such as copyright, granted by national legislation but the *exercise* of such rights may in certain circumstances infringe the prohibitory rules contained in the Treaty.[21]

Thus, the existence of copyright under the laws of the Member States is not affected but the exercise of such rights in the form of exclusive licensing or assignments, may be subject to the competition provisions of the Treaty.

(i) *Exclusive rights and Article 59*

8.60 Assignment of copyright limited to territory of Member State. In *Compagnie Generale pour la Diffusion de la Television Coditel v. Cine-Vog Films* *("Coditel No. 1"),*[22] the European Court of Justice held that the prohibition contained in Article 59 of the E.C. Treaty on restrictions upon freedom to provide services do not "preclude an assignee of the performing right in a cinematographic film in a Member State from relying upon his right to prohibit the exhibition of that film in that State, without his authority, . . . if the film . . . exhibited is picked up and transmitted after being broadcast in another Member State by a third party with the consent of the original owner of the right".[23]

In reaching its decision the Court drew a distinction between the exclusive right of reproduction of a work and the exclusive right of performance. The importance of this distinction lies in the fact that although the exclusive right of reproduction may be exhausted by the first marketing of the work within the Common Market the "owner of the copyright in a film and his assigns have a legitimate interest in calculating the fees due in respect of the authorization to exhibit a film on the basis of the actual or probable number of performances and in authorizing a television broadcast of the film only after it has been exhibited in cinemas for a certain period of time".[24] Thus, the exclusive right of performance remains unaffected and may be exercised or prohibited by the owners of such right.

---

[21] See, *e.g.* Case 78/70, *Deutsche Grammophon Gesellschaft mbH v. Metro-SB-Grossmarkte GmbH & Co. KG*: [1971] E.C.R. 487.
[22] Case 62/79: [1980] E.C.R. 881.
[23] *Ibid.*, para. [18].
[24] *Ibid.*, para. [13].

The effect of *Coditel No. 1* is that the owner of a film is able to grant exclusive licences or assignments for the exploitation of his films, and such assignment may relate to a specific territory or territories within the European Union without infringing the provisions of the Treaty as to the freedom to provide services.

(ii) *Exclusive rights and Article 85*

Article 85. Article 85 of the E.C. Treaty prohibits "all agreements **8.61** between undertakings . . . and concerted practices which may affect trade between Member States and which have as their object or effect the prevention, restriction or distortion of competition within the common market". By Article 85(2) any such agreements or decisions are automatically void. The agreements, decisions and concerted practices between undertakings[25] which are prohibited by Article 85(1) are those which are capable of having an "appreciable" or substantial effect on competition. The existence of an agreement, decision or concerted practice between undertakings is a condition precedent to the application of Article 85(1). Article 85(1) is directly applicable under the Treaty[26] and therefore enforceable in proceedings in national courts.

The case law of the European Court of Justice indicates that to come within Article 85 the exercise of the right in a film must constitute the purpose, means or result of an agreement decision or concerted practice which restricts competition. Where there is an assignment of film rights in respect of a particular territory there is no subsisting legal relationship which may restrict competition.[27] Any restriction of competition arises as a consequence of the assignment and the assertion by the new owner of his rights. On the other hand where an exclusive licence has been granted whereby the exercise of the right is licensed for a specified period to another person, the arrangement may have a bearing on competition.

In *Compagnie Generale pour la Diffusion, Coditel v. SA Cine-Vog Films*[28] **8.62** ("*Coditel No. 2*") Coditel argued that where the proprietor of the rights of exploitation of a film grants by contract to a company in another Member State an exclusive right to perform the film in that State, for a specified period, that contract is liable, by reason of the rights and obligations contained in it and the economic and legal circumstances sur-

---

[25] See *post*, para. 9.24 for meaning of "undertaking".
[26] Reg. 17: [1962] O.J. 13/204 (Art. 1) Case 13/61, *Robert Bosch GmbH v. Kleding-Verkoopbedriff de Geus un Uitdenbogerd*: [1962] E.C.R. 45; [1962] C.M.L.R. 1 (Art. 85(1) and Case 127/73, *BRT v. SABAM*: [1974] E.C.R. 313; [1974] 2 C.M.L.R. 238 (Art. 86).
[27] Case 262/81, *Compagnie Generale pour la Diffusion de la Television, Coditel v. S.A. Cine Vog Films* [1982] E.C.R. 3381 at 3409.
[28] *Ibid.*

rounding it, to constitute an agreement, decision or concerted practice which is prohibited between undertakings pursuant to Article 85(1) and (2) of the Treaty. The European Court of Justice, whilst stating that copyright in a film and the right deriving from it, namely that of exhibiting the film, are not subject to the prohibitions contained in Article 85, held that "the exercise of those rights may none the less, come within the . . . prohibitions of the Article where there are economic or legal circumstances the effect of which is to restrict film distribution to an appreciable degree or to distort competition on the cinematographic market, regard being had to the specific characteristics of the market".[29] The Court stated that is for the national courts[30] to determine whether or not the exclusive right to exhibit a film creates barriers which are artificial or unjustifiable in terms of the need of the film industry, or the possibility of charging fees which exceed a fair return on investment, or an exclusivity the duration of which is disproportionate to those requirements, and whether or not such exercise within a geographic area is such as to prevent, restrict or distort competition within the common market.[31]

However, in determining whether the exercise of exclusive right prevents, restricts or distorts competition "the mere fact that the owner of the copyright in a film has granted to a sole licensee the exclusive licensee the right to exhibit that film in the territory of a Member State and, consequently, to prohibit, during a specified period, its showing by others, is not sufficient to justify the finding that such a contract must be regarded as the purpose, the means or the result of an agreement, decision or concerted practice prohibited by the Treaty."[32]

(iii) *Pre-recorded video-cassettes*

8.63   Where video-cassettes are sold by the author in one Member State his rights are exhausted[33] in respect of the issuing of copies to the public by sale and they may be purchased in one Member State and sold in another Member State.[34] Where, however, national legislation confers on an author the specific right to hire out video-cassettes the fact that an author has put video-cassettes into circulation in a Member State which does nor provide specific protection for the right to hire them does not exhaust the author's rental rights[35] conferred by another Member

---

[29] *Ibid.*, para. [17].
[30] It should be noted, however, that the E.C. Commission has a concurrent jurisdiction under Reg. 17.
[31] Case 262/81: [1982] E.C.R. 3381, para. [19]; see also *Re, German TV Films*: [1990] 4 C.M.L.R. 841.
[32] *Ibid.*, para. [15].
[33] See *post*, para. 12.53.
[34] Case 158/86, *Warner Brothers Inc. v. Erik Viuff Christiansen*: [1988] E.C.R. 2605.
[35] See *post*, paras. 12.15–12.32.

State.[36] Thus, where A purchases a pre-recorded video-cassette in Member State X, which grants no exclusive rental rights in its national legislation, and imports it into Member State Y, which does grant such exclusive right, the author of the film comprising the video-cassette is entitled to restrain the rental in Member State Y.

---

[36] Case 158/86, *Warner Brothers Inc. v. Erick Viuff Christiansen*: [1988] E.C.R. 2605.

CHAPTER 9

MUSIC

1. Copyright in Lyrics, Musical Works and Sound Recordings

9.01 Copyright in musical works, lyrics and sound recordings distinguished.
A "musical work" is defined in the Copyright, Designs and Patents Act
1988 ("the 1988 Act") as a "work consisting of music, exclusive of any
words or action intended to be sung, spoken or performed with the
music,"[1] and a literary work ("the lyrics") as any work, other than a dramatic or musical work, which is written, spoken or sung.[2] A sound
recording is defined as:

(a) a recording of sounds, from which sounds may be produced; or

(b) a recording of the whole or any part of a literary, dramatic or
musical work, from which sounds reproducing the work or part
may be produced,

regardless of the medium on which the recording is made or the
method by which the sounds are reproduced or produced.[3] Thus, any
means of sound recording now existing or which may be invented from

---

[1] Copyright, Designs and Patents Act 1988, s.3(1).
[2] *Ibid.*, s.3(1).
[3] *Ibid.*, s.5(1).

which sounds may be produced will qualify as a sound recording and such sound recording will have a separate copyright from the works which form the subject matter of the recording.

The effect is, therefore, that there is a separate and distinct copyright in the music and the lyrics in a song. Additionally, there is a separate copyright in any sound recording incorporating such musical work and lyrics. The fact that the music and words are combined together for the purposes of performance or recording does not cause the separate and distinct copyrights to merge. Thus, where X writes the words and Y composes the music, X will be the first owner[4] of copyright in the lyrics and Y the owner of the copyright in the music. If the song is then recorded by X and Y, copyright will subsist in the sound recording which may or may not belong to X and Y depending on the contractual relationship entered into with their record company.

Thus, where words are set to music and a sound recording is made of that composition, the musical work, the lyrics (*i.e.* the literary work) and the sound recording remain distinct works for copyright purposes.[5] The fact that the copyright in the lyrics, musical work and sound recording remain separate and distinct has important consequences in respect of the manner in which the exclusive rights in the musical work, lyrics and sound recording are exploited.[6]

However, it is a pre-condition of the subsistence of copyright in the musical and literary work that it be "recorded, in writing or otherwise"[7] but it is immaterial whether the work is recorded by or with the permission of the author.[8] Therefore, where, for example, X composes a musical work it is not necessary for him to write down that work or to make a sound recording to create copyright in the musical work. It will be sufficient if he orally communicates the work to Y who writes it down or makes a sound recording of it. Similarly, where X creates a musical work but does not reduce it to writing or other recording, copyright in the work will subsist if and when X plays the musical work in a recording studio for the purposes of making a sound recording notwithstanding the fact that the sound recording is made by his recording company. In both instances, a separate copyright will exist in the sound recording and the musical work where the author is a qualified person or the work is first published in a qualifying country. **9.02**

---

[4] See *ante*, para. 7.07.
[5] See Copyright, Designs and Patents Act 1988, s.3(1).
[6] See *post*, paras. 9.15–9.20.
[7] Copyright, Designs and Patents Act 1988, s.3(2).
[8] *Ibid.*, s.3(3).

(a) *Qualified person and qualifying country*

9.03 In order that copyright may subsist,

(a) the author of the sound recording must be a "qualified person"[9]: when the lyrics, musical work or sound recording was "made".[10] In the case of published lyrics or music when first published or if the author died before that time immediately before his death. Where the lyrics or music is unpublished the material time is when it was made; or

(b) the lyrics, musical work or sound recording must be first published in the United Kingdom, or a country specified in The Copyright (Application to other Countries) Order 1993[11];

Publication for these purposes means the issue of copies to the public[12] of any of the three categories of the work. In respect of lyrics and musical works it also means making the work available to the public by means of an electronic retrieval system.[13] However, "publication" does not include:

(a) in respect of lyrics and musical works, the performance of the work or the broadcasting or its inclusion in a cable programme service[14];

(b) in respect of a sound recording, the work being played or shown in public, or its broadcasting or inclusion in a cable programme service.[15]

Where, however, the work is first "published" in a non-convention country and is subsequently published within 30 days in a convention country it is regarded as first published simultaneously in the qualifying country.[16]

(b) *Period of copyright*

(i) *Lyrics and musical works*

9.04 **General.** Copyright in the lyrics and music expire at the end of 50 years from the end of the calendar year in which the author dies.[17] This rule is, however, subject to three exceptions in relation to (1) works of unknown authorship,[18] (2) computer generated works[19]; and (3) works of joint authorship.[20]

---

9 For the meaning of "qualified person", see *ante*, para. 8.07.
10 Copyright, Designs and Patents Act 1988, s.154(5)(a).
11 *Ibid.*, s.155(1). See *post*, Appendix A.
12 For the meaning of "issue copies to the public", see *post*, paras. 12.14–12.32.
13 Copyright, Designs and Patents Act 1988, s.175(1).
14 *Ibid.*, s.175(4)(a).
15 *Ibid.*, s.175(4)(c).
16 *Ibid.*, s.155(3).
17 *Ibid.*, s.12(1). See Art. 1(1) of Directive 93/98: [1993] O.J. L290/9.
18 *Ibid.*, s.12(2).
19 *Ibid.*, s.12(3).
20 *Ibid.*, s.12(4).

Works of unknown authorship. If the work is of unknown author-   **9.05**
ship,[21] copyright expires at the end of 50 years from the end of the
period of 50 years from the end of the calendar year in which it is first
made available to the public. Copyright in such works expires 50 years
after the work is made available to the public.[22] However, if the author
becomes known prior to the expiration of the 50 year period prescribed
by the 1988 Act the copyright period will be the life of the author plus 50
years.[23] If the identity of the author becomes known after the end of the
50 year period in which the work is first made available to the public the
copyright period is not extended to the life of the author plus 50 years
although the author is still alive or died less than 50 years previously.[24]
For these purposes a work is of unknown authorship if the identity of
the author cannot be ascertained by reasonable inquiry but if his identity is once known it is not subsequently to be regarded as unknown.[25]

Computer generated works. The 1988 Act draws a distinction between   **9.06**
works which are "generated by computers" and other computer aided
works. A work is generated by a computer where there is no human
author of the work.[26] Thus, where the computer program is no more than
the tool by which an author creates a work, the ownership and duration
of copyright will fall to be determined by the general principles. Where
however, the computer programme creates the work without the operator assisting the computer in any way other than starting the sequence of
necessary commands, it would appear that such a work is computer
generated and the copyright subsists in it for a period of 50 years from the
end of the calendar year in which the work was made.[27]

Works of joint authorship. The period of copyright of a musical or lyri-   **9.07**
cal work of joint authorship[28] is measured by reference to the last of the
joint authors to die.[29] Thus, if X and Y were to be joint authors of a
musical composition and Y were to die in 1993 but X did not die until
1995 the copyright would continue in the joint work for 50 years from
the death of X.

---

[21] *Ibid.*, s.9(4).
[22] *Ibid.*, s.12(2)(a). Pursuant to Directive 93/98 the term of copyright runs for 70 years after
the work is made available to the public. Where a pseudonym adopted by the author
leaves no doubt as to his identity, or if the author discloses his identity during the
initial 70 years the term of copyright is 70 years plus the life of the author.
[23] *Ibid.*, s.12(2).
[24] *Ibid.*, s.12(2).
[25] *Ibid.*, s.9(5).
[26] *Ibid.*, s.178.
[27] *Ibid.*, s.12(3).
[28] *Ibid.*, s.10(1): "A work of joint authorship is a work produced by the collaboration of
two or more authors in which the contribution of each author is not distinct from that of
the other author or authors."
[29] *Ibid.*, s.12(4).

(ii) *Sound recordings*

9.08 Copyright in a sound recording expires at the end of the period of 50 years from the end of the calendar year in which it was made, or if it is released before the end of that period, 50 years from the end of the calendar year in which it is released.[30] For these purposes, a sound recording is "released" when it is first published, broadcast or included in a cable programme service, or in the case of a film sound track is first shown in public with the permission of the author.[31] Thus, where a sound recording is made in 1990 but is not released, copyright would expire at the end of 50 years from 1990. If, however, it is released in the year 2000 copyright would expire 50 years from the year 2000.

(c) *Ownership of copyright*

(i) *Musical or literary work*

9.09 The author,[32] and the first owner of copyright, in relation to a musical or literary work is the composer or lyricist.[33] However, where the composer or lyricist creates the relevant work as an employee during the course of his employment, his employer is the first owner of any copyright in the work subject to any agreement to the contrary.[34] There is, however, no similar provision in the 1988 Act relating to sound recordings.

(ii) *Sound recordings*

9.10 In the case of sound recordings, the author, and therefore the first owner of the copyright, is the person "by whom the arrangements necessary for making the recording . . . are undertaken".[35] In general, this will be the record company which makes the arrangements for the recording of the performance.

(iii) *Computer generated work*

9.11 Where a literary or musical work is computer generated in circumstances where there is no human author of the work,[36] the author, and thus the first owner of any copyright in it, is the person by whom "the arrangements necessary for the creation of the work are undertaken".[37]

---

[30] *Ibid.*, s.13(1).
[31] *Ibid.*, s.13(2). See *ante*, para. 8.06 in respect of copyright accorded to a film sound track.
[32] *Ibid.*, s.9(1).
[33] *Ibid.*, s.9(1), s.11(1).
[34] *Ibid.*, s.11(2). For meaning of "employee", see *ante*, para. 8.34, n.66.
[35] *Ibid.*, s.9(2)(a). For a discussion of the meaning of "the person by whom the arrangements necessary for the making of the recording are undertaken" in relation to "Films", see *ante*, paras. 8.03–8.04.
[36] *Ibid.*, s.178.
[37] *Ibid.*, s.9(3).

(d) *Restricted acts*

(i) *Lyrics and musical work*

Restricted acts. The author of lyrics and musical works has the exclusive   **9.12**
rights to do any of the following acts in the United Kingdom.

(a) to copy the work[38];

(b) to issue copies of the work to the public[39];

(c) to perform, show or play the work in public[40];

(d) to broadcast the work or include it in a cable programme ser-
     vice[41];

(e) to make an adaptation of the work or do any of the above in rela-
     tion to an adaptation.[42]

The law relating to these exclusive rights are the subject of consideration elsewhere in this work.[43]

(ii) *Sound recordings*

Restricted acts. The author of a sound recording has the exclusive rights   **9.13**
to do any of the following acts in the United Kingdom:

(a) to copy the work[44];

(b) to issue copies of the work to the public[45];

(c) to perform, show or play the work in public[46];

(d) to broadcast the work or include it in a cable programme ser-
     vice.[47]

(e) *Secondary infringement*

Infringement of the rights in a sound recording may take place by: **9.14**

(a) importing an infringing copy;

(b) possessing or dealing with an infringing copy;

(c) providing means for making infringing copies;

(d) permitting use of premises for infringing performance;

---

[38] *Ibid.*, s.17. See *post*, paras. 12.09–12.10.
[39] *Ibid.*, s.18. See *post*, para. 12.14.
[40] *Ibid.*, s.19. See *post*, para. 12.53.
[41] *Ibid.*, s.19. See *post*, para. 10.26 and para. 12.39.
[42] *Ibid.*, s.21.
[43] See *post*, paras. 12.39–12.43.
[44] Copyright, Designs and Patents Act 1988, s.17. See *post*, paras. 12.08 and 12.13.
[45] *Ibid.*, s.18. See *post*, paras. 12.14–12.32.
[46] *Ibid.*, s.19. See *post*, paras. 12.33–12.34.
[47] *Ibid.*, s.19. See *post*, para. 10.26 and para. 12.39.

(e) provision of apparatus for infringing performance;

The law relating to these infringing activities are the subject of consideration elsewhere in this work.[48]

2. The Collecting Societies

9.15 General. The copyright ownership and commercial exploitation of lyrics, musical works and sound recordings have traditionally been divided between music publishers and recording companies. The music publishing companies usually own or are exclusive licensees of all rights in the lyrics and musical work, except performing rights which are vested in the Performing Rights Society Limited (PRS).[49] The right to reproduce on record the music and lyrics ("the mechanical rights") are, in general, exercised by the Mechanical Copyright Protection Society Limited (MCPS) as agent for the publishers and composers. The recording companies, however, own the copyright in the sound recording of the particular music and lyrics which are the subject of the recording, and the right to perform those sound recordings in public is usually controlled by Phonographic Performance Limited (PPL) on behalf of the record companies. The performing and broadcasting rights in promovideos are vested in the majority of cases in Video Performance Limited (VPL)

(a) *Mechanical rights*

9.16 Reproduction on records: the mechanical rights. Section 48(1) of the Copyright Act 1956 provided that "reproduction" of lyrics and musical works included reproduction in the form of a sound recording. The 1988 Act, however, simply provides that copying in relation to lyrics and musical works means reproducing the work in any material form.[50] It has been suggested that the change of expression has not altered the law in this respect.[51] Thus, the reproduction in the form of sound recordings continues to be a restricted act within the meaning of "to copy the work". Therefore, record companies, or other persons, who wish to reproduce lyrics and musical works on records require the licence of the copyright owner.

---

[48] See *supra*, n.43.
[49] For a detailed survey of the Articles and Constitution of the Performing Right Society see Cotterell, L., *Performance: The Business and Law of Entertainment* (Sweet & Maxwell, 3rd ed., 1993) p. 499 *et seq.*
[50] Copyright, Designs and Patents Act 1988, s.17.
[51] See *Copinger & Skone James on Copyright* (Sweet & Maxwell, 13th ed., 1991), para. 8–18.

Exercise of the mechanical rights. The right to reproduce lyrics and   **9.17**
musical works on records is customarily referred to in the music industry as the "mechanical rights". Where a composer has entered into a
publishing agreement such rights are generally subject to a future
assignment of copyright[52] which vests ownership in the publisher
upon the work coming into being. Generally, musical publishers[53]
appoint the Mechanical Copyright Protection Society (MCPS) as their
agents for the grant of licences of the mechanical rights and the collection of fees relating to the exercise of such rights. The MCPS is therefore
a licensing body within section 116(2) of the 1988 Act.[54]

The television and radio companies, BBC and the commercial broadcasters, and the MCPS have concluded blanket agreements whereby the
companies are licensed, in accordance with the blanket licence agreement, to record, for broadcasting, the music which the MCPS administers on behalf of the publishers.

The MCPS also has affiliation agreements with foreign collecting
societies. Such agreements give it effective control over the recording,
reproduction, importation and distribution rights in the majority of
records made, imported or distributed in the United Kingdom.

(b) *Performing Rights*

Performing rights. An assignment to a music publisher, whether of   **9.18**
existing or future copyright in a lyrics and musical composition will
generally reserve to the composer the right of public performance,
broadcasting and film synchronisation rights in the composition. As a
member of the PRS, the lyricist and composer will be subject to a Deed
of Assignment whereby he assigns the existing and future performing
rights in his work to the PRS. The rights reserved to the composer as
against the music publisher will therefore automatically be assigned to
the PRS who will exercise those "performing rights" on his behalf. The
term "performing rights" in relation to a musical work[55] is defined in
the PRS's Articles of Association as meaning the right, to the extent that
such rights exist under the laws of the United Kingdom or any other

---

[52] See generally "Agreements between Copyright Owners and Licensees", *ante*, para.
7.07.

[53] It should be noted that the MCPS is also open to membership by individual composers.
There are approximately 5,000 members of whom over half consist of individual
composers.

[54] See generally "The Copyright Tribunal", *post*, para. 16.16 *et seq.*

[55] "Musical work" is defined in the Society's Articles of Association as including:

(a) any part of a musical work; (b) any vocal or instrumental music in films; (c) any
musical accompaniment to non-musical plays; (d) any words or music of monologues
having a musical introduction or accompaniment; (e) any other words (or part of words)
which are associated with a musical work (even if the musical work itself is not in
copyright, or even if the performing right in the musical work is not administered by
the Society).

country, to perform the work in public or broadcast the work, or include it in a cable programme service or authorise other persons to do so.

It therefore follows that any performance in public of lyrics or musical works, or their broadcast or inclusion in a cable programme service will require a licence from the PRS for such performance. A typical example, of such an occasion would be the performance in a public house of a sound recording. The manager of the public house may require a licence in respect of the sound recording from the PPL but he will also require a licence from the PRS in respect of the lyrics and music included in the sound recording.

The PRS also administers film synchronisation rights[56] on behalf of its members. This right vests in the PRS in respect of every work composed or written by a member of the PRS primarily for the purpose of a particular film or films which were in contemplation when the work was commissioned.

9.19 **Grand rights.** As a general rule, the PRS does not administer the "grand rights" nor does it control the performing rights to son-et-lumiere productions. Grand rights in general comprise performance, in whole or part, of dramatico-musical works[57] and ballets.[58] However, the PRS will, in general, control grand rights where they are performed by means of a film produced for cinema exhibition.

(c) *Performing rights: sound recordings*

9.20 **Exercise of performing rights in sound recordings.** The exclusive rights to perform the work in public, and to broadcast or include it in a cable programme service, represent important sources of recurring revenue for a record company. The task of licensing the performing rights, administering such licences and collecting performing rights royalties is generally performed on behalf of the record companies by Phonographic Performances Limited (PPL). The members of PPL assign to it the performing rights in respect of the sound recordings owned by such members, including the public performance and broadcast rights in respect of such recordings. PPL then licenses the right to broadcast and publicly perform such copyright sound recordings. It therefore follows that any public performance of copyright sound recording in places

---

[56] For the meaning of "film synchronisation", see *ante*, para. 8.43.
[57] The PRS Articles of Association defines a dramatico-musical work as "an opera, operetta, musical play, review or pantomime in so far as it consists of words and music written therefore".
[58] The PRS Articles of Association defines a "ballet" as a "choreographic work having a story plot or abstract idea devised or used for the purpose of interpretation by dancing and/or miming but does not include country or folk dancing nor tap dancing nor precision dance sequences".

such as discotheques, pubs and in television and radio broadcasts requires a licence from PPL.

As with the MCPS and the PRS, the PPL is a licensing body within the meaning of section 116(2) of the 1988 Act and thus subject to the jurisdiction of the Copyright Tribunal.[59]

3. Competition Law and Collecting Societies

(a) *Copyright Tribunal*

This subject is dealt elsewhere in this work.[60]

9.21

(b) *European Community law*

General. In this section of this work it is proposed to deal with European Community law only in so far as it relates to the exclusive rights accorded to an owner of copyright in a work. For a detailed examination of general competition law reference should be made to a standard work dealing with European Community law.

9.22

Exhaustion of rights and performance. Although the receipt of a fee in respect of the manufacture or sale of a sound recording may exhaust the right to restrict the sale of the recordings, it does not exhaust the performance rights in the lyrics and musical work, or the sound recording itself.[61] The copyright owner in such works has the exclusive right to authorise both the reproduction, by manufacture and sale, and its public performance, and these two rights may be exercised by him separately and cumulatively.[62] Thus, Articles 30 and 59 of the E.C. Treaty do not preclude the application of national legislation, which treats as an infringement of copyright the public performance of musical works by means of sound recordings without payment of a royalty in a case where a royalty in respect of the manufacture and sale of the sound recordings has already been paid in another Member State.[63] However, the exercise of the performing rights may in certain circumstances infringe Articles 85 and 86 of the E.C. Treaty.

9.23

(i) *Article 85*

General. All agreements between undertakings, decisions by associations of undertakings and concerted practices which may affect trade between member States and which have as their object or effect the pre-

9.24

---

[59] See "Copyright Tribunal", *post*, para. 16.16 *et seq.*
[60] See *post*, Chap. 16.
[61] Case 158/62, *Warner Brothers v. Erik Viuff Christiansen*: [1988] E.C.R. 2605, para. [13].
[62] *Ibid.*
[63] Case C-395/87, *Ministere Public v. Tournier*: [1991] 4 C.M.L.R. 248, para. [15].

vention or distortion of competition within the common market are prohibited by the E.C. Treaty and are automatically void.[64] An undertaking is not confined solely to companies. In *BRT v. SABAM*[65] the principle was described thus: "the application of competition law is not affected to any great extent by the legal mould in which the undertaking is cast. If it has its own legal personality no particular attention is paid to the legal form adopted, namely whether it is a commercial, co-operative or civil company, or even an association . . . Article 85 . . . thus applies to an undertaking exercising economic activity, in other words, indulging in any transactions, whether involving goods or services". Thus, a collecting society is an "undertaking" for the purposes of Article 85.

9.25 **Reciprocal representation contracts.** A reciprocal representation contract is "a contract between two national copyright management societies concerned with musical works whereby the societies give each other the right to grant, within the territory for which they are responsible, the requisite authorizations for any public performance of copyrighted musical works of members of the other society and to subject those authorizations to certain conditions in conformity with the laws of the country in question".[66] Both the MCPS and the PRS operate reciprocal representation contracts (more often referred to as affiliation agreements). Such agreements are not in themselves restrictive of competition within the meaning of Article 85(1). However, reciprocal representation contracts may amount to a concerted practice restrictive of competition and capable of affecting trade between Member States if they have as their effect the denial to users established in other Member States of direct access to the repertoires of collecting societies established in another Member State.[67] Thus, it would prima facie be restrictive of competition if an agreement between a collecting society in the United Kingdom and France were to provide that a user of recorded music in France could not obtain a licence from the United Kingdom collecting society for music in its repertoire.

9.26 **Mechanical rights.** The manufacture of sound recordings does not necessarily take place in the territory in which the collecting society issuing the licence is situated. A record company may decide that it is commercially advantageous to sub-contract the pressing to a company in another Member State. In such circumstances a mechanical rights

[64] E.C. Treaty, Art. 85.
[65] Case 127/73, Advocate General Mayras: [1974] E.C.R. 313 at 322.
[66] Case C-395/87, *Ministere Public v. Tournier*: [1991] 4 C.M.L.R. 248.
[67] *Ibid.*

licence granted in one Member State is valid throughout the Community, and authorises manufacture in any Member State.[68]

(ii) *Article 86*

General. Article 86 prohibits any "abuse", in so far as it affects trade **9.27**
between member States, committed:

(a) by one or more undertakings;

(b) occupying a dominant position;

(c) within the common market or in a substantial part of it.

An organisation whose object is to exploit and manage copyrights for profit[69] pursues a business activity consisting in the "supply of services in respect of composers, authors and publishers, as well as users of music.[70] Thus, collecting societies are undertakings within the meaning of Article 86 and subject to the restrictions prescribed by Article 86. A collecting society occupies a dominating position within the Common Market, or in a substantial part of it, if the particular market (*e.g.* the U.K.) is of relative importance to the Common Market as a whole.[71] However, the prohibition contained in Article 86 applies not to the mere existence of a dominant position but to its "*abuse*" in so far as it may affect trade between Member States. Although Article 86 gives a number of examples as to what may amount to an "abuse", no comprehensive definition is given. What amounts to abuse must therefore be determined according to the circumstances of each particular case: the test whether such 'abuse' has occurred is an objective one.[72] Thus, it matters not what the intended effect was of the act of which complaint is made.

(a) *Abuse of a dominant position in relation to members of society*

Discrimination against nationals of other Member States. In *Re Gema*,[73] **9.28**
the Commission found that Gema, a collecting right society, was an undertaking occupying a dominant position in Germany, which constituted a substantial part of the Common Market. The Commission held that the Gema abused its dominant position by discriminating against

---

[68] *Re Gema* [1985] 2 C.M.L.R. 1.
[69] See Case 7/82, *GVL v. Commission* [1983] E.C.R. 483 where it was stated by the Commission that a collecting society may be an "undertaking" within Art. 86 where the rights were not managed for profit.
[70] Case 71/224, *Re Gema*: [1971] C.M.L.R. D35; Case C-395/87, *Ministere Public v. Tournier*: [1991] 4 C.M.L.R. 248.
[71] Case 127/73, *Belgische radio en Televisie and Societie belge des autteurs, compositeurs et editeurs v. SV SABAM*: [1974] E.C.R. 51.
[72] Case 40/70, *Sirena S.R.L. v. Eda S.R.L.*: [1971] E.C.R. 69.
[73] [1971] C.M.L.R. D35.

nationals of other Member States by reason of the fact that a German composer, wherever his residence, was entitled to become a voting member of Gema, whereas that possibility was not open to a national of another Member State unless he had a fiscal residence in Germany. Further abuse of a dominant position was found by the Commission in the fact that a foreign publisher was not entitled to become an ordinary member of Gema.

9.29 **Discrimination amongst members in distribution of income.** The payment by a collecting society of loyalty bonuses by way of supplementary fees only to certain members constitutes an abuse of a dominant position where the payments are made from contributions of all members, including members from other countries.[74]

9.30 **Binding members by unnecessary obligations.** A collecting society in a dominant position may abuse that position by binding its member with obligations which were "not objectively justified and which, in particular, unfairly complicate the movement of its members to another society".[75] In *Re Gema* such unnecessary obligations were to be found in the fact that Gema required members to assign to it all rights for all categories of exploitation in the work and for the whole world. The Commission expressed the view that such obligations would not be unjustified in respect of the territories in which Gema carried on "direct activity". Further, where a collecting society has a dominant position it may not refuse its services to a foreign performer who wishes to exercise his rights in that market.[76]

9.31 **Excluding recourse to courts to settle disputes.** Any restriction by a collecting society in a dominant position which seeks to restrict the right of a member to have recourse to the courts to settle disputes between himself and the collecting society, is an abuse of a dominant position.[77] In such circumstances it is not sufficient that the collecting society is subject to internal regulation, for such control does not guarantee to each member that individual account will be taken of his rights in calculating the payment due to him.

(b) *Abuse of dominant position with regard to users of musical works*

9.32 **Extending copyright to non-copyright works by contractual means.** In *Re Gema* the Commission examined the principal contract between Gema and German record manufacturers. The contract provided that

---

[74] Case 71, 224, *Re Gema*: [1971] C.M.L.R. D35.
[75] *Ibid.*
[76] Case 7/82, *GVL v. Commission*: [1983] E.C.R. 483.
[77] Case 71/224, *Re Gema*: [1971] C.M.L.R. D35.

Gema would be paid full fees for the sides of records on which Gema works accounted for only part of the recording, whether the non-Gema works reproduced were in the public domain or had not been placed by their authors under Gema control. Thus, for example, if only one-tenth of a side of a record contained Gema material, Gema claimed one third of the fee. Where it comprised 34 per cent. and upwards Gema demanded the full fee, as if the whole side of the record comprised works on the Gema list. The Commission concluded that this arrangement was an abuse by Gema of its dominant position by "extending by contractual means to unprotected works the copyrights which it administers" and that "such a regulation would not have been accepted by the producers of records if GEMA did not enjoy a dominant position".

Royalty rates charged to users. The royalty rates charged to discotheques by collecting societies has been the subject of two decisions by the European Court of Justice. In *Basset v. SACEM*[78] the Court had to decide whether a "supplementary mechanical reproduction fee", permitted by national legislation, in addition to a performance royalty, on the public performance of sound recordings, was permissible even where such supplementary fee was not provided for in the Member State where those sound recordings were lawfully placed on the market. The Court held that such additional fee was not in itself abusive conduct within the meaning of Article 86. Analysis of the "supplementary mechanical fee" showed it to be in respect of the performance of the sound recording and not on the basis of the number of the records bought and sold. However, the Court stated that the amount of royalty, or of the combined royalties so charged by the collecting society, may amount to abusive conduct, in particular by imposing unfair conditions within the terms of Article 86. The question whether the fees were excessive was acknowledged as being for the determination of the national court. Consequently, no meaningful guidance was given by the Court as to what would amount to an excessive royalty fee.

9.33

However, some guidance is to be found in *Ministere Public v. Tournier*[79] as to the criteria to be used in determining whether the level of fee charged amounts to an abuse of a dominant position. The Court stated that a prima facie abuse of a dominant position, within the meaning of Article 86, will occur where charges made by a collecting society in respect of a particular usage are, "when compared on a consistent basis", appreciably higher than those charged in other Member States. In such circumstances the burden would be on the collecting society to

---

[78] Case 402/85: [1987] E.C.R. 1717.
[79] Case C-395/87: [1991] 4 C.M.L.R. 248.

justify the level of royalty which it charges by reference to "objective and relevant dissimilarities between copyright management in the member State concerned and copyright management in the other member States".[80]

---

[80] *Ibid.*, para. [46].

CHAPTER 10

BROADCAST, SATELLITE AND CABLE TELEVISION

1. Broadcast

Broadcast. "Broadcast" is defined by the Copyright, Designs and **10.01** Patents Act 1988 as a transmission by wireless telegraphy of visual images (*e.g.* a film) sounds (*e.g.* a radio broadcast) or other information (*e.g.* Teletext or Oracle) which is:

(a) capable of being lawfully received by members of the public[1]; or

(b) is transmitted for presentation to members of the public.[2]

It therefore follows that if the transmission by wireless telegraphy is capable of being lawfully received by the public it will be a "broadcast" and it does not matter, in such circumstances, that the person making the transmission did not intend it for public reception.

---

[1] Copyright, Designs and Patents Act 1988, s.6(1)(a).
[2] *Ibid.*, s.6(1)(b).

10.02   A transmission "for presentation to members of the public" will include circumstances where, for example, a football match or boxing event is transmitted to a particular place or places for reception and presentation to an audience and not to the public at large. A broadcast will include circumstances where visual images, sound or information are the broadcast and are intended, *inter alia*, to be relayed by a telecommunications system to members of the public.[3] Thus, if a cable programme provider picks up the signals of the broadcast of, for example, the local independent television licensee and relays it by means of cable to its subscribers, the broadcast will not lose its quality of being a broadcast by reason of the fact that its reception by subscribers is not by wireless telegraphy.

Where the transmission is encrypted it is regarded as capable of being lawfully received by members of the public, and thus a broadcast, only if decoding equipment has been made available to members of the public by, or with the authority of the person making the transmission or the person providing the contents of the transmission.[4]

"Wireless telegraphy" for these purposes means the sending of electro-magnetic energy over paths not provided by a material substance constructed or arranged for that purpose.[5] Thus, with the exception of a broadcast relayed by a telecommunications system, where programming is provided by means of a physical material, for example fibre-optic cables, the programmes so delivered will not be a broadcast within the meaning of the 1988 Act.

10.03   **Broadcaster.** The person making the broadcast or, in the case of a broadcast which relays another broadcast by reception and immediate retransmission, the person making that other broadcast, is the owner of the copyright in the broadcast.[6] Under the 1988 Act the "broadcaster" of the visual images, sounds or other information is the person transmitting the programme, if he has responsibility to any extent for its contents, and any person providing the programme who makes with the person transmitting it the arrangements necessary for its transmission.[7] Thus, the BBC and the 15 independent television licensees will be the broadcaster and the owner of the copyright in the broadcasts they make. However, where, a person (*e.g.* British Telecom) provides the

---

[3] *Ibid.*, s.6(5). "Telecommunication system" means a system for conveying visual images, sounds or other information by electronic means. "Electronic means" in this context means actuated by electronic, magnetic or electrochemical energy. An example would be a fibre optic cable but also includes such systems when using wireless telegraphy.

[4] *Ibid.*, s.6(2).

[5] *Ibid.*, s.178.

[6] *Ibid.*, s.9(2)(b), s.11. See *ante*, para. 8.07. The broadcaster must come within one of the listed categories to qualify for copyright protection when the broadcast was made.

[7] *Ibid.*, s.6(3).

means of transmission of the programme signals and acts as a common carrier without being responsible for the contents of the programme it will not be a joint owner of the copyright in the broadcast.

Duration of copyright. Copyright in a broadcast or cable programme **10.04** expires at the end of the period of 50 years from the end of the calendar year in which the broadcast was made or the programme was included in a cable programme service.[8] However, copyright in a repeat broadcast or cable programme expires at the same time as the copyright in the original broadcast or cable programme.[9] Thus, no copyright arises in respect of a repeat broadcast or cable programme which is broadcast or included in a cable programme service after the expiry of the copyright in the original broadcast or cable programme. For these purposes a repeat broadcast or cable programme means one which is a repeat either of a broadcast previously made or of a cable programme previously included in a cable programme service.[10]

2. Satellite Television

Definition and place of broadcast under 1988 Act. The definition of **10.05** "broadcast" includes broadcasting by satellite.[11] However, difficulties may arise as to the place from which the broadcast is made. The 1988 Act expressly provides that a satellite broadcast is made from the place from which the signals carrying the broadcast are transmitted to the public.[12] Thus, if U.K. Films Ltd. transmits the signals for its satellite programme service from the United Kingdom to a satellite for re-transmission to the households within the footprint of the satellite signals, the broadcast will take place from the United Kingdom notwithstanding the fact that the signals from the United Kingdom to the satellite were not capable of being received by the public. Thus, satellite broadcasters who transmit the up-link of their programme services from the United Kingdom come within the legal framework set down by the Copyright, Designs and Patents Act 1988.

Infringing acts. The infringing acts in respect of a satellite broadcast are **10.06** the same as in respect of broadcast.[13]

---

[8] *Ibid.*, s.14(1).
[9] *Ibid.*, s.14(1).
[10] *Ibid.*, s.14(3).
[11] See *supra*, paras. 10.01–10.02 and nn.1–5, "Broadcast".
[12] Copyright, Designs and Patents Act 1988, s.6(4).
[13] See *post*, paras. 10.20–10.26.

Satellite Television and E.C. law

10.07   **General.** Council Directive 93/83[14] sets out certain rules on the co-ordination of copyright and rights related to copyright applicable to satellite broadcasting.

"Satellite" is defined by the Directive as, "any satellite operating on frequency bands which, under telecommunications law, are reserved for the broadcast of signals for reception by the public or which are reserved for closed, point to point[15] communication. In the latter case . . . the circumstances in which individual reception of the signals take place must be comparable to those which apply in the first case."[16] "Comparable" in this context would appear to mean that the programme signals must be received simultaneously by individual households, whether by means of retransmission by a cable system or otherwise, but without alteration of the contents of the broadcast. Thus, the Directive seeks to ensure that "an end should be put to the differences of treatment of the transmission of programmes by communications satellite which exist in Member states, so that the vital distinction throughout the Community becomes whether works and other protected subject matter are communicated to the public". Which expression means "the act of introducing, under the control and responsibility of the [broadcaster] . . . the programme carrying signals intended for reception by the public into an uninterrupted chain of communication leading to the satellite and down towards the earth."[17] Thus, the applicable test for the purposes of the Directive is whether the satellite broadcast is "communicated to the public".[18]

10.08   **Place of broadcast.** The place of broadcast of a satellite programme is the place from which the programme carrying signals intended for reception by the public are transmitted in an "uninterrupted chain of communication leading to the satellite and down towards the earth".[19] If the programme carrying signals are encrypted, there is, nevertheless, communication to the public by satellite if the means of decrypting the broadcast are provided to the public by the broadcaster or with its consent.[20] This accords with the position under the 1988 Act. However,

---

[14] [1993] O.J. L248/15. Members States are required to bring into force before January, 1 1985, laws necessary to comply with the Directive.
[15] This is a communication service via satellite between earth stations at fixed points. The programme carrying signals are transmitted to the satellite which transmits the signal back to an earth station from where the programme signals are normally distributed by a cable system to individual homes.
[16] Directive 93/83 [1993] O.J. L248/15, Art. 1.
[17] *Ibid.*, Art. 2(a).
[18] *Ibid.*, Recital 13. Broadly similar to the definitions in the C.D.P.A. 1988.
[19] *Ibid.*, Art. 2(a).
[20] *Ibid.*, Art. 2(c). See also *ante*, para. 10.02.

if the up-link station is not situated in a Member State but a broadcaster established in a Member State has commissioned the act of communication to the public by satellite, that act is deemed to have occurred in the Member State in which the broadcaster has its head office or principal place of business.[21]

These provisions have two important consequences. First, the act of transmission of a broadcast takes place from the place from which the programme signals originate, and it is this transmission which is the decisive event for purposes of the application of the copyright and related rights. Secondly, a broadcasting organisation located in, for example, the United Kingdom will not avoid the need to obtain the authorization of the author, or to pay a single equitable remuneration to the performers, for use of the work, by transmitting the signals to the satellite from a non-Member State for reception in a Member State.

Exclusive right to broadcast by satellite. Member States are required to **10.09** provide an exclusive right for the "author" to authorize the communication to the public by satellite of copyright works.[22] This exclusive right currently exists under the 1988 Act but the definition of "author" differs from that provided in the Act in that the "author" under the 1988 Act is generally considered, in the case of a film, to be the person by whom the arrangements for the making of the film are undertaken.[23] The Directive, however, stipulates that the principal director of a "cinematographic or audiovisual work shall be considered as its author or one of its authors. Member States may provide for others to be considered as its co-authors."[24]

Thus, the exclusive right to authorize a satellite broadcast will be exercisable by the director and any additional person who is also designated by the United Kingdom enacting legislation. Where the rights to broadcast by satellite are acquired in the country of origin of emission of the programme signals, no fees will be payable by the broadcaster in respect of the reception of the programmes in the country of reception. In recognition of this rule "in arriving at the amount of the payment to be made for the rights acquired, the parties should take account of all

---

[21] *Ibid.*, Art. 1(2)(b): "Communication" for these purposes means the act of introducing the programme-carrying signals intended for reception to by the public into an uninterrupted chain of communication leading to the satellite and down towards the earth".

[22] Directive 93/83, Art.2.

[23] Copyright, Designs and Patents Act 1988, s.9(2)(a). See also *ante*, paras. 8.03–8.04.

[24] Directive 93/83, Art. 1(5). Where an agreement for the exploitation of a work has been entered into prior to 1 January 1995 but does not expire until after 1 January 2000 the director does not acquire authorisation rights in respect of the satellite exploitation of such works until 1 January 2000: *ibid.*, Art. 7(2).

aspects of the broadcast, such as the actual audience, the potential audience and the language version."[25]

The exclusive right to authorize communication to the public by satellite of copyright works may be acquired only by agreement.[26]

10.10   **Rights of performers and phonogram producers.** Where communication to the public by satellite occurs, performers have an exclusive right to authorise a satellite broadcast of their live performance.[27] Where a phonogram is broadcast by satellite to the public, a "single equitable remuneration"[28] is payable by the broadcaster and is to be shared between the relevant performers and the phonogram producers.[29]

10.11   **Rights of broadcasting organisations.** Broadcasters have the exclusive right to authorize or prohibit the re-broadcasting by satellite of their broadcasters, as well as the communication to the public of their broadcasts, if such communication is made in places accessible to the public against payment of an entrance fee.[30]

10.12   **Transmission by satellite of co-productions.** A co-production is a film produced between a number of producers whereby each contributes finance, creative and organisational facilities. Such productions are often between producers of different countries and will generally provide for the division of exploitation rights along geographical and/or language boundaries.

The Directive makes specific transitional provisions for circumstances where a co-production agreement concluded before January 1995 between a co-producer from a Member State and one or more co-producers from other Member States or third countries expressly provides for a system of division of exploitation rights between the co-producers by geographical areas for all means of communication to the public, without distinguishing the arrangement applicable to communication to the public by satellite from the provisions applicable to the other means of communication. In such circumstances where communication to the public by satellite would prejudice the exclusivity, in particular the language exclusivity, of one of the co-producers or his assignees in a given territory, the authorization by one of the co-producers or his assignees for a communication to the public by satellite requires the prior consent of the holder of that exclusivity, whether

---

[25] *Ibid.*, Recital 17.
[26] *Ibid.*, Art. 3(1).
[27] *Ibid.*, Art. 4. For "live performances", see *post*, para. 14.04.
[28] Directive 92/100: [1992] O.J. L346/61, Art. 8(2). See *post*, paras. 12.28–12.31.
[29] Directive 93/83, Art. 4.
[30] *Ibid.*, Art. 4.

co-producer or assignee.[31] Thus, if A (U.K.), B (France) and C (Germany) co-produce a film, and divide the exploitation rights along geographical and language lines corresponding to the respective territories without making any provision as to satellite broadcasting, C would not be entitled without the prior consent of A or his assignees to transmit the film to the United Kingdom.

This provision may be of particular use to those who co-produced films prior to the rapid growth in satellite technology. However, producers have, since the early 1980s, generally included provisions in their co-production agreements relating to satellite broadcasts. This provision of the Directive may, therefore be of limited value.

3. Cable Programme Service

Definition. A cable programme[32] service is defined by the 1988 Act as meaning a service which consists wholly or mainly in sending visual images, sounds or other information by means of a telecommunication system, otherwise than by wireless telegraphy, for reception[33]:   **10.13**

    (a) at two or more places for simultaneous reception, or at different times in response to requests by different user[34]; or

    (b) for presentation to members of the public.[35]

Thus, where a cable transmission is made according to a set programme schedule it will come within the meaning of cable programme service. Similarly, where subscribers to the service are able to request the provision of the programmes at times which suit their requirements rather than at a fixed time dictated by the service provided. It is to be noted, however, that a cable programme service in order to qualify as such must be transmitted via a telecommunications system which means a system for conveying visual images, sounds or other information by electronic means. "Electronic means" in this context means actuated by electronic, magnetic, electromagnetic or electrochemical energy. An example would be physical matter such as fibre optic cable. Presentation to the public within this context will typically include circumstances where a boxing match or a concert is sent by a telecommunications system to a stadium for viewing by a paying audience but which is not available to the public at large. The definition   **10.14**

---

[31] Directive 89/552 [1989] O.J. L293/23, Art. 7(3).
[32] A "cable programme" is any item included in a cable programme service: Copyright, Designs and Patents Act 1988, s.7(1).
[33] *Ibid.*, s.7(1). For the meaning of "telecommunications system", see *ante*, para. 10.02, n.3.
[34] *Ibid.*, s.7(1)(a).
[35] *Ibid.*, s.7(1).

of cable programme service does not, however include any of the following:

(a) services which have the essential feature that while visual images, sounds or other information are being conveyed by the person providing the service, the person receiving them can use the same system or the same part of it (other than for the purposes of the operation or control of the services) for sending information for reception by the person providing the service or other persons receiving it.[36] Thus, a cable telephone system would not come within the meaning of cable programme service nor would a video conferencing system operated by cable;

(b) a service run for the purposes of a business where the signals are conveyed solely for the purposes of the internal running of the business and the system is not connected to any other telecommunications system[37];

(c) a service run by a single individual where the apparatus comprised in the system is under his control, the signals or information contained in the system are solely for his domestic use and the system is not connected to any other telecommunications system[38];

(d) a service in which the apparatus comprising the system connects, or is situated in premises which are (a) in single occupation, and (b) the system is not connected to any other telecommunications system.[39] However, where the apparatus satisfies (a) and (b) but is part of the amenities provided for residents or inmates of premises run as a business, it will be a cable programme service.[40] Thus, a service in a state run hospital or prison would not be a cable programme service, but such a system run, for example, by Group 4 in a privatised prison, might be a cable programme service;

(e) services which are run for persons providing broadcasting or cable programme services, or providing programmes for such services.[41]

10.15   **Owner of copyright in cable programme.** The author, and thus the owner of the copyright in a cable programme, is the person providing the cable programme service in which the programme is included.[42]

---

[36] *Ibid.*, s.7(2)(a).
[37] *Ibid.*, s.7(2)(b).
[38] *Ibid.*, s.7(2)(c).
[39] *Ibid.*, s.7(2)(d).
[40] *Ibid.*, s.7(2)(d).
[41] *Ibid.*, s.7(2)(e).
[42] *Ibid.*, s.9(2)(c). See also *ante*, para. 10.03, n.6.

This does not, however, affect the copyright of the person supplying the programme to the cable broadcaster. His rights of ownership and exploitation by other media will, subject to the terms of the agreement with the service provider, be exercisable without the permission of the service provider.

For these purposes no copyright will subsist in a cable programme if it is included in a cable programme service by reception and immediate re-transmission of a broadcast, or if it infringes, or to any extent that it infringes, the copyright in another cable programme or in a broadcast.[43]

Duration of copyright. For a discussion of duration of copyright, see **10.16** *ante*, paragraphs 10.01 to 10.03, "Broadcast".

Reception and retransmission of broadcast in a cable programme ser- **10.17** **vice.** Where a broadcast made from a place in the United Kingdom is, by reception and immediate re-transmission, included in a cable programme service, copyright in the broadcast or cable programme is not infringed in two circumstances. First, where the inclusion is in pursuance of a requirement imposed under section 13(1) of the Cable and Broadcasting Act 1984[44] and secondly, to the extent that the broadcast is made for reception in the area in which the cable programme service is provided and is not a satellite transmission or an encrypted transmission.[45]

Cable retransmission and E.C. law

Meaning of cable retransmission in E.C. Law. Cable retransmission for **10.18** these purposes is "the simultaneous, unaltered and unabridged retransmission by cable or microwave system for reception by the public of an initial transmission from another Member State, by wire or over the air, including that by satellite, television or radio programmes intended for reception by the public."[46] Thus, for example, where a cable operator in the United Kingdom receives and simultaneously retransmits satellite programmes emanating from the Netherlands for reception by individual households, cable retransmission within the meaning of Directive 93/83[47] will occur, and the retransmission will thus come within the regime laid down by the Directive.

---

[43] *Ibid.*, s.7(6). For the meaning of "cable programme", see *ante*, para. 10.13, n.32.
[44] *Ibid.*, s.73(2)(a). The duty imposed by the Cable and Broadcasting Act 1984 is a general duty of reception and immediate re-transmission of broadcasts of the programmes included in a programme service provided by the BBC or a licensee for reception in the area for which the cable programme service provider has been granted a licence.
[45] Copyright, Designs and Patents Act 1988, s.73(2)(b).
[46] Directive 93/83: [1993] O.J. L248/15, Art. 1(3).
[47] It is a requirement of the Directive that Member States bring into force before January 1, 1995, laws necessary to comply with these requirements (Art. 12).

10.19   Where a cable retransmission takes place, the Member State in whose territory the retransmission occurs is under a duty to ensure, first, that the applicable copyright and related rights[48] are observed, and secondly, that such retransmission takes place on the basis of individual or collective contractual agreements between copyright owners, holders of related rights,[49] and cable operators.[50] Thus, for example, a cable operator is not entitled to receive and retransmit satellite emissions from a Member State without permission from the owners of copyright and related rights. The cable service provider may not retransmit the broadcast until such time as agreement is reached with the collecting society in respect of the terms on which the broadcast is to be retransmitted. Directive 93/83 provides that such authorization must take place through a collecting society, and sets down a mechanism which provides a means by which a party may not unreasonably prevent the granting of authorization. Article 12 specifically provides that "Member States shall ensure by means of civil or administrative law . . . that the parties enter and conduct negotiations regarding authorization for cable transmission in good faith and do not prevent or hinder negotiation without valid justification." It is difficult, however, to envisage the manner in which such an undertaking may be enforced and what quantifiable loss will flow from a breach, since in the majority of cases there will be no quantifiable loss.[51] It is probable that the United Kingdom will grant the Copyright Tribunal jurisdiction in cases where the parties are unable to reach agreement as to the terms on which such rights are to be exercised.

It is to be noted that the requirement that cable retransmission rights be exercised through a collecting society does not apply to a broadcasting organisation in respect of its own transmission, irrespective of whether the rights concerned are its own or have been transferred to it by other copyright owners and/or holders of related rights.[52]

4. Infringement of Copyright in Broadcast and Cable programme

10.20   The restricted acts in a broadcast[53] or cable programme are:

    (a) copying the broadcast or cable programme[54];

    (b) issuing copies of it to the public[55];

---

[48] *e.g.* performer's rights.
[49] *e.g.* performers.
[50] Directive 93/83, Art. 8(1).
[51] *cf. Walford v. Miles* [1992] A.C. 128, H.L. See also *ante*, paras. 1.09–1.10.
[52] Directive 93/83, Art. 10.
[53] For these purposes "Broadcast" includes satellite.
[54] Copyright, Designs and Patents Act 1988, s.17.
[55] *Ibid.*, s.18. See also *post*, para. 12.14.

   (c) showing or playing it in public[56];

   (d) broadcasting or including it in a cable programme service.[57]

An infringement of copyright will occur where any of these restricted acts are carried out by an unauthorised person as to the whole or any substantial part of it, either directly or indirectly.[58]

(a) *Copying broadcast or cable programmes*

In addition to the general definition of copying,[59] the 1988 Act also pro- **10.21**
vides that copying, in relation to a film, television broadcast or cable
programme, includes making a photograph of the whole or any substantial part of any image-forming part of the film, broadcast or cable
programme.[60] Thus, the unauthorised copying of a "still" frame from a
broadcast will constitute copying.[61] However, the 1988 Act provides an
exception to this rule by providing that the making for private and
domestic use of a photograph of the whole or any part of an image forming part of a television broadcast or cable programme does not infringe
any copyright in the broadcast or cable programme or any film included
in it.[62]

(b) *Issuing copies to the public*

For a discussion of this infringing activity see *post*, paragraphs 12.14 to **10.22**
12.32.

(c) *Performance in public of broadcast or cable programme*

Infringement of broadcast or cable programme. It is an infringement of **10.23**
the copyright in a broadcast or cable programme, where a person, without the authority of the owner, shows the whole or a substantial part of
such a work in "public" to a paying audience without the authority of the
owner, but where no payment is made by the audience for admission to
the place where the broadcast or programme is seen or heard, the showing or playing in public does not infringe copyright in (a) the broadcast
or cable programme or (b) any sound recording or film included in it.[63]
Thus, where, for example, customers pay for entrance to a venue to watch
the broadcast of a football match, an infringement of the copy-

---

[56] *Ibid.,* s.19. See also *post*, para. 12.33.
[57] *Ibid.,* s.20.
[58] *Ibid.,* s.16(3).
[59] See also *post*, paras. 12.03–12.13.
[60] Copyright, Designs and Patents Act 1988, s.17(4). But see "Permitted Acts", *post*, paras. 10.27–10.32.
[61] *Spelling Goldberg Productions Inc. v. BPC Publishing Ltd.* [1981] R.P.C. 283.
[62] Copyright, Designs and Patents Act 1988, s.71.
[63] *Ibid.,* s.19(3), s.72(1).

right in the broadcast or cable programme will take place unless the managers of the venue have obtained a licence from the broadcaster. There will also be an infringement of any rights in any sound recording, musical work and lyrics, and film incorporated in the broadcast. Where a licence has been obtained from the copyright owner of the broadcast the managers of the venue will nevertheless be required to obtain a licence from the PRS in respect of musical compositions included in the broadcast or sound recordings. A PPL licence is not required, however, in respect of the performance of a sound recording by means of radio or television to a paying audience. Where the audience is not a paying audience there will be no infringement in the sound broadcast, cable programme or sound recording by showing it in public to the audience. There will, nevertheless, be a requirement to obtain a PRS licence in respect of any musical composition included in the broadcast.

10.24 **Meaning of paying audience.** An audience is treated as having paid for admission to a place in either of two circumstances. First, if they have paid for admission to a place of which that place forms part,[64] or secondly, if goods or services are supplied at that place, or a place of which it forms part, and those goods are supplied:

(a) at prices which are substantially attributable to the facilities afforded for seeing or hearing the broadcast or programme[65]; or

(b) at prices exceeding those usually charged there and which are partly attributable to the facilities.[66]

Thus, for example, where a public house charges its customers for admission to a part of the public house there to view a particular football match, or where the public house increases the prices of the alcohol on the occasion of the provision of the facilities to view the match, the audience will be a "paying audience" in either of those circumstances.

Paying for admission is not treated as having taken place where broadcasts and cable programmes are relayed (a) to residents or inmates of places[67] (*e.g.* homes for the elderly or hospitals) or (b) to members of clubs or societies where the payment is for membership of the club or society and the provision of facilities for seeing and hearing broadcasts or programmes is only incidental to the main purpose of the club.[68]

10.25 **Persons responsible for infringement by showing works in public on television or radio.** Where copyright in a work is infringed by its being performed, played or shown in "public" by means of television or

---

[64] *Ibid.*, s.72(2)(a).
[65] *Ibid.*, s.72(2)(b)(i).
[66] *Ibid.*, s.72(2)(b)(ii).
[67] *Ibid.*, s.72(3)(a).
[68] *Ibid.*, s.72(3)(b).

radio, the person by whom the visual images or sound are sent, and in the case of a performance the performers, are not to be regarded as responsible for the infringement of copyright.[69] Thus, for example, where a broadcast of a musical concert is shown by the proprietor of a public house to his customers without obtaining a PRS licence, the proprietor and not the broadcaster will be regarded as infringing the copyright in the music lyrics or any sound recording used in such concert.

(d) *Infringement by Broadcasting or including work in a cable programme service*

The broadcasting[70] of a work or inclusion in a cable programme ser- **10.26**
vice,[71] without the authority of the copyright owner, is an act restricted by the copyright in a literary, dramatic, musical or artistic work,[72] a sound recording or film,[73] or a broadcast or cable programme.[74] It is to be noted, however, that copyright does not subsist in a live event; consequently the transmission of such events without the authority of the promoter is not an infringement of copyright.

5. Permitted Acts

Reference should be made to *post*, paragraphs 12.68 to 12.86 for a **10.27**
detailed treatment of acts which are permitted in relation to broadcast and cable transmissions, and works included in such transmissions. The following are, however, of particular relevance.

(a) *Incidental inclusion of copyright works*

Copyright in a work is not infringed by its incidental inclusion in a **10.28**
broadcast or cable programme.[75] However, a musical work, (*i.e.* words spoken or sung with music, or so much of a sound recording, broadcast or cable programme as includes a musical work or such words) is not to be regarded as incidentally included if it is deliberately included.[76]

Thus, for example, where background music is selected and included by a producer in a documentary or television programme, such inclusion is deliberate and thus not incidental. If, however, a documentary

---

[69] *Ibid.*, s.19(4). For the meaning of "public" see *post*, paras. 12.14–12.32.
[70] See *ante*, para. 10.01 *et seq.*
[71] For meaning of "cable programme service", see *ante*, para. 10.13.
[72] Copyright, Designs and Patents Act 1988, s.20(a).
[73] *Ibid.*, s.20(b).
[74] *Ibid.*, s.20(c).
[75] *Ibid.*, s.31(1). See also *post*, para. 12.76.
[76] *Ibid.*, s.31(3).

is made in, for example, a public house or discotheque, and the music from loudspeakers in such places is captured on the sound-track of the film, such inclusion would not normally come within the definition of "deliberately included". Nor would the live broadcast of a football match at which music is played by the stadium managers at the stadium and the broadcast of the event includes sounds of that music.

(b) *Incidental recording for purposes of broadcast or cable programmes*

10.29 A person authorised to broadcast or include in a cable programme a literary, dramatic or musical work, or an adaptation of such a work,[77] an artistic work,[78] or a sound recording or film, has the following rights:

(a) in the case of a literary, dramatic or musical work or an adaptation of such a work he has right to make a sound recording or film of the work or an adaptation[79];

(b) in the case of an artistic work, to take a photograph or make a film of it[80];

(c) in the case of a sound recording or film to make a copy of it.[81]

10.30 However, such recording, film, photograph or copy may not be used for any other purpose than that licensed,[82] and must be destroyed within 28 days of being first used for broadcasting the work or, where applicable, being included in a cable programme service.[83] Where either of these conditions are not complied with, the recording, film or photograph is to be regarded as an infringing copy.[84] These rights enable a person who has a right to broadcast a work to make a copy of the work for the purposes of enabling it to exercise the right granted to it. However, the right is somewhat restricted in that such copies cannot be retained for a period exceeding 28 days. In practice, such rights will be of limited applicability due to the fact that it is generally the practice of broadcasters to obtain the necessary rights without any limitations as to destruction and use. Where such rights are not obtained at the time of the contract, either through omission or because the copyright owner refuses, the limited rights set out above will apply.

---

[77] *Ibid.*, s.68(1)(a).
[78] *Ibid.*, s.68(1)(b).
[79] *Ibid.*, s.68(2)(a).
[80] *Ibid.*, s.68(2)(b).
[81] *Ibid.*, s.68(2)(d).
[82] *Ibid.*, s.68(3)(a).
[83] *Ibid.*, s.68(3)(b).
[84] *Ibid.*, s.68(4).

(c) *Time-shift recording for private and domestic use*

The recording of television programmes by individuals for their per-   **10.31**
sonal viewing at a later time or date is a widespread and commonly
accepted activity. The 1988 Act recognises such activity by providing
that the making for private and domestic use of a recording of a broadcast or cable programme solely for the purpose of enabling it to be
viewed or listened to at a more convenient time does not infringe any
copyright in the broadcast or cable programme or in any film included
in it.[85]

The recording of radio broadcasts, although not as a common as the
recording of television broadcasts, is also included in this exemption.
However, the exemption applies only in so far as (a) the recording is for
private and domestic purposes and (b) it is to enable it to be viewed or
listened to at a more convenient time. This would tend to imply that
there is no exemption where a recording is made at the time that the
individual is watching the programme as transmitted but whether or
not this is the intention of the provision the policing of such recordings
is extremely difficult and consequently only in rare circumstances will it
arise for consideration before the courts.

(d) *Fair dealing*

For a discussion of fair dealing see *post*, paragraphs 12.68 to 12.75.   **10.32**

6. Unauthorised Decoders for Encrypted Services

Encrypted Transmissions. Where a person (a) makes charges for the   **10.33**
reception of programmes included in a broadcasting or cable programme service provided from a place in the United Kingdom; or
(b) sends encrypted transmissions of any other description from a place
in the United Kingdom, he is entitled to the same rights and remedies
as a copyright owner[86] has in respect of infringements of copyright
against a person who (a) makes, imports or sells or lets for hire any
apparatus or device designed or adapted to enable to assist persons to
receive the programmes or other transmissions when they are "not
entitled to do so"; or (b) publishes any information which is calculated
to enable or assist persons to receive the programmes or other transmissions when they are not entitled to do so.[87]

The persons being enabled or assisted to receive programmes or
other encrypted transmissions include all persons within the footprint

---

[85] *Ibid.*, s.70.
[86] See *post*, Chap. 13.
[87] Copyright, Designs and Patents Act 1988, s.298.

of the transmission who are capable with the necessary decoders of receiving such programmes or transmissions.[88] Thus, a person is not entitled without the authorization of the provider of programmes who makes charges for their reception or the sender of the encrypted transmissions to make, import or sell or let for hire equipment designed or adapted to enable or assist persons to receive the programmes or encrypted transmissions. The effect of section 298(2) is to "regulate the conduct of makers and sellers of decoders in the United Kingdom in a way which may have consequential effects on television users outside the United Kingdom".[89] Thus, a person may not manufacture or provide within the United Kingdom, without the authority of the person providing the service, any equipment or information which enables or assists a person to receive the programmes included in the service and it matters not that the result is that he is prohibited from selling equipment to viewers outside the jurisdiction.[90] However, the protection afforded by the section to programme providers in relation to television users in other countries can readily be bypassed by decoders being made and sold by persons in countries outside the United Kingdom without any liability under the 1988 Act.[91]

---

[88] *B.B.C. Enterprises Ltd. v. Hi-Tech Xtravision Ltd.* [1991] A.C. 327 at 337.
[89] *Ibid.* at 337.
[90] *Ibid.* at 337.
[91] *Ibid.* at 337.

CHAPTER 11

THEATRE PRODUCTIONS

Introduction

In this section it is proposed to deal in outline with the underlying   **11.01**
rights in respect of live presentations in the theatre of plays, musicals,
operas and ballets. The acquisition of underlying rights for the presentation of these productions do not markedly differ from those for films,
save that in general licenses are granted in respect of such rights rather
than assignments.

Literary and dramatic works

Prior to the creation and presentation of live play or musical presen-   **11.02**
tations it will be necessary for a producer or impresario to acquire the
rights in the literary or dramatic work on which the work is based.[1] The
rules as to the use of plots and ideas in relation to theatrical and ballet
productions are the same as those applying to film productions.[2]

Music

Reference should be made to the section of this work relating to music.   **11.03**
It should be noted, however, that the rules relating to licensing and the
use of performing rights in respect of opera and ballet productions differ from those of the productions in which music forms a part.[3] Such
rights are often referred to as "grand rights" and are generally retained
by the composer or his publisher from whom the necessary performing
rights will have to be obtained.[4]

---

[1] See "Films", *ante*, paras. 8.23–8.26 for an examination of the law relating to the use and
adaptation of these works.
[2] See *ante*, paras. 8.23–8.26. See also *Corelli v. Gray* (1913) T.L.R. 116; *Holland v. Vivian Van
Damm Productions Ltd.* [1936–45] MacG.Cop.Cas. 69.
[3] See "Music", *ante*, Chap. 9.
[4] For the meaning of "grand rights", see *ante*, para. 9.19.

Dance, choreography and mime

11.04 Where such a work is recorded in writing or otherwise[5] it will qualify as a dramatic work[6]: if it is not so recorded in writing or otherwise it will also acquire copyright protection if filmed at the time of performance.

Scenic effects[7]

11.05 Where such works are the subject of drawings they will attract protection as artistic works. In such circumstances, if the designer is commissioned under a contract for services[8] he will be the first owner of copyright in the designs. Where the designer is employed by the commissioner, the first owner of the copyright in the designs will be the commissioner.[9]

Performers

11.06 The law relating to rights of performers in respect of live performances is discussed in Chapter 14.[10]

Consumer protection and the theatre

Reference should also be made to the consumer protection sections at Chapters 36 and 37 of this work.

---

[5] "Writing" includes any form of notation or code, whether by hand or otherwise and regardless of the method by which, or medium in or on which, it is recorded: Copyright, Designs and Patents Act 1988, s.178(1).

[6] *Ibid.* s.3(1).

[7] See *ante*, para. 8.37.

[8] See *ante*, para. 8.34, n.66 and text for meaning of contract for services.

[9] Copyright, Designs and Patents Act 1988, s.11(2).

[10] See also Cotterell, L., *Performance: The Business and Law of Entertainment* (Sweet & Maxwell, 3rd ed., 1993) which has a useful examination of theatrical contracts relating to artists directors and others.

CHAPTER 12

INFRINGEMENT OF COPYRIGHT IN FILMS SOUND RECORDINGS AND MUSIC

1. Introduction

Distinction between primary and secondary infringement. Primary 12.01
infringement takes place where a person does any of the acts restricted
by the copyright in the work or authorises another so to do.[1] In general,
innocence is no defence to a primary infringement. Secondary infringement, in outline, consists of the importing, possessing or dealing in
infringing copies, providing means for making infringing copies or
permitting use of premises for infringing performance. In such cases

---

[1] Copyright, Designs and Patents Act 1988, s.16(2).

the infringer must know or have reason to believe that the act is an infringing act.[2]

2. Primary Infringement

12.02 **Acts restricted by copyright.** The owner of the copyright in work has the exclusive right to do any of the following acts in the United Kingdom[3]:

(a) to copy the work[4];

(b) to issue copies of the work to the public[5];

(c) to perform, show or play the work in public[6];

(d) to broadcast the work or include it in a cable programme service[7];

(e) to make an adaptation of the work or to do any of the above in relation to an adaptation.[8]

These are also the "acts restricted by the copyright".[9] The 1988 Act provides that an act restricted by copyright in a work is the doing of it in relation to the whole of a work or "any substantial part of it,"[10] whether that copying is done directly or indirectly,[11] and it is immaterial whether any intervening acts themselves infringe copyright.[12] Where, therefore, any person carries out, or authorises another to do, any of the "acts restricted by copyright" without licence of the copyright owner, he commits an act of primary infringement of the copyright in the work.[13]

In this context "authorises" means "a grant or purported grant, which may be express or implied, of the right to do the act complained of".[14] However, it would appear that an act is not authorised by a person who "merely enables or possibly assists or even encourages another to do that act, but does not purport to have authority which he can grant to justify the doing of the act."[15]

---

[2] *Ibid.*, ss.22–26.
[3] *Ibid.* s.16(1).
[4] *Ibid.*, s.16(1)(a).
[5] *Ibid.*, s.16(1)(b).
[6] *Ibid.*, s.16(1)(c).
[7] *Ibid.*, s.16(1)(d).
[8] *Ibid.*, s.16(1)(e).
[9] *Ibid.*, s.16(1).
[10] *Ibid.*, s.16(3)(b).
[11] *Ibid.*, s.16(3)(a).
[12] *Ibid.*, s.16(3).
[13] *Ibid.*, s.16(2).
[14] *C.B.S. Songs Ltd. v. Amstrad Plc.* [1988] 1 A.C. 1013.
[15] *C.B.S. Inc. v. Ames Records & Tapes Ltd.* [1982] Ch. 91 *per* Whitford J., approved *C.B.S. Songs Ltd. v. Amstrad Plc.* [1988] 1 A.C. 1013 at 1055, H.L.

(a) *Infringement by copying*

(i) *Copying of literary, dramatic or musical works*

Meaning of copying. Copying in relation to a literary, dramatic or **12.03** musical works means "reproducing the work in any material form".[16] Two questions of interpretation immediately arise out of this definition of copying in relation to literary, dramatic or musical works. First, the meaning of "reproduction" and secondly the meaning of "in any material form". In order to constitute a "reproduction" of a literary dramatic or musical work there must be present two elements: first, there must be sufficient objective similarity between the infringing work and the copyright work, or "substantial part" of it, and secondly, the copyright work must be the source from which the infringing work is derived.[17] Whether there is such objective similarity and causal connection is a question of fact but " . . . [w]here there is a substantial degree of objective similarity, this of itself will afford prima facie evidence to show that there is a causal connection between the plaintiff's and the defendants' work; at least, it is a circumstance from which the inference may be drawn".[18]

The 1988 Act expressly states that reproducing the work "in any material form" includes storing the work in any "electronic medium"[19] and the making of copies which are "transient or incidental to some other use".[20] There is, however, no further assistance in the 1988 Act as to the meaning of "any material form". It is clear from the use of the words "in any material form" that an infringement by copying is not limited to a reproduction which is in the same medium as the copyright work. Thus, for example, the making of a film of a dramatic work or a sound recording of a musical work would be a "reproduction in a material form".

Substantial part. "Reproduction" may also occur where there is, first, an **12.04** objective similarity between a substantial part of the allegedly infringing work and the copyright work and, secondly, a causal connection between the infringing work and copyright work. Whether a part is "substantial" is a matter of fact and degree.[21] No precise test can thus be formulated but

---

[16] Copyright, Designs and Patents Act 1988, s.17(2).
[17] *Francis Day and Hunter Ltd v. Bron* [1963] Ch. 587, C.A.; *Purefoy Engineering Co. Ltd. v. Sykes Boxall & Co. Ltd.*, [1955] 72 R.P.C. 89, C.A.; *William Hill (Football) Ltd. v. Ladbrokes (Football) Ltd.* [1964] 1 W.L.R. 273.
[18] *Francis Day and Hunter Ltd. v. Bron* [1963] 1 Ch. 587 at 614, C.A.
[19] Copyright, Designs and Patents Act 1988, s.17(2).
[20] *Ibid.*, s.17(6). Transient or incidental uses may in specified circumstances come within one of the "Permitted acts": see also *ante*, paras. 10.28–10.30.
[21] *Ladbroke (Football) Ltd. v. William Hill (Football) Ltd.* [1964] 1 W.L.R. 273, H.L.

what is substantial is generally determined by the quality of what is copied rather than the quantity.[22] This is illustrated by *Fernald v. Jay Lewis Productions Ltd.*[23] where the defendant reproduced in his film, *The Gift Horse*, four pages out of the plaintiff's 126 page novel, *Destroyer From America*. The incident which the defendant was alleged to have reproduced was found, as a matter of fact, comprise five to six minutes of the film but the court nevertheless found that the four pages were a substantial part of the plaintiff's original work.

However, the reproduction of a part which by itself has no originality will not normally be a substantial part of the copyright and will not be protected.[24]

12.05 **Innocence.** Once the two elements of sufficient objective similarity and causal connection are established, it is no defence that the infringer was unaware, and could not have been aware, that what he was doing infringed the copyright in the work.[25]

12.06 **Direct and indirect copying.** Copying may take place directly or indirectly and it matters not that an intervening act may itself have infringed copyright.[26] Thus, for example, where an infringing copy of a work is made of an infringing work made under licence from the copyright owner it will be an infringement of copyright.

12.07 **"Subconscious copying".** "Subconscious copying" would appear to comprise three elements. First, an objective similarity between the copyright work and the alleged infringing work; secondly a causal connection between the copyright work and the alleged infringing work; thirdly, the author of the infringing work believed, and may have had reasonable grounds for believing, that there was no causal connection.[27] The first two, if established, would amount to an infringement of copyright but the third is irrelevant to liability, although it may be relevant in establishing a defence of innocence under section 97 of the Copyright, Designs and Patents Act 1988.[28] However, such defence would be available only up to the point that the infringer became aware of the alleged infringement.[29]

---

[22] *King Features Syndicate Inc. v. O. & M. Kleeman Ltd.* [1941] A.C. 417 at 424; *Ladbroke (Football) Ltd. v. William Hill (Football) Ltd.* [1964] 1 W.L.R. 273, H.L.; *Leco Instruments (U.K.) v. Land Pyrometers* [1982] R.P.C. 1430.

[23] [1975] F.S.R. 499.

[24] *Ladbroke (Football) Ltd. v. William Hill (Football) Ltd.* [1964] 1 W.L.R. 273 at 293, H.L.; *Warwick Productions Ltd. v. Eisinger* [1969] 1 Ch. 508.

[25] *Francis Day & Hunter Ltd. v. Bron* [1963] 1 Ch. 587, C.A. See also *post,* para. 13.27.

[26] Copyright, Designs, and Patents Act 1988, s.16(3)(b). See also *ante,* para. 12.04, nn.11–13.

[27] *Francis Day & Hunter Ltd. v. Bron* [1963] 1 Ch. 587, C.A.

[28] *Ibid.*

[29] *E.M.I. Music Publishing Ltd. v. Papathanasiou* [1993] E.M.L.R. 306.

Parody and burlesque. If a parody or caricature does no more than con- **12.08**
jures up the idea of a copyright work, no infringement of copyright will
occur. If, however, the parody or caricature reproduces the copyright
work or a substantial part of it, there is no defence that the infringing
work was intended as a parody or caricature.[30] The fact that the infringer may himself have employed labour and produced something
original or some part of his work is original matters not if the defendant
reproduces the plaintiff's copyright work without his licence.[30a]

Copying of a literary work. The general principles in relation to copy- **12.09**
ing of a literary work have been discussed at *supra*, paragraphs 12.03 to
12.08. It is therefore not proposed to deal at any length with this work
individually. For the purposes of the entertainment industry it should,
however, be noted that a literary work will include the lyrics for a song
and a reproduction of such lyrics in a material form will comprise the
making, for example, of a sound recording incorporating such lyrics. In
determining whether there has been an infringement of copyright in
lyrics the general principles in relation to copying set out in *supra*, paragraphs 12.03 to 12.08 will apply.

For the application of the general principles to films, reference should
be made to *ante*, paragraphs 8.26 to 8.33.

Copying dramatic works. For the application of the general principles **12.10**
in *supra*, paragraphs 12.03 to 12.08 to films and theatre, reference should
be made to *ante*, paragraphs 8.26 to 8.33.

Copying musical works. The general test of infringement of a musical **12.11**
work is the same as for a literary work though more difficult of application owing to the more complicated nature of the subject-matter.

Determining whether one musical work is a copy of another often
present difficulties by reason of the form of such copying. Guidance on
the proper approach to the question of infringement in music copyright
cases is to be found in the judgments of Wilberforce J. at first instance
and Wilmer L.J., in the Court of Appeal in the case of *Francis Day &
Hunter Ltd. v. Bron*.[31] In his judgment Wilberforce J. observed that:

"In endeavouring to reach an approach which is neither too super-
ficial nor unduly academic or technical, I think I must to some

---

[30] *Schweppes Ltd. v. Wellingtons Ltd.* [1987] F.S.R. 97; *Williamson Music Ltd. v. Pearson
Partnership Ltd.* [1987] F.S.R. 97.
[30a] *Schweppes Ltd. v. Wellingtons Ltd.* [1984] F.S.R. 210. In so stating Falconer J. expressed
the view that the headnotes of *Joy Music Ltd. v. Sunday Pictorial Newspapers (1920) Ltd.*
[1960] 2 Q.B. 60, which appeared to conflict with his judgment, was incorrect in that it
did not properly reflect the decision of the court in *Joy Music Ltd.*
[31] [1963] 1 Ch. 587; see also *D'Almaine v. Boosey* (1835) 1 Y. & C. 288 where the same
approach was adopted.

extent rely on my aural judgment, instructed as it has been by these various experts. As it was put by Professor Neiman, 'The public has a purer approach to music than the critics.' That, of course, does not mean that one must discount the help that the critics can give, but I think I must rely on the ear as well as on the eye, and on the spoken words of the witnesses.''[32]

Wilmer L.J., in the Court of Appeal, appeared to adopt this approach when he observed in the course of his judgment:

" . . . when the two songs were played to us, it was immediately apparent, to me at any rate, that the effect on the ear was one of noticeable similarity. This is a matter which is not without importance, for, as was pointed out by Astbury J. in *Austin v. Columbia Gramophone Co. Ltd.*,[33] 'infringement of copyright in music is not a question of note for note comparison', but falls to be determined by the ear as well as by the eye.''[34]

12.12   Thus, in the final analysis it is a matter for the judge's aural and visual perception as to whether there is sufficient objective similarity between two works.

Where only a part of a musical work has been taken the test of whether such part is "substantial" is illustrated by *Hawkes & Son (London) Ltd. v. Paramount Film Service Ltd.*,[35] where the defendant had distributed to cinemas newsreels recording a film of the scene at the public opening of a new school, together with 28 bars, without his authorization, of the plaintiff's musical composition entitled "Colonel Bogey". It was held that though the plaintiff's composition would take four minutes to play and the part reproduced on the newsreel comprised 20 seconds of the composition, nevertheless it was a substantial and vital part of the plaintiff's composition.

(ii) *Copying a sound recording*

12.13   It is an infringement[36] of copyright to copy, directly or indirectly,[37] the whole or a substantial part[38] of a sound recording. It is to be noted that "copying" of sound recording is not accorded the extensive definition accorded to literary, dramatic and musical works; in particular, the stipulation that such works are copied if reproduced in any material

---

[32] *Francis Day & Hunter Ltd. v. Bron* [1963] 1 Ch. 587 at 594.
[33] (1923) MacG.C.C. (1917–1923).
[34] *Francis Day & Hunter Ltd. v. Bron* [1963] 1 Ch. 587 at 608.
[35] [1934] 1 Ch. 593.
[36] Copyright, Designs and Patents Act, s.17(1).
[37] *Ibid.*, s.16(3)(b).
[38] *Ibid.*, s.16(3)(a).

form or stored in any electronic medium. However, it would appear that what must be copied is the recording itself, whether by means of vinyl or digital recording or other means. See also under "Lyrics, Musical Works and Sound Recordings", Chapter 9, paragraph 9.01 *et seq.*

(b) *Infringement by issuing copies to the public*

(i) *Issuing copies to the public*

It is an infringement of copyright in a work to "issue to the public" copies of the work, without the authority of the owner.[39] To "issue to the pub-lic" copies means to put into circulation copies of a work not previously in circulation in the United Kingdom or elsewhere, but does not include any subsequent distribution, sale or hiring or loan of those copies,[40] or any subsequent importation of those copies into the United Kingdom.[41] Thus, where copies of the work have been issued to the public in the United States by X, who is the copyright owner of a work created in the United Kingdom, Y will not infringe X's exclusive right to issue copies to the public by buying copies of the work and importing them into the United Kingdom for the purposes of sale in the course of business. The act of importing may, however, be a secondary infringement.[42]

(ii) *Rental rights*

United Kingdom rental rights

Prior to the 1988 Act, when the owner parted with the film or sound recording by way of, for example, sale, the purchasers were at liberty to hire them out without the permission of the copyright owner. It is now expressly provided by the 1988 Act that in relation to sound recordings and films the restricted act of issuing copies to the public includes "rental" of copies to the public.[43] "Rental" for these purposes means an arrangement under which a copy of a work is made available for pay-ment[44] or in the course of business as part of services or amenities for which payment is made on the terms that it will be returned.[45] Conse-quently, an infringement of the owner's exclusive right to issue copies to the public will occur where sound recordings and films are (a) issued to the public for the first time anywhere in the world without the auth-ority of the owner or (b) where copies are rented to the public without

12.14

12.15

---

[39] *Ibid.*, s.18(1).
[40] *Ibid.*, s.18(2)(a).
[41] *Ibid.*, s.18(2)(b).
[42] See *post*, paras. 12.50–12.53.
[43] Copyright, Designs and Patents Act 1988, s.18(2). The rental right does not apply to any copy of a film or sound recording acquired by a person prior to the commencement of the 1988 Act for the purpose of renting to the public: *ibid.*, s.170, Sched. 1, para. 14.2.
[44] *Ibid.*, s.178.
[45] *Ibid.*, s.178.

the authority of the copyright owner. Thus, where X, the copyright owner, issues copies of a film to the public by, for example, sale on video-cassettes, but does not hire the film on video-cassette nor authorise such hiring, Y will infringe X's rental rights if he purchases a copy of the film on video-cassette and hires the same to the public without X's licence.

The rental right is conferred by the 1988 Act upon the person by whom the arrangements necessary for the making of the recording are made.[46] Thus, performers, composers and directors are not vested with any rental rights under the 1988 Act.

E.U. rental rights

12.16 **General.** E.C. Directive 92/100[47] seeks to harmonise the laws of the European Union by conferring exclusive "rental and lending rights" on authors, composers, performers and producers throughout the Member States. The Directive was adopted on November 19, 1992, by the Council of Ministers. Member States are required to pass legislation implementing the Directive by July 1, 1994.

12.17 **Coming into effect of rental rights.** The rental rights apply in respect of "all copyright works, performances, phonograms . . . and first fixations of films . . . which are, on 1 July 1994, still protected by the legislation of the Member States in the field of copyright and related rights or meet the criteria for protection under the provisions of [the] Directive on that date."[48] Therefore, if the enumerated categories are protected by the 1988 Act on July 1, 1994 they will be entitled to rental rights in the United Kingdom. The fact that a work may not qualify for copyright protection in the United Kingdom on July 1, 1994, does not however, deprive it of rental rights in another Member State if the work has copyright protection in that Member State. Alternatively, rental rights will apply if the criteria for protection under the Directive are met.

The application of rental rights does not, however, have retrospective effect in respect of exploitation performed prior to July 1, 1994.[49] Thus, for example, any rental which has occurred prior to July 1, 1994, is not subject to the payment of an equitable remuneration to the performer or author, but an equitable remuneration would be payable in respect of any rental which occurs thereafter, subject to the right of a Member State to stipulate the date on which payment is to commence.[50]

---

[46] See *ante*, paras. 8.03–8.04 for a discusion of the meaning of "the person by whom the arrangements necessary for the making of the recording or film are undertaken".
[47] [1992] O.J. L346/61.
[48] *Ibid.*, Art. 13(1).
[49] *Ibid.*, Art. 13(2).
[50] See "Equitable remuneration" *post*, para. 12.28.

Article 13(3) of the Directive makes specific provision for cases where **12.18** one of the objects (*e.g.* a film) of rental rights have been acquired prior to July 1, 1994 by a third party with a view to renting or lending it. In such cases, Member States have the right to implement the Directive so as to provide that the persons entitled to rental rights are deemed to have given their authorization to the rental or lending of the object. The Member State may, however, in such circumstances nevertheless provide that an "equitable remuneration" should be paid where such rental or lending occurs.

Definition of rental and lending rights. For the purposes of the Direct- **12.19** ive "rental" is defined as "making available for use, for a limited period of time and for direct or indirect economic or commercial advantage".[51] "Lending" is defined as "making available for use, for a limited period of time and not for direct economic or commercial advantage, when it is made through establishments which are accessible to the public."[52]

The typical form of rental will occur, within the meaning of the Directive, where an individual rents a pre-recorded videocassette in return for a fee payable in respect of each rental. Rental will, also occur, however, where there is an indirect commercial advantage. Thus, where the works are made available for a limited period of time and the consideration is, for example, publicity provided to the renter which has the effect of improving the commercial standing of his business an "indirect economic or commercial advantage" will have accrued.

Recital 13 to the Directive provides that "it is desirable, with a view to **12.20** clarity" to exclude from the defined concepts of rental and lending "certain forms of making available," and cites two examples of such exceptions one of which is the making available of records or films for the purpose of public exhibition. It would appear, therefore, that the "making available" for "a limited period" for *public exhibition* would not come within the meaning of rental as defined by the Directive.

Persons and works to which the right relates. The rental right is an **12.21** exclusive right to authorize or prohibit rental and lending.[53] By Article 2(1) of the Directive this right is conferred on:

  (a) an author in respect of the original copies of his work;

  (b) a performer in respect of the first recording of his performance;

---

[51] Directive 92/100, Art. 1(2).
[52] *Ibid.*, Art. 1(3).
[53] *Ibid.*, Arts. 1(1) and 2(1).

(c) a record producer[54] in respect of his records; and

(d) the producer[55] of the first recording of a film in respect of the original copies of his film

12.22   Article 2(2) of the Directive provides that the "principal director of a film is to be considered as its author or one of its authors". The absolute terms of Article 2(2) would indicate that where a director is employed under a contract of employment by, for example, a television company, he would also be entitled to a rental right together with the right to receive an equitable remuneration. Member States are given a discretion as to the date from which Article 2(2) will apply, provided that that date is no later than July 1, 1997.[56] However, a Member State, in implementing the Directive, will be entitled to exclude the application of Article 2(2) to films created before July 1, 1994.[57] The effect, therefore, is that if a Member State were to interpret its obligation restrictively it would be entitled to restrict a director's rental rights to films created after July 1, 1997.

It will be readily seen that the Directive, when implemented, will have a marked effect on the nature of the exclusive rental rights accorded to copyright owners under United Kingdom law in that composers, performers and directors will be entitled to exercise a rental right in parallel with the author of a record or film.

12.23   Transmission of rental rights. The rights conferred by the Directive "may be transferred, assigned or subject to the granting of contractual licences".[58]

12.24   Presumption of transfer. Article 2(5) of the Directive provides that subject to contractual provisions to the contrary "when a contract concerning film production is concluded, individually or collectively, by performers with a film producer, the performer covered by the contract shall be presumed . . . to have transferred his rental right". This presumption is, however, subject to the retention by the performer of the right to receive an "equitable remuneration for the rental". By Article 2(6), a Member State may, in implementing the Directive, provide for a similar presumption in respect of the "principal director of the film".

Article 2(5) makes provision for the contract to be concluded "individually or collectively". The conclusion of individual contracts pres-

---

[54] The term "producer" as used in the Directive would appear to bear the same meaning as "author" in s.9(2) of the 1988 Act.
[55] See *supra*, n.54.
[56] Directive 92/100.
[57] *Ibid.*, Art. 13(5).
[58] *Ibid.*, Art. 2(4).

ents little difficulty in this context. However, the reference to the conclusion of contracts "collectively" is not entirely without difficulty. This expression would appear to be a reference to the conclusion of "blanket" agreements between industry unions acting on behalf of performers and producers' associations acting on behalf of film producers. Such agreements do not, in practice, result in any concluded contract between a performer and a producer in respect of a particular film but merely provide a framework for the conclusion of individual agreements. They are, however, almost invariably expressly incorporated into the terms agreed by the producer and the performer. Consequently, any contrary terms contained in such industry agreements will rebut the presumption.

As an alternative to the rebuttable presumption of transfer of rental **12.25** rights, Article 2(7) permits Member States to "provide that the signing of a contract concluded between a performer and a film producer has the effect of authorizing rental, provided that such a contract provides for an equitable remuneration". The adoption of this alternative by a Member State would have the effect that a performer would have no right to reserve his rental rights and would, on the signing of the contract, be entitled only to receive an "equitable remuneration".

It is to be noted that the presumption of transfer is limited only to contracts "concerning film production". The term "film" is defined in Article 2(2) as meaning "cinematographic or audiovisual work or moving images, whether or not accompanied by sound", and is thus wide enough to encompass a film made for the cinema, television or solely for exploitation on video. A contract "concerning film production" would therefore appear to mean any contract between any performer, including a musical performer, for the film recording of his performance and its use in any media of exploitation.

Presumption of transfer in respect of records. There is some doubt as to **12.26** whether a presumption of transfer applies in relation to contracts concerning record production. If such a presumption is available under the terms of the Directive it would appear that it is permissible only to the extent that it is compatible with the Rome Convention.[59]

Presumed transfer by contracts entered into prior to July 1, 1994. Subject to the equitable right of remuneration, a Member State may, in implementing the Directive, provide that where a person entitled to **12.27**

---

[59] *Ibid.*, Recital 19 (Second Part). But see Reinbothe, J. and von Lewinski, S. *The E.C. Directive on Rental and Lending Rights and Piracy* (Sweet & Maxwell, 1993), who express the view that the Directive permits no presumption of transfer other than that concerning film production.

rental rights under the national provisions adopted in implementation of the Directive has, before July 1, 1994, given his consent for exploitation, he is presumed to have transferred his rental rights.[60] It is to be noted that, subject to the right to equitable remuneration, nothing in the Directive affects any right acquired under a contract entered into prior to November 19, 1992.[61]

12.28   **Equitable remuneration.** "Where an author[62] or performer has transferred or assigned his rental right concerning a phonogram or an original or copy of a film to a phonogram or film producer, that author or performer shall retain the right to obtain an equitable remuneration for the rental".[63] It would appear that "author" in this context includes the "principal director" but does not include the producer of the phonogram or film. It is clear from the general tenor of the Directive and this provision that the payment which is envisaged is an "equitable remuneration *for the rental*".

Thus, it would appear that such remuneration must specifically relate to the rental of the phonogram or the film, and not to the remuneration payable in respect of the performer's performance. "Equitable remuneration" is not defined by the Directive. However, Recital 17 provides guidance as to the assessment of such remuneration. Recital 17 provides that "equitable remuneration must take account of the importance of the contribution of the authors and performers concerned to the phonogram or film". Remuneration would therefore depend upon an assessment of "the importance of contribution" of each author and performer in relation to each other; in other words it will depend upon the facts of each particular case and the meaning given to "contribution". However, difficulties may arise in applying this test. For example, a cameo appearance, of very limited duration, by an international star may give a film or phonogram a boost in the number of rentals. In such circumstances, is it to be said that "contribution" is to be assessed by reason of the artistic contribution of the performer, the length of his performance or his contribution to the financial success of the phonogram or film? It is submitted that all these factors, will be important in assessing the "equitable remuneration".

12.29   Recital 16 to the Directive provides that the remuneration for the rental may be paid "on the basis of one or several payments at any time on or after the conclusion of the contract". Thus, for example, an assess-

---

[60] *Ibid.,* Art. 13(7).
[61] *Ibid.,* Art. 13(6).
[62] "Author" in this context includes the "principal director".
[63] Directive 92/100, Art. 4(1).

ment of an equitable remuneration for rental may be made at the time of the conclusion of the contract and paid to the author or performer at its conclusion or thereafter.

It has been suggested[64] that Recital (16) only prescribes a method of payment. The fact of such payment does not absolve the producer from the requirement to pay the author or performer "an equitable remuneration". If, therefore, the rental of the phonogram or film proves to be more successful than is envisaged at the time of the assessment on which the initial payment is made further payments would have to be made to comply with the duty to provide an "equitable remuneration" is described in Recital (15) and Article 4(2) as unwaivable. If a flat rate payment, at or after the conclusion of the contract, is capable of amounting to full payment for the rental rights notwithstanding the success of the phonogram or film, its acceptance by the author or performer would, contrary to the provision of the Directive, amount to a waiver of an equitable remuneration.

Date from which remuneration payable. Article 13(8) provides that **12.30** Member States "may determine the date . . . from which the unwaivable right to an equitable remuneration . . . exists, provided that that date is no later than July 1, 1997". Thus, a Member State may determine that the right of equitable remuneration may take effect on any date from July 1, 1994, to July 1, 1997.

If, for example, the United Kingdom should provide that the right should be operative from July 1, 1995, only acts of rental occurring on or after that date, pursuant to contracts entered into before or after that date, will be subject to the rental rights. However, in the case of contracts concluded before July 1, 1994, "the unwaivable right to an equitable remuneration . . . [applies] only where authors or performers or those representing them have submitted a request to that effect before January 1, 1997".[65] In the absence of agreement concerning the level of remuneration, Member States may fix the level of equitable remuneration.[66]

Collection of "equitable remuneration". The right to obtain an equit- **12.31** able remuneration "may be entrusted to collecting societies representing authors or performers".[67] However, Member States in implementing the Directive, may require that the remuneration be collected through a collecting society and that such collection be from a party other than the producer (*e.g.* the rental outlet).[68]

---

[64] Rienbothe and von Lewinski, *op. cit.*, pp. 70–74.
[65] Directive 92/100, Art. 13(9).
[66] *Ibid.*, Art. 13(9). See Reinbothe & von Lewinski, *op cit.*, p. 128 where it is suggested that "Member State" includes judicial authorities.
[67] *Ibid.*, Recital 15, Art. 4(3).
[68] *Ibid.*, Art. 4(4).

12.32   **Duration of rental rights.** The term of the rental rights accorded to an "author" by the Directive is the life of the author plus 70 years.[69] In the case of performers, and phonogram and film producers, the rental rights will last at least until the end of a period of 50 years computed from the end of the year in which the performance was recorded.[70]

(c) *Infringement by performance, showing or playing of work in public*

(i) *Protected works*

Literary, dramatic or musical work

12.33   **General.** The "performance" in "public" of a literary, dramatic, or musical work, without the authority of the copyright owner, is an infringement of the copyright in that work.[71] For the purposes of the entertainment industry, the important forms of performance in public will, in general include any form of visual or acoustic presentation of the work, including presentation by means of a sound recording, film, broadcast or cable programme.[72] The protection afforded by this provision is particularly important in the context of the entertainment industry in that the public performance of a work represents an important source of revenue for composers, music publishers, film producers and record companies.[73] Its effect is that the playing, for example, of a sound recording in a discotheque, is a performance in public of the lyrics (*i.e.* a literary work) and music of a composition and the sound recording notwithstanding the fact that the sound recording of the lyrics and the music may have been made with the authority of the copyright owner. The person playing such sound recording in public will therefore require a licence from the PRS in respect of the lyrics and music, and from the PPL in respect of the sound recording.

Sound recording or film

12.34   It is an infringement of the copyright in a sound recording, or film, where a person without the authority of the owner shows the whole or a substantial part of such works in "public" without the authority of the owner.[74] However, copyright in such works is not infringed where they

---

[69] Directive 93/98: [1993] O.J. L290/9, Art. 2. See *ante*, para. 8.07, n.11.
[70] *Ibid.*, Art. 3.
[71] Copyright, Designs and Patents Act 1988, s.19(1).
[72] *Ibid.*, s.19(2)(b).
[73] Such public performing rights are, in general, controlled by the collecting societies on behalf of the copyright owners. For a description of such societies see *ante*, paras. 9.15–9.20.
[74] Copyright, Designs and Patents Act 1988, s.19(3).

are included in a broadcast or cable programme which is shown or played in public to an audience which has not paid for admission.[75] Therefore, where X shows a broadcast of "Top of the Pops" to the non-paying customers of his public house, insofar as such broadcasts consists of sound recordings he will not infringe the copyright in the sound recording. He will, however, require a licence from the PRS in respect of the underlying musical and literary works in the sound recording.

Broadcast or cable programme

Infringement of broadcast or cable programme. This subject is dealt **12.35** with under "Broadcast and Cable", *ante*, paragraphs 10.23 to 10.25.

(ii) *Performance in public*

The expression "in public" has no statutory definition in the context of **12.36** copyright law. It has, however, been the subject of a number of judicial decisions which have sought to set out the approach to defining the scope and extent of the private, as opposed to public, performance of a work.

The question of what is a performance "in public" involves both law in the sense that the true meaning of the words "in public" must be ascertained as a matter of law, and fact in the sense that it must be determined whether the facts of the case do or do not fall within that meaning.[76] In deciding whether a performance is "in public", the character of the audience is the decisive factor.[77] Where the performance is given to an audience which has certain features pointing to the performance being in public and other features pointing to the performance in private, for example, performances given to members of clubs[78] and performances given by employers to employees,[79] there is a relationship between the giver of the performance and the audience which raises the possibility of the performance being treated as being in private and the court has to decide whether the public or private features prevail. The correct approach to determining whether a

---

[75] *Ibid.*, s.72(1)(b). See also *ante*, paras. 9.15–9.20.
[76] *Jennings v. Stephens* [1936] 1 Ch. 469, C.A.; *Ernest Turner Electrical Instruments Ltd. v. Performing Right Society Ltd.* [1943] 1 Ch. 167, C.A.
[77] *Jennings v. Stephens* [1936] 1 Ch. 469; *Ernest Turner Electrical Instruments Ltd. v. Performing Right Society Ltd.* [1943] Ch. 167; *Performing Right Society v. Harlequin Shops* [1979] 1 W.L.R. 851.
[78] *Jennings v. Stephens* [1936] 1 Ch. 469.
[79] *Ernest Turner Electrical Instruments Ltd. v. Performing Right Society Ltd.* [1943] 1 Ch. 167; *Performing Right Society v. Hammond's Bradford Brewery Co. Ltd.* [1934] Ch. 121, C.A.

performance is "in public" or private and domestic was set out in by Greene L.J. in *Jennings v. Stephens*,[80] when he observed:

> "The question may . . . be usefully approached by inquiring whether or not the act complained of as an infringement would, if done by the owner of the copyright himself, have been an exercise of the statutory right conferred upon him. In other words, the expression "in public" must be considered in relation to the owner of the copyright himself. If the audience considered in relation to the owner of the copyright may be properly described as the owner's 'public; or part of his 'public', then in performing the work before that audience he would in my opinion be exercising the statutory right conferred upon him; and any one who without his consent performed the work before that audience would be infringing his copyright."

12.37   Thus, in determining whether a performance is in public, where there are certain features pointing to the performance being in public and other features pointing to the performance being in private, the primary matter to consider is the "relationship of the audience to the owner of the copyright rather than the relationship of the audience to the performer"[81] and in that determination the effect which the performance has on the value of the copyright owner's exclusive rights in the work is a consideration of "great importance".[82] Therefore, where a person organises a private party in his own home it is reasonable to assume that use of the copyright work is not redounding to the financial disadvantage of the owner of the copyright, since the selected audience is not enjoying the work under conditions in which they would normally pay for the privilege in one form or another and a performance of the work in such conditions would ordinarily be in private.

Where, however, the proprietors of a factory relayed to their employees who numbered about 600 while they were at work, programmes of music broadcast by the BBC and also records which were played at the factory and relayed by loudspeakers the performance was held to be "in public". Such persons being part of "the owner's public or part of his public". An important consideration being the effect on the value of the exclusive rights of the copyright owner if such performances were to be allowed to take place at any factory without the con-

---

[80] *Jennings v. Stephens* [1936] 1 Ch. 469, C.A., approved *Erest Turner Electrical Instruments Ltd. v. Performing Right Society Ltd.* [1943] 1 Ch. 166, C.A.; *Performing Right Society Ltd. v. Rangers F.C. Supporters Club* [1975] R.P.C. 626.

[81] *Jennings v. Stephens* [1936] 1 Ch. 469, C.A., approved *Ernest Turner Electrical Instruments Ltd. v. Performing Right Society Ltd.* [1943] 1 Ch. 166, C.A.; *Performing Right Society Ltd. v. Rangers F.C. Supporters Club* [1975] R.P.C. 626.

[82] *Ernest Turner Electrical Instruments Ltd. v. Performing Right Society Ltd.* [1943] 1 Ch. 166, C.A.; *Performing Right Society Ltd. v. Rangers F.C. Supporters Club* [1975] R.P.C. 626.

sent of the copyright owner.[83] On these principles, performance of copyright works in hotel rooms for the enjoyment of guests would, it is submitted, amount to performance "in public".[84]

Where, however, a performance is given in circumstances which, on any normal meaning of the words, could not be treated as anything but "in public" the expression is to be given its ordinary usage and is not to be defined by a special meaning which they would not bear in such ordinary usage.[85] This is illustrated by *Performing Right Society Ltd. v. Harlequin Record Shops Ltd*,[86] where a performance given to an audience consisting of persons present in a shop which the public at large were permitted to enter without payment or invitation, with a view of increasing the shop owner's profit was held to be "only properly be described as a performance 'in public'" within the ordinary usage of the word. **12.38**

(d) *Infringement by broadcasting or including work in a cable programme service*

The broadcasting[87] of the work, or its inclusion in a cable programme service[88] is an act restricted by the copyright in a literary, dramatic, musical or artistic work,[89] a sound recording or film,[90] or a broadcast or cable programme.[91] **12.39**

(e) *Infringement by adaptations*

General. Literary, dramatic and musical works are the raw material of the entertainment industry. Consequently, an important aspect of the industry is the adaptation of such works so as to create the final product of a film, sound recording or a dramatic production in the theatre. **12.40**

Exclusive right to make adaptation. The owner of the copyright in a work has the exclusive right to make an adaptation of a work or to copy the adaptation, issue copies of it to the public, perform it in public, broadcast or include it in a cable programme service.[92] Thus, for **12.41**

---

[83] *Ernest Turner Electrical Instruments Ltd. v. Performing Right Society Ltd.* [1943] 1 Ch. 166, C.A.
[84] *Rank Film Production Ltd. v. Dodds* [1983] 2 N.S.W.L.R. 553.
[85] *Performing Right Society Ltd. v. Harlequin Record Shops Ltd.* [1979] 1 W.L.R. 851, *per* Browne-Wilkinson J.; see also *Canadian Admiral Corporation Ltd. v. Rediffusion Inc.* [1954] Ex.C.R. 382.
[86] [1979] 1 W.L.R. 851.
[87] For the meaning of "Broadcasting" see *ante*, para. 10.01.
[88] For meaning of "cable programme service" see *ante*, para. 10.13.
[89] Copyright, Designs and Patents Act 1988, s.20(a).
[90] *Ibid.*, s.20(b).
[91] *Ibid.*, s.20(c).
[92] *Ibid.*, ss. 16(1)(e), 21(1). See also *ante*, para. 10.26.

example, the copyright owner of a novel has the exclusive right to make, or authorize, an adaptation of the novel in the form of a screen or stage play. Thus, where X, a film producer, wishes to produce a film of Y's novel, an infringement of the exclusive right of adaptation will take place if X, without the authority of Y, commissions Z to write a screenplay. Such an infringement will take place even though X's intention is to solicit finance to produce the film whereupon he intends to negotiate with Y for the acquisition of the film rights.

12.42 **Adaptation of literary or dramatic work.** Adaptation in relation to literary and dramatic works, in so far as is relevant to the entertainment industry, means:

(a) a translation of the work[93]; or

(b) a version of a dramatic work in which it is converted into a non dramatic form, or vice versa.[94]

For these purposes an adaptation is made when it is recorded, in writing or otherwise.[95]

12.43 **Adaptation of musical work.** The adaptation of musical works means an arrangement or transcription of the work.[96]

3. Secondary Infringement

(a) *Introduction*

12.44 **General.** The 1988 Act sets out five categories of secondary infringement of copyright which may be committed by a person:

(a) infringement by importing an article which he knows or has "reason to believe" is an "infringing copy"[97];

(b) infringement by possessing or dealing with an article which "he knows or has reason to believe" is an "infringing copy"[98];

(c) infringement by providing an article specifically designed or adapted for making copies of a specific work "knowing or having reason to believe" that it is to be used to make "infringing copies"[99];

---

[93] *Ibid.*, s.21(3)(i).
[94] *Ibid.*, s.21(3)(a)(ii). See *ante*, para. 8.26 *et seq.*
[95] *Ibid.*, s.21(1).
[96] *Ibid.*, s.21(3)(b).
[97] *Ibid.*, s.22.
[98] *Ibid.*, s.23.
[99] *Ibid.*, s.24.

(d) infringement by permitting the use of premises for infringing performance unless when he gave permission he "believed on reasonable grounds" that the performance would not infringe copyright[1]; and

(e) infringement,[2]   **12.45**

    (i) by the provision of apparatus for infringing performances when "he knew or had reason to believe" at the time he supplied the apparatus that it would be used to infringe copyright[3]; or

    (ii) in the case where the normal use of the apparatus involves public performance, playing or showing he "did not believe on reasonable ground" that it would not be used to infringe copyright[4]; or

    (iii) by giving permission for apparatus to be brought onto the premises "when he knew or had reason to believe" that the apparatus was likely to be used to infringe copyright[5]; or

    (iv) by supplying a copy of a sound recording or film used to infringe copyright when he "knew or had reason to believe" that what he supplied or a copy made directly or indirectly from it, was likely to be used to infringe copyright.[6]

As will be readily seen it is a requirement of all categories of secondary infringement that some degree of knowledge is possessed by the alleged infringer that the copy or activity constituted an infringement of copyright in the work. In addition, it is a common feature of (a), (b) and (c) that the infringing act consists in dealing with an "infringing copy" of the work.

(i) *Degree of "knowledge" of infringement required*

"Did not believe on reasonable grounds". Reference should be made to   **12.46**
post, paragraph 14.16 for a discussion of this requirement.

"Knew or had reason to believe". It has been suggested[7] that the   **12.47**
change of wording from "if to his knowledge" as appeared in the equivalent provisions under the Copyright Act 1956[8] to "knew or had reason to believe" in the 1988 Act has not materially affected the pre-1988 Act law as regards the degree of knowledge except "to render liable

---

[1] *Ibid.*, s.25.
[2] *Ibid.*, s.26.
[3] *Ibid.*, s.26(2).
[4] *Ibid.*, s.26(2)(b).
[5] *Ibid.*, s.26(3).
[6] *Ibid.*, s.26(4).
[7] *Copinger and Skone James on Copyright* (Sweet & Maxwell, 13th ed., 1991), para. 9–18.
[8] Copyright Act 1956, ss.5(2), (3); 16(2), (3).

a defendant who has negligently failed to make inquiry".[9] Under the 1956 Act the requisite degree of knowledge on the part of the defendant which fell to be proved was actual not constructive knowledge.[10] This is subject, however, to a number of limiting principles.

First, a person who deliberately refrains from inquiry and shuts his eyes to that which is obvious, cannot be heard to say that he lacked the requisite knowledge.[11]

Secondly, actual knowledge may be inferred on the "part of a particular person on the assumption that such person has the ordinary understanding expected of persons in his line of business. In other words, the true position is that the court is not concerned with the knowledge of a reasonable man but is concerned with reasonable inferences to be drawn from a concrete situation as disclosed in the evidence as it affects the particular person whose knowledge is in issue."[12]

Thus, where it is proved by evidence that the particular person habitually participates in the line of business or has opportunities for knowledge and there is nothing to indicate that there are obstacles to the particular person acquiring the relevant knowledge there is some evidence from which the court can conclude that such a person has the knowledge.

12.48   However, "[u]nless a defendant has some degree of specific knowledge about a specific [infringing copy], his general knowledge that a [copy] is quite likely to be a pirate does not . . . fix him with knowledge sufficient for these provisions that the [copy] was made in breach of copyright."[13] Thus, where the proprietor of a shop hiring pre-recorded video-cassettes knows that a proportion of the video-cassettes are infringing copies but does not know which although he has the expertise to find out, such general knowledge is insufficient to fix him with the requisite degree of knowledge. The general knowledge possessed in such circumstances is equally consistent with a specific video tape being an infringing or a legitimate copy.

12.49   **Burden of proof.** The burden of proof is upon the plaintiff to show "belief on reasonable grounds" or actual knowledge. Where there is no, or not sufficient, evidence to establish such knowledge, it is customary

---

[9] *Copinger and Skone James on Copyright* (13th ed.), para. 9–18.
[10] *Politechnika v. Dallas Print Transfers Ltd.* [1982] F.S.R. 529; *Hoover plc v. George Hulme Ltd.* [1982] F.S.R. 565; *Columbia Pictures Inc. v. Robinson* [1987] 1 Ch. 38.
[11] *Columbia Pictures Inc. v. Robinson* [1987] 1 Ch. 38.
[12] *R.C.A. Corporation v. Custom Cleared Sales Pty. Ltd.* [1978] F.S.R. 576; approved in *Hoover plc. v. George Hulme Ltd.* [1982] F.S.R. 565; cf. *Infrabrics Ltd. v. Jaytex Shirt Co. Ltd.* [1978] 451 at 464–465 where Whitford J. was of the opinion that "knowledge" means notice which would put a reasonable man on inquiry.
[13] *Columbia Pictures Inc. v. Robinson* [1987] 1 Ch. 38.

practice to serve notice upon the party dealing in the infringing copy notifying him of the specific article which it is alleged is an infringing copy. After sending such a notice an alleged infringer is entitled to a "reasonable opportunity of making inquiries" whether the work infringes copyright or not.[14] What amounts to a reasonable time is a question of fact.[15] If after the expiration of such reasonable time the alleged infringer carries on the infringing activity he will be fixed with the requisite degree of knowledge.

(ii) *Meaning of "infringing copy"*

An article is an infringing copy in either of two circumstances[16]: First, if **12.50** its making constituted an infringement of the copyright in question.[17] Secondly, if:

(1) the article has been or is proposed to be imported into the United Kingdom,[18] and

(2) its making in the United Kingdom would have constituted an infringement of the copyright in the work in question, or a breach of an exclusive licence agreement relating to that work.[19]

The first category presents little difficulty. The second, however, requires further analysis.

In determining whether an imported copy of a work is an infringing copy it is necessary to enquire whether, first, there is exclusive licence agreement relating to the alleged infringing article and or, secondly, had that article been manufactured in the United Kingdom whether it would have been an infringement of copyright.

Exclusive licensee. The first limb of this enquiry has the consequence **12.51** that if an exclusive licence has been granted of the exclusive rights for the United Kingdom in respect of the manufacture and distribution in the United Kingdom, any unauthorised importation into the United Kingdom of an article, the subject of the exclusive licence, would make the imported article an infringing copy. Thus, where an exclusive licence has been granted to Y to manufacture and distribute a sound recording in the United Kingdom, the importation by X of sound

---

[14] *Van Dusen v. Kritz* [1936] 2 K.B. 176 at 182.
[15] *Ibid.* at 182.
[16] In relation to an article made on or after June 1, 1957 but before commencement of the 1988 Act, "infringing copy" is to be determined by the 1956 Act. Where the article was made before June 1, 1957 "infringing copy" is to be determind by reference to the 1911 Act.
[17] Copyright, Designs and Patents Act 1988, s.27(2).
[18] *Ibid.*, s.27(3)(a).
[19] *Ibid.*, s.27(3)(b).

recordings which form the subject matter of the exclusive licence would constitute such sound recordings infringing copies.

12.52 **Hypothetical manufacturer test.** The second limb of the enquiry gives rise to the "hypothetical manufacturer" test. Namely, "Would the hypothetical making of the article in the United Kingdom have been an infringement? In determining this question the actual maker and not the importer of the alleged infringing article is treated as the hypothetical maker in the United Kingdom.[20]

Therefore, where, for example, Wild Records Ltd., which is the owner of the copyright in a sound recording, grants an exclusive licence to Gentle Records Inc., for the manufacture and distribution of the sound recording in the United States and X buys such records in the United States and imports them into the United Kingdom for sale, Gentle Records Inc., being the manufacturer of the sound recordings in the United States is treated as the hypothetical manufacturer in the United Kingdom. Due to the fact that Gentle Records Inc. has only rights to the United States manufacture and distribution of the sound recording such hypothetical manufacture is an infringement of Wild Record's copyright. The copies imported by X will consequently be "infringing copies". However, it would appear that where, for example, Wild Records itself manufactures and distributes the sound recordings in the United Kingdom and exports them into the United States, the purchase in the United States and importation of such sound recordings into the United Kingdom by X would not constitute the articles infringing copies, unless there was a United Kingdom exclusive licence agreement extant, because the actual and hypothetical manufacturer and the copyright owner are the same.

12.53 **Parallel import.** Where, however, Wild Records Ltd. (U.K.) manufactures and distributes sound recordings in Germany and X purchases such recordings in Germany and imports them into the United Kingdom with a view to sale, such sound recordings will not amount to infringing copies.[21] In such circumstances, Wild Records will have exhausted its rights in the sound recordings within the European Union in so far as the sale of the sound recordings is concerned, and will not be entitled to prohibit the purchase and importation into any other Member State. The exhaustion of rights in these circumstances will not, however, exhaust the right of the copyright owner to prohibit

---

[20] *C.B.S. United Kingdom Ltd. v. Charmdale Record Distributors Ltd.* [1981] Ch. 91.
[21] Copyright, Designs and Patents Act 1988, s.27(5).

the unauthorised rental or performance rights in the sound recording, or as the case may be a film, following such purchase.[22]

(b) *Infringement by importing infringing copy*

The copyright in a work is infringed by a person who, without the licence of the copyright owner, imports into the United Kingdom, otherwise than for his private and domestic use an article which is, and which he knows, or has reason to believe, is an infringing copy of the work.[23] **12.54**

Infringing copy. Reference should be made to *supra*, paragraphs 12.50 to 12.53 for the meaning of "infringing copy". **12.55**

Knowledge. Reference should be made to *ante*, paragraph 12.47 for the requisite degree of knowledge. **12.56**

"Private and domestic use". No definition is provided in the 1988 Act. It is submitted, however, that a useful approach to determining this question is that adopted in relation to the determination of performance "in public".[24] The defendant bears the burden of proving, on a balance of probabilities, that the importation was for private and domestic use. **12.57**

(c) *Infringement by possessing or dealing with infringing copy*

A person infringes the copyright in a work in any of four circumstances where, without the licence of the copyright owner, he deals with an article which is, and which he knows or has reason to believe is, an infringing copy of the work.[25] These circumstances occur where the person: **12.58**

(a) possesses the article in the course of business;

(b) sells or lets it for hire, or offers or exposes it for sale or hire;

(c) in the course of a business exhibits the article in public or distributes it; or

(d) distributes it otherwise than in the course of business to such extent as to affect prejudicially the owner of the copyright.

It therefore follows, for example, that where the owner of a video rental outlet has in his possession a video-cassette, which he knows or has reason to believe is an infringing copy, he infringes the rights of the

---

[22] Case 78/70, *Deutsche Grammophon v. Metro*: [1979] E.C.R. 487; Case 158/86, *Warner Brothers Inc. v. Erik Viuff Christiansen*: [1988] E.C.R. 2625; Case 341/87, *EMI Electrola GmbH v. Patricia Im-und Export*: [1989] E.C.R. 72.
[23] Copyright, Designs and Patents Act 1988, s.22.
[24] See *ante*, paras. 12.36–12.38.
[25] Copyright, Designs and Patents Act 1988, s.23.

owner by exposing or letting it for hire within (a), (b), (c). An infringement is likely to take place within (d) where an infringing article is distributed in such a manner as to deprive the copyright owner of licence fees or sales.

(d) *Providing means for making infringement copies*

12.59   **Infringement by specially adapted equipment.** A person who, without the licence of the copyright owner, makes, imports into the United Kingdom, possesses or sells or lets for hire, or offers for sale or hire "an article specifically designed or adapted for making copies of that work, knowing or having reason to believe that it is to be used to make infringing copies" infringes the copyright in the work.[26] It is submitted that this provision is not intended to reverse the effect of *C.B.S. Songs Ltd. v. Amstrad Consumer Electronics Plc*,[27] in that the provision is intended to have effect in respect of equipment and master recordings which are designed or adapted for the specific purpose of copying a work. Where, therefore the equipment or article is capable of infringing and non-infringing purposes, it would appear not to come within the provision.

12.60   **Infringement by recipient of telecommunications signals.** The use of a telecommunication system[28] to transmit a work, without the licence of the copyright owner, to a place within the United Kingdom or elsewhere, knowing or having reason to believe that infringing copies of the work will be made by means of the reception of the transmission, amounts to an infringement of copyright in the work.[29] Thus, where X, situated in the United Kingdom, uses a satellite or other telecommunications system to transmit sound recordings or films to Y in France, with the intention that on receipt Y will copy the works, an infringement will take place notwithstanding the fact that the copying takes place in France and not the United Kingdom. What matters is that the person transmitting the signal via the system does so from the United Kingdom and knows or has reason to believe that infringing copies will be made by means of the reception.

(e) *Permitting use of premises for infringing performance*

12.61   Where the copyright in a literary, dramatic or musical work is infringed by a performance at a place of public entertainment, the person who gave permission for that place to be used for the performance is also

---

[26] *Ibid.*, s.24(1).
[27] [1988] 1 A.C. 1013.
[28] A "telecommunication system" means a system for conveying visual images, sounds or other information by electronic means: Copyright, Designs and Patents Act 1988, s.178.
[29] Copyright, Designs and Patents Act 1988, s.24(2).

liable for the infringements, unless when he gave permission he believed on reasonable grounds that the performance would not infringe copyright.[30] In order to found liability the plaintiff will have to prove first that copyright is infringed by the performance and secondly that the person gave permission for the performance at the place of public entertainment and thirdly that he believed on reasonable grounds that the performance would infringe copyright.

Place of public entertainment. The expression "place of public enter- **12.62** tainment" includes premises which are occupied mainly for other purposes but are from time to time made available for hire for the purposes of public entertainment.[31] A place of public entertainment will therefore not only include a place such as a theatre or discotheque but will also include a private club which is hired out from time to time.

Permission. In order to succeed in establishing liability in respect of the **12.63** granting of permission the plaintiff must adduce evidence of permission given by the defendant that "particularly relates to the work the performance which is complained of".[32] However, the court may infer an authorization or permission from acts which fall short of being direct and positive "for indifference, exhibited by acts of commission or omission, may reach a degree from which authorization or permission may be inferred".[33] It is, however, a question of fact in each case what is the true inference to be drawn from the conduct of the person who is said to have permitted the use of the place of entertainment for the performance complained of.

(f) *Provision of apparatus for infringing performance, etc.*

General. The 1988 Act provides that three different categories of per- **12.64** sons are liable for infringement where copyright in a work is infringed by a public performance of the work, or by the playing or showing of the work in public, by means of apparatus for:

(a) playing sound recordings;

(b) showing films; or

(c) receiving visual images or sounds conveyed by electronic means, the following persons are liable for infringement of copyright.

These persons are as follows.

---

[30] *Ibid.*, s.25(1).
[31] *Ibid.*, s.25(2).
[32] *Performing Right Society v. Ciryl Theatrical Syndicate* [1924] 1 K.B. 1 at 13, 15.
[33] *Ibid.* at 9, *per* Bankes L.J.

12.65 Supplier of apparatus. A supplier of the apparatus, or any substantial part of it, is liable for infringement in either of two circumstances. First, if when he supplied the apparatus or part of it he knew or had reason to believe that the apparatus would be used to infringe copyright.[34] Secondly, in the case of apparatus whose normal use involves a public performance, playing or showing, he did not believe on reasonable grounds that it would not be so used to infringe copyright.[35] The first type of infringing activity might typically occur where a sound system is supplied and utilised for a "rave" and a common example of the second type of infringing activity is the provision of karaoke machines for the use in public houses and clubs where the proprietor has not obtained a PRS licence.

12.66 Occupier of premises. An occupier of premises infringes copyright where he gives permission for the apparatus to be brought on to the premises if, when he gave permission, he knew or had reason to believe the apparatus was likely to be used to infringe copyright.[36] Thus, where the owner or manager of a public house allows a karaoke machine onto his premises without himself holding or obtaining a PRS licence it is likely that he will be held to know "or had reason to believe the apparatus was likely to be used to infringe copyright".

12.67 The supplier of the sound recording or film. The supplier of a copy of a sound recording or film used to infringe copyright is also liable for the infringement if when he supplied it he knew or had reason to believe that what he supplied, or a copy made directly or indirectly from it, was likely to be used to infringe copyright.[37] Thus, if X supplies a sound recording for use at a "rave" knowing or having reason to believe that no licence has been obtained from PRS or PPL by the organiser of the "rave", he will have supplied a copy of a sound recording used to infringe copyright.

4. Permitted Acts

12.68 General. Chapter III of the Copyright Act 1988 sets out in forty-nine sections the acts permitted in relation to copyright works. For the purposes of this work it is proposed to consider only those exceptions which are particularly relevant to the entertainment industry. Where a

---

[34] Copyright, Designs and Patents Act 1988, s.26(2)(a).
[35] *Ibid.*, s.26(2)(b).
[36] *Ibid.*, s.26(1).
[37] *Ibid.*, s.26(4).

particular permitted act is not considered in detail in this work reference should be made to a standard work[38] on copyright.

The permitted acts which are set out in Chapter III of the 1988 Act are
acts which may be done notwithstanding the subsistence of copyright.
They relate only to the question of infringement of copyright and do not
affect any other right or obligation restricting the doing of any specified
acts.[39] For example, where copyright works have been communicated in
confidence, such communication may be impressed with an "obligation
of confidence".[40] In such circumstances the mere fact that the doing of
an act in relation to that work is a permitted act under Chapter III of the
1988 Act does not prevent that act from amounting to a breach of confidence.

(a) *Fair dealing*

In relation to the entertainment industry the "fair dealing" exception   **12.69**
provided by Chapter III represents the most important of the permitted
acts. The 1988 Act provides that "fair dealing" for the purposes of
research, or private study,[41] criticism, or review[42] and the reporting of
current events[43] does not infringe any copyright. Fair dealing in relation to criticism or review and the reporting of current events can, however,   only   be   relied   upon   if   accompanied   by   "sufficient
acknowledgement.[44] No acknowledgement is, however, required in
connection with the reporting of current events by means of a sound
recording, film, broadcast or cable programme.[45]

Fair dealing. "Fair dealing" is a matter of impression, fact and degree.[46]   **12.70**
Among the relevant factors to be taken into consideration in deciding
whether the dealing is "fair" will be "the number and extent of the quo-
tations and extracts . . . [T]he use made of them. If they are used as a
basis for comment, criticism or review that may be fair dealing. If they
are used to convey the same information as the author for a rival purpose that may be unfair. Next, you must consider the proportions. To

---

[38] See *Copinger and Skone James on Copyright* (13th ed., 1991), Chap. 10.
[39] Copyright, Designs and Patents Act 1988, s.28(2).
[40] For the rights and liabilities arising in such circumstances see "Breach of confidence",
post, para. 17.01 *et seq.*
[41] Copyright, Designs and Patents Act 1988, s.29(1); but note that this exception is limited
to literary, dramatic, musical or artistic works.
[42] *Ibid.*, s.30(1).
[43] *Ibid.*, s.30(2). See *post*, para. 12.74 for the meaning of "current events".
[44] *Ibid.*, s.30(1), (2). For meaning of "sufficient acknowledgement", see, *infra*, para. 12.72.
[45] *Ibid.*, s.30(3).
[46] *Hubbard v. Vosper* [1972] 2 Q.B. 84, C.A.; *Sillitoe v. McGraw-Hill Book Co. (U.K.) Ltd.*
[1983] F.S.R. 545; *British Broadcasting Corporation Ltd. v. British Satellite Broadcasting Ltd.*
[1992] Ch. 141.

take long extracts and attach short comments may be unfair. But short extracts and long comments may be fair".[47]

An unpublished work is not automatically excluded from the defence of fair dealing but the fact that it may have been leaked is an important factor in determining whether the dealing with it is fair.[48]

12.71   The fair dealing must be for the approved purpose,[49] namely criticism, review or the reporting of current events, and any oblique motive may render the dealing unfair.[50] But, if a programme is a genuine reporting of current events or criticism or review it would appear to matter not that the inclusion of the work may also serve other purposes, such as making the programme attractive to viewers.[51] The fact, for example, that the broadcaster using the material and claiming the benefit of the fair dealing defence is a commercial rival of the copyright owner does not, *ipso facto*, take the case outside fair dealing. It is a factor to be taken into consideration whether there has been fair dealing, and in some cases it may be of great importance, but "it is no more than a factor".[52]

12.72   Sufficient acknowledgement. A "sufficient acknowledgement" will take place where there is an acknowledgement identifying the work used by its title or other description and identifying the author if known.[53] In *Sillitoe v. McGraw-Hill Book Co. (U.K.) Ltd.*[54] it was said that in order to amount to "sufficient acknowledgement" for these purposes an acknowledgement must recognise the position or claims of the copyright holder.

Criticism or review and reporting of current events

12.73   Criticism or review. "Fair dealing" with a work for the purposes of criticism or review of that or another work, or performance of a work, does not infringe any copyright in the work provided that it is accompanied by "sufficient acknowledgement".[55] This category of "fair dealing" is of particular importance to television broadcasters in that it

---

[47] *Hubbard v. Vosper* [1972] 2 Q.B. 84 at 94, C.A.; followed *Sillitoe v. McGraw-Hill Book Co. (U.K.) Ltd.* [1983] F.S.R. 545 and *British Broadcasting Corporation Ltd. v. British Satellite Broadcasting Ltd.* [1992] Ch. 141.
[48] *Beloff v. Pressdram Ltd.* [1973] 1 All E.R. 241.
[49] *Ibid.* at 262.
[50] *Johnstone v. Bernard Jones Publications Ltd.* [1938] Ch. 599 at 607.
[51] *British Broadcasting Corporation v. British Satellite Broadcasting Ltd.* [1992] Ch. 141.
[52] *Ibid.; cf. Independent Television Publications Ltd. v. Time Out Ltd. v. Time Out Ltd.* [1984] F.S.R. 64.
[53] Copyright, Designs and Patents Act 1988, s.178.
[54] [1983] F.S.R. 545.
[55] Copyright, Designs and Patents Act, s.30(1).

permits the use of clips from films and excerpts from a sound recording for the purposes of, *inter alia*, creating review programmes.

For example, it would be permissible within the terms of this defence for a broadcaster to create a programme whose purpose is to review new films or plays. In so doing, the broadcaster may use clips from the films without the consent of the owner so as to create the review programme subject to the "fair dealing"[56] defence, and provided that there is "sufficient acknowledgement" in relation to such clips.

The same principles apply with regard to criticism. A programme which has as its purpose the review of films or a dramatic performance in the theatre will inevitably also contain criticism of the film or dramatic performance, for only in so doing will it be able to assist its intended public in making an informed choice.

Reporting of current events. "Fair dealing" with a work, other than a **12.74** photograph, for the purpose of reporting current events does not infringe any copyright in the work provided that it is accompanied by "sufficient acknowledgement".[57] However, no acknowledgement is required if the reporting is by means of a sound recording, film, broadcast or cable programme.[58] What constitutes "current events" is not capable of a succinct or precise definition. As a general principle, however, the reporting must be of a current as opposed to a historical event, but there may be cases where the publication of historical material may be necessary to report current events. This was graphically illustrated in *Associated Newspapers plc. v. News Group Ltd.*[59] by Walton J. where he observed:

> "One has only to think, for example, of correspondence dealing with nuclear reactors which have just blown up or have a core melt down: that might date from a very considerable period previous to the event happening, but would be of a topical nature in order to enable a report on what had actually happened to be properly prepared."

This defence is not, however, restricted to the reporting of current **12.75** events within the context of general news programmes such as, for example, the BBC News, but may also include programmes solely concerned with reporting current sport events or other particular categories of current events.[60] Thus, any programme which has as its purpose the

---

[56] As to what amounts to "fair dealing", see *ante*, para. 12.70, "Fair dealing".
[57] Copyright, Designs and Patents Act, s.30(1).
[58] *Ibid.*, s.30(3).
[59] [1986] R.P.C. 515.
[60] *British Broadcasting Corporation v. British Satellite Broadcasting Ltd.* [1992] Ch. 141.

reporting of current events relating to any particular subject is capable of coming within the meaning of "reporting of current events".

The use of photographs is excluded from this fair use exception. This exception recognises that for some photographers the taking and licensing of the use of such photographs for reporting current events is the basis of their business and consequently any use without licence and payment will prejudicially affect such enterprises.

(b) *Incidental inclusion of copyright works*

12.76   Copyright in a work is not infringed by its incidental inclusion in a sound recording, film, broadcast or cable programme.[61] If, therefore, in making a "fly on the wall' documentary in a family's home a producer should film the family while it is watching television the inclusion of the television broadcast would be incidentally included. However, a musical work, words spoken or sung with music, or so much of a sound recording, broadcast or cable programme as includes a musical work or such words is not to be regarded as incidentally included if it is deliberately included.[62]

Thus, for example, where background music of the song "Money" is included by a producer in a documentary or television programme about money or finances such inclusion will not be incidental because it has been deliberately included. If, however, a documentary is made in, for example, a public house or discotheque and the music from loudspeakers in such places is captured on the soundtrack of the film such inclusion would not normally come within the definition of "deliberately included".

(c) *Notes and recordings of spoken words*

12.77   **General.** Where a record of spoken words is made, in writing or otherwise, for the purpose of "reporting current events"[63] or "of broadcasting or including in a cable programme service" the whole or part of the work,[64] it is not an infringement of any copyright in the words as a literary work to use the record or material taken from it (or to copy the record, or any such material, and use the copy) for "that purpose" providing:

(a) the record is a direct record of the spoken words and is not taken

---

[61] Copyright, Designs and Patents Act 1988, s.31(1).
[62] *Ibid.*, s.31(3).
[63] *Ibid.*, s.58(1)(a). See also *ante*, para. 12.74–12.75 for meaning of "current event".
[64] *Ibid.*, s.58(1)(b).

from a previous record or from a broadcast or cable programme[65];

(b) the *making* of the record was not prohibited by the speaker and, where copyright already subsisted in the work, did not infringe copyright[66];

(c) the use made of the record or material taken from it is not of a kind prohibited by or on behalf of the speaker or copyright owner *before* the record was made[67];

(*d*) the use is by or with the authority of a person who is lawfully in possession of the record.[68]

This defence is of particular relevance to the interviewing of individuals and the inclusion of such matters in news programmes and commentaries. It would appear, however, that to avail itself of the defence a broadcaster, for example, would have to show first that the conditions were satisfied and secondly that the material was used for "that purpose" for which it was recorded.

Making not prohibited by the speaker. The most important of the conditions is that "the making of the record was not prohibited by the speaker". It would appear that there is no duty placed on, for example, a broadcaster to seek the permission of the speaker for the making of the recording. Thus, the onus is on the speaker expressly to prohibit the recording before it is made if the broadcaster is to be deprived of the defence. If it was not so expressly prohibited prior to making the record, it would appear that the broadcaster may use it for the purpose for which it was made whether or not the speaker subsequently objects. **12.78**

Use of recorded material. The 1988 Act specifically refers to "use the record or material . . . for that purpose". It would appear therefore that the purpose for which the material may be used by the maker of the recording is limited to the purpose for which it was made, namely for one of the defined purposes (*i.e.* reporting of current events or of broadcasting or including in a cable programme service). Where the speaker does not completely prohibit the use of the recording but prohibits certain uses, for example the use in documentary programmes, although made in general for reporting current events, the defence is not available where the recording is subsequently incorporated in a documentary dealing with current events. **12.79**

---

[65] *Ibid.*, s.58(2)(a).
[66] *Ibid.*, s.58(2)(b).
[67] *Ibid.*, s.58(2)(c).
[68] *Ibid.*, s.58(2)(d).

(d) *Playing sound recordings for the purposes of non profit making clubs*

12.80 It is not an infringement of the copyright in a sound recording to play it as part of the activities of, or for the benefit, of a club, society or other organisation provided that the following conditions are met[69]:

(a) the organisation is not established or conducted for profit and its main objects are charitable or are otherwise concerned with the advancement of religion, education or social welfare[70]; and

(b) the proceeds of any charge for admission to the place where the sound recording is to be heard are applied solely for the purpose of that organisation.[71]

Thus, where the conditions are satisfied, the club, society or other organisation is under no obligation to obtain a licence from PPL in respect of the sound recording. The defence does not, however, apply to any musical work (or composition) included in such a sound recording in which copyright subsists. Consequently, there will be an infringement of the musical work incorporated in the sound recording unless a licence is obtained from the PRS in respect of the public performance of such musical works by the means of the sound recording.

(e) *Broadcast and cable programmes*

(i) *Incidental recording for purposes of broadcast or cable programmes*

12.81 A person authorised to broadcast or include in a cable programme a literary, dramatic or musical work, or an adaptation of such a work,[72] an artistic work,[73] or a sound recording or film has the following rights:

(a) in the case of a literary, dramatic or musical work or an adaptation of such a work he has right to make a sound recording or film of the work or an adaptation[74];

(b) in the case of an artistic work, to take a photograph or make a film of it[75];

(c) in the case of a sound recording to make a copy of it.[76]

---

[69] *Ibid.*, s.67(1).
[70] *Ibid.*, s.67(2)(a).
[71] *Ibid.*, s.67(2)(b).
[72] *Ibid.*, s.68(1)(a).
[73] *Ibid.*, s.68(1)(b).
[74] *Ibid.*, s.68(2)(a).
[75] *Ibid.*, s.68(2)(b).
[76] *Ibid.*, s.68(2)(d).

However, such recording, film, photograph or copy may not be used   **12.82**
for any other purpose than that licensed,[77] and must be destroyed
within 28 days of being first used for broadcasting the work or where
applicable, being included in a cable programme service.[78] Where
either of these conditions are not complied with the recording, film or
photograph is to be regarded as an infringing copy.[79] These rights
enable a person who has a right to broadcast a work to make a copy of
the work for the purposes of enabling it to exercise the right granted to
it. However, the right is somewhat restricted in that such copies cannot
be retained for a period exceeding twenty-eight days. In practice, such
rights will be of limited applicability due to the fact that it is generally
the practice of broadcasters to obtain the necessary rights without any
limitations as to destruction and use. Where such rights are not
obtained at the time of the contract, either through omission or because
the copyright owner refuses, the limited rights set out above will apply.

(ii) *Time-shift recording for private and domestic use*

This subject is discussed at *ante*, paragraph 10.31.   **12.83**

Free public showing or playing of broadcasts or cable programmes.   **12.84**
Reference should be made to *ante*, paragraphs 10.23 to 10.24 for a discussion of this defence.

Public interest. Where the enforcement of copyright would be such as   **12.85**
to prevent the disclosure of "iniquity" the courts may permit the publication of such copyright material notwithstanding the copyright
owner's refusal to authorise publication. For a discussion of the circumstances in which the court will so permit publication, see *post*, paragraphs 17.17 to 17.19.

(f) *Other statutory exemptions*

Additional exemptions in relation to public administration,[80] recording   **12.86**
or recitation of literary or dramatic works in public,[81] abstracts of scien-
tific and technical articles[82] artistic works[83] are set out in the 1988 Act.

---

[77] *Ibid.*, s.68(3)(a).
[78] *Ibid.*, s.68(3)(b).
[79] *Ibid.*, s.68(4).
[80] *Ibid.*, ss.45–50.
[81] *Ibid.*, s.59.
[82] *Ibid.*, s.60.
[83] *Ibid.*, ss.62–65.

REMEDIES FOR INFRINGEMENT OF COPYRIGHT

1. Jurisdiction

13.01 Copyright under the provisions of the Copyright, Designs and Patents Act 1988 is closely defined by territory.[1] The statutory right which is granted in respect of copyright is to do certain acts exclusively in the United Kingdom. Only acts done in the United Kingdom in contravention of those rights constitute an infringement, either direct or indirect, capable founding an action in England.[2] Thus, where a work which is protected under United Kingdom copyright law is the subject of reproduction in a foreign country and such reproduction would be an infringement if it were done in the United Kingdom, the matter is not justiciable in an English court. Furthermore, disputes arising under a foreign copyright law fall exclusively within the jurisdiction of the courts of the country by the law of which those rights were created.[3] It therefore follows, for example, that where X, a United Kingdom resident, infringes, in the United States, the copyright in a work created in the United Kingdom by Y, a United Kingdom resident, the English courts have no jurisdiction to determine whether the acts in the United States by X is or is not an infringement of Y's rights.

---

[1] See, *e.g.* Copyright, Designs and Patents Act 1988, ss.16, 17, 18, 19, 20, 21.
[2] *Deff Lepp Music v. Stuart-Brown* [1986] R.P.C. 273.
[3] *Tyburn Productions Ltd. v. Conan Doyle* [1990] 1 All E.R. 909.

Period of limitation. An action in respect of infringement of copyright **13.02**
may not be commenced after the expiration of six years after the
infringement.[4] However, where there is a recurring infringement successive limitation periods may apply.

2. Presumptions as to Copyright and Title

The United Kingdom does not possess the relatively sophisticated sys- **13.03**
tem of copyright registration operated through the Library of Congress
in the United States of America. Consequently, one of the difficulties in
any litigation involving the alleged infringement of copyright in a work
is the establishment of the plaintiff's title and the subsistence of copyright. A plaintiff is now considerably assisted in this task by the creation in the Copyright, Designs and Patents Act 1988 of certain
statutory presumptions which will apply in proceedings. These presumptions, in general, relate to ownership and subsistence of copyright
in works. A pre-condition of the availability of these presumptions is
that there be some form of notice or label on the copyright work.

(a) *Presumptions in relation to musical, literary and dramatic works*

Author named on work. Where a name purporting to be that of the **13.04**
author[5] appears on copies of the work as published or on the work
when it is made, the person whose name appears is to be presumed,
until the contrary is proved, to be the author[6] and it is to be presumed
that such works have not been made in the course of employment.[7] A
like presumption is applicable in respect of a work alleged to be of joint
authorship.[8]

Author not named on work. Where no name purporting to be that of **13.05**
the author appears on copies of the work as published, or when it is
made, but the work qualifies by reason of having been first published
in a qualifying territory[9] and a name purporting to be that of the publisher appeared on copies of the work when first published, the person
whose name so appeared is presumed, until the contrary is proved, to
have been the owner of copyright at the time of publication.[10]

---

[4] Limitation Act 1980, ss.2, 36(1).
[5] "Author" in this context is to be taken to mean the owner of the copyright.
[6] Copyright, Designs and Patents Act 1988, s.104(2)(a).
[7] *Ibid.*, s.104(2)(b).
[8] *Ibid.*, s.104(3). For the meaning of "joint authorship" see *ante*, para. 9.07, n.28.
[9] For meaning of "qualifying territory" see *ante*, paras. 8.07–8.08. For the meaning of "published", see *ante*, para. 8.06.
[10] Copyright, Designs and Patents Act 1988, s. 104(4).

13.06   Author dead or identity cannot be ascertained. If the author of a work is dead or his identity cannot be ascertained by reasonable inquiry, it is to be presumed, in the absence of evidence to the contrary, that the work is an original work and that the plaintiff's allegations as to the date and place of first publication are correct.[11]

(b) *Presumptions relating to sound recordings*

13.07   Where copies of a sound recording when issued to the public bear a label or other mark stating:

   (a) that a named person was the owner of copyright in the recording at the date of issue of the copies; or

   (b) that the recording was first published in a specified year or in a specified country,

the label or mark is admissible as evidence of the facts stated and is to be presumed correct unless the contrary is proved.[12] These presumptions apply equally to proceedings relating to an infringement alleged to have occurred before the date on which the copies were issued to the public.[13] Thus, where the work is made and the label or other mark attached but, before being issued to the public by the copyright owner, an infringer issues copies to the public, the presumption will apply notwithstanding the fact that at the date of infringement no copies of the legitimate copies had been placed on the market.

(c) *Presumptions relating to the films*

13.08   **Films issued to the public.** Where copies of a film when issued to the public bear a statement that:

   (a) a named person was the author or director[14] of the film[15]: or

   (b) a named person was the owner of the copyright in the film at the date of issue of the copies[16]; or

   (c) that the film was published in a specified year or in a specified country,[17]

the statement is admissible as evidence of the facts stated and it is to be presumed to be correct unless the contrary is proved.[18] This presump-

---

[11] *Ibid.*, s.104(5).
[12] *Ibid.*, s.105(1).
[13] *Ibid.*, s.105(4).
[14] This will be of importance in relation to the moral rights of the director.
[15] Copyright, Designs and Patents Act 1988, s.105(2)(a).
[16] *Ibid.*, s.105(2)(b).
[17] *Ibid.*, s.105(2)(c).
[18] *Ibid.*, s.105(2).

tion applies equally to proceedings relating to an infringement alleged to have occurred before the date on which the copies were issued to the public.[19]

Film shown in public, broadcast or included in a cable programme ser- **13.09**
vice.[20] Where a film which is shown in public, broadcast or included in a cable programme service bears a statement that:

(a) a named person was the author or director of the film[21]; or

(b) that a named person was the owner of copyright in the film immediately after it was made,[22]

the statement will be admissible as evidence of the facts stated and shall be presumed to be correct unless the contrary is proved.[23] This applies equally in proceedings relating to an infringement alleged to have occurred before the date on which the film was first shown in public, broadcast or included in a cable programme service.[24]

3. Remedies of Copyright Owner

Infringements of copyright are actionable at the suit of the copyright **13.10**
owner.[25] In such actions all such relief, by way of damages, injunction, account or otherwise is available to the plaintiff as is available in respect of any other property right.[26] However, it is clear that an owner in equity of copyright is entitled to move for an interlocutory injunction but cannot obtain a permanent injunction or other remedy without joining the legal owner of copyright.[27]

(a) *Damages*

Measure of damages. The measure of damages in an action for infringe- **13.11**
ment of copyright "is the depreciation caused by the infringement to the value of the copyright as a chose in action".[28] The heads of damage

---

[19] *Ibid.*, s.104(4).
[20] *Ibid.*, s.105.
[21] *Ibid.*, s.105(5)(a).
[22] *Ibid.*, s.105(5)(b).
[23] *Ibid.*, s.105(5).
[24] *Ibid.*, s.105(5).
[25] See *ante*, paras. 13.21–13.24 for rights of exclusive licensee.
[26] Copyright, Designs and Patents Act 1988, s.96.
[27] *Performing Right Society Ltd. v. London Theatre of Varieties Ltd.* [1924] A.C. 1, H.L.; *Merchant Adventurers Ltd. v. M. Grew & Co. Ltd.* [1972] 1 Ch. 242 at 252. See also *ante*, para. 7.05.
[28] *Sutherland Publishing Co. Ltd. v. Caxton Publishing Co. Ltd.* [1936] 323 at 336, *per* Lord Wright C.A; *Infabrics Ltd. v. Jaytex Shirt Co. Ltd.* [1984] R.P.C. 405 at 457; *Patterson Zochonis Ltd. v. Merfarken Packaging Ltd.* [1983] F.S.R. 273 at 281, 287, 294.

will generally fall into one of three categories.[29] First, a loss of reputation occurring as a result of the publication of the infringing work. Secondly, the loss of sales as a result of customers being diverted to the infringing article[30]; and thirdly damages on the basis of licence fees which would have been charged in respect of the infringing copies.[31] The second and third categories are of particular application in the entertainment industry where the copyright owner or exclusive licensee's income is derived from the sale or licensing of copyright works.

13.12   Diversion of customers to the defendant. Where the plaintiff claims damages on the basis of a diversion of customers to the defendant and consequently lost sales the burden of proof is on the plaintiff but the court does not require certainty of proof of the sale lost. Once it is shown that the sale or rental of infringing copies has taken place, some loss of legitimate sales may be properly assumed.[32] Where reasonable commercial expectations for the copyright work, for example, a film, are established by evidence, and where (a) in relation to other comparable films, the film has done poorly and (b) the presence of the infringing copies upon the market has been established, the copyright owner is entitled as against the infringer, in the absence of any other explanation for the lack of success of the film, to attribute the shortfall to the activities of the infringer.[33] Quantification of damages requires an estimate to be made of the number of lost sales; the maximum cannot in practice exceed the difference between the number actually sold and the number that would have needed to be sold to justify the commercial expectations, and the minimum will be the number of infringing copies that can be shown to have been sold.[34] Where, between these two extremes, the estimate of lost sales should fall, will depend on all the circumstances of the case, and in particular on the weight of the evidence of the legitimate commercial expectations. However, where there is no comparative evidence comparing the sales of the copyright work in question with sales of other such works, such an approach will not be a reliable guide to the loss caused by the sale or rental of infringing copies.

---

[29] *Lewis Trusts v. Bambers Stores Ltd.* [1983] F.S.R. 453 at 469.
[30] *Birn Bros Ltd. v. Keene & Co. Ltd.* [1918] 2 Ch. 281. See also *Pike v. Nicholas* (1869) 5 Ch.App. 251, 260; *Colburn v. Simms* (1843) 2 Hare 543 at 560; *Delfe v. Delamotte* (1857) 3 K. & J. 581.
[31] *Performing Right Society Ltd v. Bradford Corpn.* (1917–23) MacG.Cop.Cas. 309; *Lewis Trusts v. Bambers Stores Ltd.* [1983] F.S.R. 453 at 469.
[32] *Columbia Pictures v. Robinson* [1988] F.S.R. 531.
[33] *Ibid.*
[34] *Ibid.*

Licence fee which would have been charged. An alternative basis for **13.13**
assessing damages is to award such sum as would be a fair remuneration or royalty as would have been paid to the copyright owner for a
licence to use the copyright for the purpose for which it was used.[35]
Where there is an established licence fee for the use of a work, as in the
case of PRS and PPL, such fees would, prima facie, be a fair fee or
royalty for the use of such work.

"Additional damages". Section 97(2) of the 1988 Act provides that: **13.14**

> "(2) The court may in an action for infringement of copyright hav-
> ing regard to all the circumstances, and in particular to—
> (a) the flagrancy of the infringement, and
> (b) any benefit accruing to the defendant by reason of the
> infringement,
> award such additional damages as the justice of the case may
> require."

This provision confers a discretion on the court to award damages
which would not usually be recoverable under the normal rules relating
to remoteness and proof of damage.[36] There is, however, no clear test as
to the circumstances in which such damages will be awarded.[37]
"Flagrancy" of the infringement and its benefit to the defendant are
expressly mentioned as material but the court must have "regard to all
the circumstances". It has been suggested that "[t]hese include such
matters as the defendants' conduct with regard to the infringement and
the motive for it, injury to the plaintiff's feeling for suffering insults,
indignities and the like; and also the plaintiff's corresponding behaviour".[38] Thus, in *William v. Settle*,[39] additional damages were awarded
where the defendant, who was commissioned to take photographs of
the plaintiff's wedding, subsequently sold certain of those photographs
to a newspaper following the murder of plaintiff's father. The photographs were subsequently prominently displayed in a national newspaper to the distress of the plaintiff. Sellers L.J. observed that "it was a
flagrant infringement of the right of the Plaintiff, and it was scandalous
conduct and in total disregard not only of the legal rights of the Plaintiff
regarding copyright but of his feelings and his sense of family dignity
and pride".

---

[35] *Performing Right Society Ltd. v. Bradford Corpn.* (1917–23) MacG.Cop.Cas. 309; *Stovin-
Bradford v. Volpoint Properties Ltd.* [1971] 1 Ch. 1007 at 1016, 1020; *Lewis Trusts v. Bambers
Stores Ltd.* [1983] F.S.R. 453 at 469.
[36] *Mondaress Ltd. v. Bourne Hollingsworth Ltd.* [1981] F.S.R. 118.
[37] See, however, *McGregor on Damages* (15th ed. 1988) para. 1716.
[38] *Beloff v. Pressdram Ltd.* [1973] 1 All E.R. 241 at 267.
[39] [1960] 1 W.L.R. 1072.

In *Nichols Advanced Vehicle System Inc. v. Rees Oliver*[40] Templeman J. awarded additional damages to the plaintiff on the basis that the defendants had acted treacherously and "by stealing a march based on infringement received benefits and inflected humiliation and loss".

Thus, it would appear that the attitude of the court is that additional damages are most appropriate in circumstances where the breach has resulted in some distress or emotional consequence. This would appear to be correct in principle for in the ordinary course the plaintiff would receive damages according to the normal measure.

(b) *Injunction*

13.15   Reference should be made to *post*, paragraph 20.01 *et seq.* where this subject is discussed.

(c) *Account of profits*

13.16   Where an infringement of copyright has occurred, the copyright owner may seek an account of profits. He is not, however, entitled to both an account of profits and damages; he must elect which remedy he will have,[41] because damages and account are incompatible remedies since a claim for an account condones the infringement.[42] The remedy is an equitable discretionary remedy based upon the proposition that, in equity, the profit belongs to the copyright owner. There is, however, a deterrent effect provided by the remedy in that the infringer is not permitted to retain a profit made by means of his own wrongdoing.[43] In many cases involving the pirating of films and records the amount of the profit will be known only to the infringer. However, where such an account is ordered by the court the defendant must make out his account and unless the court otherwise directs verify it by an affidavit to which the account must be exhibited.[44] This remedy is therefore of particular assistance to the plaintiff in that he is not placed under a duty to prove his loss.

(d) *Delivery up*

13.17   Section 97 of the 1988 Act grants to the owner of copyright in a work the right to apply to the court for an order that the infringing copy or article be delivered up to him or such other person as the court may direct.[45]

---

[40] [1979] R.P.C. 127.
[41] *Neilson v. Betts* [1871] L.R. 5 H.L. 1; *De Vitre V. Betts* (1873) L.R. 6 H.L. 319.
[42] *Neilson v. Betts* [1871] L.R. 5 H.L. 1; *De Vitre v. Betts* (1873) L.R. 6 H.L. 319; *Caxton Publishing Co., Ltd. v. Southern Publishing Ltd.* [1939] A.C. 178 at 198.
[43] *Attorney-General v. Guardian Newspapers Ltd. (No. 2)* [1990] 1 A.C. 107.
[44] R.S.C. Ord. 43, r.4.
[45] Copyright, Designs and Patent Act 1988, s.99(1).

The right to make such an application is, however, only available where a person:

(a) has an infringing copy of a work in his possession, custody or control in the course of business[46]; or

(b) has possession, custody or control of an article specifically designed or adapted for making copies of a particular copyright work, knowing or having reason to believe that it has been, or is to be, used to make infringing copies.[47]

An order for delivery up must not, however, be made unless the court also makes, or it appears to the court that there are grounds for making, an order for the disposal of the infringing copy or article.[48] A person to whom an infringing copy or article is delivered up in pursuance of an order must retain it pending the making of an order, or the decision not to make an order, as to the disposal of the infringing copy or other article.[49] The power to make an order is not, however, available where a defendant undertakes to take a licence of right where such licence is available,[50] and an application for delivery up may not be made after the end of the period of six years from the date that the infringing copy or article was made.[51]

(e) *Seizure without order of court*

Principals on which right is to be exercised. The copyright owner or a **13.18** person authorised by him may, without order of the court, seize and detain an infringing copy of a work[52] which is found exposed or otherwise immediately available for sale or hire and in respect of which he would be entitled to apply for an order[53] for delivery up.[54] The exercise of the right of seizure is however subject to the following conditions:

(1) the right to seize and detain is subject to any decision of the court relating to forfeiture and disposal[55];

(2) before anything is seized, notice of the time and place of the proposed seizure must be given to a local police station[56];

(3) A person may, for the purpose of exercising the right of seizure,

---

[46] *Ibid.*, s.99(1)(a).
[47] *Ibid.*, s.99(1)(b).
[48] *Ibid.*, s.99(2).
[49] *Ibid.*, s.99(3).
[50] *Ibid.*, s.98.
[51] *Ibid.*, ss.99(2), 113(1).
[52] For meaning of infringing copy see *ante*, paras. 12.50–12.53.
[53] *i.e.* pursuant to Copyright, Designs and Patents Act, to s.99.
[54] *Ibid.*, s.100(1).
[55] *Ibid.*, s.100(1).
[56] *Ibid.*, s.100(2).

enter premises[57] to which the public have access but may not seize anything in the possession, custody or control of a person at a permanent or regular place of business of his, and may not use force[58]; and

(4) at the time when anything is seized there must be left at the place where it was seized a notice in the prescribed form[59] containing the prescribed particulars as to the person by whom or on whose authority the seizure is made and the grounds on which it is made.[60]

13.19   The restriction contained in (3) above means that the right may not be exercised against an infringer who conducts business from a regular and permanent place of business. The provision therefore recognises the reality that the vast majority of those involved in this type of activity in respect of sound recordings and films are generally itinerant or operate from temporary premises, and that in such circumstances a swift form of action is necessary to assist copyright owners.

(f) *Forfeiture*

13.20   An application may be made to the court for an order that an infringing copy or other article:

(a) delivered up following an order of the court[61]; or

(b) seized without such an order,[62]

be forfeited to the copyright owner, or destroyed or otherwise dealt with as the court orders.[63] Likewise an application may be made that no such order be made.[64] The High Court has jurisdiction to make such orders on application by originating summons, or by summons or notice in a pending action.[65]

4. Remedies of Exclusive Licensees

13.21   **Nature of exclusive licensees remedies.** In an action for infringement of copyright, the exclusive licensee has, except against the owner of the copyright, the same rights and remedies in respect of matters occurring

---

[57] *Ibid.*, s.100(5) "Premises" includes land buildings, movable structures, vehicles, vessels, aircraft and hovercraft.
[58] *Ibid.*, s.100(3).
[59] As to the "prescribed form", see S.I. 1989 No. 1006.
[60] Copyright, Designs and Patents Act 1988, s.100(4).
[61] Pursuant to *ibid.*, ss.99 or 108.
[62] Pursuant to *ibid.*, s.100.
[63] *Ibid.*, s.114.
[64] *Ibid.*, s.114.
[65] *Ibid.*, s.115(3). See R.S.C., Ord. 93, r. 24.

after the grant of the licence as if the licence had been assignment.[66] Such rights and remedies are concurrent with those of the owner,[67] and in an action brought by the exclusive licensee a defendant may avail himself of any defence which would have been available to him if the action had been brought by the copyright owner.[68]

Exercise of concurrent rights of action. Where an action for infringe- **13.22** ment brought by the copyright owner or an exclusive license, relates to an infringement in respect of which they have concurrent rights of action, the copyright owner, or where applicable, the exclusive licensee, may not without the leave of the court proceed with the action unless the other is joined as plaintiff or added as a defendant. The court may, however, give the exclusive licensee leave to proceed with his action without the joinder of the copyright owner as either plaintiff or defend- ant.[69] These requirements do not, however, affect the granting of inter- locutory relief on the application by a copyright owner or exclusive licensee alone.[70]

Principles to be applied by court in award of damages or account of **13.23** **profits.** In an action relating to an infringement of copyright where the copyright owner and the exclusive licensee have or had concurrent rights of action, the court, in assessing damages, is required to take into account the terms of the licence granted to the licensee[71] and any pecu- niary remedy already awarded or available to either of them in respect of the infringement.[72]

No account of profits may be directed if an award of damages has been made, or an account of profits has been directed, in favour of the copyright owner and exclusive licencees in respect of the infringe- ment[73] but where the court does direct an account of profits it is required to apportion the profits between them as it considers just, sub- ject to any agreement between the parties.[74]

These rules are applicable whether or not the copyright owner and the exclusive licensee are both parties to the action.[75]

---

[66] *Ibid.*, s.101(1). See also *ante*, para. 7.18.
[67] *Ibid.*, s.101(2).
[68] *Ibid.*, s.101(3).
[69] *Ibid.*, s.102(1).
[70] *Ibid.*, s.102(3). See *ante*, para. 13.10 as to the conduct of the action after interim proceedings.
[71] *Ibid.*, s.102(4)(a)(i).
[72] *Ibid.*, s.102(4)(a)(ii).
[73] *Ibid.*, s.102(4)(b).
[74] *Ibid.*, s.102(4)(b).
[75] *Ibid.*, s.102(4)(c).

13.24 **Delivery up or seizure.** Prior to exercising any right of seizure or applying for an order for delivery up, the copyright owner is under an obligation to notify any exclusive licensee having concurrent rights.[76] The licensee is entitled in such circumstances to apply to the court and the court may make such order in respect of delivery up or, in the case of a proposed seizure without order of the court, permit or prohibit the exercise by the copyright owner of the right of seizure, as it thinks just having regard to the terms of the licence.[77] This provision provides an important safeguard to the exclusive licensee in ensuring that the copyright owner acts in accordance with the licence agreement and does not seize legitimate copies, thus destroying the confidence of the licensee's customers in his business.

5. Defendants to the action

13.25 **General.** The persons liable to be sued are primary infringers and secondary infringers. In addition, where two or more persons act in concert with one another pursuant to a common design in the infringement they may be liable as joint tortfeasors.[78]

13.26 **Directors of companies.** The mere fact that a person is a director of a limited company does not *per se* render him liable for its torts, but where he has ordered or procured such tortious acts he may be personally liable.[79] In every case where it is sought to make a director liable for his company's torts, it is necessary to examine with care what part he played personally with regard to the act or acts complained of.[80]

Defences

13.27 **Innocence.** Neither intention to infringe, nor knowledge, on the part of the defendant, that he was infringing copyright is a necessary ingredient in the cause of action for infringement of copyright. Once the two elements of sufficient objective similarity and causal connection are established, it is no defence that the defendant was unaware, and could not have been aware, that what he was doing infringed the copyright in the plaintiff's work. This is expressly recognised in section 97(1) of the 1988 Act which restricts the remedies available against an innocent infringer but recognises his liability. Thus, under section 97(1) the

---

[76] *Ibid.,* s.102(5).
[77] *Ibid.,* s.102(5).
[78] *C.B.S. Songs Ltd. v. Amstrad Consumer Electronics plc.* [1988] 1 A.C. 1013, H.L.
[79] *Performing Rights Society v. Ciryl Theatrical Syndicate Ltd.* [1924] 1 K.B. 1; *Evans & Sons Ltd. v. Spritebrand Ltd.* [1985] F.S.R. 267.
[80] *Evans & Sons Ltd. v. Spritebrand Ltd.* [1985] F.S.R. 267.

defendant is not liable in damages where he shows that he "did not know, and had no reason to believe" that copyright subsisted in the work. This does not, however, deprive the plaintiff of his other remedies. Such relieving of liability in respect of damages is "without prejudice to any other remedy".[81]

To obtain relief from liability in damages under section 97(1) the **13.28** defendant must show that he did not know and had no reason to believe that copyright *subsisted* in the work to which the action relates. It would appear that in the absence of any knowledge or information as to the origin of the work and any action taken by the defendant to satisfy himself about the matter, the mere fact of the existence of the work affords a sufficient ground for him to suspect that copyright subsists in it.[82] Where the defendant knows or suspects the subsistence of copyright in work but makes a mistake as to the owner of the copyright, and under that mistake obtains authority from a person who is not in fact the owner, the defence is not available, for that is a mistake as to the owner and not as to *subsistence* of copyright.[83] Nor is it available where he takes a mistaken view of the law, as, for example, where he forms a mistaken view as to whether the work is a proper subject matter of copyright.[84]

6. Transitional Provisions

Infringements. In general, infringements taking place before the 1988 **13.29** Act are governed by the Copyright Act 1956 and those taking place after the 1988 Act are governed by the 1988 Act.

Delivery up and seizure. The remedies of delivery up and seizure of **13.30** infringing copies without court order apply to infringing copies and other articles made before or after commencement of the 1988 Act.[85]

Exclusive licensees. Section 100 and 102 (rights and remedies of the **13.31** exclusive licensee) of the 1988 Act apply where sections 96 to 100 (rights and remedies of copyright owner) of the 1988 Act apply (*i.e.* where there are concurrent rights).[86] Section 19 of the 1956 Act continues to apply

[81] Copyright, Designs and Patents Act 1988, s.97(1).
[82] *Pytram Ltd. v. Models (Leicester) Ltd.* [1930] 1 Ch. 639; Kirk v. Fleming (1928–30) MacG.Cop.Cas. 44; *J. Whittaker & Sons Ltd. v. Publishers Circular Ltd.* (1946–47) MacG.Cop.Cas. 10.
[83] *Byrne v. Statist Company* [1914] 1 K.B. 622 at 628.
[84] *Pytram Ltd. v. Models (Leicester) Ltd.* [1930] 1 Ch. 639; *J. Whittaker & Sons Ltd. v. Publishers Circular Ltd.* (1946–47) MacG.Cop.Cas. 10.
[85] Copyright. Designs and Patents Act 1988, Sched. 1, para. 31(2).
[86] *Ibid.*, Sched. 1, para. 31(3).

where section 17 or 18 of the 1956 Act applies.[87] Sections 101 and 102 of the 1988 Act do not apply to a licence granted before June 1, 1957.[88]

13.32 Presumptions. Sections 104 to 106 of the 1988 Act (the presumptions) apply only to proceedings to which the 1988 Act apply and section 20 (proof of facts in copyright cases) of the 1956 Act continues to apply in proceedings brought by virtue of the 1956 Act.[89]

---

[87] *Ibid.*, Sched. 1, para. 31(3).
[88] *Ibid.*, Sched. 1, para. 32.
[89] *Ibid.*, Sched. 1, para. 31(4).

CHAPTER 14

RIGHTS IN PERFORMANCES

1. Introduction

Part II of the Copyright, Designs and Patents Act 1988 creates and con- **14.01** fers rights on:

(a) a performer by requiring his consent to the exploitation of his "performances"[1]; and

(b) those having "recording rights in relation to a performance, in relation to recordings made without his consent or that of the performer".[2]

These rights are independent of any other right including copyright in, or moral rights relating to, any work performed or any film or sound recording of, or broadcast or cable programme including, the performance.[3]

---

[1] Copyright, Designs and Patents Act 1988, s.180(1)(a).
[2] *Ibid.*, s.180(1)(b).
[3] *Ibid.*, s.180(4).

2. Performers' Rights

14.02 **The right conferred.** The protection conferred on a performer by Part II of the 1988 Act in respect of his performances arises where:

(a) his performance is a "live" dramatic (including dance or mime) or musical performance, or a reading or recitation of a literary work or a performance of a variety act or any similar presentation[4]; and

(b) it is a qualifying performance.[5]

(a) *"Performer" and "Performance"*

14.03 **Performer.** "Performer" is not defined by the 1988 Act. However, the categories of performances set out by the 1988 Act would have the effect of categorising, as a performer, anyone giving a performance falling within one of the listed categories of performances. This has the consequent effect that sportsmen and women taking part in a sports event are not performers within the meaning of the 1988 Act, but would be performers if they were to take part in a dramatic reconstruction of an event in which they previously participated. The position of other individuals such as figure skaters participating in a sporting event is not, however, without difficulty. The figure skater renders what could be called a dramatic performance in the form of dance although it is in a competitive arena and receives marks based upon the quality of the dramatic performance. It is submitted therefore that such persons would be performers within the meaning of the Act.

14.04 **Performances.** For the purposes of the 1988 Act, a "performance" means a live[6] performance given by one or more individuals and falling within one of the following categories:

(a) dramatic performance (which includes dance and mime)[7];

(b) a musical performance[8];

(c) a reading or recitation of a literary work[9]; or

(d) a performance of a variety act or similar presentation.[10]

"Live" for these purposes would appear to mean a performance which can be heard or seen during the occurrence of the performance.

---

[4] *Ibid.*, s.180(2).
[5] *Ibid.*, s.182.
[6] *Ibid.*, s.180(2).
[7] *Ibid.*, s.180(2)(a).
[8] *Ibid.*, s.180(2)(b).
[9] *Ibid.*, s.180(2)(c).
[10] *Ibid.*, s.180(2)(d).

Thus, a recording of a live performance (*e.g.* a pop concert) would not, it is submitted, be a live performance within the context of section 180(2) of the 1988 Act. The performance which is the subject-matter of the recording would be a live performance for the purposes of section 180(2) and capable of attracting performers' rights.

Dramatic and musical performances. The 1988 Act does not define the **14.05** meaning of a dramatic or musical performance. The determination of what is a dramatic as opposed to a musical performance is not without difficulty. For, example, is an opera singer, or the lead in a musical, rendering a dramatic performance or a musical performance? The answer would appear to be that such performances would come within the category of dramatic performances. However, the persons providing the accompanying music would appear come within the category of "musical performance". Where, however, a musician performs in a production in which he gives a dramatic performance which requires him to play a musical instrument, it would be artificial to seek to draw a distinction between his dramatic performance and his musical performance. In such circumstances his performance would, it is submitted, be dramatic.

No clear test can be laid down for discerning what is dramatic and what is musical. It is submitted that "dramatic performance" and "musical performance" should be given their ordinary English usage: it is a question of fact in each case which category most fits the performance. There will of course be clear cases such as a performance at a pop concert, or an actor in a film, which will present little difficulty.

It is to be noted that the 1988 Act does not require that the performance of a dramatic or musical performance be of a "work". It would therefore appear that any dramatic (including dance and mime) or musical performance will attract protection for the purposes of performance rights whether they are performance of "works" or improvised.

Reading or recitation of a literary work. This is the only category of per- **14.06** formance to which the word "work" is applied in respect of rights in performances. In this case to a "literary work". It therefore follows that unless the reading or recitation is of a literary work the performer will acquire no performance rights.

Variety acts or any similar presentation. The term "variety acts" is com- **14.07** monly used in the entertainment industry to refer to persons connected with music hall and theatrical entertainments. However, modern usage of "variety acts" would include performances in working men's clubs and comedy theatres. A typical presentation of a variety performance will generally comprise a "variety" of acts in the form of, for example, comedians, singers and dancers and magicians. The wording of the 1988 Act does not confine the protection afforded to occasions on which they are given in a variety performance show comprising other similar performers. Thus, it would appear that if the performance of a "variety act" is given, for example, during the interval of a play or film, such a performance would qualify for protection. If this is correct, the performance, for example, of a clown, who often will be found in variety acts, would also be entitled to protection in respect of his performance given during the presentation of a circus.

(b) *Qualifying performances*

14.08 The rights conferred on a performer by the 1988 Act subsists only in so far as the performance is a "qualifying performance". For these purposes a performance is a qualifying performance if it is given by a "qualifying individual" or takes place in a "qualifying country".[11]

(i) *Qualifying individual*

14.09 A qualifying individual is a citizen or subject[12] of, or an individual resident in, a qualifying country.[13]

(ii) *Qualifying country*

14.10 This subject is dealt with at *ante*, paragraphs 8.07 and 8.08.

14.11 **Countries enjoying reciprocal protection.** See *ante*, paragraphs 8.07 and 8.08 for the meaning of reciprocal protection and countries enjoying such protection.

14.12 **British vessels and the continental shelf.** The rights in performances conferred by Part II of the 1988 Act also applies to things done on a British ship,[14] aircraft[15] or hovercraft,[16] or in the United Kingdom

---

[11] Copyright, Designs and Patents Act 1988, s.181.
[12] *Ibid.*, s.206(a)(b): "Citizen or subject" of a "qualifying country" is to be construed in relation to the U.K. as reference to his being a British citizen and in relation to a colony of the U.K. as a reference to his being a British Dependent Territories' citizen by connection with that colony. Whether a person is a citizen or subject of another country is to be determined according to the law of that country.
[13] *Ibid.*, s.206(1).
[14] *Ibid.*, s.210(2): "British ship" means a ship which is a British ship for the purposes of the Merchant Shipping Acts otherwise than by virtue of registration in a country outside the United Kingdom.
[15] *Ibid.*, s.210(2): British aircraft and British hovercraft mean an aircraft or hovercraft registered in the United Kingdom.
[16] *Ibid.*, s.210(1).

sector[17] of the continental shelf on a structure or vessel which is present there for purposes directly connected with the exploration of the sea bed or subsoil, or the exploration of their natural resources, as it applies to things done in the United Kingdom.[18]

3. Infringement of Performers' Rights

(a) *Making recording without consent*

A performers' rights are infringed where a person without the performer's consent makes a recording, otherwise than for his private and domestic use, of the whole or a substantial part of a qualifying performance.[19] Thus, an infringement of a qualifying performance will occur where, for example, a person makes a recording at a concert of a qualifying performance given within the United Kingdom with the intention of hiring or exposing for sale records of such performance. Where, however, a recording is made with consent the person making such a recording may exploit that recording without the further consent of the performer: no further consent being necessary to enable records to be made from such a recording.[20] **14.13**

Meaning of "Recording". A recording for these purposes means a film or sound recording, of the whole or any substantial part of a qualifying performance,[21] made: **14.14**

(1) directly from the live performance[22];

(2) from a broadcast of, or cable programme including, the performance[23];

(3) directly or indirectly from another recording of the performance.[24]

No guidance is provided in Part II of the Act as to the scope and extent of "any substantial part" in the context of Rights in Performances. However, it is submitted that the like principles as apply in relation to restricted acts in copyright would apply in determining whether any substantial part of a performance has been used in any of

---

[17] The U.K. sector means the areas designated by order under s.1(7) of the Continental Shelf Act 1964.
[18] Copyright, Designs and Patents Act 1988, s.209(2).
[19] *Ibid.*, s.182(1)(a).
[20] *Mad Hat Music Ltd. v. Pulse 8 Records Ltd.* [1993] E.M.L.R. 172 at 179.
[21] Copyright Designs and Patents Act 1988, s.182(1)(a).
[22] *Ibid.*, s.180(2)(a). See *ante*, para. 14.04 for meaning of "live performance".
[23] *Ibid.*, s.180(2)(b). See *ante*, paras. 10.01 and 10.13 for "broadcast" and "cable programme service".
[24] *Ibid.*, s.180(2)(b).

the prohibited ways. Thus, it is submitted the court will, in general, look to the quality of what has been taken rather than the quantity.[25]

14.15   **"Private domestic use"**. A person is taken not to have infringed the performer's rights where the recording is for "private and domestic use". No guidance as to the meaning of this phrase is given in the 1988 Act but it would appear to bear the meaning of recording for the purposes of being used for the private use in a person's home as opposed to, for example, the private use in an hotel room, which although private would not be domestic. However, it would appear that where a recording is made for private and domestic use and is subsequently shown or played or broadcast in public without the consent of the performer, an infringement of the performers rights will occur.

14.16   **Reasonable grounds for belief that consent given.** It is expressly provided by the 1988 Act that both in respect of making a recording, and the broadcast live or inclusion live in a cable programme service, damages are not to be awarded against a defendant who shows that at the time of the infringement he "believed on reasonable grounds that consent had been given" to make a recording of the whole or a substantial part of a qualifying performance.[26] The existence of "reasonable grounds" and the belief founded on it is a question of fact.[27] It follows that the burden is on the defendant to adduce evidence to show that he actually believed and that the grounds on which he formed that belief were such as would induce a reasonable person to believe.[28] If the defendant is able to establish a belief based on reasonable grounds, the plaintiff may, in such circumstances, nevertheless be entitled to an injunction restraining the defendant from using the recording, or an order for delivery up or forfeiture and destruction.

(b) *Live transmission*

14.17   It is an infringement of a performer's right in his performances if the whole or a substantial part of his performance is broadcast[29] "live", or included "live" in a cable programme service, without his consent.[30] It is submitted, that "live" in this context means broadcast or inclusion in a cable programme service simultaneously with the occurrence[31] of the

---

[25] *L.B. Plastics v. Swish Products Ltd.* [1979] R.P.C. 551 at 622. See also *ante*, para. 12.04.

[26] Copyright, Designs and Patents Act 1988, s.182(2).

[27] *Inland Revenue Commissioners v. Rossminster Ltd.* [1980] A.C. 952, H.L.

[28] *Nakkuda Ali v. Jayaratne* [1951] A.C. 66, P.C.; *Inland Revenue Commissioners v. Rossminster Ltd.* [1980] A.C. 952, H.L.

[29] For the meaning of "Broadcast" see *supra*, n. 23.

[30] Copyright, Designs and Patents Act 1988 s.183(a).

[31] *cf.* the definition in the O.E.D. which defines a live broadcast as "heard or seen during the occurrence of an event not recorded or edited".

performance. The fact that there may be a few seconds delay between the performance and the transmission does not, it is submitted, affect the simultaneous nature of the transmission.

Reasonable grounds for believing consent given. Reference should be   **14.18**
made to *supra*, paragraph 14.16.

(c) *Use of recordings without performer's consent*

An infringement of the performer's rights will also occur where,   **14.19**

(a) a recording of the whole or a substantial part of the qualifying performance is shown, or played in public, or broadcast or included in a cable programme service without the performer's consent[32]; and

(b) the person carrying out such acts, or any of them, knew or had reason to believe, at the time of carrying out the acts, that the recording was made without the performer's consent.[33]

Thus, in order to constitute an infringement of the performer's rights by the use of a recording without consent, the consent must be lacking both when the recording was first made and at the time of the infringing act.[34]

It would appear, therefore, that where consent has been given for the recording, a showing in public of the recording or the inclusion in a television programme service without the further consent of the performer is not an infringement of the performer's rights, notwithstanding that a limitation on such further uses may have been imposed by the performer in the original consent for the recording. Where no consent was given for the recording but consent is given prior to the performance by means of the recording, no infringement will occur.

Knows or had reason to believe. Where consent is lacking on either of   **14.20**
these occasions and the plaintiff cannot show that the defendant had actual or constructive knowledge that consent was not given for the recording, the defendant will not be liable for the infringement.[35]

(d) *Importing, possessing and dealing with illicit recordings*

This category of infringing activity corresponds to secondary infringe-   **14.21**
ment of copyright. In order to succeed in establishing a secondary infringement falling within this category a performer must show that a person, without his consent:

---

[32] Copyright, Designs and Patents Act 1988, s.183.
[33] *Ibid.,* s.183.
[34] *Ibid.,* s.183.
[35] *Ibid.,* s.183.

(a) imported a recording into the United Kingdom, otherwise than for his private and domestic use,[36] a qualifying performance[37]; or

(b) in the course of business possessed, sold or let for hire, offered or exposed for sale or hire, or distributed a recording[38];

(c) which that person knows or had reason to believe, is an illicit recording.[39]

For these purposes the only consent that is relevant, for the purposes of determining whether infringement has occurred, is that of the performer. If the consent is present there can be no infringement.

14.22 **Illicit recording.** For these purposes an "illicit recording" is a recording of the whole or any substantial part of a performance which is made otherwise than for private purposes without the consent of the performer.[40] Further, where a recording comes within one of the acts permitted under Schedule 2 to the 1988 Act,[41] but is subsequently "dealt with" by means of being "sold or let for hire, or offered or exposed for sale or hire", it is treated as an illicit recording for the purposes of that dealing, and for all subsequent dealings, if that dealing infringes the rights of the performer and those having recording rights in his performances.

4. Recording Rights

14.23 **Recording rights.** In the pop music industry it is the common practice for performers to make contracts granting their exclusive services to recording companies. However, prior to 1988 the courts proved reluctant to grant protection to record companies in respect of recording rights in performances where a person made a recording of a performance subject to an exclusive recording contract.[42] The 1988 Act expressly creates "recording rights" which may be granted to a person under an exclusive recording contract, and sets out specific statutory

---

[36] See *ante*, para. 14.14 for "private and domestic".
[37] Copyright, Designs and Patents Act 1988, s.184(1)(a).
[38] *Ibid.*, s.184(1)(b).
[39] *Ibid.*, s.184(1).
[40] *Ibid.*, s.197(2).
[41] *i.e.* a recording of a performance:
   (a) made for the purposes of instruction or examination; or
   (b) by an educational establishment for educational purposes; or
   (c) recordings of performance in electronic form retained on transfer of principal recordings; or
   (d) for purposes of broadcast or cable programme.
[42] See *Ex parte Island Records Ltd.* [1978] Ch. 122; *Lonrho Ltd. v. Shell Petroleum Co. Ltd. (No. 2)* [1982] A.C. 173; *RCA Corp. v. Pollard* [1983] 1 F.S.R. 9.

protection for such rights. Recording rights in a performance may be conferred upon a person in any of three ways.

(1) By a "qualifying person" being a party to and having the benefit of an exclusive recording contract to which the performance is subject.[43]

(2) By the benefit of an "exclusive recording contract" being assigned to a "qualifying person".[44] or

(3) Where the person who has the benefit of an exclusive recording contract is not a qualifying person the person having recording rights may be,

    (i) any person who is licensed by the person having the benefit of the exclusive recording contract to make recordings of the performance with a view to commercial exploitation[45];

    (ii) or to whom the benefit of such a licence has been assigned and who is a qualifying person.[46]

It therefore follows that, provided that the person who exercises the recording rights, by licence or assignment of the benefit of the exclusive recording contract, is a qualifying person, it matters not that the person having the benefit of the exclusive recording contract is not a qualified person.

Exclusive recording contract. "Recording rights" are protected under **14.24** the 1988 Act only in so far as there is an exclusive recording contract between the performer and another person. The 1988 Act defines an "exclusive recording contract" as meaning "a contract between a performer and another person under which that person is entitled to the exclusion of all other persons (including the performer) to make recordings of one or more of his performances with a view to their commercial exploitation".[47]

The 1988 Act does not lay down any requirement that the exclusive recording contract be concluded between the performer and record or film company. Thus, an exclusive recording contract may be concluded between a performer and a record company or between a performer and a personal manager. In the latter case, the record company would be able to obtain the recording rights by an assignment of the benefit of the exclusive recording contract from the personal manager. Further, the contract may be exclusive although its subject-matter may be only

---

[43] Copyright, Designs and Patents Act 1988, s.185(2)(a). See *post*, para. 14.27 for the meaning of "qualifying person".

[44] *Ibid.*, s.185(2)(b).

[45] *Ibid.*, s.185(3)(a).

[46] *Ibid.*, s.185(3)(b).

[47] *Ibid.*, s.185.

one performance. Thus, the recording of a performance for one film or one pop record may be the subject of an exclusive recording contract.

"With a view to commercial exploitation" is defined by the 1988 Act as meaning "with a view to the recordings being sold or let for hire, or shown or played in public".[48] It is submitted that the question whether the exclusive contract is, with a view to commercial exploitation, must be determined objectively from the terms of the exclusive recording contract.

14.25 **Qualifying person and qualifying country.** A "qualifying person", for the purposes of determining the ownership of recording rights, is a qualifying individual,[49] or a body corporate or other body, for example, a partnership, which is:

(a) formed under the law of a part of the United Kingdom or another "qualifying country"[50]; and

(b) has in any qualifying country a place of business at which substantial business activity is carried on.[51]

The 1988 Act directs that in determining whether a substantial business activity is carried on at a place of business in any country, account is not to be taken of dealings in goods which are at all material times outside that country.[52] A qualifying country will include the United Kingdom, Member States of the European Union and countries which are designated by Order under section 208.

(a) *Infringement of recording rights*

(i) *Recording of performance subject to exclusive contract*

14.26 Recording rights will be infringed where a person makes a recording[53] of the whole, or a substantial part of a performance without the consent[54] of the performer, or a person having recording rights.[55] In such circumstances the recordings which the person makes are not recordings reproducing the recordings of the person entitled to the recording rights. They are records of the live performance made by the person himself, or by someone else who was present at, for example, the concert at which the performer gave the performance, or who made a recording of a live broadcast of that concert without the consent of the

---

[48] *Ibid.*, s.185(4).
[49] For meaning of "qualifying individual" see *ante*, para. 14.09.
[50] Copyright, Designs and Patents Act 1988, s.206(1).
[51] *Ibid.*, s.206(1).
[52] *Ibid.*, s.206(1).
[53] For the meaning of "recording" see *ante*, para. 14.14.
[54] Copyright, Designs and Patents Act 1988, s.193: no particular form for the giving of such consent is prescribed by the 1988 Act.
[55] *Ibid.*, s.186(1).

performer, or the person having recording rights. In such circumstances, an infringement of the recording rights will occur and it matters not that the performances, the subject of the exclusive recording contract, are not qualifying performances.

However, where the recording is made by a third party with the consent of the performer, the third party is entitled to rely on that consent, notwithstanding the fact of the exclusive recording contract. The person or company having the benefit of the exclusive recording contract would in such circumstances have to rely on its contractual remedies against the performer under the exclusive recording contract and, if the third party was aware of the exclusive recording contract, on any remedy he may have in tort against such third party. **14.27**

No infringement of the recording rights will occur, however, where the recording of the performance is for the purposes of "private and domestic" use.[56]

Further, it is to be noted that where a live broadcast or inclusion in a cable programme service of a "live" performance takes place there will not be an infringement of the recording rights.

(ii) *Use of recording made without consent*

An infringement of recording rights occurs where a person, without the consent of the person(s) having the recording rights, or in the case of a qualifying performance, the consent of the performer, shows or plays in public, or broadcasts, or includes in a cable programme service, the recording of the whole or a substantial part of the performance by means of a recording.[57] However, in order to establish liability the person having recording rights must show that the person alleged to have infringed his rights knew, or had reason to believe, at the time of the infringing act, that the recording was made without the consent of the performer or the person who at the time the consent was given had recording rights in relation to the performance.[58] **14.28**

Thus, there will be an infringement unless there is consent at the stage at which the recording is made or at the time at which the recording is performed, but any consent by the performer in this respect will be ineffective to negate an infringement of recording rights if the performance was not a qualifying performance.[59]

---

[56] *Ibid.*, s.186(1). For a discussion of the meaning of "private and domestic", see *ante*, para. 14.15.
[57] *Ibid.*, s.187(1).
[58] *Ibid.*, s.187(1), (2).
[59] *Ibid.*, s.187(1).

(iii) Importing possessing or dealing with illicit recording

14.29 The infringing act and the protection accorded to a person having exclusive recording rights in respect to this category of infringement is similar to that accorded to performers.[60] There are, however, two
differences. First, an "illicit recording" for the purposes of "recording
rights" is defined as one which is made otherwise than for private purpose *without the consent of the performer or the person having recording
rights*.[61] Secondly, to constitute an infringement of the recording rights
by importing, possessing or dealing in an illicit recording it is necessary
that:

    (a) the person making use of the recording "knows or has reason to
    believe" that the recording was made *without the consent of the
    performer or the person or persons who had recording rights*; and

    (b) the use of such recording so as to show, play in public, broadcast,
    or include in a cable programme service, the whole or a substan-
    tial part of the performance was also *without either the consent of
    the performer or the person having the recording rights*.

14.30 However, any consent given by the performer under (b) will be ineffective to negate an infringement of recording rights if the performance
was not a qualifying performance.[62] Once again the protection which is
accorded is to the recording rights which have been granted under the
exclusive recording contract and the right to exploit commercially any
recordings made under that contract. The recordings in which the
infringer deals are not recordings reproducing the record companies
recordings in which copyright subsists. They are recordings made by
someone from a live performance, live broadcast or cable programme
service or from an illicit recording made from such performances.

(b) *Consent*

(i) *General*

14.31 **Previous consent binding.** Where a performance right passes to another
person, any consent binding on the person previously entitled to the
performance right in question binds the person to whom the right
passes in the same way as if the consent had been given by him.[63] A
person having recording rights is bound by any consent given by a
person through whom he derives his rights under an exclusive

---

[60] *Ibid.*, s.188.
[61] *Ibid.*, s.197(3).
[62] *Ibid.*, s.187(1).
[63] *Ibid.*, s.193(3).

recording contract or licence in the same way as if the consent had been given by him.[64]

Form and nature of consent. The 1988 Act specifies no particular form in which the consent of the performer need be given. Thus, the consent may be given orally or by conduct, such as by the performer attending at a recording studio for a recording of his performance to be made.[65] Where consent is given, it may be in respect of a specified performance, a specified description of performances or performances generally, and may relate to past or future performances.[66] **14.32**

Consent following death. On the death of a person entitled to the performer's rights, the rights pass to any person he may by testamentary disposition specifically direct,[67] and if no such person is specifically directed, the rights are exercisable by his personal representatives.[68] Where such testamentary disposition vests the performer's rights in more than one person, any one of such persons may give consent.[69] **14.33**

(ii) *Power of Copyright Tribunal to give consent*

Jurisdiction of the Tribunal. The Copyright Tribunal has jurisdiction, on the application of a person wishing to make a recording from a previous recording of a performance, to give consent in a case: **14.34**

(a) where the identity or whereabouts of a performer[70] cannot be ascertained by reasonable inquiry[71]; or

(b) where a performer[72] unreasonably withholds his consent.[73]

The jurisdiction of the Tribunal does not, however, extend to granting consent to show or play in public, or broadcast, or include in a cable programme service a recording of a performance. Nor does the Tribunal have jurisdiction to grant consent on behalf of a person having recording rights whose identity or whereabouts cannot be ascertained.

---

[64] *Ibid.*, s.193(2).
[65] *Mad Hat Music Limited v. Pulse 8 Records Limited* [1993] E.M.L.R. 172.
[66] Copyright, Designs and Patents Act 1988, s.193.
[67] *Ibid.*, s.192(2)(b).
[68] *Ibid.*, s.192(2)(b).
[69] *Ibid.*, s.192(2)(b).
[70] "Performer" would appear to include the owner of the performance right for the time being. See *Ex parte Sianel Pedwar Cymru* [1993] E.M.L.R. 251, where the Tribunal granted consent on behalf of the personal representatives of a deceased performer whose identity was known but the identity of whose personal representatives could not be ascertained.
[71] Copyright, Designs and Patents Act 1988, s.190(1)(a).
[72] See *infra*, n.78.
[73] Copyright, Designs and Patents Act 1988, s.190(1)(b).

14.35 **Pre-conditions to granting consent.** The Tribunal may not give its consent to the making of a recording from a previous recording where the identity or whereabouts of a performer cannot be ascertained by reasonable inquiry, except after the service or publication of notices required by its general procedural rules,[74] or such notices as the Tribunal may in any particular case direct.[75]

Where the Tribunal is requested to grant consent in a case where the performer is said to have unreasonably withheld his consent, the Tribunal is enjoined not to give consent unless it is satisfied that the performer's reasons for withholding consent do not include the protection of a "legitimate interest of his".[76] The onus is placed by the 1988 Act on the performer to show what his reasons are for withholding consent, and in default of evidence as to his reasons the Tribunal is entitled to draw such inferences as it thinks fit.[77]

14.36 What is a "legitimate interest" is undefined by the 1988 Act. However, it is submitted that such interest will include the protection of a performer's reputation and future employment where the performer can show that consent would have an adverse influence on such matters. If, however, "performer" is to include the owner of the performance rights for the time being, and thus possibly a personal representative, future employment would obviously not be a legitimate interest in such circumstances. The question of whether reputation divorced from the possibility of future performances would be a "legitimate interest" in such circumstances would, however, be a matter which is more difficult to resolve. A performer lives by his reputation with the public. It is that reputation that generates further work and any matter which diminishes his reputation also diminishes his future employment. There is, therefore, a strong argument that where the performer has died the reputation is not a sufficient legitimate interest to enable the Tribunal to withhold consent.

14.37 **Factors to be taken into account when considering application.** The Tribunal is further required to take into account two matters. First, whether the original recording was made with the performer's consent and is lawfully in the possession or control of the person proposing to make the further recording.[78] Secondly, whether the making of the further recording is consistent with the obligations of the parties to the

---

[74] Pursuant to Copyright, Designs and Patents Act 1988, s.150. See S.I. 1989 No. 1129 for the applicable rules.
[75] Copyright, Designs and Patents Act 1988, s.190(3).
[76] *Ibid.*, s.190(4).
[77] *Ibid.*, s.190(4).
[78] *Ibid.*, s.190(5)(a).

arrangements under which, or is otherwise consistent with the purposes for which, the original recording was made.[79]

An example of the second factor is where a performer enters into an agreement for the appearance in a film or a series of films. The making of such films naturally results in a large amount of film footage, some of which is not used for the final film as exhibited to the public. If the agreement between the producer and the performer is for the particular film and the producer should at some later date wish to make a completely new film which comprises the "out-takes"[80] and "clips"[81] from the original recordings, he will need the consent of the performer, or failing that, the Tribunal. In such circumstances, the new film will not be consistent with the terms of the agreement between the producer and the performer. It is submitted that in such a case the Tribunal should tend towards refusal of consent where the performer objects, or should only grant consent on such terms as would provide compensation to the performer which reflects the market value of the recording to the producer.

Nature and terms of consent. Any consent given by the Tribunal has **14.38** effect as if given by the performer[82] and may be made subject to any conditions specified in the Tribunal's order granting consent,[83] including, in default of agreement between the applicant and the performer, terms as to the payment to be made to the performer in consideration of consent being given.[84]

5. Transmission of Performance Rights

Rights in performances are not assignable or transmissible.[85] There are, **14.39** however, a number of exceptions to this general rule. First, on the death of a person entitled to the performer's rights the rights pass to any person he may by testamentary disposition specifically direct,[86] and if no such person is specifically directed, the rights are exercisable by his personal representatives.[87] Where such testamentary disposition vests the performers' rights in more than one person, any one of such persons

---

[79] *Ibid.*, s.190(5)(b).
[80] *i.e.* film footage which comprise not only film which at the time of the shooting was unsatisfactory but also sequences which, though satisfactory, were discarded in the process of editing.
[81] *i.e.* excerpts from the final film as exhibited to the public.
[82] Copyright, Designs and Patents Act 1988, s.190(2).
[83] *Ibid.*, s.190(2).
[84] *Ibid.*, s.190(6).
[85] *Ibid.*, s.192(1).
[86] *Ibid.*, s.192(2)(b).
[87] *Ibid.*, s.192(2)(b).

may give consent.[88] Secondly, a person may become the owner of a recording right by reason of the assignment or licence of the benefit of an exclusive recording contract.[89]

6. Duration of Performance Rights

14.40 Performance rights continue to subsist for a period of 50 years from the end of the calendar year in which the performance takes place.[90]

7. Permitted Acts

14.41 **General.** Schedule 2 to the 1988 Act specifies acts which may be done in relation to a performance or recording, notwithstanding the performance rights conferred by the Act.[91] Three matters are to be borne in mind when considering the permitted acts. First, permitted acts relate only to the question of infringement of performance rights and do not affect any other right or obligation restricting the doing of any specified acts.[92] Secondly, it is not permissible to draw an inference from the permitted acts as to the scope of the performance rights granted by the 1988 Act. Thirdly, the fact that a permitted act does not specifically fall within one category does not mean that it does not fall within another category.

The permitted acts are those which can be done in relation to copyright, save that there is no restriction relating to time shifting and off-air recording of photographs for private purposes. For a discussion of such permitted acts reference should be made to the Chapter 12 of this work entitled "Infringement of Rights".

8. Remedies for Infringement

14.42 **Damages.** Infringement of any of the performance rights is actionable by the person entitled to the right as a breach of statutory duty.[93] Where the infringement is in the form of:

(a) the broadcast or inclusion in a cable programme service[94]; or

(b) a programme broadcast and re-transmitted as a programme in a cable programme service[95],

---

[88] *Ibid.*, s.192(2)(b).
[89] *Ibid.*, s.192(4).
[90] *Ibid.*, s.191.
[91] *Ibid.*, Sched. 2, para. 1(1).
[92] *Ibid.*, Sched. 2, para. 1(1).
[93] *Ibid.*, s.194. See also, *post*, para. 15.37 *et seq.*
[94] *Ibid.*, Sched. 18(4).
[95] *Ibid.*, Sched. 19(2).

the court is required, in assessing damages for the infringement, to take into account the fact that it was heard or seen by the public by the reception of the broadcast or programme.[96] Such factors, it is submitted, would require the court to consider the number of audience reached and the fee that would have been payable had consent been given in consideration of a fee.

14.43 The court may not, however, award damages in the case of the infringement of the performer's rights, or the rights of a person having recording rights, where the defendant shows that at the time of the infringement he believed on reasonable grounds that consent had been given.[97] Where the infringement is in the form of the importing, possessing or dealing with illicit copies, and the defendant shows that the illicit recording was innocently acquired by him or a predecessor in title, damages are limited to a sum not exceeding a reasonable payment in respect of the act complained of. For these purposes "innocently acquired" means that the person acquiring the recording did not know, and had no reason to believe, that it was an illicit recording.

Any damages recovered by personal representatives in respect of an infringement after a person's death devolves as part of his estate as if the right of action had subsisted and been vested in him immediately before his death.[98]

14.44 **Order for delivery up.** In addition to the power to award damages the court has power to make an order for delivery up. Where such an order is made, the person to whom the illicit recordings are delivered up in accordance with the order must retain them pending an order of the court as to the disposal, or the decision of the court not to make an order.[99] An order may not be made more than six years after the illicit recording was made.[1] If, however, during the whole or part of that period the person entitled to apply for the order was under a disability[2] or is prevented by fraud or concealment from discovering the facts entitling him to apply, an application may be made by him at any time before the end of the period of six years from the date on which he ceased to be under the disability or, as the case maybe, could with reasonable diligence have discovered those facts.[3] Further, no order

---

[96] *Ibid.*, Sched. 18(4) and 19(2).
[97] *Ibid.*, s.182(2). See *ante*, paras. 12.46–12.48.
[98] *Ibid.*, s.192(5).
[99] *Ibid.*, s.195(3).
[1] *Ibid.*, s.195.
[2] "Disability" has the same meaning as in the Limitation Act 1980.
[3] Copyright, Designs and Patents Act 1988, s.203.

may be made unless it appears to the court that there are grounds for making an order as to disposal of the illicit recordings.[4]

14.45 **Seizure of illicit recordings.** Illicit recordings of a performance exposed for sale, or immediately available for sale or hire, in respect of which a person would be entitled to apply for an order for delivery up, may be seized and detained by him subject to the following conditions[5]:

    (a) before seizure notice of the time and place of the proposed seizure must be given to the local police station;

    (b) he may not seize anything in the possession, custody or control of a person at a permanent or regular place of business of his;

    (c) he may not use force; and

    (d) at the time when anything is seized he must leave a notice in the prescribed form setting out the prescribed particulars.[6]

14.46 **Order as to disposal of illicit recording.** Where an order for delivery up has been made or illicit recordings seized, an application may be made to the court that the illicit recording be forfeited to the performer or the person having the recording rights, or that they be destroyed or otherwise dealt with as the court directs.[7] The court is required when deciding what order, if any, should be made, to consider whether other remedies available in an action for infringement of the performance rights would be adequate to compensate the persons entitled to the rights and to protect their interests.[8]

Where there is more than one person interested in a recording, the court may make such order as it thinks just. It may, in particular, direct that the recording be sold, or otherwise dealt with, and the proceeds divided.[9]

14.47 A person is entitled to appeal against an order whether or not he appeared. To give effect to this requirement the 1988 Act provides that an order is not to take effect until the end of the period within which the notice of an appeal may be given or, if before the end of that period notice is duly given, until the final determination of the appeal.[10]

Where no order is made by the court for forfeiture or disposal, the person in whose possession, custody or control the recording was before being delivered up, or seized, is entitled to its return.[11]

---

[4] *Ibid.,* s.195(2).
[5] *Ibid.,* s.196.
[6] For the "prescribed form", see S.I. 1989 No. 1006.
[7] Copyright, Designs and Patents Act 1988, s.204.
[8] *Ibid.,* s.204(2).
[9] *Ibid.,* s.204.
[10] *Ibid.,* s.204(3)(b).
[11] *Ibid.,* s.204(5).

9. Transitional Provisions

The rights in performances created by the 1988 Act apply to perfor-   **14.48**
mances taking place before commencement of the 1988 Act[12] but no act
done before commencement of the Act, or in pursuance of arrangements made before commencement, is to be regarded as an infringement. Therefore, a performance given in 1980 will be subject to
performance rights which will expire at the end of 50 years from 1980,
and until such time is capable of being infringed by any of exploitation
of the performance occurring after commencement.[13]

---

[12] August 1, 1989.
[13] Copyright, Designs and Patents Act 1988, s.180(3).

CHAPTER 15

MORAL RIGHTS

1. Introduction

15.01 General. Article 6 *bis* of the Paris text of the Berne Convention[1] expressly recognises the existence of two moral rights: the moral right to be identified[2] and the right to object to derogatory treatment[3] by providing:

> "(1) Independently of the author's economic rights, and even after the transfer of the said rights, the author shall have the right to claim authorship of the work and to object to any distortion,

---

[1] Berne Copyright Convention (Paris Revision, 1971), Cmnd. 5002.
[2] Commonly referred to as the "right of paternity".
[3] Commonly referred to as the "right of paternity".

mutilation or other modification of, or other derogatory action in relation to the said work, which would be prejudicial to his honour or reputation.

(2) The rights granted to the author in accordance with the preceding paragraph shall, after his death, be maintained, at least until the expiry of the economic rights, and shall be exercisable by the persons or institutions authorised by the legislation of the country where protection is claimed . . .

(3) The means of redress for safeguarding the rights granted by this Article shall be governed by the legislation of the country where protection is claimed."

The Copyright Designs and Patents Act 1988[4] incorporates into the laws of the United Kingdom the right to be identified[5] and the right to object to derogatory treatment[6] set out in the Berne Convention, together with the moral rights to object to false attribution[7] and the right to privacy of certain photographs and films.[8]

2. Right to be Identified

Right to be identified. The right to be identified means the right to be **15.02** identified, in certain specified circumstances where the right has been asserted,[9] as the author of the whole or any substantial part[10] of a copyright literary, dramatic, musical or artistic work or as director of the whole or any substantial part[11] of a copyright film.[12]

(a) *Circumstances in which right arises*

Literary or dramatic work. The author of a literary work, other than **15.03** words intended to be sung or spoken with music (*i.e.* lyrics), or a dramatic work has the right to be identified whenever the whole or any substantial part[13] of the work is:

---

[4] Copyright, Designs and Patents Act 1988, ss.77–84.
[5] *Ibid.*, s.77.
[6] *Ibid.*, s.80.
[7] *Ibid.*, s.84.
[8] *Ibid.*, s.85.
[9] As to the "assertion", see *post*, para. 15.11.
[10] Copyright, Designs and Patents Act 1988, s.89(2).
[11] *Ibid.*, s.89(2).
[12] *Ibid.*, s.77(1).
[13] *Ibid.*, s.89(1). See *ante*, para. 12.04 for the meaning of "substantial part".

(a) published commercially, performed in public,[14] broadcast[15] or included in a cable programme service[16]; or

(b) copies of a film or sound recording including the work are issued to the public.[17]

15.04 **Musical work.** Where the work consists of a musical work, or a literary work consisting of words intended to be sung with music (*i.e.* lyrics), the author has the right to be identified:

(a) whenever the whole or any substantial part[18] of the work is published commercially[19]; or

(b) whenever copies of a sound recording of the whole or any substantial part[20] of the work is issued to the public[21];

(c) whenever a film of which the sound-track includes the whole or any substantial part[22] of the work is shown in public or copies of such films are issued to the public.[23]

15.05 It is to be noted that, in contrast to the position of an author of literary works, the author of a musical work has no statutory right to be identified as author where a musical work is performed in public, broadcast or included in cable programme service. Where, however, a sound-track of a film includes the work, and the film is shown in public, or copies issued to the public the author has a right to be identified subject to such right being asserted.

For these purposes "commercial publication" means issuing copies to the public at a time when copies made in advance of the receipt of orders are generally available to the public, or making the work available to the public by means of an electrical retrieval system.[24] Thus, for example, the placing in a shop of the sheet music of a composition, for which no orders have been received or making a film available by means of video on demand, with the intention of satisfying any demand that may arise, will amount to commercial publication of a musical work.

---

[14] For "performed in public", see *ante*, para. 12.36 *et seq.*
[15] For the meaning of "broadcast" see *ante*, para. 10.01.
[16] Copyright, Designs and Patents Act 1988, s.77(2)(a). For the meaning of "cable programme service", see *ante*, para. 10.13.
[17] *Ibid.*, s.77(2)(b). See *ante*, para. 12.14 for "issue to public".
[18] *Ibid.*, s.89(1).
[19] *Ibid.*, s.77(3)(a).
[20] *Ibid.*, s.89(1).
[21] *Ibid.*, s.77(3)(b).
[22] *Ibid.*, s.89(1).
[23] *Ibid.*, s.77(3)(c).
[24] *Ibid.*, s.175(2).

Artistic work. For the purposes of entertainment law the author of an **15.06**
artistic work has the right to be identified whenever:

(a) a visual image of the whole of the work or any substantial part of
it is broadcast or included in a cable programme service[25]; or

(b) a film including a visual image of the whole of the work, or any
substantial part of it, is shown in public, or copies of such a film
are issued to the public.[26]

Adaptation. Where any of the events occur where identification ought **15.07**
to be accorded, in relation to an adaptation of a literary, dramatic or
musical work, the right to be identified also includes the right to be
identified as author of the work from which the adaptation was made.[27]

Thus, for example, where a film is based upon a screenplay, the
author of the screenplay, if he writes the screenplay under a contract for
services, has a right to be identified in the screen credits of the film as
the author of the dramatic work, where the right has been asserted,
when the film is issued to the public. The same principle would apply
where the film is broadcast or included in a cable programme service.

Director of film. A director has the right to be identified whenever the **15.08**
whole or any substantial part[28] of the film is shown in public, broadcast
or included in a cable programme service, or copies of the film are
issued to the public.[29]

(b) *What amounts to identification*

Where a film or sound recording is issued to the public, or a musical **15.09**
work or lyrics are published commercially, the author or director is to
be identified in or on each copy or, if that is not appropriate, in some
manner likely to bring his identity to the notice of a person acquiring a
copy.[30] In any other case, such as a theatrical presentation, the right is to
be identified in a manner likely to bring his identity to the attention of
the person seeing or hearing the performance, exhibition, showing,
broadcast or cable programme in question.[31] Such forms of identification are, however, subject to the overriding requirement that the
identification must in each case be clear and reasonably prominent.[32]
Whether the identification is reasonably prominent will be a question

---

[25] *Ibid.*, s.177(4)(a).
[26] *Ibid.*, s.77(4)(b).
[27] *Ibid.*, s.77(2). See *ante*, paras. 12.42–12.43 for "adaptation".
[28] *Ibid.*, s.89(1).
[29] *Ibid.*, s.77(6).
[30] *Ibid.*, s.77(7)(a).
[31] *Ibid.*, s.77(7)(c).
[32] *Ibid.*, s.77(7).

of fact to be decided in each particular case. Thus, in the case of a film sold on video-cassette it may be sufficient if the director and screenplay writer are given prominent screen credits. However, it is arguable that the identification must be such that the "person acquiring a copy" must be made aware of the identity of the director and author prior to viewing the film.

(c) *Assertion of right to be identified*

15.10 **No infringement of right where not asserted.** A pre-condition of the right to be identified is the "assertion" of the right by the author or director.[33]

15.11 **Nature and extent of assertion.** The right to be identified may be asserted generally, or in relation to any specified act or description of acts.[34] Thus, an author or a director may assert the right in relation only to cinema exhibition of a film incorporating his work or he may assert his right in respect of all cases permitted by the 1988 Act. The 1988 Act provides for two ways in which the right may be asserted. First, it may be asserted on an assignment of copyright in the work, by including in the document effecting the assignment a statement that the author, or director, as the case may be, asserts in relation to that work his right to be identified.[35] Secondly, it may be asserted by a formal or informal document signed by the author or director.[36] In an action for infringement of the right to be identified the court is required to take into account any delay in asserting the right.[37]

In the case of a work of joint authorship, a right to be identified as a joint author must be asserted by each joint author in relation to himself.[38]

15.12 **Persons bound by assertion.** Where the assertion is contained in a document effecting an assignment of the copyright, the assignee and anyone claiming through him are bound by the assertion, whether or not he has notice of the assertion.[39] Where, however, the assertion is not contained in the assignment of copyright, a person is not bound by such assertion unless it has been brought to his notice.[40]

---

[33] *Ibid.*, s.78.
[34] *Ibid.*, s.78(2).
[35] *Ibid.*, s.78(2)(a).
[36] *Ibid.*, s.78(2)(b).
[37] *Ibid.*, s.78(5).
[38] *Ibid.*, s.88(1). "A work of joint authorship" is a work produced by the collaboration of two or more authors in which the contribution of each author is not distinct from that of the other author or authors. See also *ante*, para. 8.36.
[39] *Ibid.*, s.78(4)(a).
[40] *Ibid.*, s.78(4)(b).

Thus, where the assertion is contained in a licence it would appear that a sub-licensee is not bound by such an assertion unless it has been brought to his notice, but where it is contained in an assignment a person claiming through the assignee is bound whether or not he has notice. For example, where an author licences the film rights in his novel to a producer and asserts his right to be identified and at the same time grants the producer a right to sub-licence, a sub-licensee will not be bound by the assertion of rights if the assertion is not brought to his notice by the original licensee when entering into the sub-licence.

(d) *Exceptions to right to identify*

Section 79 of the 1988 Act sets out a number of exceptions to the right to be identified. For the purposes of this work the following are of importance. **15.13**

Acts done with authority of copyright owner. The right does not apply to anything done by or with the authority of the copyright owner where copyright originally vested in: **15.14**

(a) the author's employer, by reason of the fact that it is produced under a contract of service[41]; or

(b) the director's employer, by reason of such employer undertaking the arrangements necessary for the making of the film.[42]

Thus, the right will not apply where a scriptwriter or composer is a "staff" writer. Nor will it apply where, for example, the director's employer as defined above authorises a broadcaster to broadcast without the inclusion of identification.

Reporting of current events. The right does not apply in relation to any work made for the purpose of reporting current events.[43] Thus, the director of a current affairs documentary or news programme would have no right to be identified. **15.15**

Acts which would not infringe copyright. The right of identification is not infringed by an act falling within any of the following categories which would not infringe copyright: **15.16**

(a) fair dealing so far as it relates to the reporting of current events by means of sound recording, film, broadcast or cable programme[44];

---

[41] *Ibid.*, s.79(3)(a). See *ante*, para. 8.34, n. 58 for distinction between contract of service and contract for services.
[42] *Ibid.*, s.79(3)(b). See also *ante*, paras. 8.03–8.04.
[43] *Ibid.*, s.79(5). See *ante*, paras. 12.74–12.75 for "current events".
[44] *Ibid.*, s.79(4)(a). For an examination of the "fair dealing" provision see *ante*, para. 12.69.

(b) incidental inclusion of work in sound recording, film, broadcast, or cable programme[45];

(c) anonymous or pseudonymous works: acts permitted on assumptions as to expiry of copyright or death of author.[45a]

3. Right to Object to Derogatory Treatment

(a) *Introduction*

15.17 The right to object to derogatory treatment is the second of the two moral rights recognised by the Berne Convention and is often referred to as the right to integrity. By section 80 of the 1988 Act the author of a copyright literary, dramatic, musical or artistic work and the director of a copyright film "has the right not to have [the whole or any part of][46] his work subjected to derogatory treatment". The right to object to derogatory treatment extends to treatment of parts of a work resulting from a previous treatment by a person other than the author or director, if those parts are attributed to, or likely to be regarded as the work of the author or director.[47] Where the work is one of joint authorship, the right is a right of each author and his right is satisfied if he consents to the treatment in question.[48]

In contrast to the right to be identified, the right to object to derogatory treatment is not subject to the assertion by the author or director of the right.

(b) *What amounts to derogatory treatment*

15.18 First, one must determine whether there has been a "treatment". Secondly, whether that treatment is "derogatory". What is "treatment" is dealt with in section 80(2)(a) of the 1988 Act which provides that:

> " 'treatment' of a work means any addition to, deletion from or alteration to or adaptation of the work, other than (i) a translation of a literary or dramatic work, or (ii) an arrangement or transcription of a musical work involving no more than a change of key or register".

What is derogatory treatment is described by the 1988 Act as follows:

---

[45] *Ibid.*, s.79(4)(b). See also *ante*, para. 10.28.
[45a] *Ibid.*, s.79(4)(h).
[46] *Ibid.*, s.89(2).
[47] *Ibid.*, s.80(7).
[48] *Ibid.*, s.88(2).

"the treatment of a work is derogatory if it amounts to distortion or mutilation of the work or is otherwise prejudicial to the honour or reputation of the author or director".[49]

Thus, it is submitted that in determining whether a treatment is dero- **15.19** gatory the following approach is applicable. First, where the treatment amounts to a "distortion or mutilation of the work" it is derogatory and thus prima facie prejudicial to the honour and reputation of the author or director. Secondly, where the treatment is not a distortion or mutilation but is "otherwise prejudicial to the honour or reputation of the author or director" it is prima facie derogatory. The expression "otherwise prejudicial to the honour and reputation" is, in this context, closely analogous to the phraseology of defamation.

It is submitted that on this analogy and the context in which the words are used it would imply the application of an objective rather than a subjective test in determining whether treatment is prejudicial to the author or director's honour and reputation, and thus derogatory within the second category of derogatory treatment. If it were otherwise, the practical effect in respect of the entertainment industry might be destructive of the production of films and sound recordings. A script, for example, is altered many times during the production of a film. Such changes are not always to the detriment of the professional reputation of the author but dramatic creation is a precious business and consequently the author may nevertheless, and often does, object because he feels that his intended meaning has been changed or destroyed to his detriment. A subjective interpretation would leave the producer exposed in such circumstances.

However, it is unclear whether such prejudice must be to the honour **15.20** or reputation of the author or director as author or director, or in their position as members of society. It is submitted that in this context the former approach is to be preferred.

Whether a treatment is derogatory within the meaning of the above provision is a question of fact for the court.[50] Such treatment may, for example, occur where the out-takes from a serious dramatic film are used to create a comedic film advertised as the work of the director of the dramatic film, or where lyrics have been modified by means of part taken from their context and put into a different context. It may also be derogatory of a newly created religious musical work for it to be performed as a pop recording.

---

[49] *Ibid.*, s.80(2)(b).
[50] *Morrison Leahy Music Ltd. v. Lightbond Ltd.* [1993] E.M.L.R. 144.

(c) *Circumstances in which right is available*

15.21 There can be no infringement of the right, and thus no right to object to derogatory treatment, until such time as the work is exposed to the public in one of the forms set down by the 1988 Act in respect of each category of work. These forms are as follows in respect of each of the following works.

15.22 **Literary, dramatic or musical work.** In the case of a literary, dramatic or musical work the right is infringed by a person who:

(a) publishes commercially,[51] performs in public, broadcasts or includes in a cable programme service a derogatory treatment of the work[52]; or

(b) issues to the public copies of a film or sound recording of, or including, a derogatory treatment of the work.[53]

15.23 **Artistic work.** In the case of an artistic work the right is infringed by a person:

(a) broadcasting or including in a cable programme service a visual image of a derogatory treatment of the work[54]; or

(b) showing in public a film including a visual image of a derogatory treatment of the work.[55]

15.24 **Film.** In the case of a film, the right is infringed by a person who shows in public, broadcasts, or includes in a cable programme service,[56] or issues to the public, copies of a derogatory treatment of the film.[57] Additionally, the right is infringed where a person, along with the film, plays in public, broadcasts or includes in a cable programme service, or issues to the public copies of, a derogatory treatment of the film soundtrack.[58]

(d) *Exceptions to the right*

15.25 **Reporting of current events.** The right does not apply in relation to any work made for the purpose of reporting current events.[59]

---

[51] For the meaning of "commercially published", see *ante*, para. 15.05.
[52] Copyright, Designs and Patents Act 1988, s.80(3)(a). See *ante*, paras. 10.01, 10.13 and 10.23 for "broadcast", "cable programme service" and "performs in public" respectively.
[53] *Ibid.*, s.80(3)(b).
[54] *Ibid.*, s.80(4)(a).
[55] *Ibid.*, s.80(4)(b).
[56] *Ibid.*, s.80(6)(a).
[57] *Ibid.*, s.80(6)(b).
[58] *Ibid.*, s.80.
[59] *Ibid.*, s.81(3).

Consumer protection. The right is not infringed by anything done to **15.26** the work for the purpose of avoiding the commission of an offence,[60] or complying with a duty imposed by or under an enactment[61] such as, for example, complying with the ITC Programme Guidelines.[62] Additionally, no infringement occurs where the BBC does any act in relation to the work for the purpose of avoiding the inclusion in a programme broadcast by it of anything which offends against good taste or decency or which is likely to encourage or incite to crime or to lead to disorder or to be offensive to public feeling.[63] In such circumstances, where the author or director is identified at the time of the act or has previously been identified in or on published copies of the work, a "sufficient disclaimer" must be included. "Sufficient disclaimer" for these purposes means a clear and reasonably prominent indication given at the time of the act (*e.g.* the broadcast of the film) and if the author or director is then identified, appearing along with the identification, that the work has been subjected to treatment to which the author or director has not consented.[64] These provisions do not, however, affect the right of an author or director to negotiate contractual terms which limit or restrict the right of a broadcaster or exhibitor to edit a film.[65]

(e) *Limitations on the right*

The right to object to derogatory treatment does not apply to anything **15.27** done in relation to a work by or with the authority of the copyright owner where a work is produced:

(a) by an author in the course of his employment and the copyright thereby vests in his employer[66]; or

(b) where the director's employers undertook the arrangements necessary for the making of the film and the employer is thereby the author.[67]

However, in such circumstances, where the author or director is identified at the time of the act (*e.g.* an exhibition in public with deletions which in the ordinary course might amount to derogatory treatment) or has previously been identified in or on published copies of the work

---

[60] *Ibid.*, s.81(6)(a).
[61] *Ibid.*, s.81(6)(b).
[62] See under Consumer Protection for the ITC Programme Guidelines *post*, Chap. 32.
[63] Copyright, Designs and Patents Act 1988, s.81(6)(c).
[64] *Ibid.*, s.81(6).
[65] See, *e.g. Frisby v. British Broadcasting Corporation* [1967] Ch. 932.
[66] Pursuant to Copyright, Designs and Patents Act 1988, s.11(2).
[67] *i.e.* pursuant to *ibid.*, s.9(2).

(for example, on previous public exhibitions) a "sufficient disclaimer" must appear.[68]

(f) *Secondary infringement right*

15.28 The right to object to derogatory treatment also arises where a person does any of the following specified acts in respect of an article of which he has actual or constructive knowledge that it is an infringing article[69]:

(a) possesses it in the course of business; or

(b) sells or lets it for hire, or offers or exposes it for sale or hire; or

(c) in the course of a business exhibits it in public or distributes it; or

(d) distributes it otherwise than in the course of business so as to affect prejudicially the honour or reputation of the author or director.

An infringing article for these purposes means a work or a copy of a work which has been subjected to derogatory treatment and has been or is likely to be subject to any of the acts which give rise to the right to object to derogatory treatment[70] (*e.g.* issuing copies to the public).

4. Right to Object to False Attribution of Work

(a) *What amounts to false attribution*

15.29 A false attribution occurs where, contrary to fact, an express or implied statement is made by a person whereby the whole or any part[71] of (a) a literary dramatic, musical or artistic work is falsely attributed to a person as author, or (b) a film is falsely attributed to a person as director.[72] Additionally, a false attribution occurs where an express or implied statement is made whereby a literary, dramatic or musical work is falsely represented as being an adaptation of the work of a person.[73] Thus, for example, a composer has the right to object to lyrics or music being falsely attributed to him, whether such attribution is made expressly or by means of an implied statement and an author will be similarly protected where a film is made and is falsely stated to be based upon an adaptation of his novel.

---

[68] *Ibid.*, s.82(2). For meaning of "sufficient disclaimer", see *supra*, para. 15.26.
[69] Copyright, Designs and Patents Act 1988, s.83(1).
[70] *Ibid.*, s.83(2).
[71] *Ibid.*, s.89(2).
[72] *Ibid.*, s.84(1).
[73] *Ibid.*, s.84(8). See *Moore v. News of the World Ltd.* [1972] 2 W.L.R. 419, C.A.

The right to object to false attribution is in addition to any remedy that a person may have at common law.[74]

(b) *Circumstances in which the Right is Infringed*

For the purposes of the subject matter of this work the right is infringed   **15.30** by a person who:

    (a) issues to the public copies of a literary or dramatic work or a film in or on which there is a false attribution[75]; or

    (b) in the case of a literary, dramatic or musical work, performs a work in public, broadcasts it or includes it in a cable programme service as being the work of a person[76]; or

    (c) in the case of a film, shows it in public, broadcasts it, or includes it in a cable programme service as being directed by a person[77]; or

    (d) issues to the public or displays in public material containing a false attribution in connection with any of the acts set out in (a), (b) and (c) above[78]; or

    (e) possesses, sells, lets for hire, offers or exposes for sale or hire, exhibits in public or distributes a copy of a literary, dramatic, musical work or film in or which there is a false attribution.[79]

In the case of infringements (a), (b) and (c) there is a requirement that   **15.31** the person committing the infringing act has actual or constructive knowledge that the attribution is false. With regard to infringement (e) the requirement is that such acts are committed "knowing or having reason to believe" that there is such an attribution and that it is false.

An example, of infringement (d) would occur where a cinema exhibits advertising material falsely attributing a person as director of the film exhibited at the cinema.

Infringement of the right also occurs where the acts set out in (a) to (e) above are accompanied by any false statement as to the authorship of a work of joint authorship, and by the false attribution of joint authorship in relation to a work of sole authorship.[80] In such circumstances the false attribution infringes the right of every person to whom authorship of any description is, whether rightly or wrongly, attributed.[81]

---

[74] See *post*, para. 18.06 *et seq* and para. 21.54.
[75] Copyright, Designs and Patents Act 1988, s.84(2)(a).
[76] *Ibid.*, s.84(3)(a).
[77] *Ibid.*, s.84(3)(b).
[78] *Ibid.*, s.84(4).
[79] *Ibid.*, s.84(4)(a).
[80] *Ibid.*, s.88(3).
[81] *Ibid.*, s.88(3).

5. Consent and Waiver of Moral Rights

15.32   An author or director may consent to any specific act which would otherwise be an infringement of his moral rights.[82] He may also waive his moral rights in respect of a specific work, works of a specified description, or to works generally,[83] and the waiver may be conditional or unconditional and may be expressed to be subject to revocation.[84] Where the waiver is made in favour of the owner or prospective owner of copyright in the work or works to which it relates, it is presumed to extend to the copyright owners' licensees and successors in title unless a contrary intention is expressed.[85]

The waiver must be in writing and signed by the person giving up the right[86]: where there are joint authors or directors a waiver by one of them does not affect the rights of the other.[87] However, lack of such writing does not exclude the operation of the general law of contract or estoppel in relation to an informal waiver or other transaction in relation to the moral rights.[88] It therefore follows that where an author or director leads another person, by words or conduct, to believe that his moral rights will not be insisted upon, the author or director may be estopped from insisting upon his strict legal rights notwithstanding that he has not waived his rights by an instrument in writing signed by him. Thus, for example, where a director attends the editing of a film with a producer and complies without reservation with the producer's instructions as to the manner in which the film should be edited he may be estopped from asserting his strict legal rights.

6. Transmission of Moral Rights

15.33   **Right to be identified and right to object to derogatory treatment.** Moral rights are not assignable.[89] However, the 1988 Act makes provision for the transmission in certain specified circumstances of moral rights upon the death of the author or director. First, the person entitled to a right to be identified and a right to object to derogatory treatment, may, on his death, by testamentary disposition, pass such rights to such person as he may direct.[90] Secondly, where no such testamentary disposition has

---

[82] *Ibid.*, s.87(1).
[83] *Ibid.*, s.87(2)(3)(a).
[84] *Ibid.*, s.87(3)(b).
[85] *Ibid.*, s.87(3).
[86] *Ibid.*, s.87(2).
[87] *Ibid.*, s.88(3), (5). A film is "jointly directed" if it is made by the collaboration of two or more directors and the contribution of each director is not distinct from that of the other director or directors: *ibid.*, s.86(5).
[88] *Ibid.*, s.87(4).
[89] *Ibid.*, s.94.
[90] *Ibid,*, s.95(1)(a).

been made but the copyright in the work in question forms part of his estate, the right passes to the person to whom the copyright passes.[91] If and to the extent that the rights are not transmitted in either of the above circumstances, it is exercisable by the author or director's personal representatives.[92]

Where the copyright forming part of a person's estate passes in part to another (*e.g.* the right to do one or more, but not all, of the things the copyright owner has the exclusive right to do, or authorise) any moral right which passes with the copyright is correspondingly divided.[93] Thus, if the film rights in a literary work pass to one person and the remaining rights to a second person, the person possessing the film rights will be entitled to exercise moral rights in respect of the film rights.

Special provisions are laid down in the 1988 Act in respect of the exercise of the right where it becomes exercisable by more than one person by virtue of a testamentary disposition, or where there is no such disposition and the copyright in the work forms part of the author's or director's estate, and the right passes to the persons to whom the copyright passes. Where this occurs, the right of identification may be asserted by any of such persons[94] and in the case of the right to object to derogatory treatment the right is exercisable by each of them and satisfied in relation to any of them if one consents to the treatment or act in question.[95] A waiver by one of them does not, however, affect the rights of others,[96] but a consent or waiver previously given or made binds any person to whom the right has passed.[97] **15.34**

False attribution. The right to object to false attribution is enforceable by the personal representatives of the person upon whom the right is conferred.[98] **15.35**

7. Duration of Moral Rights

The right to be identified as author or director and the right to object to derogatory treatment of the work subsist so long as the copyright subsists in the work,[99] whereas the right to object to false attribution **15.36**

---

[91] *Ibid.,* s.95(1)(b).
[92] *Ibid.,* s.95(1)(c).
[93] *Ibid.,* s.95(2).
[94] *Ibid.,* s.95(3)(a).
[95] *Ibid.,* s.95(3)(b).
[96] *Ibid.,* s.95(3)(c).
[97] *Ibid.,* s.95(4).
[98] *Ibid.,* s.95(5).
[99] *Ibid.,* s.86(1).

continues to subsist until 20 years after the death of the person upon whom the right is conferred.[1]

8. Remedies for Infringement

15.37 An infringement of a person's moral rights is actionable as a breach of statutory duty[2] owed to the person entitled to the right.[3] Where the action relates to the infringement of the right to be identified, the court is required by the 1988 Act, in considering remedies, to take into account any delay in asserting the right. Thus where, for example, a director has delayed unconscionably in asserting his right of paternity and the producer has struck prints of the film for exhibition and the director then asserts his rights, the court would be entitled to take the delay into account and simply award damages and not injunctive relief.

Where the proceedings relate to the right to object to derogatory treatment of work, the 1988 Act provides that the court may, if it thinks it is an adequate remedy in the circumstances, grant an injunction on terms prohibiting the doing of any act unless a disclaimer is made in such terms and in such manner as may be approved by the court, dissociating the author or director from the treatment of the work.[4]

9. Transitional Provisions

15.38 No act is actionable as an infringement of the moral rights where they took place before commencement.[5] Further, the right to be identified and the right to object to derogatory treatment do not apply in relation to a literary, dramatic, musical and artistic work the author of which died before commencement, nor to a film made before commencement.[6]

Schedule 1, paragraph 23(3) further provides that the rights conferred by section 80 in relation to an existing literary, dramatic, musical or artistic work do not apply where (a) copyright first vested in the author, to anything which by reason of the assignment of copyright or licence granted before the commencement may be done without infringing

---

[1] *Ibid.*, s.86(2).
[2] For "statutory duty" generally see *Clerk & Lindsell on Torts* (Sweet & Maxwell, 16th ed. 1989) Chap.14.
[3] Copyright, Designs and Patents Act 1988, s.103(1).
[4] *Ibid.*, s.103(2).
[5] *Ibid.*, Sched. 22(1).
[6] *Ibid.*, Sched. 23(2). Commencement: August 1, 1989.

copyright, or (b) copyright first vested in a person other than the author, to anything done by or with the licence of the copyright owner.

Section 43 of the Copyright Act 1956 continues to apply to false attribution in respect of acts done before the commencement of the 1988 Act.[7]

---

[7] *Ibid.*, Sched. 22(2).

THE COPYRIGHT TRIBUNAL

1. Jurisdiction of the Copyright Tribunal

16.01 In so far as is relevant to the areas of Entertainment and Broadcasting Law, the Copyright Tribunal has jurisdiction[1] to hear and determine:

(a) references of proposed and existing "licensing schemes"[1a];

(b) applications with respect to entitlement to licences under existing licensing schemes[2];

(c) references or applications with respect to licensing by a "licensing body"[3];

(d) applications to settle a royalty or other sum payable for the rental of sound recording or film[4];

(e) applications to give consent to the making of a recording from a previous recording of a performance on behalf of a performer

---

[1] Copyright, Designs and Patents Act 1988, s.149.
[1a] *Ibid.*, ss.118, 119, 120; and see *post*, paras. 16.02 and 16.04–16.05.
[2] *Ibid.*, ss.149, 121, 122. See *post*, paras. 16.08–16.15.
[3] *Ibid.*, ss.125, 126, 127. See *post*, paras. 16.03 and 16.16–16.22.
[4] *Ibid.*, s.142. See *post*, para. 16.23.

whose identity or whereabouts cannot be traced or who unreasonably withholds his consent[5];

(f) applications to determine the royalty or other remuneration to be paid to the trustees for the Hospital for Sick Children in respect of the use of the play *Peter Pan* by Sir James Barrie[6];

(g) applications to settle the terms of payment under a compulsory licence in respect of programmes listings[7];

(h) applications to settle the terms of payment in, or as to the reasonableness of any condition in relation to compulsory or statutory licences for "needletime".[8]

Licensing schemes. A "licensing scheme" is defined by the 1988 Act as **16.02** meaning a scheme, tariff or any other general terms setting out:

(a) the classes of case in which the operator of the scheme, or the person on whose behalf he acts, is willing to grant copyright licences; and

(b) the terms on which licences would be granted in those classes of case.[9]

An example of a licensing scheme is the publication by the Mechanical-Copyright Protection Society of standard terms for licensing rights which it administers.

Licensing body. A licensing body is a society or other organisation **16.03** which has as its main object, or one of its main objects, the negotiation or granting, either as owner or prospective owner of copyright or as agent for him, of copyright licences, and whose objects include the grant of licences covering works of more than one author.[10] For these purposes, a copyright licence is a licence to do, or authorise the doing of, any of the acts restricted by copyright.[11] A licensing body will therefore include collecting societies and agencies such as MCPS, PRS, PPL and VPL who have as their main object the administration and granting of copyright licences for the use of the works of their members.

---

[5] *Ibid.*, s.190. See *ante* paras. 14.34–14.38.
[6] *Ibid.*, Sched. 6, para. 5. See *post*, para. 16.25.
[7] Broadcasting Act 1990, Sched. 17, paras. 5, 6, 7(1).
[8] Copyright, Designs and Patents Act 1988, ss.135D, 135E and 135F as inserted by Broadcasting Act 1990, s.175. See *post*, paras. 16.31–16.34.
[9] *Ibid.*, s.116(1).
[10] *Ibid.*, s.116(2). It is to be noted that a single collective work or collective works of which the authors are the same or works made by employees of or commissioned by a single individual, firm, company or group of companies do not come within the meaning of licensing schemes or licences covering more than one author.
[11] *Ibid.*, s.116(3). See *ante*, para. 12.02 for acts restricted by copyright.

(a) *Licensing scheme*

(i) *Jurisdiction*

16.04 Literary, dramatic, musical, artistic works and films. The Tribunal has jurisdiction in respect of licensing schemes operated by licensing bodies in relation to the copyright in literary, dramatic, musical or artistic works or films (or film sound-tracks when accompanying a film) covering the works of more than one author so far as they relate to licences for copying the work, performing, playing or showing the work in public, or broadcasting, or including it in a cable programme service.[12] Consequently, only schemes operated collectively in relation to literary, dramatic, musical, artistic works or films are referable to the Tribunal. It is, therefore, not within the Tribunal's remit to consider any schemes that may be operated by individual authors in respect of literary, dramatic, musical, or artistic works and films.

16.05 Sound recordings, broadcasts or cable programmes. Where the subject matter of the licensing scheme is the copyright in sound recording (other than film sound tracks when accompanying a film), broadcasts or cable programmes, the jurisdiction of the Tribunal is not limited to schemes operated collectively. In such circumstances it may receive and consider references relating to *all* licence schemes whether operated by a licensing body or by an individual copyright owner.[13]

16.06 Rental of sound recordings and films. All licensing schemes relating to the rental of sound recordings and films, whether individually or collectively operated, are subject to the jurisdiction of the Tribunal.[14]

(ii) *Reference of licensing scheme to the Tribunal*

16.07 Proposed scheme. The terms of a licensing scheme proposed to be operated by a licensing body may be referred to the Tribunal by an organisation claiming to be a representative of persons claiming that they require licences in cases of a description to which the proposed scheme would apply.[15] Thus, in relation to a *proposed* scheme the Tribunal has no jurisdiction to entertain a reference from an individual nor from an organisation which does not represent persons claiming that they require licences coming within the scheme. In such circumstances the Tribunal, of its own motion, or any other organisation may take objection to an applicant's credentials to make a reference.[16]

---

[12] *Ibid.*, s.117(a).
[13] *Ibid.*, s.117(b).
[14] *Ibid.*, s.117(c).
[15] *Ibid.*, s.118(1).
[16] The Copyright Tribunal Rules 1989 (S.I. 1989 No. 1129), rr. 5 and 6.

Where a reference is made by an organisation, the Tribunal is required first to consider "whether to entertain the reference, and may decline to do so on the basis that the reference is premature".[17] The basis on which the Tribunal is entitled to decline to entertain a reference would appear to be limited to the prematurity of the references. The fact that an applicant may not have the necessary *locus standi* does not appear to be a relevant factor at this stage in the Tribunal's determination because rules 5 and 6 of the Copyright Tribunal Rules provide a procedure for objecting to an applicant's credentials.

Existing scheme. Where a licensing scheme is in operation and a dispute arises between the operator of the scheme and a person claiming that he requires a licence in a case of a description to which the scheme applies, or an organisation claiming to be a representative of such persons, that person or organisation may refer the scheme to the Tribunal in so far as it relates to cases of that description.[18] The reference of an existing scheme would appear to differ from a reference in respect of a proposed scheme in that both individuals and organisations may refer an existing scheme to the Tribunal. However, the reference in the case of existing schemes is limited to the licences of the particular description in respect of which the dispute arises, whereas references in respect of proposed schemes may take place "either generally or in relation to any description of case". **16.08**

Where a reference has been made in respect of an existing scheme, that scheme remains in operation until proceedings on the reference are concluded. It therefore follows that where the dispute arises by reason of the desire of the operator of the scheme to charge a higher licence fee, such higher fee cannot be imposed during the currency of the proceedings and its subsequent imposition is subject to the order of the Tribunal.

Further reference of scheme to Tribunal. Where a proposed or existing scheme has previously been referred to the Tribunal and it has made an order with respect to that scheme, a subsequent reference may be made during the currency of the order in respect of cases of the descriptions to which it relates.[19] The persons eligible to make such a subsequent reference are the operator of the scheme, the person claiming that he requires a licence in a case of the description to which the order applies, or an organisation claiming to be representative of such persons.[20] **16.09**

However, a licence scheme may not be so referred, except with

---

[17] Copyright, Designs and Patents Act 1988, s.118(2).
[18] *Ibid.*, s.119(1).
[19] *Ibid.*, s.120(1).
[20] *Ibid.*, s.120(1)(a), (b), (c).

special leave of the Tribunal, in respect of the same description of cases within 12 months from the date of the order on the previous reference, or if the order was made so as to be in force for 15 months or less, until the last three months before its expiry.[21] These time limits provide a sufficient period for the practical effects of the scheme to be judged. If at the end of the period it is seen to be working to the detriment of either party the provision entitling further references provides a means of seeking a remedy in that the Tribunal is given powers to either confirm, vary, or further vary the scheme.[22]

16.10 **Application for grant of licence in connection with licensing scheme.** Where a licensing scheme is in operation an application may be made to the Tribunal either:

(a) by a person who claims that the operator of the scheme has refused to grant him, or procure the grant to him of, a licence in accordance within the scheme, or has failed to do so within a reasonable time after being asked[23]; or

(b) by a person who claims, in a "case excluded" from a licensing scheme, that the operator of the scheme either:

(i) has refused to grant him a licence, or procure the grant within a reasonable time of being asked, and that in the circumstances it is unreasonable that a licence should not be granted[24]; or

(ii) proposes terms which are unreasonable.[25]

16.11 A case is excluded from a licensing scheme if it is expressly excluded by the scheme[26] or is so similar to those in which licences are granted under the scheme that it is unreasonable that it should not be dealt with in the same way.[27] If the Tribunal determines that the applicant's claim is well founded it is required to make an order declaring that the applicant is entitled to a licence on such terms as the Tribunal may determine applicable in accordance with the scheme or, as may be reasonable in the circumstances.[28]

An applicant may apply to the Tribunal to review its order.[29] Where such review is sought, the requirements as to leave are identical to

---

[21] *Ibid.*, s.120(2).
[22] *Ibid.*, s.120(4).
[23] *Ibid.*, s.121(1).
[24] *Ibid.*, s.121(2)(a).
[25] *Ibid.*, s.121(2)(b).
[26] *Ibid.*, s.121(3)(a).
[27] *Ibid.*, s.121(3)(b).
[28] *Ibid.*, s.121(4).
[29] *Ibid.*, s.122(1).

those in respect of a further reference in respect of a licensing scheme.[30] Where the Tribunal proceeds to review its order its powers are identical to those in the proceedings in which the original order was made.[31]

(iii) *Powers of the Tribunal on a reference of a proposed or existing scheme*

Power to make order confirming or varying

On a reference to the Tribunal it has power "to make such order, either confirming or varying the proposed scheme . . . as the Tribunal may determine to be reasonable in the circumstances"[32] and such order "may be made so as to be in force indefinitely or for such period as the Tribunal may determine."[33] The language of the power granted to the Tribunal makes it clear that "the decision is to confirm or vary as appears to [the Tribunal] to be reasonable. There is no presumption in favour of a referred scheme. Nor is there a presumption that a referred scheme should be varied".[34]   **16.12**

Effect of order as to licensing scheme

Duration of the scheme. A proposed or existing licensing scheme that has been confirmed or varied by the Tribunal continues in force so long as the order relating to it remains in force.[35]   **16.13**

Copyright infringement. During the period of the scheme a person who is in a class to which the order applies is in the same position as regards infringement of copyright as if he had at all material times been the holder of a licence from the owner of the copyright in the work if he[36]:   **16.14**

(a) pays the operator of the scheme the charges payable under the scheme in respect of a licence or, where the amount payable is unascertained, undertakes to pay when it is ascertained[37]; and

(b) who complies with the licence terms.[38]

Date from which order takes effect. Where the Tribunal varies the amount of charge payable under a proposed or existing licensing scheme it may direct that the order has effect from a date before the order was made.[39] However, such date must not be earlier than the date   **16.15**

---

[30] *Ibid.*, s.122(2). See *ante*, para. 16.09.
[31] *Ibid.*, s.122(3).
[32] *Ibid.*, ss.118(3), 119(3).
[33] *Ibid.*, ss.118(4), 119(4).
[34] *The British Phonographic Industry Limited v. Mechanical-Copyright Protection Society Limited (No. 2)* [1993] E.M.L.R. 86 at 99.
[35] Copyright, Designs and Patents Act 1988, s.123(1).
[36] *Ibid.*, ss.123(2), 123(5).
[37] *Ibid.*, s.123(2)(a).
[38] *Ibid.*, s.123(2)(b).
[39] *Ibid.*, s.123(3).

on which the reference was made, or, if later, the date on which the scheme came into operation.[40] The effect, therefore, is that the Tribunal has power to backdate the amount of the charge payable to the date of the reference where the scheme was existing, and to the date it came into operation where it was a proposed scheme. Where the amount of the charge is varied and backdated the parties are required to make any necessary repayments, or further payments in respect of the charges already paid.[41] Thus, if, in respect of an existing scheme, the Tribunal should raise the charges and backdate such charges to the date of the references the licensee would be required to make such additional payments to take account of his shortfall in payment since the date of reference and the date of the order.

(b) *References and applications with respect to licensing by licensing bodies*

(i) *Jurisdiction of Copyright Tribunal*

16.16 The Tribunal has jurisdiction in respect of licences granted by a licensing body in relation to:

(1) the copyright in literary, dramatic, musical or artistic works, or films (or film sound-tracks when accompanying a film) covering the works of more than one author so far as they relate to licences for copying the work, performing playing or showing the work in public or broadcasting or including it in a cable programme service.[42]

(2) any licences relating to the copyright in a sound recording (other than a film sound-track when accompanying the film) broadcast or cable programme[43];

(3) all licences in relation to the copyright in sound recordings and films so far as they relate to the rental of copies to the public.[44]

Only individual licences granted by a licensing body which do not come within a licensing scheme come within this particular jurisdiction.

16.17 **Proposed licence.** Where a proposed licence is the subject of the dispute only the individual licensee has the necessary *locus standi* to refer the proposed terms to the Tribunal.[45] As in the case of a proposed licensing

---

[40] *Ibid.*, s.123(3).
[41] *Ibid.*, s.123(3)(a).
[42] *Ibid.*, s.124(a).
[43] *Ibid.*, s.124(b).
[44] *Ibid.*, s.124(c).
[45] *Ibid.*, s.125(1).

scheme, the Tribunal has to first decide whether the reference is premature,[46] and where it entertains the reference it has power to make an order either confirming or varying the terms as it may consider reasonable in the circumstances.[47] The benefit of an order made by a Tribunal under its powers may, if not prohibited by the order, be assigned.[48]

Existing licences. Where the subject matter of a reference is an existing licence which is due to expire by the affluxion of time or by notice given by the licensing body, the individual licensee may apply to the Tribunal on the ground that it is unreasonable in the circumstances that the licence should cease to be in force.[49] Such application may not, however, be made until the last three months before the licence is due to expire,[50] but where it is so made the licence remains in operation until proceedings on the reference are concluded.[51] If the Tribunal finds that it would be unreasonable that the licence should cease to be in force it must make an order declaring that it is to continue in force on such terms as it may determine to be reasonable.[52] If the assignment was not prohibited under the terms of the original licence, the benefit of an order extending the licence may be assigned.[53]   **16.18**

Application for review of order. An applicant may apply to the Tribunal to review its order.[54] Where such a review is sought, the requirement as to leave is identical to those in respect of a further reference in respect of a licensing scheme.[55] Where the Tribunal proceeds to review its order its powers are identical to those in the proceedings in which the reviewed order was made.[56]   **16.19**

(ii) *Effect of order as to licensing scheme*

Duration of scheme. A proposed or existing licensing scheme that has been confirmed or varied by the Tribunal continues in force so long as the order relating to it remains in force.[57]   **16.20**

---

[46] *Ibid.*, s.125(2).
[47] *Ibid.*, s.125(3).
[48] *Ibid.*, s.128(2)(a).
[49] *Ibid.*, s.126(1).
[50] *Ibid.*, s.126(2).
[51] *Ibid.*, s.126(3).
[52] *Ibid.*, s.126(4).
[53] *Ibid.*, s.128(2)(b).
[54] *Ibid.*, s.127(1).
[55] *Ibid.*, s.127(2). See *ante*, para. 16.09.
[56] *Ibid.*, s.127(3). See *ante*, paras. 16.17–16.18.
[57] *Ibid.*, s.128(1).

16.21 Copyright infringement. During the period of the scheme a person who is in a class to which the order applies is in the same position as regards infringement of copyright as if he had at all material times been the holder of a licence from the owner of the copyright in the work if he[58]:

(a) pays to the licensing body any charges payable in accordance with the order or, where the amount payable is unascertained undertakes to pay when it is ascertained[59]; and

(b) who complies with the other terms specified in the order.[60]

16.22 Date from which order takes effect. Where the Tribunal varies the amount of charge payable under a proposed or existing licence it may direct that the order has effect from a date before the order was made.[61] However, such date must not be earlier than the date on which the reference was made or, if later, on which the licence was granted, or as the case may be, was due to expire.[62] Where the charges are backdated any necessary repayments, or further payments must then be made in respect of charges already paid.[63]

(c) *Settling royalty in respect of rental right*

16.23 In respect of sound recordings and films, the exclusive rights of copyright owners to issue copies to the public include any rental of copies to the public.[64] Section 66 of the 1988 Act provides for compulsory licensing, by order of the Secretary of State, of sound recordings and films, in such cases as may be specified in the order, of the rental to the public of copies of sound recordings, subject only to the payment of a reasonable royalty or other payment as may be agreed between the parties, in default of agreement, as may be determined by the Tribunal.[65] Where the parties fail to reach agreement as to the reasonable royalty or payment to be made, the Tribunal, on an application to settle the royalty payable, must make such order as to the charges payable as it determines to be "reasonable in the circumstances".[66]

Either party may subsequently apply to the Tribunal to vary the order[67] but such an application may not be made, except with special leave of the Tribunal, within 12 months from the date of the original

---

58 *Ibid.*, s.123(2), 123(5).
59 *Ibid.*, s.128(1)(a).
60 *Ibid.*, s.128(1)(b).
61 *Ibid.*, s.123(3).
62 *Ibid.*, s.128(3).
63 *Ibid.*, s.128(3)(a).
64 *Ibid.*, s.18(2). See *ante*, paras. 12.13–12.32.
65 *Ibid.*, s.66(1).
66 *Ibid.*, s.142(2).
67 *Ibid.*, s.142(3).

order, or of the order on a previous application.[68] Where such an application is duly made, the Tribunal has a discretion whether to confirm or vary the original as it may consider to be reasonable in the circumstances.[69] An order made on a subsequent application cannot, however, be backdated. It must take effect from the date on which the order is made or, if so specified by the Tribunal, a later date.[70]

(d) *Consent on behalf of performers*

16.24 This subject is dealt with under "Rights in Performances" at *ante*, paragraphs 14.34 to 14.38.

(e) *Settling royalty payable in* Peter Pan

16.25 Section 301 of the 1988 Act confers on the trustees for the benefit of the Hospital for Sick Children, Great Ormond Street, a right to a royalty in respect of the public performance, commercial publication, broadcasting or inclusion in a cable programme service of the play *Peter Pan* by Sir James Matthew Barrie, or any adaptation of the work notwithstanding the expiry of copyright. Where the parties fail to reach agreement as to the reasonable royalty or payment to be made to the trustees the Tribunal, on an application to settle the royalty payable, must make such order as to the charges payable as it determines to be "reasonable in the circumstances".[71]

Either party may subsequently apply to the Tribunal to vary the order,[72] but such an application may not be made, except with special leave of the Tribunal, within 12 months from the date of the original order, or of the order on a previous application.[73] Where such an application is duly made, the Tribunal has a discretion whether to confirm or vary the original as it may consider to be reasonable in the circumstances.[74] An order made on a subsequent application cannot, however, be backdated. It must take effect from the date on which the order is made or, if so specified by the Tribunal, at a later date.[75]

(f) *Settlement of terms for television listings information*

16.26 **Right to publish listings information.** Under section 176 of the Broadcasting Act 1990, providers of television and national radio services are

---

[68] *Ibid.*, s.142(3).
[69] *Ibid.*, s.142(3).
[70] *Ibid.*, s.142(5).
[71] *Ibid.*, Sched. 6, para. 5(1).
[72] *Ibid.*, Sched. 6, para. 5(2).
[73] *Ibid.*, Sched. 6, para. 5(3).
[74] *Ibid.*, Sched. 6, para. 5(2).
[75] *Ibid.*, Sched. 6, para. 5(4).

obliged to make available information as to the date, time and title of programmes to any person who wishes to publish such information.

16.27 Conditions for the exercise of the right. A publisher wishing to avail himself of the right is required to give notice of his intention to the person providing the programme service, asking that person to propose terms of payment.[76] Where the terms proposed by the programme provider appear unreasonably high, or no terms are proposed after a reasonable period, the publisher may proceed to publish the information subject to two conditions.

First he must give notice to the programme service provider of the date on which he proposes to begin publishing the information and the terms of payment in accordance with which he intends to do so.[77]

Secondly, before exercising the right to publish the information, the publisher must give reasonable notice to the Tribunal of his intention to exercise his right to publish, the date on which he proposes to begin to do so, and apply to the Tribunal to settle the terms of payment.[78]

16.28 Jurisdiction of Tribunal. The jurisdiction of the Tribunal is wide and unfettered. Schedule 17, paragraph 5(1) of the Broadcasting Act 1990 provides that:

> "On an application to settle the terms of payment, the Copyright Tribunal shall consider the matter and make such order as it may determine to be reasonable in the circumstances."

In determining what is reasonable no matters are expressly excluded from consideration in contrast, for instance, to the provisions dealing with the powers of the tribunal in respect of "needletime".

16.29 Order of the Tribunal. Where such an application is made the Tribunal may make such order as it determines "to be reasonable in all the circumstances,"[79] and such order takes effect from the date the applicant begins to publish the information.[80] A subsequent application may be made for a review of the order. However, such an application may not be made without special leave of the Tribunal within 12 months from the date of the order on the previous application, or if the order was

---

[76] Broadcasting Act 1990, Sched. 17, para. 3(1).
[77] *Ibid.,* Sched. 17, para. 3(1)(b).
[78] *Ibid.,* Sched. 17, para. 3(2).
[79] *Ibid.,* Sched. 17, para. 5(1).
[80] *Ibid.,* Sched. 17, para. 5(2).

made so as to be in force for 15 months or less, or as a result of a decision on a previous application is due to expire within 15 months of that decision, until the last three months before its expiry.[81] Where such further references are duly made, the Tribunal is given power to either confirm, vary or further vary the scheme,[82] and where varied such variation takes effect from the date on which the order is made or such later date as directed by the Tribunal.[83]

Principles applied in settlement of terms. In *News Group Newspapers* **16.30** *Limited v. Independent Television Publications Limited*[84] the Tribunal exercised its jurisdiction so as to promote the policy and objects of the Broadcasting Act 1990. It concluded that that policy was to ensure diversity in broadcasting and the services connected with it, and fair and effective competition. Consequently, when setting the terms of payment it would appear that the Tribunal will have regard to the encouragement of the widest dissemination of, and easy access to, programme material, even if this involves financial detriment to the interests of the broadcasters as the copyright holders. In general the Tribunal considers that such wide dissemination and easy access to programme information "will be best achieved if the terms of payment are moderate from the publishers' viewpoint and not unreasonably in excess of the Broadcasters' costs".[85]

(g) *Needletime*

The Broadcasting Act 1990[86] amends the Copyright, Designs and **16.31** Patents Act 1988 by inserting into the 1988 Act sections 135A to 135G. The effect of these sections is to entitle broadcasters to a compulsory licence to broadcast Phonographic Performance Limited's repertoire and to abolish its right to impose needletime restrictions on broadcasters. The 1988 Act, as so amended, gives to any broadcaster, on fulfillment of certain conditions,[87] the right to a compulsory licence "allowing unlimited needletime or such needletime as demanded"[88] to broadcast sound recordings, and if need be, to pay for that copyright use in accordance with terms of payment notified by the broadcaster to

---

[81] *Ibid.*, Sched. 17, para. 6(1).
[82] *Ibid.*, Sched. 17, para. 6(3).
[83] *Ibid.*, Sched. 17, para. 6(4).
[84] [1993] E.M.L.R. 1.
[85] *Ibid.* at 19.
[86] c. 42, s.175.
[87] Copyright, Designs and Patents Act 1988, s.135B.
[88] *Ibid.*, s.135A(2), (3). "Needletime" means the time in any period (whether determined as number of hours in the period or a proportion of the period, or otherwise) in which any recordings may be included in a broadcast or cable programme service: *ibid.*, s.135A(5).

the licensing body.[89] Before exercising this right the broadcaster must first give reasonable notice to the Tribunal of his intention to exercise the right, and of the date on which he proposes to begin to do so,[90] and, secondly, must apply to the Tribunal to settle the terms of payment.[91]

16.32 On an application[92] to the Tribunal to settle the terms of payment it is the duty of the Tribunal to "consider the matter and make such Order as it may determine to be reasonable in the circumstances".[93] The same duty is imposed in relation to the licensing body's proposed licence conditions and its requirements as to information to be provided to it by the broadcaster.[94] In determining what is "reasonable" in both cases two matters are relevant. First, the Tribunal is required to "exercise its powers so as to secure that there is no unreasonable discrimination between persons exercising [a right to a compulsory or statutory licence] against the same licensing body".[95] This has been interpreted to mean that any Order of the Tribunal should not cause "unreasonable discrimination" between broadcasters who take a compulsory or statutory licence in relation to the copyright of PPL.[96] Thus, the Tribunal may discriminate between applicants or groups of applicants provided that such discrimination is on reasonable criteria.

16.33 Where a broadcaster does not broadcast needletime under a compulsory licence the provision as to unreasonable discrimination does not apply. Nevertheless, under section 129 of the 1988 Act the Tribunal is under a duty "to secure that there is no unreasonable discrimination between licensees . . . under the scheme or licence to which the reference or application relates and licensees under other schemes operated by, or other licences granted by, the same person." Thus, in circumstances where there is a reference or application it matters not whether the licence is compulsory or otherwise there must be no "unreasonable discrimination".

16.34 Secondly, in settling the terms of payment, the Tribunal "shall not be guided by any order it has made under any enactment other than . . . section [135D]" of the 1988 Act.[97] Consequently the Tribunal may not base its decision, to any extent, on an order made under previous legis-

---

[89] Copyright, Designs and Patents Act 1988, ss.135B(1), 135C.
[90] *Ibid.*, s.135B(3)(a).
[91] *Ibid.*, s.135(3)(b); s.135C.
[92] Pursuant to *Ibid.*, s.135D.
[93] *Ibid.*, s.135D(1).
[94] *Ibid.*, s.135E.
[95] *Ibid.*, s.135G(1)(b).
[96] *The Association of Independent Radio Companies Ltd. v. Phonographic Performance Ltd.*; [1993] E.M.L.R. 181.
[97] Copyright, Designs and Patents Act 1988, s.135G(2).

lation. However, it has been held that this does not require the Tribunal to "ignore any previous order, and in our view we are free to refer to such an order as an essential part of the history of the matter".[98]

(h) *Factors to be taken into account by the Tribunal in its determination*

(i) *General factors to be taken into account by Copyright Tribunal in all proceedings*

In all classes of case within its jurisdiction, the Tribunal is given a **16.35** power either to make such order as it "may determine to be reasonable in the circumstances".[99] In determining what is "reasonable in the circumstances" on a reference or application, the Tribunal is under a general duty to have regard to "all relevant considerations".[1] Subject to this general and overriding duty, section 129 expressly makes "comparables" relevant in that it directs the Tribunal to have regard to:

"(a) the availability of other schemes, or the granting of other licences, to persons in similar circumstances; and

(b) the terms of those schemes or licences".

Further, section 129 directs the Tribunal to exercise its powers so as to secure that there is no unreasonable discrimination between licensees, or prospective licensees, under the scheme or licence to which the reference or application relates, and licensees under other schemes operated by, or other licences granted by the same person. It therefore follows that the Tribunal may exercise its powers so as to cause discrimination between licensees or prospective licensees provided such discrimination is based on reasonable criteria.

No further guidance is provided by the 1988 Act as to the factors to be **16.36** taken into account in determining what is reasonable in the circumstances. In *Association of Independent Radio Contractors v. Phonographic Performance*,[2] Harman J. considered section 25(5) of the Copyright Act 1956[3] which required the Performing Right Tribunal to "consider the matter in dispute and . . . and . . . make such order . . . as the Tribunal may determine to be reasonable in the circumstances". He concluded that the "language used by Parliament does not suggest that Parliament was creating a Tribunal to decide what were open market values".

---

[98] *The Association of Independent Radio Companies Ltd. v. Phonographic Performance Ltd.*; [1993] E.M.L.R. 181 at 227.
[99] Copyright, Designs and Patents Act 1988, s.118(3), 119(3), 120(4), 121(4), 122(3), 125(3), 127(3), 142(2), (3), Sched. 6, para. 5(1).
[1] *Ibid.*, s.135.
[2] Unreported; 1986.
[3] Copyright Act 1956, s.25(5).

In *News Group Newspapers Limited v. Independent Television Limited*[4] the Tribunal applied Harman J.'s observations. It would therefore appear that open market values is not a relevant consideration.

16.37   The general philosophy underlying the protection of intellectual property by copyright law in the United Kingdom includes the need to provide an adequate reward for creative effort and an incentive to continue creative activity and as such would appear to be "a circumstance of the case"[5] In determining an adequate reward for creative effort the level of profitability of a licensee is an important, but not determinative, relevant consideration in determining what level of fee is to be charged.[6] In *Association of Independent Radio Contractors v. Phonographic Performance*,[7] the approach in applying this criterion was stated thus:

> "If this [the 'guideline' consisting of the financial performance of the broadcasting companies] means that the Tribunal is entitled to say 'Look, these people make large profits . . . so let us charge them a high royalty', that would be . . . a wrong approach and an error of law. On the other hand it must be proper for the Tribunal to consider 'Are the companies solvent and making profits or are they struggling and unable to afford any substantial sum?", since this must affect what is 'reasonable'. It could not be reasonable to charge a royalty that would put the broadcasting companies out of business."

16.38   However, this does not mean that high profitability is not a relevant factor where it is clearly referable to the licence in issue but such casual connection will not always be easy to establish. As was observed in *The British Phonographic Industry Limited v. Mechanical-Copyright Protection Society Limited (No. 2)*[8]:

> " . . . profits available are a relevant consideration but should by no means be regarded as determinative. High profitability in a licensee may be due to a variety of causes and it would not be right for a high royalty to follow automatically . . . ".

---

[4] [1993] E.M.L.R. 1.
[5] *News Group Newspapers Ltd. v. Independent Television Ltd.* [1993] E.M.L.R. 1 at 19; *The British Phonographic Industry Ltd. v. Mechanical-Copyright Protection Society Ltd. (No. 2)* [1993] E.M.L.R. 86 at 125.
[6] *Association of Independent Radio Contractors v. Phonographic Performance* (unreported; 1986); *The British Phonographic Industry Limited v. Mechanical-Copyright Protection Society Limited (No. 2)* [1993] E.M.L.R. 86.
[7] Unreported; 1986.
[8] [1993] E.M.L.R. 86.

(ii) *Particular factors to be taken into account in particular classes of case*

Sound recordings films

Licences relating to sound recordings, films, broadcasts or cable pro- **16.39**
grammes which include, or are to include, any entertainment or other
event. In proceedings in respect of licences relating to sound recordings, films, broadcasts or cable programme which include any entertainment or other event the Tribunal is required to have regard to any
conditions imposed by the promoters of the entertainment or event.[9] In
particular, the Tribunal is directed not to hold a refusal or failure to
grant a licence in respect of such works to be unreasonable if such
licence could not have been granted consistently with the conditions
imposed by the promoter of the entertainment or event.[10] However, the
Tribunal is not required to have regard to any such conditions in so far
as they:

(a) purport to regulate the charges imposed by the owner of the
work in respect of the grant of licences[11]; or

(b) relate to payments to be made to the promoters of any event in
consideration of the grant of facilities for making the recording,
film, broadcast or cable programme.[12]

Thus, for example, where a television producer is given broadcast
rights to a pop concert and it is a condition of the licence permitting the
recording of the event that the recording is not exhibited in the cinema,
the Tribunal is not to hold such provision unreasonable. The imposition of such a duty on the Tribunal enables an impresario effectively
to exploit the rights in the entertainment or event by licensing broadcast television, video rights and other media separately, thus maximis-
ing his revenue.

Licences to reflect payment in respect of underlying rights. Where a **16.40**
reference or application relates to:

(a) licences for rental to the public of copies of sound recordings or
films[13]; or

(b) in such cases where the Secretary of State by Order specifies, the
rental to the public of sound recordings shall be treated as
licensed by the copyright owner subject only to the payment of

---

[9] Copyright, Designs and Patent Act 1988, s.132(2).
[10] *Ibid.*, s.132(2).
[11] *Ibid.*, s.132(3)(a).
[12] *Ibid.*, s.132(3)(b).
[13] *Ibid.*, s.133(1)(a).

such reasonable royalty as may be agreed or determined in default of agreement by the Tribunal,[14]

the Tribunal is required to take into account any reasonable payments which the owner of the copyright in the sound recording or film is liable to make in consequence of the granting of the licence, or of the acts authorised by the licence to "owners of copyright in works included in that work".[15] Payments which the copyright owner may be "liable to make in consequence of the granting of the licence" will include any sums payable by way of royalty for rental rights in respect of copyright material such as sound recordings, dramatic or musical works incorporated in the sound recording or film.[16]

16.41   In the cases where the reference to the Tribunal relates to licensing in respect of the copyright in sound recordings, films, broadcasts or cable programmes, a similar principle applies as to payments, save that in such cases the payment to be taken into account by the Tribunal is that payable "in respect of any performance included in the recording, film, broadcast or cable programme".[17] Thus, for example, if the owner of the copyright is obliged to make a royalty payment (more often referred to in the entertainment industry as a "residual" payment) to performers in respect of each, or a set number of, video-cassette(s) of a film sold such payment is to be taken into account in fixing the licence fee.

16.42   **Licences in respect of works included in re-transmissions.** The 1988 Act sets out special provisions in respect of references to the Tribunal relating to licences to include literary, dramatic, musical, artistic works or sound records or films in a broadcast or cable service where one broadcast or cable programme ("the first transmission") is, by reception and immediate re-transmission, to be further broadcast or included in a cable programme service ("the further transmission"). In so far as the further transmission is to the same area as the first transmission, the Tribunal is directed, when deciding what charges if any should be paid for licences for either transmission, to have regard to the extent to which the copyright owner has already received or is entitled to receive payment for the other transmission which adequately compensates him in respect of transmissions to that area.[18] The effect of such a requirement is that in general a copyright owner will not be able to recover twice in respect of the transmission to the same area of the same material.

---

[14] *Ibid.*, s.133(1)(b).
[15] *Ibid.*, s.133.
[16] *Ibid.*, 133(2).
[17] *Ibid.*, 133(2).
[18] *Ibid.*, s.134(2).

Where further transmissions are made to an area outside that to **16.43**
which the first transmission was made, the Tribunal is not to have
regard to and shall leave out of account the further transmission in considering what charges if any should be paid for licences for the first
transmission.[19] However, where the Tribunal is satisfied that the
requirements imposed under the Cable and Broadcasting Act 1984[20]
will result in the further transmission being to areas part of which fall
outside the area to which the first transmission is made it is required to
exercise its powers so as to secure that the charges payable for licences
for the first transmission adequately reflect that fact.[21]

2. Appeal to the High Court on point of Law

An appeal lies on any point of law arising from the decision of the Tri-   **16.44**
bunal to the High Court.[22] In exercising its powers under the 1988 Act
the Tribunal is enjoined to make such order "as the Tribunal may determine to be reasonable in the circumstances".[23] In such circumstances
the Tribunal can only err in law if it does something which no Tribunal,
if it thought about the matter, could have regarded as reasonable.

Irrationality could, in theory, be demonstrated in two ways. First, the
royalty fixed by the Tribunal might be so large or so small that no
rational Tribunal could have arrived at such as figure. Secondly, the
reasons given by the Tribunal pursuant to rule 17 of the Copyright Tribunal Rules 1989, might disclose some *non sequitur* which invalidates
the reasoning.[24]

---

[19] *Ibid.*, s.134(3).
[20] *Ibid.*, s.13(1).
[21] *Ibid.*, s.134(4).
[22] *Ibid.*, s.152. There is no restriction on further appeal from the decision of the Court.
[23] *Ibid.*, ss.118(3), 119(3), 120(4), 121(4), 122(3), 125(3), 127(3), 142(2), Sched. 6, para. 5(1). See
also *ante*, para. 16.35.
[24] *The Performing Right Society Ltd. v. The British Entertainment and Dancing Association Ltd.*
[1993] E.M.L.R. 325.

Part III

EQUITABLE REMEDIES

CHAPTER 17

BREACH OF CONFIDENCE

1. Introduction

Elements of action of breach of confidence. "[T]hree elements are nor-   **17.01**
mally required if, apart from contract, a case of breach of confidence is
to succeed. First, the information itself . . . must have the necessary
quality of confidence about it. Secondly, that information must have
been imparted in circumstances importing an obligation of confidence.
Thirdly, there must be an unauthorised use of that information to the
detriment of the party communicating it".[1]

(a) *Necessary quality of confidence*

Information in public domain. The public accessibility of the infor-   **17.02**
mation sought to be protected by the duty of confidence is an important
factor in determining whether information has the necessary quality of
confidence. In general, information which is public property and public
knowledge is not confidential. However, "something that has been constructed solely from materials in the public domain may possess the

---

[1] *Coco v. A.N. Clark (Engineers) Ltd.* [1969] R.P.C. 41 at 437, *per* Megarry J., summarising
the principles to be elicited from *Saltman Engineering Co. Ltd. v. Campbell Engineering
Co. Ltd.* (1948) 65 R.P.C. 203, C.A.; approved *Dunford & Elliott v. Johnston* [1978] F.S.R.
143, 148, C.A.; *Yates Circuit Foil v. Electrofoils Ltd.* [1976] F.S.R. 345 at 385;
Commonwealth of Australia v. John Fairfax & Sons Ltd. (1980) 147 C.L.R. 39 at 50–51;
Stephens v. Avery [1988] Ch. 449 at 452; *Talbot v. General Television Corporation Pty Ltd.*
[1981] R.P.C. (Australia S.C. of Victoria); *Attorney-General v. Guardian Newspapers Ltd
(No. 2)* [1990] A.C. 109.

necessary quality of confidentiality: for something new and confidential may have been brought into being by the application of the skill and ingenuity of the human brain. Novelty depends on the thing itself, and not upon the quality of its constituent parts".[2] This has the consequence that the whole result of the application of such skill and ingenuity will qualify as confidential athough the separate features may have been published.

Thus, the question whether the public accessibility of the information sought to be protected is fatal to an attempt to restrain the use or disclosure of the information by enforcing a duty of confidence cannot be answered in absolute terms. The answer will depend upon the circumstances of the particular case and will depend upon the nature of the information, the nature of the interest sought to be protected, the relationship between the plaintiff and the defendant, the manner in which the defendant has come into possession of the information and the circumstances in which and the extent to which the information has been made public.[3] Further, where the confider discloses the information to a limited part of the public, the information will not necessarily be public property or public knowledge by means of this disclosure. It is a question of degree depending on the particular case, but if relative secrecy remains the information will be confidential.[4]

(b) *Duty of confidence*

17.03   A duty of confidence arises when confidential information comes to the knowledge of a person in circumstances where he has notice, or is held to have agreed, that the information is confidential, with the effect that it would be just in all the circumstances that he should be precluded from disclosing the information to others.[5] "Knowledge" in this context includes circumstances where the confidant has deliberately closed his eyes to the obvious.[6] Such a duty often arises by reason of either an

---

[2] *Thomas Marshall (Exports) Ltd. v. Guinle* [1979] 1 Ch. 227; see also *Saltman Engineering Co. Ltd. v. Campbell Engineering Co. Ltd.* (1948) 65 R.P.C. 203 at 215; *Coco v. A.N. Clark (Engineers) Ltd.* [1969] R.P.C. 41 at 47; *O. Mustad & Son v. Dosen* (Note) [1964] 1 W.L.R. 109; *Seager v. Copydex Ltd.* [1967] 1 W.L.R. 923; *Under-Water Welders & Repairers Ltd. v. Street & Longthorne* [1968] R.P.C. 498 at 506–7; *Attorney-General v. Guardian Newspapers (No. 2)* [1990] 1 A.C. 109.

[3] *Saltman Engineering Co. Ltd. v. Campbell Engineering Co. Ltd.* (1948) 65 R.P.C. 203 at 215, per Lord Greene M.R.; *O. Mustad & Son v. Dosen* (Note) [1964] 1 W.L.R. 109; *Seager v. Copydex Ltd.* [1967] 1 W.L.R. 923; *Attorney-General v. Guardian Newspapers (No. 2)* [1990] A.C. 109. "Novelty" is an important element where the component parts are in the public domain. Without such novelty it will be difficult to persuade the court that the information was not known to the public.

[4] *Franchi v. Franchi* [1967] R.P.C. 149 at 152–153, per Cross. J; *Attorney-General v. Guardian Newspapers Ltd. (No. 2)* [1990] 1 A.C. 109.

[5] *Seager v. Copydex Ltd.* [1967] 1 W.L.R. 923 at 931; *Attorney-General v. Guardian Newspapers (No. 2)* [1990] 1 A.C. 109 at 281, per Lord Goff, H.L.

[6] *Attorney-General v. Guardian Newspapers (No. 2)* [1990] 1 A.C. 109 at 281.

expressed or an implied term of a contract but it is well settled that the
duty does not depend on any contract, express or implied, between the
parties but depends on the broad principle of equity that he who has
received information in confidence shall not take unfair advantage of
it.[7]

The application of this principle is not without difficulty, however,
where the information is partly private and partly public, for then the
recipient must take care to separate out the two types of information
and although free to use the latter he is under a disability in that he
must take no advantage of the former. This is often referred to as the
"springboard" principle or doctrine. The principle can be stated thus:

> " . . . the essence of this branch of the law . . . is that a person who
> has obtained information in confidence is not allowed to use it as a
> spring-board for activities detrimental to the person who made the
> confidential communication, and spring-board it remains when all
> the features have been published or can be ascertained by actual
> inspection by a member of the public".[8]

The duration of the restraint upon the confidant and the circumstances in which it is removed is not without difficulty especially in the
light of the fact that the confidant may be placed under a severe commercial disadvantage as a result of the restraint.[9] It would appear, however, that the restraint is removed where the information is disclosed by
the confider[10] or a third party.[11]

Further: "Although a man must not use such information to get a
start over others nevertheless that springboard does not last for ever. If
he does use it a time may come when so much has happened that he can
no longer be restrained."[12] It would appear that what is envisaged in
such circumstances is a communication to the public by the confidant
himself. It is submitted that in such circumstances a question of degree
to what extent the information has become public knowledge. Where
the information has been released to the public generally by the confidant and restraint upon the confidant will serve no further useful purpose the confider ought to be left to is remedy in damages.[13] The duty of

---

[7] *Seager v. Copydex Ltd.* [1967] 1 W.L.R. 923; *Fraser v. Evans* [1969] 1 Q.B. 349; *Attorney-General v. Guardian Newspapers* [1987] 1 W.L.R. 1248 at 1265; *Attorney-General v. Guardian Newspapers (No. 2)* [1990] 1 A.C. 109.
[8] *Terrapin Ltd. v. Builders' Supply Co. (Hayes) Ltd.* [1967] R.P.C. 375; *Seager v. Copydex Ltd.* [1967] 1 W.L.R. 923, C.A.
[9] See *Coco v. A.N. Clark (Engineers) Ltd.* [1969] R.P.C. 41.
[10] *O. Mustad & Son v. Dosen* (Note) [1964] 1 W.L.R. 109.
[11] *Attorney-General v. Guardian Newspapers Limited (No. 2)* [1990] 1 A.C. 109.
[12] *Potters-Ballotini Ltd. v. Weston-Baker* [1977] R.P.C. 202 at 206–207; see also *Attorney-General v. Guardian Newspapers Limited (No. 2)* [1990] 1 A.C. 109.
[13] *Attorney-General v. Guardian Newspapers Limited (No. 2)* [1990] 1 A.C. 109.

confidence does not, however, extend to information which is useless or trivial.[14] Nor does it extend to confidential information, disclosure of which is required in the public interest, because there is no duty of confidence as to the disclosure of iniquity.[15]

(c) *Detriment*

17.04 Although detriment or potential detriment to the plaintiff will nearly always form part of a plaintiff's case it is an open question whether detriment is necessary to found an action for breach of confidence. Dicta in *Attorney-General v. Guardian Newspapers Ltd. (No. 2)*[16] would suggest, however, that detriment may not always be necessary and where necessary it is a sufficient detriment to the confider that information given in confidence is to be disclosed to persons whom he would prefer not to know of it, even though the disclosure would not be harmful to him in any positive way.[17]

(d) *Duty imposed on third parties*

17.05 A duty of confidence will not necessarily lie on every third party who comes into possession of the confidential information. For it to do so, the circumstances must be such as to raise an "obligation of conscience"[18] affecting the third party. A third party who receives information from a person bound by an obligation of secrecy or confidence, and who knows that the information has been passed to him by his informant in breach of that obligation, becomes automatically prima facie bound by a like obligation of secrecy or confidence which will prevent him disseminating or using the information any further, or

---

[14] *McNicol v. Sportsman's Book Stores* [1930] MacG. C.C. 116.; *Coco v. A.N. Clark (Engineers) Ltd.* [1969] R.P.C. 41 at 48; *Attorney-General v. Guardian Newspapers Ltd. (No. 2)* [1990] 1 A.C. 109.

[15] *Gartside v. Outram* (1857) 26 L.J.Ch. 113 at 114, *per* Sir William Page Wood V.-C.; *Initial Services Ltd. v. Putterill* [1968] 1 Q.B. 396; *Fraser v. Evans* [1969] 1 Q.B. 349; *Attorney-General v. Guardian Newspapers (No. 2)* [1990] 1 A.C. 109. See *post*, para. 17.17.

[16] [1990] 1 A.C. 109 at 282, *per* Lord Goff of Chieveley. His Lordship was of the view however that detriment may not always be necessary but wished to keep the question whether it is an essential ingredient of an action for breach of confidence. Lord Griffiths appeared to be of the view that detriment or potential detriment is necessary: *ibid.* at 269. No views were expressed by Lord Brightman and Lord Jauncey on this aspect of breach of confidence. See also *Coco v. Clark (Engineers) Ltd.* [1969] R.P.C. 41 at 48 where Megarry J. gave examples of cases where there need be no detriment to succeed in an action for breach of confidence; *Dunford v. Johnson* [1978] F.S.R. 143 at 148 and *Jarman & Platt v. Barget* [1977] F.S.R. 260 at 277 assume detriment necessary, *cf. Nichrotherm v. Percy* [1956] R.P.C. 272 at 273.

[17] *Attorney-General v. Guardian Newspapers Ltd. (No. 2)* [1990] 1 A.C. 109 at 256, *per* Lord Keith of Kinkel.

[18] *Fraser v. Thames Television Ltd.* [1984] Q.B. 44.

making use of it without the consent of the person to whom the obligation of secrecy or confidence was owed by the informant.[19]

The circumstances in which such an obligation of conscience will arise in a commercial context was considered in *Schering Chemicals Ltd. v. Falkman Ltd.*[20] where the plaintiffs marketed a drug by the name of "Primodos". Confidential information about the drug was supplied by the plaintiff to the second defendant, Elstein, for the purposes of public relations work, which the first defendant was to carry out for the plaintiff. The second defendant wanted to use that confidential information in a television programme to be made by Thames Television, the third defendant. An interlocutory injunction restraining the second and third defendants, pending trial, from using the information, was granted at first instance. The Court of Appeal dismissed the appeal. In considering the position of the confidee and confider *inter se*, Shaw L.J. said:

> "As I see the position, the communication in a commercial context of information which at the time is regarded by the giver and recognised by the recipient as confidential, and the nature of which has a material connection with the commercial interests of the party confiding that information, imposes on the recipient a fiduciary obligation to maintain that confidence thereafter unless the giver consents to relax it."[21]

Having established the principles governing the duty of the confidee with regard to the information Shaw L.J. went on to consider the position of the third party: **17.06**

> "While it is true that Thames were not the direct recipients of the confidential information conveyed in a fiduciary situation, it is not in controversy that they were at all times aware of the circumstances in which Mr. Elstein first became possessed of it. If Mr. Elstein was in breach of duty in seeking to use it at all, Thames cannot be entitled to collaborate with him by taking advantage of his repudiation of his fiduciary obligations."[22]

In *Fraser v. Thames Television Ltd.*[23] Hirst J. stated the guiding principle thus:

> " . . . in order to be fixed with an obligation of confidence, a third party must know that the information was confidential; knowledge

---

[19] *Schering Chemicals Ltd. v. Falkman Ltd.* [1982] Q.B. 1; *Fraser v. Thames Television Ltd.* [1984] Q.B. 44; *Attorney-General v. Guardian Newspapers Ltd. (No. 2)* [1990] 1 A.C. 109.
[20] [1982] Q.B. 1.
[21] *Ibid.*, at 27.
[22] See *ibid*, at 40, *per* Templeman L.J.
[23] [1984] Q.B. 44.

of a mere assertion that a breach of confidence has been committed is not sufficient".

The extent to which such "obligation of conscience" arises in relation to a third party without notice is, however, unclear. It has been suggested that a purchaser for value without notice of confidential information is in a like position to that of an innocent user in that if he subsequently receives notice he is liable to be restrained.[24] Although no clear basis for according protection has been enunciated the preponderance of judicial authority would indicate that a purchaser for value without notice is not impressed with an obligation of confidence and thus necessarily liable to be restrained if he should subsequently learn of the confidential nature of the information.[25]

In *Stevenson, Jordan & Harrison Ltd. v. McDonald & Evans*[26] Evershed M.R. expressed the view, obiter, that it would be

"somewhat shocking if reputable publishers, who discovered that there was in some work which they had acquired a gross breach of faith, publication of which would involve the ruin of some business, yet nevertheless could say, having discovered that fact before they had published or incurred any substantial expense, that they were entitled to insist on going on with their publication".

Although the Master of the Rolls' formulation may have been coloured by the extreme circumstances he had in mind, it is submitted that the formulation provides a useful basis for determining whether it would be equitable to restrain a third party purchaser for value without notice who subsequently learns of its confidential nature. The application of the formulation would require not only the third party to have expended moneys on the purchase or development of the information. He must, to avoid restraint, either have published the information or expended or incurred "substantial expense" in respect of the information. Prima facie, such expense could take the form of paying a substantial purchase price and/or the post purchase expenditure of moneys in developing the information into a commercial product.

---

[24] *Stevenson, Jordan & Harrison Ltd. v. McDonald & Evans* [1952] R.P.C. 10 at 16; *Wheatley v. Bell* [1984] F.S.R. 16; *Fraser v. Evans* [1969] 1 Q.B. 349 at 361, *per* Lord Denning M.R., C.A.
[25] *Morison v. Moat* (1851) 9 Hare 241 at 263 where Turner V.-C. said that "the purchaser for value of a secret without notice . . . might be in a different position from a volunteer"; *Attorney General v. Guardian Newspapers Ltd.* [1987] 3 All E.R. 316 at 328, *per* Browne-Wilkinson V.-C: "The equitable interest of the confider would . . . be enforceable against the whole world save the bona fide purchaser for value without notice the confider's right to confidentiality"; *Attorney-General v. Observer Ltd.*, Court of Appeal (Civil Division) Transcript No. 696 of 1986).
[26] [1952] R.P.C. 10.

The duty imposed on a third party cannot, however, be determined **17.07** in all circumstances by whether he was a mere volunteer or a purchaser for value without notice. Where a duty of confidence is sought to be enforced against a broadcaster who has come into possession of the information, as a third party, knowing it to be confidential, the duty of the broadcaster will not, in such circumstances, necessarily be co-terminus with the duty on its informant.[27] The existence and scope of the alleged duty will, where the broadcaster contends that the information should be published in the public interest, depend on the relative weight of the public or private interests for the protection of which the duty is claimed, on the one hand, and of the public or private interests to be served by the disclosure of the information on the other hand.

No obligation of conscience will ordinarily arise where the third party comes into possession of information which, although once confidential, has ceased to be so otherwise than through the agency of the third party.[28]

2. Categories of Confidential Information of Importance to the Entertainment Industry

The following categories of confidential information are of particular **17.08** relevance to the entertainment industry.

(a) *Confidential information included in news and current affairs*

Protection of sources of information. How far and in what circum- **17.09** stances a court may compel a broadcaster to disclose confidential[29] sources of information is governed by section 10 of the Contempt of Court Act 1981. This section provides as follows:

> "No court may require a person to disclose, nor is any person guilty of contempt of contempt for refusing to disclose, the source of information contained in a publication for which he is responsible, unless it be established to the satisfaction of the court that disclosure is necessary in the interests of justice or national security or for the prevention of disorder or crime."

In *X Ltd. v. Morgan-Grampian plc.*[30] Lord Oliver observed that the

---

[27] *Attorney-General v. Guardian Newspapers Ltd. (No. 2)* [1990] 1 A.C. 109 at 156. For the application of this principle see under "Confidential information contained in news and current affairs", para. 17.09 *et seq.*

[28] *Schering Chemicals Ltd. v. Falkman Ltd.* [1982] Q.B. C.A.; *Attorney General v. Guardian Newspapers Ltd. (No. 2)* [1990] A.C. 109 at 216, C.A.; *ibid.* on appeal, H.L. unaffected on this point.

[29] See *British Steel Corpn. v. Granada Television Ltd.* [1981] A.C. 1096, particularly at 1174, where it was recognised that this involved a question of the situations in which a journalist will be compelled to breach confidence *viz.* sources of information.

[30] [1990] 2 W.L.R. 1000 at 1018, H.L.

sense of the section is that the "court is not permitted to require the disclosure of a journalistic source unless it is satisfied that one or more of the four enumerated considerations (*i.e.* **the interests of justice, etc.**) are of such preponderating importance in the individual case that the ban on disclosure imposed by the opening words of the section really needs to be overridden".

17.10   The restriction on disclosure applies not only to direct orders to disclose the identity of a source but also to an order for disclosure of material which will indirectly identify the source, and applies notwithstanding that the enforcement of the restriction may operate to defeat rights of property vested in the party who seeks to obtain that material.[31] Secondly, it applies to information contained in a publication or intended publication.[32] This expression, by virtue of section 19 of the interpretation section to the Act, bears the meaning assigned to it in section 2(1) which deals with the strict liability rule. It is there defined as including "any speech, writing, broadcast or other communication in whatever form, which is addressed to the public at large or any section of the public". Although in section 2(1) this definition is introduced by the words "includes" rather than "means", the context in which it appears in that subsection speaks of "publications" in the plural and makes it clear that it is intended as a complete and comprehensive definition of the terms.[33]

Provided that it is addressed to or intended for the public at large, or any section of it, the source of every information so addressed falls within the section and is entitled to the protection granted by it unless the publication falls within one of the express exceptions introduced by the word "unless". The onus of proving that an order of the court has or may have the consequence of disclosing the source of information and falls within any of the exceptions lies upon the party by whom the order is sought[34] and it must be established that disclosure is "necessary".[35]

17.11   Whether such necessity has or has not been established is a question of fact based on the evidence adduced in any particular case.[36] The use of the word "necessary" involves not so much a discretion as a value judgment but such a judgment nearly always involves the consideration of factors which will be relevant to the exercise of a discretion. This

---

[31] *Secretary of State for Defence v. Guardian Newspapers Ltd.* [1985] A.C. 339 at 349–350, H.L.; *X Ltd. v. Morgan-Grampian plc.* [1990] 2 W.L.R. 1000 at 1006, H.L.
[32] *X Ltd. v. Morgan-Grampian plc.* [1990] 1000 at 1007, H.L.
[33] *Secretary of State for Defence v. Guardian Newspapers Ltd.* [1985] 1 A.C. 339, H.L.
[34] *Ibid.* at 348.
[35] *Ibid.* at 350; *X Ltd. v. Morgan-Grampian plc.* [1990] 2 W.L.R. 1000 at 1007, H.L.
[36] *Secretary of State for Defence v. Guardian Newspapers Ltd.* [1985] 2 A.C. 339 at 350; *X Ltd. v. Morgan-Grampian plc.* [1990] 2 W.L.R. 1000 at 1007.

involves the necessity of striking a balance between, on the one hand, the public importance attached to the preservation of the confidentiality of the source which is enshrined in the statutory prohibition, and, on the other hand, the relative public importance of the interests of justice in the particular case.[37]

Where non-disclosure of a source of information will imperil national security or enable a crime to be committed which might otherwise be prevented, the application of this approach will often require disclosure. These two public interests are of such overriding importance that once it is shown that disclosure will serve one of those interests, the necessity of disclosure follows almost automatically; though even here if a judge were asked to order disclosure of a source of information in the interests of the prevention of a crime, he "might properly refuse to do so if, for instance, the crime was of a trivial nature".[38]

Where the question under consideration is disclosure in the "interests of justice", the task is one of weighing the importance of enabling the ends of justice to be attained in the circumstances of the particular case on the one hand, against the importance of protecting the source on the other hand.[39] There is no comprehensive test as to how this balancing exercise should be carried out but in *X Ltd. v. Morgan-Grampian plc.*[40] Lord Bridge indicated the "kind of factors" which will require consideration: **17.12**

"In estimating the importance to be given to the case in favour of disclosure there will be a wide spectrum within which the particular case must be located. If the party seeking disclosure shows, for example, that his very livelihood depends upon it, this will put the case near one end of the spectrum. If he shows no more than that what he seeks to protect is a minor interest in property, this will put the case at or near the other end. On the other side the importance of protecting a source from disclosure in pursuance of the policy underlying the statute will also vary within a wide spectrum. One important factor will be the nature of the information obtained from source. The greater the legitimate public interest in the information which the source has given to the publisher or intended publisher, the greater will be the importance of protecting the source. But another and perhaps more significant factor which will very much affect the importance of protecting the source will be the manner in which the information was itself obtained by the source. If it appears to the court that the information was obtained

---

[37] *X Ltd. v. Morgan-Grampian plc.* [1990] 2 W.L.R. 1000, H.L.
[38] *Ibid.* at 1008.
[39] *Ibid.* at 1008, 1009.
[40] *Ibid.*

legitimately this will enhance the importance of protecting the source. Conversely, if it appears that the information was obtained illegally, this will diminish the importance of protecting the source unless, of course, this factor is counterbalanced by a clear public interest in the publication of the information, as in the classic case where the source has acted for the purpose of exposing iniquity."[41]

In weighing these competing matters the expression "interests of justice" is not to be confined to the technical sense of the administration of justice in a court of law.[42]

17.13   **Broadcasting of state and government secrets.** Where the government asserts a private law interest in the confidentiality of its information, such information is likely to relate to the conduct of national affairs. In such circumstances a conflict readily arises between the public interest in preserving the confidentiality of the information and the public interest in the freedom of speech and of the media. The law provides no entrenched guarantee of freedom of speech or the media. The rule is that any broadcaster may broadcast anything it wishes unless there is some legal reason why they should not. This means that a government seeking an order to restrain future publication of a government or state secret must show,

"(a) that such publication would be a breach of confidence; (b) that the public interest requires that publication be restrained, and (c) that there are no other facets of the public interest contradictory to and more compelling than that relied upon. Moreover, the court, when asked to restrain such a publication, must closely examine the extent to which relief is necessary to ensure that restrictions are not imposed beyond the strict requirement of public need."[43]

Accordingly, the court will determine the government's claim to confidentiality by reference to the public interest. Unless the disclosure is likely to injure the public interest the court will not restrain the dissemination of the information.

The common law places the burden on the party seeking to restrain publication to show cause why restraint is necessary. Where national security is relied upon, the burden imposed on the government by the

---

[41] *Ibid.* at 1010.
[42] *Ibid.*
[43] *Attorney-General v. Jonathan Cape Ltd.* [1976] Q.B. 752 at 770–771; *Commonwealth of Australia v. John Fairfax & Sons Ltd.* (1980) 147 C.L.R. 39; *Attorney-General v. Guardian Newspapers (No. 2)* [1990] 1 A.C. 109.

foregoing principle is a light one.[44] Once the factual basis is established by evidence so that the court is satisfied that the interest of national security is a relevant factor to be considered in the determination of the case, the court will accept the opinion of the Crown or the responsible officer as to what is required to meet it, unless it is possible to show that the opinion was one which no reasonable minister advising the Crown could in the circumstances reasonably have held.[45]

However, the further the case is from the paradigm national security **17.14** case the more real will be the court's balancing function: in such circumstances the court's approach will not, because of the competing interests involved, be the same as that in a private dispute between citizen and citizen.[46] The court will not prevent the publication of information which merely throws light on the past workings of government, even if it is not public property, so long as it does not prejudice the community in other respects. If, however, it appears that disclosure will be inimical to the public interest because national security, relations with other countries, or the ordinary business of government will be prejudiced, disclosure will be restrained.[47]

The essence of the matter is a weighing, on a balance, of the two public interests, that of the nation or the public service in non-disclosure and that of the public interest in the disclosure of the documents.[48] The rationale behind this rule is that although in the case of private citizens there is a public interest that the confidential information should as such be protected, in the case of government secrets the mere fact of confidentiality does not alone support such a conclusion, because in a free society there is a continuing public interest that the workings of government should be open to scrutiny and criticism.[49]

The maintenance of the doctrine of joint responsibility within the **17.15** cabinet is in the public interest and the application of that doctrine might be prejudiced by premature disclosure of the views of individual Ministers expressed during Cabinet meetings. In such circumstances

---

[44] *Council of Civil Service Unions v. Minister for the Civil Service* [1985] A.C. 374 at 412, H.L.; *Attorney-General v. Guardian Newspapers Ltd. (No. 2)* [1990] 1 A.C. 109, H.L.
[45] *Council of Civil Service Unions v. Minister for the Civil Service* [1985] A.C. 374; *Attorney-General v. Guardian Newspapers Ltd.* [1990] 1 A.C. 109.
[46] *Attorney-General v. Jonathan Cape Ltd.* [1976] Q.B. 752; *Commonwealth of Australia v. John Fairfax & Sons Ltd.* 147 C.L.R. 39 at 51–52; *Attorney-General v. Guardian Newspapers Ltd.* [1990] 1 A.C. 109.
[47] *Commonwealth of Australia v. John Fairfax & Sons Ltd.* (1980) 147 C.L.R. 39, approved, *Attorney-General v. Guardian Newspapers Ltd. (No. 2)* [1990] A.C. 109 at 257, 270, 283, H.L.
[48] *Attorney-General v. Jonathan Cape Ltd.* [1976] Q.B. 752; *Commonwealth of Australia v. John Fairfax & Sons Ltd.* (1980) 147 C.L.R. 39; *Attorney-General v. Guardian Newspapers (No. 2)* [1990] 1 A.C. 109.
[49] *Attorney-General v. Guardian Newspapers (No. 2)* [1990] 1 A.C. 109 at 283 *per* Lord Goff.

the court may restrain the improper publication of such opinions, and also of information received in confidence by a cabinet minister, but should only do so "in the clearest of cases where the confidentiality of the material can be demonstrated".[50] However, the obligation of confidence imposed on ministers does not extend to advice given by civil servants and ministerial observations on the capacity of such civil servants.[51]

This approach records with Article 10 of the Convention for the Protection of Human Rights and Fundamental Freedoms which, in so far as is relevant, provides:

> "1. Everyone has the right to freedom of expression. This right shall include freedom to hold opinions and to receive and impart information and ideas without interference by public authority and regardless of frontiers . . . 2. The exercise of these freedoms, since it carries with it duties and responsibilities, may be subject to such formalities, conditions, restrictions or penalties as are prescribed by the law and are necessary in a democratic society, territorial integrity or public safety, for the prevention of disorder or crime, for the protection of health or morals, for the protection of the reputation or rights of theirs for preventing the disclosure of information received in confidence, or for maintaining the authority and impartiality of the judiciary."

The decisions of the European Court of Human Rights establish that the limitation of free expression in the interests of national security should not be regarded as "necessary" unless there is a "pressing social need" for the limitation and unless the limitation is appropriate to the legitimate aims pursued".[52] The United Kingdom courts have interpreted "pressing social need" as requiring that prior restraint of publication of a matter of public interest should only be ordered where there is a "substantial risk of grave injustice".[53]

17.16   In *Attorney-General v. Guardian Newspapers Ltd.*[54] four of their Lordships[55] referred to the Convention and none suggested that its terms were in conflict with the common law. In *Attorney-General v. Guardian Newspapers Ltd. (No. 2)*[56] the same approach was adopted by the

---

[50] *Attorney-General v. Jonathon Cape Ltd.* [1976] 1 Q.B. 752 at 771, C.A.
[51] *Ibid.* at 771.
[52] *The Sunday Times v. United Kingdom* (1979) 2 E.H.R.R. 245; *Lingens v. Austria* (1986) 8 E.H.R.R. 407; *Attorney-General v. Guardian Newspapers Ltd. (No. 2)* [1990] 1 A.C. 109.
[53] *Attorney-General v. British Broadcasting Corporation* [1981] A.C. 303 at 362, H.L.
[54] [1987] 1 W.L.R. 1248, H.L.
[55] *Ibid.*, Lord Bridge of Harwich at 1286; Lord Brandon of Oakbrook at 1307; Lord Templeman at 1296–1299; and Lord Ackner at 1307.
[56] [1990] 1 A.C. 109.

majority of the House of Lords with Lord Goff of Chieveley considering it to be his "duty" when free to do so "to interpret the law in accordance with the obligations of the Crown under this treaty".[57] From these authorities can be derived an evolving general principle that can be stated thus: interference with the freedom of speech is permissible only where the party seeking such restraint is able clearly[58] to show that it is necessary in the interests of national security, for protecting the reputation and rights of others, for preventing the disclosure of information received in confidence or for maintaining the authority and impartiality of the judiciary having regard to the facts of the specific case.[59]

The iniquity defence. The so called "iniquity defence" has the effect of   **17.17**
negating a duty of confidence if the subject-matter of the information is something inimical to the public interest.[60] Care must, however, be taken in defining what is in the public interest, for there is a wide difference between what is interesting to the public and what it is in the public interest to make known.[61]

In origin, the iniquity defence was narrowly stated on the basis that a man cannot be made the confidant of a crime or a fraud.[62] However, it is clear that the principle extends to matters of which disclosure is required in the public interest and is not limited to cases in which there has been crime or fraud or other wrong-doing on the part of the plaintiff.[63] The guiding principle was stated by Ungoed-Thomas J., in *Beloff v. Pressdram Ltd.*[64]:

> "The defence of public interest clearly covers and, in the authorities does not extend beyond, the disclosure, which as Lord Denning M.R. emphasised must be disclosure justified in the public interest, of matters carried out or contemplated, in breach of the country's security, or in breach of law, including statutory duty, fraud, or

---

[57] *Ibid.* at 283. See also *Attorney-General v. British Broadcasting Corporation* [1981] A.C. 303 at 352, where Lord Fraser of Tullybelton made similar observations.

[58] *Cambridge Nutrition Ltd. v. British Broadcasting Corporation* [1990] 3 All E.R. 523, C.A.; *Secretary of State for the Home Department v. Central Broadcasting Ltd.* [1993] E.M.L.R. 253, C.A.

[59] *Attorney-General v. Guardian Newspapers Ltd.* [1987] 1 W.L.R. 1248 at 1297.

[60] *Gartside v. Outram* (1857) 26 L.J. Ch. 113 at 114; *Initial Services Ltd. v. Putterill* [1968] 1 Q.B. 396, C.A.; *Lion Laboratories Ltd. v. Evans*, per Griffiths L.J. [1985] Q.B. 526 at 550; *Beloff v. Pressdram Ltd.* [1973] 1 All E.R. 241 at 260; *Attorney-General v. Guardian Newspapers (No. 2)* 109 at 159, 202, 222, 282.

[61] *Beloff v. Pressdram* [1973] 1 All E.R. 240; *British Steel Corporation v. Granada Television Ltd.* [1981] A.C. 1096 at 1168, H.L.

[62] *Gartside v. Outram* (1857) 26 L.J. Ch. 113 at 114; see also *Initial Services Ltd. v. Putterill* [1968] 1 Q.B. 396, C.A.

[63] *Lion Laboratories Ltd. v. Evans*, per Griffiths L.J. [1985] Q.B. 526 at 550, C.A.; *Attorney-General v. Guardian Newspapers (No. 2)* 109 at 202, 222, 282, H.L.

[64] [1973] 1 All E.R. 241, 260; approved *Attorney-General v. Guardian Newspapers Ltd.* [1990] 1 A.C. 109, H.L.; see also *Lion Laboratories Ltd. v. Evans* [1985] Q.B. 526, C.A.

otherwise destructive of the country or its people, including matters medically dangerous to the public; and doubtless other misdeeds of similar gravity. Public interest, as a defence in law, operates to override the rights of the individual (including copyright) which would otherwise prevail and which the law is also concerned to protect."

17.18   The iniquity defence is, however, subject to two limiting principles. First, where public interest grounds exist for disclosing iniquity, it does not follow that the public interest will require disclosure to the media, or to the public by the media. If, for example, the public interest would equally be served by disclosing the information to the police or a professional disciplinary body it may not always be permissible to disclose the information to the public at large.[65] This exception has been categorised as "disclosure . . . to one who has a proper interest to receive the information".[66] The principle is illustrated by *Francome v. Mirror Group Newspapers Ltd.*[67] where unidentified persons tapped telephone conversations to and from the home of the plaintiff. The *Daily Mirror* acquired the tapes and the plaintiff sued for an injunction to restrain their publication. The *Daily Mirror* had notice of their private and confidential character and the injunction was sought on the ground that the *Daily Mirror* was under a duty to preserve the confidentiality of the conversations. The *Daily Mirror's* defence was that disclosure was justified in the public interest on the ground that the tapes revealed breaches by the plaintiff of the rules of racing.

The Court of Appeal declined, pending trial of the action, to allow the contents of the tapes to be disclosed to the public at large but were prepared to allow disclosure to the police and to the stewards of the Jockey Club. The iniquity defence therefore had the effect of limiting the duty of confidence. The duty would have been broken by disclosure to the public. It would not have been broken by disclosure to the police or to the Jockey Club. Thus, the existence of a procedure for inquiry or complaint will be an important factor having a bearing on the need, in the public interest, for wider dissemination of the confidential information but there may be cases where notwithstanding the availability of such a procedure "the misdeed is of such a character that the public interest may demand, or at least excuse, publication on a broader field, even to the press".[68] Whether the misdeed is of such a character would appear to be a question of fact.

---

[65] *Initial Services Ltd. v. Putterill* [1968] 1 Q.B. 396; *Francome v. Mirror Group Newspapers Ltd.* [1984] 1 W.L.R. 892; *Attorney-General v. Guardian Newspapers Ltd. (No. 2)* [1990] 1 A.C. 109.

[66] *Initial Services Ltd. v. Putterill* [1968] 1 Q.B. 396 at 405, *per* Lord Denning M.R.

[67] [1984] 1 W.L.R. 892.

[68] *Initial Services Ltd. v. Putterill* [1968] 1 Q.B. 396 at 405–406.

The second limiting principle is that the duty of confidence is not **17.19**
overridden or ousted by the mere making of allegations of iniquity.
Such an allegation will only suffice if, following such investigations as
are reasonably open to the recipient, and having regard to all the circumstances of the case, the allegation in question can reasonably be
regarded as being a credible allegation from an apparently reliable
source.[69]

(b) *Ideas for plays and films*

It is common practice in the entertainment industry that ideas, in par- **17.20**
ticular for films and television programmes, are communicated to producers and television companies so as to solicit finance for their
production as a film or television series. The general practice of the television and film sectors of the industry is that where such ideas are communicated the receiver of the communication will not make use of the
idea without the consent of the communicator. The authorities establish
that the existence of such a practice is a factor of considerable weight in
deciding whether an obligation of confidence exists in such circumstances.[70]

In *Fraser v. Thames Television Ltd.*[71] the existence of such practice was
accepted by the court and it was there stated that where an idea which
is original, clearly identifiable, of potential commercial value and sufficiently well developed to be capable of commercial realisation is communicated in confidence, the recipient of the information is under an
obligation not to use the idea without the maker's permission.[72] In
identifying the applicable principles, Hirst J. stated that in order to succeed the plaintiffs had to establish,

"not only that the occasion of communication was confidential, but
also that the content of the idea was clearly identifiable, original, of

---

[69] *Attorney-General v. Guardian Newspapers Ltd.* [1987] 1 W.L.R. 1248, C.A.; *Attorney-
General v. Guardian Newspapers (No. 2)* [1990] 1 A.C. 109 at 223, 283.
[70] *Saltman Engineering Co. Ltd. v. Campbell Engineering Co. Ltd.* 65 R.P.C. 203; *Thomas
Marshall (Exports) Ltd. v. Guinle* [1979] Ch. 227; *Fraser v. Thames Television Ltd.* [1984] 1
Q.B. 44.
[71] [1984] 1 Q.B. 44.
[72] *Fraser v. Thames Television Ltd.* [1984] Q.B. 44; see also *Gilbert v. Star Newspaper Co. Ltd.*
(1894) 11 T.L.R. 4; *Moore Edwards* [1901–4] MacG.Cop.Cas. 44; *Fraser v. Edwards*
[1905–10] MacG.Cop.Cas. 10; *Talbot v. General Television Broadcasting Corporation Pty.
Ltd.* [1981] R.P.C. 1. (Supreme Court of Victoria); *cf. Times Newspapers Ltd. v. MGN Ltd.*
[1993] E.M.L.R. 443 which appears to lay down no new principle of law which would
affect the application of this principle in that in the latter case the circumstances of the
case were entirely novel and thus there was no established usage which would raise an
obligation of confidence.

potential commercial attractiveness and capable of being realised in actuality".[73]

17.21   On the facts of the case it was clear that the information had been imparted in confidence. However, no clear test arises from *Fraser v. Thames Television Ltd.* as to what is a "clearly identifiable" idea so as to satisfy the second requirement. It would appear that whether the idea is "clearly identifiable" is a question of fact. Hirst J. observed:

> "No doubt both the communication and the content of an oral idea may be more difficult to prove than in the case of a written idea, but difficulties of proof should not affect the principle any more than in any other branches of the law where similar problems arise."[74]

The idea once identified must have some "significant element of originality" not already in the realm of public knowledge. Where one is dealing with an idea for a film or television programme, this "significant element of originality" may consist in a significant twist or slant to a well known concept.[75]

17.22   In assessing the potential commercial attractiveness and capability of the idea being realised the court has regard to whether the idea is "sufficiently developed, so that it would be seen to be a concept which has at least some attractiveness for a television programme and which is capable of being realised as an actuality." This requirement does not necessitate "in every case a full synopsis. In some cases the nature of the idea may require extensive development in a synopsis or treatment to meet the criteria of potential commercial attractiveness. But in others the criteria may be met by a short unelaborated statement of the idea."[76]

It would appear that "sufficiently developed" requires no more than that the idea in the form that it is expressed is capable of forming the basis of a film or television programme. The degree of development will vary, as in the case of a game show where little elaboration is needed for a potential exploiter of the product to judge its commercial viability, to a major film where a high degree of working out of the idea may be required to demonstrate its potential. However, if, in fact, the idea does so form the basis of a film or television programme, that is of itself

---

[73] *Fraser v. Thames Television Limited* [1984] 1 Q.B. 44 at 66.
[74] *Ibid.* at 65.
[75] *Ibid.* at 66; see also at 67 where Hirst J. stated that the fact of the creation of a series of programmes based on the idea is "eloquent testimony" of its originality. *Saltman Engineering Co. Ltd. v. Campbell Engineering Co. Ltd.* 65 R.P.C. 203; *Coca v. A.N. Clark (Engineers) Ltd.* [1969] R.P.C. 41.
[76] *Fraser v. Thames Television Limited* [1984] 1 Q.B. 44 at 65H–66B.

cogent evidence that it is sufficiently developed to be of commercial attractiveness and ability to be realised in actuality.[77]

(c) *Publicised persona contrary to private persona*

A performer who seeks publicity to present himself to the public in his **17.23** most favourable light so that audiences will come to hear and support him cannot be heard to complain if a servant or agent discloses the truth about him. If the image which they fostered was not a true image, it is in the public interest that it should be corrected. Thus, in *Woodward v. Hutchins*,[78] where an individual was employed as a public relations officer and consultant for the purpose of ensuring that certain pop artistes received favourable publicity and that their activities were shown to the public in the most favourable light and on the termination of his employment he wrote articles for a newspaper in which he "tells" the secrets about the group, an injunction was refused restraining him from breaching his undertaking of confidence. Lord Denning explained the rationale of the court's decision as follows:

"There is no doubt whatever that this pop group sought publicity. They wanted to have themselves presented to the public in a favourable light so that audiences would come to hear them and support . . . If a group of this kind seek publicity which is to their advantage, it seems to me that they cannot complain if a servant or employee of theirs afterwards discloses the truth about them. If the image they fostered was not a true image, it is in the public interest that it should be corrected. In these cases of confidential information it is a question of balancing the public interest in maintaining the confidence against the public interest in knowing the truth . . . In this case the balance comes down in favour of the truth being told, even if it should involve some breach of confidential information."

It is not an invariable rule that disclosure will not be restrained but it **17.24** would appear that the balance will, except in an exceptional case, come down in favour of disclosing the truth rather than upholding the publicised persona. This is in accord with the courts approach to restraints on the freedom of expression and would appear to be merely the application of that principle.

---

[77] *Ibid.* at 67.
[78] [1977] 1 W.L.R. 760; see also *Lennon v. News Group Newspapers Ltd. & Twist* [1978] F.S.R. 573.

3. Remedies for Misuse of Confidential Information

17.25 **Account.** It is well settled that an account is a possible and alternative form of relief to damages[79] and is available against all persons involved in the wrongful act.[80] If confidential information of a commercial character is misused, the account of profits serves to compensate the owner of the information for the unauthorised use that has been made of it. The profit in equity belongs to the owner of the information. Where, however, the confidential information consists of information about the affairs of state or activities of the security services, or does not serve any useful commercial purpose, an account of profits may be possible but only in so far as it ensures that the wrongdoer does not benefit from his wrongdoing.[81]

17.26 **Damages.** The measure of damages is such sum as would put the plaintiffs in the position they would have been in if the defendants had not wrongly obtained and used the confidential information.[82] However, in applying this test the method of assessment of the loss sustained by the plaintiff will depend upon the facts of the particular case.[83] In *Dowson v. Mason*[84] Slade L.J., referring to *McGregor on Damages*,[85] drew a distinction between damages where the confidant would himself have made the product to which the confidence related for profit, and a case where he would merely have allowed third parties to use his confidential information under licence for royalties. In the former case, the basis of the assessment is lost profits from the sale of the manufactured product, and in the latter, lost royalty profit.

Where, for example, the confidential information is in the form of a concept for film or television it would appear that one permissible basis of assessment of loss would be loss of chance of obtaining a contract to produce a film or television programme or series embodying the idea even though it was not certain that the plaintiff would have secured such a contract.[86]

---

[79] *Peter Pan Manufacturing Corporation v. Corsets Silhouette Ltd.* [1962] R.P.C. 45 at 58, *per* Pennycuick J.; *Attorney-General v. Guardian Newspapers Ltd. (No. 2)* [1990] 1 A.C. 109; *Neilson v. Betts* (1870) L.R. 5 H.L. 1 at 22; *De Vilne v. Betts* (1873) L.R. 6 H.L. 319, 321.

[80] *House of Spring Gardens Ltd. v. Point Blank Ltd.* [1985] F.S.R. 327.

[81] *Attorney-General v. Guardian Newspapers Ltd. (No. 2)* [1990] 1 A.C. 109.

[82] *Dowson & Mason Ltd. v. Potter* [1986] 1 W.L.R. 1419, 1421.

[83] *Talbot & General Television Corporation Pty. Ltd.* [1981] R.P.C. 1 (Supreme Court of Victoria) where *Seager v. Copydex* [1969] 1 W.L.R. 809 is treated as laying down no general principle; see also *Dowson v. Mason* [1986] 1 W.L.R. 1419 where the majority of the Court of Appeal were also of this view.

[84] [1986] 1 W.L.R. 1419, C.A., distinguishing *Seager v. Copydex Ltd. (No. 2)* [1969] 1 W.L.R., C.A.

[85] *McGregor on Damages* (14th ed., 1980), paras. 1453 to 1455.

[86] *Talbot v. General Television Corporation Pty. Ltd.* [1981] R.P.C. 1 (Supreme Court of Victoria).

Injunctions generally. If the plaintiff shows that a defendant has   **17.27**
infringed his legal rights and intends to continue doing so, the plaintiff
will ordinarily be entitled to an injunction to restrain the defendant's
unlawful conduct in future unless the plaintiff can be adequately compensated in damages. However, where the defendant has already
disclosed the confidential information the injunction will ordinarily not
be granted.[87]

Interlocutory injunctions. Where the breach of the confidential infor-   **17.28**
mation results in the commercial use of the information, damages may
be an adequate remedy where an undertaking is given by the defendant
to keep an account of the receipts from the exploitation of the information and either to pay into court or a joint account the monies
received pending the outcome of the trial. Where there is confidentiality of information and that is in conflict with a public interest, for
example, the public interest in the publication of an iniquity, an award
of damages to either party would be unlikely to provide an adequate or
appropriate remedy for any wrongs suffered pending trial.[88] In such circumstances the court should, other things being equal, favour the
preservation of confidentiality unless convinced that the other public
interest outweighs it: the reason being the difficulty in quantifying the
loss which will have been suffered by the plaintiff by the publication of
the information.[89]

Delivery up. Subject to the provisions of section 10 of the Contempt of   **17.29**
Court Act 1981,[90] a court may order that a third party to whom confidential information and or documents have been disclosed assist the
person who is entitled to the benefit of the information by giving him
full information and disclosing the identity of the person who disclosed
the information and or documents.[91]

---

[87] *Williams v. Williams* (1817) 3 Merriv. 157 at 160; *Attorney-General v. Guardian Newspapers Ltd. (No. 2)* [1990] 1 A.C. 109.
[88] *Attorney-General v. Guardian Newspapers Ltd.* [1987] 1 W.L.R. 1248; *Schering Chemicals Ltd. v. Falkman Ltd.* [1982] Q.B. 1; *Cambridge Nutrition Ltd. v. British Broadcasting Corporation* [1990] 3 All E.R. 523.
[89] *Attorney-General v. Guardian Newspapers Ltd.* [1987] 1 W.L.R. 1248; *Schering Chemicals Ltd. v. Falkman Ltd.* [1982] Q.B. 1.
[90] See *ante*, para. 17.09 *et seq.* for the operation of this section in relation to such disclosures.
[91] *British Steel Corpn. v. Granada Television Ltd.* [1981] A.C. 1096.

PASSING OFF

1. Elements of Passing Off

18.01 Minimum requirements of a passing-off action. The minimum requirements necessary to create a valid cause of action for passing off of goods and services were summarised by Lord Diplock and Lord Fraser in *Erven Warnink Besloten Vennootschap v. J. Townend & Sons (Hull) Ltd.*[1] In Lord Diplock's formulation he identifies five characteristics which must be present to create a valid cause of action for passing off:

"(1) a misrepresentation (2) made by a trader in the course of trade (3) to prospective customers of his or ultimate consumers of goods or services supplied by him (4) which is calculated to injure the business or goodwill of another trader, in the sense that this is a reasonably foreseeable consequence, and (5) which causes actual damage to a business or goodwill of the trader by whom the action is brought or, in a quia timet action, will probably do so".

18.02 Lord Fraser's formulation[2] requires the plaintiff to show at least the following facts:

"(1) that his business consists of, or includes, selling in the United Kingdom a class of goods to which the particular trade name

---

[1] *Erven Warnink Besloten Vennootschap v. J. Townend & Sons (Hull) Ltd.* [1979] A.C. 731 at 742, with which three other members of the court agreed, although they also agreed with Lord Fraser's formulation .

[2] *Ibid.* at 755, 756.

applies; (2) that the class of goods is clearly defined, and that in the minds of members of the public, or of a section of the public, in the United Kingdom the trade name distinguishes that class from other similar goods; (3) that because of the reputation of the goods, there is goodwill attached to that name; (4) that he, the plaintiff, as a member of the class of those who sell the goods is the owner of goodwill in the United Kingdom which is of substantial value; (5) that he has suffered, or is really likely to suffer, substantial damage to his property in the goodwill by reason of the defendant's selling goods which are falsely described by the trade name to which the goodwill is attached".

These two passages are to be read together since Lord Fraser concentrates on what conditions have to be satisfied by the plaintiff, whereas Lord Diplock concentrates on what the defendant must have done.[3]   **18.03**

The fact that the characteristics are present does not necessarily mean that a valid cause of action will exist.[4] However, the "presence of those characteristics is enough, unless there is also present in the case some exceptional feature which justifies, on the grounds of public policy withholding from a person who has suffered injury in consequence of the deception practised on prospective customers or consumers of his product a remedy in law against the deceiver".[5] The principles enunciated in *Erven Warnink Besloten Vennootschap v. J. Townend & Sons (Hull) Ltd.* can be stated thus[5a]: the plaintiff must establish a goodwill or reputation attached to the goods or services which he supplies in the mind of the purchasing public by association with the identifying get-up (whether that is identified by brand name packaging or label) under which his particular goods or services are offered to the public, such that the get-up is recognised by the public distinctive specifically as the plaintiff's goods or services.

Secondly, he must demonstrate a misrepresentation by the defendant to the public (whether or not intentional) leading or likely to lead the public to believe the goods or services offered by him are the goods or services of the plaintiff.

---

[3] *Pete Waterman Ltd. v. CBS United Kingdom Ltd.* [1993] E.M.L.R. 27, *per* Sir Nicolas Browne-Wilkinson V.-C.; see also *British Broadcasting Corpn. v. Talbot Motor Car Co. Ltd.* [1981] F.S.R. 228 at 232, *per* Megarry V.-C.; *Anheuser-Busch v. Budejovicky Budvar* [1984] F.S.R. 413 at 463.

[4] *Erven Warnink Besloten Vennootschap v. J. Townend & Sons (Hull) Ltd.* [1979] A.C. 731 at 742, H.L., *per* Lord Diplock.

[5] *Ibid.* at 748.

[5a] The following passage is based upon the judgment of Nourse L.J. in *Consorzio del Prosciutto di Parma v. Marks and Spencer plc* [1991] R.P.C. 351, C.A., and Lord Jauncey in *Reckitt & Colman Products Ltd. v. Borden Inc.* [1992] 1 All E.R. 873, H.L.; see also *Fortnum & Mason plc v. Fortnum* [1994] F.S.R. 438.

Thirdly, he must demonstrate that he suffers or, in a *quia timet* action, that he is likely to suffer damage by reason of the erroneous belief engendered by the defendant's misrepresentation that the source of the defendant's goods or services is the same as the source of those offered by the plaintiff.

18.04 Right protected by passing off action. This proprietary right recognised by the law is not a right in the name, mark or get-up itself. It is a right in the reputation or goodwill of which the name, mark or get-up is the badge or vehicle.[6] A person who engages in commercial activities may acquire a valuable reputation in respect of the goods in which he deals, or of the services which he performs, or of his business as an entity. The law regards such a reputation as incorporeal property, the integrity of which the owner is entitled to protect. However, the owner of such property is not entitled to protection against legitimate competition. Thus if X's goods have acquired a reputation in the market connected with a particular name, mark or get-up, X cannot complain if the value of that reputation is depreciated by Y coming onto the market with similar goods which acquire a reputation. X can, however, complain if Y in the course of his operation uses in connection with his goods the name, mark or get up associated with Y's goods, or one so closely resembling it as to be likely to lead to confusion on the market between the goods of X and those of Y. By so doing Y wrongfully appropriates to himself part of the reputation or goodwill belonging to X and so infringes the integrity of X's property in that reputation or goodwill.

(a) *Goodwill*

18.05 Goodwill. The concept of "goodwill" is in law a broad one and has been defined as "the benefit and advantage of the good name, reputation, and connection of a business. It is the attractive force which brings in custom."[7] It has been said to embrace "every circumstance which contributes to the success and value of the business to which it

---

[6] *Singer Manufacturing v. Loog* (1882) 18 Ch.D. 395 at 412, and on appeal (1882) 8 App.Cas. 15 at 26, 27, 38, 39; *Reddaway v. Banham* [1896] A.C. 199 at 209, H.L.; *Burberry's v. Cording* (1909) 26 R.P.C. 693 at 701; *A.G. Spalding Bros. v. A.W. Gamage Ltd.* (1915) 32 R.P.C. 273 at 284, H.L.; *H.P. Bulmer Ltd. and Showerings Ltd. v. J. Bollinger S.A.* [1978] R.P.C. 79 at 94, 95, C.A.; *Erven Warnink Besloten Vennootschap v. J. Townend & Sons (Hull) Ltd.* [1979] A.C. 731 at 740, 741, H.L.; *Star Industrial Co. Ltd. (trading as New Star Industrial Co.) v. Yap Kwee Kor* [1976] F.S.R. 256 at 269, P.C.
[7] *Inland Revenue Commissioners v. Muller & Co.'s Margarine Ltd.* [1901] A.C. 217 at 223–224; see also *Trego v. Hunt* [1896] A.C. 274, H.L. "The whole advantage, whatever it may be, of the reputation and connection of the firm."

relates".[8] However, "goodwill", as the subject of proprietary rights, has no independent existence apart from the business to which it is attached.[9] So that when the business is abandoned the goodwill perishes with it although if the plaintiff can show that there is, notwithstanding abandonment, some residual goodwill, he may be able to maintain a cause of action.[10]

Locality of the goodwill. The international nature of the entertainment **18.06** industry means that it is of some importance for foreign entertainment companies to know what form of activity on its part is required before it can be said that it has a "business" in the United Kingdom[11] to which goodwill can attach. Prior to the decision of *Alain Bernardin et Cie v. Pavilion Properties Ltd.*,[12] a foreign trader who had established goodwill in the United Kingdom through the sale of his goods or services directly, or through his agents, to customers, but had no place of business, in the United Kingdom would acquire a goodwill which would be protected by the English courts.[13] *Alain Bernardin et Cie v. Pavilion Properties Ltd.* cast some doubt upon this principle in that it appeared to establish that even if the foreign trader has customers in the United Kingdom he cannot protect his reputation unless he has conducted some business here. The decision has had a mixed reception.[14] In *Anheuser-Busch Inc. v. Budejovicky Budvar NP*[15] the majority of the Court of Appeal treated the presence of a local goodwill as being essential to the right to protection. However, it would appear that the Court treated the absence of customers in this country as decisive of whether or not the plaintiff was carrying on business here thus having a local goodwill.

In *Pete Waterman Ltd. v. C.B.S. United Kingdom Ltd.*[16] the **18.07**

---

[8] *H.P. Bulmer and Showerings Ltd. v. J. Bollinger S.A.* [1978] R.P.C. 79 at 95, C.A.
[9] *Inland Revenue Commissioners v. Muller & Co.'s Margarine Ltd.* [1901] A.C. 217 at 223–224; *Star Industrial Co. Ltd. v. Yap Kwee Kor* [1976] F.S.R. 256, P.C.
[10] *Ad-Lib Club Ltd. v. Granville* [1972] R.P.C. 673; *Berkeley Hotel Co. Ltd. v. Berkeley International (Mayfair) Ltd.* [1972] R.P.C. 237.
[11] There is no difference between the law of England and Wales and that of Scotland with regard to passing off.
[12] [1967] R.P.C. 581.
[13] *S.A. des Anciens Etablissements Panhard et Levassor Motor Co. Ltd.* (1901) 18 R.P.C. 405; *Poiret v. Jules Poiret Ltd.* (1920) 37 R.P.C. 177; *Sheraton Corp. of America v. Sheraton Motels Ltd.* [1964]; *Pete Waterman Ltd. v. C.B.S. United Kingdom* [1993] E.M.L.R. 27 at 51.
[14] Criticised in *C. & A. Modes v. C. & A. (Waterford) Ltd.* [1978] F.S.R. 126, where the court refused to follow it; *Baskin-Robbins Ice Cream Co. v. Gutman* [1976] F.S.R. 545, and *Maxim's Ltd. v. Dye* [1977] 1 W.L.R. 1115, where Graham J. treated cases of international goodwill as depending not on the situs of the goodwill but on the use of the name or mark in the U.K.
[15] [1984] F.S.R. 413.
[16] [1993] E.M.L.R. 57.

authorities[17] were reviewed. The plaintiffs claimed to be entitled to the exclusive use in the United Kingdom of the name or description "The Hit Factory". In February 1990 the defendant, C.B.S., announced that it was proposing to refurbish its recording studios in London and rename them "The Hit Factory". The plaintiff claimed that "The Hit Factory" had become distinctive of its organisation including its studios. C.B.S., on the other hand claimed that The Hit Factory Inc. in New York had before and after 1987 enjoyed a reputation and goodwill in this country by contracting with United Kingdom customers for the use of the studios in New York. They therefore claimed to be entitled to by reason either of prior use or concurrent use with the plaintiff of the name "The Hit Factory" in the United Kingdom. The argument advanced by the plaintiff was that since The Hit Factory had neither had any place of business in this country, nor rendered any services as a recording studio here, it had never had any goodwill capable of being protected in the courts of this country. Sir Nicolas Browne-Wilkinson V.-C., in giving judgment suggested, that *Alain Bernardin et Cie v. Pavilion Properties Ltd.* was wrongly decided and concluded that:

> "The presence of customers in this country is sufficient to constitute the carrying on of business here whether or not there is otherwise a place of business here and whether or not services are provided here. Once it is found that there are customers, it is open to find that there is a business here to which local goodwill is attached."

It is submitted therefore that in so far as *Alain Bernardin et Cie v. Pavilion Properties Ltd.* purported to set down a rule that it is not sufficient to have customers in the United Kingdom to acquire protectable goodwill it is unlikely to be followed in the future cases.

18.08   **Goodwill may be acquired though trade not commenced.** The nature of entertainment products and services requires an entertainment company to expend considerable sums on the advertising of, for example, a record or film before the date on which it will become available to the consumer. In such cases there is always the risk that a rival may seek to

---

[17] *Commissioners of the Inland Revenue v. Muller & Co.'s Margarine Ltd.* [1901] A.C. 217; *Panhard et Levassor SA v. Panhard Levassor Motor Co. Ltd.* (1901) 18 R.P.C. 405; *Poiret v. Jules Poiret Ltd.* (1920) 37 R.P.C. 177; *R.J. Reuter Co. Ltd. v. Muhlens* (1953) 70 R.P.C. 235; *T. Oertli A.G. v. E.J. Bowman (London) Ltd.* [1957] R.P.C. 389; *Sheraton Corp. of America v. Sheraton Motels Ltd.* [1964] R.P.C. 202; *Baskin-Robbins Ice Cream Co. v. Gutman* [1976] F.S.R. 545; *Maxim's Ltd. v. Dye* [1977] 1 W.L.R. 1115; *Star Industrial Company Ltd. v. Yap Kwee Kor* [1976] F.S.R. 269; *C. & A. Modes v. C. & A. (Waterford) Ltd.* [1978] F.S.R. 126; *Erven Warnink B.V. v. J. Townend & Sons Ltd.* [1979] A.C. 731, H.L.; *Metric Resources Corp. v. Leasemetrix Ltd.* [1979] F.S.R. 571; *Athlete's Foot Marketing Associates Inc. v. Cobra Sports Ltd.* [1980] R.P.C. 343; *Lego v. Lego M. Lemelstrich* [1983] F.S.R. 155.

pre-empt the success of such a record or film by placing on the market a product which trades on such advertising or reputation. In such circumstances an action in passing off may be available if the existence of sufficient goodwill can be established by showing that definite and substantial preparations had been made with a view to putting goods and intended services before the public under some suitable name or mark, and that a substantial number of persons knew of and desired to acquire when available, the goods or services under that name.[18]

Thus, in *British Broadcasting Corporation v. Talbot Motor Company Ltd.*[19] where the BBC had received publicity in the press on television and at the motor show in respect of a traffic information system under the name of CARFAX which had not been launched, the court restrained the defendant from using CARFAX in respect of a motor vehicle spare parts business. The court was of the view that although the BBC had not yet launched the system at the date of seeking inter-locutory relief it had built up goodwill because a significant part of the public knew about the name CARFAX as distinctive to the BBC's system. A producer may therefore acquire a substantial reputation and goodwill in respect of a film, record or theatre play by advance publicity notwithstanding the fact that the film is not on general release to the public, and would be entitled to protection of such goodwill if another producer should seek to release a film which seeks to trade on the reputation which the film has acquired. Whether such a reputation and goodwill has been established is a question of fact in each case.

(b) *Misrepresentation*

Misrepresentation essential. Although injury to a trader's goodwill is a **18.09** necessary ingredient of a cause of action in passing off, it is not alone sufficient to give rise to such a cause of action. The plaintiff "must demonstrate a misrepresentation by the defendant to the public (whether or not intentional) leading or likely to lead the public to believe that the goods or services offered of the plaintiff".[20] Whether the public is aware of the plaintiff's identity as the manufacturer or supplier of the goods or services

---

[18] *W.H. Allen & Co. v. Brown Watson Ltd.* [1965] R.P.C. 191; *British Broadcasting Corpn. v. Talbot Motor Co. Ltd.* [1981] F.S.R. 228; *My Kinda Bones Ltd. (trading as Chicago Rib Shack) v. Dr. Pepper's Stove Co. Ltd. (trading as Dr. Pepper's Manhattan Rib Shack)* [1984] F.S.R. 289; *Elida Gibbs Ltd. v. Colgate-Palmolive Ltd.* [1983] F.S.R. 95; *Mirage Studios v. Counter-Feat Clothing Company Ltd.* [1991] F.S.R. 145 at 159.

[19] [1981] F.S.R. 228.

[20] *Reckitt & Colman Properties Ltd. v. Borden Inc.* [1990] 1 W.L.R. 491 at 499, H.L. See also *H.P. Bulmer Ltd and Showerings Ltd. v. J. Bollinger S.A.* [1978] R.P.C. 79, C.A.; *Newsweek Inc. v. British Broadcasting Corporation* [1979] R.P.C. 441 at 447 C.A.; *Cadbury-Schweppes Pty. Ltd. v. Pub Squash Co. Pty. Ltd.* [1981] 1 W.L.R. 193, P.C.

is immaterial, as long as they are identified with a particular source which is in fact the plaintiff.[21] For example, if the public is accustomed to rely upon a particular brand name in purchasing goods of a particular description, it matters not that there is little or no public awareness of the identity of the proprietor of the brand.

18.10 **Confusion.** In deciding whether confusion is likely to result, the test is whether a substantial number of ordinary sensible members of the public would be confused. It is not sufficient that the only confusion would be to a very small, unobservant section of the public.[22] If a plaintiff can show that the defendant has had the intent to mislead members of the public, the court will readily infer that deception or confusion has indeed resulted or is likely to result.[23] While it is not essential to establish fraudulent intention in order to obtain relief in a passing off action, proof of such an intent to deceive lightens the burden of proof of misrepresentation.[24]

18.11 **Common field of activity.** "The expression 'common field of activity' is not a term of art but merely a convenient shorthand term for indicating . . . the need for a real possibility of confusion which is the basis of the action".[25] In determining the question of confusion the court will look to see whether there is any kind of association, or could be in the minds of the public any kind of association, between the fields of activities of the plaintiff and the fields of activities of the defendant. Where such a common field of activity is found it is a cogent factor to be taken into account in considering whether the misrepresentation is calculated to deceive, or is likely to lead to deception.[26] However, there is no requirement that in order to succeed in an action for passing off the plaintiff and the defendant must compete in the same line of business. It would appear to be sufficient if the plaintiff establishes that what is

---

[21] *Reckitt & Colman Properties Ltd. v. Borden Inc.* [1990] 1 W.L.R. 490, H.L.

[22] *Singer Manufacturing Co. v. Wilson* (1876) 2 Ch.D. 434 at 447, C.A.; *Henry Thorne & Co. Ltd. v. Sandow* (1912) 29 R.P.C. 440 at 453; *Newsweek Inc. v. British Broadcasting Corporation* [1979] R.P.C. 441 at 447, C.A.

[23] *Slazenger & Sons v. Feltham & Co.* (1889) 6 R.P.C. 531 at 538; *Reddaway v. Banham* (1895) 12 R.P.C. 83 at 89, C.A.; *Claudius Ash, Son & Co. Ltd. v. Invicta Manufacturing Co. Ltd.* (1912) 29 R.P.C. 465 at 475, H.L.; *Office Cleaning Services Ltd. v. Westminster Window and General Cleaners Ltd.* (1946) 63 R.P.C. 39 at 42; *Parker-Knoll Ltd. v. Knoll International Ltd.* [1962] R.P.C. 265 at 278, H.L.; *Cadbury-Schweppes Pty. Ltd. v. Pub Squash Co. Pty. Ltd.* [1981] 1 W.L.R. 193 at 203; *R.H.M. Foods Ltd. v. Bovril Ltd.* [1983] R.P.C. 275 at 278, 281.

[24] *Cellular Clothing Co. Ltd. v. Maxton and Murray* [1899] A.C. 326 at 334.

[25] See *Lyngstad v. Anabas Products Ltd.* [1977] F.S.R. 62 at 67.

[26] *Annabel's (Berkeley Square) Ltd. v. Schock (trading as Annabel's Escort Agency* [1972] R.P.C. 838 at 844; *Henderson v. Radio Corp. Pty. Ltd.* [1969] R.P.C. 218; *Nationwide Building Society v. Nationwide Estate Agents Ltd.* [1987] F.S.R. 579 at 588.

done represents the defendant's goods to be the same as, or connected or associated with, the plaintiff's business in such way as to lead a substantial number of people to accept them on the faith of the plaintiff's reputation,[27] but where the fields of activity are very dissimilar it may be difficult to prove a misrepresentation[28] or damage.[29] In determining whether there is a likelihood of confusion between the plaintiff's goods or business and the goods and activities of the defendant, the court may have regard not only to the pre-existing goods or business activities of the plaintiff but also to the natural and potential expansion into "allied fields of activity to which [the plaintiff's] business might reasonably be extended or at least thought to extend".[30]

Passing off by similarity of get-up. "Get-up" is the badge of the plain- **18.12** tiff's goodwill, that which associates the goods with the plaintiff in the mind of the public.[31] Passing off may occur, therefore, where the get-up of the defendant's goods bears a similarity to that of the plaintiff's although there is no property in a get-up. It is, however, a factor which the court may take into account in determining whether there is a likelihood of confusion. But confusion resulting from the lawful right of another trader to employ, as indicative of the nature of his goods, terms which are common to the trade, gives rise to no cause of action.[32]

To succeed, however, in establishing deception and the likelihood of confusion the plaintiff must demonstrate more than simply the use of the get-up. He must demonstrate that it has become so closely associated with his goods as to acquire the secondary meaning not simply of goods of that description but specifically goods of which he alone is the source.[33] In such circumstances, the test for determining whether confusion is likely to occur from similarity of get-up is "how far the defendants" trade mark bears such a resemblance to that of the plaintiffs, as to

---

[27] *H.P. Bulmer Ltd. v. J. Bollinger SA* [1978] R.P.C. 79, *per* Goff L.J., C.A.; *Lego System AS v. Lego M. Lemelstrich Ltd.* [1983] F.S.R. 155; *Mirage Studios v. Counter-Feat Clothing Ltd.* [1991] F.S.R. 145.

[28] *Annabel's (Berkeley Square) Ltd. v. Schock (trading as Annabel's Escort Agency)* [1972] R.P.C. 838.

[29] *Stringfellow v. McCain Foods (G.B.) Ltd.* [1984] R.P.C. 501.

[30] *Sterwin A.G. v. Brocades (Great Britain) Ltd.* [1979] R.P.C. 481 at 490; see also *Dunlop Pneumatic Tyre Co. Ltd. v. Dunlop Lubricant Co.* (1898) 16 R.P.C. 12 at 15; *Crystalate Gramophone Record Manufacturing Co. Ltd. v. British Crystalite Co. Ltd.* (1934) 51 R.P.C. 315 at 322.

[31] *Reckitt & Colman Properties Ltd. v. Borden Inc.* [1990] 1 W.L.R. 491, H.L.

[32] *Hennessy & Co. v. Keating* (1908) 25 R.P.C. 361, H.L.; *J.B. WIlliams Co. v. Bronnley & Co. Ltd.* 26 R.P.C. 765, C.A.; *Reckitt & Colman Properties Ltd. v. Borden Inc.* [1990] 1 W.L.R. 491, H.L.

[33] *Reddaway v. Banham* [1896] A.C. 199 at 210; *Reckitt & Colman Properties Ltd. v. Borden Inc.* [1990] 1 W.L.R. 491 at 506, H.L.

calculated to deceive the incautious purchaser".[34] The test must be applied, however, against the background of the type of market in which the goods are sold, and the habits and characteristics of the purchasers in that market. Where, however, a defendant who adopts a get-up similar to that of the plaintiff's takes sufficient steps to see that his "goods can be really distinguished"[35] from those of the plaintiff, this may negate the similarity of get-up.[36]

(c) *Damage*

18.13 The plaintiff must also demonstrate that he suffers, or, in a *quia timet* action, that he is likely to suffer, damage by reason of the erroneous belief engendered by the defendant's misrepresentation that the source of the defendant's goods or services is the same as the source of those offered by the plaintiff.[37] The type of damage suffered by the plaintiff will vary with the subject-matter of the goodwill.

Generally, where the misrepresentation is such to induce the public to believe that the defendant's business is connected with the plaintiff's business in some way this may cause damage to the plaintiff both by way of loss of business to the defendant and by reason of the fact that the "quality of the goods [the defendant sells], the kind of business [he] do[es], the credit or otherwise which [he] enjoys are all things which may injure the [plaintiff] who is wrongly assumed to be associated with [the defendant]".[38]

For example, in the case of merchandising rights the damage will be of two kinds. First, the plaintiff will lose royalties. The goods which would have been manufactured under licence from them will go elsewhere and also the amount of royalties that they can seek to get from those who do take licences from them is likely to be reduced, since the market will not be an exclusive one.[39]

The second type of damage the plaintiff will suffer will be loss of control over the quality of the goods on which the name, character or likeness is reproduced. Where the value of a name character or likeness is

---

[34] *R. Johnston & Co. v. Archbald Orr Ewing & Co.* (1882) 7 App.Cas. 219 at 229, *per* Lord Kingsdown, H.L.; *per* Lord Blackburn *Leather Cloth Co. Ltd. v. American Leather Cloth Co. Ltd.* (1865) 11 H.L. Cas. 523, 539; approved *Reckitt & Colman Properties Ltd. v. Borden Inc.* [1990] A.C. 491, H.L. *Cf. Schweppes Ltd. v. Gibbens* (1905) 22 R.P.C. 601 at 606–607.

[35] *Payton & Co. Ltd. v. Snelling, Lampard & Co. Ltd.* 17 R.P.C. 48 at 56; *Reckitt & Colman Properties Ltd. v. Borden Inc.* [1990] 1 W.L.R. 491 at 508, H.L.

[36] *Reckitt & Colman Properties Ltd. v. Borden Inc.* [1990] 1 W.L.R. 491 at 509, H.L.

[37] *Ibid.*; *H.P. Bulmer Ltd. and Showerings Ltd. v. J. Bollinger S.A.* [1978] R.P.C. 79, C.A.; *Erven Warnink BV v. J. Townend & Sons (Hull) Ltd.* [1979] A.C. 731.

[38] *Ewing v. Buttercup Margarine Co. Ltd.* [1917] 2 Ch. 1 at 13.

[39] See *Mirage Studios v. Counter-Feat Clothing Ltd.* [1991] F.S.R. 145; similar principles will apply where the goodwill is not attached to merchandising. In such a case the plaintiff will lose revenue from sales which he would otherwise have obtained but for the passing off.

linked to maintaining the quality of the goods to which it is attached, if the goods go down market or are of inferior quality[40] that will affect the value of the copyright in the character and thereby reduce its value.[41]

2. Passing Off in the Entertainment Industry

(a) *Merchandising Rights*

Nature of character merchandising. Character merchandising is an **18.14** industry which has grown in sophistication over comparatively recent times.[42] It generally consists in the owners of the copyright in a film, television series or cartoon characters licensing the use of the name, mark, get-up or fictitious characters appearing in such films, television series and cartoons, for the reproduction on merchandise and goods by licensees. The return to the owner of the copyright, the creator of the character, is normally in the form of royalty payments. Such merchandising rights are extremely valuable in a case where the underlying film or television series has been successful. Consequently, merchandising rights, and their protection, are of great importance to the entertainment industry. There is a developing body of law relating to the protection afforded to such rights in a passing off action. Uncertainty remains, however, as to the test to be applied in determining whether protection is to be afforded, and, secondly, whether the test is the same in respect of a fictional character to which copyright protection may be accorded and a name as to which there is prima facie no copyright protection.

Fictitious characters from books films and television series. *Tavener* **18.15** *Rutledge Ltd. v. Trexapalm Ltd.*[43] was the first of a line of authorities which sought to set down the appropriate test for protection in passing off in character merchandising. In that case the plaintiff used the word "Kojakpops" as brand name for its lollipops, had done so on a large scale for several months prior to the commencement of proceedings, and had built up a considerable goodwill and reputation doing so. "Kojak" was the name of a television series, the leading character being

---

[40] It is an actionable injury to pass off goods known not to be the plaintiffs as and for the plaintiff's even though not inferior: *Singer Manufacturing Co. v. Loog* (1882) 8 App.Cas. 15, 30 H.L. See also *Blofeld v. Payne* (1833) 4 B & Ad 410; *Edelsten v. Edelsten* (1863) 1 De GJ & Sm 185.
[41] See *Mirage Studios v. Counter-Feat Clothing Ltd.* [1991] F.S.R. 145.
[42] See *Mirage Studios v. Counter-Feat Clothing Ltd.* [1991] F.S.R. 145; *In re American Greetings Corpn.* [1984] 1 W.L.R. 189 at 191, where the House of Lords was willing to accept that character merchandising has become a "widespread practice in various countries, including the United Kingdom".
[43] [1977] R.P.C. 275.

a detective who had the habit of sucking lollipops. The plaintiff company did not have a licence from the owners of the series to use the name and the defendant, who claimed that it had such a licence, began to sell lollipops under the brand name "Kojak lollies". The plaintiff commenced an action for passing off and was granted an interlocutory injunction restraining the defendant from using the name. The defendant contended that because of the growth of the merchandising industry the members of the public would take it that, if the word "Kojakpops" was used the right to use that name had been licensed by whoever was the owner of the rights in the series "Kojak", that moreover they have insisted upon a certain standard of quality and that, therefore, anybody who uses the word "Kojakpops" is to some extent taking advantage of the good name of the copyright. Walton J. in giving judgment said:

> "I regret to say that I am wholly unimpressed by any such argument. Certainly it is not established by the evidence that it has yet arisen and I think that it is a good long way off, if in fact it ever does arise, but there may come a time when the system of character merchandising will have been so well known to the man in the street that immediately he sees Kojakpops he will say to himself: 'They must have a licence from the person who owns the rights to the television series': but that by itself, so far as I can see would not be of any assistance to [the defendant] because that does not carry him home. What he would have to go on to show is that it had become so well known that people in the situation of the licensors of these names exercised quality control over any product bearing their name, so that as soon as anybody in the street came to the conclusion that a product was licensed by the owners of some series . . . he would say to himself not only. 'This must have been licensed by them', but also: 'and that is a guarantee of quality' ".

18.16   He then went on to lay down the test to be applied in determining whether merchandising rights would be entitled to protection under passing off:

> "It appears to me that therefore one would have to prove three things, first that a reference to "Kojakpops" inevitably carried the man in the street back to the person . . . who was the owner of the television series; secondly, that the owners of all licensing rights automatically included provision for quality control in their agreements and thirdly, that all automatically saw that those were carried out. Unless all these matters are satisfied it cannot be said that there is any relevant overlap in any of the activities of the plaintiff and the owner of the character or television series."

This three-fold test was approved in *Lyngstad v. Anabas Products Ltd.*[44] where Oliver J. stated that in essence the test is whether there was a "real possibility of confusion" that reasonable people might suppose that there was some sort of association between the plaintiff's activities and the goods or business of the defendant's and that the plaintiff's exercised some sort of control over the quality of the defendant's products.

The test laid down by Walton J. In *Tavener Rutledge v. Trexapalm* and **18.17** approved in *Lyngstad v. Anabas* arose out of cases which were heard at a time when the merchandising industry was in its infancy. As such it was unlikely that the ordinary member of the public would, at that time, have associated an article or garment bearing a fictitious character with the owner of the character or name. However the growth of the industry has meant that there has been an increasing perception on the part of the public as to the origins of such products. The courts too have shown a willingness to accept that merchandising is a widespread and common activity,[45] and it has now been accepted as arguable that the public will assume that the owner of a fictitious character appearing on an article or garment has been licensed by the owner.[46]

The authorities were reviewed by Sir Nicolas Browne-Wilkinson **18.18** V.-C. in *Mirage Studios v. Counter-Feat Clothing Co. Ltd.*[47] in the light of the growth in the merchandising industry since the earlier decisions.[48] This case concerned the merchandising of the Teenage Mutant Ninja Turtles ("Turtles").

The "Turtles" were fictitious cartoon characters conceived in the United States by the first plaintiffs who were the owners of the copyright in the drawings of these characters in the form of a comic strip. The first plaintiff did not manufacture or market any goods themselves, the major part of their business consisting of creating and marketing cartoons videos and films of the Turtles. However, part of their business included the licensing of the reproduction of characters on goods sold by third parties and a major part of their income was derived from royalties received from such licensing activities. The second plaintiffs were the first plaintiff's worldwide licensing agents and the third plaintiff's the licensing agents for the United Kingdom. The contractual requirements with third parties included provisions as to the quality

---

[44] [1977] F.S.R. 62.
[45] *In re American Greetings Corpn.* [1984] 1 W.L.R. 189 at 191, H.L.; *Mirage Studios v. Counter-Feat Clothing Co. Ltd.* [1991] F.S.R. 145.
[46] *IPC Magazines Ltd. v. Black and White Music Corp.* [1983] F.S.R. 348.
[47] [1991] F.S.R. 145.
[48] *viz. Tavener Rutledge Ltd. v. Trexaplam Ltd.* [1977] R.P.C. 275; *Lyngstad v. Anabas Products Ltd.* [1977] F.S.R. 62; *Wombles Ltd. v. Wombles Skips Ltd.* [1977] R.P.C. 99.

control of the goods to which the reproductions of Turtle were attached. At the time of the application for an injunction over 150 licences had been granted in the United Kingdom and elsewhere as a character concept among children and teenagers.

The first defendant had made drawings of humanoid turtle characters similar in appearance to those of the plaintiffs, utilising the concept of the Turtles rather than actual drawings of Turtles. The defendant began licensing those drawings to various garment manufacturers for reproduction on T-shirts and jogging clothes and the plaintiffs commenced an action for passing off and sought an interlocutory injunction to restrain them from so doing.

18.19   In granting an injunction Sir Nicholas Browne-Wilkinson V.-C. readily found that "the critical evidence" in the case was that a substantial number of the buying public now expected and knew that where a famous cartoon or television character is reproduced on goods, that reproduction is the result of a licence granted by the owner of the copyright or owner of other rights in that character. The evidence which gave rise to this conclusion is not entirely clear from a reading of the judgment. However, it would appear that some reliance was placed on an informal survey conducted by the plaintiffs which revealed that out of 20 people shown the defendant's drawing 11 identified the turtles in question as being those seen on television or in other ways related back to the plaintiff's Turtles. In this respect therefore the finding satisfied the test laid down in previous cases[49] that reasonable people must suppose that there was some sort of association between the plaintiff's activities and goods or business and the defendant's.

18.20   Secondly, the Vice-Chancellor found that a remedy in passing off is not limited to those who market or sell the goods in question. If the public was misled in a relevant way as to the features or quality of the goods as sold, that was sufficient to found a case of action in passing off brought by those with whom the public associated that feature or that quality which had been represented. Thus, a licensor who does not produce or sell goods may bring an action against a defendant who does so sell or produce goods which are passed off as the licensor's goods, and may also bring a similar action against a defendant licensor who does not himself produce or sell goods but is a licensor of merchandising rights. The goodwill that the licensor is entitled to protect is the merchandising right which the public might associate with the licensor and it matters not that he does not manufacture or sell the goods himself. It therefore follows that a "common-field" of activity, in the sense

---

[49] *Tavener Rutledge v. Trexapalm Ltd.* [1977] R.P.C. 275; *Lyngstad v. Anabas Products* [1977] F.S.R. 62.

of being a manufacturer or seller of the goods, was not considered necessary.

Thirdly, although there was a provision in the merchandising agree-   **18.21**
ments entered into by the plaintiff with third parties which required
the maintenance of quality control, there was no clear finding by the
Vice-Chancellor that there was an awareness in the public that the
plaintiff was concerned to uphold the quality of the goods. Indeed,
the Vice-Chancellor[50] went so far as to say with regard to the judgment
in *Tavener Rutledge v. Trexapalm Ltd.*[51] that:

> "Walton J. made certain remarks about the need to show an aware-
> ness in the public that licensors of characters were concerned to
> uphold the quality of the goods on which the characters appear. At
> the moment I am afraid I do not understand why that is an essential
> characteristic of passing off."

The decisions in *Tavener Rutledge Ltd. v. Trexapalm Ltd.*,[52] *Lyngstad v.*   **18.22**
Anabas Products Ltd.,[53] *Wombles Ltd. v. Wombles Skips Ltd.*[54] were
distinguished on two bases. First, that they did not touch on a case such
as *Mirage Studios v. Counter-Feat Clothing Co. Ltd.*, where the plaintiff's
clearly had copyright in the drawings and was in business on a large
scale in the United Kingdom in licensing the use of the copyright in the
drawing. Secondly, in so far as those cases related to the use of the name
of characters and personalities "[t]here is no copyright in a name . . . it
is hard to see what business the plaintiffs could have been carrying on
in licensing the copyright in the name and the name alone. Here . . . the
plaintiffs are carrying on the business of licensing the copyright in the
drawings of the Ninja Turtles in which copyright does exist".[55] However, it is difficult to see why copyright should underpin the rights
licensed. The subject-matter of protection in a passing off action is
goodwill. If this is present it should not matter that the goodwill is
unsupported by copyright. Some support for this proposition can be
found in *Shaw Bros. (Hong Kong) Ltd. v. Golden Harvest (HK)*,[56] where
the court decided that a film producer who had a licence to use the story
creating the character can build up a goodwill which may be protected
in a passing off action although he may not be the owner of the copyright.

---

[50] *Mirage Studios v. Counter-Feat Clothing Co. Ltd.* [1991] F.S.R. 145 at 158.
[51] [1977] R.P.C. 275.
[52] *Ibid.*
[53] [1977] F.S.R. 62.
[54] [1977] R.P.C. 99.
[55] *Mirage Studios v. Counter-Feat Clothing Ltd.* [1991] F.S.R. 145 at 157–158.
[56] [1972] R.P.C. 559 (Hong Kong).

18.23   *Mirage Studios v. Counter-Feat Clothing Co. Ltd.* is significant to the
extent that it shows a recognition by the court of the rapid growth of
character merchandising since the late 1970s. Nevertheless, some
evidence must be before the court, albeit it would seem not a great deal
of such evidence, showing that the public associates the goods with the
licensor. Further, it would tend to indicate that the plaintiff's merchandising rights will only be entitled to protection if he has at the date
of the action established a business licensing such rights.

     In the light of the review of the authorities in *Mirage Studios v.
Counter-Feat Clothing Ltd.*, it is submitted that in a passing off action the
following principles are applicable in relation to fictional characters.

18.24   First, a plaintiff will have to show that reasonable people would suppose that there was some association between the defendant's goods,
services or activities, and that the plaintiff was licensed by him.[57] The
court will readily find such association where there is some evidence to
this effect before it.[58]

     Secondly, the plaintiff must show that reasonable people assumed an
association as a result of a misrepresentation by the defendant. Where
the court finds on the evidence that such an association has been made
by reasonable people it will readily find that to "market goods which
the public mistake for the genuine article necessarily involves a misrepresentation to the public that they were genuine" and further that the
belief that they are genuine involves the further misrepresentation that
they are licensed by the plaintiff.[59]

18.25   Thirdly, *Tavener Rutledge Ltd. v. Trexapalm Ltd.*,[60] *Anabas Products
Ltd.*,[61] and *Wombles Ltd. v. Wombles Skips Ltd.*[62] require that the plaintiff
must show that the public placed some reliance on the licensor to
uphold the quality of the goods on which the characters appear. However, there is some doubt as to whether this requirement is applicable
in the law of passing off as applied to character merchandising.[63] It is
submitted that there is no basis in law for imposing such a require-

---

[57] *Tavener Rutledge Ltd. v. Trexapalm Ltd.* [1977] R.P.C. 275; *Lyngstad v. Anabas Products
   Ltd.* [1977] F.S.R. 62; *Wombles Ltd. v. Wombles Skips Ltd.* [1977] R.P.C. 99; *Children's
   Television Workshop Inc. v. Woolworths (New South Wales) Limited* [1981] R.P.C. 187;
   Mirage Studios v. Counter-Feat Clothing Limited [1991] F.S.R. 145.
[58] *Mirage Studios v. Counter-Feat Clothing Co. Ltd.* [1991] F.S.R. 145; it would appear that in
   this case such an association was inferred from an informal survey with a sample as
   little as 20 people.
[59] *Mirage Studios v. Counter-Feat Clothing Co. Ltd.* [1991] F.S.R. 145; *Children's Television
   Workshop Inc. v. Woolworths (New South Wales) Limited* [1981] R.P.C. 187.
[60] [1977] R.P.C. 275.
[61] [1977] F.S.R. 62.
[62] [1977] R.P.C. 99.
[63] *Mirage Studios v. Counter-Feat Clothing Co. Ltd.* [1991] F.S.R. 145.

ment. The fact of the customer believing the goods to be licensed by the plaintiff would of itself be an assurance of and reliance on the genuiness and quality of such goods.

Fourthly, the misrepresentation must cause actual damage to a business or to the goodwill of the licensor. Where the public associates the goods with the creator of the characters the depreciation of the image by fixing the characters to inferior goods and inferior material will generally first reduce the royalty by diverting business, and secondly reduce the value of the merchandising rights by diminishing the reputation of the licensor.[64]

Name and likeness of groups or individuals. Where the name or like-   **18.26**
ness of a performer is used by the defendant to endorse a product, or is placed without the performer's authority, the authorities would tend to indicate that it is difficult for the artiste or performer to succeed in an action for passing off where the goods or services are not in some way associated with the area of activity in which the artiste or performer has established his reputation. This approach is illustrated by *McCulloch v. Lewis A. May (Produce Distributors), Ltd.*[65] where the plaintiff who was a well-known broadcaster of children's programme who used the name of "Uncle Mac" for such broadcasts. He also used this name in his activities which included charity appeals, the writing of children's books, the making of records, association with road safety campaigns, the giving of lectures and the opening of fetes. The defendants commenced the distribution of puffed wheat under the name "Uncle Mac's Puffed Wheat". The carton containing the product also carried the words "Uncle Mac loves children and children love Uncle Mac! Uncle Mac has a wonderful way of brightening any table to which he has been invited". The plaintiff commenced an action for passing off and an injunction. The court refused an injunction on the basis that as the plaintiff was not in any way involved in producing or marketing puffed wheat there was no field of activity common to the plaintiff and the defendant and therefore no proprietary right which could have been invaded. This decision was criticised in *Henderson v. Radio Corp. Pty.*[66] as placing an over reliance on the principle of "common field of activity", but was approved by Oliver J., in *Lyngstad v. Anabas Products Ltd.*, who observed that criticism was based on a misconception as to what was meant by the term a "common field of activity" as used in *McCulloch v. Lewis A. May (Produce Distributors) Ltd.*

---

[64] *Ibid.*
[65] [1947] 2 All E.R. 845; *cf. Henderson v. Radio Corpn. Pty. Ltd.* [1969] R.P.C. 218 at 236, 244 (Aust.), where a photograph of ballroom dancers was placed on a record sleeve in such a way to suggest that they had sponsored or recommended the music.
[66] [1969] R.P.C. 218 at 236, Oliver J. said that the case followed a whole line of respectable English authorities.

18.27   The requirement for a "common field of activity" or "the need for a real possibility for confusion" would appear to have been a significant factor in the decision in *Lyngstad v. Anabas Products Ltd.*, where the defendants manufactured, *inter alia*, badges and transfers for pillows, slips and T-shirts bearing the pictures of the members of the Abba pop group. The plaintiffs contended that the defendants were making use of the group's reputation for their own commercial gain and were therefore liable for passing off since the public were likely to suppose that Abba were somehow associated with the defendants having licensed or endorsed their products. At the time of the application the plaintiffs had not established any business in the sale of the offending articles. Oliver J. in dismissing the application for an interlocutory injunction observed that:

> "The plaintiff is not complaining of the possibility of confusion between the defendants' activities as singers but that their activities as singers have generated a public interest which has enabled the Defendants to exploit for their own purposes the use of the plaintiff's photographs name".

and concluded "there is no business of the plaintiff here which in my judgment the defendants' goods could possibly be confused."

18.28   In *Lyngstad v. Anabas Products Ltd.*, there was no evidence of substantial exploitation by merchandising by the use of Abba's name and likeness. There was, however, evidence of their intention to licence the right to reproduce such name and likeness. It has been suggested,[67] however, that if the right evidence were before the court on a future occasion this case may call for future reconsideration. It would appear that the evidence required would be proof of active licensing of the merchandising rights in the name and or likeness of the group or individual, and the connection in the public mind with group or individual with the product bearing the likeness and name of the group or individual with such persons or definite and substantial preparations so to do and that a substantial number of persons knew of and desired to acquire the goods bearing the name and likeness. On the same principle, the decision in *McCulloch v. Lewis A. May (Produce Distributors) Ltd.* would also fall for reconsideration and it is doubtful whether it now represents the state of the law where the name or likeness of a performer appears on goods or services.

It is clear that in the latter case the plaintiff had made extensive use of his name outside his broadcasting activities and allowed it be associated with a number of professional activities and campaigns. As such

---

[67] *Mirage Studios v. Counter-Feat Clothing Ltd.* [1991] F.S.R. 145, *per* Sir Nicolas Browne-Wilkinson V.-C.

he had established a goodwill in that name which on the trend of modern authorities may be protectable under the law of passing off if similar facts were to arise for consideration.

It is submitted that on the authorities two approaches are open for the protection of the names and likeness of a performer under the law of passing off.

First, it is clear that modern conditions cannot wholly be equated   **18.29** with that which obtained at the time of *McCulloch v. Lewis A. May (Produce Distributors) Ltd.* was decided. The developments in the field of advertising and marketing has opened up a new area of gainful employment which is now a natural extension of the trade of performers who, by their fame, have found themselves in a position to earn substantial sums of money by lending their recommendation or sponsorship to goods and services. It is clear that a trader[68] is entitled to protect not only his reputation in a particular trade but also a potential trade in allied fields to which his business might reasonably be extended or at least be thought to extend.[69]

It is submitted that this principle is equally applicable to a performer with regard to the use of his name, likeness and voice[70] in the areas of marketing, advertising, sponsorship and endorsement of products.

Secondly, where the performer is able to show that he has established   **18.30** a business which actively licenses the use of his name and likeness for affixing to goods or for advertising, sponsoring or marketing goods, he may be entitled to protection of the goodwill in that business even if he does not manufacture or produce goods himself.

Some support for this proposition can be found in *Mirage Studios v. Counter-Feat Clothing Ltd.*, where identifying a business to which the goodwill attached was considered to be the "critical question" in the case, and where it was found that there was a business which licensed the rights to which the goodwill attached.

It is submitted that if the performer can satisfy either of the foregoing and can further establish that reasonable people assumed an association as a result of a misrepresentation by the defendant and the misrepresentation causes, or is likely to cause, damage to the performer's goodwill an action in passing off will lie.

---

[68] "Trader" in this respect includes a performer: see *Hines v. Winnick* [1947] 1 Ch. 708.
[69] *Dunlop Pneumatic Tyre Co. Ltd. v. Dunlop Lubricant Co.* (1898) 16 R.P.C. 12 at 15.
[70] See *Sim v. H.J. Heinz Co. Ltd.* [1959] 1 All E.R. 547, *per* Hodson L.J., C.A., where it was said that it is arguable that the voice of an actor is part of his stock-in-trade and therefore is something which he is entitled to protect as part of his goods.

(b) *Fictional characters from books, films and television series*

18.31 **Names of characters.** There is, as yet, no English authority which bears on the question as to whether a fictional character from a film or television series is protectable by a passing off action where a defendant seeks to use the name and essential characteristics of such characters in a series not authorised by the author or producer who owns the rights to such a character.

However, television, radio and film have given numerous examples of parts in serial programmes which have been played for a time by one actor and subsequently by another actor. The newcomer often brings his own interpretation to the part but the character remains essentially the same. If that character still attracts the listener or viewer and induces him to continue to watch the programme it is submitted that there is the goodwill which has attached to the programme and constitutes the property in the character.[71] Some support for this proposition can be found in dicta of May L.J. in *O'Neill v. Paramount Pictures Corporation*[72]:

> "Whilst I agree that there is presently no copyright in fictional characters in books, films or plays, I am by no means satisfied that an author of such works, particularly when consisting of a series of books about the same character, who has become widely known, has no form of proprietary interest in that character. Indeed, in their recent decision in *Cadbury-Schweppes Pty. Ltd. v. Pub Squash Pty. Ltd.* . . . the Privy Council clearly held that the true basis of the cause of action of passing off is that the offending acts injure right of property in the plaintiff, namely, in that case, his right to the goodwill of his business; the equivalent in the literary world is an author's right to the goodwill in a character whom he has created. The essence of any goodwill, whether in a product or a character, is that the public recognises such product or character as the property of the proprietor."

18.32 It is therefore submitted that a producer may acquire a reputation and goodwill in the name and characteristics of a character depicted in a film[73] if the public recognises such a product or character as the property[74] of the producer.[75] Any unauthorised use by a second

---

[71] *Shaw Bros (Hong Kong) Ltd. v. Golden Harvest (HK)* [1972] R.P.C. 559 (Hong Kong) where it was held that goodwill was capable of existing in a character from a film.

[72] [1983] C.A.T. 235; [1984] N.L.J. 338.

[73] *Shaw Bros (Hong Kong) Ltd. v. Golden Harvest (HK)* [1972] R.P.C. 559 (Hong Kong).

[74] A film producer who has a licence to use the story creating the character can build up a goodwill which may be protected in a passing-off action although he may not be the owner of the copyright: *Shaw Bros (Hong Kong) Ltd. v. Golden Harvest (HK)* [1972] R.P.C. 559 (Hong Kong).

[75] *O'Neill v. Paramount Pictures Corporation* [1983] C.A.T. 235; [1984] N.L.J. 338 *per* May L.J.; *Hexagon Pty. Ltd. v. Australian Broadcasting Commission* [1976] R.P.C. 328, 628 (Supreme Court of New South Wales).

producer of that character may in such circumstances amount to passing off if first the public associates the character, secondly, the association is a result of a misrepresentation by the infringer with the owner and, thirdly, that damage has occurred or is likely to occur as a result.

(c) *Performers' names*

Where a performer has acquired a reputation under an invented name   **18.33**
he is entitled to protect that name under the law of passing off.[76] Further, where a fictional name is given by a producer to an individual in a television programme, series, or theatrical or musical production by a producer and that name becomes part of the individual's stock in trade and identified with him by the public such name becomes, in the absence of agreement to the contrary, his property, and it is not open to the producer or the television company to make use of that name in connection with any person other than the individual.[77] It is submitted, however, that this principle will extend only to those rare cases where the performer acquires a professional reputation from a production and earns his living not only from the production by which he has acquired the reputation, but through appearances elsewhere under the name.

(d) *Title of a film*

Use of the name of novel or play as title of film. The owner of the copy-   **18.34**
right in a novel or play of which there exists no film version can maintain a passing-off action against the producer of a film for representing to the public, contrary to fact, that his film is a film version of the novel or play.[78] Thus, in *Samuelson v. Producers' Distributing Co., Ltd.*[79] the plaintiff, professionally known as Laurie Wylie, was the owner of copyright in a sketch called *The New Car*. It had been performed under licence by George Clarke, a well known comedian, at a Royal Command Performance. The defendants made a film entitled *His First Car* featuring George Clarke. The plaintiffs claimed that the defendants had issued advertisements likely to deceive members of the public into thinking that their film was a version of the sketch. The advertisements stated "The man who made the Queen laugh. George Clarke in *His First Car*. come and see the P.D.C. Talkie Version." An injunction was granted. Lawrence L.J., in giving judgment, stated:

---

[76] *Fleetwood Mac Promotions Ltd. v. Clifford Davis Management Ltd.* [1975] F.S.R. 150.
[77] *Hines v. Winnick* [1947] 1 Ch. 708; *Forbes v. Kemsley Newspapers Ltd.* [1951] 2 T.L.R. 656.
[78] *Samuelson v. Producers' Distributing Co., Ltd.* [1932] 1 Ch. 201.
[79] [1932] 1 Ch. 201; *Raleigh v. Kinematograph Trading Co., Ltd.* (1914) 31 R.P.C. 143; *Twentieth Century Fox Film Corpn. v. Gala Film Distributors Ltd.* [1957] R.P.C. 105.

"It is said that what the appellants did was not 'passing-off' and that therefore the action ought to have been dismissed. The argument was that, as the plaintiff had not yet made a film version of his sketch and therefore had no goods in respect of which the defendants could have represented their goods to be his, their acts would not be termed 'passing-off'. In my judgment that argument is not well founded . . . If the plaintiff had stood by, his exclusive right to make a film version of his sketch would have been rendered valueless, and he is not bound to wait until that damage to his property, which in all probability would have been irreparable had accrued before bringing his action."[80]

18.35   However, there will be no passing off where the same title is used but there is no immediate prospect of any film version of the plaintiff's play or novel being produced in public and further there is no representation that the film is a film version of the novel or play.[81] Additionally, if the title adopted by the plaintiff "is really a hackneyed one, and one which many people might quite well have used as the title of films dealing with quite different subjects", it will be difficult for him to succeed in an action for passing off.[82]

These principles would appear to be equally applicable where the title of a novel is used as the title of a play.

18.36   **Passing off song or composition as title of film or play.** Where a producer uses the title of a song or composition as the title of a film or play no action in passing off will lie at the suit of the owner of the copyright in that song or composition.

Thus, in *Francis Day & Hunter, Ltd. v. Twentieth Century Fox Corpn., Ltd.*[83] the appellants, part owner of the copyright in a song consisting of words and music entitled "The Man Who Broke the Bank at Monte Carlo", commenced an action in which they claimed that the performance in public in Canada of a motion picture entitled *The Man Who Broke the Bank at Monte Carlo* was a passing off of their song. Apart from the fact that the title of the song and the motion picture were the same, no part of the actual words or music of the song were used in the film. Lord Wright, in delivering the judgment of the Privy Council held that there had been no passing off by the exhibition of the motion picture bearing the same title as the song, said:

---

[80] *Samuelson v. Producers' Distributing Co., Ltd.* [1932] 1 Ch. 201 at 298, 209.
[81] *O'Gorman v. Paramount Film Service, Ltd.* [1937] 2 All E.R. 113.
[82] *Houghton v. Film Booking Offences Ltd.* (1931) 48 R.P.C. 329: see also *Loew's Incorporated v. Littler, The Times,* May 11, 1955.
[83] [1940] A.C. 112.

"The member of the public who is supposed to be likely to be deceived, must, to start with, be assumed to know what he was wanting to see or hear. Thus, in the present case he must be presumed to know that what he wanted was to hear the song 'The Man Who Broke the Bank at Monte Carlo.' It seems inconceivable that when, or if, he bought a ticket for the motion picture, he imagined he was going to hear a performance of the familiar song. The two things are completely different, and incapable of comparison in any reasonable sense. The thing said to be passed off must resemble the thing for which it is passed off . . . In Canada, what was advertised was the film. There was no hint that the song was going to be sung."

The thing said to be passed off, and the song, and the motion picture were completely different and incapable of comparison in any reasonable sense.

CHAPTER 19

UNDUE INFLUENCE

19.01   The general principles applicable to the doctrine of undue influence with particular reference to entertainers' contracts have been discussed in Chapter 6 of this work following Restraint of Trade, since the two principles commonly arise together in cases involving entertainers.

The doctrine is noted here in Part III as a relevant inclusion in this review of equitable remedies available. Readers are directed to the following sections for further detail:

19.02

CHAPTER 20

INJUNCTIONS

1. Interlocutory Injunctions

Jurisdiction of court to grant injunction. An injunction is a remedy *in*   **20.01**
personam. The English court has jurisdiction to grant injunctions so as
to restrain the individual, company or agent within the jurisdiction
from doing acts, either here or abroad, in breach of a contract governed by English law,[1] although in many cases the court will be reluctant to exercise such jurisdiction in relation to the defendant's
activities outside the jurisdiction.[2] Where the subject matter of an
application is the alleged infringement of copyright in a foreign
country which would otherwise be an infringement if done in the
United Kingdom, the court has no jurisdiction to grant an injunction
because only acts done in the United Kingdom constitute infringement, either direct or indirect, of copyright.[3] Furthermore, an English
court has no jurisdiction to grant an injunction in respect of disputes
over title to rights arising under the copyright laws of a foreign
country although both parties to that dispute may reside within the
jurisdiction of the courts.[4]

Nature of interlocutory injunctions. "A right to obtain an interlocutory   **20.02**
injunction is not a cause of action. It cannot stand on its own. It is
dependent upon there being a pre-existing cause of action against the
defendant arising out of an invasion, actual or threatened by him, of a
legal or equitable right of the plaintiff for the enforcement of which the

---

[1] *Hospital For Sick Children (Board of Governors) v. Walt Disney Productions Inc.* [1968] 1 Ch. 52.
[2] *Def Lepp Music v. Stuart-Brown* [1986] R.P.C. 273 at 277.
[3] *Ibid.* at 277.
[4] *Tyburn Productions Ltd. v. Conan Doyle* [1990] 1 All E.R. 909.

defendant is amenable to the jurisdiction of the court."[5] The object of the interlocutory injunction is to protect the plaintiff against injury by violation of his right for which he could not be adequately compensated in damages recoverable in the action if those rights were vindicated at trial; but the plaintiff's need for such protection must be weighed against the corresponding need of the defendant to be protected against the injury resulting from his having been prevented from exercising his legal rights for which he could not be adequately compensated under the plaintiff's undertaking in damages if the uncertainty were resolved in his favour at trial. The court must weigh one need against the other and determine where the "balance of convenience lies".[6] Its grant is to preserve the "status quo" pending the ascertainment by the court of the rights of the parties and the grant to the plaintiff of the relief to which his cause of action entitles him, which may or may not include a final injunction[7] and as such it is both a temporary and discretionary remedy.[8]

(a) *Prohibitory injunctions*

(i) *Principles applied by the court in exercising its discretion*

20.03 **Serious question to be tried.** In considering the grant of an interlocutory injunction the court must first be satisfied that there is a "serious question to be tried".[9] In setting out the guiding principle with regard to this aspect of exercising its discretion Lord Diplock,[10] with whom all the other members of the House of Lords agreed, said:

> "The use of such expressions 'as a probability', 'a prima facie case', or 'a strong prima facie case' in the context of a discretionary power to grant an interlocutory injunction leads to confusion as to the object sought to be achieved by this form of temporary relief. The court no doubt must be satisfied that the claim is not frivolous or vexatious; in other words, that there is a serious question to be tried.
>
> It is no part of the court's function at this stage of the litigation to try to resolve conflicts of evidence on affidavit as to facts on which the claims of either party may ultimately depend nor to decide difficult questions of law which call for detailed argument and mature considerations. These are matters to be dealt with at the trial."

---

[5] *Siskina v. Distos Compania Naviera S.A.* [1979] A.C. 210 at 256.
[6] *American Cyanamid Co. v. Ethicon ltd.* [1975] A.C. 396 at 406.
[7] *Siskina v. Distos Compania Naviera S.A.* [1979] A.C. 210 at 256.
[8] *American Cyanamid Co. v. Ethicon ltd.* [1975] A.C. 396 at 405.
[9] *Ibid.* at 407, H.L.; *Dimbleby & Sons Ltd. v. National Union of Journalists* [1984] 1 W.L.R. 427 at 430, H.L.; *Garden Cottage Foods Ltd. v. Milk Marketing Board* [1984] A.C. 130, H.L.
[10] *American Cyanamid Co. v. Ethicon Ltd.* [1975] A.C. 396 at 407.

Thus the plaintiff does not have to establish that he has a prima facie **20.04** case or a probability of success at trial: what must be shown is that there is a serious question to be tried. A serious question in this context would appear to include a conflict of evidence, as appearing from the affidavits, which is not on the face of it implausible. This approach was adopted by the Privy Council in *Eng Mee Yong v. Letchumanan*,[11] where Lord Diplock in delivering judgment observed:

> "Their Lordships must therefore turn to the evidence that was before the High Court on the hearing of the application, bearing in mind that if there appears to be any conflict of evidence which is not on the face of it implausible, such conflict ought not to be disposed of on affidavit evidence only. It leaves a serious question to be tried."[12]

This approach was also adopted by the Court of Appeal in *Cayne v.* **20.05** *Global Natural Resources plc*.[13] where the court decided that for the purposes of an application for an interlocutory injunction there is a serious question to be tried if there is some supporting material for the case advanced and the outcome of the trial is uncertain. Eveleigh L.J., with whom all the other members of the court agreed, stated:

> " . . . if this is to be approached as one in which a triable issue has to be established, I myself would come to the conclusion that there was here a triable case. The plaintiffs' evidence . . . clearly pointed to the inference which they asked the court to draw. Global's evidence, if true and accepted, of course clearly destroyed that inference. But the great question that has to be determined is whether the defendants' case is accepted or not. The mere fact it is deposed to does not make it incontrovertible. Therefore, when the evidence is not accepted by the plaintiffs, I am left in doubt as to the outcome of the trial on that issue. If I am in doubt and if the issue seems to be one that is not frivolous, in other words is one for which there is some supporting material, then I would conclude there is a triable issue."

It would appear, however, that where there are no issues of fact involved, the principles enunciated in *American Cyanamid Co. v. Ethicon Ltd.* are not applicable: in such circumstances the court ought to resolve the dispute before deciding whether or not to grant the injunction.[14]

---

[11] [1980] A.C. 331.
[12] *Ibid.* at 338.
[13] [1984] 1 All E.R. 225.
[14] *Bradford City Metropolitan Council v. Brown* (1986) 84 L.G.R. 731, C.A.

20.06 **Adequacy of damages.** If the court is satisfied that the plaintiff's claim raises a serious question to be tried the court must next consider whether if the plaintiff were to succeed in his claim for a permanent injunction at trial he would be adequately compensated by an award of damages for the loss he would have sustained as result of the defendant's continuing to do what was sought to be enjoined between the time of the application and the time of the trial. If damages in the measure recoverable at common law would be an adequate remedy and the defendant would be in a financial position to pay them, or if there is no substantial risk of damage to the plaintiff, the court will normally refuse to grant an interlocutory injunction however strong the plaintiff's claim.[15] If damages would not provide an adequate remedy for the plaintiff in the event of his succeeding at trial the court must then consider whether the defendant, if he were to succeed at trial, would be adequately compensated under the plaintiff's cross-undertaking in damages for the loss which the defendant would have sustained before trial by being prevented from doing the acts sought to be restrained. "If damages in the measure recoverable under [the] cross-undertaking would be an adequate remedy and the plaintiff would be in a financial position to pay them there would be no reason upon this ground to refuse an interlocutory injunction."[16]

20.07 **Balance of convenience.**[17] "It is where there is doubt as to the adequacy of the respective remedies in damages available to either party or to both, that the question of the balance of convenience arises."[18] In determining where the balance of convenience lies, "the court must weigh one need against another".[19] It must weigh the need "to protect the plaintiff against injury by violation of his right for which he could not be adequately compensated in damages recoverable in the action if the uncertainty were resolved in his favour at the trial; but the plaintiff's need for such protection must be weighed against the corresponding need of the defendant to be protected against injury resulting from his having been prevented from exercising his own legal rights for which he could not be adequately compensated under the plaintiff's

---

[15] *American Cyanamid Co. v. Ethicon Ltd.* [1975] A.C. 396; *Garden Cottage Foods Ltd. v. Milk Marketing Board* [1983] 2 All E.R. 770, H.L.
[16] *American Cyanamid Co. v. Ethicon Ltd.* [1975] A.C. 396 at 408, H.L., *per* Lord Diplock.
[17] This expression has received some criticism from the Court of Appeal where for example in *Cayne v. Global Natural Resources plc* [1984] 1 All E.R. 225 at 237, May L.J. preferred the phrase "the balance of risk of doing injustice" because this better described the process involved. In *Francome v. Mirror Group Newspapers Ltd.* [1984] 1 W.L.R. 892 at 898, Sir John Donaldson M.R. said that the balance of convenience was an unfortunate expression since the business of the court was justice not convenience and the court should seek a "balance of justice, not of convenience".
[18] *American Cyanamid Co. v. Ethicon Ltd.* [1975] A.C. 396 at 408, H.L.
[19] *Ibid.*

undertaking in damages if the uncertainty were resolved in the defendant's favour at trial".[20]

However, in laying down this guideline, the House of Lords in *American Cyanamid Co. v. Ethicon Ltd.* declined to specify the factors to be taken into account in carrying out this balancing exercise on the basis that the factors and the weight to be given to them would vary from case to case. Lord Diplock, however, indicated that the extent to which the disadvantages to each party would be incapable of being compensated in damages in the event of his succeeding at the trial is always a significant factor in assessing where the balance of convenience lies.[21] If "extent of the uncompensatable disadvantage to each party would not differ widely, it may not be improper to take into account in tipping the balance the relative strength of each party's case as revealed by the affidavit evidence adduced on the hearing of the application",[22] but this may only be done where it is apparent upon the facts disclosed by the evidence, as to which there is no credible dispute, that the strength of one party's case is disproportionate to that of the other party.[23] He added: "I would reiterate that, in addition to those to which I have referred, there may be many other special factors to be taken into consideration in the particular circumstances of individual cases."[24]

In *N.W.L. Ltd. v. Woods,*[25] Lord Diplock said that there was nothing in   **20.08**
the decision in *American Cyanamid. Co. v. Ethicon Ltd.* to suggest that in considering whether or not to grant an interlocutory injunction the judge ought not to give full weight to all the practical realities of the situation to which the injunction would apply. *N.W.L. Ltd. v. Woods* was exceptional, he said, in that the grant or refusal of an injunction at that stage would in effect dispose of the action finally in favour of whichever party was successful on the application, because there would be nothing left on which it was in the unsuccessful party's interest to proceed to trial. In such an exceptional case there is brought into the balance of convenience an important additional element: when the grant or refusal of an interlocutory injunction will have the practical effect of putting an end to the action because the harm that will have

---

[20] *American Cyanamid Co. v. Ethicon Ltd.* [1975] A.C. 396 at 406, H.L.; *Fellowes & Son v. Fisher* [1976] Q.B. 122, C.A.; *Hubbard v. Pitt* [1976] Q.B. 142 at 161, C.A.
[21] *American Cyanamid Co. v. Ethicon Ltd.* [1975] 1 A.C. 396, 409.
[22] *Ibid.* at 409.
[23] *Ibid.* at 409.
[24] *Ibid.* 396 at 408–9.
[25] [1979] 1 W.L.R. 1294 at 1306–7; *Cambridge Nutrition Ltd. v. British Broadcasting Corporation* [1990] 3 All E.R. 523; *Lansing Linde Ltd. v. Kerr* [1991] 1 W.L.R. 251, C.A.; but *cf. Cayne v. Global Natural Resources plc.* [1984] 1 All E.R. 225 and *Cambridge Nutrition Ltd. v. British Broadcasting Corporation* [1990] 3 All E.R. 523 where it was stated by Kerr L.J. that where an interlocutory injunction would finally dispose of the matter the established guidelines requiring the court to look at the balance of convenience do not apply.

been already caused to the losing party by its grant or refusal is complete, and of a kind for which nothing can constitute any worthwhile recompense, then the degree of likelihood that the plaintiff will have succeeded in establishing his right to an injunction if the action had gone to trial is a factor to be brought into the balance of convenience by the judge in deciding the application one way rather than the other.

Thus it would appear that "properly understood",[26] the "special factors" alluded to in *American Cyanamid Co. v. Ethicon Ltd.* are not factors which would take the case outside the guidelines there set out but factors which may be of an exceptional nature which ought to be part of the balancing exercise and which by their nature may be of overriding importance.

20.09 Status quo. Where the factors appear to be evenly balanced, the court should take such steps as are calculated to preserve the status quo until the matter in issue between the parties can be finally disposed of.[27] For these purposes, the "status quo" is

> "[the] state of affairs existing during the period immediately preceding the issue of the writ claiming the permanent injunction or, if there be unreasonable delay between the issue of the writ and the motion for an interlocutory injunction, the period immediately preceding the motion. The duration of that period since the state of affairs last changed must be more than minimal, having regard to the total length of the relationship between the parties in respect of which the injunction is granted; otherwise the state of affairs before the last change would be the relevant status quo."[28]

20.10 Cross-undertaking in damages. At the time that an interim injunction is granted it is not possible for the court to be absolutely certain that the plaintiff will succeed at the trial in establishing his legal right to restrain the defendant from doing what he was threatening to do. If he should fail to do so the defendant may have suffered loss as a result of having been prevented from doing it while the interim injunction was in force. It is to mitigate this risk that the court refuses to grant an interlocutory injunction unless the plaintiff is willing to furnish an undertaking by himself or by some other willing and responsible person "to abide by an order the court may make as to damages in case the court shall hereafter be of the opinion that the defendant shall have sustained any

---

[26] *Ibid.* at 1306.
[27] *American Cyanamid Co. v. Ethicon Ltd.* [1975] A.C. 396 at 408 H.L.; *Garden Cottage Foods Ltd. v. Milk Marketing Board* [1984] 1 A.C. 130 at 140, H.L.
[28] *Garden Cottage Foods Ltd. v. Milk Marketing Board* [1984] 1 A.C. 130 at 140, H.L.; *cf. Graham v. Delderfield* [1992] F.S.R. 313, C.A. and *Alfred Dunhill v. Sunoptic S.A.* [1979] F.S.R. 337, where Browne L.J. said that the status quo may well vary in different cases.

damages by reason of this order '(sc., the interim injunction)' which the plaintiff ought to pay".[29]

The nature and effect of such an undertaking was explained by Lord Diplock in *Hoffman-La Roche & Co. A.G. v. Secretary of State for Trade and Industry* thus:

> "The court has no power to compel an applicant for an interim   **20.11**
> injunction to furnish an undertaking as to damages. All it can do is
> to refuse the application if he declines to do so. The undertaking is
> not given to the defendant but to the court itself. Non-performance
> of it is contempt of court, not breach of contract, and attracts the
> remedies available for contempt, but the court exacts the undertak-
> ing for the defendants benefit. It retains a discretion not to enforce
> the undertaking if it considers that the conduct of the defendant in
> relation to the obtaining or continuing of the injunction or the
> enforcement of the undertaking makes it inequitable to do so, but if
> the undertaking is enforced the measure of the damages at which
> the principles to be applied are fixed and clear. The assessment is
> made upon the same basis as that upon which damages for breach
> of contract would be assessed if the undertaking had been a con-
> tract between the plaintiff and the defendant and the plaintiff
> would *not* prevent the defendant from doing that which he was res-
> trained from doing by the terms of the injunction."[30]

A plaintiff outside the jurisdiction will generally be required by the court to give security, whether by himself or some person within the jurisdiction,[31] towards implementing any liability he may incur under his cross-undertaking in damages.[32]

(b) *Interlocutory mandatory injunctions*

Grant at interlocutory stage. The principles enunciated in *American*   **20.12**
Cyanamid Co. v. Ethicon Ltd. do not apply to the case of mandatory injunctions.[33]

Generally, a mandatory injunction will not be granted on an inter-locutory application unless the applicant's case is unusually strong and clear so that the court can feel a high degree of assurance that at the trial it will appear that the injunction was rightly granted.[34] This principle

---

[29] *Hoffman-La Roche & Co. A.G. v. Secretary of State for Trade and Industry* [1975] A.C. 295, 361.
[30] *Ibid.* at 361.
[31] *Anglo-Danubian Co. Ltd. v. Rogerson* (1867) L.R. 4 Eq. 3.
[32] *Harman Pictures N.V. v. Osborne* [1967] 1 W.L.R. 723 at 739.
[33] *Locabail Finance Ltd. v. Agroexport* [1986] 1 All E.R. 901 at 906; *Film Rovers International v. Cannon Film Sales Ltd* [1986] 3 All E.R. 772 at 780.
[34] *Shepherd Homes Ltd. v. Sandham* [1971] 1 Ch. 340; *Leisure Data v. Bell* [1988] F.S.R. 367.

would appear, however, to be subject to two exceptions. First, notwith-standing the requirement that this "high degree of assurance" has not been shown, the court will take the steps necessary, for whichever party should succeed at the trial, to preserve in the meantime, the value of an asset in relation to which the parties are in dispute. In *Leisure Data v. Bell*,[35] Dillon L.J. stated the principle thus:

20.13   "The court is required . . . to give full weight to the practical reali-ties of the situation and weigh the respective risks that injustice may result from a decision one way or another. The court has to keep firmly in mind the risk of injustice to either party. Beyond that, there are many cases where there is a salvage element involved, and where it is necessary that some form of mandatory order shall be made to deal with a situation which cannot on the practical realities of the situation be left to wait until the trial. Here the court will act whether or not the high standard of probability of success . . . is made out."[36]

Secondly, "if it appears to the court that, exceptionally, the case is one in which withholding a mandatory injunction would in fact carry a greater risk of injustice than granting it, even though the court does not feel a 'high degree of assurance' about the plaintiff's chances of estab-lishing his right, there cannot be any rational basis for withholding the injunction".[37]

2. Injunctions: Performance of Personal Service by Artistes

20.14   **General.** As a general proposition, injunctive relief will not be granted to enforce performance of an artiste's negative obligations in a contract for personal services inseparable from the exercise of some special skill or talent if enforcement will effectively compel the artiste to perform his obligations under the contract.[38]

In *Warren v. Mendy*[39] the Court of Appeal, in a single judgment delivered by Nourse L.J., reviewed the authorities in this area of the law and laid down the appropriate approach where an injunction is sought against a performer to enforce negative covenants.

The Court considered *Warner Brothers Pictures Inc. v. Nelson*[40] to be a

---

[35] *Leisure Data v. Bell* [1988] F.S.R. 367; see also *Beggars Banquet Records Ltd. v. Carlton Television Ltd.* [1993] E.M.L.R. 349.
[36] *Leisure Data v. Bell* [1988] F.S.R. 367.
[37] *Films Rover International Ltd. v. Cannon Film Sales Ltd.* [1986] 3 All E.R. 772 at 781.
[38] *Warren v. Mendy* [1989] 1 W.L.R. 853; see also *Page One Records v. Britton* [1968] 1 W.L.R. 157 at 166.
[39] [1989] 1 W.L.R. 853.
[40] [1937] 1 K.B. 209.

case both turning on its own particular facts which laid down no general principle of law and which was against the general thrust of authorities prevailing at the time it was decided. In explaining the basis of the decisions in which injunctions had previously been granted against performers Nourse L.J. commented:

" . . . the most significant feature of each of those in which an injunction was granted before *Warner Brothers Pictures Inc. v. Nelson* was that the term of the engagement was short, in none of them exceeding 20 weeks. In *Lumley v. Wagner* itself the contractual period was three months of which there were less than two to run when the injunction was granted . . . Although it is impossible to state in general terms where the line between short and long term engagements ought to be drawn, it is obvious that an injunction lasting for two years or more . . . may practically compel performance of the contract".

Thus as a starting point it would appear that a court will prima facie **20.15** refuse to grant an injunction restraining the breach of a negative covenant in a contract for personal services inseparable from some special skill or talent where that would require enforcement of a term of two years or more. However, merely because the term may be under two years does not necessarily mean that such an injunction will be granted. The skill possessed by the performer may be such that a short period of six-months may be such as will affect that skill and as such should not, on the principles of *Warren v. Mendy*, be granted.

Applicable principles when injunction sought against artiste. The prin- **20.16** ciples set out in *Warren v. Mendy*[41] are now to be considered the authoritative approach to be taken when considering the grant or refusal of an injunction against an artiste or a third party who has induced a breach of contract by an artiste. In applying these principles a distinction is to be drawn between those whose services are inseparable from some special skill and talent and those whose services cannot be so described. Nourse L.J. stated the underlying rationale thus:

"It is well settled that an injunction to restrain a breach of contract for personal services ought not to be granted where its effect will be to decree performance of the contract. Speaking generally, there is no comparable objection to the grant of an injunction restraining the performance of particular services for a third party, because, by not prohibiting the performance of other services, it does not bind the servant to the contract. But a difficulty can arise, usually in the entertainment or sporting worlds, where the services are

---

[41] [1989] 1 W.L.R. 853.

inseparable from the exercise of some special skill or talent, whose continued display is essential to the psychological and material, and sometimes to the physical well being of the servant. The difficulty does not reside in any beguilement of the court into looking more tenderly on such who breach their contracts, glamorous though they often are. It is that the human necessity of maintaining the skill or talent may practically bind the servant to the contract, compelling him to perform it."[42]

20.17 Persons whose services are inseparable from some special skill or talent would include actors, musicians, composers, writers and directors. Where such persons are concerned, the following general principles are applicable to the grant or refusal of an injunction to enforce performance of negative obligations in a contract for personal services inseparable from the exercise of some special skill or talent[43]:

(1) the court ought not to enforce the performance of the negative obligations if their enforcement will effectively compel the servant to perform his positive obligations under the contract;

(2) compulsion is a question to be decided on the facts of each case, with a realistic regard for the probable reaction of an injunction on the psychological and material, and sometimes the physical, need of the servant to maintain the skill or talent;

(3) the longer the term for which an injunction is sought, the more readily will compulsion be inferred[44];

(4) compulsion may be inferred where the injunction is sought not against the servant but against a third party if either the third party is the only available master[45] or if it is likely that the master will seek relief against anyone who attempts to replace him;

(5) an injunction will less readily be granted where there are obligations of mutual trust and confidence, as in the case of a musician and his manager, more especially where the servant's trust in the master may have been betrayed or his confidence in him has genuinely gone.

---

[42] *Ibid.* at 857.

[43] *Ibid.* at 867.

[44] *Ibid.*: see the comments of the court at 865H–866A (quoted above) where it is said that an injunction lasting two years or more may practically compel the performance of the contract. It is submitted, however, that the period must depend upon the age of the artiste and his reputation and the effect of even a period as short as six-months would have on his ability to return to his calling.

[45] "Master" is used here solely for the sake of convenience and not to denote the legal relationship between the artiste and the third party with whom he may contract.

However, in applying these principles the court should   **20.18**

" . . . scrutinise most carefully, even sceptically, any claim by the artiste that he is under the human necessity of maintaining the skill or talent and thus will be compelled to perform the contract, or that his trust in the master has been betrayed or that his confidence in him has genuinely gone. But if, having done that, the judge is satisfied that the grant of an injunction will effectively compel performance of the contract, he ought to refuse it."[46]

Injunctions against third parties restraining them from entering into **20.19**
agreement with artiste. Where injunctions are sought against third parties, who for present purposes must be taken to have induced a breach of contract by the artiste, the material considerations will not be exactly the same as in a case where the relief is sought directly against the servant. Most significantly, the court must take account not only of the availability of other third parties with whom the servant may be able to contract, but also of the likelihood or not that the plaintiff will take similar proceedings against them which would ultimately have the effect of forcing the artiste to perform his contract or remaining idle.[47]

Adequacy of damages in cases involving artistes. As a general rule the   **20.20**
court will not grant an injunction to restrain a breach of contract if it is shown that the plaintiff could be compensated by damages. It would appear that in cases where the activity sought to be restrained is an artiste entering into a contract with a third party or, for example, the distribution of a film or record the title to which is disputed it would be open to the court to refuse injunctive relief on an undertaking to keep full and proper account of income from the activity and to pay a proportion into court or a joint account. This approach was set out by Nourse L.J. as follows:

"In most of the decided cases it is assumed that the damages will not be an adequate alternative remedy to the grant of an injunction and the point is not much discussed. Thus in *Lumley v. Wagner* itself it was assumed that the mere chance of any damages which a jury might give was not worth very much. Now that these damages are invariably assessed by a judge or master we do not think that it can be assumed that they will always be an inadequate remedy. For example, in a case like the present it would be open to the court to refuse injunctive relief at the interlocutory stage on an undertaking by the defendant to keep full and proper accounts of his receipts from acting on behalf of the servant and to pay a specified propor-

---

[46] *Warren v. Mendy* [1989] 1 W.L.R. 853 at 867H–868B.
[47] *Ibid.* at 867.

tion into court or into a joint account. An arrangement such as that would achieve the twin objectives of going some way to quantify the plaintiff's damages and preserving funds to meet any award which might be made later."[48]

3. Injunctions: Broadcasting

20.21 The *American Cyanamid* principles do not lend themselves readily to cases where the subject matter of an application concerns the transmission by a broadcaster of a matter of public interest whose value and impact depends on its timing. In such circumstances the balancing exercise requires the court to put on one side the right of free speech and the public interest in the transmission of the programme, and this right will only be counter-balanced on the otherside where there is clear evidence supporting the right asserted by the plaintiff.[49]

This principle is illustrated by *Cambridge Nutrition Ltd. v. British Broadcasting Corporation*[50] where the BBC prepared a programme in close co-operation with the plaintiff dealing with a low calorie diet marketed by the plaintiffs. After completion of the programme, but prior to the broadcast, the plaintiffs became concerned about the tone and content of the programme and sought an interlocutory injunction restraining the BBC from broadcasting the programme, alleging that there was an agreement between the BBC and the plaintiffs that the former would not broadcast the programme until after the publication of a government report into low calorie diets. The BBC denied that they were so contractually bound.

In the absence of clear evidence that the BBC had entered into the alleged contract the court held that it should not be restrained from transmitting the programme which was on a matter of public interest. "[T]he whole case would be different if the BBC had in fact entered into a binding contract from which they now sought to resile. In that event, but only in that event, would there have to be a competing balance of public interest"[51]; which would balance any right to freedom of speech.

20.22 There is a developing general principle which holds that expression of opinion and conveyance of information, whether by a private individual, a public body or a broadcaster will not be restrained "save on

---

[48] *Ibid.* at 868.
[49] *Cambridge Nutrition Ltd. v. British Broadcasting Corporation* [1990] 3 All E.R. 523 (C.A.)
[50] [1990] 3 All E.R. 523, C.A., approved *Secretary of State for the Home Department v. Central Broadcasting Limited* [1993] E.M.L.R. 253.
[51] *Ibid.* at 534.

pressing grounds,"[52] or in "the most extreme circumstances".[53] "Pressing grounds" for these purposes being a risk of "irreparable"[54] damage or a "substantial risk of grave injustice".[55] This approach was adopted in *R. v. Advertising Standards Authority Ltd., ex parte Vernons Organisations Ltd.*[56] and follows the principles laid down in Article 10 of the Convention for the Protection of Human Rights and Fundamental Freedoms, which has been ratified but not incorporated into the domestic law of the United Kingdom. Article 10, in so far as is relevant for present purposes, provides:

"1. Everyone has the right to freedom of expression. This right shall include freedom to hold opinions and to receive and impart information and ideas without the interference by public authority and regardless of frontiers . . . 2. The exercise of these freedoms, since it carries with it duties and responsibilities, may be subject to such formalities, conditions, restrictions or penalties as are prescribed by the law and are necessary in a democratic society, in the interests of national security, territorial integrity or public safety, for the prevention of disorder or crime, for the protection of health or morals, for the protection of the reputation or the rights of others, for preventing the disclosure of information received in confidence, or for maintaining the authority and impartiality of the judiciary."

Thus to be valid under the Convention any restriction must accord- **20.23** ingly be prescribed by law and necessary in a democratic society for one at least of the purposes mentioned. In *The Sunday Times v. United Kingdom*[57] the majority of the European Court of Human Rights held that:

"The court has noted that, whilst the adjective 'necessary', within the meaning of article 10(2), is not synonymous with 'indispensable', neither has it the flexibility of such expressions as 'admissible', 'ordinary', 'useful', 'reasonable' or 'desirable' and that it implies the existence of 'pressing social need'."[58]

---

[52] *R. v. Advertising Standards Authority Ltd., ex parte Vernons Organisation Ltd.* [1992] 1 W.L.R. 1289; see also *Re X* [1975] 1 All E.R. 697 (C.A.); *Attorney-General v. Jonathan Cape Ltd.* [1976] Q.B. 752, 770–771; *Commonwealth of Australia v. John Fairfax & Sons Ltd.* (1980) 47 C.L.R. 39, 52.

[53] *Slater v. Raw* [1977] C.A. Transcript 374C.

[54] *R. v. Advertising Standards Authority Ltd., ex parte Vernons Organisation Ltd.* [1992] 1 W.L.R. 1289 at 1294.

[55] *Attorney-General v. British Broadcasting Corporation* [1981] 1 A.C. 303, 362.

[56] *R. v. Advertising Standards Authority Ltd., ex parte Vernons Organisation Ltd.* [1992] 1 W.L.R. 1289: see in particular 1294.

[57] (1979) 2 E.H.R.R. 245 at 275, para. 59.

[58] Affirmed *Lingens v. Austria*, 8 E.H.R.R. 407.

In *Attorney-General v. British Broadcasting Corporation*[59] Lord Scarman observed:

" . . . the prior restraint of publication, though occasionally necessary in serious cases, is a drastic interference with freedom of speech and should only be ordered where there is a substantial risk of grave injustice. I understand the test of 'pressing social need' as being exactly that."[60]

20.24   In *Attorney-General v. Guardian Newspapers Ltd.*[61] four of their Lordships referred to the Convention and none suggested that its terms were in conflict with the common law. Lord Fraser of Tullybelton has, however, observed that where the common law is unclear:

"This House, and other courts in the United Kingdom, should have the regard to the provisions of the Convention for the Protection of Human Rights and Fundamental Freedoms (1953) (Cmnd. 8969) and to the decisions of the Court of Human Rights in cases, of which this is one, where our domestic law is not firmly settled."[62]

This approach was followed by three of their Lordships in *Attorney-General v. Guardian Newspapers Ltd. (No. 2)*,[63] where Lord Goff observed:

" . . . I conceive it to be my duty, when I am free to do so, to interpret the law in accordance with the obligations of the Crown under this treaty".[64]

20.25   It is submitted that this approach does not differ to any real extent from that adopted in *Cambridge Nutrition Ltd. v. British Broadcasting Corporation*, discussed above. Indeed in *Secretary of State for the Home Department v. Central Broadcasting Ltd.*[65] Hirst L.J., expressed the view that "the *Cambridge Nutrition* case is fully in line with Article 10 of the Convention for the Protection of Human Rights and Fundamental Freedom".

Thus, it is submitted that although there is no entrenched guarantee of freedom of speech or the media, the evolving general rule is that prior restraint of the freedom of speech of a broadcaster is permissible only where the party seeking such restraint is able to show clear prima facie of evidence[66] of "pressing social need," or in other words a

---

[59] [1981] A.C. 303.
[60] *Ibid.* at 362.
[61] [1987] 1 W.L.R. 1248, H.L.
[62] *Attorney-General v. British Broadcasting Corporation* [1981] A.C. 303 at 352.
[63] [1990] 1 A.C. 107 at 256, 273, 283, H.L.
[64] *Ibid* at 283.
[65] [1993] E.M.L.R. 253 at 274.
[66] *Cambridge Nutrition Ltd. v. British Broadcasting Corporation* [1990] 3 All E.R. 523, C.A.

substantial risk of grave injustice, giving rise to a need for a prior restraint of publication by the courts.[67] Generally, such "pressing social need" will be found in "conditions, restrictions or penalties . . . prescribed by the law and [which] are necessary in a democratic society, in the interests of national security, territorial integrity or public safety, for the prevention of disorder or crime, for the protection of health or morals, for the protection of the reputation or the rights of others, for preventing the disclosure of information received in confidence, or for maintaining the authority and impartiality of the judiciary."[68]

However, where the transmission consists of a film for general entertainment where no public interest arises, the *American Cyanamid* principles will apply.

4. *Anton Piller* Order

Generally. The court has the inherent jurisdiction,[69] and jurisdiction by the rules of court,[70] to make an order requiring the defendant to allow the plaintiff to enter his premises for the purposes of (a) the preservation of evidence essential to the plaintiff's case which might otherwise be removed, destroyed or concealed,[71] or (b) after judgment for the purpose of eliciting documents which are essential to the execution, and which would otherwise be unjustly denied to the execution creditor.[72] An application for an order is made *ex parte.* Where the order is granted, the obligation placed on the defendant to allow entry and search does not arise until after a reasonable period of time has been given for legal advice to be obtained.[73] Where after taking legal advice the defendant successfully applies to have the order set aside no penalty is likely to be imposed by the court. Where, however, he fails and there is reason to believe that, in the period between the time when the order has been served on him and the time when he eventually complies with the order, he has taken steps which are inconsistent with the order, such steps may justify a finding of contempt, but technical breaches will not justify such a finding.[74]

20.26

---

[67] *Attorney-General v. British Broadcasting Corporation* [1981] A.C. 303 at 352.
[68] See also *ante*, paras 17.13–17.19 for restraint in respect of confidential information.
[69] *Anton Piller K.G. v. Manufacturing Processes Ltd.* [1976] Ch. 55 at 61.
[70] R.S.C., Ord. 29, r. 2.
[71] *Crest Homes plc. v. Marks* [1987] 1 A.C. 829, H.L.
[72] *Distributori Automatici Italia SpA v. Halford General Trading Co. Ltd.* [1985] 1 W.L.R. 1066.
[73] *Bhimji v. Chatwani* [1991] 1 All E.R. 705.
[74] *WEA Records Ltd. v. Visions Channel 4 Ltd.* [1983] 1 W.L.R. 721 at 725, C.A.; *Bhimji v. Chatwani* [1991] 1 All E.R. 705.

20.27   Pre-conditions to grant of order. "There are three essential pre-conditions for the making of such an order . . . First, there must be an extremely strong prima facie case. Secondly, the damage, potential or actual must be very serious for the plaintiff. Thirdly, there must be clear evidence that the defendants have in their possession incriminating documents or things, and that there is a real possibility that they may destroy such material before any application *inter partes* can be made."[75]

20.28   Safeguards for the defendant. In *Columbia Picture Industries Inc. v. Robinson*[76] Scott J. laid down five essential criteria which should be observed in relation to the grant of an *Anton Piller* order. First, they must be drawn to extend no further than the minimum extent necessary to achieve the purpose of which they are granted, namely the preservation of documents or articles which might otherwise be destroyed or concealed. Secondly, a detailed record of the material taken should always be required to be made by the solicitors who execute the order before the material is removed from the respondent's premises. Thirdly, no material should be taken from the respondent's premises by the executing solicitors unless it is clearly covered by the terms of the order. Fourthly, it is inappropriate that seized material the ownership of which is in dispute, such as allegedly pirate tapes, should be retained by the plaintiff's solicitors pending trial. If the proper administration of justice requires such matters to be seized they should be held by a neutral officer of the court charged with custody of the material, and if one cannot be found, returned to the defendants' solicitors on their undertaking for its safe custody and production, if required, in court. Fifthly, the affidavits in support of applications for the order ought to err on the side of excessive disclosure.

In *Universal Thermosensors Ltd. v. Hibben*,[77] Sir Donald Nicholls V.-C. approved the judgment of Scott J. in *Columbia Pictures v. Robinson* and emphasised the following additional safeguards:

20.29   (a) the order should normally contain a term that before complying with the order the defendant may obtain legal advice. In order to make this possible orders should only be permitted to be executed on working days in office hours;

          (b) if the order is to be executed at a private house and it is at all likely that a woman may be in the house alone the solicitor serving the order must be, or must be accompanied by, a woman;

---

[75] *Anton Piller K.G. v. Manufacturing Processes Ltd.* [1976] Ch. 55 at 62; *Ex. p. Island Records Ltd.* [1978] 3 All E.R. 824 at 837, C.A.
[76] [1987] Ch. 38.
[77] [1992] 1 W.L.R. 840 at 860–861.

(c) orders should provide that, unless this is seriously impracticable, a detailed list of the items being removed should be prepared at the premises before they are removed and the defendant should be given an opportunity to check the list at the time it is prepared;

(d) orders should provide that, unless there is good reason for doing otherwise, the order should not be executed at business premises save in the presence of a responsible officer of the company or trader in question;

(e) a director, or other officer or employee of the plaintiff company should not conduct or take part in the search of the defendant's premises bearing in mind that they may be competitors;

(e) judges should give serious consideration to the desirability of **20.30** providing by suitable undertakings or otherwise:

    (i) that the order should be served, and its execution supervised, by a solicitor other than a member of the firm of solicitors acting for the plaintiff in the action;

    (ii) that he or she should be an experienced solicitor having some familiarity with the workings of *Anton Piller* orders and with judicial observations on the subject;

    (ii) that the solicitor should prepare a written report on what occurred when the order was executed;

    (iv) that a copy of the report should be served on the defendants; and

    (v) that in any event and within the next few days the plaintiff must return to the court and present the report at an *inter partes* hearing preferably to the judge who made the order.

Self incrimination. Section 72 of the Supreme Court Act 1981 provides **20.31** that:

"(1) In any proceedings to which this subsection applies a person shall not be excused, by reason that to do so would tend to expose that person . . . to proceedings for a related offence or for the recovery of a penalty—(a) from answering any question put to that person in the first mentioned proceedings; or (b) from complying with any order made in those proceedings. (2) Subsection (1) applies to the following proceedings in the High Court, namely— (a) proceedings for infringement of rights pertaining to any intellectual property or for passing off; (b) proceedings brought to obtain disclosure of information relating to any infringement of such rights or for passing off: (c) proceedings brought to prevent any apprehended infringement of such rights or any apprehended passing off. (3) Subject to subsection (4), no statement or admission made by a person—(a) in answering a question put to him in any proceedings to which subsection (1) applies; or (b) in complying with any order made in such proceedings, shall, in any proceedings for any related offence or for the recovery of any related penalty, be admissible in evidence against that person . . . (4) Nothing in subsection (3) shall render any statement or admission made by a person as there mentioned admissible in evidence against that person in proceedings for perjury or contempt of court."

20.32   Section 72 was passed in order to meet the difficulty caused by the fact that the circumstances in which intellectual property rights are infringed frequently involve the commission of a criminal offence or subject the defendant to statutory penalties. Where they do, save for section 72, the defendant would be able to claim that the privilege against self incrimination entitles him to have any order for discovery or production set aside (*e.g.* an *Anton Piller* order). In order to meet this situation section 72 deprives the defendant, in proceedings to which it relates, of his right to claim to be excused from answering questions or complying with an order of the court on grounds that the answers or compliance might expose him to proceedings of a penal nature and as a quid pro quo, safeguards his position by providing that no statement made or answer given shall be admissible as evidence in such proceedings. The privilege against self incrimination is withdrawn only so far as the answer or compliance with the order would expose the defendant to proceedings for a "related offence". To be a "related offence" the offence must be one which is committed by the very act of infringement complained of or one committed in the course of carrying out that infringement or it must be an offence involving fraud or dishonesty which is committed in connection with the infringement complained of, or an offence revealed by the facts on which the plaintiff relies in the proceedings.[78]

---

[78] *Crest Homes plc. v. Marks* [1987] A.C. 829.

DEFAMATION

CHAPTER 21

DEFAMATION

1. Introduction

General. The tort of defamation consists in the publication, to a person **21.01** other than the plaintiff, of a statement of and concerning the plaintiff, where such statement is untrue in substance and in fact, and is defamatory in nature. Such statement may take the form of libel or slander. It is proposed to deal with these subjects in this work only insofar as is relevant to film, television and music.

Libel and slander distinguished. If the statement is in any permanent **21.02** and visible form, it is known as libel. If it is in a transitory form it is known as slander. There are two further distinctions of importance between libel and slander. First, libel may be a criminal offence as well as a tort, whereas slander is actionable as a criminal offence only in certain specified circumstances. Secondly, whereas libel is in all cases actionable *per se*, slander is with certain exceptions, only actionable if it is proved that the plaintiff sustained special damage as a result of the publication of the slander.

For the purposes of the law of libel and slander as it applies to England, Wales and Northern Ireland, the publication of words in any programme included in a programme service is treated as publication in a permanent form and thus a libel.[1] Similarly, the publication of words in the course of the performance of a play is treated as publication in a permanent form,[2] except where the performance is given on a domestic occasion in a private dwelling,[3] or for the purpose of (a) rehearsal[4]; (b) to enable a record or film to be made from or by means of the performance[5]; (c) enabling the performance to be broadcast; or (4) enabling the performance to be transmitted to subscribers to a diffusion service.[6]

2. Statement "Defamatory In Nature"

21.03 "Judges and textbook writers alike have found difficulty in defining with precision the word 'defamatory'."[7] Consequently, there are varying formulations of the appropriate test to be applied in determining whether a statement is defamatory.

In *Sim v. Stretch*,[8] Lord Atkin adopted the test "would the words tend to lower the plaintiff in the estimation of right thinking members of society generally?". Although this test has become generally accepted, other tests are also used. Prominent amongst these alternative tests is that a statement is defamatory if it brings the plaintiff into hatred, ridicule, or contempt,[9] or if it tends to make the plaintiff be shunned and avoided[10] or to injure his reputation in relation to his office or profession or trade. It has been said that these "definitions are cumulative so that any imputation falling within any of them is defamatory".[11]

However, whichever test is applied, it is an objective test[12] in that the words "must tend to disparage [the plaintiff] in the eyes of the average sensible citizen. Words are not actionable as defamatory, however much they may damage a man in the eyes of a section of the community, unless they also amount to disparagement of his reputation in the eyes of right thinking men generally."[13] Hence it is no defence to

---

[1] Broadcasting Act 1990, s.166(1).
[2] Theatres Act 1968, s.4(1).
[3] *Ibid.*, s.7(1).
[4] *Ibid.*, s.7(2)(a).
[5] *Ibid.*, s.7(2)(b)(i).
[6] *Ibid.*, s.7(2)(b)(iii).
[7] *Sim v. Stretch* [1936] 2 All E.R. 1237 at 1240, H.L.
[8] *Ibid.*
[9] *Parmiter v. Coupland* (1840) 6 M. & W. 105 at 108; *cf. Sims v. Stretch* [1936] 2 All E.R. 1237, where Lord Atkin considered that this test was too narrow.
[10] *Youssoupoff v. Metro-Goldwyn-Mayer* (1934) 50 T.L.R. 581 at 587, C.A.
[11] Lewis, P., *Gatley on Libel and Slander* (Sweet & Maxwell, 8th ed., 1981) Chap. 2, p. 13.
[12] *E. Hulton v. Jones* [1910] A.C. 20.
[13] *Tolley v. J.S. Fry & Sons Ltd.* [1930] 1 K.B. 467 at 479; on appeal [1933] A.C. 333.

say that the statement was not intended to be defamatory of the plaintiff.[14]

Construction of the language used

Natural and ordinary meaning of words. In actions for libel "the question is what the words would convey to the ordinary man: it is not one of construction in the legal sense".[15] What the ordinary man would infer without special knowledge has generally been called the natural and ordinary meaning of the words. But that expression can be misleading, in that it conceals the fact that there are two elements in it. The defamatory meaning may be in the words themselves, as where, for example, the plaintiff says of an actor or actress that he or she is incompetent.[16] Often, however, the defamatory meaning is not so much in the words themselves as in what the ordinary man will infer from them, and that is also regarded as part of the natural meaning.[17] The opinions of the ordinary man are liable to vary as to the meaning to be attached to particular words. In *Lewis v. Daily Telegraph Ltd.*,[18] Lord Reid formulated the test of ascertaining what meaning the ordinary man would put on the words as follows:

> "Ordinary men and women have different temperaments and outlooks. Some are unusually suspicious and some are unusually naive. One must try to envisage people between these two extremes and see what is the most damaging meaning they would put on the words in question."[19]

Ultimately, in making this judgment, what the ordinary man, so defined, would read into the words complained of must be a matter of impression.

Innuendo. "The word 'innuendo' has given rise to confusion in that it was, and sometimes is, used in a general sense embracing not only the genuine innuendo supported by extrinsic facts but also any implication that leads to identification of the libel with the plaintiff."[20] The word

21.04

21.05

---

[14] *Capital and Counties Bank v. Henty* (1882) 7 App.Cas. 741 at 772; *E. Hulton v. Jones* [1910] A.C. 20, H.L.

[15] *Lewis v. Daily Telegraph Ltd.* [1964] A.C. 234 at 258 H.L.; *Capital and Counties Bank Ltd. v. George Henty & Sons* (1882) 7 App.Cas. 741 at 772, H.L.; *Slim v. Daily Telegraph Ltd.* [1968] 2 Q.B. 157 at 171, C.A.

[16] *Duplany v. Davis* (1886) 3 T.L.R. 184.

[17] *Lewis v. Daily Telegraph Ltd.* [1964] A.C. 234 at 258, H.L.; *Capital and Counties Bank Ltd. v. George Henty & Sons* (1882) 7 App.Cas. 741 at 772, H.L.; *Slim v. Daily Telegraph Ltd.* [1968] 2 Q.B. 157 at 171, C.A.

[18] [1964] A.C. 234, H.L. See also *Capital and Counties Bank Ltd. v. Henty & Sons* (1882) 7 App.Cas. 741 at 745, H.L.; *Nevill v. Fine Art & General Insurance Co. Ltd.* [1897] A.C. 68 at 72, 73, H.L.

[19] *Lewis v. Daily Telegraph Ltd.* [1964] A.C. 234 at 259, H.L.

[20] *Grubb v. Bristol United Press Ltd.* [1963] 1 Q.B. 309 at 328.

"innuendo" is, however, properly used to described an alternative or additional libel which occurs by reason of the fact that, in the light of some extrinsic evidence, the words bear to the reader some meaning defamatory of the plaintiff which, without such evidence, the words would not bear in their ordinary and natural meaning.[21]

Thus, any innuendo, in its proper sense, cannot rely on a mere interpretation of the words of the libel itself but must be supported by extrinsic facts or matters. It matters not that in publishing the words the defendant did not know of the extrinsic facts or matters which enabled some persons to whom the libel was published, to draw an inference defamatory of the plaintiff.[22] It is sufficient if any reasonable man with such knowledge would interpret the words in a defamatory sense.[23]

3. Defamation Must Be Of and Concern the Plaintiff

21.06   It is important to observe that in order to make anyone liable in an action based on defamation, it must be proved that he made a defamatory statement of and concerning the plaintiff. This does not necessarily mean that the plaintiff must be referred to by name, or that the plaintiff need actually be the person to whom it was intended to refer.[24] All that is necessary is that the words are "such as would reasonably lead persons acquainted with the plaintiff to believe that he was the person referred to".[25] This principle is illustrated by *Yousoupoff v. Metro-Goldwyn-Mayer Pictures Ltd.*,[26] where the defendant produced a film which dealt with the alleged circumstances in which the influence exercised by Rasputin on the Czar and Czarina brought about the destruction of Russia. In the film it was represented that a lady had illicit relations with Rasputin. The plaintiff brought an action alleging that reasonable people would understand that she was the woman who was represented as having had the relations and it was found that although the defendants did not use the name of the plaintiff, they used a description of her that could apply to no one but the plaintiff. *Youssoupoff v. Metro-Goldwyn-Mayer* concerned the dramatisation and embellishment of historical facts. Thus the likelihood of characters in the film

---

[21] *Grubb v. Bristol United Press Ltd.* [1963] 1 Q.B. 309, C.A.; *Lewis v. Daily Telegraph Ltd.* [1964] A.C. 234 at 277, H.L.
[22] *Cassidy v. Daily Mirror Newspapers Ltd.* [1929] 2 K.B. 331 C.A., but see "Unintentional Defamation", *post*, para. 21.10 *et seq.*
[23] *Tolley v. J.S. Fry & Sons, Ltd.* [1931] A.C. 333; *Hough v. London Express Newspapers Ltd.* [1940] 2 K.B. 507, C.A.; *Astaire v. Campling* [1966] 1 W.L.R. 34, C.A.
[24] *Newstead v. London Express Newspapers Ltd.* [1940] 1 K.B. 377.
[25] *Knupffer v. London Express Newspapers Ltd.* [1944] A.C. 116, H.L.; *E. Hulton & Co. v. Jones* [1910] A.C. 20, H.L.; *Morgan v. Odhams Press Ltd.* [1971] 1 W.L.R. 1239, H.L.
[26] (1934) 50 T.L.R. 581, C.A.

being associated with real life characters was a real possibility. However, the principle goes further.

A statement defamatory of a named person believed by the author of the statement to be a fictitious person and never intended to refer to the plaintiff might nevertheless be defamatory of him if reasonable people acquainted with him would be led to believe that the plaintiff was the person was referred to.[27] Thus it matters not that the defendant in creating the character believed that it was entirely fictitious and had no parallel in real life. It will be defamatory if reasonable people would identify the description, name, or character of the fictitious character with the plaintiff.[28] This is an area which is of particular concern to those in the film, television and theatre sectors of the entertainment industry for it is clear that although an author may intend a character in a film or television programme to be fictitious and not based upon a real life character the film may nevertheless be defamatory. **21.07**

4. Publication

What is publication. "What is the meaning of 'publication'? The making known the defamatory matter after it has been written to some person other than the person of whom it is written."[29] The indispensable quality of publication is therefore the communication of the defamatory material to a person other than the person of whom it concerns. **21.08**

Requirement for publication. "I would go by the principle, which is well established, that in defamation . . . the cause of action is the *publication* of defamatory words of and concerning the plaintiff. The cause of action arises when those words are *published* to the person by whom they are read or heard. The cause of action arises then not later."[30] The principle can be stated thus: in defamation a cause of action arises as soon as the words are published to a person then knowing all the material facts; if there are extrinsic facts, he must know them at the time of publication.[31] It therefore follows that the publication of words cannot be made into a cause of action by reason of facts subsequently coming to the knowledge of the reader or hearer. **21.09**

---

[27] *E. Hulton & Co. v. Jones* [1920] A.C. 20, H.L.
[28] *Ibid.*
[29] *Pullman v. Hill & Co.* [1891] 1 Q.B. 524 at 527.
[30] *Grappelli v. Derek Block Ltd.* [1981] 1 W.L.R. 822 at 825, C.A.; see also *Powell v. Gelston* [1916] 2 K.B. 615 at 619.
[31] *Grappelli v. Derek Block Ltd.* [1981] 1 W.L.R. 822, C.A.; see also *Powell v. Gelston* [1916] 2 K.B. 615 at 619.

Each communication of a libel is a separate publication in respect of which a civil action may be brought.[32]

5. Defences

(a) *Unintentional defamation*

21.10 **General.** The principle that "liability for libel does not depend on the intention of the defamer; but on the fact of defamation"[33] means, for example, that if a person depicts an individual so that others reasonably believe that the character drawn is the plaintiff, it is no answer to say that the character was in the author's mind merely fictional. This was described as "adding a terror to authorship"[34] and was consequently of some concern to, *inter alia*, dramatists, and film producers. The effect of this principle has, however, to some extent, been ameliorated by section 4 of the Defamation Act 1952.

Defamation Act 1954, Section 4

21.11 **Innocent publication.** Section 4(1) provides that a person who has published words alleged to be defamatory of another person "may, if he claims that the words[35] were published by him innocently in relation to that other person, make an offer of amends". For the purposes of the Act words are treated as published by one person innocently in relation to another person "if and only if" the following conditions are satisfied[36]:

    (a) that the publisher did not intend to publish them of and concerning that other person and did not know of circumstances by virtue of which they might be understood to refer to him; or

    (b) that the words were not defamatory on the face of them, and the publisher did not know of circumstances by virtue of which they might be understood to be defamatory of that other person; and

    (c) in either case, that the publisher exercised reasonable care in relation to the publication.

---

[32] *Duke of Brunswick v. Harmer* (1849) 14 Q.B. 185; *"Truth" (N.Z.) Ltd. v. Holloway* [1960] 1 W.L.R. 997.

[33] *Cassidy v. Daily Mirror Newspapers, Ltd.* [1929] 2 K.B. 331 at 354, C.A.

[34] *Knuppfer v. London Express Newspapers, Ltd.* [1943] 1 K.B. 80 at 89.

[35] For the purposes of the Act "words" includes "reference to pictures, visual images, gestures and other means of signifying meaning": Defamation Act 1952, s.16(1).

[36] Defamation Act 1954, s.4(5).

"Offer of amends". An "offer of amends" means an offer: **21.12**

(a) to publish or join in the publication of a suitable correction of the words complained of, and a sufficient apology to the party aggrieved in respect of those words[37];

(b) where copies of a document or record containing the words have been distributed by or with the knowledge of the person making the offer, to take such steps as are reasonably practicable on his part for notifying persons to whom the copies have been so distributed that the words are alleged to be defamatory of the party aggrieved.[38]

The "offer of amends" must be expressed to be made for the purposes of section 4 of the Defamation Act 1952 and be accompanied by an affidavit specifying the facts relied upon by the person making it to show that the words in question were published by him innocently in relation to the party aggrieved.[39] Where such an offer has been made, accompanied by an affidavit in this prescribed form, and the offer is rejected by the party aggrieved, no evidence, other than evidence of facts specified in the affidavit, is admissible on behalf of that person, at a subsequent trial of the action, to prove that the words were published innocently.[40] Particular care must therefore be taken in the drafting of such an affidavit: if the aggrieved person should reject the offer no further facts may be adduced at the trial of the action.

Acceptance of offer of amends. If the offer is accepted by the party   **21.13**
aggrieved and duly performed, no proceedings for libel or slander may be taken or continued by that party against the party making the offer in respect of the publication in question.[41] This does not, however, affect the right of the party aggrieved to take or continue proceedings against any other party jointly responsible for the publication.[42] Where the offer is so accepted any question as to the steps to be taken in fulfillment of the offer must, in default of agreement between the parties, be referred to and determined by the High Court, whose decision is final.[43]

Further, on the acceptance of the offer the power of the High Court to make orders as to costs in proceedings by the party aggrieved against the person making the offer in respect of the publication, or in respect of steps to be taken in fulfillment of the offer, include power to order

---

[37] *Ibid.*, s.4(3)(a).
[38] *Ibid.*, s.4(3)(b).
[39] *Ibid.*, s.4(2).
[40] *Ibid.*, s.4(2).
[41] *Ibid.*, s.4(1)(a).
[42] *Ibid.*, s.4(1)(a).
[43] *Ibid.*, s.4(4)(a).

payment by the person making the offer to the party aggrieved of costs on an indemnity basis and any costs reasonably incurred or to be incurred by that party in consequence of the publication.[44] Where no such proceedings are taken, the High Court has a like power upon the application of the party aggrieved.[45]

21.14 **Rejection of offer of amends.** If an offer of amends is not accepted by an aggrieved party it is a defence in any proceedings by him for libel or slander against the person making the offer in respect of the publication, to prove that the words complained of were published by the defendant innocently in relation to the plaintiff and that the offer was made as soon as practicable after the defendant received notice that they were or might be defamatory of the plaintiff, and has not been withdrawn.[46] This defence is not available, however, in relation to publication by any person of words of which he is not the author unless he proves that the words were written by the author without malice.[47]

(b) *Justification*

21.15 When facts are stated which can be justified as true, although defamatory of and concerning the plaintiff, no remedy will lie for publication of the defamatory statement. The burden is upon the defendant[48] to prove the words were true in substance and in fact. This requirement has been expressed as requiring that "the sting of the libel or, if there is more than one, the stings of the libel should be made out" and it matters not if there are "mistakes here and there in what has been said"[49] which make no substantial difference to the quality of the alleged libel or in the justification pleaded for it.

Thus, for example, if X publishes words to the effect that, on January 12, Y took a painting from the drawing room of X's house and sold it the next day and pocketed the money all without notice to X and that in X's opinion Y stole the painting, and if the facts are found to be that Y did not take the painting from the drawing room but from the hall, and that he did not sell it the following day but a week afterwards, without X's knowledge or consent and did indeed pocket the proceeds, the whole sting of the libel will be justified notwithstanding the errors of detail.

21.16 Where a defence of justification is being considered, section 5 of the Defamation Act 1952 may be applicable where the defamatory words contain two or more distinct charges against the plaintiff. Section 5 of

---

[44] *Ibid.*, s.4(4)(b).
[45] *Ibid.*, s.4(4)(b).
[46] *Ibid.*, s.4(1)(b).
[47] *Ibid.*, s.4(6).
[48] *Beevis v. Davison* [1957] 1 Q.B. 195, C.A.
[49] *Sutherland v. Stopes* [1925] A.C. 47 at 73, H.L.

the Act provides that "[i]n an action for libel or slander in respect of words containing two or more distinct charges against the plaintiff, a defence of justification shall not fail by reason only that the truth of every charge is not proved if the words not proved to be true do not materially injure the plaintiff's reputation having regard to the truth of the remaining charges." The section requires the distinct charges against the plaintiff to be founded on separate words, and these must be contained in the passages of which the plaintiff complains.[50] A defendant is not to fail in his defence of justification simply because he cannot prove every distinct charge to be true: if he proves the greater part of the libel to be true, then even though there is a smaller part not proved, nevertheless the defendant is entitled to succeed as long as the part not proved does not do the plaintiff much more harm.[51]

(c) *Privilege*

It is a good defence to show that the occasion on which a statement is made is privileged. Privilege is of two kinds. Absolute privilege and qualified privilege. Such privilege may either arise out of common law or be conferred by statute in respect of particular proceedings. It is proposed to deal with these privileges in so far only as they are relevant to broadcasting and the provision of programme services. **21.17**

(i) *Absolute Privilege*

By section 3 of the Law of Libel Amendment Act 1888,[52] a fair and accurate report in any broadcast or programme service, provided by means of a broadcasting station in the United Kingdom, of proceedings publicly heard before any court exercising judicial authority in the United Kingdom[53] is, if published contemporaneously with such proceedings, privileged. "[W]henever something is done in the course of proceedings which is in any way related to the proceedings as such, and can be done in the proceedings, that may properly be said to be "proceedings publicly heard", and a report of it may be protected"[54] though the report contains matter of a defamatory kind which is injurious to individuals. **21.18**

Thus, for example, the evidence of witnesses, or anything said by counsel or by the judge may be reported. However, by contrast, if a

---

[50] *Polly Peck (Holdings) plc. v. Trelford* [1986] 2 All E.R. 84.
[51] *Moore v. News of the World Ltd.* [1972] 1 Q.B. 441, C.A.; *Polly Peck (Holdings) plc. v. Trelford* [1986] 2 All E.R. 84, C.A.
[52] As amended by the Defamation Act 1952, s.9(2).
[53] *Ibid.*, s.8.
[54] *Farmer v. Hyde* [1937] 1 K.B. 728 at 742, C.A.

man, who is not sworn[55] as a witness and is making no application to the court, should state in open court that part of the plaintiff's testimony is little short of perjury, such words would form no part of the proceedings: a report of such statement would therefore not attract privilege under section 3.[56]

21.19   "Contemporaneously" in this context should not be taken in its literal meaning but should be construed widely to include broadcast on the evening of the proceedings or as soon as reasonably practicable after the proceedings the subject of the broadcast.

The section does not state whether the privilege is absolute or qualified but the authorities and textbook writers indicate the privilege so conferred is absolute and not qualified privilege.[57]

(ii) *Qualified Privilege*

21.20   We are here mainly concerned with the reporting of proceedings of judicial, quasi-judicial and domestic tribunals and public meetings. In all such circumstances qualified privilege, whether at common law or by statute, is granted to a United Kingdom broadcaster who publishes a defamatory statement at such proceedings. However, notwithstanding the accuracy of the report the privilege will be lost, both at common law and under statute, in cases where it is proved by the plaintiff that the publication is made with malice.[58]

"Malice" in this context is often referred to as "express malice" and broadly means malice in the popular sense of a desire to injure the person who is defamed. To destroy the privilege the desire to injure must be the dominant motive for the defamatory publication; knowledge that it will have that effect is not enough if the broadcaster is nevertheless acting in accordance with the rights accorded to it at common law or by statute.[59]

An example of a situation in which express malice might be found would be where a news editor publishes proceedings of a court trial not because it is of public concern and for the public benefit but because he wishes to give vent to his personal spite or ill towards the person who has been defamed in the proceedings. The court will, however, in such

---

[55] Where he has been sworn as a witness but has completed his evidence but interrupts when out of the witnesses box his statement may attract privilege: *Hope v. Sir W.G. Leng & Co. (Sheffield Telegraph) Ltd.* 23 T.L.R. 243, C.A.

[56] *Farmer v. Hyde* [1937] 1 K.B. 728, C.A.

[57] See *Gatley on Libel and Slander* (8th ed., 1981) para. 631, n.51; *Farmer v. Hyde* [1937] 1 Q.B. 728, C.A.; *McCarey v. Associated Newspapers Ltd.* [1964] 1 W.L.R. 855.

[58] Defamation Act, s.7(1).

[59] *Horrocks v. Lowe* [1975] A.C. 135.

circumstances be slow to draw the inference that the dominant motive for the publication is the desire to injure.[60]

In *Horrocks v. Lowe*[61] Lord Diplock stated the principle thus: **21.21**

"Qualified privilege would be illusory, and the public interest that it is meant to serve defeated, if the protection which it affords were lost merely because a person, although acting in compliance with a duty or in protection of a legitimate interest, disliked the person whom he defamed or was indignant at what he believed to be that person's conduct and welcomed the opportunity of exposing it. It is only where his desire to comply with the relevant duty or to protect the relevant interest plays no significant part in his motives for . . . publishing that "express malice" can properly be found."

(a) *Common law*

Judicial proceedings. At common law "where there are judicial pro- **21.22** ceedings before a properly constituted judicial tribunal exercising its jurisdiction in open Court, then the publication, without malice, of a fair and accurate report of what takes place before that tribunal is privileged".[62] The privilege extends to proceedings before superior and inferior[63] courts which are open to the public. It will not, however, extend to reports of tribunals which are not open to the public nor to domestic tribunals,[64] but will attach to the publication of the decision of the domestic tribunal which is in the terms which the tribunal bona fide embodied it and in the publication chosen by the parties as the means of communication between the tribunal and the section of the public interested.[65] The report of the proceedings must, however, "be strictly confined to the actual proceedings in court, and must contain no defamatory observations or comments from any quarter whatever, in addition to what forms strictly and properly legal proceedings".[66]

---

[60] *Ibid.*
[61] *Ibid.* at 150–51, *per* Lord Diplock, H.L.
[62] *Kimber v. Press Association, Ltd.* [1893] 1 Q.B. 65, 68 (C.A.).
[63] *McCarey v. Associated Newspapers Ltd.* [1964] 1 W.L.R. 855 (coroner's court); *Kimber v. Press Association, Ltd.* [1893] 1 K.B. 65 (*ex. parte* hearing before magistrates' court).
[64] *Chapman v. Ellesmere* [1932] 2 K.B. 431 at 475. Qualified privilege will extend to reports of the General Medical Council. By reason of the "duty of the council towards the public . . . this report stands on principle in the same position as a judicial report": *Allbutt v. General Council of Medical Education* (1889) 23 Q.B.D. 400 at 410.
[65] *Chapman v. Ellesmere* [1932] 2 K.B. 431 at 475.
[66] *Delegal v. Highley* (1837) 3 Bing. N.C. 950 at 960. See under "Absolute privilege", *ante*, para. 21.18 for the term to like effect.

21.23   Qualified privilege will also extend to reports of foreign judicial proceedings where such proceedings "throw light upon, or [is] related to or
connected with, the administration of justice in England".[67]

21.24   **Parliamentary debates.** The publication, without malice, of a fair and
accurate report of proceedings in Parliament is likewise protected at
common law by qualified privilege.[68]

(b) *Statutory protection*

21.25   The Defamation Act 1952[69] extends qualified privilege to two categories
of statements of which reports are broadcast from a transmitter in the
United Kingdom as part of a programme service. The categories are as
follows:

  (a) statements privileged without explanation or contradiction; and

  (b) statements privileged subject to explanation or contradiction.

21.26   **Statements privileged without explanation or contradiction.** These
statements are set out in the Schedule to the Defamation Act 1952. A
broadcaster is under no duty to publish either a contradiction or an
explanation in the words of a letter or terms put forward by a person
who alleges that he has been libelled in such statements. The statements
are as follows:

  (1) a fair and accurate report of any proceedings in public of the
      legislature of any part of Her Majesty's dominions outside Great
      Britain;

  (2) a fair and accurate report of any proceedings in public of an
      international organisation of which the United Kingdom or Her
      Majesty's Government in the United Kingdom is a member, or of
      any international conference to which that government sends a
      representative;

  (3) a fair and accurate report of any proceedings in public of an
      international court;

  (4) a fair and accurate report of any proceedings before any court
      exercising jurisdiction throughout any part of Her Majesty's
      dominions outside the United Kingdom, or of any proceedings
      before a court-martial held outside the United Kingdom under
      the Naval Discipline Act, the Army Act or the Air Force Act;

  (5) a fair and accurate report of any proceedings in public of a body

---

[67] *Webb v. Times Publishing Co. Ltd.* [1960] 1 Q.B. 535.
[68] *Wason v. Walter* (1868) L.R. 4 Q.B. 73.
[69] Defamation Act 1952, s.7.

or person appointed to hold a public inquiry by the government or legislature of any part of Her Majesty's dominions outside the United Kingdom;

(6) a fair and accurate copy of or extract from any register kept in pursuance of any Act of Parliament which is open to inspection by the public, or of any other document which is required by the law or any part of the United Kingdom to be open to inspection by the public;

(7) a notice or advertisement published by or on the authority of any court within the United Kingdom or any judge or officer of such court.

Statements privileged subject to explanation or contradiction. In an action for libel in respect of the publication of a report which is privileged subject to explanation or contradiction, the Defamation Act 1952 provides no defence if it is proved that the defendant has been requested by the plaintiff to broadcast a reasonable statement by way of explanation or contradiction, and has refused or neglected to do so, or has done so in a manner not adequate or not reasonable having regard to all the circumstances.[70] A general letter asking for a full apology does not amount to a "request" to broadcast a statement by way of explanation or contradiction.[71]   **21.27**

It would appear therefore that the plaintiff must, in order to bring himself within section 7 of the Act, specify the terms of the explanation or contradiction which he requests the broadcaster to transmit. The statements privileged subject to explanation or contradiction are as follows.

Domestic tribunals.   **21.28**

"(8) a fair and accurate report of the findings or decision of any of the following associations, or any committee or their governing body:

(a) an association formed in the United Kingdom for the purpose of promoting or encouraging the exercise of or interest in any art, science, religion or learning, and empowered by its constitution to exercise control over or adjudicate upon matters of interest or concern to the association, or actions or conduct of any persons subject to such control or adjudication;

(b) an association formed in the United Kingdom for the purpose of promoting or safeguarding the interests of any trade,

---

[70] *Ibid.*, s.7(2).
[71] *Khan v. Ahmed* [1957] 2 Q.B. 149.

business or profession, or of the persons carrying on or engaged in any trade, business, industry or profession, and empowered by its constitution to exercise control over or adjudicate upon the matters connected with the trade, business, industry or profession, or the actions or conduct of those persons;

(c) an association formed in the United Kingdom for the purpose of promoting or safeguarding the interests of any game, sport or pastime to the playing or exercise of which members of the public are invited or admitted, and empowered by its constitution to exercise control over or adjudicate upon persons connected with or taking part in the same, sport or pastime,

being a finding or decision relating to a person who is a member of or is subject by virtue of any contract to the control of the association."

Thus, whereas no protection is given at common law in respect of reports of domestic tribunals, statutory protection is now available under the Schedule 2, paragraph 8 of the Defamation Act 1952. This protection is a qualified privilege and is subject to "explanation and contradiction".

21.29 **Public meetings.** "A fair and accurate report of the proceedings at any public meeting held in the United Kingdom, is privileged subject to explanation and contradiction.[72] A "public meeting" for these purposes is "a meeting bona fide and lawfully held for a lawful purpose and for the furtherance or discussion of any matter of public concern, whether the admission to the meeting is general or restricted". Whether a meeting is a "public meeting" is a question of law.[73] However, even if a meeting is a public meeting, no privilege will attach to the publication of any matter which is prohibited by law, or any matter which is not of public concern *and* for the public benefit.[74]

A meeting held for the sole purpose of libelling a person and in breach of the peace is neither bona fide nor lawfully held and thus no privilege will attach to the reporting of such an event.

21.30 **Miscellaneous meetings and sittings.** Privileged statements comprise a fair and accurate report of the proceedings at any meeting or sitting in any part of the United Kingdom of:

(a) any local authority or committee of local authorities;

(b) any justice or justices of the peace acting otherwise than as a court exercising judicial authority;

---

[72] Defamation Act 1952, Sched. para. 9.
[73] *Khan v. Ahmed* [1957] 2 Q.B. 149.
[74] *Kelly v. O'Malley* (1889) 6 T.L.R. 62.

(c) any commission, tribunal, committee or person appointed for the purposes of any inquiry by Act of Parliament, by Her Majesty or by a Minister of the Crown;

(d) any person appointed by a local authority to hold a local inquiry in pursuance of any Act of Parliament;

(e) any other tribunal, board, committee or body constituted by or under, and exercising functions under, an Act of Parliament,

not being a meeting or sitting admission to which is denied to representatives of broadcasters and other members of the public.[75]

Meetings of companies. Privilege within the terms of Part II of the Schedule to the Defamation Act 1952 applies to a fair and accurate report of proceedings at a general meeting of any company or association constituted, registered or certified by or under any Act of Parliament or incorporated by Royal Charter, not being a private company within the meeting of the Companies Act 1948. **21.31**

Notices. Privilege within the terms of Part II of the Schedule to the Defamation Act 1952 applies to a fair and accurate report or summary of any notice or other matter issued for the information of the public by or on behalf of any government department, officer of state, local authority or chief officer of police. **21.32**

(d) *Fair comment*

Fair comment distinguished from privilege. Fair comment does not come within the category of "privileged occasion". "A privileged occasion is one on which the privileged person is entitled to do something which no one who is not within the privilege is entitled to do on that occasion. A person in such a position may say or write about another person things which no other person in the kingdom can be allowed to say or write. But in the case of [fair comment] every person in the kingdom is entitled to do exactly the same things, and therefore the occasion is not privileged."[76] **21.33**

Circumstances giving rise to defence. Where it is alleged that published words are defamatory it is a defence for the defendant to show that such words are a fair comment on matters of public interest. The defendant who raises this defence does not have to show that the comments are true. What he must show is (a) that the comment is an expression of opinion not an assertion of facts; (b) that the comment was fair; and (c) that such comment was with regard to a matter of public interest. **21.34**

---

[75] Part II, para. 10, Schedule to Defamation Act 1952.
[76] *Merivale v. Carson* (1887) 20 Q.B.D. 275 at 280, C.A.

(i) *Comment not fact*

21.35 A comment is an expression of opinion based upon identified facts. Thus in order to qualify as comment there must "in all cases [be] a sufficient substratum of fact stated or indicated in the words which are the subject matter of the action".[77] But it is unnecessary that all the facts on which the comment is based is stated, provided that the facts are sufficiently and not incorrectly or untruthfully stated[78] and not so mixed up with the comment that the reader or listener cannot distinguish between facts and comment.[79] However, it is not always easy to distinguish, in the words complained of, between the expression of opinion and the statement of fact. In *Kelmsley v. Foot*[80] Lord Porter stated the distinction thus:

> "It often depends on what is said in the rest of the article. If the defendant accurately states what some public man has really done, and then asserts that 'such conduct is disgraceful', this is merely the expression of his opinion, his comment on the plaintiff's conduct. So, if without setting it out, he identifies the conduct on which he comments by a clear reference . . . But if he asserts that the plaintiff has been guilty of disgraceful conduct, and does not state what that conduct was this is an allegation of fact for which there is no defence but privilege or truth. The same considerations apply where a defendant has drawn from certain facts an inference derogatory to the plaintiff. If he states the bare inference without the facts on which it is based, such an inference will be treated as an allegation of fact. But if he sets out the facts correctly, and then gives his inference, stating it as his inference from those facts, such an inference will as a rule, be deemed a comment."

(ii) *Fair comment*

21.36 The second limb of the ingredients necessary to establish the defence requires that the comment be (a) fairly and honestly made[81]; (b) on facts truly stated[82]; and (c) the comment must not convey imputations of evil or corrupt motives except in so far as the facts truly stated warrant the imputation.[83]

---

[77] *Kelmsley v. Foot* [1952] A.C. 345.

[78] *Ibid.*

[79] *Hunt v. Star Newspapers Co. Ltd.* [1908] 2 K.B. 309 at 319, C.A.

[80] [1952] A.C. 345 at 356–357, citing and approving a passage from *Odgers on Libel and Slander* (6th ed., 1929).

[81] *Merrivale v. Carson* (1887) 20 Q.B.D. 275; *Silkin v. Beaverbrook Newspapers Ltd.* [1958] 1 W.L.R. 743; *Slim v. Daily Telegraph Ltd.* [1968] 2 Q.B. 157, C.A.

[82] *Joynt v. Cycle Trade Publishing Co.* [1904] 2 K.B. 292 at 294; *Hunt v. Star Newspaper Company Ltd.* [1908] 2 K.B. 309 at 320, C.A.

[83] *Campbell v. Spottiswoode* 3 B. & S. 769; *Hunt v. Star Newspapers Co. Ltd.* [1908] 2 K.B. 309 at 320.

Comments fairly and honestly made. The comment must be fair in the   **21.37**
sense that it must be the honest opinion of the person making the comment and not actuated by malice. If a comment is made with a malicious
motive it will be unfair although viewed objectively it is prima facie
fair.[84] The true test is "was this an opinion, however exaggerated, obsti-
nate or prejudiced, which was honestly held by the writer?"[85]

Facts truly stated. A comment cannot be fair which is based upon facts   **21.38**
which are not truly stated.[86] Thus, at common law where the facts "are
fully set out in the alleged libel, each fact must be justified and if the
defendant fails to justify one, even if it be comparatively unimportant,
he fails in his defence".[87] However, this rule has been modified by section 6 of the Defamation Act 1952 which provides that:

> "In an action for libel or slander in respect of words consisting
> partly of allegations of fact and partly of expression of opinion, a
> defence of fair comment shall not fail by reason only that the truth
> of every allegation of fact is not proved if the expression of opinion
> is fair comment having regard to such of the facts alleged or
> referred to in the words complained of as are proved."

Thus, the defence will not fail if the comment is fair "having regard to
such facts" as are proved. However, "(1) fair comment is a defence to
comment only and not to defamatory statements of fact, and . . . section
6 has not altered the law in this respect (2) that where there is any defamatory sting in any of the facts on which the comment is based these
defamatory statements of fact can only be defended by a successful plea
with now the benefit of section 5 of the Defamation Act, 1952".[88]

"If a statement made by a witness is fairly and accurately reported,   **21.39**
and attributed by the witness who made it, then, no doubt, although
the evidence given by the witness is afterwards shown to be false, the
statement reported can be made the subject of fair comment."[89] Similarly, in a report of proceedings in Parliament. If a speaker in a debate

---

[84] *Thomas v. Bradbury, Agnew & Co.* [1906] 2 K.B. 627; *Broadway Approvals Ltd. v. Odhams Press Ltd. (No. 2)* [1965] 1 W.L.R. 805 at 816.
[85] *Silkin v. Beaverbrook Newspapers Ltd.* [1958] 1 W.L.R. 743 at 747; see also *Merivale v. Carson* (1887) 20 Q.B.D. 275, C.A.; *Turner v. M.G.M. Pictures Ltd.* [1950] 1 All E.R. 449, H.L.
[86] *Joynt v. Cycle Trade Publishing Co.* [1904] 2 K.B. 292; *Hunt v. Star Newspaper Co. Ltd.* [1908] 2 K.B. 309, C.A.; *Kemsley v. Foot* [1952] A.C. 345.
[87] *Kemsley v. Foot* [1952] A.C. 345 at 357, 358, H.L. See also *Carr v. Hood* (1908) 1 Camp. 357; *Hunt v. Star Newspapers Co. Ltd.* [1908] 2 K.B. 309, C.A.
[88] *Truth (N.Z.) Ltd. v. Avery* [1959] N.Z.L.R. 274; applied *Broadway Approvals Ltd. v. Odhams Press Ltd.* [1965] 1 W.L.R. 805, C.A.; *London Artists Ltd. v. Littler* [1969] 2 Q.B. 375 at 391, C.A. See also Dias, R.W.M., *Clerk & Lindsell on Torts* (Sweet & Maxwell, 16th ed., 1989).
[89] *Grech v. Odhams Press Ltd.* [1958] 2 Q.B. 275 at 285.

"got his facts entirely wrong or was actuated by the most express of malice" neither the reporter nor the broadcaster is liable as long as the report was fair and the reporter himself was not actuated by malice.[90]

21.40 **Imputations of evil or corrupt motives.** "Comment must not convey imputations of an evil sort except so far as the facts truly stated warrant the imputation."[91] In this context "warrant the imputation" means that the imputation must "be a reasonable inference" from the facts so stated upon which it purports to be a comment.[92] Whether the facts can be reasonably inferred is a question of law for the judge: if he finds that the inference is capable of being reasonably drawn it is for the jury to determine whether in that particular case it ought to be drawn.[93] Thus, it is insufficient to show that the imputation was made in good faith as the honest expression of the opinion which the defendant held on facts truly stated and is such that a fair minded man might in good faith hold upon those facts. Such an imputation is an assertion of fact and thus must be justified.

(iii) *Public Interest*

21.41 "There is no definition in the books as to what is a matter of public interest. All we are given is a list of examples, coupled with the statement that it is for the judge and not the jury . . . Whenever a matter is such as to affect people at large, so that they may be legitimately interested in, or concerned at what is going on; or what may happen to them or to others; then that is a matter of public interest on which everyone is entitled to make fair comment."[94]

Thus, it is clear that no exhaustive list can be given as to what matters may be commented on. Examples of instances in which fair comment may be made include the administration of justice, parliamentary proceedings, the conduct of central and local government and the conduct of those in public life. Where public criticism is invited by the presentation of a film or play to the public, fair comment may also be made of such works but not so as to mount an "attack upon [the author's] character unconnected with his authorship".[95]

---

[90] *Cook v. Alexander* [1974] 1 Q.B. 279 at 288.

[91] *Hunt v. Star Newspaper Co. Ltd.* [1908] 2 K.B. 309, C.A.; *Campbell v. Spottiswoode* 3 B & S. 769; *Dakyl v. Labouchere* [1908] 2 K.B. 325n; *Homing Pigeon Co. Ltd. v. Racing Pigeon Co. Ltd.* (1913) T.L.R. 389.

[92] *Dakhyl v. Labouchere* [1908] 2 K.B. 325n; *Campbell v. Spottiswoode* 3 B. & S. 769; *Hunt v. Star Newspapers Co. Ltd.* [1908] 2 K.B. 309.

[93] *Dakhyl v. Labouchere* [1908] 2 K.B. 325n; *Campbell v. Spottiswoode* 3 B. & S. 769; *Hunt v. Star Newspapers Co. Ltd.* [1908] 2 K.B. 309; *Homing Pigeon Co. Ltd. v. Racing Pigeon Co. Ltd* (1913) T.L.R. 389. For contrary view see *Gatley on Libel and Slander* (8th ed.) paras. 723–724.

[94] *London Artists Ltd. v. Littler* [1969] 2 Q.B. 375 at 391, C.A.

[95] *Carr v. Hood* (1808) 1 Camp. 357.

6. **Remedies**

(a) *Damages*

General principle. In an action for defamation the wrongful act is   **21.42**
damage to the plaintiff's reputation. The injuries he sustains for which
damages are awarded may be classified under two heads. First, the consequences of the attitude adopted towards him by other persons as a
result of the diminution of the esteem in which they hold him because
of the defamatory statement, and secondly, the grief or annoyance
caused to the plaintiff himself by the defamatory statement.[96] Damages
under both heads are compensatory and at large.[97]

Damages under the first head may, where the plaintiff pleads and
proves such loss,[98] include special damages arising as a direct result of
the defamatory statement: such loss may for example include loss of
employment, or inability to obtain fresh appointments. However, the
major award under the first head of damage will be in respect of the
social consequences of the defamatory words.

The extent of the damages under the second head may depend not   **21.43**
merely on the wrongful act itself but upon the manner in which, or it
may be, the motives with which, it is done and which may make it
appropriate that the compensation for the plaintiff's injured feelings are
greater than otherwise would be the case; that is, the damages may be
"aggravated" for one or other or both of these reasons. There may, however, be cases where, for example, a broadcaster or a film producer[99]
deliberately publishes a defamatory statement in the expectation of
increasing its viewing figures or audience by an amount which would
exceed any damages awarded by way of compensation alone. In such
circumstances, exemplary damages within the second category laid
down in *Rookes v. Barnard*[1] can properly be awarded "to teach a wrongdoer that tort does not pay".[2]

(b) *Mitigation of damages*

Evidence of plaintiff's bad character. It is permissible to call evidence of   **21.44**
the plaintiff's bad character in mitigation of damages. The rational for
this rule is that a person should not recover damages for injury to a
character that he is generally known not to possess.[3] For these purposes

---

[96] *McCarey v. Associated Newspapers Ltd. (No. 2)* [1965] 2 Q.B. 86, C.A.
[97] *Ibid.*
[98] *Bluck v. Lovering* (1885) 1 T.L.R. 497; *McCarey v. Associated Newspapers Ltd. (No. 2)* [1965]
    2 Q.B. 86 at 105, 111, C.A.
[99] See, *e.g. Youssoupoff v. Metro-Goldwyn-Mayer* (1934) 50 T.L.R. 581, C.A.
[1] [1964] A.C. 1129 at 1226, H.L.
[2] *Ibid.* at 1226.
[3] *Plato Films Ltd. v. Speidel* [1961] A.C. 1090, H.L.

"character" is to be taken to mean the character which the plaintiff bears in the public estimation.[4] A defendant may not, however, adduce evidence of "rumours and suspicions to the same effect as the defamatory matter complained of,"[5] nor evidence of particular facts tending to show the disposition of the plaintiff unless those particular facts are of sufficient notoriety to be likely to contribute to the plaintiff's reputation.[6] Particular criminal convictions may, however, be adduced in mitigation of damages if they are relevant in the sense that they must be convictions in the "relevant sector of his life and have taken place within a relevant period such as to affect his current reputation".[7] Thus, in such circumstances, the nature and date of the conviction are of crucial importance in determining the admissibility of the conviction. Where the conviction occurred some considerable time before the alleged defamatory statement and is irrelevant, it would, in such circumstances be inadmissible.

21.45 **Repetition.** Evidence may be given in mitigation of damages that the defamatory statement was obtained from another source and that that source was stated in the defamatory statement itself.[8] However, where the defamatory statement is made as though it were a fact and no source is stated, the defendant may not adduce evidence in mitigation of damages to show that the information was obtained from another source.[9]

Evidence may also be adduced that the alleged libel was copied from another source in order to negative or diminish express malice and with a view to mitigating the damages.[10]

21.46 **Previous publication.** The plaintiff may not adduce evidence in mitigation of damages to show that the same libel has been published by newspapers or other providers of programme services.[11]

21.47 **Evidence of other damages recovered.** In any action for libel or slander the defendant may give evidence in mitigation of damages that the plaintiff has recovered damages, or has brought actions for damages, for libel or slander in respect of a publication of words to the same effect as the words on which the action is founded, or has received, or agreed to receive, compensation in respect of any such publication.[12]

---

[4] *Ibid.* at 1128.
[5] *Ibid.* at 1129, 1130.
[6] *Ibid.* at 1130, 1131.
[7] *Goody v. Odhams Press Ltd.* [1967] 1 Q.B. 333 at 341, C.A.
[8] *Mullett v. Hulton* (1809) 4 Esp. 248.
[9] *Mills v. Spencer* (1817) Holt 533.
[10] *Saunders v. Mills*; 6 Bing. 213; *Dingle v. Associated Newspapers Ltd.* [1964] A.C. 371, H.L.
[11] *Saunders v. Mills*, 6 Bing. 213; *Dingle v. Associated Newspapers Ltd.* [1964] A.C. 371, H.L.
[12] Defamation Act 1952, s.12.

This is intended to deal with the situation where, for example, similar libels have been published by two different persons and an action has been brought against each in respect of the defamatory statement published by each of them. In such circumstances the jury "ought . . . to be directed that in considering the evidence . . . they should consider how far the damage suffered by the plaintiffs can reasonably be attributed solely to the libel with which they are concerned and how far it ought to be regarded as the joint results of the two libels. If they think that some part of the damage is the joint result of the two libels they should bear in mind that the plaintiff ought not to be compensated twice for the same loss."[13]

(c) *Injunction*

The following principles relating to the grant of interim injunctions in   **21.48**
defamation actions may be derived from the authorities.

First, no injunction will be granted if the defendant raises the defence of justification.[14] However, an injunction may be granted where the Attorney-General seeks to restrain further publication of the defamatory statement as being in contempt of court, and he is able to show that there is substantial risk that the course of justice in the proceedings in question will be seriously impeded or prejudiced justice.[15]

Secondly, no injunction will be granted if the defence raises privilege, unless the evidence of malice is so overwhelming that the judge is driven to the conclusion that no reasonable jury could find otherwise; that is, that it would be perverse to acquit the defendant of malice.[16]

Thirdly, the principles enunciated in *American Cyanamid Co. v. Ethicon Ltd.*[17] are not applicable to defamation actions.[18]

7. Instances of Defamatory Imputations Relevant to Entertainment Industry

General. It is not proposed to give an exhaustive list of circumstances   **21.49**
which may give rise to an action for defamation. As has been pointed out, the question of whether particular facts and matters are defamatory is a question of fact depending upon the circumstances of the publi-

---

[13] *Lewis v. Daily Telegraph Ltd.* [1964] A.C. 234 at 261, H.L.
[14] *Bonnard v. Perryman* [1891] 2 Ch. 269.
[15] *Attorney-General v. News Group Newspapers Ltd.* [1986] 2 All E.R. 833, C.A.
[16] *William Coulson & Sons v. James Coulson & Co.* (1887) 3 T.L.R. 846, C.A.; *Harakas v. Baltic Mercantile and Shipping Exchange Ltd.* [1982] 1 W.L.R. 958, C.A.; *Herbage v. Pressdam* [1984] 2 All E.R. 769, C.A.
[17] [1975] A.C. 396.
[18] *J. Trevor & Sons. v. Salomon* (1977) 248 E.G. 779; *Herbage v. Pressdam Ltd.* [1974] 2 All E.R. 769, C.A.

cation and the place and state of opinion. The examples given below are therefore only a selection of specific instances that might give rise to an action in defamation.

Defamation of artistes

(i) Actors and actresses

21.50 **Incompetence.** It is defamatory of an actor or actress to state that he or she is incompetent and unfitted to be an actor.[19]

21.51 **Credit or billing.** An actor or actress may be libelled by being "billed" or advertised on playbills or in programmes in a manner which is incompatible with his or her professional reputation. Thus in *Russell v. Notcutt*[20] where the defendant engaged the plaintiff to sing at a concert and placed her name in a comparatively obscure position among the list of artistes, it was held that advertising her in this manner was calculated to injure her professional reputation. Lord Esher M.R. observed:

> "That order might have no meaning at all in itself under ordinary circumstances, but here a particular class of people and a particular publication were being dealt with, and evidence was given by persons of the greatest experience in such matters that the order in which names were placed had a particular meaning. It was stated in evidence that the first place was a sign of superior reputation . . . and that the beginning and the end in such announcements as these were superior positions as compared with the middle."

21.52 The observations of the Master of the Rolls now reflects the custom in respect of credits in the cinema, theatre and on television. It is therefore possible, for example, for an actor or actress to be libelled by being given a screen credit which does not accord to his or her professional reputation either because it is placed in an obscure position or because it is below that of someone whose reputation is not on a par with his or hers. Such a libel would, however, be rare in modern times due to the fact that it is the practice for actors and actresses to stipulate with precision, as a contractual term, the screen credit that they will receive. Disputes arising as a result of incorrect credits are therefore more likely to give rise to a contractual dispute rather than an action in defamation.

(ii) Authors, Dramatists and Composers

21.53 **Attack on works.** A comment, by, for example a critic, upon the work of an author, dramatist or composer may amount to a libel if there is a misdescription of the work such as to lead to a conclusion that an impu-

---

[19] *Duplany v. Davis* (1886), 3 T.L.R. 184.
[20] (1896) 12 T.L.R. 195, C.A.; *Elen v. London Music Hall Ltd.*, *The Times*, May 31, June 1, 1906.

tation was cast upon the character of the authors, or where the criticism is made under the guise of criticism with an indirect and dishonest intention to injure the author.[21]

Publishing under the name of author. Defamation may occur where a **21.54** person publishes a record, film or play under the name of a performer, director or producer or established reputation if it is shown that the work was of inferior quality.[22]

---

[21] *Merrivale v. Carson* (1887) 20 Q.B.D. 275.
[22] *Ridge v. English Illustrated Magazine Ltd.* (1913) 29 T.L.R. 592; *Moore v. News of the World* [1972] 2 W.L.R. 419, C.A.; see also "Passing Off", *ante*, para. 18.06 and "Moral Rights", *ante*, para. 15.29.

PART V

REGULATION OF TELEVISION AND RADIO

CHAPTER 22

THE BRITISH BROADCASTING CORPORATION

1. Introduction

The British Broadcasting Corporation ("BBC") was established in 1926 **22.01** by Royal Charter. The Charter was renewed in 1937, 1947, 1952 and 1964 and was last renewed in 1981[1] and expires on December 31, 1996. The duties of the BBC with regard to the provision of programmes is laid down in the Licence and Agreement between the BBC and Her Majesty's Secretary of State for the Home Department.[2]

It is important to underline the important differences between the Independent Television Commission, the Radio Authority, the BBC, the theatre and the cinema as sources of entertainment. The duties of the Independent Television Commission and the Radio Authority are set out in a statute and are thus subject to judicial review: the duties of the other sources of entertainment are not. Consequently save in certain limited circumstances where programme standards[3] are in issue, the decisions of the Board of Governors with regard to programming and the conduct of the affairs of the BBC are not subject to judicial review. Where there is a breach of the Licence Agreement such breach is a matter of contract matter between the Board of Governors of the BBC and the Secretary of State for National Heritage.

2. Duties of the BBC

By Clause 13(1), the BBC's primary and general duty is to provide pro- **22.02** grammes in the home and external services.

More specific duties inlcude:

---

[1] See Cmnd. 8313; as amended July 13, 1983, Cmnd. 9013. The Government has announced its intention to renew the Charter and Licence for a period of 10 years from January 1, 1997: "The Future of the BBC," Cmnd. 2621.

[2] Cmnd. 8233.

[3] See *post*, para. 32.44 *et seq.*

(a) a duty to refrain from sending any broadcast matter expressing the opinion of the BBC on current affairs or matters of public policy other than broadcasting and matters contained in programmes which consist of proceedings in either Houses of Parliament or proceedings of a local authority[4];

(b) a duty to treat controversial subjects with due impartiality in the BBC's news services and in the general field of programmes dealing with matters of public policy, and so far as is possible to ensure that programmes in general do not offend against good taste or decency or are likely to encourage or incite to crime or lead to disorder or be offensive to public feeling[5];

(c) a duty to refrain from sending any subliminal images which may affect the minds of viewers without their being fully aware of what is being done.[6]

3. Government control of BBC services

22.03 The Secretary of State may from time to time by notice in writing require the BBC to refrain from sending any matter, or matters, of any class specified in the notice: when complying with the notice the BBC may in its discretion announce, or refrain from announcing, that such notice has been given, or has been varied, or revoked.[7] This power was invoked by the Secretary of State to require, *inter alia*, the BBC to refrain from broadcasting the voices of representatives of certain specified terrorist organisations.[8]

4. Jurisdiction of the Broadcasting Complaints Commission and the Broadcasting Standards Council

22.04 The BBC is subject to the jurisdiction of both the BCC and the BSC.[9]

---

[4] Licence Agreement between Her Majesty's Secretary of State and the Home Department and the BBC: Cmnd. 8233, art. 13(7).

[5] *Ibid.*, Annex, which sets out the undertaking given by the then Chairman of the Board of Governors, Lord Normanbrook, in a letter dated June 13, 1964. For a discussion of this duty see *post*, para. 32.44.

[6] *Ibid.*, art. 13(3).

[7] *Ibid.*, art. 13(4).

[8] See *post*, para. 32.20 *et seq.* for a discussion of the order and the challenge thereto in *R. v. Secretary of State, ex. parte Brind*.

[9] Broadcasting Act 1990, ss.143(2), 152(3). See *post*, Chaps. 33 and 34 for jurisdiction of BCC and BSC.

CHAPTER 23

INDEPENDENT TELEVISION SERVICES

1. Television Programme services

Independent Television Services are all those services which are not **23.01** provided by the BBC or the Welsh Authority. The following are therefore within the meaning of Independent Television Services.

Television broadcast service. Television broadcast services are services **23.02** which broadcast television programmes for general reception in the whole of the United Kingdom or any area of it, including a domestic satellite service.[1] The fact that a service is encrypted to any extent is for these purposes irrelevant and it is to be regarded as a television broadcast service.[2] A television broadcast service does not, however, include teletext or any service in which the visual images broadcast in the service consist wholly or mainly of non-representational images.[3] Thus, still pictures will come within the definition of television broadcast but signals for the actuation or operation of equipment or computers will not.

Non-domestic satellite service. This subject is dealt with elsewhere in **23.03** this work.[4]

---

[1] Broadcasting Act 1990, s.2(5). See *post*, para. 25.01 *et seq.* for the meaning of "domestic" and "non-domestic" satellite services.
[2] *Ibid.*, s.202(5).
[3] *Ibid.*, s.2(6).
[4] See *post*, para. 25.06.

23.04 **Licensable programme service.** A licensable programme service is the provision of relevant programmes[5] transmitted by a "telecommunications system".[6] The transmission must be received in two or more houses in the United Kingdom or in two or more places in the United Kingdom. It will not be a licensable programme service where the reception is by persons having a business interest[7] in the reception of the programme.[8] However, where the service is received by a group, it will be licensable if some or all of those receiving it do not have a business interest in so receiving it.[9] It is irrelevant, for these purposes, whether the telecommunications system is run by the person providing the programme or by some other person and whether the service is only provided on demand.[10]

23.05 **Additional services.** Any service where telecommunications signals[11] are transmitted by wireless telegraphy using the spare capacity within the signals will be an additional service.[12] Such services would normally include teletext, subtitling, automatic video programming, stereo sound, data broadcasting and test signals. Additional services will not be available on frequencies used to transmit local delivery services[13] but they will be available on the other frequencies used by services licensed by the Commission.[14]

23.06 **Local delivery services.** This is a service which uses a telecommunications system[15] for the purpose of delivering simultaneously in two or

---

[5] Broadcasting Act 1990, s.2(6): a "relevant programme" means a television programme capable of being seen as a moving picture and does not include for example teletext which is an additional service.

[6] *Ibid.*, s.46(1). A "telecommunications system" is a system for the conveyance, through the agency of electric, magnetic, electro-magnetic, electro-chemical or electro-mechanical energy of speech, music and other sounds, signals serving for the impartation of any other matter otherwise than in the form of sounds and visual images or signals serving for the actuation of machinery or apparatus (for example fibre optic cable, telephone, microwave): *ibid.*, s.202(1) applying s.4(1), Telecommunications Act 1984.

[7] *Ibid.*, s.46(5). A person has a "business interest" in receiving programmes if he has an interest in receiving them for the purpose of his business trade profession or employment.

[8] *Ibid.*, s.46(1)(a).

[9] *Ibid.*, s.46(1)(b).

[10] *Ibid.*, s.46(1). See *post*, Chap. 27 for a fuller description of Licensable Programme Service.

[11] *Ibid.*, s.48(6): telecommunication signals means any of speech, music and other sounds, visual images, signals serving for the impartation (whether as between persons and persons, things and things or persons and things) of any matter otherwise than in the form of sounds or visual images, or signals serving for the actuation or control of machinery or apparatus.

[12] *Ibid.*, s.48(1).

[13] *Ibid.*, s.48(1)(a).

[14] *Ibid.*, s.48(2).

[15] See *ante*, para. 22.02, n.6.

more dwelling houses in the United Kingdom[16] any television broadcasting service, whether provided by a holder of a licence granted by the Commission, the BBC or the Welsh Authority,[17] any non-domestic satellite service,[18] or any licensable programme service.[19] It will also include any service of a particular class or description as specified by Order of the Secretary of State.[20]

2. Regulation of Independent Television Services

(a) *The regulatory duties of the Independent Television Commission ("The Commission")*

The Duty. The Commission has a duty to regulate all television programme services[21] which are provided from places within the United Kingdom irrespective of the method by which they are delivered.[22] This duty also extends to additional services which are provided from places in the United Kingdom[23] and local delivery services.[24]   **23.07**

The Nature of the Duty. The general duty imposed upon the Commission under the Broadcasting Act 1990 is to do "all they can to secure" that standards of broadcasting are maintained; to ensure that licences are only held by appropriate persons; to ensure that consumers are protected; and to control advertising.[25] Where in the Act the Commission is required to "do all that they can to secure," there is a duty imposed on it to use the powers granted to it by the 1990 Act to "adopt methods of working, or a system, which, in their opinion [is] best adapted to securing the requirements set out".[26] Where such a system has been instituted and operated by the Commission any challenge to the exercise by the Commission of its duties would involve satisfying the court that the Commission had misdirected themselves as to the duty, or, which would amount to the same thing, that no reasonable   **23.08**

---

[16] Broadcasting Act 1990, s.72(1)(a).
[17] *Ibid.*, s.72(2)(a).
[18] *Ibid.*, s.72(2)(b). For the meaning of "non-domestic satellite services", see *post*, para. 25.06 *et seq.*
[19] *Ibid.*, s.72(2)(c).
[20] *Ibid.*, s.72(1)(b).
[21] *Ibid.*, s.2. The duty does not extend to services broadcast by the BBC or Welsh Authority, s.2(1)(a).
[22] *Ibid.*, s.2(1)(a).
[23] *Ibid.*, s.2(1)(b).
[24] *Ibid.*, s.2(1).
[25] See, *e.g. ibid.*, ss.3(3), 5, 6, 7(1), 9.
[26] See *R. v. Independent Broadcasting Authority, ex parte Whitehouse, The Times,* April 4, 1985, C.A., discussing the analogous provision under the Broadcasting Act 1981, s.4.

body of members properly directing themselves as to the duty could have devised and operated the system in fact adopted.[27]

Further, the Commission is required, where the licensee fails to comply with any legitimate directions given by it, to take such action as is within its powers to ensure compliance. Such powers may include an escalating range from informal letters to formal direction not to repeat the programme, to the imposition of a financial penalty, the shortening of the licence, or ultimately the revocation of the licence. This follows from the mandatory requirement to do "all they can to secure" compliance. It is therefore not within the discretion of the Commission to, for example, allow an infringement of the consumer protection provisions of the 1990 Act without any action on its part.

Some support for this analysis can be obtained from the statements during the examination of the Bill in committee where it was said that the expression was deliberately all embracing so as to encourage "the Commission to use informal correspondence and meetings as well as the formal written licence conditions to ensure that the licensee understands and complies with the relevant requirements".[28]

23.09   The Commission is also under a duty to ensure that a wide range of services is available throughout the United Kingdom, and to ensure fair and effective competition in the provision of such services and services connected with them.[29] This duty is, however, framed in terms requiring the Commission to fulfil them *in the manner which they consider best calculated* to achieve those objectives. This discretion would appear to involve a high degree of subjective judgment. It follows that it will be difficult to mount an effective challenge on what may be called the conventional ground of *Wednesbury* unreasonableness.[30] Irrationality short of extremes of bad faith, improper motive or manifest absurdity will therefore be insufficient to mount an effective challenge.[31] Consequently, the Commission has a wide discretion in the manner in which it proceeds but it is submitted that it must nevertheless adopt a system which although it may be flexible must be capable of enabling it to fulfil this aspect of its duties.

23.10 **Summary of the Duties.** There are numerous aspects of the Commission's duties. Broadly speaking, the duties can be placed in the following categories:

(a) the duty to ensure that market forces are free to operate;

---

[27] See *Ibid.*
[28] David Mellor, Minister of State, Home Office: Standing Committee F, January 30, 1990.
[29] Broadcasting Act 1990, s.2(2).
[30] *Associated Picture Houses Ltd v. Wednesbury Corporation* [1948] 1 K.B. 223.
[31] *R. v. Parliamentary Commissioner, ex parte Dyer* [1994] 1 W.L.R. 626.

(b) the duty to ensure that licences are held by qualified persons;

(c) the duty to ensure consumers are protected;

(d) the duty to control advertising;

(e) the duty to monitor and carry out research.

The operation of market forces. The Act grants the Commission a wide   **23.11**
discretion in the allocation of licences. However, the Commission must
exercise that discretion to stimulate competition. There are two aspects
in which this is relevant: the provision of a wide range of services
throughout the United Kingdom and the free competition between
licence holders at any particular stage.

To boost consumer choice, the Commission is to licence services in a
manner which is best calculated to ensure that a wide range of services
is available throughout the United Kingdom.[32] This may in some circumstances require the Commission to require the provision of particular services to particular communities within a regional Channel 3
licence area.

Once a wide range of services has been provided, the Commission must   **23.12**
ensure that there is fair and effective competition in the provision of
such services and any services connected with them.[33] There are two
elements to the obligation. First, it will extend to intervening to protect
one licensee from the anti-competitive practices of one or more other
licensees. Second, it will also extend to intervening where a non-
licensee is adversely affected. Therefore, the Commission would, for
example, have the power to intervene in a complaint made by a satellite
broadcaster which wished to advertise on a regional Channel 3 service
but is prohibited from so doing by the licensee or a charge is made
which discriminates between the satellite service and other advertisers.

The Commission's competition obligations do not preclude the
powers or functions of the Director General of Fair Trading, the
Secretary of State or the Monopolies and Mergers Commission.[34]
Further, an aggrieved party would have a remedy in E.C. law if the
requirements of Articles 85 or 86 were made out.[35] In the case of an
aggrieved party being located in another Member State, it is submitted
that the more appropriate remedy may be a recourse to the provisions
of the Treaty of Rome.

---

[32] Broadcasting Act 1990, s.2(a)(i).
[33] *Ibid.*, s.2(2)(a)(ii).
[34] *Ibid.*, s.2(3).
[35] See Bellamy & Child *Common Market Law of Competition* (Sweet & Maxwell, 4th Ed.,
1993) for a discussion of the applicable principles.

23.13 Quality, tastes and interests. The Commission must ensure that in discharging their licensing duties the licensed services, taken as a whole, are of high quality and offer a wide range of programmes calculated to appeal to a variety of tastes and interests.[36] There is no definition of "high quality" and the term creates some difficulty. It can be contrasted with the formula used in the 1981 Act which required: "a high general standard in all respects (and in particular in respect of their content and quality)".[37] The reduction of the duty, from ensuring that there was a high standard in all respects, would suggest that the Commission will fulfil its duty if they ensures that when all the broadcast services are taken together the programme output is of high quality. Thus it would be a proper exercise of the Commissioner's power to balance the high quality of Channels 3 and 4 against the lower standards of other services if, in the final analysis, the programmes as a whole are of a high quality.

23.14 Qualified persons. The Commission must not grant a licence to provide any independent television service unless they are satisfied that the applicant is a "fit and proper person to hold it".[38] Where the licence has been granted and subsequently the person ceases to be fit and proper the Commission must do all they can to secure that the licence is no longer held by that person.[39] Thus the duty is present not only at the point at which the licence is awarded but is a continuing duty throughout the period of the licence.

The concept of a "fit and proper person" is undefined in the 1990 Act and is to be determined by the Commission. It is submitted that when considering whether a person is a fit and proper person the Commission is under a duty to act in the public interest in reaching a decision. Thus a person may not be a "disqualified person"[40] within the meaning of the Act but he may nevertheless fail to qualify as a fit and proper person because of his past business or personal history. However, in reaching a decision as to whether a person is fit and proper the Commission must act in accordance with the principles laid down in *Associated Provincial Picture Houses Ltd. v. Wednesbury Corporation*.[41]

23.15 The Commission are under a duty to do all they can to secure that a person does not become or remain a licence holder if he is a "disqualified person" in relation to that licence[42] and that any requirements imposed to prevent (a) an accumulation of interests in licensed services

---

[36] Broadcasting Act 1990, s.2(2)(b).
[37] Broadcasting 1981 Act, s.2(2)(b).
[38] Broadcasting Act 1990, s.3(3)(a).
[39] *Ibid.*, s.3(3)(b).
[40] See *post*, para. 32.02 *et seq.* for the meaning of "disqualified person".
[41] [1948] 1 K.B. 223.
[42] Broadcasting Act 1990, s.5(1)(a).

(b) an accumulation of controlling interests in both newspapers and licensed services and (c) the holding of licence by operators of public telecommunications system are complied with.[43]

Consumer protection requirements.[44] The Commission must "do all   **23.16** that they can to secure"[45] that every licensed service complies with the consumer protection requirements of the Act.[46] The consumer protection requirements are licence conditions.

There are two aspects of the duty. First, the Commission must do all that it can to ensure that programmes presented are impartial. Second, the Commission must do all that it can to ensure that the public is protected from violent and other offensive material.

Impartiality

As part of the duty to protect the consumer, the Commission must seek to ensure that the services provided are impartial. The Commission must draw up and review a code giving guidance as to the rules to be observed in connection with the application of the requirement for due impartiality in relation to a licensed services.[47]

The rules specified in the Code must take account: **23.17**

(a) that due impartiality should be preserved by a person providing a service as respects major matters of political or industrial controversy or relating to current public policy[48];

(b) that due impartiality is provided in a service (taken as a whole) as respects matters of political or industrial controversy or relating to public policy[49]; and

(c) the need to determine what constitutes a series of programmes.[50]

The rules in the Code must, in addition, indicate, to the extent that   **23.18** the Commission considers appropriate:

(a) what due impartiality does and does not require, either generally or in relation to particular circumstances[51];

---

[43] *Ibid.*, s.5(1). For a Full examination for these restrictions see *post*, Chap. 30.
[44] See *post*, Chap. 32.
[45] See *ante*, para. 23.08 as to the requirements of this duty.
[46] Broadcasting Act 1990, s.6(1).
[47] *Ibid.*, s.6(3)(a).
[48] *Ibid.*, s.6(5)(a).
[49] *Ibid.*, s.6(5)(a).
[50] *Ibid.*, s.6(5)(b). For meaning of "series of programmes" see *post*, para. 32.32.
[51] *Ibid.*, s.6(6)(a).

    (b) the ways in which due impartiality may be achieved in connection with programmes of particular descriptions[52];

    (c) the Code must indicate the timescale within which programmes must be included if impartiality is to be achieved over a series. This is to be achieved by requiring the Commission to indicate the period within which a programme should be included in a licensed service if its inclusion is intended to ensure that due impartiality is achieved for the purposes of section 6(1)(c)[53] in connection with that programme and any programme previously included in that service taken together.[54]

    (d) in relation to any inclusion in a licensed service of a series of programmes which is of a description specified in the Code the dates and times of the other programmes comprised in the series should be announced at the time when the first programme in the series is included in the service[55] or if that is not practicable, that advance notice should be given by other means of subsequent programmes in the series which include material intended to secure or assist in securing that due impartiality is achieved in connection with series as a whole.[56]

23.19   The Code must indicate that due impartiality does not require absolute neutrality on every issue or detachment from fundamental principles.[57]

Further, the Commission are "to do all that they can to secure"[58] that the provisions of the Code are observed.[59] As the provisions of the Code can be incorporated as licence conditions, this will amount to ensuring that the Commission utilises its enforcement powers.

As part of the requirement for impartiality, the Commission must "do all that they can to secure" that there are excluded all expressions of the views and opinions of the service provider on matters, other than the provision of programme services, which are of political or industrial controversy or relate to current public policy.[60]

---

[52] *Ibid.*, s.6(6)(b);

[53] *i.e.* for the purposes of preserving due impartiality in respects of matters of political or industrial controversy or relating to current public policy.

[54] Broadcasting Act 1990, s.6(6)(c).

[55] *Ibid.*, s.6(6)(d)(i).

[56] *Ibid.*, s.6(6)(d)(ii).

[57] *Ibid.*, s.6(6).

[58] As to the nature and extent of this duty, see *ante*, para. 23.08 and *post*, paras. 32.03–32.06.

[59] Broadcasting Act 1990, s.6(3)(b).

[60] *Ibid.*, s.6(4).

General Code for programmes

The Act envisages that the consumer will be protected from material   **23.20**
which is or may be offensive. To this end the Commission must draw
up and review a code giving guidance as to the rules to be observed
with respect to:

   (a) the showing of violence, or the inclusion of sounds suggestive of
       violence, in programmes included in licensed services, particu-
       larly when large numbers of young children and young persons
       may be expected to be watching the programmes[61]

   (b) the inclusion in such programmes of appeals[62]; and

   (c) such other matters concerning standards and practice for such
       programmes as the Commission may consider suitable for inclu-
       sion in code.[63] In considering what "other matters" ought to be
       included in the Code the Commission must have special regard
       to programmes included in licensed services in circumstances
       such that large numbers of children and young persons may be
       expected to be watching the programmes.[64]

When drawing up and revising the Code the Commission must take   **23.21**
into account the international obligations of the United Kingdom. More
specifically these international obligations will include the Council of
Europe's Convention on Transfrontier Television and the European
Community's Directive on broadcasting[65] and the Broadcasting Standards Council's code.[66] The Commission's duty with regard to the code
is to "do all that they can to secure" that the provisions of the Code are
observed in the provision of licensed services.[67]

General duties in relation to advertisements and sponsorship. The   **23.22**
Commission must "do all that they can to secure"[68] that a licensed service does not include:

   (a) any advertisement which is inserted by or on behalf of any body
       whose objects are wholly or mainly of a political nature[69];

---

[61] *Ibid.,* s.7(1)(a).
[62] *Ibid.,* s.7(1)(b).
[63] *Ibid.,* s.7(1)(c).
[64] *Ibid.,* s.7(2).
[65] Directive 89/522: [1989] O.J. L298/23.
[66] Broadcasting Act 1990, s.7(3).
[67] *Ibid.,* s.7(1). See also *ante, para.* 23.08 and *post,* paras. 32.03–32.06.
[68] See *ante,* para. 23.08 for nature and content of this duty.
[69] *Ibid.,* s.8(1), (2)(a). See *post,* para. 30.07, n.15 for the meaning of "body of a political
nature". This prohibition does not, however, prohibit the inclusion in a licensed
service of any party political broadcast which complies with the rules made by the
Commission for such broadcasts: *ibid.,* s.8(3).

(b) any advertisement which is directed towards any political end[70]; or

(c) any advertisement which has any relation to any industrial dispute, other than an advertisement of a public service nature inserted by or on behalf of a government department.[71]

It is clear that in (a) and (b) there are two tests for the prohibition of advertising. The first, in section 8(2)(a)(i), refers to the identity of the advertiser. The second, in section 8(2)(ii), refers to the intent and content of the advertisement. A body may find a general ban imposed upon it under section 8(2)(a)(i) because its objects are wholly or mainly of a political nature.

It is noteworthy that this prohibition applies whether or not the body proposes advertisements which have a political end: the fact that the body is of a political nature without more engages the prohibition. A body which does not come within the first category will come within section 8(2)(a)(ii) where it seeks to promote a political cause in the form of a particular advertisement.

A number of difficulties arise as to the meaning of "objects", "wholly or mainly" and "political".

"Objects" is capable of meaning, by analogy with corporate bodies, the trade or purpose, as opposed to the powers, of the body as set down in its governing document or constitution. However, section 201 of the Act envisages that a "body" is capable of meaning a "body of persons whether incorporated or not and includes a partnership". Thus, it is submitted that, "objects" in the context of section 8(2) of the 1990 Act is also capable of meaning the objects of that "body of persons" as can be discerned from its activities where its "objects" have not been recorded, formally or otherwise, in a document.

The phrase "wholly or mainly" qualifies the words which immediately precede and follow them and are thus of some importance within the context of the prohibition imposed on a licensed service. There is no difficulty in the word "wholly" but the use of the word "mainly" is not without difficulty. Although, in some cases "mainly" has been interpreted to mean more than half[72] this is an unsatisfactory test when dealing with unquantifiable subject matter such as objects.

It is submitted that the correct approach to the resolution of the meaning of "mainly" is to be found by analogy with the manner in which the main objects of corporate bodies are determined.[73] In some

---

[70] *Ibid.*, s.8(2)(a)(ii). See n.68.
[71] *Ibid.*, s.8(2)(a)(iii).
[72] See, *e.g. Fawcett Properties Ltd. v. Buckingham County Council* [1961] A.C. 636 at 669, H.L.
[73] See *North of England Zoological Society v. Chester Rural District Council* [1959] 3 All E.R. 116.

cases it may be clear from the constitution or governing document of the body what are its main objects. In which case there will be no need to go further. If, however, there is any ambiguity or the objects cannot for whatever reason be so discerned it is permissible to look at the actual activities of the body to construe the document or, in the absence of a governing document, to ascertain its main objects.

The meaning of "political" is not defined by the 1990 Act. In the committee stage of the Broadcasting Bill, David Mellor stated that "political" covers any material that is aimed at securing a change in some aspect of public policy.[74] This would appear to be too wide in definition in that, prima facie, it is capable of encompassing any matter which does not depend upon the policy of the government or statute.[75] This is to be contrasted with the definition of "political", as an objective, to be found in the speech of Lord Diplock in *Cheng v. Pentonville Prison (Governor)*[76] where he stated:

> "Policies are about government. "Political" as descriptive of an objective to be achieved must, in my view, be confined to the object of overthrowing or changing the government of a state or inducing it to change its policy or escaping from its territory the better so to do."

This statement was in the context of a case concerning extradition. Therefore some caution must be observed in seeking to apply it as a general definition. It would appear to be too narrow in that if policies are about government political as an objective is not confined to the objects enumerated by Lord Diplock but would also include the object of inducing a government to adopt a policy in an area in which it hitherto had no policy. Thus a body whose objects are wholly or mainly of a political nature may include bodies which are not political parties, or which do not have political objects in the narrower sense of party political objects, but which act as pressure groups having as its whole or main object the advancement of the interests it represents by inducing changes in government policy or the adoption by government of particular policies or by the enactment of statutes.

The Commission must also ensure that in the acceptance of advertisements for inclusion in a licensed service there must be no unreasonable discrimination either against or in favour of any particular advertiser.[77] Thus, it would be unreasonable for a Channel 3 licence holder to refuse to accept advertisements from a satellite channel which advertises the **23.23**

[74] David Mellor, Minister of State, Home Office Committee F, col. 429.
[75] See, e.g. *In the Estate of Hall, Hall v. Knight & Baxter* [1914] P. 1 at 5, C.A.
[76] [1973] 2 All E.R. 204.
[77] Broadcasting Act 1990, s.8(2)(b).

latter channel. There is no prohibition in the 1990 Act in respect of sponsorship.

However, the Commission is under a duty to ensure that a licence holder does not, without the previous approval of the Commission, include a programme which is sponsored by any person whose business consists wholly or mainly in the manufacture or supply of a product or service which the licence holder is prohibited from advertising by reason of the Commission's Advertising and Sponsorship Code.[78] There is no prohibition on religious advertising but such advertising would have to satisfy the consumer protection requirements.

Advertising and Sponsorship Code

23.24   In an analogous manner to the duty to draw up consumer protection codes, the Commission must draw up and review an advertising and sponsorship code and do all that they can to ensure that the provisions of the Code are observed in the provision of licensed services.[79] Unlike the other codes, prior to drawing up and publishing the Code the Commission must consult, as it thinks fit, with:

(a) the Radio Authority[80];

(b) every Commission licence holder except a local delivery services licence holder[81];

(c) bodies or persons as may appear to the Commission to represent viewers, advertisers and professional organisations qualified to give advice in relation to the advertising of particular products.[82]

The Act recognises that there are commercial interests in the contents of advertising and that those interests must be heard before regulation is imposed.

23.25   The Code must set out rules:

(a) governing standards and practice in advertising and in the sponsorship of programmes[83]; and

(b) prescribing the advertisements and methods of advertising or sponsorship to be prohibited, or to be prohibited in particular circumstances.[84]

The Code may make different provision for different kinds of

---

[78] *Ibid.*, s.8(3).
[79] *Ibid.*, s.9(1)(b).
[80] *Ibid.*, s.9(2)(a).
[81] *Ibid.*, s.9(2)(b).
[82] *Ibid.*, s.9(2)(c).
[83] *Ibid.*, s.9(1)(a)(i).
[84] *Ibid.*, s.9(1)(a)(ii).

licensed services.[85] The Commission therefore has a discretion to vary the degree of control it exercises over the advertisements contained in different kinds of services. In drawing up, revising and enforcing the Code the Commission must take account of such international obligations as the Secretary of State may notify to it.[86]

The Commission may impose methods of control of advertisements **23.26** or methods of advertising or sponsorship which go beyond the requirements imposed by the Code.[87] These methods of control include a power to give directions to a licence holder with respect to the classes and descriptions of advertisements and methods of advertising sponsorship to be excluded or to be excluded in particular circumstances[88] or the exclusion of a particular advertisement, or its exclusion in particular circumstances.[89] Additionally, the Commission may also give directions to persons holding any class of licences with respect to the times when advertisements are to be allowed[90] but in so doing it must take into account the international obligations of the United Kingdom.[91] Any or all of these directions may be either general or specific and qualified or unqualified.

Where the directions relate to the times when advertisements are to **23.27** be allowed such directions may relate to the maximum amount of time to be given to advertisements in any hour or other periods,[92] the minimum interval which must elapse between any two periods given over to advertisements and the number of such periods to be allowed in any programme or in any hour or day,[93] and the exclusion of advertisements from a specified part of a licensed service.[94] Such directions may make different provisions for different parts of the day, different days of the week, different types of programmes or for other differing circumstances.[95]

Monitoring of programmes. In order to assist the Commission in main- **23.28** taining supervision over the programmes included in the licensed services the Commission may make recordings of those programmes or

---

[85] *Ibid.*, s.9(1).
[86] *Ibid.*, s.9(9): these international obligations are currently contained in the Council of Europe's Convention on Transfrontier Television and the European Community's Directive on Broadcasting, 89/522: [1989] O.J. L298/23.
[87] *Ibid.*, s.9(5).
[88] *Ibid.*, s.9(6)(a).
[89] *Ibid.*, s.9(6)(b).
[90] *Ibid.*, s.9(7).
[91] *Ibid.*, s.9(9). See also *ante*, para. 23.24, n.80.
[92] *Ibid.*, s.9(8)(a).
[93] *Ibid.*, s.9(8)(b).
[94] *Ibid.*, s.9(8)(c).
[95] *Ibid.*, s.9(8).

any part of such programmes.[96] To further assist it in its regulatory duties and the BCC and the BSC in the consideration of complaints the Commission is under a duty to include licence conditions requiring the following:

   (a) the licence holder must retain for a period not exceeding 90 days, a recording of every programme included in the service[97];

   (b) at the request of the Commission to produce to the Commission such recording for examination or reproduction[98];

   (c) at the request of the Commission, to produce to them any script or transcript of a programme included in the licensed service which he is able to produce.[99]

23.29   Section 11(3) expressly provides that the power to make and use recordings of programmes for the purposes of its regulatory duties does not imply a duty on the part of the Commission to preview programmes before transmission. The general scheme of the Act places the obligations on the licence holder to ensure that its programme service complies with the licence conditions and Codes. The Commission's regulatory powers come into effect after an offending programme has been included in a programme service. However, if it should come to the Commission's attention that an offending programme is to be transmitted by the licensee there does not appear to be any provision of the Act which would prevent the Commission from intervening to preview the programme before transmission. Indeed, it is arguable that in such circumstances the Commission will not have done all that it can to secure the observance of consumer protection requirements if it does not preview the programme to ensure that it is not in breach of the Commission's code.[1]

23.30   **Audience research.** The Commission is under a duty to make arrangements for ascertaining:

   (a) the state of public opinion concerning programmes included in a licensed services[2] and any effects of those programmes on the attitudes or behaviour of viewers[3]; and

   (b) for the purpose of assisting the Commission in the performance of their duties in relation to Channels 3, 4 and 5 and for ascertain-

---

[96] *Ibid.,* s.11(1).
[97] *Ibid.,* s.11(2)(a).
[98] *Ibid.,* s.11(2)(b).
[99] *Ibid.,* s.11(2)(b).
[1] See *ante,* para. 23.08 and *post,* paras. 32.03–32.06.
[2] Broadcasting Act 1990, s.12(1)(a)(i).
[3] *Ibid.,* s.12(1)(a)(ii).

ing the types of programmes that viewers would like to be included in licensed services.[4]

These arrangements must ensure that so far as reasonably practicable, any research in pursuance of the foregoing objectives is undertaken by people who are neither members nor employees of the Commission[5] and include provision for full consideration by the Commission of the results of the research.[6]

(i) *Powers and duties of Commission in relation to licences*

Power to vary licences. The Commission has power to vary the licence   **23.31**
period by notice provided that the licence holder (in an analogy with the law of contract) consents.[7] However such an agreement does not affect the power of the Commission to vary the licence without the consent of the licence holder under its powers under section 41(1)(b)[8] of the Act nor does it affect licence conditions requiring the payment of the cash bid or additional payments for Channels 3 and 5, domestic satellite services and additional services.[9] Variation may, for example, be imposed as a penalty for a breach of a licence condition: in such a case the consent of the licence holder is not required. The licence may also be varied where it is agreed that a variation is preferable to any other penalty that the Commission may wish to impose.

Consent of the Commission required for transfer of licence. A licence   **23.32**
granted to any person is not transferable without the previous consent in writing of the Commission.[10] The consent of the Commission may only be given if two conditions are satisfied. First, the Commission must be satisfied that the proposed transferee would be in a position to comply with all the pre-existing licence conditions for the remainder of the licence period.[11] Second, the prospective transferee must be a fit and proper person to hold the licence.[12] Where these two conditions are satisfied it is difficult to envisage circumstances in which the Commission would be entitled to refuse permission to transfer the licence

---

[4] *Ibid.*, s.12(1)(b).
[5] *Ibid.*, s.12(2)(a).
[6] *Ibid.*, s.12(2)(b).
[7] *Ibid.*, s.(3)(4)(a).
[8] Such powers could only be exercised after giving the licence holder a reasonable opportunity of replying to the matters complained of. This rule would include the provision of all the information on which the Commission based its actions and the opportunity to meet any points raised by the Commission on the basis of that information.
[9] Broadcasting Act 1990, s.3(5).
[10] *Ibid.*, s.3(6).
[11] *Ibid.*, s.3(6). See Clause 22 of the Standard Form of Regional Channel 3 Licence.
[12] *Ibid.*, s.3(3). See also *ante*, para. 23.14 *et seq.* as to meaning of "fit and proper person". See also Clause 34(3)(g) of the Standard Form of Regional Channel 3 Licence.

and any such refusal would be liable to challenge on grounds of rationality.

(ii) *Powers of Commission to impose general licence conditions*

23.33   **General scheme of regulatory powers of Commission.** The licence, on a purely contractual analysis, is the record of the basis upon which the licensee tendered for the licence. The licence is in part a contract between the parties and will therefore be subject to the normal rules as to its existence and enforceability.

The Commission has broad powers to draw up and include conditions in licences for the purpose of exercising its statutory functions. The overriding principle in relation to licence condition is that the Commission may include those conditions which appear to be appropriate having regard to the duties imposed on it, or the licence holder, by or under the 1990 Act.[13] These provisions apply to all regulated services. Any provision in the Act which specifies particular conditions which may or must be included by the Commission in a licence is not to be taken as a derogation from this general power.[14]

Thus, for example, the Act requires particular terms to be included in a licence but in addition to those specific terms the Commission may impose such additional terms as will enable it to devise and institute a system which enables it to ensure that the activities of the licensees reflect the requirements of the Act. Thus, for example, under Clause 18(8) of the Standard Form of Regional Channel 3 licence the Commission is entitled to require a licence holder to attend meetings with the Commission at such intervals as it may require to conduct periodic reviews of the performance by the licensee of his obligations under the Licence. The general power enables the Commission to have a certain degree of flexibility in the carrying out of its duties and to impose terms which are able to meet changing conditions in a rapidly changing business.

(b) *Government control over licensed services*

23.34   The Secretary of State or any other Crown Minister may, where he considers it necessary or expedient, issue a notice requiring the Commission to direct the holders of any licence specified in the notice to publish in their licensed service, at the times specified in the notice, a specified announcement, with or without visual images of any picture, scene or object mentioned in the announcement[15] or to direct the holders of any licence specified in the notice to refrain from including in

---

[13] *Ibid.*, s.4(1)(a).
[14] *Ibid.*, s.4(6).
[15] *Ibid.*, s.10(1).

the programmes included in their licensed services any matter or classes of matter specified in the notice.[16] Where such a notice is given the Commission must comply.[17]

However, when the licence holder publishes the announcement he may announce that he is doing so as a result of a direction.[18] The discretionary power of the Secretary of State to give directions to the broadcasting authorities is subject to judicial review. However, the courts may not substitute their own views for the informed view of the Secretary of State. What the court is permitted to do is to consider whether the Secretary of State has taken into account all relevant matters and has ignored irrelevant matters. If these conditions are satisfied, then the court can only interfere by way of judicial review if the decision is irrational or perverse. This power was invoked by the Government to impose a prohibition upon the broadcasting of statements by specified terrorist groups. Its use was challenged in *R. v. Secretary of State for the Home Department, ex parte Brind*[19] where it was held that the Secretary of State had not exceeded his discretion nor acted unreasonably in making the proscription order.

Listed Events

The Commission is under a duty to do all that it can to secure that any **23.35** programme which consists of or includes the whole or any part of a listed event is not included on pay-per-view terms in any service licensed by it.[20] For these purposes a listed event is a sporting or other event of national interest which is included on a list drawn up by the Secretary of State. A programme is included in any service on pay-per-view if any payments made by subscribers to the service will or may vary according to whether the programme is or is not actually received by them.[21]

The listed events at the time of writing are:

- Cricket Test Matches involving England;
- The Derby;
- The Grand National;
- The FIFA World Cup Final;
- The F.A. Cup Final;
- The Olympic Games;

---

[16] *Ibid.*, s.10(3).
[17] *Ibid.*, s.10(1), (3).
[18] *Ibid.*, s.10(2).
[19] *R. v. Secretary of State for the Home Department, ex parte Brind* [1991] 2 W.L.R. 588. See also *post*, para. 32.20 *et seq.*
[20] Broadcasting Act 1990, s.182.
[21] *Ibid.* s.182(2).

- Finals Weekend of Wimbledon;
- The Scottish F.A. Cup Final (Scotland only).

Currently, there is no pay-per-view service available to viewers, but it is envisaged that, in the near future, this will become a significant aspect of broadcasting.

CHANNELS 3, 4 AND 5

1. Channel 3

Establishment of Channel 3. The Commission is required by the Broad-   **24.01**
casting Act 1990 to do all that it can to secure the provision of a nationwide system of television broadcasting services, structured on a
regional basis,[1] to be known as Channel 3.[2]

Regional Channel 3 service. The Act grants the Commission a dis-   **24.02**
cretion to determine the geographical area for each regional service[3] but
the discretion is limited to the extent that the Commission cannot
designate the whole of either England or Scotland as the area in which a
Channel 3 service will broadcast.[4] In the exercise of its discretion the
Commission has maintained and granted licences in respect of the 15
regional areas which existed prior to the 1990 Act.

Commission discretion. The Act envisages that Channel 3 will be rep-   **24.03**
resentative of various sectors of the population. That representative
capacity will theoretically extend to the provision of services to individual communities in so far as the Commission decides that provision is
necessary in the exercise of its discretion. Two points arise.
    First, the Commission in exercising its discretion will be forced to
analyse what the service should represent. That analysis has three

---

[1] Broadcasting Act 1990, s.14(6).
[2] *Ibid.*, s.14(1).
[3] *Ibid.*, s.14(2).
[4] *Ibid.*, s.14(7).

aspects. First, as a matter of definition, what a community is (or could be) poses some difficulty. Although it will be a simple matter to decide that (for example) Welsh speakers in a certain area count as a "community".

However, what other groups in the area would count as a community? The analogous problems arise in Race Relations legislation over the definition of "ethnic group". Secondly, even if there are groups that are readily identifiable as communities, the Commission will have to decide how large a community is to be before it merits its own programming. Thirdly, it is submitted that some regard must be had to the needs of the community. If the test were to be purely numerical that would erode the concept of representative television by giving programmes to those who (as a result of, *inter alia*, ratings concerns) are already catered for. It follows that any test which is devised will be as much based on policy considerations as demographics.

24.04   Fourthly, the allocation will be judicially reviewable. However, in order to obtain leave to move for judicial review, the applicants will have to demonstrate that they as a group possess sufficient *locus standi* to raise the challenge. On one view (see *R. v. Secretary of State for the Environment ex parte Rose Theatre Trust*[5]) mere pressure groups do not possess *locus standi* to maintain an application for judicial review. It would follow that it is possible to envisage a certain type of community which would not be defined as a community by the Commission and not possess sufficient *locus standi* for a judicial review challenge.

24.05 Establishment of Channel 5. The Commission is under a duty to "ensure that they do all they can to secure" the provision of a Channel 5 service for such minimum area of the United Kingdom as they shall determine.[6] In determining the minimum area for which Channel 5 is to be provided the Commission must so far as is reasonably practicable make the most effective use of the frequencies on which the service is to be provided.[7] Whether or not the provision of a service is reasonably practicable is a question of fact. It therefore follows that the duty under section 28(1) will be eroded by the Commission's conclusions as to what is reasonably practicable. Further, the duty will vary over time. As the duty under section 28(1) is a continuing duty, the Commission will be obliged to reconsider the position as and when the resources and/or technology require it.

---

[5] [1990] 1 Q.B. 504.
[6] Broadcasting Act 1990, s.28(1).
[7] *Ibid.*, s.28(2).

(a) *Licensing of Channel 3 and 5 services*

Procedure to be applied in awarding Channel 3 and 5 licences

Consideration of applications. The Commission must undertake a two   **24.06**
stage process in awarding and renewing licences.[8] First, the applicant
must demonstrate that its service passes the quality threshold. Second,
the Commission must, subject to the exercise of its discretion where
exceptional circumstances exist, award the licence to the highest cash
bid.

The quality threshold

Passing the quality threshold is a condition precedent to the Com-   **24.07**
mission's consideration of whether to award an applicant a licence on
the basis of his cash bid.[9] The quality threshold has two limbs. First, the
proposed service must comply with either the regional or the national
requirements set out in section 16(2) and (3) ("the first limb")[10] and
secondly that the applicant must demonstrate that he would be able to
maintain that service throughout the duration of the licence ("the
second limb").[11] The Commission has a discretion to adjust the criteria
for meeting the quality threshold having regard to the nature of the service to be provided.[12] Therefore the Commission has vires to dispense
with, for example, the news and current affairs requirements, where a
Channel 5 breakfast licence holder is concerned.

The first limb. The Commission must be satisfied that an applicant's   **24.08**
service accords a "sufficient amount of time" to news and current
affairs, programmes, non-news and current affairs programmes,
religious programmes and regional programmes[13]: the regional programmes taken as a whole must be calculated to appeal to a variety of
tastes and interests.[14] Additionally a "proper proportion" of programmes included in the service must be of a European origin and 25
per cent. of the time allocated to the broadcasting of qualifying programmes in the service is to be allocated to independent productions.[15]
In deciding whether an applicant's proposed service complies with the
first limb the Commission must take into account any representations

---

[8] *Ibid.,* s.20(4)(a)(ii).
[9] *Ibid.,* s.16(1).
[10] *Ibid.,* s.16(1)(a).
[11] *Ibid.,* s.16(b).
[12] *Ibid.,* ss.16(3), 29(3).
[13] *Ibid.,* s.16.
[14] *Ibid.,* s.16(2)(f).
[15] *Ibid.,* s.16(2).

made to it by the public following the publication of the details of the application.[16]

24.09 European programmes. A "proper proportion" is not defined. However, the European Directive on Broadcasting[17] specifies that Member States must "where practicable and by appropriate means" ensure that broadcasters reserve for "European works" the greater proportion of their transmission time excluding the time allocated for news, sports events, games and advertising and teletext services.[18] The greater proportion is to be achieved progressively on the basis of suitable criteria. The requirements in the Directive and the European Convention on Transfrontier Television are to be put into practice by the Commission and the BBC. The Directive requires that when a majority of European programming cannot be achieved, the proportion of European work be achieved by a State's broadcasters should not fall below the 1988 level.

24.10   A European work is one falling in any of the following categories:

(a) works originating from Member States of the European Union;

(b) works originating from European countries who are party to the European Convention on Transfrontier Television and which are:
   (i) made by one or more producers established in one or more of such states; or
   (ii) production of the works is supervised and actually controlled by one or more producers established in two or more of those states; or
   (iii) the contribution of co-producers of those states to the co-production costs is preponderant and the co-production is not controlled by one or more producers established outside those states;

(c) works originating from other European countries made exclusively or in co-production with producers established in one or more European Union States by producers established in one or more non-E.U. countries with which the European Union will conclude agreements in accordance with the procedures in the Treaty if those works are mainly made with authors and workers residing in one or more European States.

24.11   Works which are not European works within the above definition but made mainly with authors and workers residing in one or more states of the European Union may nevertheless qualify as European to an extent

---

[16] Pursuant to Broadcasting Act 1990, s.15(6)(b).
[17] Directive 89/552: [1989] O.J. L298/23.
[18] *Ibid.*, Art. 4(1).

corresponding to the proportion of the contribution of European Union
co-producers to the total production costs.[19]

Application of the first limb. "A sufficient amount of time" is given no
definition. The expression implies the minimum necessary to pass the
quality threshold. The requirement must, however, be read in conjunction with the obligation to ensure that the programmes are of high quality (see the Commission general duty in section 2(2)(b)). Three
difficulties arise.

    First, the precise relationship between the two elements is unclear.
On one reading, the Commission could decide that all programmes in a
certain category must be of high quality. However, it is submitted that
"high quality" is, by definition, a standard that cannot be reached in all
the programmes that are broadcast. It follows that the Act envisages that
there will be a number of "flagship programmes" and the rest of the
output will be of good but not high quality. That reading would be
consistent with the underlying thesis of the Act that the market will
determine what programming is acceptable.

    Secondly, the test is extremely subjective. Taken across the broad
spectrum of consumers the test could have a multiplicity of meanings.
As the Commission is one of the bodies with the most experience in the
area, it follows that the Commission may well be the sole arbiter of the
standard required. Therefore, the Act appears to have made the Commission both the creator of the standard and the regulatory authority
applying that standard.

    Thirdly, the Commission's decision is judicially reviewable. How-
ever, it will be difficult to mount a successful challenge to the Commission's decision. The Commission has a very wide discretion to
apply a subjective test as it sees fit. Further, the Commission is a benchmark authority on whether or not programming reaches the required
standard. Therefore, it is unlikely that a rejected applicant will be able
to persuade a court that the Commission's decision should be quashed
because it failed to take into account relevant facts. It is submitted that
irrationality, short of extremes of bad faith, improper motive or manifest absurdity, will be insufficient to mount an effective challenge.

    The first limb only lays down content requirements in three areas: the
need to cater for a wide variety of taste and interests, the inclusion in
the programmes of a suitable proportion of European programmes and
the independent production quota. The rationale for these requirements is firstly the Commission's obligation to take into account its

24.12

24.13

24.14

---

[19] *Ibid.,* Art. 4.

international obligations on programming content.[20] Both the Council of Europe's Convention on Transfrontier Television and the European Community's Directive on Broadcasting require that the majority of programming should be European where practicable.

Secondly, Channel 3 services are designed to be regional and therefore more responsive to local needs than a national service. Therefore the applicant must broadcast material which caters for the local audience and must state[21] what regional facilities he would use. The specialised and responsive nature of Channel 3 services is emphasised by the power given to the Commission to relax the requirements where a national Channel 3 service is to be provided. Only those requirements which the Commission deems to be necessary will apply to the national services.[22]

24.15 **The Second limb.** The Commission must be satisfied that the applicant would be able to maintain the service throughout the period for which the licence would be in force.[23] The grounds on which the Commission makes that decision are unspecified. This will require the Commission to consider the nature of the licence service and the projected revenues against its own estimates. It therefore will again be a matter for the exercise of the Commission's discretion in reaching a decision on rational grounds.

24.16 **Highest cash bid.** The general principle is that the Commission awards the licence to the applicant who has satisfied both limbs of the quality threshold and submitted the highest cash bid.[24] The requirement to take the highest bid is subject to two provisos relating to exceptional circumstances and the source of the funds for the licence.

24.17 **Exceptional circumstances.** The Commission may disregard the requirement to award to the highest cash bidder and award the licence to an applicant who has not submitted the highest bid if it appears to it that there are "exceptional circumstances", which make it appropriate for it to award the licence to it.[25] The Act does not define "exceptional circumstances" but it does provide an instance of when this might occur. The Act specifically provides that the Commission may award the licence to an applicant who has not submitted the highest bid where it appears to the Commission that the quality of his proposed service is

---

[20] Broadcasting Act 1990, s.16(4).
[21] Pursuant to Broadcasting Act 1990, s.15(3)(e).
[22] *Ibid.*, s.16(3).
[23] *Ibid.*, s.16(1)(b).
[24] *Ibid.*, s.17(1).
[25] *Ibid.*, s.17(1).

exceptionally high[26] and is also substantially higher than that of the highest bidder or bidders.[27] The decision to apply this element of the exceptional circumstances rule will again depend upon a subjective analysis of the quality of proposed service. As such, it will be difficult to challenge.[28] Further, the Commission's discretion to apply or disapply the exceptional circumstances requirement is unfettered by its previous decisions to apply or disapply the requirement.[29]

Source of funds not in the public interest. The Commission may not **24.18** grant a licence to a party which it has grounds for suspecting proposes to fund the instalments of the cash bid[30] and the appropriate qualifying percentage of qualifying revenue[31] or for otherwise financing[32] the proposed service from sources of finance such that it would not be in the public interest for a licence to be awarded to that person. In such circumstances the Commission must refer the application to the Secretary of State together with a copy of all documents submitted to it by the applicant[33] and a summary of its deliberations on the application.[34] The Secretary of State must approve the grant unless he is satisfied that the source of funds is such that it would not be in the public interest for the licence to be awarded.[35]

Grant of the licence. Any licence granted to the applicant will be subject **24.19** to two sets of conditions. First, the body of the licence at clause 7 and following rehearses the statutory provisions governing programme content. Clause 7 repeats the consumer protection requirements, clause 9 requires the licence holder to broadcast high quality news services which are to be provided by a nominated news provider, clause 12 requires the licence holder to ensure that sufficient provision is made for subtitling for the deaf and clause 15 imposes advertising control provisions under E.C. and domestic law on the holder. These conditions cannot be varied by the Commission unless the licence itself is varied. If these conditions are breached, the Commission may require the licence holder to broadcast a correction or apology. Failure to do so will result in a financial penalty being imposed or the licence being revoked.

---

[26] *Ibid.*, s.17(4)(a).
[27] *Ibid.*, s.17(4)(b)(i), (ii).
[28] See *R. v. Independent Television Committee, ex parte Television South West, The Times,* March 30, 1992.
[29] Broadcasting Act 1990, s.17(4).
[30] *Ibid.*, s.17(7)(a).
[31] *Ibid.*, s.17(7)(a).
[32] *Ibid.*, s.17(7)(b).
[33] *Ibid.*, s.17(5)(a)(i).
[34] *Ibid.*, s.17(5)(ii).
[35] *Ibid.*, s.17(5).

24.20   Secondly, the first part of the Annex to the licence includes conditions reflecting the proposals submitted by the licensee as to the service to be provided as set out in the information supplied to the Commission. The conditions will be subject to modification by the Commission with the consent of the licensee as permitted under section 33 of the Act, to take account of networking arrangements adopted before the start of broadcasting. Section 5(2) of the Act gives the Commission the discretionary power to make the grant of a licence conditional upon an applicant who is not fully in conformity with any requirements imposed by or under Parts III to V of Schedule 2[36] to the Act taking steps to bring himself within those requirements.

Fees payable by a licence holder

24.21   **Commission fee.** The Commission may include conditions requiring the payment by a licence holder to the Commission (whether on the grant of the licence or at such times afterwards as may be determined by or under the licence or both) of a fee or fees of an amount to be determined by the Commission.[37] The amount of any fee must be in accordance with a tariff from time to time fixed, and which represents what appears to the Commission to be an appropriate contribution of the holder of a licence towards meeting the sums which the Commission regards as necessary to at least enable it to meet its obligations and discharge its functions under the Act.[38]

Additional payments

24.22   In addition to the Commission fee, a Channel 3 licence must include conditions requiring the licence holder to pay to the Commission additional payments that fall into two categories.

24.23   **The cash bid payments.** A licence holder must pay in respect of the first complete calendar year falling within the period for which the licence is in force, the amount specified in his cash bid[39] and in respect of each subsequent year falling wholly or partly within that period the cash bid as increased by the "appropriate percentage".[40]

---

[36] For the terms of these provisions see *post*, Chap. 30.
[37] Broadcasting Act 1990, s.4(1)(b).
[38] *Ibid.*, s.4(3).
[39] *Ibid.*, s.19(1)(b).
[40] *Ibid.*, s.19(1)(b). The "appropriate percentage", in any relevant year is the percentage corresponding to the percentage increase between the Retail Prices Index published by the Central Statistical Office of the Chancellor of the Exchequer for the November in the year preceding the first complete calendar year falling within the period for which the licence is in force and the retail prices index for the November in the year preceding the relevant year: Broadcasting Act 1990, s.19(10).

Qualifying revenue payments. The third category of payment by a   **24.24**
licence holder is an amount representing such percentage of the
qualifying revenue for that accounting period as was specified in the
notice proposing to grant a Channel 3 licence.[41] For these purposes the
"qualifying revenue" for any accounting period of the licence holder is
calculated by reference to all payment received by him or by any connected person in consideration of the inclusion in Channel 3 service in
that period of advertisements or other programmes[42] or in respect of
charges made in that period for the reception of programmes included
in that service.[43]

There are four anti-avoidance elements to the calculation. First, any   **24.25**
payment to a person connected with the licence holder qualifies.
Secondly, if the licence holder obtains an indemnity as opposed to
direct payments,[44] from an advertiser to cover the qualifying revenue
payments made to the Commission the amount of that indemnity must
be taken into account in calculating the qualifying revenue payments.[45]
Thirdly, any sums received as a result of a sponsorship arrangement
with an advertising agent[46] representing a payment by the advertiser
minus any commission gained by the agent (subject to any amounts
over 15 per cent. being irrecoverable)[47] must be included.[48] Fourthly, if
the licence holder derives, in relation to any programme included in a
Channel 3 service, any financial benefit (whether direct or indirect)
from payments made by any person, by way of sponsorship, for the
purpose of defraying or contributing towards the costs incurred or to be
incurred in connection with that programme, that benefit must be
included in the qualifying revenue for that accounting period.[49]

The Channel 3 licence includes conditions enabling the Commission   **24.26**
to estimate before the beginning of an accounting period the amount
due for that period as a percentage of qualifying revenue[50] and requires
the licence holder to pay the estimated amount by monthly instalments
throughout that period.[51] The Commission is authorised to revise any
estimate on one or more occasions and to adjust the instalments payable

---

[41] *Ibid.*, s.19(1)(c).
[42] *Ibid.*, s.19(2)(a).
[43] *Ibid.*, s.19(2)(b).
[44] The direct payments would have to have been pursuant to s.19(2)(a) to be caught by
this provision.
[45] *Ibid.*, s.19(3).
[46] *Ibid.*, s.19(4)(b).
[47] *Ibid.*, s.19(5).
[48] *Ibid.*, s.19(4).
[49] *Ibid.*, s.19(6).
[50] *Ibid.*, s.19(7)(a).
[51] *Ibid.*, s.19(7).

by the licence holder to take account of the revised estimate[52] and providing for the adjustment of any over or under payment.[53]

24.27   **Disputes as to qualifying revenue.** The Commission is under a duty to draw up and from time to time review and publish a statement setting out the principles to be followed in ascertaining the qualifying revenue[54] for any accounting period or any year. The statement may set out different principles for different licence holders.[55] In the event of any disagreement as to the amount of the qualifying revenue for an accounting period or any year or the amount of any qualifying revenue payment or instalment of such payment the amount will be as determined by the Commission.[56] Any determination made by the Commission with regard to this matter is only subject to challenge by judicial review.[57]

Duration and renewal of Channel 3 licences

24.28   **Duration.** Subject to the Commission's power of revocation, a Channel 3 licence continues in force for 10 years.[58]

24.29   **Renewal.** An application for the renewal of a licence can be made by the licence holder no earlier than four years before the date on which it would otherwise cease to be in force and no later than the "relevant date".[59] The "relevant date" is the date which the Commission determines as that by which it would need to publish a proposal notice pursuant to section 15(1) if it were to grant, as from the date on which that licence would expire, a fresh licence to provide the Channel 3 service formerly provided under that licence.[60]
         On application, the Commission may only refuse to renew if it is not satisfied that the service provided by the licence holder would, if the licence were to be renewed, comply with the conditions included in the licence as originally imposed or as varied[61] by the Commission or meet the quality threshold[62] or where it proposes to restructure Channel 3[63] or where the licensee's source of finance would be against the public

---

[52] *Ibid.*, s.19(8)(a).
[53] *Ibid.*, s.19(8)(b).
[54] *Ibid.*, Sched. 7, Part I, para. 1(1).
[55] *Ibid.*, Sched. 7, Part I, para. 1(2).
[56] *Ibid.*, Sched. 7, Part I, para. 2(1).
[57] *Ibid.*, Sched. 7, Part I, para. 2(2).
[58] *Ibid.*, s.20(1).
[59] *Ibid.*, s.20(2).
[60] *Ibid.*, s.20(10).
[61] *Ibid.*, pursuant to s.33(3).
[62] *Ibid.*, s.20(4)(ii).
[63] *Ibid.*, s.20(40)(b).

interest.[64] Otherwise the licence must be renewed.[65] On renewal the Commission is obliged to determine a revised cash bid[66] and have a discretion to set a new percentage of qualifying revenue payable by the licence holder.[67] The licence cannot be formally renewed until the licensee has been notified of these matters and notified the Commission that he consents to the licence being renewed on these terms.[68] The revised cash bid is calculated by the Commission's estimating the amount which would be payable to it if the licence were open to competitive tender.[69]

Provision of news services for Channel 3

Provision of news services. As a result of the licence conditions requir-   **24.30**
ing the provision of news, Channel 3 licence holders will be required to contract with a nominated news provider. The Act does not fetter the nominated news provider's powers to charge for its services. It follows that the remedies open to an aggrieved licence holder will be the usual competition law remedies. Under English law, a complaint can be made to the Office of Fair Trading. A further complaint could be made under Articles 85 and 86 of the Treaty of Rome. That complaint will only be viable if the nominated news provider enjoyed a dominant position in the provision of news to the United Kingdom and such provision affected the flow of trade between Member States. Assuming that those preconditions were made out and that there was evidence of anti-competitive behaviour, the aggrieved licence holder could either avoid any contract which it had entered into with the news provider or maintain an action for breach of statutory duty.

A licence holder is free to contract with a non-nominated news provider in respect of non-peak time news coverage.

Nomination of a news provider. The 1990 Act imposed on the Com-   **24.31**
mission a duty to nominate at least one news provider prior to the publishing of a Channel 3 proposal notice.[70] ITN has been nominated by the Commission as news providers. The duration of the nomination is a period of 10 years and may be renewed by the Commission for a further period of 10 years at the expiration of the first term.[71] The 1990 Act creates a presumption that any company that is qualified to provide a high quality news service must be nominated as a news provider.

---

[64] *Ibid.*, s.20(5).
[65] *Ibid.*, s.20(1).
[66] *Ibid.*, s.20(6)(a).
[67] *Ibid.*, s.20(6)(b).
[68] *Ibid.*, s.20(8).
[69] *Ibid.*, s.20(7).
[70] *Ibid.*, s.32(1).
[71] *Ibid.*, s.32(3).

A qualified company is one that is effectively equipped and adequately financed to provide such service and is not disqualified[72] under the ownership rules. A company may apply to the Commission with or without invitation to be a nominated news provider.[73]

24.32   On application, the Commission can only reject the application if it decides that the company is not qualified to be a news provider[74] or if to grant the application, given the number of subsisting nominated news providers, would be prejudicial to the provision of high quality news programmes in regional Channel 3 services taken as a whole.[75] Where nomination has been refused on this basis, the performance of the actual nominations must be reviewed "from time to time". The times of the review are to be set by the Commission in the exercise of its discretion. On review, if the Commission is satisfied that another non-nominated company would offer a higher quality news service than the nominated news service provider the Commission must by notice terminate the nomination and nominate the qualified news service provider which is in a position to provide a better service.[76]

However, prior to such termination the Commission must give the company whose nomination is to be terminated a reasonable opportunity of making representations to them about the proposed nomination[77] and must consult every Channel 3 licence holder in respect of such termination and nomination of a news provider.[78] Other than in this particular case there is no duty imposed on the Commission to review the performance of the nominated news provider. However, the Commission is under a duty (subject to the requirements of natural justice) to terminate a nomination if at any time it is dissatisfied with the service provided and decides that to terminate the nomination would not be prejudicial to the provision of high quality news services across all Channel 3 services.[79]

Networking Arrangements

24.33   All Channel 3 licensees are required to participate in a nationwide television service which is capable of competing with other nationwide services.[80] Such an arrangement is generally referred to as "the networking arrangements". The arrangements mean that programmes

---

[72] As to "disqualified persons", see *post*, Chap. 30.
[73] Broadcasting Act 1990, s.32(2)(a).
[74] *Ibid.*, s.32(2)(b).
[75] *Ibid.*, s.32.
[76] *Ibid.*, s.31(4).
[77] *Ibid.*, s.32(6).
[78] *Ibid.*, s.32(7).
[79] *Ibid.*, s.32(5).
[80] *Ibid.*, s.39(1)(a).

made, commissioned or acquired by or on behalf of one or more of the holders of one Channel 3 licence are to be available for broadcasting in all regional Channel 3 services.[81] The Act leaves the detail of the networking arrangements to be settled by the market subject to the approval of the Commission[82] and the regulatory powers of the Director General of Fair Trading.[83] Network arrangements are organised with the Independent Television Association (ITVA) which is the trade body of the independent television companies. The overall programme strategy, network hours and budgets are to be determined by the ITVA Council. A Chief Executive and Network Director have day to day responsibility for scheduling and for commissioning programmes: that is, the commitment to the acquisition or financing of programmes on behalf of the network. These two executives together with support staff are known as the Network Centre.

As initially drawn the Guidelines for the commissioning of programmes from independent producers for the network required the independent producer to contract with a licensee and directly with the Network Centre. The standard terms and conditions of such licences required the independent producer to transfer to the ITVA United Kingdom broadcasting rights for a period of 10 years with an option for the ITVA to extend for another five years.

Following the approval of these arrangements by the Commission the **24.34** networking arrangements were referred to the Director General of Fair Trading under section 39 of the Broadcasting Act 1990 and subsequently to the Monopolies and Mergers Commission ("MMC"). The consequent effect is that the network arrangements have been modified with regard to independent producers. It is a requirement of any arrangement whereby a programme is supplied for broadcast on the network that there be a tri-partite agreement between the independent producer, the network centre and a network licensee. The independent producer contracts with the network centre for the production and delivery of the programme. The sole function of the network licensee as a contracting party is to ensure that the programme supplied by the independent producer complies with the network licensees' contractual obligations to the Commission as regard, *inter alia*, consumer protection.

Additionally, the MMC ordered that requirement that independent producers grant broadcasting rights to programmes for a period of 10 years with an option to extend for another five years be removed from the standard term contract. No specific term is indicated by the MMC but the Network centre may only acquire the United Kingdom broad-

---

[81] *Ibid.*, s.39(1)(b).
[82] *Ibid.*, s.39(1).
[83] *Ibid.*, s.39(3).

casting rights. The period of the rights, options for further programmes being subject to negotiation between the parties but must not be more onerous than the terms contained in the Network Programme Licence and the ITVA General Terms and Conditions applicable to an ITVA Network Programme Licence.

2. Channel 4

24.35 **Establishment of the Channel Four Television Corporation.** The 1990 Act[84] establishes the Channel Four Television Corporation ("the Corporation"). The Corporation is to replace the Channel Four Television Company in providing the services previously provided by Channel 4.[85]

However, unlike the Channel Four Television Company (whose shares vested in the Corporation on January 1, 1993),[86] the Corporation is not a subsidiary of the Commission. Therefore the Corporation is more than merely a commissioning, purchasing and editing body in that it is now responsible for its own programme schedule and advertising time under a Commission licence[87] lasting for 10 years: the Commission have a power to renew it on one or more occasions.[88] It is an independent broadcasting company which is to broadcast to so much of England, Scotland and Northern Ireland as is "reasonably practicable".[89]

(a) *Conditions to be included in Channel 4 licence*

24.36 **Complementary service to Channel 3.** The Commission must ensure that Channel 4 contains a "suitable proportion of matter calculated to appeal to tastes not generally catered for by Channel 3" by the insertion of licence conditions to that effect.[90] Innovation and experiment in programme form and content are to be encouraged.[91] Generally Channel 4 is to be given a distinctive character of its own.[92]

It is clear that Channel 4 is not intended to be a direct competitor with

---

[84] *Ibid.*, s.23(1).
[85] *Ibid.*, s.24(1).
[86] *Ibid.*, s.24(2).
[87] *Ibid.*, s.24(4).
[88] *Ibid.*, s.24(4).
[89] *Ibid.*, s.24(3): the Corporation's duty to broadcast is not subject to limitations in principle but to technical limitations. It therefore follows that the duty to broadcast will vary over time. The Corporation will therefore be under a duty to ascertain whether at any particular time the technical limitations which then apply alter the area to which the Corporation should broadcast.
[90] *Ibid.*, s.25(1)(a).
[91] *Ibid.*, s.25(1)(b).
[92] *Ibid,*. s.25(1).

Channel 3. It is to cater for different tastes and to provide a distinctive service. However, it is unclear what precisely Channel 4 is to do. The problem is in part definitional. Innovation, experimentation, tastes and a "suitable proportion" are not defined in the Act and are *per se* very general terms. Therefore the Act has created a general conceptual framework and avoided the conceptual difficulties by placing the onus on the parties to decide, in agreeing licence conditions, that which is meant by all and each of the terms. It is submitted that solution is unacceptable for several reasons.

The solution centres on two limbs: an analysis of taste and an analysis **24.37** of a suitable proportion. In analysing tastes, although, in a general sense it is easy to see that Channel 4 may exist to provide programmes for tastes which are not "mainstream",[93] it is suggested that it is difficult to give the duty an empirical meaning. It would be necessary to define tastes, then to see what tastes are presently catered for and then not make provision for those tastes in the schedule.

Further, what is a suitable proportion will be a matter of fact in any particular case and at any particular time. Further, as the issue will arise from questions of taste, any decision reached will be a matter of subjective analysis of subjective facts. The factors which may be taken into account in deciding what is a suitable proportion are unlimited. The only limits will be the discretion of the officers of the Corporation at any time and the conditions of the licence.

Each of those limits raises further complexities. The officers of the Corporation will owe duties as company directors to act in the financial interests of the company and to ensure that the Corporation's transactions are carried out in order to further the Companies' financial interests.[94] Broadcasting programmes which only cater for minority interests will have an immediate impact on the companies' advertising revenue and therefore potentially upon its profitability. It follows that in analysing, a suitable proportion, questions of profitability will have to be taken into account. The immediate difficulty is carrying out the comparative exercise of deciding when financial considerations will curtail the Corporation's duty to cater for varied interests.

There are similar difficulties with regard to the terms of the licence **24.38** conditions imposed. Any licence condition imposed will face one of two conceptual complications. The parties could either agree a con-

---

[93] Although if those tastes are the tastes of a "community" Channel 3 broadcasters will be under a duty to cater for them. By implication Channel 4 would therefore not broadcast to communities.

[94] See *Rolled Steel Products v. BSC* [1986] Ch. 246 at 288; *Hogg v. Cramphorn* [1967] Ch. 254; *Re Smith & Fawcett* [1942] Ch. 304. The interests of the company are to be objectively determined (see *Howard Smith v. Ampol Petroleum* [1974] A.C. 821).

dition which repeats the statutory provision. Such a condition would potentially be void for uncertainty at common law as it would not define the circumstances in which the Corporation would be in breach.

At the other extreme, a licence condition listing the amounts of time which could be given to particular tastes would fetter the Corporation's discretion to programme flexibly. Further, if what is a suitable proportion varies over time, a contractual condition fettering the Corporation's discretion for 10 years could well be *ultra vires* the statute.

In keeping with the analogy with Channel 3 services, parallel conditions apply to the Channel 4 licence placing it under parallel duties to provide news services of a high quality and to broadcast European programmes. It is also under three other duties.

24.39 **Public service duties.** The Commission is also required to include conditions requiring that Channel 4 is provided as public service for disseminating information, education and entertainment.[95] So far as education is concerned Channel 4 is required to ensure that a suitable proportion of its programmes are of an educational nature but the compliance with such a requirement does not by itself fulfil the Channel's public service duty to disseminate education.[96]

24.40 **Quality and range of programmes.** The licence shall include conditions requiring the Channel service to maintain (a) a high "general standard" in respect of the service and in particular in respect of the content and quality of the programmes[97] and (b) a wide range in the subject-matter such programmes having regard both to the programmes as a whole and also the days of the week on which and the times of the day at which the programmes are broadcast.[98] The requirement for a high "general standard" means that the programmes on the service must be considered as a whole rather than individually. This obligation is to be read in conjunction with the requirements as to catering for particular tastes and providing for innovation and experiment. As these requirements are conjunctive, it is to be presumed that the service as a whole across all its programmes will meet this requirement not that all individual programmes will do so.

24.41 **Independent productions.** The licence must also include a condition requiring the Corporation not to be involved in the making of programmes to be broadcast on Channel 4 except to the extent that it is permitted so to do by the Commission.[99] This condition preserves Channel

---

[95] Broadcasting Act 1990, s.25(2)(a).
[96] *Ibid.*, s.25(2)(a).
[97] *Ibid.*, s.25(2)(b).
[98] *Ibid.*, s.25(2)(b)(ii).
[99] *Ibid.*, s.25(5).

4's remit as a publisher-broadcaster and effectively means that all its programmes are obtained from independent producers, other broadcasters or acquired in the form of ready made material. However, in so doing it must ensure that a minimum proportion of 25 per cent. of the "qualifying programmes" are from independent producers as defined by the Secretary of State.[1]

(b) *Funding of Channel 4*

Levy. As a statutory corporation under the 1990 Act Channel 4 is relatively autonomous. However, the Act provides a financial safety net. Revenue deficits of the Corporation are to be funded by Channel 3 licensees. This safety net is calculated first by the Commission estimating,[2] starting before January 1993 and in each subsequent year, (a) Channel 4's qualifying revenue[3] for that year (b) the total television revenues for all Channel 3 or 5 licence holders, the Welsh Authority and Channel 4 itself[4] and (c) Channel 4's prescribed minimum income for that year at 14 per cent.[5] of the total television revenues.[6] Should the aggregate of Channel 4's qualifying revenue and reserves,[7] for any year, fall below 14 per cent. of total television revenue as estimated by the Commission, a levy will be imposed in respect of the difference on the Channel 3 licence holders.[8] The levy may not exceed 2 per cent. of total television revenues and is to be apportioned amongst the licence holders as the Commission considers appropriate: different sums may be set in respect of different licensees.[9] A failure to pay the levy will be a breach of the licence conditions. **24.42**

Application of excess "levy" receipts. If in any year the Commission imposes a levy and the aggregate amount of the levy receipts forwarded to Channel 4 exceeds the "relevant amount" the Commission is under a duty to notify Channel 4 of that fact and Channel 4 is under a duty to repay the excess as soon as is reasonably practicable.[10] "Relevant amount" **24.43**

---

[1] *Ibid.*, s.25(2)(f). For the meaning of "independent producer", see *post*, Chap. 28.
[2] The Commission may on one or more occasions revise the estimate: Broadcasting Act 1990, s.26(1).
[3] In accordance with *ibid.*, s.19(2)–(6); *ibid.*, s.26(9). For the manner in which "qualifying revenue" is calculated pursuant to these provisions see *ante*, para. 24.24.
[4] *Ibid.*, s.26(1)(b).
[5] *Ibid.*, s.26(10): the Secretary of State may by order substitute a different percentage but no such order may be made before the end of 1997.
[6] *Ibid.*, s.26(1)(c).
[7] See *post*, para. 24.44.
[8] *Ibid.*, s.26(3).
[9] *Ibid.*, s.26(4).
[10] *Ibid.*, s.25(7).

is defined as the amount by which the aggregate of qualifying revenue and the reserve fund is less than the prescribed amount.[11] The effect of this section is that if a levy of £1,750 is imposed and paid over to Channel 4 and the "prescribed amount" is £1,500 but the aggregate of the qualifying revenue and the reserve fund is £1,250 the "relevant amount" would be £250 and Channel 4 would have to repay £1,500. This would mean that the prescribed income only would be received by Channel 4.

24.44 **Application of Channel 4's Excess revenue.** When Channel 4's qualifying revenue[12] for any year exceeds the prescribed minimum income[13] for that year, it must pay one half of the excess to the Commission[14] and carry one quarter to the credit of the reserve fund.[15] It may apply the remaining quarter towards meeting current expenditure incurred by it in the provision of the Channel 4 service but where it is not so applied it must be carried to the reserve fund.[16] Where the Commission receives one half of the excess it must distribute it between Channel 3 licence holders in such a way that each receives such proportion as corresponds to the proportion of the aggregate amount which it would in the opinion of the Commission have been required to pay had a levy been imposed.[17]

Channel 4 may determine the management and application of the reserve fund but any application must be for Channel 4 purposes.[18] However, the Secretary of State, with Treasury approval, may give to Channel 4 directions with respect to the management and application of the fund including directions requiring the whole or part of it to be paid into the Consolidated Fund and Channel 4 must comply.[19] No directions may, however, be given by the Secretary of State to Channel 4 with respect to the application of any money standing to the credit of the reserve fund which has been taken into account by the Commission in assessing whether to impose a levy[20] or in determining whether there has been an excess of levy payment which should be refunded.[21]

---

[11] *Ibid.*, s.25(8).
[12] See *ante*, para. 24.24 for the meaning of "qualifying revenue".
[13] See *supra*, para. 24.43.
[14] Broadcasting Act 1990, s.27(1)(a).
[15] *Ibid.*, s.27(1)(b).
[16] *Ibid.*, s.27(3)(b).
[17] *Ibid.*, s.27(2).
[18] *Ibid.*, s.27(4).
[19] *Ibid.*, s.27(5).
[20] *Ibid.*, s.27(4).
[21] Broadcasting Act 1990, s.27(4): see *ante*, para. 24.43 for the rules relating to repayment where there has been an excess levy payment.

3. Channel 5

Licensing

The competitive tendering procedure applicable to Channel 3 also **24.45**
applies to Channel 5 as does the requirement to make additional
payments.[22] The quality threshold requirements are, however, modified to the extent that there is no requirement to provide regional programming on the service.[23]

Returning of equipment by Channel 5 licence holder

Licence conditions: duty to retune. A Channel 5 licensee is under an **24.46**
obligation to ensure that his transmissions do not interfere with pre-
existing relevant equipment[24] and therefore will be obliged to retune
any such equipment used wholly or mainly for domestic purposes[25] at
the request of its owner,[26] without charge,[27] in a proper manner[28] and
completed within such a period as is specified in the licence. The Commission will be the arbiter of the standard to which the work is carried
out.[29] Once the licence holder has retuned the equipment and any
equipment connected to and dependent on it[30] he can be placed under
no further obligation to retune or modify the equipment.[31] Where
equipment is brought into the Channel 5 broadcast area subsequent to
the commencement of the broadcast Channel 5 will be under no obligation to retune that equipment.

---

[22] *Ibid.*, s.29(1).
[23] *Ibid.*, s.29(2).
[24] *Ibid.*, s.30(7): "relevant equipment" is any equipment capable of transmitting self
generated electro-magnetic signals for reception by a television set connected to it and
liable, if used without being returned or otherwise modified, to suffer interference
caused by the transmission of Channel 5.
[25] *Ibid.*, s.30(3)(a).
[26] *Ibid.*, s.30(a)(i).
[27] *Ibid.*, s.30(1)(a)(ii).
[28] *Ibid.*, s.30(1)(b)(i).
[29] *Ibid.*, s.30(1)(c).
[30] *Ibid.*, s.30(6).
[31] *Ibid.*, s.30(3).

CHAPTER 25

SATELLITE TELEVISION

Licensing and Regulation of Satellite Television Services

25.01 General. The Broadcasting Act 1990 draws a distinction between three categories of satellite television services. These categories are domestic satellite television services, and non-domestic satellite services, which come within the licensing regime of the Broadcasting Act 1990, and non-domestic satellite services which do not. The latter is referred to in this Chapter as "Foreign Satellite Services".

(a) *Domestic satellite services*

25.02 Definition. A "domestic satellite" service is a television broadcasting service where the television programmes included in the service are transmitted by satellite from a place in the United Kingdom on an "allocated frequency" for reception in the United Kingdom by members of the public.[1] An "allocated frequency" is a frequency allocated to the United Kingdom for Broadcasting by satellite.[2] This system is commonly referred to Direct Broadcasting by Satellite (DBS). Five frequencies were allocated to the United Kingdom and subsequently licensed to British Satellite Broadcasting but since the merger of that company with Sky Television the allocated frequencies have not been utilised.

25.03 Regulation of domestic satellite services. A licence is required from the Commission for the operation of a domestic satellite service. The requirements for obtaining a licence are similar to those imposed on Channel 3. The applicant must pass a quality threshold and must submit the highest cash bid but the Commission retains a residual discretion to invoke the exceptional circumstances provision of the Act.[3]

---

[1] Broadcasting Act 1990, s.43(1).
[2] *Ibid.*, s.43(4).
[3] *Ibid.*, s.44(3). See *ante*, para. 24.07.

The quality threshold requires the service to provide a proper proportion of European programmes[4] and at least 25 per cent. of the amount of the total time allocated to broadcasting of qualifying programmes must be allocated to the broadcasting of a range and diversity of independent productions. There is, however, no requirement that the service provide regional programmes or news programmes.

Similarly, the service is subject to the same enforcement provisions which are provided for Channel 3 under the provisions of the Act.[5]

Duration and renewal of domestic services licence. A domestic satellite **25.04** services licence continues in force for 15 years.[6]

Presumption in favour of renewal. If an application is made by the **25.05** licence holder the Commission may only refuse the application if they are not satisfied that the applicant would, if his licence were renewed, provide a service which complied with the conditions included in the licence as originally imposed or as varied[7] or would fail to provide a proper proportion of European programmes and or allocate to independent productions not less 25 per cent. of transmission time allocated to qualifying programmes.[8] Renewal may be on one or more occasions for a period of fifteen years beginning with the date of renewal.[9]

(b) *Non-domestic satellite services*

Definition. The Broadcasting Act creates two categories of "non- **25.06** domestic satellite service". The first category comprises the transmission of television programmes by satellite from a place in the United Kingdom, otherwise than on an "allocated frequency",[10] for general reception in the United Kingdom or in a "prescribed country",[11] or both.[12] The second category comprise a service which is not transmitted from the United Kingdom or a prescribed country but which is intended for reception in the United Kingdom. The person providing services falling within the first category will require a licence from the Commission.[13] Where there is no such person the person providing the transmission to the satellite will require the licence.

---

[4] *Ibid.*, s.44(3).
[5] *Ibid.*, s.44(3). See "Enforcement of Licences", *post*, Chap. 31.
[6] *Ibid.*, s.44(4)(d)(i).
[7] *Ibid.*, s.44(3).
[8] *Ibid.*, s.43(4).
[9] *Ibid.*, s.44(3)(a).
[10] *Ibid.*, s.43(2)(b). For the meaning of "allocated frequency", see *ante*, para. 25.05.
[11] The "prescribed countries" are Belgium, Denmark, Federal Republic of Germany, France, Greece, Ireland, Italy, Luxembourg, the Netherlands, Portugal and Spain: Broadcasting (Prescribed Countries) Order 1991 (S.I. 1991, No. 1820).
[12] Broadcasting Act 1990, s.43(2)(a)(ii).
[13] *Ibid.*, ss.43, 44.

Thus if X, who resides in France, wishes to provide programmes for transmission, by Y, from Y's up-link in London, for general reception in the United Kingdom or a prescribed country, Y will require a licence. Where services fall in the second category a licence will be required from the Commission if and to the extent that the programmes included in such service consist of material provided by a person in the United Kingdom who is in a position to determine what is included in the service so far as it consists of programme material provided by him.[14]

The differing licensing regimes in respect of the two categories of non-domestic satellite services arises by reason of the fact that under Directive 89/552[15] and the Council of Europe's Convention on Trans-frontier Broadcasting any service provided by a person in a prescribed country must be regulated under the law of that country and not the law of the receiving country.

25.07   **Granting of non-domestic satellite services licences.** A non-domestic satellite services licence may only be refused where it appears to the commission that the service which would be provided under the licence would not comply with the consumer protection requirements set out in section 6(1) of the Act.[16]

25.08   **Duration of licence.** Subject to the powers of the Commission to revoke a licence,[17] a licence to provide a non-domestic satellite service continues in force for a period of 10 years.[18]

(c) *Foreign satellite services*

25.09   **Definition.** A foreign satellite service is a service which consists wholly or mainly in the transmission by satellite from a place outside the United Kingdom of television or sound programmes which are capable of being received within the United Kingdom and which do not come within the meaning of a non-domestic satellite service.[19] These are such services which do not come within the regulatory scheme created by the Broadcasting Act. There is no general restriction on a foreign satellite service being received by viewers who have the necessary receiving equipment. Nor is there any restriction on the service being advertised or decoding equipment being sold in the United Kingdom for the reception of any encrypted foreign satellite service.

---

[14] *Ibid.*, ss.43, 45.
[15] [1989] O.J. L298/23.
[16] Broadcasting Act 1990, s.45(2). See also "Regulation of Programme Standards", *post*, Chap. 32.
[17] See *post*, para. 31.09.
[18] Broadcasting Act 1990, s.45(4).
[19] *Ibid.*, s.177(6). See *ante*, paras. 25.02–25.06 for "non-domestic satellite services".

Orders proscribing unacceptable foreign satellite services. Although **25.10** such services are generally outside the jurisdiction of the Commission and the Radio Authority, sections 177 and 178 of the Broadcasting Act 1990 contains provisions for the control of such services where it appears that "there is repeatedly contained in programmes included in the service matter which offends against good taste or decency or is likely to encourage or incite to crime or lead to disorder or to be offensive to public feeling".[20] Where the Secretary of State has been so notified by the Commission or Radio Authority, as the case may be, he may make an order proscribing a foreign satellite service (the "proscribed service") if he is satisfied that the making of the order is in the public interest and compatible with the international obligations of the United Kingdom.[21]

The principal international obligation is contained in Directive 89/ **25.11** 552 which lays down minimum rules which must be observed by Member States in respect of foreign satellite services emanating from within the European Union. Each Member State must ensure that television broadcasts transmitted by broadcasters under its jurisdiction or broadcasters who make use of a frequency or a satellite capacity granted by, or a satellite up-link situated in that Member State comply with the law applicable to broadcasts intended for the public in that Member State.[22]

Member States may not restrict the "retransmission" on their terri- **25.12** tory of television broadcasts which fall within the areas coordinated by the Directive.[23] These areas are (a) promotion and distribution of television programmes; (b) television, advertising and sponsorship; and (c) protection of minors. However, Member States may suspend re-transmission where the broadcast manifestly, seriously and gravely infringes Article 22; where during the previous 12 months, the broadcaster has infringed the same provisions on at least two prior occasions; where the Member State concerned has notified the broadcaster and the Commission in writing of the alleged infringements and of its intention to restrict retransmission should any such infringement occur again; and where consultations with the transmitting state has not produced a settlement.[24] Article 22 provides:

> "Member States shall take appropriate measures to ensure that television broadcasts by broadcasters under their jurisdiction do not include programmes which might seriously impair the physical,

---

[20] *Ibid.*, s.177(2).
[21] *Ibid.*, s.177(1), (4).
[22] Directive 89/552, Art. 2.
[23] *Ibid.*, Art. 2.
[24] *Ibid.*, Art. 22.

mental or moral development of minors, in particular those that involve pornography or gratuitous violence. This provision shall extend to other programmes which are likely to impair the physical, mental or moral development of minors, except where it is ensured, by selecting the time of the broadcast or by any technical measure, that minors in the area of the transmission will not normally hear or see such broadcasts.

Member States shall also ensure that broadcasts do not contain any incitement to hatred on grounds of race, sex, religion or nationality."

25.13 The power contained in sections 177 and 178 of the Broadcasting Act was invoked by the Secretary of State in the case of *R. v. Secretary of State for the National Heritage, ex parte Continental Television*[25] where the court upheld an order proscribing "'Red Hot Dutch". The court rejected the submission that "retransmission" as used Directive 89/552 was not applicable to transmissions which were received by the viewer directly from the satellite and preferred the view that the expression should be construed purposively in accordance with the practice of the European Court. It was therefore to be taken to include cases where the services are directly received by satellite without, for example, the intervention of a local delivery service provider.

The case has been referred to the European Court for a ruling on the meaning of "retransmission" and as to whether "except where it is ensured, by selecting the time of the broadcast or by any technical measure, that minors in the area of the transmission will not normally hear or see such broadcasts", as used in Article 22 of the Directive, is applicable to pornographic programmes or only to "other programmes". It is clear that on a strict construction of the Directive and the practice of the broadcasting industry "retransmission" in this context refers to point to point satellite transmission and subsequent delivery by cable or microwave or other means to the viewer. Direct broadcasting by satellite involves no element of retransmission except in so far as the signals are transmitted from the up-link to the satellite and from there retransmitted to houses within the footprint.

Notwithstanding the apparent meaning of "retransmision" the rapid progress of technology in the area of satellite broadcasting and the approach of the European Court in the interpretation of legislation lends weight to the approach of the United Kingdom court. Additionally, there is much force in the argument that the interpretation contended for by *Continental Television* would deprive the Directive of much of the protection accorded to minors.

---

[25] [1993] E.M.L.R. 389.

CHAPTER 26

LOCAL DELIVERY SERVICES

1. Definition and Licensing

Local delivery services is the successor under the provisions of the 1990 **26.01**
Broadcasting Act to cable franchises awarded under the Cable and
Broadcasting Act 1984. Under the provisions of the 1984 Act cable franchises were restricted to providing cable services by means of physical
material. The 1990 Act permits such services to be delivered both by the
conventional cable and by means of wireless telegraphy such as multi-
point video distribution services (MVDS). Further, it seeks to draw a
distinction, for regulatory purposes, between the provision of a local
delivery service and the making, acquiring and packaging of programmes into a programme schedule for delivery to the consumer via
such a service. In both cases a licence is required from the regulatory
authority. However, notwithstanding this apparent dichotomy, a local
delivery service operator may hold both a licensable programme
service[1] licence and a local delivery service licence.[2]

Meaning of local delivery service. A "local delivery service" is a service **26.02**
which uses a telecommunications system[3] to deliver one or more specified services for simultaneous reception in two or more dwelling houses
in an area of the United Kingdom consisting of more than 1,000 dwelling houses.[4] The "television services" are:

(a) television broadcasting services whether provided by the holder
of a licence under the 1990 Act, the BBC or the Welsh Authority[5];

---

[1] For the meaning of "licensable programme service", see *post*, para. 27.01 *et seq.*
[2] Broadcasting Act 1990, s.79(1).
[3] For the meaning of "telecommunications system", see *ante*, para. 23.04, n.6.
[4] Broadcasting Act 1990, s.72(1)(a), (b): S.I. 1990 No. 2389 as amended by S.I. 1991 No. 2188.
[5] *Ibid.*, s.72(2)(a).

395

(b) non-domestic satellite services[6];

(c) licensable programme service[7];

(d) sound broadcasting services to which section 84[8] applies or which is provided by the BBC[9];

(e) licensable sound programme services.[10]

A delivery service which delivers only BBC, Channel 3 and 4 does not come within the meaning of a local delivery service.

26.03   Thus, three elements must be present in order that a service be a local delivery service which is subject to the regulatory framework laid down in Part II of the Broadcasting Act 1990. First, the service must use a tele-communication system[11] for the delivery of the services. Secondly, it must be available in an area in the United Kingdom consisting of more than 1,000[12] homes. Thirdly, the television service transmitted over the service must be for simultaneous reception in the homes to which it is transmitted.

However, the award of a local delivery licence does not of itself permit the local delivery service to transmit programmes over its service. To do so the local delivery service operator will also require a licensable programme service licence under Chapter IV of the 1990 Act.[13]

26.04   Thus under the new statutory regime the local delivery services is not confined to delivery by means of cable but may include any form of tele-communications system which is used for the purpose of delivering the specified services. However, a service which delivers programme on demand to individual homes at a time requested by the viewer by means of a telecommunications system does not come within the meaning of a local delivery service because such programmes are not transmitted for simultaneous reception and consequently do not fall to be regulated under the provisions of the 1990 Act. Such a service would, however, require a licensable programme service licence. Thus, for example, a service providing video on demand to a subscriber at a time convenient to him would not be for simultaneous reception. Such a service would, however, require a licensable programme service licence and would be regulated by the Commission under the 1990 Act.

---

[6] *Ibid.*, s.72(2)(b).

[7] *Ibid.*, s.72(2)(c); see further *post*, Chap. 27 for "licensable programme service".

[8] As to which see "Independent Television Radio Services", *post*, Chap. 29.

[9] Broadcasting Act 1990, s.72(2)(d).

[10] *Ibid.*, s.72(2)(e).

[11] For example, cable or multi-point video distribution (MVDS), or both.

[12] Where a system delivers programmes to 1,000 or fewer homes a licence will, however, be required under the Telecommunications Act 1984.

[13] See "Licensable Programme Service", *ante*, Chap. 23.

Licensing of local delivery licences. The provisions of Sections 3 and 4 **26.05**
of the 1990 Act apply to local delivery licences.[14] Thus the Commission
may not grant a licence to a person they do not consider fit and proper[15]
to hold such licence and they must "do all they can to secure"[16] that if
they cease to be satisfied that such person is fit and proper must revoke
the licence. The Commission may also, under section 3, vary the
duration of a licence with the consent of the licence holder,[17] but has no
power to vary any conditions relating to the payment of the cash bid or
additional payments.[18]

The Act permits the Commission to include conditions in a local
delivery service licence permitting a licence holder to authorise any person who is not a "disqualified person"[19] to undertake to the provision
of the licensed service on the licence holder's behalf.[20] This provision
enables the licensee to sub-licence his right to operate the local delivery
service. However, the provisions of the local delivery licence apply in
respect of such persons as they apply in relation to the provision of the
service by the licence holder. Thus any failure by the person authorised
to operate the service will be treated as a failure by the licence holder to
comply with those conditions.[21]

Restrictions on holding licences. The Restrictions on holding of **26.06**
licences contained in sections 3, 4, 5 and Schedule 2 of the Act apply to
local delivery services granted by the Commission.[22]

Criteria for the award of licence. The 1990 Act requires the Commission **26.07**
to award the licence to the applicant who has passed the technical and
financial threshold, and submitted the highest bid.[23] However, the
Commission retains a residual discretion to disregard this requirement
and award the licence to an applicant who has not submitted the highest bid if it appears to it there are "exceptional circumstances" which
make it appropriate for them to award the licence to that applicant.[24]
"Exceptional circumstances" is undefined by the Act but two particular
circumstances are given in which exceptional circumstances may apply.

These are first, where it appears that the coverage proposed to be
achieved by the applicant to whom it is proposed to award the licence is

---

[14] Broadcasting Act 1990, s.73(3).
[15] See *ante*, para. 23.14.
[16] For the nature of this duty see *ante*, para. 23.08.
[17] See *ante*, para. 23.21.
[18] Broadcasting Act 1990, s.73(4)(c).
[19] For the meaning and categories of "disqualified persons", see *post*, Chap. 30.
[20] Broadcasting Act 1990, s.73(5), (6).
[21] *Ibid.*, s.73(7).
[22] *Ibid.*, s.73(3), (4); see "Restrictions on the Holding of Licences", *post*, Chap. 30.
[23] *Ibid.*, s.76(1).
[24] *Ibid.*, s.76(3).

substantially greater than that proposed to be achieved by the applicant who has submitted the highest bid[25] and secondly, where it appears, in the context of the licence, that any circumstances are to be regarded as exceptional circumstances. The fact that the exceptional circumstances coming within the second category has, on another occasion, been relied upon by the Commission is no bar to such circumstances being relied upon in the context of any other licences.[26] The second category of exceptional circumstances gives the Commission a wide discretion. Matters which may, prima facie, be important in the context of a licence will include the audience profile and the services to be provided to that group, cost of laying cables or providing services within that particular area.

26.08   **Source of funds.** Where the source of funds which are to finance the service or pay the cash bid is not in the public interest the Commission is prohibited from awarding the licence to that applicant. In such circumstances it must submit the details of the bid to the Secretary of State for his consideration[27] who may on such referral refuse the grant of the licence if he is satisfied that the source of funds is such that it would not be in the public interest to award the licence to that person.[28]

26.09   **Additional payments.** Analogous duties to those relating to Channel 3 in respect of additional payments are imposed on a local delivery service.[29] Under section 74(2) the Commission may set at nil the percentage of qualifying revenue that may be payable by a licence holder in any qualifying period. This may take place for example where the Commission chooses to encourage the development of a local delivery service in area which would otherwise be financially unattractive to a supplier of services.

26.10   **Duration of licence.** Subject to the variation of the licence by consent or revocation[30] a local delivery licence continues in force for a period of 15 years and may be renewed on one or more occasions for a further period of 15 years.[31]

26.11   **Renewal of licence.** An application for the renewal of a licence may be made by the licence holder not earlier than five years before the date on which it would otherwise cease to be in force and not later than the "rel-

---

[25] *Ibid.*, s.76(4).
[26] *Ibid.*, s.76(4).
[27] *Ibid.*, s.76(5).
[28] *Ibid.*, s.75(6).
[29] *Ibid.*, s.74(1)(d). See *ante*, paras. 24.22–24.27.
[30] For the Commission's powers of revocation see *post*, Chap. 30.
[31] Broadcasting Act 1990, s.78(1).

evant date".[32] Where the application is made before the "relevant date" the Commission may postpone consideration of it for so long as it thinks appropriate having regard to the requirement to grant the licence not later than the "relevant date" or if not reasonably practicable so soon thereafter as is reasonably practicable.[33] The "relevant date" is the date which the Commission determine to be that by which it would need to publish a proposal notice under section 72 if they were to grant, as from the date on which the licence would expire if not renewed, a fresh licence to provide the local delivery service formerly provided under that licence.[34]

Refusal to renew licence. When an application for renewal of a licence **26.12** has been made to the Commission it may only refuse the application for renewal in three circumstances.

First, if it proposes to grant a fresh local delivery licence for the provision of a service which would be for different area from that for which the applicant's service is provided under his licence.[35]

Secondly, in the case of an applicant who has not achieved the coverage set out in the technical plan submitted under section 74(3)(b) either because it is not satisfied that he would, if his licence were renewed, be able to achieve that coverage in accordance with the timetable indicated in the plan or the period within which it was to be achieved has expired.[36]

Thirdly, if the source of his funds for paying his cash, bid qualifying revenue or otherwise financing the service is from a source which is not in the public interest.[37]

Enforcement of licences. The provisions of sections 41 and 42 of the **26.13** 1990 Act which are applicable to Channels 3, 4 and 5 also apply to local delivery services with the following modifications.[38] First, the qualifying revenue for the purposes of section 41(1)(c) consists of all payments which are received by the licence holder, or any person connected with him[39] and are derived from the delivery in that period in accordance

---

[32] *Ibid.*, s.78(2).
[33] *Ibid.*, s.78(3).
[34] *Ibid.*, s.78(10).
[35] *Ibid.*, s.78(4)(a).
[36] *Ibid.*, s.78(4)(b).
[37] *Ibid.*, s.78(5).
[38] *Ibid.*, s.81.
[39] Persons are connected in relation to a particular licence if they are:
    (a) the licence holder;
    (b) a person who controls the licence holder;
    (c) an associate of the licence holder, or a person falling within (b);
    (d) a body which is controlled by the licence holder or any associate of the licence holder: Broadcasting Act 1990, Sched. 2, Part. IV, para. 3.

with his licence of services falling within section 72(2)[40] whether the delivery of such services is undertaken by him or a person authorised by him.[41] Secondly, the Commission may not direct an apology to be given by the licence holder.[42] Thirdly, where the Commission resolves to revoke a licence revocation is effective from the date of the notice: the Commission has no discretion to delay the revocation so as to preserve continuity of service.[43]

2. Regulation of Delivery of Foreign Programmes by Local Delivery Services

26.14 **Meaning of foreign programmes.** A "foreign satellite programme" is a programme transmitted by satellite from a place outside the United Kingdom, other than a programme transmitted from within any country specified by the Secretary of State by Order.[44]

26.15 In so far as a local delivery service consists in or includes relaying complete and unchanged any foreign satellite services provided from a non-prescribed country[45] the Commission is required to do all that it can to secure[46]:

(a) that nothing is included in its programmes which offends against good taste or decency or is likely to encourage or incite to crime or to lead to disorder or to be offensive to public feeling;

(b) that due responsibility is exercised with respect to the content of any such programmes which are religious programmes, and that in particular any such programmes do not involve:

(i) any improper exploitation of any susceptibilities of those watching the programmes; or

(ii) any abusive treatment of the religious views of and beliefs of those belonging to a particular religion or religious denominations; and

---

[40] See *ante*, para. 26.02 for a list of services.
[41] Broadcasting Act 1990, s.81(2)(a)(i).
[42] *Ibid.*, s.81(2)(a)(ii).
[43] *Ibid.*, s.81(2).
[44] *Ibid.*, s.79(5). These countries are Belgium, Cyprus, Denmark, Germany, France, Greece, Holy See, Ireland, Italy, Luxembourg, Malta, the Netherlands, Norway, Poland, Portugal, San Marino, Spain, Switzerland: Broadcasting (Foreign Satellite programmes) (Specified Countries) (Amendment) Order 1993 (S.I. 1994 No. 453). The specified countries are signatories to the European Community's Directive on Broadcasting and the Council of Europe's Convention on Transfrontier Television and under a duty to regulate the broadcasts emanating in those territories. Only in specific and limited circumstances may another country restrict the reception of such programmes by its citizens.
[45] "Non-prescribed countries" are any of those not falling within those set out in *supra*, n.44.
[46] Broadcasting Act 1990, s.79(2). For the nature and extent of this duty see, *ante*, para. 23.08.

(c) that the programmes so relayed do not include any technical device which, by using images of very brief duration or by other means, exploits the possibility of conveying a message to, or otherwise influencing the minds of, persons watching the programmes without their being aware, of what has occurred.

The ITC Programme Code[47] applies to such a foreign satellite programmes as if the delivery of those programmes constituted a licensed service.[48] The local delivery service operators are therefore under a duty to observe these requirements as licence condition.

Direction to cease relaying foreign television programmes. If the Commission is satisfied that it is appropriate to do so in pursuance of any international agreement to which the United Kingdom is a party, it may give to the holder of a local delivery licence a direction requiring him not to relay television programmes which are transmitted from a place outside the United Kingdom and are included in any service specified or described in the direction.[49] A direction may describe a service by reference to such matters as the Commission may think fit,[50] and it may have effect during a specified period or for an indefinite period.[51]   **26.16**

Advertisements. The holder of a local delivery licence is taken to be authorised by his licence to include in his licensed service advertisements which are inserted by him and are not included in any category of service within section 72(2).[52] However, where such advertisements are included by him, the provisions of sections 8 and 9 of the 1990 Act relating to advertisements have effect in respect of the regulation of such advertisements as are included by him.[53]   **26.17**

3. Transitional Arrangements

Continuation in force of existing "Prescribed Diffusion services" licences. Any licence to provide a "prescribed diffusion service"[54] granted under Part I of the Cable and Broadcasting Act 1984 ("the 1984   **26.18**

---

[47] See *post*, para. 32.08 for the terms of the *ITC Programme Code*.
[48] Broadcasting Act 1990, s.79(2).
[49] *Ibid.*, s.80(1)(a), (b).
[50] *Ibid.*, s.80(2).
[51] *Ibid.*, s.80(3).
[52] See *ante*, para. 26.02 for services falling within s.72(2)
[53] Broadcasting Act 1990, s.79(4). See *ante*, paras. 23.22–23.77 for provisions of ss.5, 8 and 9.
[54] For services provided over systems first licensed after June 1, 1986, a "prescribed diffusion service" means a diffusion service in which sound and television programmes are provided to 10,000 or more dwelling houses. Where the service is first licensed before June 1, 1986, a prescribed diffusion service means a service in which sound and television programmes are relayed direct to the home by means of a wide band cable system capable of carrying at least 16 video channels simultaneously: Cable (Prescribed Diffusion Service) Order (S.I. 1990 No. 1309).

Act") which is in force immediately before the date the assets of the Cable Authority vests in the Commission ("the transfer date"[55]) continue in force for the remainder of the period specified in the licence.[56] Where the licence continues in force the terms which were included in the licence before the transfer date similarly continue in force.[57] However, the Commission is granted a residual power to make such variations in the licence as may appear to them to be appropriate in consequence of any provisions of Schedule 12 of the 1990 Act.[58]

26.19 **Replacement of cable licences by local delivery licences.** A holder of a prescribed diffusion services[59] licence, where the closing date for the making of application for the licence under section 6 of the 1984 Act fell before November 7, 1988, may within six months beginning with the transfer date[60] request the grant to him by the Commission of a local delivery licence for the area in which the cable service is authorised to be provided under his prescribed diffusion services licence.[61] The Commission is under a duty to grant the licence applied for and on the coming into force of that licence, the prescribed diffusion services licence ceases to have effect.[62] The duration of the replacement local delivery licence is a period of 15 years beginning with the date the prescribed diffusion services licence came into force.[63] The local delivery licence may authorise the licensed service to be provided by wireless telegraphy.[64]

On the grant of the local delivery licence the Commission is not entitled to include any terms in the licence requiring the licence holder to pay any sum during the period of the replacement licence in the form of a cash bid or any amount of such income which would constitute qualifying revenue in respect of a local delivery licence granted under Part II of the Act.[65]

26.20 An application for the renewal of the replacement local delivery licence may be made by the licence holder not earlier than five years before the date on which it would otherwise cease to be in force and not

---

[55] January 1, 1991, by virtue of S.I. 1990 No. 2540.
[56] Broadcasting Act 1990, Sched. 12, Part II, para. 1(1).
[57] *Ibid.*, Sched. 12, Part II, para. 1(2).
[58] *Ibid.*, Sched. 12, Part II, para. 1(3).
[59] See *ante*, n.54 for the meaning of "prescribed diffusion service".
[60] See *ante*, n.54 for "transfer date".
[61] Broadcasting Act 1990, Sched. 12, Part II, para. 2(1).
[62] *Ibid.*, Sched. 12, Part II, para. 2(2).
[63] *Ibid.*, Sched. 12, Part II, para. 2(5).
[64] *Ibid.*, Sched. 12, Part II, para. 2(3).
[65] *Ibid.*, Sched. 12, Part II, para. 2(4).

later than the relevant date.[66] The application may only be refused if the Commission proposes to grant a fresh local delivery licence for the provision of a service which would be provided for a different area from that for which the applicant's service is provided under his local delivery licence.[67] On renewal of the licence the Commission is under a duty to determine the amount payable by the applicant in respect of the first complete calendar year falling within the period for which the licence is to be renewed[68] and may specify the percentage of qualifying revenue for each accounting period that will be payable by the applicant[69] and the Commission may in this respect specify different percentages in relation to different accounting periods and or a nil percentage in relation to such accounting periods.[70]

The Commission has no power to include provisions in a local delivery licence so granted requiring the licence holder to comply with a timetable for area coverage.[71] Except for the matters set out above all the other matters[72] relating to a local delivery license apply to a replacement and renewed local delivery licence granted to an existing licence holder.[73]

Prescribed diffusion services: grant of new licences to provide existing services. **26.21** The Commission is granted by the 1990 Act the power, after the transfer date,[74] to grant a licence to provide a new prescribed diffusion service[75] if:

(a) the new service would be authorised to be provided in the same area as that in which the existing prescribed diffusion service is authorised to be provided under a licence which is in force under Part I of the 1984 Act immediately before the transfer date[76];

(b) the licence to provide the new service would come into force on the expiry of the licence to provide the existing service[77];

---

[66] *Ibid.*, Sched. 12, Part II, para. 2(5), s.78. "Relevant date" means the date which the ITC determine to be that by which they would need to publish a notice under s.74 of the 1990 Act if they were to grant, as from the expiry date of a local delivery licence: Sched. 12, Part II, para. 4(4).
[67] *Ibid.*, Sched. 12 Part II, para. 2(5)(b), s.78(4)(a).
[68] *Ibid.*, Sched. 12, Part II, para. 2(5), s.78(6)(a).
[69] *Ibid.*, Sched. 12 para. 2(5), s.78(6)(b).
[70] *Ibid.*, Sched. 12 Part II, para. 2(5), s.78(6).
[71] *Ibid.*, Sched. 12, Part II, para. 2(8).
[72] As to these, see *ante*, paras. 26.01–26.17.
[73] Broadcasting Act 1990, Sched. 12, Part II, para. 2(9).
[74] January 1, 1991.
[75] See for the meaning of "prescribed diffusion services", *ante*, n. 54.
[76] Broadcasting Act 1990, Sched. 12, Part II, para. 3(1)(a).
[77] *Ibid.*, Sched. 12, Part II, para. 3(1)(b).

(c) the applicant for the licence to provide the new service is the holder of the licence to provide the existing service[78]; and

(d) after the expiry of the existing licence there will remain in force under Part II of the Telecommunications Act 1984 a licence which authorises the running of the telecommunication system by means of which the existing service is provided.[79]

26.22 Where a licence is so granted it must be in writing and (subject to revocation or shortening by the Commission under its statutory powers) continues in force for the period, not exceeding eight years, as may be specified in the licence.[80] The licence may include conditions necessary to enable the Commission to comply with its duties under Schedule 12,[81] conditions requiring the rendering of a payment to the Commission on the granting of the licence or during the currency of the licence, or both, of such amounts as may be determined by or under the licence[82] and conditions requiring the rendering to the Commission of such information as they require for the purpose of exercising the functions conferred on them by virtue of Schedule 12.[83] No person is entitled to hold both a new prescribed diffusion licence and a licence to provide a local delivery service on expiry of the prescribed diffusion services licence.[84]

26.23 **Cable licences to be succeeded on their expiry by local delivery licences.** The holder of a licence[85] which is in force under Part I of the 1984 Act to provide a "prescribed diffusion service"[86] may apply to the Commission for the grant from the expiry date of the licence for a licence to provide a local delivery service for the area in which the prescribed diffusion service is authorised to be provided.[87] The application must be in writing[88] and may not be made earlier than five years before the expiry date of the existing licence and not later than the "relevant date"[89]: where an application is made before the relevant date the Commission has a discretion to postpone the consideration of the application for as long as they consider appropriate but not beyond the

---

[78] *Ibid.*, Sched. 12, Part II, para. 3(1)(c).
[79] *Ibid.*, Sched. 12, Part II, para. 3(1)(d).
[80] *Ibid.*, Sched. 12, Part II, para. 3(2).
[81] *Ibid.*, Sched. 12, Part II, para. 3(3)(a).
[82] *Ibid.*, Sched. 12, Part II, para. 3(3)(b).
[83] *Ibid.*, Sched. 12, Part II, para. 3(3)(c).
[84] *Ibid.*, Sched. 12, Part II, para. 3(6).
[85] Pursuant to Part I of the Cable and Broadcasting Act 1984.
[86] See *ante*, para. 26.18, n.54 for the meaning of "prescribed diffusion services".
[87] Broadcasting Act 1990, Sched. 12, Part II, para. 4(1).
[88] *Ibid.*, Sched. 12, Part II, para. 4(2)(b).
[89] *Ibid.*, Sched. 12, Part II, para. 4(2)(a).

relevant date.[90] The application must specify the area which would be covered by the proposed local delivery service[91] and the technical means by which the service would be provided.[92] Where the application has been made in accordance with the above rules the Commission may only refuse the application if:

(a) they propose a grant, as a replacement of the existing licence, a **26.24** local delivery licence authorising the provision of a local delivery service for an area which would be different from that in which the applicant's service is authorised to be provided under the existing licence ("the franchise area")[93]; or

(b) the applicant is not, at the time when he makes the application, providing a prescribed diffusion service throughout the whole of the franchise area[94]; or

(c) it appears to the Commission that the applicant's proposed local delivery service would not cover the whole of the franchise area[95]; or

(d) it appears to the Commission that any telecommunication system proposed to be used by the applicant in the provision of the service would not be acceptable to the relevant licensing authorities.[96]

The licence granted will come into force on the expiry date of the **26.25** existing licence.[97] On the grant of the licence the Commission must determine an amount payable to it by the licence holder in respect of the first complete calendar year falling within the period for which the licence is granted ("the cash bid").[98] The sum to be paid by the applicant will be such sum as, in the opinion of the Commission, would be payable if the local delivery licence were advertised and awarded by competitive tendering according to the rules set down in sections 74 to 76 of the 1990 Act.[99]

---

[90] *Ibid.*, Sched. 12, Part II, para. 4(3).
[91] *Ibid.*, Sched. 12, Part II, para. 4(2)(b)(i).
[92] *Ibid.*, Sched. 12, Part II, para. 4(2)(b)(ii).
[93] *Ibid.*, Sched. 12, Part II, para. 4(5)(a).
[94] *Ibid.*, Sched. 12, Part II, para. 4(5)(b).
[95] *Ibid.*, Sched. 12, Part II, para. 4(5)(c).
[96] *Ibid.*, Sched. 12, Part II, para. 4(5)(d). "Relevant licensing authority" means the Secretary of State where the proposed telecommunications system is required to be licensed under the Wireless Telegraphy Act 1949. Where the telecommunications proposed would be required to be licensed under Part II of the Telecommunications Act 1984, the relevent authority is the Secretary of State and the Director General of Telecommunications: *ibid.*, Sched. 12, Part. II, para. 4(10).
[97] *Ibid.*, Sched. 12, Part II, para. 4(6).
[98] *Ibid.*, Sched. 12, Part II, para. 4(7).
[99] *Ibid.*, Sched. 12, Part II, para. 4(7), (8)(c). See *ante*, paras. 26.05–26.08.

The Commission is, therefore, under a duty to determine the cash bid value that would be put on the franchise by a bidder and it may in its discretion decide that the value of that franchise would be nil. In addition, the Commission may specify the percentage of qualifying revenue[1] for each accounting period of his that will be payable by the applicant to the Commission during the period for which the licence is to be granted.[2] The Commission may specify different percentages in relation to different accounting periods falling within the period for which the licence is to be in force and or a nil percentage in relation to any accounting period so falling.[3] A local delivery licence granted under these provisions may authorise the licensed service to be provided by wireless telegraphy to such extent as is specified in the licence.[4] In its consideration of the application and supervision of any licence granted the general duties of the Commission relating to local delivery licences apply.[5] The Commission is also under a duty to ensure that a local delivery licence is not granted to any person who is not a fit and proper person to hold it and shall do all it can to secure that if they cease to be satisfied that a licence holder is fit and proper that he does not remain a licence holder.[6]

26.26 **Non-prescribed diffusion services: continuation in force of existing licences.** Where immediately before the transfer date there is in force a licence to provide a diffusion service which is not a prescribed diffusion service but which is provided in the area in which a prescribed diffusion service is authorised to be provided the licence to provide the diffusion service continues in force for the remainder of the period specified in the licence.[7] Similarly any conditions which were included in the relevant licence by virtue of the Cable and Broadcasting Act 1984 and which were in force immediately prior to the transfer date continue in force.[8]

---

[1] For the meaning of "qualifying revenue", see *ante*, paras. 24.24–24.27.
[2] Broadcasting Act 1990, Sched. 12, Part II, para. 4(7), (8)(b).
[3] *Ibid.*, Sched. 12, Part II, para. 4(7), s.74(2).
[4] *Ibid.*, Sched. 12, Part II, para. 4(9).
[5] *Ibid.*, Sched. 12, Part II, para. 4(9).
[6] *Ibid.*, Sched. 12, Part II, para. 4(9). As to the meaning of "fit and proper person", see *ante*, para. 23.14.
[7] *Ibid.*, Sched. 12, Part II, para. 5(1).
[8] *Ibid.*, Sched. 12, Part II, para. 5(2). The Commission may, however, vary a "relevant licence" by notice if:
  (a) in the case of a variation of the period for which the licence is to continue in force, the licence holder consents; or
  (b) in the case of any other variation, the licence holder has been given a reasonable opportunity of making representations to the Commission about variation: *ibid.*, Sched. 2(4), Part III.

Where the relevant licence is due to expire[9] the Commission may **26.27**
extend the licence if it appears to them that on the expiry date there
would be in force either a licence to provide a prescribed diffusion service or a local delivery service licence for an area consisting of or including the area in which a diffusion service is for the time being provided
under the relevant licence but that on that date the holder of the
prescribed diffusion licence or local delivery licence would not be in a
position to provide his licensed service for all the dwellings for which
the service is being provided.[10]

It should be noted, however, the Commission may not specify in the
licence the period for which the licence is extended unless they have
reasonable grounds for believing that at that date the holder of the
licence to provide the local delivery service or the prescribed diffusion
service would be in a position to provide his service for all the dwelling
houses in his area.[11]

The holder of the diffusion services licence is entitled to be granted a **26.28**
local delivery licence if, on the expiry of his licence, there is no prescribed diffusion service or local delivery service consisting of or
including the area in which the diffusion service is provided or if a
licence is in force for one of those services but it appears to the
Commission that the holder is not in a position to provide his licensed
service for all the dwelling houses for which the diffusion service was
being provided immediately before the expiry date.[12] In such circumstances the Commission may not include terms in the licence requiring
the licence holder to achieve a coverage of the franchise area within a
specified period.[13]

Further, the Commission has no power to include a term in the
licence requiring the licence holder to provide the service by wireless
telegraphy and no cash bid or payment based on qualifying revenue
may be levied until the licence granted is renewed.[14]

---

[9] Which date must not exceed eight years beginning with the transfer date: *ibid.*, Sched.
12, Part II, para. 5(5). A "relevant licence" means a licence to provide a prescribed or
other diffusion service by virtue of paras. 1, 3, 5 or 8 of Sched. 12: *ibid.*, Sched. 12, Part I,
para. 1. These services are set out above under the headings: "Prescribed diffusion
services: continuation of existing licences", "Prescribed diffusion services: grant of
new licences to provide existing services", "Other diffusion services: continuation in
force of existing licences", "Other diffusion services: certain unlicensed services to be
licensed as cable services or local delivery services".
[10] *Ibid.*, Sched. 12, Part II, para. 5(4).
[11] *Ibid.*, Sched. 12, Part II, para. 5(4).
[12] *Ibid.*, Sched. 12, Part II, para. 5(8).
[13] *Ibid.*, Sched. 12, Part II, para. 5(8)(a).
[14] *Ibid.*, Sched. 12, Part II, para. 5(8)(b).

26.29   A local delivery licence granted under these provisions continues in force for a period of five years beginning with the date from which the licence is granted[15] and may be renewed for a further period of five years.[16] An application for renewal may be made by the licence holder not earlier than three years before the date on which it would otherwise cease to be in force and not later than the relevant date and where the application is made before the relevant date the Commission may postpone its consideration for so long as they consider appropriate but no longer than the relevant date.[17] Where the application is duly made the Commission must grant the application for the licence unless they propose to grant a fresh local delivery licence for the provision of a service which would be provided for a different area from that for which the applicant's service is provided.[18]

In such circumstances the Commission must determine the amount which is payable to it by the licensee in respect of the first complete calendar year falling within the period for which the licence is to be renewed[19] and may specify the percentage of qualifying revenue which will be payable to the Commission by the applicant during the period which the licence is to be renewed.[20] The qualifying percentage so specified may be in relation to different accounting periods falling within the period for which the licence would be in force and a nil percentage may be specified by the Commission in relation to any such accounting period.[21]

26.30   **Replacement of cable licences by local delivery licences.** Where immediately before the transfer date[22] there is in force under the 1984 Act a licence to provide a diffusion service which is neither a prescribed diffusion service nor a "relevant licence"[23] the licence ceases to have effect on the transfer date but the holder of the licence is entitled to be granted by the Commission as from that date a licence under Part II of

---

[15] *Ibid.,* Sched. 12, Part II, para. 5(9).
[16] *Ibid.,* Sched. 12, Part II, para. 6(4)(a).
[17] *Ibid.,* Sched. 12, Part II, para. 6(4)(b).
[18] *Ibid.,* Sched. 12, Part II, para. 6(4)(c).
[19] *i.e.* the sum ("the cash bid") that would be payable if the licence was put out to competitive tender.
[20] *Ibid.,* Sched. 12, Part II, para. 6(4)(e).
[21] *Ibid.,* Sched. 12, Part II, para. 6(4)(e).
[22] January 1, 1991.
[23] A "relevant licence" means a licence to provide a prescribed or other diffusion service by virtue of paras. 1, 3, 5 or 8 of Sched. 12: *ibid.,* Sched. 12, Part I, para. 1. These services are set out above under the headings, "Prescribed diffusion services: continuation of existing licences", "Prescribed diffusion services: grant of new licences to provide existing ervices", "Other diffusion services: continuation in force of existing licences", "Other diffusion services: certain unlicensed services to be licensed as cable services or local delivery services".

the 1990 Act to provide a local delivery licence for the area in which the diffusion service was authorised to be provided immediately before the transfer date.[24] The Commission has no power to include a term in the licence requiring the licence holder to provide the service by wireless telegraphy.[25] No timetable may be included in such licence requiring the licence holder to achieve a coverage of the franchise area within a specified period.[26] Except as provided above all the other provisions set out below apply to local delivery licences.[27]

A licence so granted continues in force for a period of five years from the transfer date.[28]

Other diffusion services: licenses to cease to have effect. The matters **26.31** set out in the previous two headings do not apply to a licence to provide a diffusion service for a single building or in an area in which there are not more than the prescribed number of dwelling houses.[29] Such licences cease to have effect on the transfer date.[30] but any liability of the licence holder which has accrued before that time under or by virtue of the licence is not affected by the licence ceasing to have effect.[31]

Unlicensed services to be licensed as cable services or local delivery **26.32** **services.** Where a diffusion service is being provided which immediately before the transfer date is being provided in an area which is comprised in the area in which a prescribed diffusion service is authorised to be provided the Commission must grant a licence to that person in respect of that diffusion service, where he applies for such a licence, if the following conditions are met by him.[32] First, the service, is one not required to be licensed by virtue of paragraph 1 of the Schedule to the Cable Programme Services (Exceptions) Order 1988[33] and secondly, it is being provided by means of a telecommunication system which has not previously been used for the purpose of providing a service licensed

---

[24] *Ibid.*, Sched. 12, Part II, para. 6(1).
[25] *Ibid.*, Sched. 12, Part II, para. 6(2).
[26] *Ibid.*, Sched. 12, Part II, para. 6(6).
[27] As to which see *ante*, paras. 26.01–26.17.
[28] Broadcasting Act 1990, Sched. 12, Part II, para. 6(4)(a).
[29] See *infra*, n. 30 for the meaning of "prescribed number of dwelling houses".
[30] Broadcasting Act 1990, Sched 12, Part II, para. 7(1): By Broadcasting (Number of Houses in an Area for the Purposes of a Diffusion Service Licence) Order 1990 (S.I. 1990 No. 2388) the Secretary of State has prescribed 1,000 as that number.
[31] *Ibid.*, Sched. 12, Part II, para. 12.
[32] *Ibid.*, Sched. 12, Part II, para. 8(1), (2).
[33] S.I. 1988 No. 1370: a licensable cable programme service consisting only of broadcasts for general reception made by the BBC or the IBA and included in the service by the reception and immediate re-transmission of the broadcasts is not required to be licensed.

under the Cable and Broadcasting Act 1984. However, in each case it must on the transfer date constitute a local delivery service.[34]

26.33   A licence so granted continues in force for the period of five years beginning with the transfer date.[35] Where the licence granted is due to expire on a particular date and it appears to the Commission that on that date there would be in force a licence to provide a prescribed diffusion service or a local delivery service for an area consisting of or including the area in which a diffusion service is being provided but it also appears to them that on that date the holder of any such licence would not be in a position to provide his licensed service for all the dwelling-houses for which the relevant service is being provided the Commission is under a duty to vary the licence so as to ensure that the licence continues in force until such time subsequent to that date as they shall by notice inform the licence holder of the service: the Commission may not, however, specify a date unless they have reasonable grounds for believing that at that time the holder of the licence would be in a position to provide his licensed service for all the dwelling houses.[36] Any such extension of the licence must not when taken with the initial grant extend the licence beyond eight years from the transfer date.[37]

26.34   If on the expiry date of the licence there is not in force a licence to provide a diffusion service for the area or a local delivery licence consisting of or including the area in which the diffusion service was being provided immediately before the expiry date or any of these licences are in force but it appears to the Commission that the holder is not in a position to provide his service for all the dwelling-houses for which a diffusion services was being provided the holder of the licence is entitled as of right to be granted as from the expiry date a local delivery licence for the area in which a diffusion service was being provided under the relevant licence immediately before that date.[38] The Commission has no power to include a term in the licence requiring the licence holder to provide the service by wireless telegraphy[39] and no timetable may be

---

[34] Broadcasting Act 1990, Sched. 12, Part II, para. 8(1), (2). A local delivery services for these purposes is a service which consists in the use of a telecommunication system (whether run by the person who uses it or not) for the purpose of the delivery of television and sound programmes for simultaneous reception in two or more dwellings in an area of more than a 1,000 dwelling houses but does not include services which transmit television and sound broadcasts and services which only deliver BBC, Channel 3, Channel 4: *ibid.*, s.72 and The Broadcasting (Local Delivery Services) Order 1990 (S.I. 1990 No. 2389).

[35] *Ibid.*, Sched. 12, Part II, para. 8(3).

[36] *Ibid.*, Sched. 12, Part II, para. 8(5).

[37] *Ibid.*, Sched. 12, Part II, para. 8(6).

[38] *Ibid.*, Sched. 12, Part II, para. 8(7), (8).

[39] *Ibid.*, Sched. 12, Part II, para. 6(2).

included in such licence requiring the licence holder to achieve a coverage of the franchise area within a specified period.[40] Except as provided above all the other provisions set out below apply to local delivery licences granted under this heading.[41] The licence so granted continues in force for a period of 15 years from the date when it is granted.[42]

Scope of relevant licences. A relevant licence[43] has effect so as to auth-   **26.35**
orise the provision of a service consisting in the use of a telecommunication system[44] for the purpose of the delivery of any of the services specified in section 72(2)[45] or any television or local sound broadcasting service provided by the Commission or the Radio Authority in accordance with Schedule 11 to the 1990 Act for simultaneous reception in the home in the area for which the licensed service is to be provided.[46]

Accordingly, the holder of any such licensed service is not subject to regulation under the Act as respects the programmes included in any service delivered by the telecommunication system in question except to the extent that he is regarded by the Act as providing any such service.[47] However, the licence holder is subject to regulation in respect of the delivery of foreign satellite programmes[48] and the Commission may give directions to the licence holder requiring him not to relay such programmes.[49] A licence granted under these provisions may not be transferred without the previous consent in writing of the Commission who must be satisfied that the transferee would be in a position to comply with all of the conditions included in the licence which would have effect during the period for which the licence is to be in force.[50]

Power of Commission to vary a relevant licence. The Commission may   **26.36**
vary a relevant licence by notice if in the case of a variation of the period for which the licence is to continue in force the licence holder consents or in the case of any other variation, the licence holder has been given a reasonable opportunity of making representations to the Commission

---

[40] *Ibid.*, Sched. 12, Part II, para. 6(6).
[41] See *ante*, paras. 26.01–26.17.
[42] Broadcasting Act 1990, Sched. 12, Part II, para. 6(4)(a).
[43] See *ante*, para. 26.27, n. 9.
[44] For the meaning of "telecommunication system" see *ante*, para. 23.04, n.6.
[45] These are television broadcasting services whether provided by the holder of an independent television licence or by the BBC or the Welsh Authority; a non-domestic satellite service; any licensable sound or programme service; any sound broadcasting service licensed by the Radio Authority or which is provided by the BBC.
[46] Broadcasting Act 1990, Sched. 12, Part III, para. 1(1).
[47] *Ibid.*, Sched. 12, Part III, para. 1(2)(a); Sched. 12, Part III, para. 1(3)(a). As, *e.g.* where he inserts his own advertisements.
[48] *Ibid.*, Sched. 12, Part III, para. 1(3)(b).
[49] *Ibid.*, Sched. 12, Part III, para. 1(5). See *ante*, para. 26.14 *et seq.*
[50] *Ibid.*, Sched. 12, Part III, para. 2(7).

about the variation.[51] The Commission may not vary the period for which a licence to provide a prescribed diffusion licence is to continue in force if that period as varied would exceed 15 years in the case of a licence to which section 4(4)(a) of the 1984 Act applied[52] immediately before the transfer date or eight years in the case of any other licence.[53] Further the Commission may not vary a licence to which paragraph 5(1)[54] or a licence to which paragraph 8(2)[55] of Schedule 12 applies[56] except where such variations are in respect of the powers conferred in paragraphs 5(4) and 8(5) of Schedule 12.[57]

26.37   **Restrictions on holding relevant licenses.** This subject is dealt with elsewhere in this work.[58]

---

[51] *Ibid.*, Sched. 12, Part III, para. 2(4).

[52] This would be a licence for the provision of a prescribed diffusion service in an area in which such service has not previously been provided or in which such service has previously been so provided but only in so much of it as in the opinion of the Cable Authority did not amount to a substantial part of it.

[53] Broadcasting Act 1990, Sched. 12, Part III, para. 2(5)(a).

[54] This is a licence to provide a diffusion service which is not a prescribed diffusion service but is provided in an area which is comprised in the area in which such service is for the time being authorised to be provided. Such licence continues in force for the remainder of the period specified in the licence. For the meaning of "prescribed diffusion service", see *ante*, para. 26.18, n.54.

[55] See *ante*, para. 26.32.

[56] Broadcasting Act 1990, Sched. 12, Part III, para. 2(5)(b).

[57] *Ibid.*, Sched. 12, Part III, para. 2(6).

[58] See *post*, Chap. 30.

CHAPTER 27

LICENSABLE PROGRAMME SERVICES

Introduction

Meaning of licensable programme service. A "licensable programme **27.01** service" means a service consisting in the provision of "relevant programmes"[1] conveyed by means of a local delivery service:

(a) for the reception in two or more dwelling houses in the United Kingdom otherwise than for the purpose of being received there by persons who have a "business interest" in receiving them[2]; or

(b) for reception at any place, or for simultaneous reception at two or more places, in the United Kingdom for the purpose of being presented there either to members of the public or to a group of persons some or all of whom do not have a business interest in receiving them.[3]

For these purposes, it is irrelevant (a) whether the telecommunication **27.02** system is run by the person providing the programmes or by some other person, and (b) whether reception of the programmes is for simultaneous viewing or for viewing at different times in response to requests made by different users of the service at different times.[4]

---

[1] Broadcasting Act 1990, s.46(5): such service will comprise television programmes other than one consisting wholly or mainly of non-representational images. Thus, services which consist solely of text will not be a licensable programme service.

[2] *Ibid.*, s.46(1)(a): a person has a "business interest" in receiving programmes if he has an interest in receiving them for the purpose of his business, trade, profession or employment: *ibid.*, s.46(5).

[3] *Ibid.*, s.46(1)(b).

[4] *Ibid.*, s.46(1).

Thus, programme services provided to local delivery services by means of video or by means of cable or microwave for showing in dwelling houses would come within the meaning of a licensable programme service. So too would the provision on a large screen, by means of a telecommunication system, of an event such as a pop concert to a paying audience at a place other than where the concert is taking place. Importantly, where reception can take place on demand by the recipient that will also constitute a licensable programme service and a licence will be required for the provision of such service.

27.03   The following services do not come within the meaning of a licensable programme service:

(a) a service where the programmes are provided for transmission in the course of the provision of a television broadcasting service or a non-domestic satellite service (*i.e.* simple relay of programmes)[5];

(b) a service where the running of the telecommunications system does not require to be licensed under Part II of the Telecommunications Act 1984[6];

(c) or a two way communications service (for example inter-active services such as video conferencing).[7]

In accordance with the general scheme of the 1990 Act a person who uses a telecommunication system for conveying television programmes[8] or runs a telecommunication system which is so used, is not to be regarded as providing a licensable programme service in respect of the programmes except to the extent that they are provided by him with a view to their being conveyed by means of that system.[9] However, where any relevant programme is provided for transmission in the course of the provision of any additional service,[10] that service is licensable under the provisions of section 47 of the 1990 Act.

(a) *Grant of licensable programme service licence*

27.04   The 1990 Act makes no provision for the grant of one licence to cover a multiple of programme services provided by a person. Each programme service requires an individual licence in respect of that service.

Section 47(1) of the 1990 Act provides that where an application is

---

[5] *Ibid.,* s.46(2)(a).
[6] *Ibid.,* s.46(2)(b).
[7] *Ibid.,* s.46(2)(c).
[8] *Ibid.,* s.46(3)(a).
[9] *Ibid.,* s.46(3).
[10] See *ante,* para. 23.05 for the meaning of "additional services".

duly made to the Commission, they may only refuse to grant the licence applied for if it appears to them that the service which would be provided under the licence would not comply with the consumer protection requirements set out in section 6 of the 1990 Act.[11] However, notwithstanding the clear wording of section 47(1) it would appear that if the applicant is not a "fit and proper person" or is a "disqualified person" in relation to that licence the Commission is under a duty not to award that licence to him.[12] Where these requirements are met by the applicant the Commission may not impose any quality threshold or competitive tendering.

Where the service is to be provided for reception only in a particular area or locality the Commission may modify the requirement as to "due impartiality"[13] to be found in section 6 by substituting a requirement that no undue prominence is given in its programmes to the views and opinions of particular persons or bodies on matters of political or industrial controversy or relating to public policy.[14] This is a less strict requirement than that imposed by the test of due impartiality and allows the service provider to place particular emphasis upon the views and preferences of the locality for which the service caters.

(b) *Duration of licence*

A licence to provide a licensable programme service continues in force   **27.05** for such period not exceeding 10 years as may be specified in the licence.[15] Thus licences may be granted for the provision of cable channels over an extended period or for a particular event such as the relaying of a pop concert to a paying audience at a venue.

(c) *Enforcement of licences*

The enforcement provisions of the 1990 Act which are applicable to   **27.06** Channels 3, 4 and 5 also apply to licensable programme services[16] with the following modifications. First, the Commission may direct an apology to be given without giving the service provider a reasonable opportunity to make representations to them about the matters complained of.[17] Secondly the maximum amount which the holder of a

---

[11] See *post*, para. 32.01 *et seq.* for the rules relating to "consumer protection" requirements and the ITC Programme Code which applies these requirements to licensees.
[12] Broadcasting Act 1990, ss.3, 5.
[13] See *post*, para. 32.29.
[14] Broadcasting Act 1990, s.47(5).
[15] *Ibid.*, s.47(3).
[16] *Ibid.*, s.47(8). See "Enforcement of Licences", *post*, Chap. 31.
[17] *Ibid.*, s.47(9).

licence may be required to pay by way of financial penalty is £50,000.[18] Thirdly, where the Commission resolves to revoke a licence such revocation takes effect on notice of revocation and may not be postponed until a date subsequent to the notice.[19]

(d) *Restrictions on ownership*

27.07   This subject is dealt with elsewhere in this work.[20]

---

[19] *Ibid.*, s.47(10).
[18] *Ibid.*, s.47(9). This sum may be changed by the Secretary of State by Order.
[20] See *post*, para. 30.16.

CHAPTER 28

INDEPENDENT PROGRAMME PRODUCTION

Duties of Commission and Broadcasters

The Commission is under a duty to ensure that the licences awarded **28.01** impose terms imposing an obligation on the licence holders to ensure that a range and diversity of independent productions is broadcast.[1] Each of the Channel 3 licence holders, Channel 4 and Channel 5 is in turn under a duty to ensure that in each year of the licence not less than 25 per cent. of the total amount of time allocated to the broadcasting of "qualifying programmes" is allocated to a range and diversity of "independent productions".

Competition duty. The Commission is under a duty to ensure that there **28.02** is fair and effective competition in the provision of licensed services and services connected with them.[2] Thus it is under a duty to ensure that the network centre and the regional licensees do not indulge in anti-competitive practices with regard to their dealings with independent producers. Such practices may, for example, manifest themselves in the form of seeking to deprive an independent producer of the exploitation rights, where it is partly funded by the television company, or in seeking to restrict the manner in which they may deal with the format rights of any programme licensed to the licensee.

Duty of BBC to include independent productions in its television ser- 28.03 vices. The BBC's duties are analogous to those imposed on the Commission. The BBC is to ensure that at least 25 per cent. of its output in any relevant period consists of independent programmes.[3] The "rel-

---

[1] Broadcasting Act 1990, s.16(2)(h).
[2] *Ibid.*, s.2(2)(b).
[3] *Ibid.*, s.186(1).

evant periods" are (a) the period beginning with the financial year beginning with January 1, 1993 and ending with March 31, 1994, and (b) the financial year beginning with April 1, 1994 and (c) each subsequent financial year.[4]

28.04   **Domestic satellite services.** A similar duty is imposed on the domestic satellite services.[5]

28.05   **The scope of the duty.** All broadcasters are under a similar duty to ensure diversity of commissioning. The duty imposed ensures that a range of independent productions in terms of cost of acquisition and types of programme is provided.[6] As a result, the broadcaster cannot confine commissioning to cheaper programmes or to one particular source of programmes (either in- or out-of-house).

Diversity is calculated by reference to the hours of "Qualifying programmes" broadcast in any given period and the "independent productions" which are to form 25 per cent. of that output. Both "qualifying programmes" and "independent productions" are programmes of the description specified in an order by the Secretary of State.[7] He may by order substitute a different percentage for the time allocated to independent productions.[8] Before making either order he must consult with the Commission and the BBC[9] and no order is to be made unless a draft of it has been approved by a resolution of each House of Parliament.[10]

28.06   **Application of the provisions.** The provisions are applied by analysing the output of qualifying programmes by a broadcaster and then ascertaining if the appropriate percentage are independently produced.

(a) *Qualifying programmes*

28.07   Any of the following are qualifying programmes[11]:

   (a) a programme which has been made by the relevant broadcaster or by a person commissioned by them[12];

   (b) a programme made by the relevant broadcaster together with any

---

[4] *Ibid.*, s.186(9).
[5] *Ibid.*, s.44(4)(b).
[6] *Ibid.*, s.16(5).
[7] *Ibid.*, s.16(5).
[8] *Ibid.*, s.16(6).
[9] *Ibid.*, s.186(2).
[10] *Ibid.*, s.16(7).
[11] The Broadcasting (Independent Productions) Order 1991 (S.I. 1991 No. 1408) art. 2(1).
[12] *Ibid.*, art. 2(1)(a). A relevant broadcaster is any of Channel 3, Channel 5, Channel 4, domestic satellite and the BBC.

other person or by a person commissioned by the relevant broadcaster together with any other person, where more than 25 per cent. of the actual production cost originates from the relevant broadcaster[13]; and

(c) a programme which includes images or images and sounds which have been provided by a person other than the relevant broadcaster or a person commissioned by him where:
  (i) the images or images and sounds provided consist of live coverage of an event;
  (ii) they do not exceed 75 per cent. of the duration of the programme; and
  (iii) the remainder of the programme (including any sound commentary added to those images or images and sounds) has been made by the relevant broadcaster or a person commissioned by him.[14]

Qualifying programmes do not include: **28.08**

(a) a programme which has previously been shown in substantially the same form by the relevant broadcaster (*i.e.* repeats).[15] This exclusion applies to programmes which were first shown on Channel 3 and are then repeated on Channel 4;

(b) a programme which consists wholly or mainly of news.[16] On Channel 3, the programmes provided by the nominated news provider will fall easily into this category;

(c) a programme which is part of a series which:
  (i) consists, wholly or mainly of news or items relevant to news;
  (ii) is presented live; and
  (iii) are usually shown on at least four days in each of the weeks when they are shown[17];

(d) a programme provided by or on behalf of the Open University or Open College; and

(e) a broadcast on behalf of a political party or any statement by a Minister of the Crown within the Ministers of the Crown Act 1975.[18]

---

[13] *Ibid.*, art. 2(1)(b): programmes which were commissioned for first showing in the cinema will be caught by this provision so as to prevent avoidance of the Order by commissioning of works for the cinema with subsequent screening on television with the minimum of editing.
[14] *Ibid.*, art. 2(1)(c).
[15] *Ibid.*, art. 2(a).
[16] *Ibid.*, art. 2(b).
[17] *Ibid.*, art. 2(c).
[18] *Ibid.*, art. 2(e).

28.09 Any qualifying programme commissioned by one Channel 3 licence holder or by the central networking commissioning unit on behalf of the other Channel 3 licence holders or some of them will qualify as a qualifying programme.[19]

28.10 **Purchased programmes as qualifying programmes.** A programme may be treated as being made by a relevant broadcaster or a person commissioned by him although more than 75 per cent. of the duration of the programme includes images or images and sounds which have been provided by some other person if the images and sounds are not broadcast live and changes of substance whether by editing or otherwise have been made to them.[20]

Therefore, if programmes are purchased for transmission by a relevant broadcaster and editing, additions, narration or other changes of substance are made, those programmes will qualify. The question of what is a change of substance would appear to be a question of fact and degree. It follows that a change which only alters 10 per cent. of the viewing time in a given programme but materially alters the nature of the purchased material may result in the programme being a qualifying programme.

(b) *Independent productions and producers*

28.11 **Meaning of independent productions.** Independent productions means any programme which:

(a) falls within any of the definitions of a qualifying programme[21];

(b) has been made by an independent producer where the programme has been commissioned from him by the relevant broadcaster or commissioned from him by the relevant broadcaster together with any other person and not less than 25 per cent. of the actual cost of production has been borne by the relevant broadcaster; or

(c) where the images and sounds consisting of live coverage of an event do not exceed 75 per cent. of the duration of the programme and which are provided by some person other than the relevant broadcaster and the remainder (including any sound commentary added to those images or images and sound) has been made by an independent producer[22];

(d) has been made in pursuance of an agreement which concerns

---

[19] *Ibid.,* art. 2(4).
[20] *Ibid.,* art. 1(3).
[21] *Ibid.,* art. 3(1)(a).
[22] *Ibid.,* art. 3(1)(b).

directly or indirectly the making of programmes (but not the use made of them[23]) and which is capable of remaining in force for a period in excess of five years and which gives the other side the right to terminate those obligations at intervals of not more than five years[24]; and

(e) the broadcaster has not required (otherwise than in pursuance of any contractual obligation arising from an earlier agreement which remains in force), the person to whom the contract is granted to agree, as a condition on which the contract is granted, to use the production facility of that broadcaster or not to use the production facilities of some other broadcaster.[25] For these purposes production facilities means any premises or equipment which may be used to make a programme and which are owned or leased by the broadcaster or are otherwise under his control[26] and any person who is employed by, or has contractual obligations with, that broadcaster in connection with the making of programmes except any person who is employed, or has contractual obligations, to be seen or heard (or both) on programmes.[27]

Independent producer. An independent producer is a producer who is   **28.12**
not an employee (whether or not on temporary leave of absence) of a broadcaster[28] or who does not have a shareholding greater than 15 per cent. in a broadcaster.[29] A company cannot be an independent producer if a broadcaster has a shareholding greater than 15 per cent. in it.[30]

In order to prevent a large company by-passing the requirement by   **28.13**
setting up a series of wholly owned subsidiary companies or related companies, the definition contains a number of anti-avoidance provisions. The definition includes a person who controls the broadcaster, an associate of either the broadcaster or person controlling the broadcaster[31] and any body controlled by the broadcaster or by an associate.[32]

An "associate" in the context means either a director or a member of the same group as the company or an individual's husband or wife and any relative or husband or wife of a relative and any company of which

[23] This would appear to exclude programme distribution agreements.
[24] The Broadcasting (Independent Productions) Order 1991, art. 3(1)(c).
[25] *Ibid.*, art. 3(3).
[26] *Ibid.*, art. 3(3)(a).
[27] *Ibid.*, art. 3(3)(b).
[28] *Ibid.*, art. 3(4).
[29] *Ibid.*, art. 3(4)(b).
[30] *Ibid.*, art. 3(4)(c).
[31] *Ibid.*, art. 3(5).
[32] *Ibid.*, art. 3(5)(c).

that individual is a director, any person acting as a trustee of a settlement and the settlor or grantor thereof and any person associated with the grantor, partners and husband, wives or relatives of any of them, any two or more persons acting together to secure control of a body corporate or other association or to secure control of any enterprise or assets.[33] This means that a person who is a relative of the producer who is employed by the broadcaster does not come within the meaning of an associate.

(c) *Specific application to the BBC*

28.14 The 1990 Act deems the BBC to be uniquely sheltered from competition. Therefore, the Act creates a system of review by the Director General of Fair Trading of the BBC's commissioning process. The Commission, its licence holders and domestic satellite services are not subject to the review.

    The Act requires the Director General to report to the Secretary of State in respect of each relevant period on the extent to which the BBC has performed its duty to commission 25 per cent. of qualifying programmes from independent producers.[34] In addition to stating whether the BBC has performed its duty the Director General may give his observations with regard to competition in connection with the production of television programmes for broadcasting by the BBC or any other matter arising out of or conducive to competition.[35] Thus if it appears to the Director General that the BBC is performing its duties he may nevertheless make observations as to any way in which the commissioning process may be improved to ensure fair and effective competition.

(d) *Reports under section 186*

28.15 **Information to be furnished by BBC for reports under section 186.** So as to enable the Director General to effectively perform his duty under section 186 he is given an express power to require the BBC to produce such documents as he may specify and which are in their custody or control specified[36] or require it to provide such information which he feels necessary to make his report.[37] However, the BBC cannot be compelled by the Director General to produce any document (or give any information) which it could not be compelled to produce (or give in evidence) before the High Court or, in Scotland, the Court of Session.[38]

---

[33] *Ibid.*, art. 3(5).
[34] Broadcasting Act 1990, s.186(3).
[35] *Ibid.*, s.186(4).
[36] *Ibid.*, s.187(1).
[37] *Ibid.*, s.187(1).
[38] *Ibid.*, s.187(2).

CHAPTER 29

INDEPENDENT RADIO SERVICES

1. Categories of "Independent Radio Services"

Independent radio services are those radio services which are not pro- **29.01** vided by the BBC. The following are therefore included within the meaning of independent radio services.

National sound broadcasting service. A national service is any sound **29.02** broadcasting service which is provided on a frequency assigned to the Radio Authority ("the Authority") for "any such minimum area of the United Kingdom as the Authority may determine".[1] In determining the minimum area the Authority is required to make effective use, so far as is reasonably practicable, of the frequency or frequencies on which the service is to be provided[2] but in so doing it must not prescribe a coverage area for the service so extensive that the costs of providing the service for the prescribed area would be likely to affect the ability of the person providing the service to maintain it.[3] It therefore follows that there is no absolute duty imposed on the Authority to ensure that a national broadcasting service covers the whole of the United Kingdom.

---

[1] Broadcasting Act 1990, s.84(2)(a).
[2] *Ibid.*, s.98(2)(a).
[3] *Ibid.*, s.98(2)(b).

29.03 **Local sound broadcasting service.** A local service is any service which is provided on a frequency assigned to the Authority by the Secretary of State "for a particular area or locality in the United Kingdom".[4] A local service sound broadcasting service includes both community and commercial local radio stations.[5]

29.04 **Restricted sound broadcasting service.** A restricted service is any service which is provided "for a particular establishment or other defined location, or a particular event, in the United Kingdom".[6] Thus a service which is provided for the transmission of horse racing commentary to betting shops or for the provision of a radio service for a hospital will be a restricted service. The fact that there may be some "leakage" of the signals so that the broadcast may be heard outside the intended establishment or location does not, it appears, make the service other than a restricted one. However, if the purpose of the radio service is intended for reception by the wider section of the community its purpose would be that of a local service and would be regulated accordingly.

29.05 **Satellite sound broadcasting services.** The 1990 Act creates two categories of independent radio satellite services which are subject to regulation by the Authority.

The first category comprises a satellite service which is a sound broadcasting service, other than one provided by the BBC, which consists in the transmission of sound programmes by satellite from a place in the United Kingdom for general reception there.[7] To the extent that the programmes included in the satellite service consists of material provided by a person in the United Kingdom who is in a position to determine what is to be included in the service (in so far as it consists of programme material provided by him) then he is regarded as providing the service whether or not the programmes are transmitted by him.[8]

The second category of satellite service comprises the transmission of sound programmes by satellite from a place outside the United Kingdom for general reception there. If and to the extent that the programmes included in the service consist of material provided by a person in the United Kingdom who is in a position to determine what is included in the service (in so far as it consists of programme material provided by him) it comes within the regulatory framework laid down

---

[4] *Ibid.*, s.84(2)(a)(ii).
[5] *Ibid.*, s.126(2).
[6] *Ibid.*, s.84(2)(a)(iii).
[7] *Ibid.*, s.84(2)(b)(i).
[8] *Ibid.*, s.84(3)(b).

by the 1990 Act.[9] Thus, where a satellite radio service is transmitted from, for example, Cyprus for reception in the United Kingdom and X, who lives in the United Kingdom, prepares the programme schedule and makes or acquires some or a part of the material for transmission the service is to be regarded as provided by him and regulated by the Authority.

Licensable sound programme service. A licensable sound programme **29.06** service is the provision of sound programmes transmitted by means of a telecommunications system.[10] To come within the regulatory framework of the Act the transmission must be for reception in two or more dwelling houses in the United Kingdom.[11] Where the service is received by a group it will be licensable if some or all of those receiving it do not have a business interest[12] in so receiving it.[13] For these purposes, it is irrelevant, in determining the nature of the service, whether the broadcaster is also the producer or commissioner of the programme or whether the service is according to a fixed schedule or provided on demand by the consumer.[14]

There are three types of service which are not licensable sound programme services.

First, a service where the programmes are provided for transmission in the course of the provision of a sound broadcasting service.[15] For example, a national or local radio service, additional service, restrictive service, satellite service.

Secondly, a service where the running of the telecommunications system does not have to be licensed under Part II of the Telecommunication Act 1984.[16]

Thirdly, a two way service.[17] A two way service is a service of which an essential feature is that there will or may be sent from each place of reception by means of the same telecommunications system visual images or sounds or both for reception by the person providing the service, for example video conferencing and home shopping.[18]

---

[9] *Ibid.*, s.84(2)(b)(ii).
[10] For the meaning of "telecommunications system", see *ante*, para. 23.04, n.6.
[11] Broadcasting Act 1990, s.112(1)(a).
[12] *Ibid.*, s.112(5): a person has a "business interest" in receiving programmes if he has an interest in receiving them for the purpose of his business, trade, profession or employment.
[13] *Ibid.*, s.112(1)(b).
[14] *Ibid.*, s.112(1).
[15] *Ibid.*, s.112(2)(a).
[16] *Ibid.*, s.112(2)(b).
[17] *Ibid.*, s.112(2)(c).
[18] *Ibid.*, s.46(2)(c).

29.07 **Additional services.** Any service where telecommunications signals for transmission are transmitted by wireless telegraphy from places in the United Kingdom by use "of spare capacity within the signals"[19] will be an additional service.[20]

2. Regulation of Independent Radio Services

Regulatory duties of the Radio Authority

(i) *Ownership duties*

29.08 **"Fit and proper" and "disqualified" persons.** The Authority is under a duty:

    (a) not grant an independent radio service licence to any person unless it is satisfied that he is a "fit and proper person" to hold it and must do, all that it can to secure, that he does not remain the licence holder if they cease to be so satisfied[21]; and

    (b) to do all it can to secure that a person does not become or remain a licence holder if he is a "disqualified person" in relation to that licence[22];

    (c) and that any requirements imposed by or under Parts III to V of Schedule 2[23] are complied with by or in relation to licence holders to whom those requirements apply.[24]

29.09 In addition to the categories of disqualified persons set out in Parts III to V of Schedule 2 of the Act[25] a person is also disqualified from holding a licence if within the last five years he has been convicted of an offence under section 1 of the Wireless Telegraphy Act 1949 which involved the making of an unlicensed transmission by wireless telegraphy,[26] an offence under the Marine, & c., Broadcasting (Offences) Act 1967[27] or an

---

[19] *Ibid.*, s.114(1): "spare capacity" means the spare capacity within the signals carrying a sound broadcasting service where that service is provided on a frequency assigned by the Secretary of State not required for the purposes of the provision of a sound broadcasting system and is determined by the Authority to be available for the provision of additional services or such frequency as the Secretary of Sate may specify when allocating such frequencies.

[20] *Ibid.*, s.114(1).

[21] *Ibid.*, s.86(4). See *ante*, para. 23.08 for the meaning of "fit and proper person", and para. 23.14 for the nature of duty "to do all it can to secure".

[22] *Ibid.*, s.88(1). For the categories and meaning of "disqualified persons" see under "Restrictions on Ownership".

[23] See *post*, Chap. 30.

[24] Broadcasting Act 1990, s.88(1)(b).

[25] See *post*, Chap. 30.

[26] Broadcasting Act 1990, s.89(1)(a).

[27] *Ibid.*, s.89(1)(b).

offence of providing an independent radio service without being authorised to do so by or under a licence provided by the Authority.[28]

So as to enable it to enforce the ownership requirements the Authority is empowered by section 88(2) of the Act to require an applicant
for a licence to provide it with such information as it may reasonably
require to determine whether he is a disqualified person[29] and to determine whether any requirements imposed by Parts III to V of Schedule 2
would preclude it from granting a licence to him[30] and if so, the steps
required to be taken by or in relation to him so that the requirements
are met.[31] This provision is analogous to that set out in section 5 in
relation to independent television services.

Relevant change. The Act requires the Authority to include, in a licence   **29.10**
granted by it, terms to ensure that where the holder is a body[32] and a
"relevant change" takes place after the grant of the licence the Authority
may revoke the licence by notice served on the holder of the licence.[33]
Such notice may not, however, be served on the licence holder unless
the Authority have given him a reasonable opportunity of making representations about the matters complained of.[34]

A "relevant change" in relation to a body which has been awarded or
granted a licence means any change affecting the nature or characteristics of the body or any change in the persons having control over or
interests in the body, being in either case a change which is such that, if
the Authority had to determine whether to award the licence to the
body in the new circumstances of the case it would be induced by the
change to refrain from awarding the licence.[35]

Where a relevant change takes place after the award but before the
grant of the licence the Authority may revoke the award.[36]

Where the relevant change occurs after the grant the Authority may   **29.11**
not serve notice revoking the licence unless they have given the body a
reasonable opportunity of making representations to them about the
matters complained of.[37] The Authority is not bound to revoke the

---

[28] *Ibid.*, s.89(1)(c).
[29] *Ibid.*, s.88(2)(a).
[30] *Ibid.*, s.88(2)(a)(ii).
[31] *Ibid.*, s.88(2)(a)(iii).
[32] *Ibid.*, s.202(1): a "body" means a body of persons whether incorporated or not and
includes a partnership.
[33] *Ibid.*, s.88(5). See *post*, Chap. 30, para. 30.37 *et seq.*
[34] *Ibid.*, s.88(5).
[35] *Ibid.*, s.88(7).
[36] *Ibid.*, s.88(2)(b).
[37] *Ibid.*, s.88(5)(b).

licence and may, after considering the representations, decide not to revoke the licence. A "relevant change" in this context may consist of a change in ownership which is not in contravention of the ownership restrictions but which raises doubts about the new owner's financial stability or consent in the dismissal or resignation of a director or programme personnel of the company who were material in inducing the Authority to award the licence to the body. A "relevant change" may also occur where a body holding a licence becomes "disqualified" in relation to the licence by virtue of any restrictions on ownership.[38] In the latter case if the Authority has exercised its powers under the provisions of the Act[39] when granting the licence it has the power to direct the licence holder to take or arrange to take any specified steps that appear to the Authority necessary to comply with Parts III to V of Schedule 2. It is envisaged that this power will be exercised in the first instance and only if there should be a failure to comply will the power to revoke be exercised.

(ii) *Consumer protection duties*

29.12   **General duties.** The Authority must do all it can to secure that every licensed service[40] complies with the requirements that:

(a) nothing is included in its programmes which offends against good taste or decency, is likely to encourage or incite to crime, to lead to disorder or to be offensive to public feeling[41];

(b) any news, given in whatever form, in its programmes is presented with due accuracy and impartiality[42]; and

(c) its programmes do not include any technique which exploits the possibility of conveying a message to, or otherwise influencing the minds of, persons listening to the programmes without their being aware, or fully aware of what has occurred.[43]

---

[38] See *post*, para. 30.02 *et seq.*

[39] In particular, s.88(2)(b) which gives it the power to impose conditions in the licence enabling it to give the licence holder directions requiring him to take, or arrange for the taking of, any specified steps to comply with the restrictions on ownership. Section 88(2)(d) also gives the Authority the power to impose conditions in the licence requiring the body corporate to give it advance notice of proposals affecting shareholdings in the body or directors of the body where such proposals are known to the body.

[40] Broadcasting Act 1990, s.90(7): these requirements do not apply to any licensed service which is an additional service. See *ante*, para. 23.08 for the nature and content of this duty.

[41] *Ibid.*, s.90(1)(a).

[42] *Ibid.*, s.90(1)(b).

[43] *Ibid.*, s.90(1)(c).

Impartiality. The Authority must, in the case of every licensed service **29.13** which is a national, local, satellite or licensable sound programme service do "all that it can to secure" that such services:

(a) that there are excluded from its programmes all expressions of the views and opinions of the person providing the service on matters, other than sound broadcasting, which are of political or industrial controversy or relate to current public policy[44];

(b) that "due responsibility" is exercised with respect to the content of any of its programmes which are religious programmes and, in particular, that programmes do not involve any improper exploitation of any susceptibilities of the programme's listeners or any abusive treatment of the religious views and beliefs of those belonging to a particular denomination.[45]

In the case of a national service the Authority must do all that it can to **29.14** secure that due impartiality is preserved by the service provider as respects matters of political or industrial controversy or relating to current public policy[46] and in preserving due impartiality series of programmes may be considered as a whole.[47]

However, where the licensed service is a local, satellite or licensable sound programme service, the requirement is that undue prominence is not given in its programmes to the views and opinions of particular persons or bodies on such matters. The undue prominence requirement is lower than that of due impartiality and admits of the expression of opinions which reflect the views of the consumers of the particular service. There is no ready formula by which the test may be measured.

It is submitted that as each licensed channel may be owned by a different individual and cater for different types of audiences undue prominence must be considered in the context of that channel without going wider.

Duty to draw up a code giving guidance on impartiality. The Authority **29.15** must draw up and from time to time review a code giving guidance as to the rules to be observed, first, in determining what constitutes a series of programmes and secondly, due impartiality in respect of a national service on matters relating to political or industrial controversy or current public policy.[48] In applying this requirement the

---

[44] *Ibid.*, s.90(2)(b).
[45] *Ibid.*, s.90(2)(c).
[46] *Ibid.*, s.90(2)(a), s.90(3)(a).
[47] *Ibid.*, s.90(4).
[48] *Ibid.*, s.90(5)(a).

programmes included in the service must be taken as a whole.[49] However, editorialising is prohibited.

29.16 **General Code for Programme standards.** The Authority must draw up a code giving guidance as to:

(a) the rules to be observed regarding the inclusion in programmes of sounds suggestive of violence, particularly in circumstances such that large numbers of children and young persons may be expected to be programme listeners[50];

(b) the rules to be observed regarding the inclusion in programmes of appeals for donations[51];

(c) such other matters concerning standards and practice for programmes as the Authority may consider suitable for inclusion in the code.[52] When considering what "other matters" ought to be included in the code, the Authority must have special regard to programmes included in licensed services in circumstances such that large numbers of children and young persons may be expected to be listening to them.[53]

Before drawing up or revising the Code the Authority must, to the extent that it considers reasonably practicable to do so, consult every licence holder.[54] It must publish the code and every revision of it, in the manner it considers appropriate and do all it can to secure that the code is observed in the provision of licensed services.[55]

29.17 **General duties in relation to advertisements and sponsorship.** The Authority must "do all it can to secure" that:

(a) a licensed service does not include any,

(i) advertisement which is inserted by or on behalf of any body whose objects are wholly or mainly of a political,[56] or

(ii) which is directed towards any political end,[57] or

(iii) which has any relation to any industrial dispute, other than

---

[49] *Ibid.,* s.90(4).
[50] *Ibid.,* s.91(10)(a).
[51] *Ibid.,* s.91(1)(b).
[52] *Ibid.,* s.90(1)(c).
[53] *Ibid.,* s.90(2).
[54] *Ibid.,* s.91(3).
[55] *Ibid.,* s.91(1), (4).
[56] *Ibid.,* s.92(2)(a)(i). See *ante,* para. 23.08 for the meaning of "political".
[57] *Ibid.,* s.92(2)(a)(ii). See *supra,* n.56 for "political".

an advertisement of a public service nature inserted by or on behalf of a government department[58];

(b) in the acceptance of advertisements for the inclusion in a licensed service there must be no unreasonable discrimination either against or in favour of any particular advertiser[59];

(c) a licensed service does not, without the Authority's prior approval, include a programme sponsored by any person whose business consists, wholly or mainly, in the manufacture of a product or the provision of a service, which the license holder is prohibited from advertising because of the provision of section 93.[60]

There is no prohibition on the inclusion in a licensed service of any party political broadcast which complies with rules made by the Authority pursuant to section 107 of the 1990 Act.[61]

Code for the control of advertisements. The Authority must draw up **29.18** and from time to time review an "advertisements and sponsorship code".[62] Prior to drawing up the code the Authority must consult with the Commission[63] and such bodies or persons as appear to the Authority to represent listeners, advertisers, professional organisations qualified to give advice in relation to particular products, such other bodies or persons who are concerned with advertising standards, as the Authority thinks fit.[64] The Authority must to the extent that it considers it reasonably practicable, consult with every licence holder.[65]

The code must govern standards and practice in advertising and the sponsoring of programmes and prescribe the advertising or sponsorship to be prohibited or to be prohibited in certain circumstances and may contain different provisions for different kinds of licensed services.[66] It must do all it can to secure that the provisions of the Code are observed in the provision of licensed services.[67] In the discharge of its general responsibility for advertisements and methods of advertising and sponsorship, the Authority may impose requirements which go beyond those imposed by the "advertisements and sponsorship code".[68] The methods of control exercisable by the Authority to ensure that the provisions of the code as well as any requirements which go

---

[58] *Ibid.*, s.92(2)(a)(iii).
[59] *Ibid.*, s.92(2)(b).
[60] *Ibid.*, s.92(4).
[61] *Ibid.*, s.92(3).
[62] *Ibid.*, s.93(1).
[63] *Ibid.*, s.93(2)(a).
[64] *Ibid.*, s.93.
[65] *Ibid.*, s.93(2)(c).
[66] *Ibid.*, s.93(1).
[67] *Ibid.*, s.93(1).
[68] *Ibid.*, s.93(5).

beyond them are complied include a power to give directions to a licence holder with respect to the classes and descriptions of advertisements and methods of advertising or sponsorship to be excluded, or excluded in particular circumstances or exclusion of particular advertisements or exclusion in particular circumstances.[69] Directions may be general, specific, qualified or unqualified.[70]

(iii) *Monitoring of programmes*

29.19   There is no duty imposed on the Authority to listen to programmes in advance of their being included in licensed services. However, the Authority may make and use recordings of programmes included in any licensed services for the purpose of maintaining supervision over them.[71] So as to enable it to carry out this duty a licence must include conditions requiring the licence holder:

   (a) to retain for a period not exceeding 42 days, a recording of each programme included in the licensed service and at the Authority's request[72];

   (b) to produce to it the recording for examination or reproduction[73]; and

   (c) at the Authority's request to produce to it any script and transcript of a programme included in the licensed service.[74]

(iv) *Government control over licensed services*

29.20   The Secretary of State or any other Minister of the Crown[75] may if it appears to him necessary or expedient to do so, in connection with his functions, by notice require the Authority to direct the holders of any specified licences to publish in their licensed services, at specified times a specified announcement and the Authority must comply with the notice and when a licence holder publishes the announcement, he may announce that he is doing so because of such direction.[76]

---

[69] *Ibid.*, s.93(6).
[70] *Ibid.*, s.93(7).
[71] *Ibid.*, s.95(1).
[72] *Ibid.*, s.95(2)(a).
[73] *Ibid.*, s.95(2)(b).
[74] *Ibid.*, s.95(2)(c).
[75] *Ibid.*, s.94(b): " . . . any other Minister of the Crown" includes the head of any Northern Ireland Department when the licensed service is provided from a place in the Northern Ireland.
[76] *Ibid.*, s.94(1), (2). Reference should be made to *ante*, para. 23.24 and *post*, para. 32.20, where the similar provision is considered.

3. Licensing of Independent Radio Services

(a) *Licensing duties of the Radio Authority*

General duty. The Authority may grant such licences to provide inde-   **29.21**
pendent radio services as it may determine.[77] The primary duty of the
Authority is to carry out its function as respects the licensing of such
services in the manner it considers best calculated to:

(a) facilitate the provision of licensed services which, taken as a
   whole, are of high quality and offer a wide range of programmes
   calculated to appeal to a variety of tastes and interests[78]; and

(b) to ensure fair and effective competition in the provision of such
   services and services connected with them.[79]

Although there is no specific programme quality requirement   **29.22**
imposed by the 1990 Act in respect of individual national or local radio
services there is a general duty imposed on the Authority to take into
account the overall quality of independent radio services when granting
licences and regulating the services. The effect is that where a licence is
being considered by the Authority any grant must be such as will
ensure that the licensed services as a whole are of a high quality. Thus,
if the grant of a licence would have the effect that the standard of service
taken as whole would fall below a "high quality" the Authority would
be entitled to award the licence to a person who does not submit the
highest bid but who submits a bid which would maintain the overall
quality of the services.

However, if the proposed licensed holders services cater for a local
community but the quality of its programmes are not high but not such
as to take the service as a whole below the quality threshold required by
the Act there will be no breach of the Authority's duty. However,
definitional difficulties arise in that it is difficult to state with any
degree of precision what constitutes "high quality". Given the envisaged large number of news stations it would appear that any assessment of quality of the services when taken as whole will not be without
difficulty not only for the Authority but for any person asserting that it
is in breach of its duty.

The duty to ensure fair and effective competition in the provision of
services is similar to the duty imposed upon the Commission. Reference should therefore be made to *ante*, paragraph 23.04 *et seq.* The
discharge by the Director General of Fair Trading, the Secretary of State
or the Monopolies and Mergers Commission of any of their functions

---

[77] *Ibid.*, s.85(1).
[78] *Ibid.*, s.85(3)(a).
[79] *Ibid.*, s.85(3)(b).

connected with competition is not affected by the Authority's duty to ensure fair and effective compeition.[80]

29.23 **Diversity in national service.** In the discharge of its licensing function the Authority is required to award licenses so as to do all it can to secure the provision within the United Kingdom of a diversity of national services. The licenses so awarded must, in respect of each national service, cater for tastes and interests different from those catered for by the others. The number of national licenses which may be awarded is not prescribed by the Act but section 85 of the 1990 Act requires that the Authority, in the award of national licenses, must ensure that one national service must, for the greater part, consist in the broadcasting of spoken material and another wholly or mainly in the broadcasting of music which is not pop music.[81]

Thus, the Act measures "diversity" by reference to the type of programme broadcast by the service. However, in defining the type of programmes which are to be broadcast by the service the Authority must have regard to the tastes and interests of the type and category of persons at which it is aimed.

29.24 **Local service duty.** The Authority's licensing duty in respect of local services is not as specifically set down as in the case of national services. The requirement is that it must do all that it can to secure the provision within the United Kingdom of a "range and diversity of local services".[82] Some assistance as to the extent and scope of this duty may be derived from section 105 of the 1990 Act. This section requires the Authority, when determining whether and to whom to grant a licence, to have regard to the extent to which any proposed service would broaden the range of programmes available by way of local services to persons living in the area or locality for which it would be provided, and, in particular, the extent to which the proposed service would cater for tastes and interests different from those already catered for by the existing local radio and the extent to which the application has local support.[83]

Thus, the Authority is given a wide discretion as to whether the services are speech based or wholly or mainly music, the language of the station and the cultural group at which it is aimed. Whereas the

---

[80] *Ibid.*, s.85(4).
[81] *Ibid.*, s.85(2)(a): "pop music" is defined as including rock music and other kinds of modern popular music which are characterised by a strong rhythmic element and a reliance on electronic amplifications for their performance (whether or not, in the case of a particular piece of rock or other such music, the music in question enjoys a current popularity as measured by the number of records sold . . . *Ibid.*, s.85(6).
[82] *Ibid.*, s.85(2)(b).
[83] *Ibid.*, s.105(b), (d).

national services duty requires the Authority to ensure that a broad category of tastes and interests is catered for the local services duty requires a closer and more detailed consideration by the Authority of the particular characteristics of the proposed audience at which the service is aimed.

Additional services duty. The Authority must do all it can to ensure that **29.25** on any frequencies assigned[84] and used for the provision of a national service and any other frequencies allocated by the Secretary of State and carrying sound broadcasting services all the spare capacity available for the provision of additional services on that frequency is used for the purposes of additional services and in accordance with the terms of the additional services licenses granted by the Authority.[85]

(b) *Licence conditions*

General conditions. The overriding discretion given to the Authority is **29.26** that a licence may include those conditions which appear to it to be appropriate, having regard to the duties which are imposed on it, or the licence holder, by or under the 1990 Act.[86] These provisions apply to all independent radio services and any provision in the Act which specifies particular conditions which may or must be included by the Authority in a licence is not to be taken as derogating from this general power.[87]

Directions to comply. The Authority may include conditions requiring **29.27** the licence holder to comply with any direction given by the Authority as to such matters as are specified in the licence or are of a description so specified[88] or (except to the extent that the Authority consents to his not doing or not doing them) not to do or to do such things as are specified in the licence or are of a description so specified.[89]

Maintenance of character of the service. The Authority is under a duty **29.28** to include in national and local licences conditions which appear to it to "be appropriate to it for securing that the character of the licensed service, as proposed by the licensed holder when making his application, is maintained during the period in which the licence is in force".[90]

Thus, the programme service which is proposed by the licensed

---

[84] *i.e.* pursuant to *ibid.*, s.84(4).
[85] *Ibid.*, s.115(1).
[86] *Ibid.*, s.87(1)(a), (6).
[87] *Ibid.*, s.86(6).
[88] *Ibid.*, s.87(2)(a).
[89] *Ibid.*, s.87(2)(a)(ii).
[90] *Ibid.*, s.106(1).

holder will be incorporated into his licence and will only be variable on one of two grounds and only with the permission of the Authority. These grounds are: first, if such variation would not narrow the range of programmes available by way of independent radio services to persons living in the area or locality for which the service is licensed to be provided[91] or secondly, it would not substantially alter the character of the service.[92] However, the Authority is under no duty to permit such variation where the changes would satisfy both requirements.

29.29 Coverage of licensed area. National and local licences include conditions requiring the licence holder to ensure that the licensed services serves so much of the area or locality for which it is licensed to be provided as is "for the time being reasonably practicable".[93] A national licence must include conditions enabling the Authority, "where it appears to them to be reasonably practicable" for the licensed service to be provided for any additional area falling outside the "minimum area" to require the licence holder to provide the licensed service for the additional area.[94] In this context reasonable practicability would appear to require not only that the technical feasibility of the provision of the service but also that the provision of the service to the additional area is commercially feasible.

29.30 Extension of local coverage. The Authority retains a discretion to authorise the holder of a local licence, by means of a variation of his licence, to provide the licensed service for any additional area or locality adjoining the area or locality for which that service has been licensed to be provided.[95] However, this discretion may be exercised only if it appears to them that the extension of the coverage area would not result in a "substantial increase" in the area or locality for which the service is provided .[96] What amounts to a substantial increase is not clear from the Act but it would appear that such extension as is permitted should firstly not encroach onto the area of a local service which is intended to cater for similar tastes and interests and secondly that the extension of coverage may be such as may permit the service to cater for tastes and interests which are on the margins of the reach of the service who are not already catered for and who are unable to receive the service without an extension of coverage.

[91] *Ibid.*, s.106(1)(a).
[92] *Ibid.*, s.106(1)(b).
[93] *Ibid.*, s.106(2).
[94] *Ibid.*, s.106(3).
[95] *Ibid.*, s.106(4).
[96] *Ibid.*, s.106(5).

News and current affairs. There is no requirement that independent **29.31** local or national services must carry news and current affairs.

Supervision and inspection. Licence conditions may enable the Auth- **29.32** ority to supervise and enforce technical standards in connection with the provision of the licensed service[97] and the right to enter upon broadcast premises and there inspect operate or test any equipment on the premises used for the broadcast.[98] It would appear that the intention of these particular provisions is to give the Authority power to prevent interference with other users of the spectrum and reflects the Authority's ability to exercise closer supervision of local stations where equipment causing such interference might be used.

(c) *Form and scope of licence*

A licence granted by the Authority must be in writing[99] and may be **29.33** granted by the Authority for the provision of either a particular service or a service of such description as is specified in the licence.[1] For example, the licence may refer to a particular service such as a national service or refer to a national service providing classical music. The licence so granted may be for the provision of service which to any extent consists in the simultaneous broadcasting of different pro- grammes on different frequencies.[2] In the case of additional services licences the Authority may grant a licence which relates to the use of spare capacity within more than one frequency.[3] The Authority may also, in respect of two or more additional services licences, grant licences to use the spare capacity within the same frequency at different times (for example by dividing the hours of the day or days of the week in which each licensee may use the frequency) or the areas in which such licences will operate (for example, as in the form of the Channel 3 system).[4]

(d) *Duration and renewal*

The maximum period that a licence to provide an independent radio **29.34** service, a licensable sound programme service and additional services can be in force is eight years.[5] No maximum period is laid down for a restricted services licence. There is no statutory presumption that licences granted by the Authority will be renewed on their expiration.

---

[97] *Ibid.,* s.87(1)(b).
[98] *Ibid.,* s.87(2)(b).
[99] *Ibid.,* s.86(1).
[1] *Ibid.,* s.86(2).
[2] *Ibid.,* s.86(2).
[3] *Ibid.,* s.115(2).
[4] *Ibid.,* s.115(2).
[5] *Ibid.,* s.86(3).

29.35 **Variation of the licence.** The Authority may vary the licence period with the consent of the licence holder.[6] In any other case it may vary the licence provided the licence holder has been given a reasonable opportunity to make representations to the Authority about the variation.[7] The Authority does not, however, have any discretion to vary the additional payments which have been specified in respect of the national services and additional services nor does it affect the right of the Authority to suspend the licence for a period of six months because of the failure of the licence holder to comply with a condition of the licence or any direction given by the Authority under Part III of the Act.[8] These provisions correspond to those in section 3 of the 1990 Act relating to independent television services.[9]

29.36 **Transfer of licence.** The prior written consent of the Authority is required for the transfer of a licence to another person.[10] The Authority's consent may only be given if two pre-conditions are satisfied.

First, the Authority must be satisfied that the proposed new licence holder would be in a position to comply with all of the pre-existing licence conditions for the remainder of the licence period.[11]

Second, the Authority must be satisfied that the prospective transferee is a fit and proper person to hold the licence.[12] It is submitted that when considering whether a person is a fit and proper person the Authority is under a duty to act in the public interest in reaching a decision. But in so doing it must act on a rational basis. Thus a person may not be "disqualified person" but he may nevertheless find that he does not qualify as a fit and proper person because of his past business or personal history.

Where these two conditions are fulfilled it is difficult to envisage circumstances are factors which could justifiably allow the Authority to refuse its permission for the transfer of the licence.

(e) *Restrictions on changes in control over holder of national licence*

29.37 During the period beginning with the date of the award of a national licence and ending on the first anniversary of it coming in to force no change in the persons controlling the national licence holder or an

---

[6] *Ibid.*, s.86(5).
[7] *Ibid.*, s.86(5).
[8] *Ibid.*, s.86(6).
[9] See *ante*, para. 23.31.
[10] Broadcasting Act 1990, s.86(7).
[11] *Ibid.*, s.86(7), (8).
[12] *Ibid.*, s.86(4).

associated programme[13] provider may take place without the prior
approval of the Authority.[14] Where such a change has taken place without prior approval the Authority may revoke the licence after giving the
licence holder a reasonable opportunity of making representations concerning the matters complained of.[15]

Sub-licensing additional services licences. An additional services   **29.38**
licence may also include provisions enabling the licence holder, subject
to such conditions as the Authority may impose, to authorise any person to provide an additional service on the spare capacity allocated by
the ice.[16] However, the person so authorised must not be a disqualified
person in relation to an additional services licence[17] and any conditions
included in the additional services licence apply in relation to the provision of such services by the licence holder.[18] Thus, any failure by the
authorised person is treated as a failure by the licence holder to comply
with those conditions.

4. Conditions Relating to Fees and Additional Payments

(a) *National and additional services*

National and additional services are required to pay to the Authority   **29.39**
fees falling within three broad categories. These are as follows.

Regulatory Fees. The Authority is required to be self financing "at the   **29.40**
earliest possible date and receive sufficient revenue thereafter to enable
them to meet their obligations and discharge their duties under the
Act."[19] In order to meet this requirement the Authority may require the
holder of a licence of a particular class or description to pay to it what
appears to the Authority to be the appropriate contribution of the
holder towards meeting the sums which the Authority regards as
necessary to discharge its functions under the Act and at the same time
be self financing.[20] In determining the tariff the Authority may specify
different fees in relation to different cases or circumstances.[21] Thus, it is

---

[13] *Ibid.*, s.103(2): "associated programme provider" means any body which is connected
with the licence holder and appears to the Authority to be, or to be likely to be, involved
to any extent in the provision of programmes for inclusion in the licensed service.
[14] *Ibid.*, s.103(1)(a).
[15] *Ibid.*, s.103(1).
[16] *Ibid.*, s.115(3).
[17] *Ibid.*, s.115(4).
[18] *Ibid.*, s.115(5).
[19] *Ibid.*, Sched. 8, para. 12(1).
[20] *Ibid.*, s.87(3).
[21] *Ibid.*, s.87(4).

under no duty to charge all licence holders the same amount and can take into consideration the financial position of the prospective payer when deciding the amount payable. This is particularly important where the prospective payer is a local community service which may not be in a position to make a payment which equality would require. As a means of enforcing this payment requirement the Authority is given a power to include conditions in national, local or additional services licence requiring the payment by the licence holder to the Authority, (on the grant of the licence or at such times thereafter, or both, as may be specified by the licence) of a fee(s)[22] in accordance with the tariff fixed from time, and published,[23] by the Authority.

29.41 **Cash bid payments.** In addition to the regulatory fees a national and additional service licence must include conditions requiring the licence holder to pay to the Authority the national and additional licence holder's cash bid payments which formed part of the prospective licensees application for the licence. These payments fall into two categories:

(1) the cash bid in respect of the first complete calendar year falling within the period for which the licence is in force[24]; and

(2) and payments in respect of each subsequent year falling wholly or partly within the licence period, the amount of the cash bid increased by the "appropriate percentage".[25]

29.42 **Qualifying revenue payments.** At the time of inviting applications for a national and additional services licence the Authority must specify that percentage of qualifying revenue for each accounting period that would be payable by the applicant if the licence were granted to him.[26] Qualifying revenue in respect of additional services means all sums referable to the right under his licence to use or to authorise other persons to use the spare capacity during the licence period whether those sums are received or to be received by the licence holder or by any connected person with him.[27] Qualifying revenue in respect of a national service for any accounting period comprises all payments received or to be received by a licence holder by him or by any connected person in con-

---

[22] *Ibid.*, s.87(1)(c).
[23] *Ibid.*, s.87(4).
[24] *Ibid.*, s.102(1)(a): national service; s.118(1)(a): additional services.
[25] *Ibid.*, s.102(1)(b) national service; s.118(1)(b) additional service. The "appropriate percentage" is the percentage corresponding to the percentage increase in the official RPI between the November in the year preceding the first complete calendar year falling within the period for which the licence is in force and the RPI for the November preceding the relevant year: Broadcasting Act 1990, s.102(10).
[26] *Ibid.*, s.98(1)(d)(ii).
[27] *Ibid.*, s.118(2).

sideration of inclusion in the national service of advertisements or other programmes[28] or in respect of charges made for the reception of programmes included in that service.[29]

Where instead of or as part of the payment for the inclusion of advertisements or charges made for reception for a programme payments are made to the licence holder or any connected person to meet the payment of the percentage of qualifying revenue payable to the Authority, such payments are treated as made in consideration of the inclusion of the programme.[30]

Thus, if agreement is reached between an advertiser and the licence holder whereby qualifying revenue is diminished by the licence holder agreeing to accept a lower unit price for the advertising space or programme in return for the advertiser providing funds to enable the licence holder to pay his dues to the Authority, which consequently will be lower, the payment so made by the advertiser will form part of qualifying revenue. Such a device would mean that the income to the Authority would be diminished to the benefit of the licence holder.

Further, if a proportion of the costs of a programme on the service is **29.43** met by the sponsoring of a programme by a third party with the result that the programme costs the licence holder less than it would otherwise the licence holder will have financially benefited to the extent of that contribution and that sum will form part of his qualifying revenue.[31] Further, if an independent producer is commissioned to provide the programme and that producer obtains sponsorship so as to lessen the cost of the programme to the licence holder he will have financially benefited, indirectly, to the extent of the sponsorship.

Where an advertisement is included in a service as a result of the agency of an advertising agency or a person connected with the licence holder a fee not exceeding 15 per cent. may be deducted by the advertising agent or connected person by way of commission and such deduction will not form part of qualifying revenue.[32] If the amount deducted by way of commission exceeds 15 per cent. of the amount paid by the advertiser, the amount of the receipt by the licence holder is taken to be the amount of the payment less 15 per cent.[33]

Disputes as to qualifying revenue. The Authority's decision shall be **29.44** final, in the event of a disagreement between the Authority and a licence holder, as to the amount of the qualifying revenue of a licence

---

[28] *Ibid.*, s.102(2)(a).
[29] *Ibid.*, s.102(2)(b).
[30] *Ibid.*, s.102(3).
[31] *Ibid.*, s.102(6).
[32] *Ibid.*, s.102(4).
[33] *Ibid.*, s.102(5).

holder for any accounting period, the amount of any payment to be made to the Authority by a licence holder in respect of such revenue or instalment of such payment.[34] The only means by which such decision of the Authority may be challenged is by judicial review.[35]

(b) *Local services*

29.45   A local service may only be required by the Authority to pay regulatory fees.[36] Local services licences are not awarded by way of cash bids.

5. Criteria for Award of Licences

(a) *National, additional and local services*

29.46   **Financial viability threshold.** The Authority needs to be satisfied that a national and local licence holder will be able to financially maintain their service for the duration of the licence period.[37] In order to assist the Authority in determining this matter an applicant's application must include details of both their present financial position and a projection of their financial position throughout the period of the licence.

29.47   **Cash bid.** Although there is no quality threshold as in the case of independent radio services it is a precondition to the considering of the cash bid in respect of a national licence that the Authority is satisfied that the proposed service:

(a) if it is to be either a speech based service or a music service, which does not consist of pop music, it is in fact such a service;

(b) if there is any existing licensed national service, that the proposed service is to be one which caters for tastes and interests different from those already catered for by any such service;

(c) that the service consists of a diversity of programmes calculated to appeal to a variety of tastes and interests;

(d) the prospective licensee would be able to maintain the service throughout the period for which the licence is in force.[38]

---

[34] *Ibid.*, Part II Sch.7, para. 2(1).
[35] *Ibid.*, Part II, Sch.7, para. 2(2).
[36] *Ibid.*, s.87(1)(c).
[37] *Ibid.*, s.99(1)(b) and s.105(a) respectively.
[38] *Ibid.*, s.99(1).

In the case of an additional services licence the Authority may not **29.48**
proceed to a consideration of the cash bid unless it appears to them[39]
that any technical plan involving the use of any telecommunication
system is acceptable to the Secretary of state and the Director General of
Telecommunications and that the services would be maintainable by
the applicant during the period of the licence.[40]

The general principle is that those applicants who satisfy these
criteria will have their cash bids considered by the Authority who will
award the licence to the applicant who submitted the highest cash
bid.[41]

Where the Authority decides that there are "exceptional circum- **29.49**
stances" it may award the licence to an applicant not making the highest bid.[42] There is no definition of what would constitute exceptional
circumstances but where it appears to the Authority in the context of
the licence that any circumstances are to be regarded as exceptional
circumstances, those circumstances may be so regarded by it despite
the fact that similar circumstances have been so regarded by it in the
context of similar licences.[43]

An important factor in determining whether there are exceptional
circumstances will be the Authority's duty to ensure the provision of
licensed services which when taken as whole are of a high quality and
offer a wide range of programmes calculated to appeal to a variety of
tastes and interests.[44] Where the programmes of an applicant who does
not offer the highest cash bid is capable of maintaining and enhancing
this general requirement but that of the highest cash bidder is not of a
similar quality it would be a proper exercise of its discretion to grant the
licence to that applicant on the basis of exceptional circumstances. Provided that the Authority acts rationally the exercise of its discretion in
such circumstances discretion will not be reviewable.

Cash bids are not a factor in the award of local service licences.

Source of funds not in the public interest. If it appears to the Authority **29.50**
that there are grounds for suspecting that any "relevant source of
funds" of an applicant who has submitted the highest bid and to whom
it is minded to award the licence in respect of an additional or national
services licence is not in the public interest it must refer his application

---

[39] *Ibid.*, s.117(2): before forming any view as to whether the technical plans are acceptable
to the Secretary of State and the Director General of Telecommunications the Authority
must consult both of them.
[40] *Ibid.*, s.117(1).
[41] *Ibid.*, s.100(1), s.117(3), applying s.100 to additional services.
[42] *Ibid.*, s.103.
[43] *Ibid.*, s.100(3).
[44] *Ibid.*, s.85(3)(a).

to the Secretary of State together with a copy of all the documents submitted to it by the applicant and a summary of the Authority's deliberations on the application and must not award the licence to the applicant unless the Secretary of State gives his approval.[45] For these purposes a "relevant source of funds" is any source of funds to which an applicant might have recourse (directly or indirectly) for the purpose of paying to the Authority the cash bid, the percentage of qualifying revenue or otherwise financing the provision of the service.[46]

It is to be noted that this provision is only applicable to national service and additional services licences. It is not clear however what the position would be if the Authority should suspect that the relevant source of funds which will be used for financing the local service is not in the public interest. When the Authority is precluded from awarding the licence to an applicant because his relevant source of funds is such that to do so would not be in the public interest, the effect is as if he had not made an application for the licence. Alternatively, the Authority may, in its discretion, publish a fresh notice proposing to grant the licence and again invite applications for it.[47]

29.51 **Diversity threshold in local services.** In awarding a local services the Authority is required to have regard to the extent which the proposed service would cater for the tastes and interests of persons living in the locality, the extent to which the proposed service would broaden the range of programmes available by way of local services to persons living in the locality for which it would be provided[48] and the extent to which the application for the licence is supported by persons living in the locality.[49]

29.52 **Technical threshold.** In the case of local licences and national licences the Authority must also be satisfied that the arrangements which the applicant proposes to make for and in connection with the transmission of the proposed service[50] are such that they are technically acceptable and would be available for the period of the licence.

The only requirement in respect of additional services is that the technical plan is acceptable to the Secretary of State and the Director General for Telecommunications.[51] If it is so acceptable and the financial criteria are passed he is entitled to have his cash bid considered.

---

[45] *Ibid.*, s.100(5), s.117(3), applying s.100 to additional services licences.
[46] *Ibid.*, s.100(6).
[47] *Ibid.*, s.100(7).
[48] *Ibid.*, s.105(b), (c).
[49] *Ibid.*, s.105(d).
[50] *Ibid.*, s.98(3)(e)(ii) in respect of national services and s.104(2)(c)(ii) in respect of local services.
[51] *Ibid.*, s.117(1)(a).

(b) *Licensable sound programme service*

Licensable sound programme service. Where an application has been **29.53**
duly made the Authority may only refuse to grant it if it appears to it
that the service which would be provided would not comply with the
consumer protection requirements.[52]

Satellite and restricted sound services. No criteria for grant of these **29.54**
licences is laid down by the Act. However, the consumer protection
requirements of section 90 apply to all independent radio services. If
therefore the applicant's proposed service does not comply with those
requirements the Authority would appear to be under a duty either to
refuse to grant a licence or grant a licence subject to the proposed
service complying with the general code for programmes drawn up by
it pursuant to section 91.

---

[52] *Ibid.*, s.113.

CHAPTER 30

RESTRICTIONS ON HOLDING LICENCES

1. Introduction

30.01 The ownership restrictions of the Act provide a comprehensive code with regard to the holding of licences. Persons who are not permitted to hold independent television or independent radio services licences broadly fall within three categories. First, "disqualified persons".[1] The Act sets out in Schedule 2, Part II, a detailed list of persons who are to be regarded as "disqualified persons" with regard to licensed services. Secondly, those who have accumulated interests in licensed services exceeding the limits set out in Schedule 2, Part III of the Act. Thirdly, persons who are not "fit and proper persons" may not hold a licence. Thus although a person may not be "disqualified" within the meaning of Schedule 2 of the Act he may nevertheless be regarded as not "fit and proper" to hold a licence.

---

[1] Broadcasting Act 1990, s.5 (independent television services); *ibid.*, s.88 (independent radio services).

2. Disqualified Persons

General duty. The Commission[2] and the Authority[3] are under a duty to   **30.02**
"do all that they can to secure"[4] first, that a person does not become the
holder of a licence if he is a disqualified person in relation to that
licence[5] and secondly that any restrictions as to the accumulation of
interest in licensed services are complied with by or in relation to persons holding licences in relation to which those requirements apply.[6]
These duties are two-fold.

First, sections 5 and 88 and Schedule 2 of the Act gives the Commission and the Authority power, and imposes a duty, to trace control
back to whoever is exercising effective over the company which holds
the licence.

Secondly, this duty is of a continuing nature in the sense that the
Commission and the Authority are required to ensure that the licence is
not awarded to a disqualified person but additionally throughout the
licence period they must establish and maintain a system whereby they
are able to monitor the ownership of the bodies holding licences so as to
ensure that the ownership rules are not breached.

In the exercise of the first of these duties the Commission[7] and the   **30.03**
Authority[8] may require the applicant for a licence, or any company proposing to takeover a licence holder, to provide it with such information
it may require to determine whether the person is "disqualified" or
whether the accumulated interests of a person in licensed services pre-
cludes him from holding a licence.[9] Where the proposed license holder
or takeover company fails to provide the information requested by the
regulatory authorities it would appear that they are entitled to draw
adverse conclusions and act upon those conclusions. In this sense therefore the burden is on the licensee or takeover company to show that
they are neither "disqualified persons" nor subject to the restrictions on
the accumulation of interests.

Categories of disqualified persons

The following categories of persons are disqualified in relation to a   **30.04**
licence granted by the Commission or the Authority.

---

[2] *Ibid.*, s.5(1).
[3] *Ibid.*, s.88(1).
[4] See *ante*, para. 23.07 *et seq.* for the scope and extent of the duty imposed by this
expression.
[5] Broadcasting Act 1990, ss.5(1)(a), 88(1)(a).
[6] *Ibid.*, ss.5(1)(b), 88(1)(b).
[7] *Ibid.*, s.5(2).
[8] *Ibid.*, s.88(2).
[9] *Ibid.*, ss.5(2), 88(2).

30.05 **Individuals.** An individual who is neither a national of a member State who is ordinarily resident within the European Union nor ordinarily resident in the United Kingdom, the Isle of Man or the Channel Islands is disqualified from holding a licence granted by the Commission or the Authority.[10]

30.06 **Body corporate.** A company which is neither a body formed under the law of a Member State which has its registered or head office or principal place of business within the European Union nor incorporated under the law of the Isle of Man or Channel Islands is disqualified from holding a licence.[11] There is no definition of the meaning of head office. The Act draws a distinction between principal office[12] and head office and it would therefore appear that the two are not necessarily the same.

Notwithstanding this apparent difference it is submitted that the two are the same within the meaning of Schedule 2, Part II, paragraph 1(1)(b) and is to be taken to mean where the business of the body corporate is managed and controlled as a whole.[13]

30.07 **Bodies having political connections.** A body[14] whose objects are wholly or mainly of a political nature ("the political body") is disqualified person in relation to a licence granted by the Commission. " 'Political' covers any material that is aimed at securing a change in some aspect of public policy".[15] Thus the restrictions are not solely confined to political parties or groups affiliated to a particular party.

The rules in respect of such groups are extremely detailed with the apparent intent of preventing circumvention of the restrictions by a body creating a sophisticated structure with many layers which disguise the party exercising effective control. In pursuance of this apparent aim the following are also disqualified persons:

(a) a local authority[16];

(b) a body whose objects are wholly or mainly of a political nature[17];

(c) a body affiliated to a body falling within (b)[18];

---

[10] *Ibid.*, Sched. 2, Part II, para. 1(1)(a).
[11] *Ibid.*, Sched. 2, Part II, para. 1(1)(b).
[12] *Ibid.*, see, *e.g.* s.199(4) where reference is made to principal office.
[13] *Garton v. Great Western Rly Co.* (1858) EB. & E. 837; *Palmer v. Caledonian Rly Co.* [1892] 1 Q.B. 823; *Clokey v. London and North Western Rly Co.* [1905] 2 I.R. 251.
[14] Broadcasting Act 1990, s.202(1): body or bodies means a body of persons whether incorporated or not and includes a partnership.
[15] See *ante*, para. 23.22 for the meaning of "wholly or mainly of political nature".
[16] Broadcasting Act 1990, Sched. 2, Part II, para. 1(1)(c).
[17] *Ibid.*, Sched. 2, Part II, para. 1(1)(c).
[18] *Ibid.*, Sched. 2, Part II, para. 1(1)(e).

(d) an individual who is an officer of a body falling within (b) or (c)[19];

(e) a company which is an associate[20] of a company falling within (b) or (c)[21];

(f) a company falling within any of (a) to (c) and (e) which is a participant[22] with more than a five per cent. interest[23];

(g) a body which is controlled[24] by a person falling within any of (a) to (e), an individual[25] or company disqualified by reason of being non-E.U. nationals,[26] or two or more such persons taken together[27];

(h) a company in which body falling within (g) other than one which is controlled[28] by a person falling within (d) or by non-E.U. individuals[29] or companies[30] or by two of such persons taken together.[31]

Religious bodies. A body whose objects are wholly or mainly of a **30.08** religious nature is a disqualified person in relation to a licence granted

---

[19] *Ibid.*, Sched. 2, Part II, para. 1(1)(f).

[20] *Ibid.*, Sched. 2, Part I, para. 1(1): "associate" in relation to a body corporate means a director of that body corporate or a body corporate which is a member of the same group as that body corporate.

[21] *Ibid.*, Sched. 1, Part II, para. 1(1)(g).

[22] *Ibid.*, Sched. 2, Part I, para. 1(2): "participant," in relation to a company means a person who holds or is beneficially entitled to shares in that body or who possesses voting power in that body.

[23] *Ibid.*, Sched. 1, Part II, para. 1(1)(h).

[24] *Ibid.*, Sched. 2, Part I, para. 1(3), (4): a person "controls" a company if:

  (a) he holds, or is beneficially entitled to, more than 50 per cent. of the equity share capital in that company or possesses more than 50 per cent. of the voting power in it ("controlling interest");

  (b) although not having controlling interest he is able, by virtue of the holding of shares or the possession of voting power in or relation to the body or any other company, to secure that the affairs of the company are conducted in accordance with his wishes and for these purposes a person may be regarded as controlling a company despite the fact that he does not have controlling interest in any such other company, any such other company does not have a controlling interest in that company or he and any such other company together do not have controlling interest in that body;

  (c) he has the power, by virtue of any powers conferred by the articles of association or other document regulating the company or any other company, to secure that the affairs of the company are conducted in accordance with his wishes.

[25] See *ante*, para. 30.05.

[26] See *ante*, para. 30.06.

[27] Broadcasting Act 1990, Sched. 1, Part II, para. 1(1)(i): persons or bodies are not to be taken as acting together unless they are acting in concert.

[28] See *supra*, n.24.

[29] See *ante*, para. 30.05.

[30] See *ante*, para. 30.06.

[31] Broadcasting Act 1990, Sched. 1, Part II, para. 1(1)(j). See *ante*, para. 26.27, n.8 for the meaning of "relevant licence".

by the Commission or Authority. This disqualification extends to:

(a) a body whose objects are wholly or mainly of a religious nature[32];

(b) a body which is controlled[33] by a religious body or by two or more bodies such bodies taken together[34];

(c) a body which controls a religious body[35];

(d) a company which is an associate[36] of a company falling within (a), (b) or (c)[37];

(e) a company in which a body falling within any of (a) to (d) is a participant with more than a five per cent. interest[38];

(f) an individual who is an officer of a religious body[39];

(g) a body controlled by an individual who is an officer of a religious body or two or more such individuals taken together.[40]

30.09 A person who is a disqualified person within the meaning of this rule may make an application to the Commission or Authority under Schedule 2, Part II, paragraph 2 for a determination by the Commission or (as the case may be) the Authority that it would be appropriate for them to hold a licence to provide a non-domestic satellite service or a licensable programme service. If the Commission (or the Authority, as the case may be) are satisfied that it would be appropriate they must make a determination that they are so satisfied. As long as the determination remains in force in relation to that person, he is not a disqualified person in relation to that licence.[41] The Commission and Authority must each publish, in the manner they consider appropriate, general guidance to applicants as to the principles to be applied by them in determining whether it is appropriate for them to hold those categories of licence.[42]

During the Committee stage of the Bill[43] this provision was described as a filter mechanism to prevent either religious cults or unacceptable religious broadcaster from taking advantage of an amelioration of the

---

[32] *Ibid.*, Sched. 2, Part II, para. 2(1)(a). See *ante*, para. 26.18, n.54 for the meaning of "prescribed diffusion service".

[33] For meaning of "controlled" see *ante*, para. 30.07, n.24.

[34] Broadcasting Act 1990, Sched. 2, para. 2(1)(b).

[35] *Ibid.*, Sched. 2, Part II, para. 2(1)(c).

[36] For meaning of "associate", see *ante*, para. 30.07, n.29.

[37] Broadcasting Act 1990, Sched. 2, Part II, para. 2(1)(d).

[38] *Ibid.*, Sched. 2, Part II, para. 2(1)(e).

[39] *Ibid.*, Sched. 2, Part II, para. 2(1)(f).

[40] *Ibid.*, Sched. 2, Part II, para. 2(1)(g).

[41] *Ibid.*, Sched. 2, Part II, para. 2(2).

[42] *Ibid.*, Sched. 2, Part II, para. 2(3).

[43] David Mellor, Minister of State, Home Office Committee F Vol. 172, col. 205.

rules for religious broadcasting. The rules are thus designed to benefit the mainstream religious groups in the United Kingdom and gives the Commission or (as the case may be) the Authority a wide discretion to use its judgment reasonably as to who to accept and who to reject where it receives applications for religious broadcasting licences.

Publicly funded bodies for radio services. A body ("publicly funded **30.10** bodies") (other than a local authority) which has in its last financial year received more than half its income from public funds is a disqualified person in relation to any licence granted by the Authority[44] other than a licence to provide a restricted service.

Further, a body which is controlled by a publicly funded body or by two or more publicly funded bodies taken together or body corporate in which the publicly funded body or the body which is controlled by a publicly funded body or two of them acting together are participants with more than five per cent interest are disqualified persons.[45] Money is received from the public funds if it is paid by a Minister of the Crown out of money provided by Parliament or out of the National Loan Funds.[46] or a Northern Ireland department of the Consolidated Fund of Northern Ireland or out of money appropriated by Measure of Northern Ireland Assembly[47] or a publicly funded body, including a body which is a publicly funded body by virtue of receiving public funds as so defined.[48] Any money paid as consideration for the acquisition of property, supply of goods or services or as remuneration, expenses, pensions, allowances or similar benefits for or in respects of a person of an office must be disregarded for the purposes ascertaining the amount of money received from public funds.[49]

Undue influence. A person is a disqualified person in relation to a **30.11** licence granted by the Commission or the Authority if he receives financial assistance or influence is otherwise exerted over his activities by a "relevant body"[50] *and* that influence has led, is leading or is likely to lead to results which are adverse to the public interest.[51] A relevant body in respect of a licence granted by the Commission is any of the following[52]:

    (a) a local authority;

---

[44] Broadcasting Act 1990, Sched. 2, para. 3(1)(a).
[45] *Ibid.*, Sched. 2, Part II, para. 3(1).
[46] *Ibid.*, Sched. 2, Part II, para. 3(2)(a).
[47] *Ibid.*, Sched. 2, Part II, para. 3(2)(b).
[48] *Ibid.*, Sched. 2, Part II, para. 3(2)(c).
[49] *Ibid.*, Sched. 2, Part II, para. 3(2).
[50] *Ibid.*, Sched. 2, Part II, para. 4(1)(a).
[51] *Ibid.*, Sched. 2, Part II, para. 4(1)(b).
[52] *Ibid.*, Sched. 2, Part II, para. 4(2).

(b) a body whose objects are wholly or mainly of a political nature;

(c) a body affiliated to the political body;

(d) an individual who is an officer of the body or its affiliate;

(e) a body corporate which is an associate of the body or its affiliate;

(f) a body which is a participant with more than five per cent. interest in the body or its affiliate;

(g) a body corporate which is a participant with more than a five per cent interest in any of the following:

   (i) a religious body;

  (ii) a body controlled by a religious body; or

 (iii) by two religious bodies taken together;

  (iv) a body which controls a religious body;

   (v) a body corporate which is an associate of a body corporate falling within (i), (ii) or (iii) above;

(h) a body controlled by a person falling within (a) to (e) above or by two or more such persons taken together.

30.12 For the purposes of a licence granted by the Authority a "relevant body" is (a) or (f) or (g) above or any body coming within those set out as disqualified under publicly funded bodies for radio services licences above or a body which is controlled as is mentioned in (h) above.

30.13 "Results which are adverse to the public interest" is undefined by the Act. The question whether a particular thing is adverse to the public interest is a question of the times and of fact. It is to be decided in the light of all the circumstances and conditions as they exist at the time it falls for consideration notwithstanding that they would not have been specifically envisaged by the legislature when this Act was passed.[53]

30.14 **Disqualification of broadcasting bodies.** The BBC, Welsh Authority, a body corporate controlled by either of these bodies or in which they are to any extent a participant or a body corporate in a body corporate controlled by them has any participation are disqualified persons for the purposes of licences granted by the Commission or the Authority.[54]

30.15 **Disqualification of advertising agencies.** An advertising agency, an associate of an advertising agency, any body controlled by the agency or its associate or by two or more such persons or any body corporate in which any of the above is a participant with more than a five per cent. interest are disqualified in relation to a licence granted by the Commission or the Authority.[55]

---

[53] *Cartwright v. Post Office* [1968] 2 All E.R. 646 at 651; affd. [1969] 1 All E.R. 421, C.A.

[54] Broadcasting Act 1990, Sched. 2, para. 5.

[55] *Ibid.*, Sched. 2, para. 6.

An advertising agency means an individual or body corporate who carries on business as an advertising agent whether alone or in partnership or has control over any body corporate which carries on business as an advertising agent. For the purposes of the Act a person is not to be regarded as carrying on business as an advertising agent, or acting as such agent, unless he carries on a business involving the selection and purchase of advertising time or space for persons wishing to advertise.[56] A person who carries on such business is to be regarded as an advertising agent irrespective of whether in law he is the agent for those for whom he acts.[57] The proprietor of a newspaper is not to be regarded as carrying on business as an advertising agent by reason only that he makes arrangements on behalf of advertisers whereby advertisements appearing in the newspaper are also to appear in one or more or other newspaper.[58] The mere fact that the articles or memorandum of association of a company authorise the activity of advertising agent does not constitute the company an advertising agent unless it carries out that activity.[59]

Local delivery licences, satellite services, licensable sound programme services and additional services. There is no restriction on a non-E.U. individual or company holding local delivery licences, a licence to provide a non-domestic satellite service, a licence to provide a non-domestic satellite radio service, a licence to provide a licensable sound programme service or a licence to provide additional services.[60] **30.16**

3. Restrictions to Prevent Accumulation of Interests in Licensed Services

Relevant Services. In the case of services licensed by the Commission the categories of relevant services for the purposes of regulating the accumulation of interests are regional and national Channel 3 services and Channel 5, domestic and non-domestic satellite services, licensable programme services, additional services and local delivery services.[61] In the case of services licensed by the Radio Authority the categories are **30.17**

---

[56] *Ibid.*, s.202(7)(a).
[57] *Ibid.*, s.202(7)(b).
[58] *Ibid.*, s.202(7)(c).
[59] *Ibid.*, s.202(7)(d).
[60] *Ibid.*, Sched. 2, Part II, para. 1(2).
[61] *Ibid.*, Sched. 2, Part III, para. 1(2).

local or national radio services, restricted radio services, satellite radio services, licensable sound programme services and additional services.[62]

(a) *Limits on the holding of licences*

30.18 **Geographical restrictions.** The maximum number of licences which may at any time be held[63] by any one person to provide a relevant service is two in the case of regional Channel 3 services, one in the case of national Channel 3 services, one in the case of Channel 5, one in the case of national radio services, 20 in the case of local radio services and six in the case of restricted radio services.[64] The provisions of the Act have now been supplemented by Order[65] of the Secretary of State under the powers granted under the 1988 Act.[66] By the Order a person may not hold licences to provide regional Channel 3 services if each of them is provided for London.[67]

There are no restrictions on a person holding licences[68] for contiguous areas.[69]

(i) *Shareholding limits*

Channel 3 and Channel 5

30.19 **Regional Channel 3 licences.** The holder of two regional Channel 3 licences may not be a participant[70] with more than a 20 per cent. interest in a third company which is the holder of another licence to provide a regional Channel 3 service.[71] Where a holder of two regional Channel 3 licences holds more than a five per cent. interest (but not more than 20 per cent.) in a third regional Channel 3 licence holder he is not allowed to hold more than a five per cent. interest in a fourth regional Channel 3 licence holder.[72]

---

[62] *Ibid.*, Sched. 2, Part III, para. 1(3).
[63] *Ibid.*, Sched. 2, Part III, para. 2(8): a person is treated as holding a licence if the licence is held by a connected person.
[64] *Ibid.*, Sched. 2, Part III, para. 2(1).
[65] Broadcasting (Restrictions on the Holding of Licences) Order 1991 (S.I. 1991 No. 1176).
[66] Broadcasting Act 1990, s.200(2).
[67] Broadcasting (Restrictions on the Holding of Licences) Order 1993 (S.I. 1993 No. 3199).
[68] *Ibid.*, art. 2(2).
[69] See Broadcasting (Restrictions on the Holding of Licences) Order 1991 (S.I. 1991 No. 1176) art. 1(4) for the meaning of "contiguous areas".
[70] For meaning of "participant", see *ante*, para. 30.07, n.22.
[71] Broadcasting (Restrictions on the Holding of Licences) Order 1991 (S.I. 1991 No. 1176) art. 5(1).
[72] *Ibid.*, art. 5(2).

National Channel 3 licences. Where a person holds a licence to provide   **30.20**
a national Channel 3 service he is prohibited from being a participant
with more than a 20 per cent. interest in a holder of a second national
Channel 3 service[73] and where the national Channel 3 licence holder is a
shareholder with more than five per cent. interest but less than 20 per
cent. in a second national Channel 3 licence holder he may not hold
more than a five per cent. interest in a third national Channel 3 licence
holder.[74]

Channel 5. A holder of a licence to provide a national Channel 5 is not   **30.21**
permitted to be a participant with more than a 20 per cent. interest in a
holder of a second national Channel 5.[75] Further, where such a national
Channel 5 licence holder is a shareholder with more than five per cent.
interest but less than 20 per cent. in a second national Channel 5 licence
holder he may not hold more than a five per cent. interest in a third
national Channel 5 licence holder.[76]

A person who is the holder of a licence to provide one of a regional
Channel 3 service, or a national Channel 3 or Channel 5 is a participant
with more than a five per cent. interest in a body corporate which is the
holder of a licence to provide a service within either of the other two
categories but is not a participant with more than 20 in such body
corporate he is not allowed to be a participant with more than a five per
cent interest in a third licence holder coming within any of the above
categories.[77]

(b) *Nominated news providers*

No person is permitted to be a participant with more than a 20 per cent.   **30.22**
interest in the nominated news provider.[78] The limit of 20 per cent.
applies to a particular participant as if he and every person connected
with him were one person.[79] A connected person for these purposes is a
person who controls the participant,[80] an associate of the participant or
person who controls the participant[81] and a body which is controlled by
the participant or any associate of the participant.[82] Further, any participants in the nominated news provider who are holders of licences to

---

[73] *Ibid.*, art. 7(1).
[74] *Ibid.*, art. 7(2).
[75] *Ibid.*, art. 8(1).
[76] *Ibid.*, art. 8(2).
[77] *Ibid.*, art. 9.
[78] Broadcasting Act 1990, s.32(9).
[79] *Ibid.*, s.32(10).
[80] *Ibid.*, s.32(10)(a).
[81] *Ibid.*, s.30(10)(b).
[82] *Ibid.*, s.32(10)(c).

provide regional Channel 3 services when taken together must have less than 50 per cent. of shares in the nominated company[83] and less than 50 per cent. of voting power in it.[84]

(c) *Radio*

30.23 **Points system.** In addition to a person being limited to holding more than one licence for national radio, 20 licences for local radio, or six licences for restricted radio services[85] further limits are prescribed by Order of the Secretary of State[86] based on a points system.[87]

TABLE

Category	Points
National radio	25
Category A local radio	15
Category B local radio	8
Category C local radio	3
Category D local radio	1
Restricted radio service otherwise for a particular event	1

30.24 A local radio service falls within category A if the number of persons over the age of 15 resident in the area for which the service is provided exceeds 4.5 million,[88] into category B if the number exceeds 1 million but does not exceed 4.5 million,[89] into category C if the number exceeds 400,000 but does not exceed 1 million[90] and into category D if the number of such persons does not exceed 400,000.[91] In the case of a service provided on AM frequency the relevant number of points applicable to the service by virtue of the table is to be reduced by one third.[92]

---

[83] *Ibid.*, s.32(b)(i).
[84] *Ibid.*, s.32(9)(b)(ii).
[85] *Ibid.*, Sched. 2, Part III, para. 2(1).
[86] Broadcasting (Restrictions on the Holding of Licences) Order 1991 (S.I. 1991 No. 1176).
[87] *Ibid.*, art. 11(1).
[88] *Ibid.*, art. 11(2)(a).
[89] *Ibid.*, art. 11(2)(b).
[90] *Ibid.*, art. 11(2)(c).
[91] *Ibid.*, art. 11(2)(d).
[92] *Ibid.*, art. 11(3).

A service which, on the day on which the licence is granted, falls into a particular category for the purposes of the table shall continue to be regarded as falling into that category as long as any increase or decrease in the relevant number of persons over the age of 15 which would otherwise take the service outside that category does not exceed 10 per cent.[93]

Points limits. A person is not permitted to hold licences to provide national, local or restricted radio services such that the total number of points applicable to such services exceeds 15 per cent. of the total number of points applicable to all such services in respect of which licences have been granted and have not ceased to have effect.[94] Such person may hold licences such that the total number of points applicable to the services to which they relate exceeds 15 per cent of the total number of points applicable to all such services if the excess is solely attributable to a reduction in the number of points applicable to all such services.[95] A person is not permitted to hold more than two licences to provide a local radio service falling into category A[96] and, subject to this restriction, not more than six licences to provide local radio services falling into category A or B.[97]   **30.25**

Additionally, a national radio service licence holder is not permitted to hold more than four licences to provide local radio services falling into category A or B.[98] A person who is a participant with more than a 20 per cent. interest in a body corporate which is the holder of a licence to provide a service falling within any of the categories set out in the table, but who does not control[99] that body shall for the purposes of the limits set out below be treated as the holder of a licence to provide a service to which one half of the points which would otherwise be applicable to such a service are ascribed.[1]

Overlapping areas. A holder of a licence to provide a local radio service is not permitted to be a participant[2] with more than a 20 per cent. interest in a company which is the holder of a licence to provide a local radio service which is provided for an area which is substantially the same as   **30.26**

---

[93] *Ibid.*, art. 11(4).
[94] *Ibid.*, art. 12(1).
[95] *Ibid.*, art. 112(2).
[96] *Ibid.*, art. 12(3).
[97] *Ibid.*, art. 12(3).
[98] *Ibid.*, art. 12(5).
[99] For the meaning of "control", see *ante*, para. 30.07, n.24.
[1] Broadcasting (Restrictions on the Holding of Licences) Order 1991 (S.I. 1991 No. 1176) art. 11(5).
[2] See *ante*, para. 30.07, n.24.

that provided by another local radio service and which is provided on the same frequency band as that service.[3]

A person who holds such a licence may be a participant with more than a 20 per cent. interest if the number of persons over the age of 15 resident in the smaller of the two areas does not exceed 10 per cent. of the number of persons resident in the larger of the areas[4] but where he does so participate in a second local radio service he may not participate with more than a 20 per cent. interest in a third company which may provide a service in substantially[5] the same area provided on the same frequency band.[6]

These rules do not, however, prevent a person from holding licences to provide local radio services if that person was immediately before the grant of the licences, a local radio contractor for an area which was substantially the same as the area in respect of which those licensed services are provided and he provided two or more different programme services on different frequencies pursuant to his contract.[7]

30.27 **Multi-channel radio services.** A "multi-channel service" means a service which to any extent consists in the simultaneous transmission of different programmes on different frequencies. Where a person holds a licence to provide a local radio service which authorises[8] the provision of a multi-channel service, he is treated for the purposes of determining whether he has exceeded the maximum permissible licences[9] as holding such number of licences to provide local radio services as corresponds to such number of channels[10] on which the service may be provided.[11] Similarly, where a person holds a licence to provide a domestic satellite service, non-domestic satellite service or a satellite radio service which authorises[12] the provision of a multi-channel service, he must be treated for the purposes of any order made in respect of any relevant service not falling within those set out above[13] as holding such number of licences to provide domestic satellite services, non-domestic satellite services or (as the case may be) satellite radio

---

[3] Broadcasting (Restrictions on the Holding of Licences) Order 1991 (S.I. 1991 No. 1176) art. 13(1).
[4] *Ibid.*, art. 13(3).
[5] *Ibid.*, art. 13(6): two areas are substantially the same if at least 50% of the persons over the age of 15 resident in the smaller area are also resident in the larger area.
[6] *Ibid.*, art. 13(4).
[7] *Ibid.*, art. 13(5).
[8] In accordance with the Broadcasting Act 1990, s.86(2).
[9] In accordance with *ibid.*, Sched. 2, Part III, para. 2(1).
[10] *Ibid.*, Sched. 2, Part III, para. 2(7): the references to the number of channels on which that service may be provided is a reference to the number of different frequencies involved.
[11] *Ibid.*, Sched. 2, Part III, para. 2(5).
[12] *Ibid.*, ss.44(2), 45(3) or 86(2).
[13] See under "Relevant service", *ante*, para. 26.35.

services as corresponds to the number of channels on which the service may be provided.[14]

4. Restrictions on Controlling Interests in both Newspapers and Licensed Services

(a) *Newspaper proprietors*

Restrictions on newspaper proprietors. The proprietors of a national or **30.28** local newspaper circulating wholly or mainly in or part of the United Kingdom may not be a participant[15] with more than a 20 per cent. interest in a body corporate which is the holder of a licence to provide a Channel 3, Channel 5 or national radio service or domestic satellite service.[16] However, a proprietor of a local newspaper may hold up to a 20 per cent. share in a company which is the holder of a licence to provide a regional Channel 3 service except where the newspaper and the service each serve an area which is to a significant extent the same as that served by the other.[17]

Newspaper proprietors are subject to the same controls upon percentage holdings as licence holders.[18]

For example, if the proprietor of X newspaper who owns 20 per cent. of Sunshine TV, a regional Channel 3 service, may not acquire an interest of more than 5 per cent in another Channel 3 service. If he already owns 4.99 per cent. of Sunshine TV but no other interest in any other service he may acquire a 20 per cent interest in any other company.

Powers of Secretary of State.[19] The Secretary of State has parallel **30.29** powers to prescribe percentage holdings as set out above. He may also by order prescribe restrictions on the extent to which the proprietor of a newspaper whether national or local may be a participant in a body corporate which is the holder of a licence to provide a relevant domestic satellite service, relevant non-domestic satellite service or a relevant satellite radio service or in two or more companies holding such licences.[20] Any order made by the Secretary of State may impose restrictions framed by reference to the number of bodies corporate in which the proprietor of a newspaper or the holder of a licence, as the case may be, or any connected third person, may be a participant.[21] This effectively

---

[14] Broadcasting Act 1990, Sched. 2, Part III, para. 2(6).
[15] See *ante*, para. 30.07, n.22.
[16] Broadcasting Act 1990, Sched. 2, Part IV, para. 2(1).
[17] *Ibid.*, Sched. 2, Part IV, para. 2(2).
[18] *Ibid.*, Sched. 2, Part IV, para. 2(4).
[19] For the Home Office.
[20] Broadcasting Act 1990, Sched. 2, Part IV, para. 2(5)(e).
[21] *Ibid.*, Sched. 2, Part IV, para. 5.

means that not only may there be restrictions as to the percentage participation but such restrictions may extend to percentage as well as the number of companies in which such participation can be held.

(b) *Holders of licences*

30.30 Restrictions on holders of licences. Licence holders are subject to identical provisions controlling the holding of interests in newspapers.[22] There are similar powers vested in the Secretary of State to alter the percentages and the applicable thresholds.

(c) *Connected persons*

30.31 Attribution of interests of connected persons. The above restrictions imposed by the Act on the proprietors of newspapers and holders of licences applies to him as if he and every person connected with him were one person.[23] For these purposes the proprietor or the person or the associate of a person who controls the proprietor or a body which is controlled by the proprietor or his associate are connected with each other in relation to a particular national or local newspaper.[24]

5. Restrictions on the Holding of Licences by Operators of Public Telecommunications Systems

30.32 A national telecommunications operator[25] who has an annual turnover exceeding £2 billion is not permitted to hold any of a Channel 3 service, Channel 5 and a domestic satellite service[26] or a licence to provide a national radio service.[27] A national public telecommunications operator may not hold a licence to provide a local delivery service[28] but this prohibition does not apply (a) where the closing date for the application falls after March 31, 1994, and immediately before the invitation for applications was published, no part of the area for which the service is authorised to be provided lay within an area in respect of which there was a local delivery licence or a licence which continued in force.[29]

---

[22] *Ibid.*, Sched. 2, Part IV, para. 3(1).
[23] *Ibid.*, Sched. 2, Part IV, para. 4.
[24] *Ibid.*, Sched. 2, Part IV, para. 1(3).
[25] *Ibid.*, Sched. 2, Part V: a "national public telecommunications operator" is a public telecommunications operator within the meaning of the Telecommunications Act 1984 who is authorised to run a telecommunication system for the whole or substantially the whole of the United Kingdom.
[26] Broadcasting (Restrictions on the Holding of Licences) Order 1991 (S.I. 1991 No. 1176) art. 16(1)(a).
[27] *Ibid.*, art. 16(1)(b).
[28] *Ibid.*, art. 16(3).
[29] *Ibid.*, art. 16(5).

Restrictions on the holding of certain relevant licences

Licences to which restrictions apply. Schedule 12 Part III paragraph 3   **30.33**
specifies certain restrictions on ownership of any relevant licence[30]
authorising the provision of a prescribed diffusion service.[31]

(i) *Disqualified persons*

The same category of persons as is disqualified from holding a Channel   **30.34**
3, 5 or domestic satellite licence is prohibited from holding a licence
under this section.[32] There are parallel restrictions on any person who is
or is an associate[33] of:

(1) a programme contractor for the provision of television pro-
    grammes or sound programmes for any area or locality[34];

(2) the holder of a licence to provide a regional Channel 3 service or a
    local radio service for any area or locality[35];

(3) the proprietor of a local newspaper circulating wholly or mainly
    in any area,[36]

if the service to be provided under the licence is to be so provided in
any part of that area or locality.[37] Further, where a Channel 5 service is
to be provided for the same area, there is to be no overlap in ownership
and control between the Channel 5 and diffusion service.

(ii) *Fit and Proper Persons*

The Commission or (as the case may be) the Authority must not grant a   **30.35**
licence to provide any service unless they are satisfied that the applicant
is a "fit and proper person to hold it".[38] Where the licence has been
granted and subsequently the person is not fit and proper, the Commission or (as the case may be) Authority must do all they can to secure
that the licence is no longer held by that person.[39] Thus the duty is present not only at the point at which the licence is awarded but is a continuing duty throughout the period of the licence.[40]

The concept of a "fit and proper person" is undefined in the 1990 Act
and is to be determined by the Commission. It is submitted that when

---

[30] For the meaning and categories of "relevant licence", see *ante*, para. 26.35.
[31] For the meaning of prescribed diffusion licence, see *ante*, para. 26.18, n.54.
[32] Broadcasting Act 1990, Sched. 12, Part III, para. 3(1).
[33] For meaning of "associate", see *ante*, para. 30.07, n.20.
[34] Broadcasting Act 1990, Sched. 12, Part III, para. 3(2)(a).
[35] *Ibid.*, Sched. 12, Part III, para. 3(2)(b).
[36] *Ibid.*, Sched. 12, Part III, para. 3(2)(c).
[37] *Ibid.*, Sched. 12, Part III, para. 3(2).
[38] *Ibid.*, s.3(3)(a); s.86(4).
[39] *Ibid.*, s.3(3)(b).
[40] *Ibid.*, s.3(3)(b).

considering whether a person is a fit and proper person the Authority is under a duty to act in the public interest in reaching a decision.

Thus a person may not be "disqualified person" within the meaning of the Act but he may nevertheless fail to qualify as a fit and proper person because of his past business or personal history. However, in reaching a decision as to whether a person is fit and proper the Commission or Authority must reach its decision on grounds which are fair and must act in accordance with the principles laid down in *Associated Provincial Picture Houses Ltd. v. Wednesbury Corporation*.[41]

6. Enforcement of Restrictions on the Holding of Licences

30.36   Both the Commission and the Authority are given wide discretion to include in licence conditions powers to revoke licence where a "relevant change" takes place after the award and grant of a licence,[42] to make the award of licence conditional on changes in the ownership structure of the proposed licence holder,[43] to impose conditions enabling them to require advance notice of proposals affecting the shareholding in or directorships of the licence holder.[44] Additionally, they may impose conditions in any licence enabling them to give the licence holder directions requiring him to take, or arrange for the taking of, any specified steps appearing to them to be required to be taken in order for any requirement on the accumulation of interests in licensed services to be complied with.[45]

30.37   **Relevant change.** Every licence must include conditions to ensure that the Commission (or the Authority as the case may be) may revoke a licence where the holder of the licence is a body and the relevant change takes place after the grant of the licence.[46] A "relevant change" may occur in either of three circumstances.

First, it may occur where a change takes place which affects the nature or characteristics of the body holding the licence.[47] This may typically occur where a new legal person takes over the licence and the licence holder is subsumed into that new person and ceases to be a legal personality.

Secondly, a change may occur where there is a change in the persons having control over or interests in the licence holder.[48] It will often be

---

[41] [1948] 1 K.B. 223.
[42] Broadcasting Act 1990, s.5(2)(b).
[43] *Ibid.*, s.5(2)(c).
[44] *Ibid.*, s.5(2)(d).
[45] *Ibid.*, s.5(2)(e).
[46] *Ibid.*, s.5(5); s.88(5).
[47] *Ibid.*, s.5(7)(a); s.88(7)(a).
[48] *Ibid.*, s.5(7)(b); s.88(7)(b).

the case that where there is a change in controlling shareholder of an existing licence holder in outward appearance the company remains the same but it may in fact materially change as a result of the new controlling shareholder. Thirdly, where the persons responsible for meeting the quality threshold who were part of the original bid for the licence. In any of these circumstances if the change is such that, if it fell to the Commission or (as the case may be) the Authority to determine whether to award the licence to the body in the new circumstances of the case, "they would be induced by the change to refrain from so awarding it".[49]

The requirement that the Commission or Authority show that "would" as opposed to "might" be induced to refrain from awarding the licence in the new circumstances places a high burden of proof on the regulatory authorities when they are seeking to justify a revocation. Unless they can show that the persons are disqualified or not fit and proper persons to hold a licence the reasons for revocation must rest upon the basis that company in the changed circumstances is such as would not have passed the quality threshold when the licence was granted. This will be extremely difficult to prove where there is no clear evidence that in the changed circumstances the company is not abiding by its programme proposals. If the basis of revocation is that the company in the changed circumstances "would" not have passed the quality threshold the Commission or the Authority would not act fairly or reasonably if it revokes the licence immediately the change takes place because it will not be immediately apparent that in the changed circumstances that body in its new guise would not abide by its programme commitments. Thus in certain circumstances relevant change appears to imply that a licensee is to have a period of probation following a relevant change.

Where the Commission or (as the case may be) the Authority proposes to revoke a licence they must give him a reasonable opportunity of making representations about the matters complained of.[50]   **30.38**

A licence granted to any person is not transferable to any other person without the previous consent in writing of the Commission.[51] The Commission must not grant its consent unless it is satisfied that the proposed licence holder would be in a position to comply with the conditions included in the licence throughout the remainder of the period for which it is to be in force.[52]

---

[49] *Ibid.*, s.5(7)(b); s.88(7)(b).
[50] *Ibid.*, s.5(6); s.88(5).
[51] *Ibid.*, s.3(6).
[52] *Ibid.*, s.3(7).

CHAPTER 31

ENFORCEMENT OF LICENCES

1. Independent Television Services

31.01 The enforcement of licence conditions is carried out by the Commission. As such, the powers exist to give effect to the Channel 3 and 4 conditions that quality thresholds are met and that licence holders comply with the consumer protection elements of the Act. There are two main sanctions which can be applied: the issuing of directions to correct or apologise and the revocation or limitation of the licence.

31.02 **Directions to apologise or correct a programme.** There are two conditions precedent to the power to issue directions. The Commission is to be satisfied that the licence holder[1] has failed to comply with any condition of the licence[2] and that failure can be appropriately remedied by the inclusion in the licensed service of a correction or apology (or both).[3] It is noticeable that the grounds on which the Commission may be satisfied are left at large. It follows that provided that it does not act perversely or take into account irrelevant facts in the reaching of its decision that the licence condition was breached, its decision will not be challengeable by judicial review.

Once the Commission is so satisfied, the requirements of natural justice require it to allow the license holder a reasonable opportunity to make representations.[4] The Commission may then direct the licence holder to include in the licensed service a correction or apology (or

---

[1] Broadcasting Act 1990, s.40(5) Channel 3, 4 and 5 services; s.45(5) non-domestic satellite services; s.47(8) licensable programme services.
[2] *Ibid.*, s.40(1)(a).
[3] *Ibid.*, s.30(1)(b).
[4] *Ibid.*, s.40(2).

both) in the form and at the time(s) that it may determine.[5] When the licence holder includes a correction or apology in the licensed service he may announce that he is doing so in pursuance of a direction.[6] Alternatively, if a programme *per se* represents a breach of a licence condition, the Commission may direct the licence holder not to repeat the programme.[7]

31.03 The powers can only be exercised after the programme has been broadcast. Reading the powers in conjunction with those given to the BCC and BSC it would follow that where a complaint can be made to the BSC and BCC that is the more appropriate form of reddress. Further, as there is no mechanism by which an individual may complain to the Commission and thereby trigger the exercise of these powers, these enforcement provisions appear to be for the benefit of the Commission as a general regulatory agency.

It follows that when these powers are to be exercised may prove to be a difficult question. It is difficult to see how, for example, the broadcasting of an apology will act as a remedy where a Channel 3 licence holder has refused to pay the Channel 4 levy. The broadcast of an apology is clearly a remedy aimed at the consumer. However, where the individual consumer has a precise complaint, the BCC and the BSC are the appropriate fora.[8] Therefore, the present powers will be used when there is a less obvious (or precisely defined) breach of the licence conditions which relate to consumer protection requirements.

31.04 Two results follow. First, the Commission could use its powers where a licence holder has failed to comply with the quality requirements. However, as the quality requirements are levied across the whole of a licence holder's output it will be difficult to support the imposition of a penalty on a particular programme and an attempt to do so would be vulnerable to a judicial review challenge as an improper exercise of the powers.

Secondly, it must follow that the powers can only be realistically exercised where, for example, there has been a breach of the guidelines by the broadcasting of a programme before the appropriate watershed. As the Commission is a benchmark authority on programme standards and the issue of a direction lies within its unfettered discretion, a licence holder will find challenging the Commission's decision to exercise its powers difficult. A challenge may well only succeed where a manifest error of law or fact has been made or *Wednesbury* grounds

---

[5] *Ibid.*, s.40(1).
[6] *Ibid.*, s.40(3).
[7] *Ibid.*, s.40(4).
[8] See *post*, Chaps. 33 and 34 for BCC and BSC.

apply. Therefore, there will be little to prevent the Commission, if it so decides, strictly enforcing the watershed requirements in the Guidelines notwithstanding the inherently subjective nature of those requirements.

(a) *Imposition of financial penalty or shortened licence period*

31.05   The powers to issue directions are reinforced by the Commission's powers, after giving the licensee a reasonable opportunity to make representations on the issue, to require the licence holder to pay, within a specified period a specified penalty to it[9] or by reducing the licence period.

31.06   **Shortening of licence.** The requirement to obtain the licence holders consent to vary the licence period[10] does not apply. The maximum period of reduction is two years[11] but the Commission may on the application of any person on whom a notice has been served shortening a licence period revoke the notice if satisfied that his conduct in relation to the operation of the licensed service has been such to justify the revocation of the notice.[12] As above, the Act leaves the Commission's discretion on this issue unfettered.

31.07   **Financial penalty.** In respect of a Channel 3 or 5 licence holder, there is a maximum financial penalty of three per cent. of his qualifying revenue for his last complete accounting period[13] for the first breach of licence conditions.[14] For subsequent breaches the penalty is five per cent. of qualifying revenue for the last complete accounting period.[15] The Commission can estimate the qualifying revenue of any person whose first complete accounting period has not yet ended.[16] However, the

---

[9] Broadcasting Act 1990, s.41(1)(a); Channel 4 by s.41(6)(a). This provision is applied to non-domestic satellite services by s.45(6); licensable programme services by s.47(8); local delivery services by s.81.

[10] Pursuant to *ibid.*, s.3(4).

[11] *Ibid.*, s.41(1)(b). The period of shortening does not apply to Channel 4: s.41(6)(a).

[12] *Ibid.*, s.41(4).

[13] This is calculated in accordance with *ibid.*, s.19(2)–(6): s.41(2)(b). The qualifying revenue for accounting period for the purposes of determining the fine to be imposed on the local delivery services differs from those used for Channel 3 and 5. The Qualifying revenue for local delivery services consists of all payments which are received or to be received by him, or by any person connected with him, and are derived from the delivery in that accounting period of television broadcast services, non-domestic satellite services, any licensable programme service, any sound broadcasting service and any licensable programme service whether their delivery is undertaken by him or by any person authorised by him who is not a disqualified person.

[14] *Ibid.*, s.41(2)(b).

[15] *Ibid.*, s.41(2)(b): the fine so imposed may be recoverable as a debt by the Commission: s.68(5).

[16] *Ibid.*, s.41(2): this provision is not applicable to non-domestic satellite services: s.45(6).

maximum amount that may be levied on a licensable programme service[17] and a non-domestic satellite service[18] is £50,000.

Combination of sanctions. The sanction of a financial penalty and **31.08**
shortening may be combined with the power to direct an apology or
correction.[19] In the case of local delivery services the Commission has
no power to impose both financial penalty and a shortening of the
licence period and must choose between those powers.[20] There is no
appeal against the penalty imposed by the Commission. It therefore follows that the aggrieved party's remedy must be by way of judicial
review. As pointed out above, the wide scope of the Commission's discretion and the very nature of the powers exercised may well mean that
obtaining a remedy by way of judicial review will prove difficult.

However, it also follows that the unfettered discretion and wide
ambit of the powers given to the Commission mean that it should scrupulously observe the requirements of natural justice in reaching any
decision.

(b) *Power to revoke independent television services licence*

Breach of licence conditions. If the Commission is satisfied that a **31.09**
licensed service is failing to comply with any licence condition[21] or with
any proper direction given by it[22] and the failure is such that, if not
remedied, it would justify the revocation of the licence[23] it must serve
on the licence holder a notice[24] specifying that there has been a breach
of condition or failure to comply with direction given by it,[25] the
respects in which, in its opinion, the licence holder is failing to comply
with any mentioned condition or direction[26] and that unless the licence
holder takes, within the period specified in the notice, specified steps to

---

[17] *Ibid.*, s.47(9): the Secretary of State may by order substitute a different sum. The order is
subject to annulment in pursuance of a resolution of either House of Parliament:
s.47(11), (12).

[18] *Ibid.*, s.45(6): the Secretary of State may by order substitute a different sum. The order is
subject to annulment in pursuance of a resolution of either House of Parliament: s.45(8),
(9).

[19] *Ibid.*, s.41(5).

[20] *Ibid.*, s.81(2)(a)(ii).

[21] Except in the case of a local delivery service timetable condition where the Commission
has not satisfied itself after consultation with the Secretary of State and the Director
General of Telecommunications that it would have been reasonably practicable for the
licence holder to comply with the requirement: *ibid.*, s.81(4).

[22] *Ibid.*, s.42(1)(a): Channel 3 and 5; domestic satellite services s.44(3)(c); non-domestic
satellite services s.45(7); licensable programme services s.47(8); local delivery licence
s.81.

[23] *Ibid.*, s.42(1)(b): as to the application to the other services, *infra*, n.21.

[24] *Ibid.*, s.42: as to the application to other independent television services, see *infra*, n.22.

[25] *Ibid.*, s.42(2)(a).

[26] *Ibid.*, s.42(2)(b).

remedy the failure the Commission will revoke the licence.[27] If at the end of the period specified in the notice the Commission is satisfied that the person on whom the notice was served has failed to take steps specified in it[28] and it is necessary in the public interest to revoke his licence, it must serve on him a notice revoking his licence.[29]

31.10   The Act does not specify the level to which any breach must be proved in order to show that there has been a breach of the licence condition. Further, there is no definition of the level of offence necessary to trigger the revocation powers. Given the draconian nature of the power and given that the Commission must act once it decides that revocation of the licence is appropriate, it is submitted that there must be strong and compelling evidence that the licence holder is in breach. Further, it is submitted that the Commission can only decide that the licence should be revoked where there is clear evidence that the licence holder is no longer an appropriate person to hold a licence.

31.11   It is submitted that the powers could only be exercised in one of three types of circumstances.

First, the licence holder has been in persistent breach of the consumer protection requirements of the Act.

Secondly, the licence holder has refused to provide services for a community or region in breach of the licence.

Thirdly, the licence holder has refused to provide a service of the quality promised in its application. In respect of the first two types of circumstance, it will be relatively simple to ensure that the licence holder complies with the direction within a certain period of time.

However, where the Commission decides that the licence holder is in breach of the quality requirements, it is submitted that for the licence holder to demonstrate compliance within a certain period will prove difficult as compliance will only occur once the licence holder has revised its schedules, altered its purchasing policy and programmes of sufficient quality have been commissioned, made and broadcast. It would follow that where the Commission decides to revoke a licence on the grounds of quality, a sufficient period would have to be given to allow the licence holder to comply.

31.12   Review of the Commission's powers will operate in one of two manners. First, it will be possible for an interested party to force the Commission to consider whether or not a licence should be revoked. A further application for mandamus could then force the Commission to

---

[27] *Ibid.*, s.42(2)(c).
[28] *Ibid.*, s.42(3)(a).
[29] *Ibid.*, s.42(b).

revoke the licence. Second, a licence holder could challenge the Commission's decision to revoke. The only grounds of that challenge would be to quash the decision that the licence holder was in breach of a licence condition or direction. Given the wide discretion vested in the Commission, that challenge would only succeed if there were to have been a breach of procedural fairness and/or *Wednesbury* unreasonableness.

Misleading information. The Commission has a further power to revoke the licence[30] if it is satisfied that the licence holder in applying for the licence, provided information which was false in a material particular[31] or withheld material information with the intention of causing the Commission to be misled.[32]   **31.13**

Financial penalties on revocation. Where the Commission revokes a Channel 3 licence in any of the above circumstances they are required to serve on the licence holder a notice requiring him to pay to them within a specified period a financial penalty of seven per cent. of the qualifying revenue for the last complete accounting period of the licence holder.[33]   **31.14**

2. Independent Radio Services

Power to require advance programme information. Parallel to the Commission's powers, the Authority has power[34] to issue a notice to a licence holder where it is satisfied that the holder of a sound broadcasting licence has failed to comply with any licence conditions or with any direction given by the Authority under or by virtue of the 1990 Act.[35] If there is another breach in the following 12 months, the Authority has power to issue a direction[36] requiring in advance of transmission such scripts and particulars of programmes to be included in the licensed service as are specified in the direction.[37] Where the programmes include recorded matter, the Authority can demand those recordings in advance for examination and reproduction.[38] The direction to provide   **31.15**

---

[30] *Ibid.*, s.42(5): this subsection is applied to domestic, non-domestic satellite services, licensable programme services, local delivery services by ss.44(3)(c), 45(7), 47(8) and 81(2)(b) respectively.

[31] *Ibid.*, s.42(5)(a).

[32] *Ibid.*, s.42(5)(b).

[33] *Ibid.*, s.18(3): the penalty is recoverable by the Commission as a debt owed by the former licence holder and any person who controls the former licence holder: s.68(5).

[34] The power applies to all services including a licensable sound service and additional services.

[35] Broadcasting Act 1990, s.109(1)(a).

[36] *Ibid.*, s.109(2).

[37] *Ibid.*, s.109(2)(a).

[38] *Ibid.*, s.109(2)(b).

preview material is to have effect for a period to be specified by the Authority in the direction but such period is not to exceed six months.[39]

The Authority's powers are wider than those exercised by the Commission as the Authority's powers are not *ex post facto* and the Authority does not have to hear representations from the licence holder before acting. Two points follow. First a court will scrutinise the exercise of these powers very carefully. Second, the main effect of these powers will be to force the holder to go through an administrative procedure before programmes are aired. The inconvenience caused will, presumably, operate as the appropriate deterrent.

31.16 **Broadcasting of correction or apology.** The Authority has similar powers to the Commission in respect of issuing directions to broadcast a correction or apology.[40]

(a) *Power to impose financial penalty, suspend or shorten licence period*

31.17 **Notice.** In the event of non-compliance with a licence condition or a direction given by the Authority, the Authority may serve (a) a notice requiring him to pay, within a specified period, a specified penalty to the Authority,[41] (b) a notice reducing the licence period by a period not exceeding two years[42] or (c) a notice suspending the licence for a period not exceeding six months.[43] The power can only be exercised after the licence holder has been afforded a chance to make representations[44] and is without prejudice to its powers to require scripts and to preview programmes or the broadcasting of a correction or apology.[45]

31.18 **Financial penalty.** The amount of any financial penalty imposed by the Authority on a licence holder other than a national licence must not exceed £50,000.[46] In the case of a national and additional licence holder the amount if such a penalty has not previously been imposed on him during any period for which the licence has been in the force, must not exceed three per cent. of the qualifying revenue[47] for his last complete

---

[39] *Ibid.*, s.109(2).
[40] *Ibid.*, ss.109(3), (4).
[41] *Ibid.*, s.110(1)(a): the authority has the same power in respect of an additional services licence: s.120(1).
[42] *Ibid.*, s.110(1)(b).
[43] *Ibid.*, s.110(1)(c).
[44] *Ibid.*, s.110(4) sound broadcasting services; s.113(3) licensable sound programme services; s.120(2) additional services licence.
[45] *Ibid.*, s.110(6).
[46] *Ibid.*, s.110(3): the Secretary of State may by order substitute a different sum. His order is subject to annulment by resolution of either House of Parliament: s.110(7).
[47] For meaning of "qualifying revenue" in respect of national "Channel 3 service", see *ante*, para. 24.24.

accounting period. If the penalty has previously been imposed in the licence period the penalty must not exceed five per cent. of the qualifying revenue for that accounting period.[48] Should the first complete accounting period fall within the relevant period not yet ended, it is three per cent. or (as the case may be) five per cent. of the amount which the Authority estimate to be qualifying revenue for the accounting period.[49]

Reduction of licence period. The Authority has similar powers as the **31.19** Commission to reduce the period of reduction on further consideration of the licence holder's conduct.[50]

(b) *Revocation of licence*

Under section 111 of the Act, the Authority is given the power to revoke **31.20** the licence if it is satisfied that there has been a breach of licence condition or direction which justifies revocation. Further the licence can be revoked if the Authority is satisfied that the misleading information was served upon it in the making of the application or information was suppressed with the intention of misleading the Authority. As with the Commission the power to revoke can only be implemented after the licence holder has been afforded the opportunity to make representations and the Authority has given the licence holder a period of time in which it is to comply with the direction or condition. It is submitted that the exercise of the power and the limits upon it are analogous to those which apply to the Commission.

There is one difference between the powers given to the Authority and those given to the Commission. The Authority has the power to ensure that the revocation takes place from a certain date in order to preserve continuous provision of a service.[51]

---

[48] Broadcasting Act 1990, s.110(2)(b) in respect of national service, and s.120(2) in respect of additional services.
[49] *Ibid.*, s.110(2).
[50] *Ibid.*, s.110(5).
[51] This power is not exerciseable in respect of a licensable sound service (*ibid.*, s.113(4)) or an additional services licence (s.120(4)).

Part VI

CONSUMER PROTECTION

CHAPTER 32

REGULATION OF PROGRAMME STANDARDS

1. Regulation of Programme Standards by the Independent Television Commission

(a) *General duty of the Commission*

The consumer protection provisions of the Broadcasting Act 1990 recog- **32.01**
nises the fact that the Independent Television Commission is a regula-
tor and not a broadcaster. Section 6 of the 1990 Act thus places a duty on
the Commission to "do all that they can to secure" that in every licensed
service,

(a) nothing is included in its programmes which offends against
good taste or decency or is likely to encourage or incite to crime
or lead to disorder or be offensive to public feeling[1];

(b) news given (in whatever form) in its programme is presented
with due accuracy and impartiality[2];

(c) due impartiality is preserved on the part of licensees as respects
matters of political or industrial controversy or relating to current
public policy[3];

(d) due responsibility is exercised with respect to the content of
religious programmes and in particular such programmes must
not involve:

(i) any improper exploitation of any susceptibilities of those
watching the programmes; or

---

[1] Broadcasting Act 1990, s.6(1)(a).
[2] *Ibid.,* s.6(1)(b).
[3] *Ibid.,* s.6(1)(c).

475

(ii) any abusive treatment of the religious views and beliefs of those belonging to a particular religion or religious denomination[4];

(e) programmes do not include any technical device which, by using images of very brief duration or by any other means, exploits the possibility of conveying a message to, or otherwise influencing the minds of, persons watching the programmes without their being aware, of what has occurred.[5]

32.02 **Pre-viewing programmes before transmission.** The expression "shall do all they can to secure that every licensed service" does not require that the members of the Commission or their staff pre-view the programmes which are included in the licensed services. Indeed, the 1990 Act expressly provides that "Nothing . . . shall be construed as requiring the Commission, in discharge of its duties . . . as respects licensed services and the programme included in them, to view such programmes in advance of their being included in such services".[6] The regulatory duty of the Commission will therefore, in general, be exercised *ex post facto*. However, if it should be brought to the attention of the Commission, by for example accurate press reviews after previews of a programme but before transmission, that the programme is likely to offend against any of requirements (a) to (e) the Commission would, it is submitted, be under a duty to take the necessary action before the transmission of the programme to ensure that the programme is in conformity with the requirements of the 1990 Act.

In such circumstances there is nothing in the 1990 Act which would prevent it from viewing the programme prior to broadcast. Indeed, the requirement to do "all they can to secure" would imply, it is submitted, that there would be a duty to pre-view the programme so as to decide whether the programme does indeed infringe section 6 of the 1990 Act.

32.03 **Adopting system to ensure compliance.** Further, the duty imposed upon the Commission by section 6 requires it to use the powers granted to it by the 1990 Act to "adopt methods of working, or a system, which, in their opinion [is] best adapted to securing the requirements set out"[7] in section 6 of the 1990 Act to ensure that the licensee is fully aware and complies with its duties as regards programme content. Where such a system has been instituted and operated by the Commission it is not open to challenge unless it can be shown that the Commission has

---

[4] *Ibid.*, s.6(1)(d).
[5] *Ibid.*, s.6(1)(e).
[6] *Ibid.*, s.11(3).
[7] See *R. v. Independent Broadcasting Authority, ex parte Whitehouse, The Times*, April 4, 1985, C.A., discussing the analogous provision under the Broadcasting Act 1981, s.4.

failed to fulfil the duty imposed by section 6 or has exceeded it. Where the system is challenged by judicial review it would involve satisfying the court that the Commission had misdirected themselves as to the duty or, which would amount to the same thing, that no reasonable body of members properly directing themselves as to the duty could have devised and operated the system in fact adopted.[8]

Duty where licensee fails to comply. Further, the Commission is **32.04** required, where the licensee fails to comply with these procedures and guideline, to take such action as is within its powers to ensure compliance. Such powers will include an escalating range from a direction not to repeat the programme, to the imposition of a financial penalty, the shortening of the licence or ultimately the revocation of the licence. This follows from the mandatory requirement to do "all they can" to ensure compliance. It is therefore not within the discretion of the Commission to allow an infringement of the consumer protection provisions of the 1990 Act without any action on its part. Some support can be obtained from this analysis from statements during the examination of the Bill in committee where it was said that the expression was deliberately all embracing so as to encourage "the ITC to use informal correspondence and meetings as well as the formal written licence conditions to ensure that the licensee understands and complies with the relevant requirements".[9]

However, the duty which is placed on the Commission as regards (a) to (e) above are not precise. They all require value judgments. It is for the Commission to decide whether these requirements have been met by a licensee. If therefore the Commission should, for example, decide to take no action in respect of matter which allegedly offends against good taste and decency the decision could not be challenged by way of judicial review unless it could be shown that the Commission misdirected themselves or came to a conclusion to which they could not reasonably come.[10] It should be noted, however, that, where the Commission have misdirected themselves or acted unreasonably, a private citizen who cannot demonstrate that he has a greater interest in, or would suffer over and above any other person from the transmission of a programme is not entitled, in the absence of the Attorney General's fiat, to seek an injunction restraining the broadcasting of the programme.[10a]

---

[8] *Ibid.,* discussing the analogous provision under the Broadcasting Act 1981, s.4.
[9] David Mellor, Minister of State at the Home Office: Standing Committee F, January 30, 1990.
[10] *Attorney-General ex rel. McWhirter v. Independent Broadcasting Authority* [1973] 1 Q.B. 629, C.A., discussing the analogous provision under the Television Act 1964.
[10a] *Attorney-General ex rel. McWhirter v. Independent Broadcasting Authority* [1973] 1 Q.B. 629, C.A.; *Holmes v. Checkland, The Times,* April 15, 1987, C.A.

32.05 **Implementation of consumer protection tduty.** As part of the system for implementing the consumer protection requirements of the 1990 Act the Commission is required to draw up a code giving guidance as to the rules to be observed, *inter alia,* with respect to the:

(a) showing of violence, or the inclusion of sounds suggestive of violence, in programmes included in licensed services, particularly when large numbers of children and young persons may be expected to be watching the programmes[11];

(b) rules to be observed with respect to the inclusion in such programmes of appeals for donations[12];

(c) observance of due impartiality by licensees as respects matters of political or industrial controversy or relating to current public policy[13];

(d) such other matters concerning standards and practice as the Commission may consider suitable for inclusion in the Code with particular regard to programmes included in licensed services in circumstances where large numbers of children may be expected to be watching the programmes.[14]

The Commission is also required to ensure that the Code "reflect the general effect" of the Broadcasting Standards Council Code for programme standards "as is relevant to the programmes in question".[15] The Code as drawn up by the Commission would appear to conform with this requirement.

32.06   There is a statutory duty imposed upon the Commission to "do all that they can to secure that the provisions of the code are observed in the provision of licensed services".[16] This duty has to some extent been satisfied by the Commission by the inclusion in each licence agreement awarded by it for Channel 3 licence holder a requirement that they comply with the provisions of the Commission Programme Code and secondly by the requirement in paragraph (e) of the Foreword to the Code which states:

"All licensees are required to ensure that any programmes that they transmit comply with this Code and to satisfy the ITC that they have adequate procedures to fulfil this requirement. They should ensure that the relevant employees and programme makers, includ-

---

[11] Broadcasting Act 1990, s.7(1)(a).
[12] *Ibid.,* s.7(1)(b).
[13] *Ibid.,* s.6(3).
[14] *Ibid.,* s.7(1)(c).
[15] Broadcasting Act 1990, s.152(3).
[16] *Ibid.,* ss.6(3)(b), 7(1).

ing those from whom they commission programmes, understand
the Code's contents. They should also have in place procedures for
ensuring that programme-makers can seek guidance on the Code
within the company at a senior level."[17]

A licensee is therefore under a contractual duty to institute internal　**32.07**
procedures which give effect to the provisions of the Code. This duty
relates not only to programmes made by the licensee but also to any
programmes commissioned by it from an independent. However, there
remains a duty on the Commission to ensure that where the Code is not
complied with it takes action to ensure that such breach does not recur.

(b) *The Programme Code*[18]

General. The Programme Code sets out in considerable detail the　**32.08**
guidelines which are to be adhered to by licensees. Due to the potentially large audience and potentially large number of licensees to which
the Code may apply it is proposed to deal with its main sections. Reference should, however, be made to Code for its full terms and narrative.
The Code is "not a complete guide to good practice"[19] but it will be
used by the Commission in assessing the performance of licensees and
reaching decisions on sanctions in relation to the Code as a whole.[20]

Services to which Code applies. The Code applies to all services　**32.09**
licensed by the Commission under Part I of the Act of 1990 and to
foreign satellite programmes included in local delivery services licensed
by the Commission under Part II of the 1990 Act.

(i) *Scheduling*

Family viewing policy. A central aspect of the Code is the rule that　**32.10**
"within the progression, 9 p.m. is normally fixed as the point up to
which licensees will regard themselves as responsible for ensuring
nothing is shown that is unsuitable for children".[21] After 9 p.m. and
until 5.30 a.m. progressively less suitable material may be shown. This
does not, however, mean that unsuitable programmes may be shown
immediately after the 9 p.m. threshold. A licensee must pay regard to
the fact that a programme which commences prior to 9 p.m. may be
such to attract family audience which may view programmes for some
time after 9 p.m. Hence, in scheduling a programme both immediately

---

[17] *ITC Programme Code*, December 21, 1992, published by the Independent Television
Commission.
[18] See *supra*, n.17.
[19] *ITC Programme Code*, para. (h), p.4.
[20] *Ibid.*, para. (j), p.4.
[21] *Ibid.*, s.1, para. 1.5.

prior to and after 9 p.m. particular regard should be had to the word "progressively". "The policy assumes a progressive decline throughout the evening in the proportion of children present in the audience. It requires a similar progression in the successive programmes scheduled from early evening until closedown; the earlier in the evening the more suitable, the later in the evening the less suitable."[22]

The Code provides a guide as to what will render material unsuitable for family viewing. Among the factors will be the portrayal of violence or sounds suggestive of violence but other factors may "include bad language, profanity, crude innuendo, explicit sexual behaviour, and scenes of extreme distress".[23]

32.11 **Encrypted services.** Where a channel is encrypted, or only available to cable customers on payment of a fee additional to the basic subscription to the service "the point at which parents may be expected to share responsibility for what is viewed may be shifted from 9 p.m. to 8 p.m. depending on the nature of the programme and [violence, bad language, profanity, crude innuendo, explicit sexual behaviour, and scenes of extreme distress]" included in the programme in question. Material of a "more adult kind" may be shown after 10 p.m. and before 5.30 a.m.

32.12 **Acquired material.** The contents of the Code apply to all acquired material. Where a British Board of Film Censors certificate exists for the version of a film proposed for transmission it may be used as a guide to scheduling but scheduling decisions are required to be made in the light of the rules set out in the Code. The following minimum rules are stipulated by the Code[24]:

(a) No "12" rating should normally start before 8 p.m.. on any service;

(b) No "15" rating should normally start before 9 p.m. (or 8 p.m. on encrypted or "additional" subscription channels, contents permitting);

(c) No "18" rating should start before 10 p.m. on any service;

(d) No "R18" rating should be transmitted at any time;

(e) No version which has been refused British Board of Film Censors certification should be transmitted at any time.

These minimum rules must be considered in the light of the requirement that nothing shown before 8 p.m. by *any* licensee should be

---

[22] *Ibid.*, s.1, para. 1.5(i).
[23] *Ibid.*, s.1, para. 1.5(i).
[24] *Ibid.*, s.1, para. 1.5(iii).

unsuitable for those aged 15 years or under. It would appear that this 8 p.m. threshold although ambiguous does not derogate from the 9 p.m. family viewing threshold.

Trailers and programme promotion clips. "Programme trailers **32.13** must . . . comply with the Family viewing policy. If it is decided to promote an . . . "adult" . . . programme before 9 p.m. the trailer must be suitable for family viewing".[25] Further, trailers should not give emphasis to violent incidents uncharacteristic of the programme as a whole.

(ii) *Offence to good taste and decency, portrayal of violence, etc.*

General duty of Commission. Section 6(1)(a) of the 1990 Act requires **32.14** that the Commission do all it can to secure that every licensed service includes "nothing[26] [in its] programmes which offends against good taste or decency or is likely to encourage or incite to crime or lead to disorder or be offensive to public feeling". This duty is reinforced by the requirement in section 7(1)(a) requiring the Commission to draw up and publish a Code giving guidance as to the rules to be observed with respect to the showing of violence or the inclusion of sounds suggestive of violence, in programmes included in licensed services, particularly when large numbers of children and young persons may be expected to be watching the programmes.

Portrayal of violence.[27] In the scheduling of the portrayal of violence **32.15** special regard must be had to the Commission family policy. The Code also stipulates that in all programmes involving the portrayal of violence the following factors must be taken into consideration:

(a) "the content of the programme schedule as a whole . . . An acceptable minimum of violence in each individual programme when considered in the context of the whole schedule may add up to an intolerable level over a period";

(b) the fact that the consequences of violence is concealed or not portrayed or is at a distance does not render the portrayal of violence acceptable;

(c) Any violence shown must be "essential to the integrity and completeness of the programme";

(d) Scenes which may unsettle the young and vulnerable or cause fear and insecurity must be handled with special care.

---

[25] *Ibid.*, s.1, para. 1.5(iv).
[26] See *Attorney-General ex rel. McWhirter v. Independent Broadcasting Authority* [1973] 1 Q.B. 629, where Lord Denning M.R. discussing a similar provision under the Television Act 1964 said "I would stress the words 'nothing is included.' Those words show that the programme is to be judged, not as a whole, but in its several parts, piece by piece."
[27] *ITC Programme Code*, s.1, para. 1.6(i).

32.16   **Language.**[28] "There is no absolute ban on the use of bad language. But when used it must be defensible in terms of context and authenticity." The Code stipulates that, in accordance with its family viewing policy, the most offensive language should not be used before 9 p.m. Its use thereafter must always be referred in advance to the licensee's most senior executive or the designated alternate for approval. In no case may bad language including profanity be used in programmes specifically designed for those 15 years and under.

32.17   **Sex and nudity.**[29] The portrayal of sexual behaviour, and of nudity, must be defensible in context and "presented with tact and discretion". The representation of sexual intercourse may not be shown until after 9 p.m. except in the case of nature films, programmes with a serious educational purpose or where the representation is non graphic and in each case must be approved by the licensee's most senior programme executive or the designated alternate.

(iii) Terrorism and crime

32.18   **General.** Specific provisions are included in the Code in respect of the filming and broadcasting of matters relating to crime and terrorism. This is in fulfilment of the Commissions duty under section 6(1)(a) of the 1990 Act when requires it to do all that it can to secure that "nothing is included in the programmes which . . . is likely to encourage or incite to crime or to lead to disorder or to be offensive to public feeling". The general rule laid down by the Code is that "any programme item which on any reasonable judgement [*sic*] would be said to encourage or incite crime or lead to disorder is unacceptable".[30]

32.19   **Demonstrations and scenes of public disturbance.** "If coverage is recorded, incidents known to have been 'manufactured' must be excluded or revealed for what they are. Where coverage is live every effort must be made to place what is being seen and heard in context, so that viewers can properly evaluate the significance of activities that have been manufactured for television cameras."[31] It would appear that "manufactured" in this context includes incidents provoked by the presence of television cameras and which would not otherwise have occurred.

---

[28] *Ibid.*, s.1, para. 1.2.
[29] *Ibid.*, s.1, para. 1.3.
[30] *Ibid.*, s.5, para. 5.1.
[31] *Ibid.*, s.5, para. 5.7.

(iv) *Terrorism in Northern Ireland*

Home Secretary's direction on specified organisations

The Direction. The BBC and all licencees are required by the Direction **32.20** of December 1990 issued by the Home Secretary pursuant section 10 of the Broadcasting Act 1990 to refrain from broadcasting any matter which consists of or includes any words spoken, whether in the course of an interview or discussion or otherwise, by a person who appears or is heard on the programme in which sounds or sounds and pictures are broadcast where:

(a) the person speaking the words represents or purports to represent a proscribed organisation;

(b) the words support or solicit or invite support for such an organisation.

With regard to what constitutes "words spoken by representative of **32.21** certain specified organisations, or words spoken in support of such organisations" the Code states:

"A member of a specified organisation or one of its elected representatives is not held to represent that organisation in all his daily activities. Accordingly, not all his words, whatever their character, are covered by the Direction. Whether at any particular instance he is representing the organisation concerned will depend upon the nature of the words spoken and the particular context. Where he is speaking in a personal capacity or purely in his capacity as a member of an organisation which does not fall under the Direction, the Direction does not apply. Where it is clear, from the context and the words, that he is speaking as a representative of an organisation falling under the Direction, his words may not be broadcast directly but can be reported. There may be borderline occasions when the licensees will require to exercise careful judgment."

There is no exemption under the Directives "for historical documen- **32.22** taries or for recordings of persons who are now dead". However, it would appear that genuine works of fiction do not come within the restrictions contained in the Directives in that a "person" does not include an actor playing a character".[32]

Similar Directives were issued by the Secretary State on October 19, 1988, pursuant to an analogous provision in section 29(3) of the Broadcasting Act 1981 and Clause 13(4) of the BBC licence. Those Directives

---

[32] *Ibid.*, s.5, para. 5.2(i).

were subject to challenge by way of judicial review in *R. v. Secretary of State for the Home Department, ex parte Brind*[33] on the grounds, *inter alia*, that they were *ultra vires* and unlawful in that (a) they contravened Article 10 of the European Convention for the Protection of Human rights and Fundamental Freedoms and (b) conflicted with the broadcasters' duty to preserve due impartiality under the 1981 Act and the BBC's licence. The House of Lords dismissed the appeal on first ground stating that section 29(3) of the 1981 Act was unambiguous as to the powers granted to the Secretary of State and there was no presumption that the exercise of his discretion under that section must be in accord with the Convention. The second ground was not taken in the House of Lords but in the Court of Appeal it was rejected on the ground that there was no duty under the 1981 Act to show due impartiality to those who support or excuse attempts to achieve political change by terrorism.[34]

32.23   Excluded statements. The Direction excludes:

(a) words spoken during proceedings in the United Kingdom Parliament but not in any other Parliament;

(b) words spoken by or in support of a candidate at a Parliamentary, European or local election pending that election;

(c) direct statements but not reported speech.

32.24   Proscribed organisations. The organisations covered by the Direction include Sinn Fein, Republican Sinn Fein and the Ulster Defence Association. The following Organisations proscribed under the Prevention of Terrorism (Temporary Provisions) Act 1989 or the Northern Ireland (Emergency Provisions) Act 1978 are also covered by the Direction:

Loyalist

Ulster Freedom Fighters
Ulster Volunteer Force
Red Hand Commandos

Republican

Irish Republican Army
Irish Nationalist Liberation Army
Cumann na Mban (The Women's Movement)
Fiann Na h'Eireann (Youth Movement)
Irish Peoples Liberation Organisation.

---

[33] [1991] A.C. 696, H.L.
[34] See *post*, para. 32.29.

(v) *Privacy and gathering of information*[35]

Filming and recording of members of the public.[36] "When coverage is   **32.25**
being given to events in public places, editors and producers must
satisfy themselves that words spoken or action taken by individuals are
sufficiently in the public domain to justify their being communicated to
the television audience without express permission being sought." It is
not clear what is meant by "in the public domain" in this context but it
would appear to mean that producers directors and editors must satisfy
themselves that such words as are spoken and recorded for broadcast
are not meant to be private conversations between private individuals.

Filming on police operations. The Code requires that when a licensee is   **32.26**
invited to film a police operation of any kind involving members of the
public the film crew should identify themselves as soon as reasonably
practicable. If they are asked to stop filming or to leave the premises
they should do so and any material filmed should only be used if
showing it would serve "the public interest". It would appear that "the
public interest" in this regard is not to be correlated with what is interesting to the public. "Public interest" in this context requires that the
showing would expose iniquity, crime or some other matter which is
detrimental to the public good.

Recorded telephone interviews. The recording of interviews by tele-   **32.27**
phones is prohibited unless the "interviewer has identified himself or
herself as speaking on behalf of a licensee seeking information to be
used in a programme, and has described the general purpose of the
programme, and the interviewee has given consent to use the
conversation in the programme".[37] In the rare cases where these
requirements cannot be met because the programme involves the
investigation of "criminal or disreputable behaviour" the consent of the
senior programme executive is required. A log of all consent must be
kept by the licensee.

Hidden microphones and cameras. Recording of individuals who are   **32.28**
not aware they are being recorded is only permissible where it is "clear
that the material so acquired is essential to establish the credibility and
authority of a story, and where the story itself is equally clearly of
important public interest". In such cases a two stage procedure must be
adhered to. First, the "explicit" consent of the senior programme executive must be obtained prior to such recording whether or not it is
intended to transmit the recording. Secondly, a further consent must be

---

[35] *ITC Programme Code*, s.2.
[36] *Ibid.*, s.2, para. 2.2
[37] *Ibid.*, s.2, para. 2.3.

obtained before any secret recording is transmitted. The Code specifically requires licensees to keep "full records of the consultation process" and cautions that the Commission will ask to see such records at
regular intervals. Where such records are not kept or are not up-to-date
"the ITC may impose a sanction for breach of the Code".[38]

(vi) *Impartiality*

32.29 **Due impartiality.** Section 6(1)(c) of the 1990 Act requires the Commission to do all that it can to secure "that due impartiality is preserved
on the part of the person providing the service as respects matters of
political or industrial controversy or relating to current policy" and in
any news service contained in programme services.[39] In *R. v. Secretary
of State for the Home Department, ex p. Brind*[40] Lord Donaldson M.R.
identified two characteristics of the duty to preserve "due impartiality".

First, it "operates in the real world in which there will be obstacles to
giving every shade of opinion equal air-time. This is well recognised in
the context of parliamentary by-elections, where it is quite impossible
to treat all candidates alike if the programme is not either to be wholly
uninformative or of inordinate length. In the result, the principal
contenders are rightly given more air time than others". Secondly, "[i]t
is for the broadcasting authorities to determine what constitutes the
appropriate degree of impartiality".

However, in determining the appropriate degree of "due impartiality", there would appear to be no duty to preserve impartiality in
respect of those who seek to effect political change by illegal means and
secondly, the Commission's duty set out in section 6(1)(a) of the 1990
Act would require it not to observe due impartiality to any views which
"offends against good taste or decency or is likely to encourage or incite
to crime or to lead to disorder or to be offensive to public feeling". No
hard and fast rule can, however, be laid down as to what constitutes
"due impartiality". It must ultimately be a question of fact depending
on the type and subject matter of the relevant programme.

The Commission has interpreted the term "due" as meaning
"adequate or appropriate to the nature of the subject and the type of
programme". The Code states that "due impartiality":

> " . . . does not mean that 'balance' is required in any simple math-
> ematical sense or that equal time must be given to each opposing
> point of view, nor does it require absolute neutrality on every
> issue".[41]

---

[38] *Ibid.*, s.2.4.
[39] Broadcasting Act 1990, s.6(1)(c).
[40] [1991] A.C. 696, H.L.
[41] *ITC Programme Code*, s.3, para. 3.2(i).

Duty of the Commission to draw up Code. The 1990 Act requires the   **32.30**
Commission to draw up a Code giving guidance as to the rules to be
observed in connection with the application of the requirements of due
impartiality on matters of political or industrial controversy or relating
to current public policy[42] and to "do all that they can to secure" that the
provisions of the code are observed in the provision of licensed services.[43]

The Code stipulates compliance is a condition of the licence[44] and
that in the event of breaches of the Code the Commission "will
normally seek appropriate remedial action in discussion with licensees".[45] It would appear therefore that the sanction that the Commission envisages, where there are breaches of the Code, is that the
infringing licensee will be required to transmit programmes which will
restore "due impartiality". The Code does not, however, require the
Commission to seek remedial action by such means. Thus, where it is
clear that there is a serious or consistent breaches of the rule by a licensee the Commission would be entitled and is under a duty to take such
measures as are in its powers to enforce compliance with the licence
and Code.

Editorialising. "If a director or officer of a licensee . . . express[es] an   **32.31**
opinion on a controversial matter, other than the provision of
programme services, in a broadcast by a licensee, it must be in a context
which makes clear that he or she is expressing a personal opinion and
not the opinion of the licensee. Speeches in Parliament are exempt from
this provision".[46] The avoidance of editorialising is regarded by the
Commission as an "integral part" of the preservation of due impartiality. This rule is, therefore, mandatory and must be observed in all
circumstances by the licensee.[47]

Impartiality over time: the "series" provision. Licensees should   **32.32**
"ensure that the principal opposing viewpoints are reflected in a single
programme or programme item where it is not likely that the licensee
will soon return to the subject or because the issues involved are of
current and active controversy. At other times, a single programme or
programme item need not express all viewpoints where the programme
consists of a programme or programme item forming part of a series of
programmes."[48]

---

[42] Broadcasting Act 1990, s.6(1)(c).
[43] *Ibid.*, s.6(3)(a).
[44] *ITC Programme Code*, s.3, Commentary (d).
[45] *Ibid.*, Commentary (h).
[46] *Ibid.*, s.3, para. 3.2(ii).
[47] *Ibid.*, Commentary (f).
[48] *Ibid.*, s.3, para. 3.3.

The Act permits a series of programmes to be considered as a whole.[49] In this context a "series of programmes" is defined by the Commission (pursuant to the powers granted by section 6(5)(b) of the Act) as "more than one programme broadcast in the same service, each one of which is clearly linked to the other/s and which deal with the same or related issues".[50] Where a series consist of programmes broadcast at regular intervals under the same title, "but which may deal with widely disparate issues from one edition to the next each programme should normally aim to be impartial in itself. Alternatively, licensees' impartiality may be achieved by dealing with the same subject-matter over two or more programmes. The intention to achieve impartiality over time should be planned in advance and, wherever practicable made clear to viewers."[51] It is not permissible to measure due impartiality by taking into account any views expressed on any other channel or any other media.[52]

32.33   In the case of personal view programmes "which are a regular fixture in the schedules, such as a nightly, weekly or monthly access programme, the views expressed on controversial matters should be kept in reasonable balance throughout the progress of the series and licensees must be able to demonstrate this".[53] Where a series takes a particular approach to a controversial issue or comprise a group of programmes presented from the same personal viewpoint which (a) may not be readily balanced the views expressed on the matters (b) the series is likely to have a long gestation period and are unlikely to be included in the schedules very long the views expressed must be kept in reasonable balance throughout the period of the licence.[54]

32.34   **"Major matters".** Section 6(5)(a) of the 1990 Act requires the Code to take particular account that due impartiality should be preserved as respects "major matters" of political or industrial controversy or relating to current public policy.[55] This is dealt with by the Commission making it a mandatory requirement that in all "major matters" of political or industrial controversy "licensees must ensure that justice must be done to a full range of significant views and perspectives during the period in which the controversy is active".[56] No definition is given in the 1990 Act as to the meaning of "major matter" but it would appear

---

[49] Broadcasting Act, s.6(6)(d)(ii).
[50] *ITC Programme Code*, s.3, para. 3.3(i).
[51] *Ibid.*, s.3, para. 3.3.
[52] *Ibid.*, s.3, para. 3.3(i).
[53] *Ibid.*, s.3, para. 3.6(i).
[54] *Ibid.*, s.3, para. 3.6.
[55] Broadcasting Act 1990, s.6(5)(a).
[56] *ITC Programme Code*, s.3, para. 3.4.

that the language of the section and the contrast which is to be drawn with section 6(1)(c) would indicate a political or industrial controversy of unusual, significant or serious importance which goes beyond what would normally prevail in respect of that subject matter.

For example, constant controversy may prevail with regard to the United Kingdom's place in the European Union but the Maastricht Treaty presented a controversy in that sphere of debate which transcended the normal day to day controversy. It is defined by the Commission as including matters of political or industrial issues of national importance or regional importance "such as a nationwide strike or significant legislation passing through Parliament".[57]

Factual programmes.[58] Due impartiality must be preserved in all factual **32.35** matters within the area of political or industrial controversy or current public policy. Programmes primarily dealing with an examination of issues already a matter of public debate "should give a fair representation of the main differing views on the matter. Those programmes which present evidence and offer a view on the authority of that evidence or which take the agenda beyond the point it has reached in existing public debate may single out one aspect of an issue for detailed examination". Programmes which seek to extend the political agenda in this way must be "fair to their subject matter".[59]

Dramatised reconstructions within factual programmes. It is a manda- **32.36** tory requirement of the Code that whenever a reconstruction is used in a documentary, current affairs or news programme it should be labelled in a manner so as to ensure that the viewer is not misled with regard to the nature of what they are viewing.[60]

News. The 1990 Act requires that any news given in whatever form **32.37** must be presented with due accuracy and impartiality.[61] "Reporting should be dispassionate" and viewers given a balanced account of events. "In reporting matters of industrial or political controversy the main differing views on the subject should be given their due weight in the period during which the controversy is active." It is for the news editor to determine whether such due impartiality is achieved within one news programme or over a series of news programmes.[62]

---

[57] *Ibid.*, s.3.4.
[58] *Ibid.*, s.3, para. 3.5.
[59] *Ibid.*, s.3, para. 3.5.
[60] *Ibid.*, s.3, para. 3.7(i).
[61] Broadcasting Act 1990, s.6(1)(b).
[62] *The ITC Programme Code*, s.3, para. 3.5(i).

32.38   Simulated news bulletins. Any stimulation of a television news bulletin or news flash included in any programme must "either be subtitled or produced in such a way that there can be no reasonable possibility that it could be taken to be an actual news bulletin".[63]

(vii) *Undue prominence in local licensable programme services*

32.39   The Commission may modify the application of the consumer protection requirements contained in section 6 of the 1990 Act in so far as it applies to licensable programme services[64] by substituting in place of section 6(1)(c) the following:

"(c) that undue prominence is not given in its programmes to the views and opinions of particular persons or bodies on matters of political or industrial controversy or relating to current public policy".[65]

The other consumer protection requirements of section 6 are unaffected.

The Commission is required to draw up and review from time to time a code giving guidance as to the application of this section 47(4).[66] Where a channel is permitted by the Commission to observe "undue prominence" rather than "due impartiality" there is a requirement imposed on the licensee to offer "an equality of opportunity" which "were it to be taken up, would result in a balance of views across the channel as a whole . . . Within this general approach there is no need for individual programmes to be balanced in order to present an impartial approach, nor for a programme presenting one specific view to be balanced by another putting forward the opposing view."[67]

(viii) *Religion*

32.40   General duty of the Commission. Section 6(1)(d) of the Broadcasting Act 1990 requires the Commission to do all it can to secure that every licensed service exercises "due responsibility" with respect to the content of religious programmes and in particular such programmes must not involve:

"(i) any improper exploitation of any susceptibilities of those watching the programmes[68]; or

(ii) any abusive treatment of the religious views and beliefs of

---

[63] *Ibid.*, s.3, para. 3.7(ii).
[64] Broadcasting Act 1990, s.47(4).
[65] *Ibid.*, s.47(5)(a).
[66] *Ibid.*, s.47(6).
[67] *ITC Programme Code*, s.3, para. 3.9.
[68] Broadcasting Act 1990, s.6(1)(d)(i).

those belonging to a particular religion or religious denomination".[69]

The Code. The Code specifies certain matters which must be observed **32.41** in respect of programmes specifically categorised as religious and, where appropriate, to general programmes which deal with religion. These rules are as follows:

(a) The identity of religious bodies featured in all programmes must be clear to the viewer, either in sound and vision.[70]

(b) Every attempt must be made to ensure that the belief and practice of religious groups are not misrepresented, and that programmes about religion are accurate and fair.[71]

(c) Religious programmes on Channel 3 and Channel 4 should reflect the worship, thought and action of the mainstream religious traditions in the United Kingdom, recognising that these are mainly, though not exclusively, Christian. Religious programmes provided for a particular region or locality should take account of the religious make-up of the area served.[72]

(d) Nothing may be included in any programme which constitutes an appeal for money by any organisation whose aims are wholly or mainly religious, unless the conditions set out in section 8 of the Code[73] are complied with. This includes appeals for funds to make programmes.[74]

(e) Religious programmes on non-specialist channels may not be designed for the purpose of recruiting viewers to any particular religious faith or denomination. Nor must programmes or follow material be used to denigrate the beliefs of other people.[75]

(f) Where published material can be seen to be closely related to a **32.42** programme and is a useful addition to the promotion of programme material.[76]

---

[69] *Ibid.*, s.6(1)(d)(ii).
[70] *ITC Programme Code*, s.9.3.
[71] *Ibid.*, s.9, para. 9.4.
[72] *Ibid.*, s.9, para. 9.5.
[73] These conditions require, *inter alia*, that "appeals for funds on behalf of religious charities may be permitted only if the charities can reliably demonstrate that any proceeds from such appeals will be devoted solely to the benefit of identified categories of disadvantaged third parties, and that the conveying of such benefit will not be associated with the promotion of any other objective (*e.g.* proselytizing)".
[74] *ITC Programme Code*, s.9, para. 9.6.
[75] *Ibid.*, s.9, para. 9.7.
[76] *Ibid.*, s.9, para. 9.8.

(g) On-air announcements permitted by section 10.3 may offer to send publications free to viewers, but may not contain any free offer.[77]

(h) Offers to provide follow up material to any religious programme must make it clear that no further contact will be made except at the instigation of the viewer. Licensees are required to satisfy themselves that follow-up material is responsible in tone and content.[78]

(i) Religious programmes must not seek to persuade or influence viewers by preying on their fears, nor by any other means engage in any improper exploitation of the susceptibilities of those watching programmes.[79]

(j) Except in the context of a legitimate investigation, religious programmes may not contain claims by or about living individuals or groups, suggesting that they have special powers or abilities, which are incapable of being substantiated.[80]

2. Radio Authority

32.43 Section 90 of the Broadcasting Act 1990 imposes on the Radio Authority similar regulatory duties to those imposed on the Commission under section 6 and 7 of the 1990 Act. However, where the licensed service is a local, satellite or licensable sound programme service the duty is to ensure that "undue prominence" is not given in programmes to the views and opinions of particular persons or bodies on such matters.[81] This reflects the general intent of the 1990 Act that such services would reflect the particular tastes and views of the community for which it is intended. Further, section 90 contains no express requirement for due impartiality in respect of "major matters".

The Authority have drawn up a Code giving guidance as to the rules to be observed respect sounds suggestive of violence and other matters. This Code generally reflects the BSC Code of practice in accordance with the requirement of section 152 of the Broadcasting Act of 1990. It is not proposed to deal with the terms of the "Authority" Code in this work.

---

[77] *Ibid.*, s.9, para. 9.9.
[78] *Ibid.*, s.9, para. 9.10.
[79] *Ibid.*, s.9, para. 9.11.
[80] *Ibid.*, s.9, para. 9.12.
[81] Broadcasting Act 1990, s.90.

3. Regulation of Programme Standards by the British Broadcasting Corporation

(a) *Programme standards*

In 1964 the BBC Board of Governors undertook that, " . . . so far as   **32.44**
possible the programme for which they are responsible should not
offend against good taste or decency, or be likely to encourage crime or
disorder or be offensive to public feeling".[82] The BBC were established
by Royal Charter and are not subject to statutory duties nor is a failure
to observe their self imposed duty with regard to decency in programme subject to judicial review.

However, the BBC is now subject to the jurisdiction of the Broadcasting Standards Council (BSC) and there is a statutory duty[83] placed on it
to reflect the BSC's Code[84] on programme standards in its own
programme code. Thus, the statutory duty imposed is with regard to the
content of the programme code. Implicit in this a duty is a duty to
ensure that the programme standards of the BBC reflect the BSC's code.
It is therefore arguable that if the BBC Code should fail to reflect such
programme standards it may be susceptible to judicial review if there is
no good reason for departing from the aspects of the BSC programme
code which it is required to reflect in its own programme code.

(b) *Impartiality*

There is no statutory duty on the BBC in respect of impartiality. Never-   **32.45**
theless Clause 13(7) of the current licence granted to it by the Secretary
of State for the Home Department contains the following proviso:

> "The corporation shall at all times refrain from sending any broad-
> cast matter expressing the opinion of the corporation on current
> affairs or on matters of public policy".

Further, a resolution of the Board of Governors of the BBC of January
8, 1981, noted by the Secretary of State and appended to the licence,
reaffirms the board's objective:

---

[82] Letter dated June 13, 1964, to the Postmaster-General from the then Chairman of the
BBC, Lord Normanbrook. The contents of the letter are noted in the prescribing
memorandum under Clause 13(4) of the BBC Licence and Agreement.
[83] Broadcasting Act 1990, s.152(3).
[84] The BSC code incorporate rules on:

(a) the family viewing 9 p.m. threshold which is discussed under regulation by the
   Independent Television Commission;
(b) portrayal of violence;
(c) sex and sexuality;
(d) taste and decency.

These rules are broadly similar to those discussed under regulation by the Independent
Television Commission.

"to treat controversial subjects with due impartiality, and they intend to continue this policy both in the corporation's news services and in the more general field of programmes dealing with matters of public policy".

32.46   This undertaking is in similar terms to that contained in the statutory duty which was imposed on the former Independent Broadcasting Authority in section 4(1)(f) of the Broadcasting Act 1981 which has now been repealed. It has been held that the failure to observe this self imposed duty is not subject to judicial review.[85] However, the matter is not entirely without doubt. In *R. v. Broadcasting Complaints Commission., ex parte Owen*[86] May L.J. said, in discussing impartiality:

"If the broadcasting authorities fail to comply with their statutory duties in so far as policy is concerned, for instance those laid down in section 4(1)(f), then the appropriate remedy lay against them and not by way of complaint to the commission. He [counsel for the commission] contended that in an appropriate case judicial review would lie against the I.B.A. for a breach of statutory duty. For my part I would also respectfully wish to reserve the question whether in similar circumstances such proceedings would not lie against the governors of the BBC. We were told that it has been decided that they would not by Hutton J. in the High Court in Belfast in *Lynch v. British Broadcasting Corporation* (unreported), 7 June 1983."

---

[85] *Lynch v. British Broadcasting Corporation*, June 7, 1983; see also *Attorney-General ex rel. McWhirter v. Independent Broadcasting Authority* [1973] 1 Q.B. 629 at 657 where Lawton J. also implies that this is indeed the case; see also *Grieve v. Douglas-Home* 1965 S.C. 315 at 338, *per* Lord Kilbrandon; *McAliskey v. British Broadcasting Corpn.* [1980] N.I. 44 at 53, *per* Murray J.

[86] [1985] 1 Q.B. 1153.

CHAPTER 33

THE BROADCASTING COMPLAINTS COMMISSION

General. The Broadcasting Act 1990 created the Broadcasting Com-   **33.01**
plaints Commission to examine and adjudicate upon complaints arising
from programmes broadcast by the independent television companies
and the BBC. The BCC's function has been preserved by the Broadcasting Act 1990.

1. Function of the BCC

The function of the BCC is set out in section 143 of the Broadcasting Act   **33.02**
1990 which states:

"143 Function of BCC

(1) Subject to the provisions of this part, the function of the BCC
shall be to consider and adjudicate upon the complaints of—
  (a) unjust or unfair treatment in programmes to which this
  Part applies, or
  (b) unwarranted infringement of privacy in, or in connection
  with the obtaining of material included in or in connection with the obtaining of material included in, such programmes."

(a) *"Unjust or unfair treatment"*

Section 150 of the 1990 Act defines "unjust or unfair treatment" as   **33.03**
including treatment which is unjust or unfair because of the way in
which material included in a programme has been selected or arranged.

495

Unjust and unfair may also, within the meaning of the 1990 Act, arise by reason of what was said or shown, or because of what was left unsaid or unshown, or because of the context in which what had been said or shown had been placed.[1] Three points arise out of this definition.

First, it is important to note that the BCC is given jurisdiction to examine only the *treatment* of a particular subject.

Secondly, the words "unjust" and "unfair" require reference to objective standards of fairness and therefore suggest that there must be a concrete person or organisation aggrieved by the treatment which can invoke those standards. It is of course possible to be unjust or unfair towards a person[2] by misrepresentation, or distortion, or, possibly, to a product, but it will be extremely rare, if at all possible, for unfair or unjust treatment of an idea, or of a theory or even of a fact to occur.

Thirdly, the 1990 Act does not refer to "inaccuracy" as an additional or separate ingredient, and therefore a programme can contain wrong or inaccurate information without, it is submitted, being unjust or unfair.

However, material inaccuracy can and often would amount to unfairness. Further, editing of material which creates inaccuracy would be subject to scrutiny under section 143.[3]

(b) *Unwarranted infringement of privacy*

33.04 **General.** The jurisdiction of the BCC to entertain a complaint in respect of an infringement of privacy depends upon the finding, first, that there was privacy capable of being infringed, secondly that the infringement was unwarranted and thirdly that the complainant is a person affected. There is an interrelationship between the first and second elements and the courts are reluctant to circumscribe the BCC's powers to act by giving a definition to the term.[4] It follows that provided the BCC does not

---

[1] *R. v. Broadcasting Complaints Commission, ex parte Owen* [1985] Q.B. 1153.

[2] Individual or corporate.

[3] Broadcasting Act 1990, s.6(1)(b) imposes obligations on the Commission to ensure (or "secure") that any news given in the programmes of a licensed service is presented with "due accuracy and impartiality". It is to be noted that within the same statute, Parliament did not give the BCC the role, even in part, of statutory policeman to ensure that "due accuracy" was acheived. However, in *R. v. Broadcasting Complaints Commission, ex parte Granada Television Limited* [1993] E.M.L.R. 426 the court held that the BCC did possess jurisdiction to examine whether or not interviews with participants were unfairly edited. It follows that although the BCC does not possess a duty to secure due impartiality it can review and adjudicate upon the achievement of due impartiality in any given case.

[4] See *R. v. Broadcasting Complaints Commission, ex parte Granada Television Ltd.* [1993] E.M.L.R. 426 at 434.

act perversely in deciding whether or not there was an infringement of privacy, its decision will not be quashed.[5]

Privacy. In English law there is no general right of action for invasion of **33.05** privacy.[6] This, together with the fact that the scope and extent of the right to privacy envisaged by the 1990 Act is not clear, renders the concept of "infringement of privacy" a subject of "considerable complexity" within the context of the 1990 Act.[7] It is submitted that the word "privacy" is capable of bearing two meanings.

First, the right to the avoidance of publicity in respect of one's activities, for in such matters as publicity there can be no privacy.

Secondly, it means the right not to have one's privacy physically disturbed by, for example, such intrusive activity as the attempt to obtain photographs of an individual at his home, for the inclusion in a programme.

However, the latter definition is qualified by the requirement that in order to obtain relief under the 1990 Act there must be a nexus or connection between the material broadcast and the infringement of privacy or in other words the infringement must have taken place in connection with the general obtaining of material which was in fact contained in the programme.[8]

Thus, for example, there would be such a nexus where a programme had as its subject complaints made by dissatisfied customers of a dating agency and where the programme investigators visited the home of the proprietor and took photographs of him with the intention of including them in the programme. If the programme is broadcast but the photographs are not included in the programme there would nevertheless be a nexus between the photograph and the subject matter of the

---

[5] See *ibid.* at 436.
[6] *Bernstein of Leigh (Baron) v. Skyviews & General Ltd.* [1978] Q.B. 479; *Kaye v. Robertson*, The Times, March 21, 1990, C.A.
[7] *Malone v. Commissioner of Police of the Metropolis (No. 2)* [1979] 2 All E.R. 620 at 649. See also Warren and Brandeis, "The Right to Privacy", (1890) 4 Harvard L. Rev. 198; Prosser, "Privacy", (1960) 48 California L. Rev. 383 where following the analysis of 600 United States tort cases the author concluded that there were four types of invasion of privacy: (1) intrusion (2) appropriation of property such as singing voice and musical style (3) false light which involves the giving of publicity concerning another which portrays the other before the public in a false light with the knowledge or reckless disregard by the communicator of the falsity of the publicised matter; (4) publicity of private facts.
[8] *R. v. Broadcasting Complaints Commission, ex parte British Broadcasting Corporation* [1993] E.M.L.R. 419 at 423. The complaint which was the subject of this case was considered under s.54(1) of the Broadcasting Act 1980 which related to "(b) unwarranted infringement of privacy in, or connection with the obtaining of material included in sound television programmes actually so broadcast". The phrase "actually broadcast" does not appear in the equivalent section in the 1990 Act.

programme and in such a case the BCC would have jurisdiction to consider the matter.[9]

Where there is an infringement of privacy within either of these two categories it matters not whether the person affected takes part or appears in the programme or subsequently hears about it.[10]

33.06   It follows from this interpretation of privacy within the context of the 1990 Act that the invasion of privacy will include:

(a) the giving of publicity concerning another which portrays the other before the public in a false light;

(b) the unwarranted giving of publicity to private and embarrassing facts;

(c) the unwarranted physical intrusion into another's home, office, car or even in a public place with the aim of acquiring material for inclusion of a programme which is eventually broadcast notwithstanding that the material is not included in such programme.

It is difficult to envisage in what circumstances the first of these infringements of privacy can be justified but in the latter two the broadcaster may escape criticism if the infringement is warranted or justified.

33.07 **"Unwarranted".** There is no definition of "unwarranted" in the 1990 Act. However, the word may be defined as meaning "unauthorized; unjustified". In this context, it would appear that few problems would arise where the infringement of privacy is "authorized" although nice questions may arise as to whether conduct or silence may give rise to authorization. Where no authorisation has been given the question arises as to whether the broadcasters actions are unjustifiable.

---

[9] *R. v. Broadcasting Complaints Commission, ex parte British Broadcasting Corporation, The Times*, October 16, 1992. The complaint which was the subject of this case was considered under s.54(1) of the Broadcasting Act 1980 which related to "(b) unwarranted infringement of privacy in, or connection with the obtaining of material included in sound television programmes actually so broadcast". The phrase "actually broadcast" does not appear in the equivalent section in the 1990 Act. See also *R. v. Broadcasting Complaints Commission, ex parte Granada Television Ltd.* [1993] E.M.L.R. 426.

[10] See *R. v. Broadcasting Complaints Commission, ex parte Granada Television Ltd.* [1993] E.M.L.R. 426, where Popplewell J. whilst stating that he was not called upon to decide whether privacy could be infringed where a matter is already in the public domain held that the BCC did not act unreasonably in taking the view that where the matter complained of is already in the public domain it may still be an infringement of privacy to subsequently include such matter in a programme.

It is submitted that an infringement will be unjustifiable where, on an   **33.08**
analysis of the specific facts, it cannot be justified on the basis of the
public interest. This will involve balancing the public interest in
upholding the right to privacy against some other public interest that is
served by the infringement of privacy. The nature of the information to
be obtained, or obtained, by the infringement of privacy will form an
important part of the circumstances that must be taken into account in
deciding whether in relation to that information the broadcaster was, or
would be, justified in infringing privacy. If the information involved
which has or will be obtained from infringing privacy would have as
one of its results the exposing of iniquity the infringement would, it is
submitted, be justifiable for to hold otherwise would be to cover up
wrongdoing.

Person affected. In relation to an unwarranted infringement of privacy   **33.09**
the "person affected" means the person whose privacy is infringed.[11]

2. Entertaining Complaints

General. Section 144 lays down the statutory limits on the making and   **33.10**
entertaining of complaints. A complaint may be made by an individual
or by a body of persons, whether incorporated or not, but may not be
entertained by the BCC unless made by "the person affected" or by a
person authorised by him to make the complaint for him.[12] Where the
person affected is an individual who has died or is for any other reason
both unable to make a complaint himself and unable to authorise
another person to do for him, a complaint may be made by the personal
representative of the person affected, or by a member of his family, or
by some other person or body closely connected with him.[13]

Where a complaint is made to the BCC by a "person affected" it may   **33.11**
not entertain or proceed with the consideration of a complaint if it
appears that:

(a) the complaint relates to the broadcasting of a programme, or its
    inclusion in a licensed service, more than five years after the
    death of the person affected[14]; or

(b) the alleged unjust or unfair treatment or unwarranted infringe-

---

[11] Broadcasting Act 1990, s.150.
[12] *Ibid.*, s.144(2).
[13] *Ibid.*, s.144(2).
[14] *Ibid.*, s.144(4)(a).

ment of privacy is either the subject of proceedings in a United Kingdom court[15]; or

(c) a matter in which the person affected has a remedy by way of proceedings in a United Kingdom court and that in the particular circumstances it is not appropriate for the BCC to consider a complaint about it[16]; or

(d) the complaint is frivolous or it appears for any reason inappropriate to entertain or proceed with its consideration.[17]

33.12   Further, the BCC may refuse to entertain a complaint if it appears to it not to have been made within a reasonable time after the programme was broadcast or included in a licensed service.[18] If it was broadcast in a licensed service within five years of the death of the person affected, the complaint must be made within a reasonable time of the programme being broadcast or included.[19] The circumstances of a particular case would determine what amounts to a reasonable time.

The BCC may also refuse to entertain a complaint of unfair or unjust treatment if the allegedly affected person was not himself the subject of the complained of treatment and it appears to the BCC that he did not have a sufficiently direct interest in the subject matter of that treatment to justify the making of the complaint with him as the affected person[20] or if the person making the complaint other than the person affected or authorised by him is not sufficiently "close" to justify making the complaint.[21]

It is important to note that section 144(2) of the 1990 Act commands the BCC *not* to entertain a complaint unless it is made by a person affected or authorised by such person. This restriction applies *before* the consideration of discretion to refuse to entertain given by section 144(7) of the Act as set out in this section.

(a) *"Person affected"*

33.13   **Person affected.** The BCC is prohibited by section 144(2) from entertaining complaints unless made by a person affected. Section 150 of the 1990 Act defines a "person affected" in relation to unwarranted infringement of privacy as the "person whose privacy was infringed".

---

[15] *Ibid.*, s.144(4)(b). See *R. v. Broadcasting Complaints Commission, ex parte Thames Television Ltd., The Times*, October 8, 1982.

[16] *Ibid.*, s.144(4)(b). See *R. v. Broadcasting Complaints Commission, ex parte British Broadcasting Corpn* (1984) 128 Sol. Jo. 384, C.A.

[17] *Ibid.*, s.144(4)(d).

[18] *Ibid.*, s.144(5).

[19] *Ibid.*, s.144(6).

[20] *Ibid.*, s.144(7)(a).

[21] *Ibid.*, s.144(7)(b).

In the context of unwarranted infringement of privacy, the application of this definition will present little difficulty in the majority of cases. However, the determination of a "person affected" in relation to unfair and unjust treatment is not without difficulty. Section 150 of the 1990 Act defines a "person affected" by unjust and unfair treatment as:

> "a participant in the programme in question who was the subject of that treatment or a person who, whether such a participant or not, had a direct interest in the subject matter of that treatment".

There are three categories of persons who have the *locus standi* to present a complaint. First, participants[22] in programmes who are the subject of the treatment, secondly, participants who had a direct interest in the subject-matter of the treatment; and thirdly, those who merely had a direct interest in the subject-matter.[23] The first category presents little difficulty but the requirement for a "direct interest" in respect of the second and third categories may prove problematical in its application.

"Direct interest" is not further defined in the 1990 Act. However, it is **33.14** submitted that if the "direct interest" provision, is to make sense within the context of the statute it must be construed narrowly. It is the stage once removed from being the *subject* of the unjust or unfair treatment. It is also clear that the "direct interest" must be an interest in the subject matter of the *treatment* not a direct interest in the subject matter of the programme. Further, the interest must be "direct" – any other interest will not do. A direct interest imports at least some connection or nexus between the complainant and the treatment complained of.[24] Although "direct interest" is not a term of art,[25] and not further defined in the 1990 Act, it is submitted that, applying public law criteria, that

---

[22] A person is a "participant" if he appeared, or his voice was heard, in programme: Broadcasting Act 1990, s.150.

[23] Note, there is no separate category for the non-participant who was nevertheless the actual subject of the unjust of unfair treatment. Such complainant is included within the "direct interest" category: *R. v. Broadcasting Complaints Commission, ex parte British Broadcasting Corporation, The Times,* May 26, 1994.

[24] *R. v. Broadcasting Complaints Commission, ex parte British Broadcasting Corporation, The Times,* May 26, 1994.

[25] See *Presho v. Insurance Officer* [1984] 2 W.L.R. 29, 34H–35B, H.L., where Lord Brandon considering s.19(1) of the Social Security Act 1975 stated that "direct interest" must be given its ordinary and natural meaning in the context which it occurs. In the context of the Social Security Act 1975 it meant those who would benefit from the trade dispute either because any agreement reached would be automatically incorporated into their contracts of employment or because it was the custom that agreements reached between the employers and employees should be applied across the board. See also *R. v. Broadcasting Complaints Commission, ex parte British Broadcasting Corporation, The Times,* May 26, 1994.

any conclusion by the BCC that a complainant has such an interest must be based on rational and reasonable grounds.[26]

33.15 **A limited class of complainant?** The 1992 Report of the BCC[27] refers to complaints from the Terence Higgins Trust, Frontliners (U.K.) Ltd, Positively Women, and the Wellcome Foundation arising from a programme which "unfairly treated the subject of AIDS" or was "one-sided and unfair". It appears that the complainants were not participants[28] in the programme. Thus, the only basis upon which the complaints could have been entertained was because the BCC concluded that those bodies had a direct interest in the subject matter of the unfair treatment.

However, that position is problematic. As previously noted it is doubtful whether there can be unfair or unjust treatment within the 1990 Act of a *subject* such as AIDS.[29] Although the Terence Higgins Trust may have had an indirect interest in the subject matter of the programme, it cannot be said to have had a direct interest in the programme itself, or in the allegedly unfair treatment of persons within that programme.[30] Thus, it is submitted that a representative body or pressure group cannot have a direct interest where an individual does not. To allow pressure groups to raise complaints as to the general presentation of ideas would be to confuse the statutory test of *direct* interest with merely being interested in the subject matter. That type of interest might well give the pressure group locus standi to challenge the BCC's decision not to hear the complaint, but that challenge should not succeed. It follows that the BCC's jurisdiction is strictly limited.

33.16   The foregoing proposition is supported by *R. v. Broadcasting Complaints Commission, ex parte Owen*[31] which outlines what the BCC's jurisdiction should be. The court accepted that David Owen as leader of the Alliance Party could present a complaint. However, the basis for the

---

[26] Note the far less precise provision in s.31(3) of the Supreme Court Act 1981 dealing with the right to apply for judicial review. There, all the applicant must demonstrate is "sufficient interest in the matter to which the application relates". Mere sufficiency of interest has permitted applications for judicial review by representative bodies and pressure groups such as Child Poverty Action Group (but without argument), and the National Union of Journalists. For an interesting analysis, see Sir Konrad Schiemann's article in Public Law 1990, p. 342.

[27] *Ibid.*, p. 19.

[28] See n.4.

[29] See *R. v. Broadcasting Complaints Commission, ex parte* [1993] E.M.L.R. 426 where the court held it was not the BCC function to ascertain whether the facts portrayed in a particular programme were correct but whether the presentation of those facts was correct at 439.

[30] If the programme had made statements about the Terence Higgins Trust there is no doubt that a section 143 complaint could have been made. However, absent that direct nexus, it is difficult to see what interest the Trust has in the presentation of programmes on general issues.

[31] [1985] 1 Q.B. 1153.

complaint was that the party itself had been unfairly treated. In deciding that the complaint could be made, the court emphasised the personal nature of the protection by the legislation of the protection afforded by the legislation. May L.J. in his analysis of the identical provisions of the 1981 Broadcasting Act stated:

> "In my opinion the purpose of Part III . . . of the Act . . . was **33.17** indeed to provide [a] . . . tribunal . . . to whom individuals or a collection of individuals could complain about the content of programmes which had been unjust or unfair to *them, either in what was said or shown, or because of what was left unsaid or unshown, or because of the context in which what had been said or shown had been placed* . . .
>
> That Parliament only had such a *limited personal type of complaint in mind* rather than a more general complaint in reality about the policy of a broadcasting organisation in relation to a programme or series of programmes is I think clear . . . [the] general tenor . . . with the references to programmes 'actually broadcast', with the requirement that the person affected or the complainant should have had a direct interest in the subject matter of the allegedly unjust or unfair treatment, with the definition of 'the relevant programme' in section 55 . . . , read in conjunction with the references to individuals and the time limits laid down . . . all [these] support the view that the type of complaint contemplated by Parliament when enacting Part III . . . of the Act of 1981 was of the personal, limited and more specified one which I have sought to describe."[32]

Further support for a narrow interpretation or the BCC's jurisdiction **33.18** can be derived from Article 23(1) of the Directive on Broadcasting which is implemented by sections 142 to 150 of the Broadcasting Act 1990.[33] That Article states:

> "Without prejudice to the other provisions adopted by the member states under civil, administrative or criminal law, any natural or legal person, regardless of nationality, whose legitimate interests, in particular reputation and good name, have been damaged by an assertion of incorrect facts in a television programme must have a right to reply or equivalent remedies."

The right is based on the "legitimate interests" of the person aggrieved. The phrase is given some meaning by the addition of "in particular reputation and good name" and the mention of those rights being damaged by "an assertion of incorrect facts". It is clear that the

---

[32] *Ibid.*, at 1173. Emphasis supplied.
[33] Directive 89/552: [1989] O.J. L298/23.

right is to be a purely personal one analogous to the private law actions of libel and slander. It is submitted that domestic law is to be interpreted, so far as possible, so as to be in harmony with E.C. legislation.[34] It is submitted therefore that the terms of Article 23(1) would support a narrow interpretation of "direct interest".

33.19   **Proper approach to section 150.** It follows from the foregoing analysis that with regard to "unjust or unfair treatment" requires, first, the identification of the treatment that is allegedly unfair. Such treatment may be in a particular part of the programme; it may be a whole programme or a series of programmes.

Secondly, when the treatment has been identified, it must be determined whether the complainant has a direct interest in the subject-matter of that treatment: there will be no direct interest unless there is at least a connection or nexus between the complainant and the treatment complained of.

Whether the treatment is fair or unfair is not a relevant consideration at this stage of the analysis. It is only if the BCC should decide that the complainant does have such a direct interest does it have jurisdiction to proceed to the next stage and consider whether the treatment contained within the subject-matter is or is not unjust or unfair.[35] This starting point is important because it avoids the temptation to proceed on the basis that if there has in fact been unjust or unfair treatment it does not matter who complains or how the complaint is activated.[36]

(b) *"Proceedings in the United Kingdom"*

33.20   **Subject of proceedings in a United Kingdom court.** Whether the alleged unjust or unfair treatment or unwarranted infringement of privacy is the subject of proceedings in the United Kingdom will present little difficulty. It is a question of fact whether the subject-matter of the proceedings is substantially the same as the subject-matter of the complaint before the BCC and where it is the BCC may not adjudicate on the complaint until the action is concluded.[37]

---

[34] *Garland v. British Railway Engineering* [1983] 2 A.C. 751 at 771, *per* Lord Diplock, H.L.

[35] *R. v. Broadcasting Complaints Commission, ex parte British Broadcasting Corporation, The Times*, May 26, 1994.

[36] *cf.* the position of the Broadcasting Standards Council which is permitted to receive complaints from anyone and can even issue complaints itself (see s.154(7)); note also the observations of Oliver L.J. in *R. v. B.C.C., ex parte B.B.C.* (1984) Sol. Jo. vol. 128 at 384.

[37] *R. v. Broadcasting Complaints Commission, ex parte Thames Television Ltd., The Times*, October 10, 1982.

Matter in respect of which remedy available in a United Kingdom **33.21**
court. Section 144(4)(c) provides that the BCC shall not entertain or proceed with the consideration of a complaint if it appears to them that
"the unjust or unfair treatment or unwarranted infringement of privacy
complained of is a matter in respect of which the person affected has a
remedy by way of proceedings in a court of law in the United Kingdom,
and that in the particular circumstances it is not appropriate for the BCC
to consider a complaint about it". The subsection imposes an obligation
on BCC to hear complaints unless in the particular case it is not appropriate. The section confers a wide discretion upon the BCC. The
decision as to whether particular circumstances make it, in the BCC's
view, inappropriate for the investigation to be entertained or to proceed
is left to it without any express guidance being provided by the 1990
Act as to the considerations which it should, or may, take into account.
Two factors may be discerned from the 1990 Act. However, these factors
pull in opposite directions.

The first factor is the absolute prohibition against proceedings with **33.22**
consideration of a complaint where the treatment complained of "is the
subject of proceedings in a court of law in the United Kingdom". This is
a relevant consideration if the circumstances are such that the BCC is of
the view that there might be a possibility of conflict between the conclusion reached by it and those reached by a court in proceedings subsequently commenced.
The existence of a legal remedy in the complainant is not, however, a
pointer against carrying out the primary statutory duty of entertaining
the complaint. It is no more than the pre-condition to the consideration
of whether there are particular circumstances which render it inappropriate for the BCC to proceed: by implication such circumstances must
in some way be related to the legal remedy. The mere existence of the
legal remedy and therefore the possibility of its being exercised cannot
itself be a "particular circumstance".[38]

The consideration on the other side of the balance is the presumption **33.23**
in favour of an investigation of a complaint. The starting point in this
analysis is that there is an absolute statutory duty to investigate a
complaint.[39] In other words where no proceedings are in fact extant it is
immaterial that the complainant may have a legal remedy for his
complaint unless the BCC consider that there are particular circumstances which renders it inappropriate for the investigation to proceed.

---

[38] *R. v. Broadcasting Complaints Commission, ex parte British Broadcasting Corporation,* C.A.
(1984; unreported).
[39] This duty arises from the Broadcasting Act 1990, ss.143(1), 145(1) and is subject only to
s.144.

Thus, what the BCC has to ask itself in such a case is whether there are "particular circumstances" connected with the existence of the complainant's remedy which are such as to dictate that the complainant should be deprived of the benefit of having his complaint investigated by the BCC in accordance with its statutory duty and left to pursue his remedy through the courts.[40] It is clear that the likelihood of proceedings being commenced is a relevant factor in that the commencement of proceedings during the BCC's investigation would be likely to bring the investigation to an end if the subject matter of the complaint is also the subject matter of the proceedings.

33.24   Where the BCC has satisfied itself that the investigation is being sought for proper motives and, *a fortiori*, where it has satisfied itself that there is no present intention on the part of a complainant to seek a remedy through the courts it would not be inappropriate for it to proceed with the inquiry, particularly where it reserves liberty to seek further clarification of the complainant's position when he appears before it.

The onus upon anyone seeking to show that there are particular circumstances which compel the BCC to find it is not appropriate to consider a complaint is a heavy one. The onus requires the party to show that the conclusion at which the BCC in fact arrived, whether or not it considered all the matters which it should have considered, was perverse and such that no reasonable BCC properly directing itself could possibly have reached it: such a finding needs to be supported by the very clearest indications and it is not sufficient that the court would or might have reached a different conclusion.[41]

3. Making of Complaints

33.25   The procedure by which complaints are to be made is laid down in section 144 of the 1990 Act. Complaints must be in writing[42] and made by a person who satisfies the tests outlined above.[43] If that person is dead, or otherwise unable both to complain himself or authorise another to do so on his behalf, a complaint may be made by his personal representative, family member or someone else closely connected with him.[44]

---

[40] *R. v. Broadcasting Complaints Commission, ex parte British Broadcasting Corporation,* C.A. (1984; unreported).
[41] *Ibid.*
[42] Broadcasting Act 1990, s.144(1).
[43] See *ante*, para. 33.10 *et seq.*
[44] Broadcasting Act 1990, s.144(3).

Examples, given by the Act, of persons closely connected are employers, or a body of which he is, or was, at death a member.[45]

4. Investigation of the Complaint

Before considering a complaint the BCC must send a copy of it to the **33.26** "relevant person"[46] and the ITC and Radio Authority if they licensed a service including the programme.[47] On receiving a copy of the complaint, the relevant person must, if required by the BCC:

(a) provide to the BCC a visual or sound recording of the programme or a specified part of it in so far as he has copy in his possession[48];

(b) make suitable arrangements for enabling the complainant to view or hear the programme or a specified part of it in so far as he has a copy of it in his possession[49];

(c) provide to the BCC and the complainant a transcript of the programme or a specified part of it in so far as he has a copy in his possession[50];

(d) provide to the BCC and the complainant copies of any correspondence about the complaint between themselves and the person affected or the complainant in connection with the complaint[51]; and

(e) furnish to the BCC and the complainant a written statement in answer to the complaint.[52]

To facilitate the operation of this provision, the BBC and Welsh Auth- **33.27** ority must retain for 90 days a recording of every television programme and for 42 days a recording of every sound programme from its broadcast such period to begin with the broadcast.[53] The ITC and Radio authority are required to include a term in the licence agreements requiring license holders to retain television programmes and sound programmes for like periods.[54]

---

[45] *Ibid.*, s.144(3).
[46] *Ibid.*, s.145(10)(a)(b): the "relevant person" means in the case where the programme was broadcast by a broadcasting body (*e.g* the BBC) that body and in the case where the programme in question was included in a licensed service (*e.g.* a channel 3 service) the licence holder.
[47] *Ibid.*, s.145(3).
[48] *Ibid.*, s.145(4)(a).
[49] *Ibid.*, s.145(4)(c).
[50] *Ibid.*, s.145(4)(c).
[51] *Ibid.*, s.145(4)(d).
[52] *Ibid.*, s.145(4)(e).
[53] *Ibid.*, s.145(5).
[54] *Ibid.*, ss.11, 95.

5. Consideration of Complaints

33.28   Every duly made complaint to the BCC must be considered by it, either at a hearing or if it thinks fit, without a hearing.[55] If there is a hearing it must be in private and the complainant, the relevant person and where the programme was included in a licensed programme service, the appropriate regulatory body, must be given an opportunity to attend to be heard.[56] Any person who appears to the BCC to have been responsible for the making or provision of the programme, such as a Channel 3 license holder for example, must also be given an opportunity to attend and make representations.[57] Any other person who the BCC consider might be able to assist at the hearing will be entitled to attend and make representations.[58]

Where the BCC or the Welsh Authority receive a copy of a complaint from the BCC, it must arrange for one or more of its governors, members or employees to attend and assist it in its consideration of the complaint.[59] Where the relevant person is a body other than a broadcasting body it must arrange for one or more of those who either take part in the management or control or are employed by it to assist them in its consideration[60] or if it is individual, either him or his employee(s).[61]

6. Sanctions

33.29   The only sanction the BCC may impose is the publication of its adjudications. The BCC cannot insist upon an apology or the correction of a false impression or provide financial redress. The upholding of a serious or repeated complaint may, however, indicate an infringement of licence conditions in which case the Commission or the Radio Authority may be under a duty to impose sanctions.

---

[55] *Ibid.*, s.145(1).
[56] *Ibid.*, s.145(2).
[57] *Ibid.*, s.145(d).
[58] *Ibid.*, s.145(e).
[59] *Ibid.*, s.145(6)(a).
[60] *Ibid.*, s.145(6)(b).
[61] *Ibid.*, s.145(6)(c).

CHAPTER 34

THE BROADCASTING STANDARDS COUNCIL

Functions of the BSC

As a result of the limited jurisdiction granted to the BCC, the 1990 Act **34.01** provides for the exercise of general supervisory powers and duties by the Broadcasting Standards Council.[1] The general nature of the powers and duties given contrast sharply with the precise scope of the BCC's jurisdiction and are in keeping with the BSC's overall function as the maintainer of standards of "taste and decency". The powers and duties fall into three categories: drawing up codes, monitoring standards and considering complaints.

(a) *The BSC Code*

The BSC must draw up, and from time to time review, a code giving **34.02** guidance on three matters:

    (a) the practices to be followed in connection with the portrayal of violence in television and song programmes broadcast by the BBC, television programmes broadcast by the Welsh Authority and television or sound programmes included in a licensed service[2];

---

[1] The Government has indicated its intention to amalgamate the BCC and the BSC into one body: see Cm. 2621.
[2] Broadcasting Act 1990, s.152(1)(a).

(b) the practices to be followed in connection with the portrayal of sexual conduct[3] in those programmes[4];

(c) the standards of taste and decency for those programmes generally.[5]

34.03   It is difficult to see how a requirement that standards of taste and decency be codified can actually be complied with. It is submitted that two results follow. First, the BSC code could be drawn up to be so vague as to be virtually meaningless and the BSC would therefore have little or no effect on programming. Second, if a set of standards could be objectified, their codification would stultify any programming which sought to challenge those standards. The unattractiveness of the latter position may given, it is submitted, lead a court to quash a BSC code which was so designed.

Before drawing up or revising the code the BSC must consult with the BBC, the Welsh Authority, the ITC, the Radio Authority[6] and such other persons as appears to the BSC appropriate.[7] The code must be published by the BSC[8] and although these bodies are not required to consult with the BSC when drawing up or revising their codes any code drawn up by the BBC, the Welsh Authority, the ITC and the Radio Authority must reflect the "general effect" of so much of the BSC code as is relevant to the programmes in question.[9] The BSC code has no direct influence on programmes, it operates on the regulators and it is the codes of the regulators that have a direct influence on programmes.

(b) *Monitoring of United Kingdom broadcast standards*

34.04   The BSC is under a duty to monitor programmes[10] so as to enable it to make reports, which it may publish, on the portrayal of violence and sexual conduct in, and the standards of taste and decency attained by, programmes generally[11] and determine whether to issue complaints about them.[12] The report may include an assessment of the attitudes of the public towards the portrayal of violence or sexual conduct in, or towards the standards of taste and decency attained by, programmes[13] and or any potential effects on the attitudes or behaviour of particular

---

[3] *Ibid.*, s.16(10): sexual conduct means any form of sexual behaviour.
[4] *Ibid.*, s.152(1)(b).
[5] *Ibid.*, s.152(c).
[6] *Ibid.*, s.152(3).
[7] *Ibid.*, s.152(5).
[8] *Ibid.*, s.152(4).
[9] *Ibid.*, s.152(3).
[10] *Ibid.*, s.202: "programmes" include advertisements.
[11] *Ibid.*, s.153(1)(a).
[12] *Ibid.*, s.153(1)(b).
[13] *Ibid.*, s.153(2)(a).

categories of people of the portrayal of violence or sexual conduct in programmes or the failure by programmes to attain those standards.[14]

(c) *Monitoring of foreign broadcasts*

The BSC is also under a duty to monitor, so far as is reasonably practicable, all television and sound programmes which are transmitted or sent from outside the United Kingdom but are capable of being received there with a view to ascertaining how violence and sexual conduct are portrayed in these programmes[15] and the extent to which those programmes meet standards of taste and decency.[16] If these programmes raise considerations of general broadcasting policy it may refer these matters to the Home Secretary.[17] **34.05**

(d) *Complaints that may be considered by the BSC*

The BSC is under a duty to consider all complaints which are in writing and which relate to the portrayal of violence or sexual conduct in programmes[18] or alleged failures by programmes to attain standards of taste and decency[19] and the BSC may itself issue a complaint in respect of these matters.[20] Where the complaint is about a television programme[21] or a sound programme[22] and the complaint is made more than two months[23] or three weeks[24] respectively after the relevant date the BSC must not entertain the complaint unless it appears to them that in the particular circumstances it would be appropriate for them so to do.[25] "Relevant date" for these purposes is the date when the programme was broadcast by the BBC or the Welsh Authority or included in a licensed service or, as the case may be, last broadcast or included.[26] There is no guidance in the Act as to what would amount to particular circumstances which would make it appropriate to consider a complaint outside the time limit. This has been interpreted by the BSC as requiring "special circumstances". It may be that where the programme was recorded for viewing or listening at a later date, the viewing at such later date outside the time limit, may qualify as a special circumstance. **34.06**

---

[14] *Ibid.*, s.153(2)(b).
[15] *Ibid.*, s.153(4)(a).
[16] *Ibid.*, s.153(4)(b).
[17] *Ibid.*, s.153(5).
[18] *Ibid.*, s.154(1)(a).
[19] *Ibid.*, s.154(1)(b).
[20] *Ibid.*, s.154(7).
[21] *Ibid.*, s.154(3)(a).
[22] *Ibid.*, s.154(3)(b).
[23] *Ibid.*, s.154(3)(a).
[24] *Ibid.*, s.154(3)(b).
[25] *Ibid.*, s.154(3).
[26] *Ibid.*, s.154(4).

(e) *Complaints the BSC may not consider*

34.07   The BSC must not entertain or proceed with the consideration of a complaint if it appears to it that the matter complained of is the subject of proceedings in a United Kingdom court[27] or it is a matter for which the complainant has a remedy by way of proceedings in a United Kingdom court, and that in the particular circumstances it is not appropriate for the BSC to consider a complaint about it[28] or the complaint is frivolous[29] or for any other reason it is inappropriate for it to entertain or proceed with the consideration of the complaint.[30]

(f) *Making and consideration of complaints*

34.08   The BSC's powers are similar to the BCC's. However, as its functions relate not to the consideration of individual complaints but to general matters of taste and decency which may be brought by members of various sections of the community, the BSC is given powers to treat complaints as constituting a single complaint.[31] If the BSC does so elect, it can then limit the persons who will be heard at the hearing of the complaint.[32]

(g) *Publication of BSC's findings*

34.09   The BSC can direct publication of its decision by the broadcaster in a similar manner to the BCC. However, in contrast to the powers of the BCC, any observations made by the BSC on its findings must be published by the broadcaster. The broadcaster may, however, make its own observations on the BSC's findings and observations in its programme service.

---

[27] *Ibid.*, s.154(5)(a).
[28] *Ibid.*, s.154(5)(b).
[29] *Ibid.*, s.154(5)(c).
[30] *Ibid.*, s.154(5)(d).
[31] *Ibid.*, s.154(6).
[32] *Ibid.*, s.155(5).

VIDEO RECORDINGS

1. Regulation of Video Recordings

The supply and distribution of video recordings is regulated by the **35.01** Video Recordings Act 1984. This Act makes it an offence to supply a video recording[1] containing a video work[2] in respect of which no classification certificate has been issued by the British Board of Film Censors unless the supply is, or would if it took place, be an exempted supply, or the video work is an exempted work.[3]

(a) *Exempted works*

Meaning of exempted work. A video work is an exempted work for the **35.02** purposes of the Video Recordings Act, if, "taken as a whole":

(a) it is designed to inform, educate or instruct[4];

(b) it is concerned with sport, religion or music[5]; or

(c) is a video game.[6]

However, such a work is not an exempted work if to "any significant extent":

---

[1] "Video recordings" means any disc or magnetic tape containing information by the use of which the whole or part of a video work may be produced: Video Recordings Act 1984, s.1(1).

[2] *Ibid.*, s.22(2): "video work" means any series of visual images (with or without sound) (a) produced electronically by the use of information contained on any disc or magnetic tape, and (b) shown as a moving picture: Video Recordings Act 1984, s.1(2)(a), (b). A video recording contains a video work for the purposes of the Act if it contains information by the use of which the whole or part of the work may be produced; but where a video work includes any extract from another video work the extract is not regarded as part of the other work.

[3] *Ibid.*, s.9(1).

[4] *Ibid.*, s.2(1)(a).

[5] *ibid.*, s.2(1)(b).

[6] *Ibid.*, s.2(1)(c).

(a) it depicts or is designed to stimulate or encourage human sexual activity or acts of force or restraint associated with such activity[7];

(b) it depicts or to any extent is designed to stimulate or encourage mutilation or torture of, or acts of gross, violence towards, humans or animals[8];

(c) it depicts human genital organs or human urinary or excretory functions.[9]

35.03   Additionally, a work will not be an exempted work where it is designed to any "significant extent" to stimulate or encourage an activity falling within category (a) above or to "any extent" is designed to stimulate or encourage an activity falling within category (b) above. The meaning of "taken as a whole" is not defined by the Act. It would appear, however, that the phrase should be taken to mean that classification is not necessary if, looked at in its entirety, the general content of the video work seeks to promote one of the exempt purposes, although there may be an isolated section which when considered by itself might not be exempt. It is clear that any inclusion, no matter how small, of material which is designed to stimulate or encourage mutilation or torture of, or acts of gross violence towards, humans or animals will deprive a video work of exempt status.

However, the interpretation of the phrase "any significant extent" in relation to the other activities is not without difficulty. The expression can have more than one meaning. It is capable, in some contexts, of meaning "more than trifling". It is submitted that it does not bear that meaning in the present context. When one considers the expression in the context of the term "taken as a whole" it would appear that a higher standard is set. How much higher cannot be stated succinctly. In deciding whether it is designed to "any significant extent" to encourage or stimulate the matters enumerated it will be important to consider, *inter alia*, the ratio between the time allotted to the offending particular matter in question and the other aspects of the video work. Secondly, the explicitness of the activity portrayed will be material.

It would appear, however, in deciding to what extent the matter is significant it is not permissible to consider the activity in the context of the alleged purpose of the video work: what must be considered is the activity in question and whether to any significant extent it depicts or stimulates such activities. However, this is not to say that other factors may not be important in respect of the individual case and it will be for

---

[7] *Ibid.*, s.2(2)(a).
[8] *Ibid.*, s.2(2)(b).
[9] *Ibid.*, s.2(2)(c).

the tribunal of fact to decide what considerations are material to each individual case and what weight to be attached to them.[10]

(b) *Exempted supplies*

If the video recording is not exempted from classification the offences of supplying, offering to supply and possessing will not be committed where the supply in question is an exempt supply or the supplier reasonably believes it to be an exempt supply.
The categories of exempt supplies are as follows:

35.04

Non-commercial supply. A supply which is neither for reward[11] nor in the course or furtherance of business.[12] Where facilities are provided on any premises for the purpose of selling video-recordings the supply by a person of a recording on those premises is to be treated as a supply in the course of furtherance of business.[13]

35.05

Supply to person who makes video recordings in course of business. A supply where the original supplier supplies a recording to a person who, in the course of business,[14] makes video works or supplies video recordings if:

35.06

(a) that the supply is not made with a view to any further supply of that recording; or

(b) if it is so made is made with a view to its eventual supply to the original supplier.[15]

Supply to person taking part in an event recorded on video recording. Where a video recording contains only a video work designed to provide a record of an event or occasion is supplied to persons who took part in it or are connected with someone who did so,[16] the supply is an exempted supply[17] provided the work does not to any significant extent[18] depict:

35.07

(a) a human sexual activity or acts of force or restraint associated with such activity;

---

[10] See *Watford Borough Council v. Private Alternative Birth Control and Education Centres Ltd.*, D.C. (1985; unreported); *Lambeth London Borough Council v. Grewal* (1986) Cr.App.R. 301, D.C.
[11] Video Recordings Act 1984, s.3(2)(a).
[12] *Ibid.*, s.3(2)(b): "business" for this purpose includes any activity carried on by a club: s.22(1).
[13] *Ibid.*, s.3(3): "premises" includes any vehicle, vessel or stall: s.22(1).
[14] The definition of "business" in this context does not include activities carried on by a club: *ibid.* s.22(1).
[15] *Ibid.*, s.3(4).
[16] *Ibid.*, s.3(3)(a).
[17] *Ibid.*, s.3(5).
[18] For meaning of "significant extent", see *ante*, paras. 35.02, 35.03.

    (b) mutilation or torture of, or other acts of gross violence towards, humans or animals;

    (c) human genital organs or human urinary or excretory functions,

or is designed to any significant extent[19] to stimulate or encourage anything falling within (a) or in the case of (b) is designed *to any extent* to do so.[20]

35.08 **Supply to premises licensed to exhibit.** The video recording is also exempted where the supply is for the purposes only of exhibition of any video work contained in it in premises licensed under legislation relating to cinemas.[21]

35.09 **Supply for use in a programme service.** Supply with a view only to its use for or in connection with broadcasting services provided by the BBC or included in a programme service licensed by the Independent Television Commission or a cable programme service which is or does not require to be licensed.[22]

35.10 **Supply for classification purposes.** The Supply of a video recording for the purpose only of submitting a video work contained in it for the issue of a classification certificate or otherwise only for purposes of arrangements made by the BBFC.[23]

35.11 **Supply for medical training.** Supply with a view only to its use in training for or carrying on any medical or related training and for the purposes connected with the National Health Services.[24]

35.12 **Re-supply to person who made exempt supply.** Re-supply otherwise than for reward for the purpose only of supplying it to a person who previously made one of the above exempted supply of it.[25]

    It is to be noted that the fact that a work has been made by, or shown on, television does not exempt it from the requirement of classification.

---

[19] *Ibid.*
[20] Video Recordings Act 1984, s.3(5)(c).
[21] *Ibid.*, s.3(6).
[22] *Ibid.*, s.3(8).
[23] *Ibid.*, s.3(9).
[24] *Ibid.*, s.3(10) which refers to use:

    (1) in training for carrying on any medical or related occupation;
    (2) for services provided in pursuance of the National Health service Act 1977; or
    (3) in training persons employed in the course of such services.

An occupation is a medical or related occupation if, to carry on the occupation, a person is required to be registered under the Professions Supplementary to Medicine Act 1960, the Nurses, Midwives and Health Visitors Act 1979 or the Medical Act 1983: Video Recordings Act 1984, s.3(11).
[25] *Ibid.*, s.3(12).

(c) *Classification of video recordings*

Designated authority. The issue of classification certificates[26] for video **35.13**
works is a function vested in the British Board of Film Censors (BBFC)
by the Secretary of State pursuant section 4 of the Act.

Meaning of classification certificate. For these purposes a "classifica- **35.14**
tion certificate" is defined by the Act as meaning a certificate issued in
respect of a video work in pursuance of the arrangements made by the
BBFC and satisfying certain specified requirements.[27] Those requirements are that the certificate must contain a statement:

(a) that the video work is suitable for general viewing and unres-
tricted supply: this statement may be issued with or without
advice as to the desirability of parental guidance with regard to
the viewing of the work by young children or as to the particular
suitability of the work for viewing by children[28]; or

(b) that the video work is suitable for viewing only by persons who
have attained a specified age (not being more than 18 years) and
that no video recording containing the work may be supplied to
any person who has not attained that age[29]; or

(c) the statement in (b) together with a statement that no video
recording containing the work may be supplied other than in a
licensed sex shop.[30]

Where any alteration is made to a video work in respect of which a
classification certificate has been issued, the certificate is not treated as
issued in respect of the altered work.[31] For these purposes "alteration"
includes addition.[32]

The system of classification and the statements as required by the Act **35.15**
are as follows[33]:

Universal: Particularly suitable for children

Universal: Suitable for all

Parental   General viewing but some scenes may be
Guidance: unsuitable for young children

---

[26] See *infra*, para. 35.15.
[27] Video Recordings Act 1984, s.7.
[28] *Ibid.*, s.7(2)(a).
[29] *Ibid.*, s.7(2)(b).
[30] *Ibid.*, s.7(2)(c).
[31] *Ibid.*, s.22(3).
[32] *Ibid.*, s.22(3).
[33] See Video Recordings (Labelling) Regulations 1985 (S.I. 1985 No. 911).

35.16 Appeal from decision of BBFC. The BBFC is required by the Act to establish a system of appeal against a determination that a video work submitted by him for certification has been either refused or placed in the wrong category.[34] The appellate panel is selected by the BBFC and presently consists of ten members. An Appeals Committee comprises five members and permits legal representation and may it in public and hear witnesses. The Appeals Committee will reconsider the matter afresh and can substitute its own decision for that of the BBFC.

2. Offences

35.17 A person commits an offence under the Video Recordings Act in the following circumstances.

35.18 No classification certificate. If he supplies or offers to supply a video recording containing a video work in respect of which no classification certificate has ben issued unless the supply is or would if it took place be, an exempted supply or the video work is an exempted work.[35]

35.19 Supply in breach of classification. Where a classification certificate issued in respect of a video work states that no video recording containing that work is to be supplied to any person who has not attained the age specified in the certificate, (*i.e.* this may not be more than 18 years of age) a person who supplies or offers to supply a video recording containing that work to a person who has not attained the specified age is guilty of an offence[36] unless the supply is exempted or would if it took place be such a supply.[37]

35.20 Recordings to be licensed only in sex shops. Where a classification certificate issued in respect of a video work states that no video recording containing that work is to be supplied other than in a licensed sex shop a person who supplies it other than at a licensed sex shop, or offers to do so, is guilty of an offence unless the supply is an exempted supply or would be such a supply if it took place.[38] It is also an offence for a person to have in his possession a video recording certificated supply in a sex shop for the purpose of supplying it at any place other than in a sex shop.[39]

---

[34] Video Recordings Act 1984, s.4.
[35] *Ibid.*, s.9.
[36] *Ibid.*, s.11.
[37] *Ibid.*, s.11(1).
[38] *Ibid.*, s.12.
[39] *Ibid.*, s.12(3).

False indication as to classification. A person is guilty of an offence if he **35.21**
supplies or offers to supply a video recording containing a video work
in respect of which no classification certificate has been issued if the
recording, spool case or anything on or in which it is kept contains any
indication that a classification certificate has been issued in respect of
the work unless the supply is an exempted supply or would be such if a
supply took place.[40]

Non-compliance with labelling requirements, etc. A person who sup- **35.22**
plies or offers to supply a video recording or any spool, case or other
thin on or in which the recording is kept which does not satisfy the
labelling requirements set out above is guilty of an offence unless the
supply is an exempted supply or would be such a supply if it took
place.[41] The Video Recording (Labelling) Regulations 1985[42] specifies
the appropriate symbols specifies that classification category must be in
the form of a label affixed to the disc, magnetic tape, spool or spine case
or cover in which the recording is kept. Such label and marking must
not be clearly legible and not obscured in any way.

---

[40] *Ibid.*, s.14(1).
[41] *Ibid.*, s.13(1).
[42] S.I. 1985, No. 911.

CHAPTER 36

OBSCENE PUBLICATIONS

1. Introduction

36.01 **Meaning of obscenity.** The Obscene Publications Act 1959 and 1964[1] provides that an article is deemed to be obscene if its effect or (where the article comprises two or more distinct items) any one of its items is, if taken as a whole, such as to tend to deprave and corrupt persons who are likely, having regard to all relevant circumstances, to read, see or hear the matter contained in it. Whether a programme or film tends to deprave and corrupt is a matter for a jury to decide as a question of fact.[2] The test is not whether the article is "obscene" but whether it has a tendency to deprave and corrupt[3] and in this context "deprave and corrupt" are not confined to sexual depravity and corruption.[4]

In determining whether it has this effect the programme or film itself is the primary consideration and not whether there is an intention on the part of the exhibitor to corrupt.[5] A programme or film which merely shocks viewers does not by that reason alone have a tendency to deprave and corrupt[6]: it is open to the broadcaster or exhibitor to show that the programme portrayed the subject matter in such an unpleasant and shocking way that it would not deprave and corrupt but rather would tend to cause people revolt from activity of that kind.[7] Neither is it obscene though it is "repulsive", "filthy", "loathsome" or "lewd"

---

[1] Obscene Publications Act 1959 and 1964, s.1(1).
[2] *R. v. Anderson* [1972] 1 Q.B. 304.
[3] *D.P.P. v. Whyte* [1972] A.C. 849 at 861.
[4] *Calder (John) (Publications) Ltd. v. Powell* [1965] 1 Q.B. 509.
[5] *Shaw v. D.P.P.* [1962] A.C. 220, H.L.
[6] *D.P.P. v. Whyte* [1972] A.C. 849 at 861.
[7] *R. v. Calder and Boyars Ltd.* [1969] 1 Q.B. 151 at 169; *R. v. Anderson* [1972] 1 Q.B. 304 at 315.

without more[8]: it must also have a tendency to deprave and corrupt a significant proportion of those likely to watch it.[9]

2. Programme Services

**Prohibition on inclusion of obscene and other material in programmes   36.02
included in programme services.** Section 162(1) Part VII of the Broadcasting Act 1990 applies the law on obscenity to programme services.[10]
It is an offence for a broadcaster to publish any obscene recorded matter
or live matter by including it in a programme service[11] whether for gain
or not or has an obscene article for publication for gain.[12]

Liability for providing live programme material. Where live pro-   **36.03**
gramme matter is included by a broadcaster in a programme which is in
turn included in a programme service and that matter has been
provided for inclusion by some other person, the Obscene Publications
Act has effect as if the matter had been included by both persons.[13]

Obscene articles kept for inclusion in programmes. Where a broad-   **36.04**
caster has an obscene article in his ownership, possession or control
with a view to the matter recorded on it being included in a relevant
programme,[14] the article is deemed for the purposes of the Obscene
Publications Act 1959 to be an obscene article had or kept by him for
publication or gain.[15] It is submitted that the wording of this provision
would indicate that if the article has not been transmitted and there is
no intention to transmit the same, no offence will have been committed.

---

[8] *R. v. Anderson* [1972] 1 Q.B. 304, 314 (C.A.).
[9] *R. v. Calder and Boyars Ltd.* [1969] 1 Q.B. 151, C.A.; see also *D.P.P. v. White* [1972] A.C.
849 at 861 where Lord Wilberforce doubted the validity of the approach which seeks the
"most likely" readers and then rejects others than the "most likely". Other categories
may be "likely" and should only be disregarded if they are numerically negligible . . .
[10] Broadcasting Act 1990, s.201: "programme service" means any of the following,
whether or not it requires to be licensed under the Broadcasting Act 1990:

   (a) any television service or other television programme service
   (b) any sound broadcasting service or licensable sound programme service;
   (c) any other service which consists in the sending, by means of a telecommunication,
      of sounds or visual images or both either
      (i) for reception at two or more places in the U.K. (whether they are sent for sim-
         ultaneous reception or at different times in response to requests made by
         different users of the service) or
      (ii) for reception at a place in the United Kingdom for the purpose of being
         presented there to members of the public of to any group of persons.
[11] Obscene Publications Act 1959 and 1964, as amended by Broadcasting Act 1990, s.162.
[12] Obscene Publications Act, s.2(1), as amended by the Obscene Publication Act 1964.
[13] Broadcasting Act 1990, Sched. 15, para. 2.
[14] *Ibid.*, Sched. 15, para. 1: a "relevant programme" means a programme included in a
programme service.
[15] *Ibid.*, Sched. 15, para. 3.

36.05 **Defences.** A person may not be convicted of an offence under section 2 of the 1959 Act for the inclusion of any matter in a programme if he proves that he did not know and had no reason to suspect that the programme would include matter rendering him liable to be convicted of the offence.[16]

36.06 **Public good.** When the publication in issue in any proceedings under the 1959 Act consists in the inclusion of any matter in a relevant programme the general defence of public good under section 4(1) of the 1959 Act does not apply.[17]

However, a person is not to be convicted of an offence under section 2 of the 1959 Act (publication of obscene matter) and an order for forfeiture cannot be made under section 3 of the 1959 Act, if it is proved that the inclusion of the matter in the programme is justified as being for the public good as being in the interests of drama, opera, ballet or any other art, science, literature or learning or any other objects of general concern.[18] The opinion of experts is admissible in determining whether publication can be justified as being in the public good on these grounds.[19]

Thus, for example, if the material in question is lewd or salacious but its dramatic content is of such a high order as to transcend or redeem the objectionable character of the subject matter it may be for the public good.[20]

3. Films and Sound Recordings

36.07 **The offence.** A person is guilty of an offence if he distributes, circulates, sells, lets on hire or offers for sale or for letting on hire or shows, plays or projects an article containing or embodying a film or sound recording which is obscene.[21]

For these purposes the exhibition of a film at a cinema would be included in this definition as would the playing of a record at a shop selling records and the hiring out of pre-recorded videocassettes.

36.08 **Public good.** Where the article in question is a moving picture film or soundtrack the general defence of public good under section 4(1) of the 1959 Act does not apply.[22] The effect of this section is that a person is

---

[16] *Ibid.*, Sched. 15, para. 5(1).
[17] *Ibid.*, Sched. 15, para. 5(2).
[18] *Ibid.*, Sched. 15, para. 5(2).
[19] *Ibid.*, Sched. 15, para. 5(3).
[20] See *D.P.P. v. Jordan* [1976] 3 W.L.R. 887, H.L.
[21] Obscene Publications Act 1959, s.1(3).
[22] *Ibid.*, s.4(1A).

not to be convicted of an offence under section 2 of the 1959 Act (publication of obscene matter) and an order for forfeiture cannot be made under section 3 of the 1959 Act, if it is proved that the publication of the film or soundtrack is justified as being for the public good because it is in the interests of drama, opera, ballet or any other art, science, literature or learning.[23]

Reference should be made to the similar heading under "Programme service" above for the operation of this section.

4. Performances of Plays

Meaning of "play". For the purposes of the Theatres Act 1968 "play"   **36.09**
means:

(a) any dramatic piece, whether involving improvisation or not, which is given wholly or in part by one or more persons actually present and performing and in which the whole or a major proportion of what is done by the person or persons performing, whether by way of speech, singing or acting, involves playing a role; and

(b) any ballet given wholly or in part by one or more persons actually present and performing, whether or not it falls within (a).[24]

The test of obscenity. For the purposes of the live performances of plays   **36.10**
in the theatre a play is deemed to be obscene if, taken as a whole, it tends to deprave and corrupt persons who were likely, having regard to all relevant circumstances, to attend it.[25] The test of obscenity is the same as that applying under the Obscene Publications Act 1959.[26]

The offence. If an obscene performance of a play is given, whether in   **36.11**
public or private, any person who, whether for gain or not, presented or directed the performance is liable on summary conviction to a fine not exceeding the prescribed sum or to imprisonment for a term not exceeding six months and on conviction on indictment to a fine or to imprisonment for a term not exceeding three years or both.[27] There is no definition in the Act as to the meaning of "director": it is submitted that the word should be given its normal accepted usage. However, for the purposes of the Theatres Act 1968 a person is treated as having

---

[23] Broadcasting Act 1990, Sched. 15, para. 5(2).
[24] Theatres Act 1968, s.18.
[25] *Ibid.*, s.2(1).
[26] See *ante*, para. 36.01 *et seq.* for the operation of the test under the Obscene Publications Act: see "Test of obscenity".
[27] Theatres Act 1968, s.2.

directed a performance of a play given under his direction although he was not present during the infringing performance.[28] Where a performer takes part in a play directed by another person that performer is treated as director if without reasonable excuse he performs otherwise in accordance with the director's instructions.[29]

It is submitted that "Presenter" as used in the Act should be taken to mean the impresario who has made the arrangements for the presentation of the play.

A person does not aid and abet an offence by the mere reason of taking part neither does the mere fact that a person takes part in a play as a performer make him the presenter.[30]

36.12 **Defence of public good.** A person may not be convicted of the offence if it is proved that the giving of the performance in question was justified as being for the public good on the ground that it was in the interests of drama, opera, ballet or any other act, or literature or learning.[31] For operation of this defence see under the similar heading under "Programme service" above.

36.13 **Exemptions from obscenity rule.** The above provisions as to obscene plays do not apply to the performance of a play given solely or primarily for a rehearsal or to enable a record or film to be made from or by means of the performance or the performance to be broadcast or the performance to be included in a programme service which is or does not require to be licensed.[32]

However, if in any proceedings under the Theatres Act 1968 relating to the performance of the play it is proved that the performance was attended by persons other than those directly connected with the giving of the performance, or the recording, filming, broadcasting or transmission, the performance must be taken not to have been given solely or primarily for one or more of the excepted purposes unless the contrary is shown.[33] In addition to the above exceptions to the Theatres Act provisions, the performances given on a domestic occasion in a private dwelling are excepted.[34]

---

[28] *Ibid.*, s.2.
[29] *Ibid.*, s.18(2).
[30] *Ibid.*, s.18(2).
[31] *Ibid.*, s.3.
[32] *Ibid.*, s.7(2).
[33] *Ibid.*, s.7(2).
[34] *Ibid.*, s.7(1).

CHAPTER 37

INCITING RACIAL HATRED

General Considerations

"Threatening, abusive or insulting". Whether words or behaviour are **37.01** threatening abusive or insulting is one of fact.[1] "It would be unwise to attempt to lay down any positive rules for the recognition of insulting behaviour as such, since circumstances in which the application of the rules would be called for are almost infinitely variable."[2] It should be noted, however, that merely because words or behaviour shows disrespect or may cause affront giving rise to resentment or protest, it is not necessarily "insulting behaviour" but where insulting behaviour as a matter of fact is found it does not lose its character of insulting behaviour by reason of the fact that persons who have witnessed it have not been thereby insulted.[3]

Meaning of "racial hatred". "Racial hatred" is defined by the Public **37.02** Order 1986, section 17 as "hatred against a group of persons in Great Britain defined by reference to colour, race, nationality (including citizenship) or ethnic or national origins".[4] In this context a group of persons defined by reference to "ethnic origins" would appear to mean a group which is a segment of the population distinguished from others by a sufficient combination of shared customs, beliefs, traditions and characteristics derived from a common or presumed past, even if not drawn from what in biological terms was a common racial stock, in that it was that combination which gave them an historically determined social identity in their own eyes, and those outside the group.[5]

---

[1] *Brutus v. Cozens* [1973] A.C. 854, H.L.
[2] *Ibid.* at 866, 867.
[3] *Parkin v. Norman* [1983] Q.B. 92.
[4] Public Order Act 1986, s.17.
[5] *Mandla v. Dowell Lee* [1983] 2 A.C. 548, H.L.

(a) *Including programmes in a programme service*

37.03 The offence. If a programme involving threatening abusive or insulting visual images or sounds is included in a programme service each of the persons providing the service, any person by whom the programme is produced or directed, and any person by whom offending words or behaviour are used, is guilty of an offence if he intends to stir up racial hatred or having regard to all the circumstances racial hatred is likely to be stirred up by such words or behaviour.[6] A producer, director or broadcaster may be liable under this provision notwithstanding the fact that he has no intention to stir up racial hatred if "having regard to all the circumstances racial hatred is likely to be stirred up".

If therefore, for example, the effect of a programme is such as to present the offending matter in a manner which is uncritical without any balancing views an offence may be committed notwithstanding the fact that there is no intention that the inclusion of the matter in the programme service should be supportive of racial hatred.

37.04 Defences: Broadcaster, Producer, Director. If the person providing the service, or a person by whom the programme was produced or directed is not shown to have intended to stir up racial hatred, it is a defence for him to prove that he did not know and had no reason to suspect that the programme would include the offending material and having regard to the circumstances in which the programme was included in a programme service, it was not reasonably practicable for him to secure the removal of the material.[7] Where the programme is provided by the network or the nominated news provider it is clear that an individual broadcaster may succeed in a defence under these provisions.

Where, however, the programme is edited and transmitted by the broadcaster's servants or agents it is difficult to envisage situations in which this defence would be available to the broadcaster. If the final edited version of the programme is supervised by the producer and the director it is submitted that the defence will not be available if the programme is transmitted in that form. If, however, the programme is edited prior to transmission by persons other than the director or producer and without their consent so as to include the offending material it is submitted that in such circumstances the producer or director will not be liable.

37.05 Producer and Director. It is a defence for a producer or director who is not shown to have intended to stir up racial hatred to prove that he did not know and had no reason to suspect that the programme would be

---

[6] Public Order Act 1986, ss.22(1), (2), as amended by Broadcasting Act 1990, s.164(3).
[7] *Ibid.*, s.22(3), as amended by Broadcasting Act 1990, s.164(3).

included in a programme service or that the circumstances in which the programme would be included in a programme service would be such that racial hatred would be likely to be stirred up.[8]

Where the programme is intended to form a part of a series of programmes which when taken together would place the offending material in a critical light but which by itself does not so do it is submitted that where the programme is transmitted by itself with no intention of the other programmes in the series being transmitted the producer and director would not be liable if they were not aware that such follow up programmes were not to be transmitted.

(b) *Possession of racially inflammatory material*

A person who has in his possession written material with a view to its **37.06** being displayed distributed or included in a programme service by himself or another or a recording of visual images or sounds with a view to its being distributed or included in a programme service whether by himself or another which are threatening abusive or insulting is guilty of an offence if he intends racial hatred to be stirred up by such material so used or, having regard to all the circumstances racial hatred is likely to be stirred up.[9] For these purposes regard is to be had to the display, distribution, showing, playing or inclusion in a programme service that he has in view.[10]

The effect of these rules is that if any person who gathers programme, whether written or recorded, which is of the nature prohibited by the Act he may be committing an offence if the programme for which he is so gathering the material is not intended to condemn or present the material in a critical manner. In proceedings for such an offence it is a defence for an accused who is not shown to have intended to stir up racial hatred to prove[11] that he was not aware of content of the written material or recording or did not suspect and had no reason to suspect that it was threatening, abusive or insulting.[12]

(c) *Use of words or behaviour or display of written material*

Scenes staged for filming purposes. Where words are spoken or there is **37.07** behaviour or displays of any written material which are threatening, abusive or insulting and which may have the effect of stirring up racial hatred such words or behaviour used or written material displayed will not constitute an offence if they are *"solely"* for the purpose of being

---

[8] *Ibid.*, s.22(4).
[9] *Ibid.*, s.23(1).
[10] *Ibid.*, s.23(2).
[11] The burden of proof may be discharged by satisfying the court on the preponderance of probability of what the accused is called to prove.
[12] Public Order Act 1986, s.23(3).

included in a programme service.[13] No definition is given within section 18(2) of the Public Order Act as to the meaning of "solely" but some assistance can be obtained from section 20(3) which provides that the matters are not solely for the purpose indicated if it is proved that persons other than those directly connected with the giving of the performance or the recording of the performance or enabling the performance to be included in the programme service. It is submitted that the restriction imposed by the words "solely" should be interpreted in the foregoing manner and it is therefore incumbent on a producer to ensure that such material is filmed in surroundings where crowds not directly related to activity are not present during the recording. Thus where the producer also intends to provide the film or programme on videocassette as an adjunct to his business of being a programme producer an offence will not be committed by him.

Thus, for example, where there is a location shoot for a film or programme which involves crowd scenes, where such words, behaviour or displays take place, no offence will be committed if the sole purpose such activities take place is for the purpose of the film or programme which is to be included in a programme service and those attending the shoot are involved in giving the performance or involved in its recording. If, however, the scenes are staged by a director or producer, in the sense that real life individuals who are not actors or performers are persuaded to utter or to carry out the infringing activities for the purposes of enabling them to be filmed, the defence may not be open to him if such persons are not directly connected with the giving of a performance to be included in a programme service.

(d) *Public performance of a play*

37.08 **The offence.** If a public performance[14] of a play is given which involves the use of threatening, abusive or insulting words or behaviour, any person who presents or directs[15] the performance is guilty of an offence if he intends to stir up racial hatred or having regard to all the circumstances, and, in particular, taking the performance as a whole, racial hatred is likely to be stirred up by the play.[16] It is submitted that "presents" in this context should be taken to mean the impresario of the play

---

[13] *Ibid.*, s.18(6). Broadcasting Act, 1990, s.164.

[14] "Public performance" includes any performance in a public place within the meaning of the Public Order Act 1936 and any performance which the public or any section thereof is permitted to attend, whether on payment or otherwise: Theatres Act 1968, s.18(1) (applied by the Public Order Act 1986, s.29(5)).

[15] A performer who takes part in a performance directed by another is treated as a person who directs if without reasonable excuse he perform's otherwise than in accordance with the person's direction: s.20(4)(b). What is a reasonable excuse is largely a question of fact: *Leck v. Epson RDC* [1922] 1 K.B. 383.

[16] Public Order Act 1986, s.20(1).

and not the individual who is employed on a contract for service as the individual producer.

Defences. A presenter or director is not guilty of the foregoing offence if **37.09** the performance is given solely or primarily for rehearsal or making a recording of the performance or enabling the performance to be included in a programme service.[17]

If, however, the performance is attended by persons other than those directly concerned with the giving of the performance or making a recording of the performance or enabling the performance to be included in a programme service or cable programme service there is a rebuttable presumption that the performance was not given solely or primarily for one of the foregoing purposes.[18] Where the presenter or director is not able to avail himself of the foregoing defence and he is not shown to have intended to stir up racial hatred, it is a defence for him to prove:

(a) that he did not know and had no reason to suspect that the performance would involve the use of the offending words or behaviour; or

(b) that he did not know and had no reason to suspect that the offending words or behaviour were threatening abusive or insulting; or

(c) that he did not know and had no reason to suspect that the circumstances in which the performance would be given would be such that racial hatred would be likely to be stirred up.[19]

(e) *Distributing, showing or playing a recording*

The offence. A person who distributes,[20] or shows or plays a record- **37.10** ing[21] of visual images or sounds which are threatening, abusive or insulting is guilty of an offence if he intends by such activities to stir up racial hatred or having regard to all the circumstances racial hatred is likely to be stirred up thereby.[22]

Defences. The offence is not committed where the showing or playing **37.11** of a recording is *"solely"* for the purpose of enabling the recording to be included in a programme service.[23] Where this defence is not available,

---

[17] *Ibid.,* s.20(3).
[18] *Ibid.,* s.20(3).
[19] *Ibid.,* s.20(2).
[20] *Ibid,* ss.21(2), 29: for these purposes, references to the distribution, showing or playing of a recording are to its distribution, showing or playing to the public or a section of the public.
[21] *Ibid.,* s.21(2): "recording" means any record from which visual images or sounds may, by any means, be reproduced.
[22] *Ibid.,* s.21(1). See *ante,* para. 37.07.
[23] *Ibid.,* s.21(4), as amended by Broadcasting Act 1990, s.164(2).

in proceedings for such an offence it is a defence for an accused who is not shown to have intended to stir up racial hatred to prove that he was not aware of the content of the recording and did not suspect, and had no reason to suspect, that it was threatening.[24]

---

[24] *Ibid.*, s.21(3).

APPENDIX A

APPENDIX A

The Copyright (Application to Other Countries) Order 1993

(S.I. 1993 No. 942)

(As amended by S.I. 1994 No. 263)

Made	*31st March 1993*
Laid before Parliament	*13th April 1993*
Coming into force	*4th May 1993*

At the Court at Buckingham Palace, the 31st day of March 1993
Present,
The Queen's Most Excellent Majesty in Council

Whereas Her Majesty is satisfied that provision has been or will be made—

   (a) in respect of literary, dramatic, musical and artistic works, films and typographical arrangements of published editions, under the law of Uganda,

   (b) in respect of sound recordings, under the laws of Bangladesh, Ghana, Malawi and Thailand,

   (c) in respect of broadcasts, under the law of Malawi,

giving adequate protection to the owners of copyright under Part I of the Copyright, Designs and Patents Act 1988(a):

Now, therefore, Her Majesty, by and with the advice of Her Privy Council, and by virtue of the authority conferred upon Her by section 159 of the said Act, is pleased to order, and it is hereby ordered as follows:—

1.—(1) This Order may be cited as the Copyright (Application to Other Countries) Order 1993 and shall come into force on 4th May 1993.

(2) In this Order—

"the Act" means the Copyright, Designs and Patents Act 1988, and "first published" shall be construed in accordance with section 155(3) of the Act.

2.—(1) In relation to literary, dramatic, musical and artistic works, films and the typographical arrangements of published editions,

533

sections 153, 154 and 155 of the Act (qualification for copyright protection) apply in relation to—

(a) persons who are citizens or subjects of a country specified in Schedule 1 to this Order or are domiciled or resident there as they apply to persons who are British citizens or are domiciled or resident in the United Kingdom;

(b) bodies incorporated under the law of such a country as they apply in relation to bodies incorporated under the law of a part of the United Kingdom; and

(c) works first published in such a country as they apply in relation to works first published in the United Kingdom;

but subject to paragraph (2) and article 5 below.

(2) Copyright does not subsist—

(a) in a literary, dramatic, musical or artistic work by virtue of section 154 of the Act as applied by paragraph (1) above (qualification by reference to author) if it was first published—
  (i) before 1st June 1957 (commencement of Copyright Act 1956(a)), or
  (ii) before 1st August 1989 (commencement of Part I of the Act) and at the material time (as defined in section 154(4)(b) of the Act) the author was not a relevant person; or

(b) in any work by virtue of paragraph (1) above if—
  (i) a date is, or dates are, specified in Schedule 1 to this Order in respect of the only country or countries relevant to the work for the purposes of paragraph (1) above, and
  (ii) the work was first published before that date or (as the case may be) the earliest of those dates;

and for the purposes of sub-paragraph (a)(ii) of this paragraph, a "relevant person" is a Commonwealth citizen, a British protected person, a citizen or subject of any country specified in Schedule 1 to this Order, or a person resident or domiciled in the United Kingdom, another country to which the relevant provisions of Part I of the Act extend or (subject to article 5 below) a country specified in Schedule 1 to this Order.

(3) Where copyright subsists in a work by virtue of paragraph (1) above, the whole of Part I of the Act (including Schedule 1 to the Act) applies in relation to the work, save that in relation to an artistic work consisting of the design of a typeface—

(a) section 54(2) (articles for producing material in particular typeface) does not apply,

(b) section 55 (making such articles not an infringement) applies as if

the words in subsection (2) from the beginning to "marketed"
were omitted, and

(c) paragraph 14(5) of Schedule 1 (transitional provision) does not
apply,

and subject also to articles 5 and 7 below.

3. In relation to sound recordings, article 2 above shall apply as it
applies in relation to films, subject to the following modifications—

(a) sections 19, 20, 26 and 107(3) of the Act (infringement by playing
in public, broadcasting or inclusion in a cable programme service
and related provisions) apply only if—

   (i) at least one of the countries relevant to the work for the purposes of article 2(1) above is specified in Schedule 2 to this
Order, or

   (ii) the sound recording in question is a film sound-track accompanying a film; and

(b) paragraph (1) of article (2) shall (subject to article 5 below) apply
as if Indonesia were specified in Schedule 1 to this Order.

4.—(1) In relation to broadcasts, sections 153, 154 and 156 of the Act
(qualification for copyright protection) apply in relation to—

(a) persons who are citizens or subjects of a country specified in
Schedule 3 to this Order or are domiciled or resident there as
they apply to persons who are British citizens or are domiciled or
resident in the United Kingdom;

(b) bodies incorporated under the law of such a country as they
apply in relation to bodies incorporated under the law of a part of
the United Kingdom; and

(c) broadcasts made from such a country as they apply to broadcasts
made from the United Kingdom;

but subject to paragraphs (2) and (3) and article 5 below.

(2) If the only country or countries relevant to a broadcast for the
purposes of paragraph (1) above are identified in Schedule 3 to this
Order by the words "television only", copyright subsists in the broadcast only if it is a television broadcast.

(3) Copyright does not subsist in a broadcast by virtue of paragraph
(1) above if it was made before the relevant date.

(4) Where copyright subsists in a broadcast by virtue of paragraph (1)
above, the whole of Part I of the Act (including Schedule 1 to the Act)
applies in relation to the broadcast, save that for the purposes of section
14(2) (duration of copyright in repeats)—

  (a) a broadcast shall be disregarded if it was made before the rel-
      evant date, and
  (b) a cable programme shall be disregarded if it was included in a
      cable programme service before the later of the relevant date and
      1st January 1985;

and subject also to article 7 below.

(5) For the purposes of paragraphs (3) and (4) above, the "relevant
date" is the date or (as the case may be) the earliest of the dates specified in Schedule 3 to this Order in respect of the country or countries
relevant to the broadcast for the purposes of paragraph (1) above, being
(where different dates are specified for television and non-television
broadcasts) the date appropriate to the type of broadcast in question.

(6) In respect of Singapore, this article applied in relation to cable
programmes as it applies in relation to broadcasts, subject to article 5
below.

5. Schedule 4 to this Order shall have effect so as to modify the application of this Order in respect of certain countries.

6. Nothing in this Order shall be taken to derogate from the effect of
paragraph 35 of Schedule 1 to the Act (continuation of existing qualification for copyright protection).

7.—(1) This article applies in any case in which—

  (a) a work was made before 1st August 1989 (commencement of Part
      I of the Act) and copyright under the Copyright Act 1956 did not
      subsist in it when it was made, or
  (b) a work is made on or after 1st August 1989 and copyright under
      the Act does not subsist in it when it is made,

but copyright subsequently subsists in it by virtue of article 2(1), 3 or
4(1) above.

(2) Where in any such case a person incurs or has incurred any
expenditure or liability in connection with, for the purpose of or with a
view to the doing of an act which at the time is not or was not an act
restricted by any copyright in the work, the doing, or continued doing,
of that act after copyright subsequently subsists in the work by virtue of
article 2(1), 3 or 4(1) above shall not be an act restricted by the copyright
unless the owner of the copyright or his exclusive licensee (if any) pays
such compensation as, failing agreement, may be determined by
arbitration.

8. The Orders listed in Schedule 5 to this Order are hereby revoked.

SCHEDULE 1   Article 2(1) and (2)

COUNTRIES ENJOYING PROTECTION IN RESPECT OF ALL WORKS EXCEPT BROADCASTS AND CABLE PROGRAMMES

(The countries specified in this Schedule either are parties to the Berne Copyright Convention and/or the Universal Copyright Convention or otherwise give adequate protection under their law.)

Algeria (28th August 1973)
Andorra (27th September 1957)
Argentina
Australia (including Norfolk Island)
Austria
Bahamas
Bangladesh
Barbados
Belgium
Belize
Benin
Bolivia (22nd March 1990)
Brazil
Bulgaria
Burkina Faso
Cameroon
Canada
Central African Republic
Chad
Chile
China
Columbia
Congo
Costa Rica
Côte d'Ivoire
Croatia
Cuba (27th September 1957)
Cyrpus, Republic of
Czechoslovakia
Denmark (including Greenland and the Faeroe Islands)
Dominican Republic (8th May 1983)
Ecuador
Egypt
El Salvador (29th March 1979)
Fiji
Finland
France (including all Overseas Departments and Territories)
Gabon
Gambia

Germany
Ghana
Greece
Guatemala (28th October 1964)
Guinea, Republic of
Guinea-Bissau
Haiti (27th September 1957)
Holy See
Honduras
Hungary
Iceland
India
Ireland, Republic of
Isreal
Italy
Japan
Kampuchea (27th September 1957)
Kenya
Korea, Republic of (1st October 1987)
Laos (27th September 1957)
Lebanon
Lesotho
Liberia
Libya
Liechtenstein
Luxembourg
Madagascar
Malawi
Malaysia
Mali
Malta
Mauritania
Mauritius
Mexico
Monaco
Morocco
Netherlands (including Aruba and the Netherlands Antilles)
New Zealand
Nicaragua (16th August 1961)
Niger
Nigeria
Norway
Pakistan
Panama (17th October 1962)
Paraguay
Peru
Philippines
Poland
Portugal
Romania
Rwanda
St. Vincent and the Grenadines

Senegal
Singapore
Slovenia
South Africa
Soviet Union (27th May 1973)
Spain
Sri Lanka
Suriname
Sweden
Switzerland
Taiwan, territory of (10th July 1985)
Thailand
Togo
Trinidad and Tobago
Tunisia
Turkey
Uganda (20th July 1964)
United States of America (including Puerto Rico and all territories and
    possessions)
Uruguay
Venezuela
Yugoslavia
Zaire
Zambia
Zimbabwe

SCHEDULE 2   Article 3(a)(i)

COUNTRIES ENJOYING FULL PROTECTION FOR SOUND RECORDINGS

(The countries specified in this Schedule either are parties to the Rome Convention for the Protection of Performers, Producers of Phonograms and Broadcasting Organisations or otherwise give adequate protection under their law.)

Argentina
Australia (including Norfolk Island)
Austria
Bangladesh
Barbados
Brazil
Burkina Faso
Chile
Colombia
Congo
Costa Rica
Czechoslovakia
Denmark (including Greenland and the Faeroe Islands)
Dominican Republic
Ecuador

539

El Salvador
Fiji
Finland
France (including all Overseas Departments and Territories)
Germany
Ghana
Greece
Guatemala
Honduras
India
Indonesia
Ireland, Republic of
Italy
Japan
Lesotho
Luxembourg
Malawi
Malaysia
Mexico
Monaco
New Zealand
Niger
Norway
Pakistan
Panama
Paraguay
Peru
Philippines
Spain
Sweden
Taiwan, territory of
Thailand
Uruguay

SCHEDULE 3   Article 4(1), (2) and (5)

COUNTRIES ENJOYING PROTECTION IN RESPECT OF BROADCASTS

(The countries specified in this Schedule either are parties to the Rome Convention for the Protection of Performers, Producers of Phonograms and Broadcasting Organisations and/or the European Agreement on the Protection of Television Broadcasts or otherwise give adequate protection under their law.)

Argentina (2nd March 1992)
Australia (30th September 1992)
Austria (9th June 1973)
Barbados (18th September 1983)
Belgium (8th March 1968—television only)
Brazil (29th September 1965)

Burkina Faso (14th January 1988)
Chile (5th September 1974)
Colombia (17th September 1976)
Congo (18th May 1964)
Costa Rica (9th September 1971)
Cyprus, Republic of (5th May 1970—television only)
Czechoslovakia (14th August 1964)
Denmark (including Greenland and the Faeroe Islands) (1st February 1962—
    television; 1st July 1965—non-television)
Dominican Republic (27th January 1987)
Ecuador (18th May 1964)
El Salvador (29th June 1979)
Fiji (11th April 1972)
Finland (21st October 1983)
France (including all Overseas Departments and Territories) (1st July 1961—
    television; 3rd July 1987—non-television)
Germany (21st October 1966)
Greece (6th January 1993)
Guatemala (14th January 1977)
Honduras (16th February 1990)
Ireland, Republic of (19th September 1979)
Italy (8th April 1975)
Japan (26th October 1989)
Lesotho (26th January 1990)
Luxembourg (25th February 1976)
Malawi (22nd June 1989)
Malaysia (1st June 1957)
Mexico (18th May 1964)
Monaco (6th December 1985)
Niger (18th May 1964)
Norway (10th August 1968—television; 10th July 1978—non-television)
Panama (2nd September 1983)
Paraguay (26th February 1970)
Peru (7th August 1985)
Philippines (25th September 1984)
Singapore (1st June 1957)
Spain (19th November 1971—television; 14th November 1991—non-television)
Sweden (1st July 1961—television; 18th May 1964—non-television)
Uruguay (4th July 1977)

SCHEDULE 4 Article 5

MODIFICATIONS

1. In respect of Indonesia, article 2(1)(a) above as applied by article 3(b) above shall apply as if the reference to persons domiciled in Indonesia were omitted.

2. In respect of Singapore—
   (a) articles 2(1)(a) and (2) and (4)(1)(a) above shall apply as if the references to persons domiciled in Singapore were omitted, and

(b) in the application of article 4(3) above in relation to cable programmes by virtue of article 4(6), the relevant date is 1st January 1985.

3. In respect of the territory of Taiwan—
(a) article 2(1)(a) and (2) above shall apply as if the reference to persons domiciled or resident in the territory of Taiwan were limited to such persons who are also citizens or subjects of China, and
(b) in the application of Part I of the Act by virtue of article 2(3) above, subsection (1) of section 21 (infringement by making adaptation) applies as if subsection (3)(a)(i) of that section (translation of literary of dramatic work) were omitted.

INDEX

Index